McGraw-Hill Reading

Wonders

McGraw Hill **Education**

Bothell, WA • Chicago, IL • Columbus, OH • New York, NY

 TextEvaluator.

ETS and the ETS logo are registered trademarks of Educational Testing Service (ETS).
TextEvaluator is a trademark of Educational Testing Service.

Cover and Title Pages: Nathan Love

www.mheonline.com/readingwonders

C

The McGraw-Hill Companies

 Education

Send all inquiries to:
McGraw-Hill Education
Two Penn Plaza
New York, New York 10121

Printed in China

7 8 9 DSS 17 16 15 14

McGraw-Hill Reading Wonders

CCSS Reading/Language Arts Program

Program Authors

Dr. Diane August
Managing Director,
American Institutes for Research
Washington, D.C.

Dr. Donald Bear
Iowa State University
Ames, Iowa

Dr. Janice A. Dole
University of Utah
Salt Lake City, Utah

Dr. Jana Echevarria
California State University, Long Beach
Long Beach, California

Dr. Douglas Fisher
San Diego State University
San Diego, California

Dr. David J. Francis
University of Houston
Houston, Texas

Dr. Vicki Gibson
Educational Consultant
Gibson Hasbrouck and Associates
Wellesley, Massachusetts

Dr. Jan Hasbrouck
Educational Consultant
and Researcher
J.H. Consulting
Vancouver, Washington
Gibson Hasbrouck and Associates
Wellesley, Massachusetts

Margaret Kilgo
Educational Consultant
Kilgo Consulting, Inc.
Austin, Texas

Dr. Jay McTighe
Educational Consultant
Jay McTighe and Associates
Columbia, Maryland

Dr. Scott G. Paris
Vice President, Research
Educational Testing Service
Princeton, New Jersey

Dr. Timothy Shanahan
University of Illinois at Chicago
Chicago, Illinois

Dr. Josefina V. Tinajero
University of Texas at El Paso
El Paso, Texas

 **Education**

Bothell, WA • Chicago, IL • Columbus, OH • New York, NY

PROGRAM AUTHORS

Dr. Diane August

American Institutes for Research, Washington, D.C.

Managing Director focused on literacy and science for ELLs for the Education, Human Development and the Workforce Division

Dr. Donald R. Bear

Iowa State University

Professor, Iowa State University

Author of *Words Their Way, Words Their Way with English Learners, Vocabulary Their Way,* and *Words Their Way with Struggling Readers, 4–12*

Dr. Janice A. Dole

University of Utah

Professor, University of Utah

Director, Utah Center for Reading and Literacy

Content Facilitator, National Assessment of Educational Progress (NAEP)

CCSS Consultant to Literacy Coaches, Salt Lake City School District, Utah

Dr. Jana Echevarria

California State University, Long Beach

Professor Emerita of Education, California State University

Author of *Making Content Comprehensible for English Learners: The SIOP Model*

Dr. Douglas Fisher

San Diego State University

Co-Director, Center for the Advancement of Reading, California State University

Author of *Language Arts Workshop: Purposeful Reading and Writing Instruction* and *Reading for Information in Elementary School*

Dr. David J. Francis

University of Houston

Director of the Center for Research on Educational Achievement and Teaching of English Language Learners (CREATE)

Dr. Vicki Gibson

Educational Consultant Gibson Hasbrouck and Associates

Author of *Differentiated Instruction: Grouping for Success, Differentiated Instruction: Guidelines for Implementation,* and *Managing Behaviors to Support Differentiated Instruction*

Dr. Jan Hasbrouck

J.H. Consulting Gibson Hasbrouck and Associates

Developed Oral Reading Fluency Norms for Grades 1–8

Author of *The Reading Coach: A How-to Manual for Success* and *Educators as Physicians: Using RTI Assessments for Effective Decision-Making*

Margaret Kilgo

Educational Consultant Kilgo Consulting, Inc., Austin, TX

Developed Data-Driven Decisions process for evaluating student performance by standard

Member of Common Core State Standards Anchor Standards Committee for Reading and Writing

Dr. Scott G. Paris

Educational Testing Service,
Vice President, Research

Professor, Nanyang Technological
University, Singapore, 2008–2011

Professor of Education and Psychology,
University of Michigan, 1978–2008

Dr. Timothy Shanahan

University of Illinois at Chicago

Distinguished Professor, Urban Education

Director, UIC Center for Literacy

Chair, Department of Curriculum &
Instruction

Member, English Language Arts Work
Team and Writer of the Common Core
State Standards

President, International Reading
Association, 2006

Dr. Josefina V. Tinajero

University of Texas at El Paso

Dean of College of Education

President of TABE

Board of Directors for the American
Association of Colleges for Teacher
Education (AACTE)

Governing Board of the National Network
for Educational Renewal (NNER)

Consulting Authors

Kathy R. Bumgardner

National Literacy Consultant

Strategies Unlimited, Inc.
Gastonia, NC

Jay McTighe

Jay McTighe and Associates

Author of *The Understanding by Design
Guide to Creating High Quality Units* with
G. Wiggins; *Schooling by Design: Mission,
Action, Achievement* with G. Wiggins;
and *Differentiated Instruction and
Understanding By Design* with C. Tomlinson

Dr. Doris Walker-Dalhouse

Marquette University

Associate Professor, Department
of Educational Policy & Leadership

Author of articles on multicultural
literature, struggling readers, and
reading instruction in urban schools

Dinah Zike

Educational Consultant

Dinah-Might Activities, Inc.
San Antonio, TX

Program Reviewers

Kelly Aeppli-Campbell
Escambia County School District
Pensacola, FL

Marjorie J. Archer
Broward County Public Schools
Davie, FL

Whitney Augustine
Brevard Public Schools
Melbourne, FL

Antonio C. Campbell
Washington County School District
Saint George, UT

Helen Dunne
Gilbert Public School District
Gilbert, AZ

David P. Frydman
Clark County School District
Las Vegas, NV

Fran Gregory
Metropolitan Nashville Public Schools
Nashville, TN

Veronica Allen Hunt
Clark County School District
Las Vegas, NV

Michele Jacobs
Dee-Mack CUSD #701
Mackinaw, IL

LaVita Johnson Spears
Broward County Public Schools
Pembroke Pines, FL

Randall B. Kincaid
Sevier County Schools
Sevierville, TN

Matt Melamed
Community Consolidated School
District 46
Grayslake, IL

Angela L. Reese,
Bay District Schools
Panama City, FL

Eddie Thompson
Fairfield City School District
Fairfield Township, OH

Patricia Vasseur Sosa
Miami-Dade County Public Schools
Miami, FL

Dr. Elizabeth Watson
Hazelwood School District
Hazelwood, MO

v

TEACHING WITH

McGraw-Hill Reading
Wonders

INTRODUCE

Weekly Concept
Grade Appropriate Topics, including Science and Social Studies

Reading/Writing Workshop

- **Videos**
- **Photographs**
- **Interactive Graphic Organizers**

TEACH

Close Reading
Short Complex Texts

Minilessons
Comprehension Strategies and Skills
Genre
Vocabulary Strategies
Writing Traits

Grammar Handbook

Reading/Writing Workshop

- **Visual Glossary**
- **Interactive Minilessons**
- **Interactive Graphic Organizers**

APPLY

Close Reading
Anchor Texts
Extended Complex Texts
Application of Strategies and Skills

Literature Anthology

- **e Books**
- **Interactive Texts**
- **Listening Library**
- **English/Spanish Summaries**

Master the Common Core State Standards!

- e Books
- Interactive Texts
- Leveled Reader Search
- Listening Library
- Interactive Activities

Leveled Readers

DIFFERENTIATE

Leveled Readers
Small Group Instruction with Differentiated Texts

- Online Research
- Writer's Workspace
- Interactive Group Projects

Collection of Texts

INTEGRATE

Research and Inquiry
Short and Sustained Research Projects

Text Connections
Reading Across Texts

Write About Reading
Analytical Writing

- Online Assessment
- Test Generator
- Reports

Weekly Assessment

Unit Assessment

Benchmark Assessment

ASSESS

Weekly Assessment

Unit Assessment

Benchmark Assessment

PROGRAM COMPONENTS

Reading/Writing Workshop

Literature Anthology

Teacher Editions

Leveled Readers

Classroom Library Tradebooks

Your Turn Practice Book

Visual Vocabulary Cards

Leveled Workstation Activity Cards

CCSS Assessing the Common Core State Standards

Sound-Spelling Cards

High-Frequency Word Cards

Response Board

Weekly Assessment

Unit Assessment

Benchmark Assessment

Go Digital

For the Teacher

 Plan
Customizable Lesson Plans

 Assess
Online Assessments
Reports and Scoring

Professional Development
Lesson and CCSS Videos

 Teach
Classroom Presentation Tools Instructional Lessons

 Collaborate
Online Class Conversations
Interactive Group Projects

Additional Online Resources
Leveled Practice
Grammar Practice
Phonics/Spelling
ELL Activities
Genre Study
Reader's Theater
Tier 2 Intervention

 Manage and Assign
Student Grouping and Assignments

 School to Home
Digital Open House Activities and Messages

For the Students

 My To Do List
Assignments
Assessment

 Words to Know
Build Vocabulary

 Read
e Books
Interactive Texts

 Play
Interactive Games

 Write
Interactive Writing

School to Home
Activities for Home
Messages from the Teacher
Class Wall of Student Work

www.connected.mcgraw-hill.com

UNIT 4 CONTENTS

Unit Planning

Weekly Lessons

Writing Process — Genre Writing: Narrative and Poetry

Model Lesson — Extended Complex Text

Close Reading Routine

Program Information

(t to b) David Frazier/Stone/Getty Images; New York Times Co./Hulton Archive/Getty Images; Michael Svoboda/the Agency Collection/Getty Images; Minden Pictures/Masterfile; Jim Cummins/Corbis

UNIT OVERVIEW
Fact or Fiction?

Text Complexity Range for Grades 4–5

	Lexile	
740	TextEvaluator™	1010
23		51

	Week 1	Week 2	Week 3

	OUR GOVERNMENT	**LEADERSHIP**	**BREAKTHROUGHS**

READING

Week 1 — OUR GOVERNMENT

ESSENTIAL QUESTION
Why do we need government?

Build Background

CCSS Vocabulary
L.4.6 *amendments, commitment, compromise, democracy, eventually, legislation, privilege, version*
Latin Roots

CCSS Comprehension
RI.4.5 Strategy: Ask and Answer Questions
Skill: Cause and Effect
Genre: Narrative Nonfiction
Analytical Writing Write About Reading

CCSS Phonics
RF.4.3a Inflectional Endings, Vowel Team Syllables

CCSS Fluency
RF.4.4a Phrasing and Rate

Week 2 — LEADERSHIP

ESSENTIAL QUESTION
Why do people run for public office?

Build Background

CCSS Vocabulary
L.4.6 *accompanies, campaign, governor, intend, opponent, overwhelming, tolerate, weary*
Idioms

CCSS Comprehension
RL.4.6 Strategy: Make Predictions
Skill: Point of View
Genre: Fantasy
Analytical Writing Write About Reading

CCSS Phonics
RF.4.3a Inflectional Endings: Changing *y* to *i*, *r*-controlled Vowel Syllables

CCSS Fluency
RF.4.4b Phrasing and Expression

Week 3 — BREAKTHROUGHS

ESSENTIAL QUESTION
How do inventions and technology affect your life?

Build Background

CCSS Vocabulary
L.4.6 *decade, directing, engineering, gleaming, scouted, squirmed, technology, tinkering*
Context Clues: Synonyms

CCSS Comprehension
RL.4.6 Strategy: Make Predictions
Skill: Point of View
Genre: Historical Fiction
Analytical Writing Write About Reading

CCSS Phonics
RF.4.3a Words with /ü/, /ū/, and /ů/, Consonant + *le* Syllables

CCSS Fluency
RF.4.4b Expression

LANGUAGE ARTS

Week 1

CCSS Writing
W.4.10 Trait: Organization

CCSS Grammar
L.4.1a Pronouns and Antecedents

CCSS Spelling
L.4.2d Inflectional Endings

CCSS Vocabulary
L.4.4b Build Vocabulary

Week 2

CCSS Writing
W.4.10 Trait: Ideas

CCSS Grammar
L.3.1a Types of Pronouns

CCSS Spelling
L.4.2d Inflectional Endings: Changing *y* to *i*

CCSS Vocabulary
L.4.5b Build Vocabulary

Week 3

CCSS Writing
W.4.10 Trait: Ideas

CCSS Grammar
L.3.1f Pronoun-Verb Agreement

CCSS Spelling
L.4.2d Words with /ü/, /ů/, and /ū/

CCSS Vocabulary
L.4.5c Build Vocabulary

 Writing Process **Genre Writing: Narrative** Fictional Narrative T344–T349

Week 4	Week 5	Week 6
WONDERS IN THE SKY	**ACHIEVEMENTS**	

Week 4 — WONDERS IN THE SKY

ESSENTIAL QUESTION
How can you explain what you see in the sky?

Build Background

CCSS Vocabulary
L.4.6 *astronomer, crescent, phases, rotates, series, sliver, specific, telescope*
Context Clues: Paragraph Clues

CCSS Comprehension
RI.4.5 Strategy: Ask and Answer Questions
Skill: Cause and Effect
Genre: Expository Text
Analytical Writing Write About Reading

CCSS Phonics
RF.4.3a Diphthongs /oi/ and /ou/, Greek and Latin Roots

CCSS Fluency
RF.4.4c Accuracy

CCSS Writing
W.4.10 Trait: Word Choice

CCSS Grammar
L.4.1g Possessive Pronouns

CCSS Spelling
L.4.2d Diphthongs /oi/ and /ou/

CCSS Vocabulary
L.4.4a Build Vocabulary

Week 5 — ACHIEVEMENTS

ESSENTIAL QUESTION
How do writers look at success in different ways?

Build Background

CCSS Vocabulary
L.4.6 *attain, dangling, hovering, triumph connotation, denotation, repetition, stanza*
Connotation and Denotation

CCSS Comprehension
RL.4.2 Literary Elements: Stanzas and Repetition
Skill: Theme
Genre: Narrative Poetry
Analytical Writing Write About Reading

CCSS Phonics
RF.4.3a Varient Vowel /ô/, Frequently Confused Words

CCSS Fluency
RF.4.4b Rate

CCSS Writing
W.4.10 Trait: Word Choice

CCSS Grammar
L.4.1g Pronouns and Homophones

CCSS Spelling
L.4.2d Varient Vowel /ô/

CCSS Vocabulary
L.4.5c Build Vocabulary

Week 6

CCSS Reader's Theater
RF.4.4b Focus on Vocabulary
Fluency: Intonation, Phrasing, Accuracy

CCSS Reading Digitally
SL.4.2 Notetaking
Skimming and Scanning
Navigating Links

CCSS Research and Inquiry
W.4.8 Relevant Facts
Unit Projects
Presentation of Ideas

Unit 4 Assessment

Unit Assessment
pages 79–105

Fluency Assessment
pages 212–221

CCSS Writing
SL.4.4 Publishing Celebrations
Portfolio Choice

Writing Process **Genre Writing: Narrative** Poetry T350–T355

UNIT OPENER

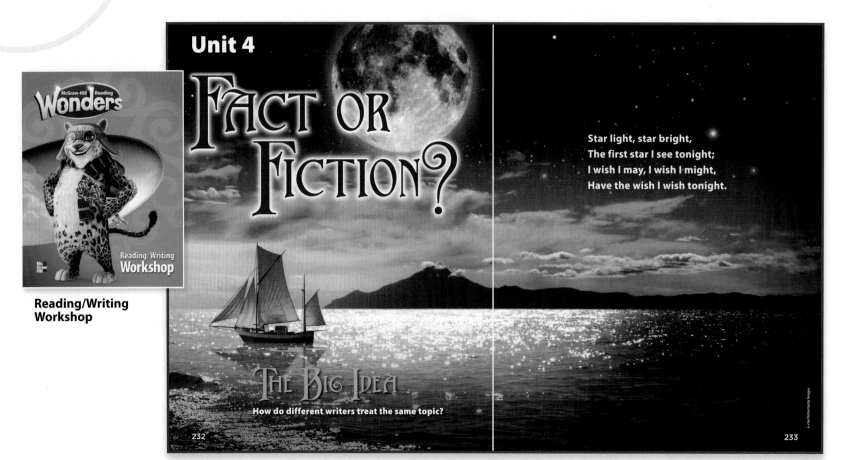

Unit 4

FACT OR FICTION?

Star light, star bright,
The first star I see tonight;
I wish I may, I wish I might,
Have the wish I wish tonight.

THE BIG IDEA
How do different writers treat the same topic?

232

233

Reading/Writing
Workshop

READING/WRITING WORKSHOP, pp. 232–233

The Big Idea *How do different writers treat the same topic?*

Talk About It

Have students read the Big Idea aloud. Ask students to think about the kinds of topics they like to read about, such as animals, sports, or history. Then have them discuss how these topics were treated differently in books, poems, articles, songs, and other texts students have read.

Ask: *Why would you read different texts about the same topic?*

Have students discuss in partners or in groups, and then share their ideas with the class.

Music Links Introduce a song at the start of the unit. Go to www.connected. mcgraw-hill.com
Resources Media: Music to find audio recordings, song lyrics, and activities.

Read the Poem: "Star Light, Star Bright"

Read the poem aloud. Ask students questions to explore the theme.

→ Who does the narrator address?

→ What does the narrator want?

Rhyme Review that many poems have lines that rhyme. Have students identify examples of rhyme in the poem.

Repetition Have students identify the repetition in the poem. Ask: *Why do you think the poet included the repetition?*

RESEARCH AND INQUIRY

Weekly Projects Each week students will produce a project related to the Essential Question. They will then develop one of these projects more fully for the Unit Research Project. Through their research, students will focus their attention on:

→ selecting and organizing relevant facts.

→ skimming and scanning techniques.

Shared Research Board You may wish to develop a Shared Research Board. Students can post questions, ideas, and information that they research about the unit theme. Students can post articles, illustrations, or information they gather as they do their research. They can also post notes with questions they have as they read the text.

WEEKLY PROJECTS

Students work in pairs or small groups.

Week 1 Create a Flow Chart, T28

Week 2 Write a Political Campaign Plan, T92

Week 3 Write a Paragraph about Plastics in Medicine, T156

Week 4 Research Eclipses, T220

Week 5 Research Narrative Poetry, T284

WEEK 6

Students work in small groups to complete and present one of the following projects.

→ Make an Educational Poster

→ Create an Illustrated Biography

→ Make a Time Line

→ Record a Newscast

→ Write a Poem

 # WRITING

Write About Reading As students read and reread each week for close reading of text, students will take notes, cite evidence to support their ideas and opinions, write summaries of text, or develop character sketches.

Writing Every Day: Focus on Writing Traits

Each week, students will focus on a writing trait. After analyzing an expert and student model, students will draft and revise shorter writing entries in their Writer's Notebook, applying the trait to their writing.

Writing Process: Focus on Narrative Writing and Poetry

Over the course of the unit, students will develop 1 to 2 longer narrative texts. Students will work through the various stages of the writing process, allowing them time to continue revising their writing, conferencing with peers and teacher.

WEEKLY WRITING TRAITS

Week 1 Strong Paragraphs, T30

Week 2 Develop Characters, T94

Week 3 Develop Plot, T158

Week 4 Figurative Language, T222

Week 5 Sensory Language, T286

GENRE WRITING: NARRATIVE AND POETIC FORMS

Choose one or complete both 2- to 3-week writing process lessons over the course of the unit.

Fictional Narrative, T344–T349

Poetry, T350–T355

COLLABORATE
Post student questions and monitor student online discussions. Create a Shared Research Board.

Go Digital! www.connected.mcgraw-hill.com

WRITER'S WORKSPACE
Ask students to work through their genre writing using the online tools for support.

WEEKLY OVERVIEW

Text Complexity Range for Grades 4–5

Lexile	
740	1010
TextEvaluator™	
23	51

McGraw-Hill Reading

Wonders

Reading/Writing Workshop

McGraw Hill

TEACH AND MODEL

CCSS **Shared Read** Genre • Narrative Nonfiction

A WORLD WITHOUT RULES

CLOSED

You may sometimes wonder if rules were made to keep you from having fun and to tell you what you to do. But what if we had no rules at all? Nobody would tell you what to do ever again! Sounds great, right? Well, let's see what it's like to inhabit a world without rules. You just might change your mind!

A Strange Morning
Let's start at home. Your alarm clock goes off. Why hurry? Without rules you don't have to go to school. **Eventually** you wander downstairs and find your little brother eating cookies in the kitchen. Since there are no rules, you can have cookies for breakfast! But you wonder if you should have something sensible like a bowl of cereal. You reach a **compromise** (KOM•pruh•mighz) and crumble the cookies over your cereal. In this new world, you will not have to brush your teeth anymore. Of course, the next time you see the dentist, you may have a cavity.

A Community in Confusion
Now, you step outside. You decide to go to the playground because there's no law saying you have to go to school. No crossing guard stands at the corner to help you across the street. Without traffic laws, cars zip by at an alarming speed honking at each other, and there is not a police officer in sight. There is no safe alternate way to cross the street. Besides, once you see the playground, you may decide it is not worth the risk of getting hit by a car. Broken swings dangle from rusty chains. Trash cans overflow with plastic bottles, snack wrappers, and paper bags. A huge tree branch lies across the sliding board. As a result of all state and federal services being gone, nobody is in charge of taking care of the playground.

 Essential Question
Why do we need government?
Read how government and laws help to protect us every day.

238   239

✔ Vocabulary

amendments
commitment
compromise
democracy
eventually
legislation
privilege
version

🔍 Close Reading of Complex Text

Shared Read "A World Without Rules," 238–241

Genre Narrative Nonfiction

Lexile 830
ⒺⓉⓈ *TextEvaluator™* 42

Minilessons

✔ **Comprehension Strategy** .... Ask and Answer Questions, T18–T19
✔ **Comprehension Skill** .... Cause and Effect, T20–T21
✔ **Genre** .... Narrative Nonfiction, T22–T23
✔ **Vocabulary Strategy** .... Latin Roots, T24–T25
✔ **Writing Traits** .... Organization, T30–T31
   Grammar .... Pronouns and Antecedents, T34–T35

✔ Tested Skills CCSS

👉 **Go**
Digital

www.connected.mcgraw-hill.com

Essential Question
Why do we need government?

APPLY WITH CLOSE READING

Literature Anthology

Complex Text

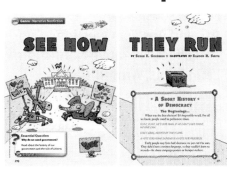

See How They Run, 270–283
Genre Narrative Nonfiction
Lexile 870
ETS *TextEvaluator* 42

PAIRED READ

"The Birth of American Democracy," 284–287
Genre Expository Text
Lexile 830
ETS *TextEvaluator* 43

Differentiated Text

Leveled Readers *Include Paired Reads*

APPROACHING
Lexile 680
ETS *TextEvaluator* 27

ON LEVEL
Lexile 820
ETS *TextEvaluator* 39

BEYOND
Lexile 890
ETS *TextEvaluator* 47

ELL
Lexile 800
ETS *TextEvaluator* 33

Extended Complex Text

A Picture Book of Harry Houdini
Genre Nonfiction
Lexile 770
ETS *TextEvaluator* 41

The Moon and I
Genre Nonfiction
Lexile 870
ETS *TextEvaluator* 38

Classroom Library

Classroom Library lessons available online.

TEACH AND MANAGE

How You Teach

INTRODUCE

Weekly Concept
Our Government

Reading/Writing Workshop
234–235

 Go Digital

Interactive Whiteboard

TEACH

Close Reading
"A World Without Rules"

Minilessons
Ask and Answer Questions, Cause and Effect, Narrative Nonfiction, Latin Roots, Writing Traits

Reading/Writing Workshop
238–241

Interactive Whiteboard

APPLY

Close Reading
See How They Run
"The Birth of American Democracy"

Literature Anthology
270–287

Mobile

How Students Practice

WEEKLY CONTRACT

PDF Online

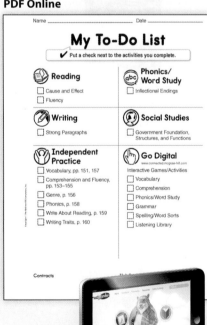

Name _____ Date _____

My To-Do List
✔ Put a check next to the activities you complete.

Reading
☐ Cause and Effect
☐ Fluency

Phonics/Word Study
☐ Inflectional Endings

Writing
☐ Strong Paragraphs

Social Studies
☐ Government Foundation, Structures, and Functions

Independent Practice
☐ Vocabulary, pp. 151, 157
☐ Comprehension and Fluency, pp. 153–155
☐ Genre, p. 156
☐ Phonics, p. 158
☐ Write About Reading, p. 159
☐ Writing Traits, p. 160

Go Digital
www.connected.mcgraw-hill.com
Interactive Games/Activities
☐ Vocabulary
☐ Comprehension
☐ Phonics/Word Study
☐ Grammar
☐ Spelling/Word Sorts
☐ Listening Library

Contracts

 **Go Digital**

Online To-Do List

LEVELED PRACTICE AND ONLINE ACTIVITIES

Your Turn Practice Book
151–160

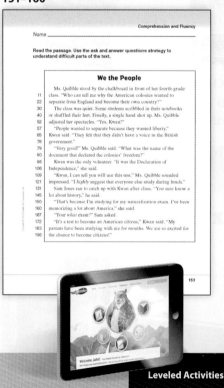

Name _____

Comprehension and Fluency

Read the passage. Use the ask and answer questions strategy to understand difficult parts of the text.

We the People

Ms. Quibble stood by the chalkboard in front of her fourth-grade class. "Who can tell me why the American colonies wanted to separate from England and become their own country?"

The class was quiet. Some students scribbled in their notebooks or shuffled their feet. Finally, a single hand shot up. Ms. Quibble adjusted her spectacles. "Yes, Kwan?"

"People wanted to separate because they wanted liberty," Kwan said. "They felt that they didn't have a voice in the British government."

"Very good!" Ms. Quibble said. "What was the name of the document that declared the colonies' freedom?"

Kwan was the only volunteer. "It was the Declaration of Independence," she said.

"Kwan, I can tell you will ace this test." Ms. Quibble sounded impressed. "I *highly* suggest that everyone else study during lunch."

Sam Jones ran to catch up with Kwan after class. "You sure know a lot about history," he said.

"That's because I'm studying for my naturalization exam. I've been memorizing a lot about America," she said.

"Your *what* exam?" Sam asked.

"It's a test to become an American citizen," Kwan said. "My parents have been studying with me for months. We are so excited for the chance to become citizens!"

153

Leveled Activities

Leveled Readers

Writer's Workspace

DIFFERENTIATE

SMALL GROUP INSTRUCTION
Leveled Readers

Mobile

INTEGRATE

Research and Inquiry
List, T28

Text Connections
Compare Reasons for
Government, T29

Analytical Writing **Write About Reading**
Write an Analysis, T29

Online Research
and Writing

ASSESS

Weekly Assessment
181–192

Online
Assessment

LEVELED WORKSTATION CARDS

16

Three Branches of Government

- Conduct research about the main responsibilities of each branch of the United States government.

- Make a three-column chart. Label the columns *Legislative, Judicial,*

SOCIAL ST

11

Organization: Strong Paragraphs

Read Colin's text. Identify the topic sentence and supporting details. Talk about what details and examples he may be missing. Revise his text.

So... ng part of a family

WRITING

More
Activities
on back

11

Latin and Greek Roots

Greek Roots   Latin Roots

- Create a Two-Pocket Foldable®. On the pockets, write *Greek Roots* and *Latin Roots*.

- On separate note cards, write the words *community, telephone, memorize, photograph, thermal* and *scribble.*

- Use a dictionary to help you define and then sort the words into the correct pockets.

- Choose two roots from the words above and write another word for each. For example, a word with the same root as *scribble* is *scribe.*

You need
20 Minutes
> Two-Pocket Foldable®
> paper
> pencils or pens
> dictionary

PHONICS/WORD STUDY

7

Cause and Effect

- Choose an informational text that you have enjoyed reading in class. As you reread, identify pairs of events that have cause-and-effect relationships.

- For each pair of events, write the cause on one side of a note card and its related effect on the other side.

- Take turns reading one side of a card and asking your partner to identify the cause or effect that goes with it.

You need
15 Minutes
> informational text
> note cards
> pencils or pens

READING

Go Digital! www.connected.mcgraw-hill.com · Interactive Games and Activities · Grade 4

DEVELOPING READERS AND WRITERS

Write About Reading • Analytical Writing

Write to Sources and Research

Summary, T20–T21

Note Taking, T25B, T25P

Summarize, T25N

Cause and Effect, T25N

Make Connections: Essential Question, T25N, T25R, T29

Key Details, T25Q

Research and Inquiry, T28

Analyze to Inform/Explain, T29

Comparing Texts, T41, T49, T53, T59

Predictive Writing, T25B

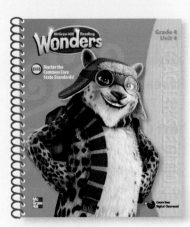

Teacher's Edition

Literature Anthology

Summarize, 283
Cause and Effect, 283

Leveled Readers
Comparing Texts
Cause and Effect

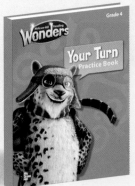

Your Turn Practice Book

Cause and Effect, 153–155
Genre, 156
Analyze to Inform, 159

Interactive Whiteboard

Writing Process • Genre Writing

Narrative Text
Fictional Narrative, T344–T349

Conferencing Routines
Teacher Conferences, T346
Peer Conferences, T347

Interactive Whiteboard

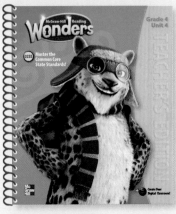

Teacher's Edition

Leveled Workstation Card
Description, Card 27

Writer's Workspace
Fictional Narrative
Writing Process
Multimedia Presentations

Writing Traits • **Write Every Day**

Writing Trait: Organization
Strong Paragraphs, T30–T31

Conferencing Routines
Teacher Conferences, T32
Peer Conferences, T33

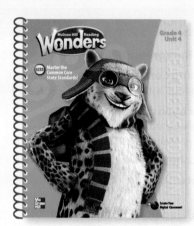

Teacher's Edition

Organization: Strong
Paragraphs,
246–247

Reading/Writing Workshop

Go Digital

Interactive Whiteboard

Strong
Paragraphs,
Card 11

Leveled Workstation Card

Organization: Strong
Paragraphs, 160

Your Turn Practice Book

Grammar and Spelling

Grammar
Pronouns and Antecedents,
T34–T35

Spelling
Inflectional Endings, T36–T37

Go Digital

Interactive Whiteboard

Teacher's Edition

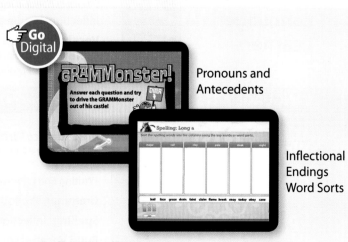

Go Digital

Pronouns and
Antecedents

Inflectional
Endings
Word Sorts

Online Spelling and Grammar Games

SUGGESTED LESSON PLAN

	DAY 1	DAY 2

READING

Whole Group

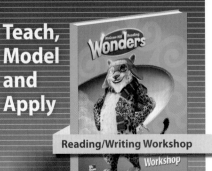

Teach, Model and Apply

Reading/Writing Workshop

DAY 1

Build Background Our Government, T10–T11

Listening Comprehension Read Aloud: "Speaking Out Against Child Labor," T12–T13

Comprehension
• Preview Genre: Narrative Nonfiction
• Preview Strategy: Ask and Answer Questions

✔ **Vocabulary** Words in Context, T14–T15

Practice Your Turn, 151

Close Reading of Complex Text "A World Without Rules," 238–241

DAY 2

✔ **Comprehension**
• Strategy: Ask and Answer Questions, T18–T19
• Skill: Cause and Effect, T20–T21
• Write About Reading ✎ Analytical Writing
• Genre: Narrative Nonfiction, T22–T23

✔ **Vocabulary** Strategy: Latin Roots, T24–T25

Practice Your Turn, 152–157

DIFFERENTIATED INSTRUCTION   Choose across the week to meet your students' needs.

Small Group

Approaching Level

DAY 1

Leveled Reader A Day in the Senate, T40–T41

Phonics/Decoding Decode Words with Inflectional Ending -ed, T42 `TIER 2`

Vocabulary
• Review High-Frequency Words, T44 `TIER 2`
• Identify Related Words, T45

DAY 2

Leveled Reader A Day in the Senate, T40–T41

Vocabulary Review Vocabulary Words, T44 `TIER 2`

Comprehension
• Identify Signal Words, T46 `TIER 2`
• Review Cause and Effect, T47

On Level

DAY 1

Leveled Reader A Day in the Senate, T48–T49

Vocabulary Review Vocabulary Words, T50

DAY 2

Leveled Reader A Day in the Senate, T48–T49

Comprehension Review Cause and Effect, T51

Beyond Level

DAY 1

Leveled Reader A Day in the Senate, T52–T53

Vocabulary Review Domain-Specific Words, T54

DAY 2

Leveled Reader A Day in the Senate, T52–T53

Comprehension Review Cause and Effect, T55

English Language Learners

DAY 1

Shared Read "A World Without Rules," T56–T57

Phonics/Decoding Decode Words with Inflectional Ending -ed, T42

Vocabulary
• Preteach Vocabulary, T60
• Review High-Frequency Words, T44

DAY 2

Leveled Reader A Day in the Senate, T58–T59

Vocabulary Review Vocabulary, T60

Writing Writing Trait: Organization, T62

Grammar Pronouns, T63

LANGUAGE ARTS   Writing Process: Fictional Narrative T344–T349   Use with Weeks 1–3

Whole Group

Writing
Grammar
Spelling
Build Vocabulary

DAY 1

✔ **Readers to Writers**
• Writing Traits: Organization/Strong Paragraphs, T30–T31
• Writing Entry: Prewrite and Draft, T32

Grammar Pronouns and Antecedents, T34

Spelling Inflectional Endings, T36

Build Vocabulary
• Connect to Words, T38
• Academic Vocabulary, T38

DAY 2

Readers to Writers
• Writing Entry: Revise, T32

Grammar Pronouns and Antecedents, T34

Spelling Inflectional Endings, T36

Build Vocabulary
• Expand Vocabulary, T38
• Review Antonyms, T38

DAY 3	DAY 4	DAY 5 Review and Assess

READING

Phonics/Decoding
• Inflectional Endings, T26
• Vowel Team Syllables, T27

Practice *Your Turn*, 158

Close Reading *See How They Run*, 270–283 • *Analytical Writing*

Literature Anthology

Fluency Phrasing and Rate, T27

Integrate Ideas • *Analytical Writing*
• Research and Inquiry, T28

Practice *Your Turn*, 153–155

Close Reading "The Birth of American Democracy," 284–287 • *Analytical Writing*

Integrate Ideas • *Analytical Writing*
• Research and Inquiry, T28
• Text Connections, T29
• Write About Reading, T29

Practice *Your Turn*, 159

DIFFERENTIATED INSTRUCTION

Leveled Reader *A Day in the Senate*, T40–T41
Phonics/Decoding Review Inflectional Endings, T42 **TIER 2**
Fluency Rate and Phrasing, T46 **TIER 2**
Vocabulary Latin Roots, T45

Leveled Reader "A New President Takes Office," T41 • *Analytical Writing*
Phonics/Decoding Practice Inflectional Endings, T43

Leveled Reader Literature Circles, T41
Comprehension Self-Selected Reading, T47
Phonics/Decoding Words with Vowel Teams, T43

Leveled Reader *A Day in the Senate*, T48–T49
Vocabulary Latin Roots, T50

Leveled Reader "A New President Takes Office," T49 • *Analytical Writing*

Leveled Reader Literature Circles, T49
Comprehension Self-Selected Reading, T51

Leveled Reader *A Day in the Senate*, T52–T53
Vocabulary
• Latin Roots, T54
• Shades of Meaning, T54 *Gifted and Talented*

Leveled Reader "A New President Takes Office," T53 • *Analytical Writing*

Leveled Reader Literature Circles, T53
Comprehension
• Self-Selected Reading, T55
• Independent Study: Plan of Action, T55 *Gifted and Talented*

Leveled Reader *A Day in the Senate*, T58–T59
Phonics/Decoding Review Inflectional Endings, T42
Vocabulary Latin Roots, T61
Spelling Words with Inflectional Endings, T62

Leveled Reader "A New President Takes Office," T59 • *Analytical Writing*
Vocabulary Additional Vocabulary, T61
Phonics/Decoding Practice Inflectional Endings, T43

Leveled Reader Literature Circles, T59
Phonics/Decoding Words with Vowel Teams, T43

LANGUAGE ARTS

Readers to Writers
• Writing Entry: Prewrite and Draft, T33

Grammar Mechanics and Usage, T35

Spelling Inflectional Endings, T37

Build Vocabulary
• Reinforce the Words, T39
• Latin Roots, T39

Readers to Writers
• Writing Entry: Revise, T33

Grammar Pronouns and Antecedents, T35

Spelling Inflectional Endings, T37

Build Vocabulary
• Connect to Writing, T39
• Shades of Meaning, T39

Readers to Writers
• Writing Entry: Share and Reflect, T33

Grammar Pronouns and Antecedents, T35

Spelling Inflectional Endings, T37

Build Vocabulary
• Word Squares, T39
• Morphology, T39

DIFFERENTIATE TO ACCELERATE

Qualitative · Quantitative
Reader and Task
TEXT COMPLEXITY

IF ▸ the text complexity of a particular selection is too difficult for students

THEN ▸ see the references noted in the chart below for scaffolded instruction to help students Access Complex Text.

	Reading/Writing Workshop 	**Literature Anthology** 	**Leveled Readers** 	**Classroom Library** 
Quantitative	"A World Without Rules" **Lexile** 830 *TextEvaluator* 42	*See How They Run* **Lexile** 870 *TextEvaluator* 42 "The Birth of American Democracy" **Lexile** 830 *TextEvaluator* 43	**Approaching Level** **Lexile** 680 *TextEvaluator* 27 **Beyond Level** **Lexile** 890 *TextEvaluator* 47 **On Level** **Lexile** 820 *TextEvaluator* 39 **ELL** **Lexile** 800 *TextEvaluator* 33	*A Picture Book of Harry Houdini* **Lexile** 770 *TextEvaluator* 41 *The Moon and I* **Lexile** 870 *TextEvaluator* 38
Qualitative	**What Makes the Text Complex?** • **Connection of Ideas** Real World T17 • **Purpose** Entertain and Inform T23 **ACT** *See Scaffolded Instruction in Teacher's Edition T17 and T23.*	**What Makes the Text Complex?** • **Connection of Ideas** Illustrations T25A; Synthesize T25C, T25K • **Sentence Structure** T25E • **Specific Vocabulary** Strategies T25G, T25Q • **Genre** Text Features T25I • **Purpose** Inform and Persuade T25L • **Prior Knowledge** History T25O **ACT** *See Scaffolded Instruction in Teacher's Edition T25A–T25R.*	**What Makes the Text Complex?** • **Specific Vocabulary** • **Prior Knowledge** • **Sentence Structure** • **Connection of Ideas** • **Genre** **ACT** *See Level Up lessons online for Leveled Readers.*	**What Makes the Text Complex?** • **Genre** • **Specific Vocabulary** • **Prior Knowledge** • **Sentence Structure** • **Organization** • **Purpose** • **Connection of Ideas** **ACT** *See Scaffolded Instruction in Teacher's Edition T360–T361.*
Reader and Task	The Introduce the Concept lesson on pages T10–T11 will help determine the reader's knowledge and engagement in the weekly concept. See pages T16–T25 and T28-T29 for questions and tasks for this text.	The Introduce the Concept lesson on pages T10–T11 will help determine the reader's knowledge and engagement in the weekly concept. See pages T25A–T25R and T28–T29 for questions and tasks for this text.	The Introduce the Concept lesson on pages T10–T11 will help determine the reader's knowledge and engagement in the weekly concept. See pages T40–T41, T48–T49, T52–T53, T58–T59, and T28–T29 for questions and tasks for this text.	The Introduce the Concept lesson on pages T10-T11 will help determine the reader's knowledge and engagement in the weekly concept. See pages T360-T361 for questio

Monitor and *Differentiate*

IF you need to differentiate instruction

THEN use the Quick Checks to assess students' needs and select the appropriate small group instruction focus.

 Quick Check

Comprehension Strategy Ask and Answer Questions T19

Comprehension Skill Text Structure: Cause and Effect T21

Genre Narrative Nonfiction T23

Vocabulary Strategy Latin Roots T25

Phonics/Fluency Inflectional Endings T27

If No →
| Approaching Level | Reteach T40–T47 |
| ELL | Develop T56–T63 |

If Yes →
| On Level | Review T48–T51 |
| Beyond Level | Extend T52–T55 |

Level Up with Leveled Readers

IF students can read their leveled text fluently and answer comprehension questions

THEN work with the next level up to accelerate students' reading with more complex text.

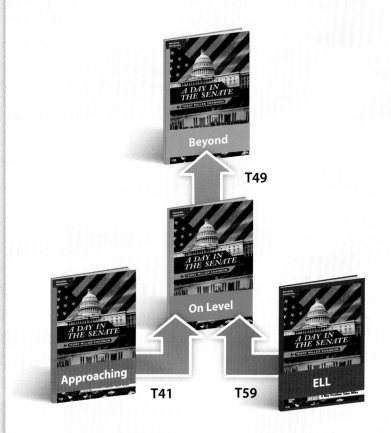

T49 T41 T59

 ENGLISH LANGUAGE LEARNERS
SCAFFOLD

IF ELL students need additional support **THEN** scaffold instruction using the small group suggestions.

Reading/Writing Workshop "A World Without Rules" T56–T57	Leveled Reader *A Day in the Senate* T58–T59 "A New President Takes Office" T59	Additional Vocabulary T61 citizen history issues rules services	Using Latin Roots T61	Writing Organization T62	Spelling Words with Inflectional Endings T62	Grammar Pronouns T63

Note: Include ELL Students in all small groups based on their needs.

→ Introduce the Concept

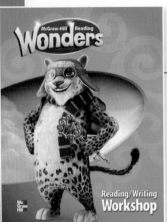

Reading/Writing Workshop

OBJECTIVES

 Paraphrase portions of a text read aloud or information presented in diverse media and formats, including visually, quantitatively, and orally. **SL.4.2**

 Follow agreed-upon rules for discussions and carry out assigned roles. **SL.4.1b**

ACADEMIC LANGUAGE

- *democracy, legislation*
- Cognates: *democracia, legislación*

MINILESSON
10 Mins

Build Background

ESSENTIAL QUESTION
Why do we need government?

Have students read the Essential Question on page 234 of the **Reading/Writing Workshop**. Tell them that our government is a **democracy,** which means that it is run by the citizens of our country.

Discuss the photograph of the court with students. Focus on the roles of government and why we need it. Have students paraphrase what is happening in the photograph.

→ Why is it important to have **legislation**, or laws?

→ The justice system is an example of government at work. What is another example of government at work?

→ What does your state government do? What services does it provide?

Talk About It

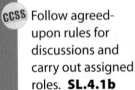
COLLABORATE

Ask: *What are the different roles government plays in our lives? Why do we need government?* Have students discuss in pairs or groups.

→ Model using the Concept Web to generate words and phrases related to the role of government. Add students' contributions.

→ Have partners continue the discussion by sharing what they have learned about government. They can complete the Concept Web, generating additional related words and phrases.

Collaborative Conversations

Take Turns Talking As students engage in partner, small-group, and whole-class discussions, encourage them to

→ wait for a person to finish before they speak. They should not speak over others.

→ quietly raise their hand to let others know they would like a turn to speak.

→ ask others in the group to share their opinions so that all students have a chance to share.

Go Digital

Discuss the Concept

Watch Video

Government
Use Graphic Organizer

Weekly Concept Our Government

Essential Question
Why do we need government?

Go Digital!

JUSTICE FOR ALL

The justice system is an example of government at work. Judges are appointed by elected officials or are elected directly by the voters. Juries are made up of citizens who listen to the evidence presented by both sides.

▶ What is another example of government at work?

▶ What services does your state government provide?

▶ What might happen if there were no government?

Talk About It

Write words that describe the different roles that government plays. Then talk to your partner about why we need government.

Government

234   235

READING/WRITING WORKSHOP, pp. 234–235

ELL ENGLISH LANGUAGE LEARNERS SCAFFOLD

Beginning	Intermediate	Advanced/High
Use Visuals Point to the picture on pages 234–235. Say: *This is a court. A court is part of the government. The government helps people.* Have students complete the sentence frame: *The government helps _____.* (people) Correct students' pronunciation as needed.	**Describe** Have students describe the picture. Ask: *How does the picture show government at work?* Elicit from students that the picture shows the justice system whose job it is to settle disputes. Repeat students' responses, correcting for grammar and pronunciation as needed.	**Discuss** Ask students to discuss the role of government. Ask: *How does government help us? Why do we need government?* If necessary, explain that the government provides many services, including free parks and education. Encourage students to use concept and vocabulary words.

GRAPHIC ORGANIZER 62

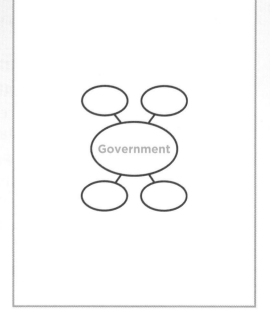

Government

→ Listening Comprehension

MINILESSON
10 Mins

Interactive Read Aloud

Go Digital

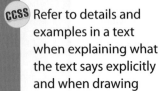

OBJECTIVES

CCSS Refer to details and examples in a text when explaining what the text says explicitly and when drawing inferences from the text. **RI.4.1**

CCSS Paraphrase portions of a text read aloud or information presented in diverse media and formats, including visually, quantitatively, and orally. **SL.4.2**

- Listen for a purpose.
- Identify characteristics of narrative nonfiction.

ACADEMIC LANGUAGE
narrative nonfiction, ask and answer questions

Connect to Concept: Our Government

Tell students that government helps protect people and improve their lives. Let students know that you will be reading aloud a passage about a time when the United States government passed laws that helped children who worked instead of going to school. Explain that their purpose in listening is to gain information.

View Photos

Preview Genre: Narrative Nonfiction

Explain that the passage you will read aloud is narrative nonfiction. Discuss features of narrative nonfiction:

→ is in the form of a story told by a narrator

→ presents information in a logical order

→ may express the author's opinion about the subject

→ often includes text features

Preview Comprehension Strategy: Ask and Answer Questions

Point out that readers can ask questions before, during, and after reading to help them understand important information in a text. When reading informational text, such as narrative nonfiction, it is helpful to ask questions such as, "Do I understand the information presented in this part of the text?"

Use the Think Alouds on page T13 to model the strategy.

Respond to Reading

Think Aloud Clouds Display Think Aloud Master 1: *I wonder . . .* to reinforce how you used the ask and answer questions strategy to understand content.

I wonder...

Model Think Alouds

Genre Features With students, discuss the elements of the Read Aloud that let them know it is narrative nonfiction. Ask them to think about other texts that you have read or they have read independently that were narrative nonfiction.

Genre	Features

Fill in Genre Chart

Summarize Have students restate the most important information from "Speaking Out Against Child Labor" in their own words.

Speaking Out Against Child Labor

It is a typical day. Your mom drops you off at school on her way to work. For a moment, you think, "I wish I could go to work instead of school."

You are heading toward the school door when you notice a new sign on the building where the name of the school used to be. The words "Garvin's Mill" are on the sign. "That's weird," you think. Inside, it gets even weirder. The building is filled with loud machines stretching white fibers and spinning them onto large spools. You see kids your age, and some even younger, working at the machines. **1**

In the early 1900s, millions of children, some as young as seven, worked long hours in places such as textile mills, factories, and coal mines. Employers liked hiring kids because they didn't have to pay them as much. For a typical twelve-hour day in a mill, a child might earn 25- to 50-cents. Workers could take few breaks, and they were often forced to eat their lunches while working. With no air conditioning and sometimes few windows, the rooms grew unbearably hot from the constantly running machines. **2**

The jobs were often dangerous ones. The mills used large machines to spin cotton fibers into threads and weave them into cloth. A machine's moving parts could easily catch a child's sleeve and pull him or her into it with deadly results. Mill workers breathed in the tiny fibers of cotton that floated in the air. Over time, many people developed breathing problems, which sometimes led to death.

Some people began to speak out against using child laborers. They argued that it was dangerous for the children and it kept them from going to school to get an education and have a better life. Finally, in 1938, a law was passed that limited work hours and set a minimum age for children who worked. **3**

As you wake up from your dream, you are thankful that child labor laws were passed. Suddenly, spending your day at school doesn't seem so bad.

1 Think Aloud Two **questions** I want to **ask** after reading this section are, "What kind of school is this?" and "Why do the words on the sign say 'Garvin's Mill'"?

2 Think Aloud As I read this paragraph, I **asked** myself, "Why didn't people take a stand against child labor?" Based on the title of the piece, my **question** will probably be answered later in the text.

3 Think Aloud In this section, I read that people spoke out against child labor. That **answers** my **question**. A law was passed in 1938 to limit work hours and set a minimum age for children who worked.

→ Vocabulary

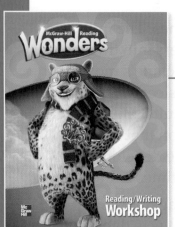

Reading/Writing Workshop

OBJECTIVES

CCSS Acquire and use accurately grade-appropriate general academic and domain-specific words and phrases, including those that signal precise actions, emotions, or states of being (e.g., *quizzed, whined, stammered*) and that are basic to a particular topic (e.g., *wildlife, conservation,* and *endangered* when discussing animal preservation). **L.4.6**

ACADEMIC LANGUAGE

- *democracy, legislation*
- Cognates: *democracia, legislación*

MINILESSON 10 Mins

Words in Context

Model the Routine

Introduce each vocabulary word using the Vocabulary Routine found on the Visual Vocabulary Cards.

Visual Vocabulary Cards

Vocabu...
Define:
Example:
Ask:

Vocabulary Routine

<u>Define:</u> A **democracy** is a government that is run by the people who live under it.

<u>Example:</u> In a democracy, it is important for people to vote during an election.

<u>Ask:</u> How is a democracy different from a government ruled by a king?

Definitions

→ **amendments** **Amendments** are formal changes made according to official procedures.

→ **commitment** A **commitment** is a sense of obligation toward something.

→ **compromise** To **compromise** means to reach agreement by having each side give up part of its demands.

→ **eventually** **Eventually** means in the end or finally.

→ **legislation** **Legislation** means laws that are made or passed.
Cognate: *legislación*

→ **privilege** A **privilege** is a special right or benefit held by a certain group of people.
Cognate: *privilegio*

→ **version** A **version** is an account given in a particular way.
Cognate: *versión*

Talk About It

Have partners look at each picture and definition. Ask them to choose three words and write questions for their partner to answer.

Go Digital

democracy

Use Visual Glossary

CCSS Words to Know

Vocabulary

Use the picture and the sentences to talk with a partner about each word.

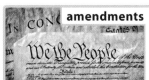

amendments

One of the **amendments** to the Constitution gave women the right to vote.

Why do we need amendments?

commitment

The two boys made a **commitment** to practice their song for the talent show.

What is a commitment you have made?

compromise

Sam and his dad agreed to **compromise** on when Sam would mow the lawn.

Describe a situation in which you felt you had to compromise.

democracy

In a **democracy**, it is important for people to vote during an election.

How is a democracy different from a government ruled by a King?

eventually

Grace knew that **eventually** the rain would finally stop.

What is a place that you would like to visit eventually?

legislation

Congress passed **legislation** protecting workers who are injured on the job.

Why might it be important to pass new legislation?

privilege

My grandmother feels that going out to dinner with her family once a week is a **privilege** she deserves.

What is a privilege you wish you had?

version

For this **version** of the movie *Cinderella*, we had to wear 3-D glasses.

What are some things that may have different versions?

Your Turn COLLABORATE

Pick three words. Write three questions for your partner to answer.

Go Digital! *Use the online visual glossary*

236

237

READING/WRITING WORKSHOP, pp. 236–237

ELL ENGLISH LANGUAGE LEARNERS SCAFFOLD

Beginning

Use Visuals *Let's look at the picture for* democracy. *The people in the picture are voting.* Gesture casting a vote. *They are voting to choose their leaders.* Ask: *Do people vote in a democracy?* (yes) Have students complete the frame: *People vote in a _____ .* (democracy) Correct students' pronunciation as needed.

Intermediate

Describe Have students describe the picture for *democracy*. Help them pronounce the word. Ask: *What makes a democracy special? Turn to a partner and explain why democracy is important.* Elicit details to support students' responses. Remind students that *democracy* in Spanish is *democracia*.

Advanced/High

Discuss Ask students to talk about the picture for *democracy* and use the word in a sentence. Ask: *Why is it important for people to vote in a democracy?* Have students discuss with a partner and share their ideas with the class. Correct responses for meaning when needed.

ON-LEVEL PRACTICE BOOK p. 151

democracy	commitment	privilege	legislation
version	eventually	amendments	compromise

Use a word from the box to answer each question. Then use the word in a sentence. Possible responses provided.

1. What word might describe an agreement reached by two different sides?
   compromise; I have a big family, so we often have to *compromise* to keep everyone happy.

2. What is a system of government where the people decide what happens?
   democracy; In the United States we are fortunate to have a *democracy.*

3. If there are formal changes made to a law, what are the changes called?
   amendments; Students should be familiar with the laws and *amendments* of our country.

4. What is another word for *finally*? _eventually_; After two hours of traveling, we *eventually* made it home.

5. If a community creates its own laws, what is it responsible for? _legislation_; The government passed *legislation* that gave its citizens equal rights.

6. What is another word for *a sense of obligation*? _commitment_; We made a *commitment* to meet every week until we completed the project.

7. What do you call a special right that a person has? _privilege_; Being able to use the school pool is a *privilege* for all students.

8. What is another word for *an account given in a particular way*?
   version; The Spanish *version* of the book has different pictures.

APPROACHING	BEYOND	ELL
p. 151	p. 151	p. 151

CCSS Shared Read Genre • Narrative Nonfiction

A WORLD WITHOUT RULES

? Essential Question

Why do we need government?

Read how government and laws help to protect us every day.

238

You may sometimes wonder if rules were made to keep you from having fun and to tell you what to do. But what if we had no rules at all? Nobody would tell you what to do ever again! Sounds great, right? Well, let's see what it's like to inhabit a world without rules. You just might change your mind!

A Strange Morning

Let's start at home. Your alarm clock goes off. Why hurry? Without rules you don't have to go to school. **Eventually** you wander downstairs and find your little brother eating cookies in the kitchen. Since there are no rules, you can have cookies for breakfast! But you wonder if you should have something sensible like a bowl of cereal. You reach a **compromise** (KOM•pruh•mighz) and crumble the cookies over your cereal. In this new world, you will not have to brush your teeth anymore. Of course, the next time you see the dentist, you may have a cavity.

A Community in Confusion

Now, you step outside. You decide to go to the playground because there's no law saying you have to go to school. No crossing guard stands at the corner to help you across the street. Without traffic laws, cars zip by at an alarming speed honking at each other, and there is not a police officer in sight. There is no safe alternate way to cross the street. Besides, once you see the playground, you may decide it is not worth the risk of getting hit by a car. Broken swings dangle from rusty chains. Trash cans overflow with plastic bottles, snack wrappers, and paper bags. A huge tree branch lies across the sliding board. As a result of all state and federal services being gone, nobody is in charge of taking care of the playground.

239

Reading/Writing Workshop

READING/WRITING WORKSHOP, pp. 238–239

Shared Read

Lexile 830   *TextEvaluator*™ 42

Connect to Concept: Our Government

Explain that "A World Without Rules" will give more information about why we need our government. Read "A World Without Rules" with students. Note the vocabulary words previously taught are highlighted in the text.

Close Reading

Reread Paragraph 2: Tell students that you are going to take a closer look at the section "A Strange Morning." Reread the paragraph together. Ask: *In a world without rules, why might it be bad to eat whatever you like?* Model how to cite evidence to answer the question.

I can use information from the text combined with my own knowledge to answer the question. The author says that in a world with no rules, no one can tell you what to do. So if you eat cookies for breakfast, you won't need to brush your teeth. The bad part is you could get a cavity from eating sugary foods and not brushing your teeth.

Reread Paragraph 3: Model how to ask and answer questions about the third paragraph. Remind students that asking and answering questions can help them understand the text.

The text says that in a world without laws, there's no school. What is so bad about not having laws? As I read on, I see that the playground is a mess and nobody has taken care of it. All of the swings are broken, and kids are not able to play.

Now think about trying to do all the other things you love. Want to go to the beach? The lifeguards will not be there to keep you safe. Want to play soccer in the park? Your state and local governments are not around to maintain the parks, so you'll never find a place to play. Feel like eating lunch outside? As a result of pollution, the air quality is so bad that you will probably have to wear a gas mask every day.

Have you ever thought about our country being invaded by another country? Remember, the government runs the army. Without the government, there is no army to protect us if another country decided to take over our country.

Back to Reality

Thankfully, that **version** of our world isn't real. We live in a **democracy** (di•MOK•ruh•see) where we have the **privilege** (PRIV•uh•lij) of voting for the people that we want to run the country. Our elected government passes **legislation** (lej•is•LAY•shuhn), or laws, meant to help and protect us. If the country outgrows an old law, then the government can pass **amendments** to the law. Community workers such as crossing guards, police officers, and lifeguards all work to keep you safe, while government agencies such as the Environmental Protection Agency have made a **commitment** to inspect the air and water for pollution. And don't forget the armed forces, which were created to protect our nation.

Our government and laws were designed to keep you safe and ensure you are treated as fairly as everyone else. Without them, the world would be a different place.

Make Connections
Talk about how government helps us maintain order and helps preserve our freedom.
ESSENTIAL QUESTION

What are some ways that the government protects you every day? TEXT TO SELF

240

241

READING/WRITING WORKSHOP, pp. 240–241

Make Connections

ESSENTIAL QUESTION

Encourage students to go back into the text for evidence as they talk about how government helps maintain order and protects people's freedom. Ask students to think of other ways government helps them and to explain why voting is important.

Continue Close Reading

Use the following lessons for focused rereadings.

→ Ask and Answer Questions, T18–T19

→ Text Structure: Cause and Effect, T20–T21

→ Narrative Nonfiction, T22–T23

→ Latin Roots, T24–T25

A C T Access Complex Text

▶ **Connection of Ideas**

Students may need help understanding the transition back to the real world in the section "Back to Reality" on page 240. Reread that section with students.

→ *What does the heading "Back to Reality" tell you?* (Now we're back in the real world.)

→ *What is the main difference between the real world and the other version?* (The real world has rules, but the other version does not.)

→ Explain that the author uses the last section to show how things are a lot better than they would be without laws.

Comprehension Strategy

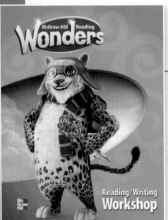

Reading/Writing Workshop

OBJECTIVES

CCSS Refer to details and examples in a text when explaining what the text says explicitly and when drawing inferences from the text. **RI.4.1**

CCSS Explain events, procedures, ideas, or concepts in a historical, scientific, or technical text, including what happened and why, based on specific information in the text. **RI.4.3**

Ask and answer questions about difficult sections of text to increase understanding.

ACADEMIC LANGUAGE

ask and answer questions, narrative nonfiction

MINILESSON
10 Mins

Ask and Answer Questions

1 Explain

Explain that when students read narrative nonfiction, they may come across unfamiliar words, facts, and ideas. Remind students that they can ask questions before, during, and after they read to help them understand and remember the information in the text. They can use what they know, along with information in the text, to answer their questions.

→ Good readers ask questions about something they do not understand and then look for answers.

→ When they encounter a difficult section of text, students can ask questions to help them understand it. They may need to reread to find the answers to their questions.

→ Often, students will find that asking and answering questions will improve their comprehension of informational texts.

Point out that the process of asking questions and looking for answers will help students focus on important information and details in a text.

2 Model Close Reading: Text Evidence

Model how asking and answering questions can help students understand the role of the Environmental Protection Agency. Reread the first paragraph under "Back to Reality" on page 240 of "A World Without Rules." Explain that one of the EPA's roles is to inspect our air and water and make sure they are clean.

3 Guided Practice of Close Reading

COLLABORATE

Have students work in pairs to answer this question: Why do we have traffic laws? Direct them to the first paragraph under "A Community in Confusion" on page 239 to find the answer. Then have partners come up with two more questions of their own and reread to find the answers.

Go Digital

View "A World Without Rules"

Comprehension Strategy

Ask and Answer Questions

When you read informational text, you may come across facts and ideas that are new to you. Stop and ask yourself questions to help you understand and remember the information. Then read the text closely to find the answers.

 Find Text Evidence

When you first read the "Back to Reality" section in a "A World Without Rules," you may have asked yourself what role the Environmental Protection Agency has in keeping people safe.

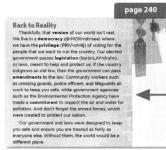

page 240

Back to Reality
  Thankfully, that **version** of our world isn't real. We live in a **democracy** (di•MOK•ruh•see) where we have the **privilege** (PRIV•uh•lij) of voting for the people that we want to run the country. Our elected government passes **legislation** (lej•is•LAY•shuhn), or laws, meant to help and protect us. If the country outgrows an old law, then the government can pass **amendments** to the law. Community workers such as crossing guards, police officers, and lifeguards all work to keep you safe, while government agencies such as the Environmental Protection Agency have made a **commitment** to inspect the air and water for pollution. And don't forget the armed forces, which were created to protect our nation.
  Our government and laws were designed to keep you safe and ensure you are treated as fairly as everyone else. Without them, the world would be a different place.

As I read on, I found the answer to my question. The Environmental Protection Agency's role is to inspect our air and water and make sure that they are clean.

Your Turn COLLABORATE

Think of two questions about "A World Without Rules." Then read to find the answers. As you read, remember to use the strategy Ask and Answer Questions.

242

READING/WRITING WORKSHOP, p. 242

 ENGLISH LANGUAGE LEARNERS SCAFFOLD

Beginning	Intermediate	Advanced/High
Actively Engage Point to and say *Environmental Protection Agency.* Explain that the agency is part of the government that helps inspect our air and water for pollution. Define the words *inspect* and *pollution.* Have students role play inspecting the air and water. Ask: *Is pollution good or bad?*	**Describe** Reread "Back to Reality." Have students find the Environmental Protection Agency in the text. Ask: *What is the Environmental Protection Agency? What does the agency do?* Point out why the text is difficult. The author describes the agency's responsibilities to show how it helps keep communities safe and why we need the agency.	**Discuss** Have partners reread "Back to Reality." Elicit why the text is difficult. Ask: *Why does the author mention the Environmental Protection Agency? How does the agency help communities? Turn to a partner and explain.* If necessary, ask additional questions to help students understand the agency's role.

 **Monitor and Differentiate**

 Quick Check

Do students ask and answer questions about sections of text they do not understand? Do they reread to answer their questions?

Small Group Instruction

If No →	Approaching Level	Reteach p. T40
	ELL	Develop p. T56
If Yes →	On Level	Review p. T48
	Beyond Level	Extend p. T52

ON-LEVEL PRACTICE BOOK pp. 153–154

Read the passage. Use the ask and answer questions strategy to understand difficult parts of the text.

We the People

11	Ms. Quibble stood by the chalkboard in front of her fourth-grade
22	class. "Who can tell me why the American colonies wanted to
30	separate from England and become their own country?"
40	The class was quiet. Some students scribbled in their notebooks
52	or shuffled their feet. Finally, a single hand shot up. Ms. Quibble
57	adjusted her spectacles. "Yes, Kwan?"
65	"People wanted to separate because they wanted liberty,"
78	Kwan said. "They felt that they didn't have a voice in the British government."
79	"Very good!" Ms. Quibble said. "What was the name of the
90	document that declared the colonies' freedom?"
96	Kwan was the only volunteer. "It was the Declaration of
106	Independence," she said.
109	"Kwan, I can tell you will ace this test." Ms. Quibble sounded
121	impressed. "I *highly* suggest that everyone else study during lunch."
131	Sam Jones ran to catch up with Kwan after class. "You sure know a
145	lot about history," he said.
150	"That's because I'm studying for my naturalization exam. I've been
160	memorizing a lot about America," she said.
167	"Your *what* exam?" Sam asked.
172	"It's a test to become an American citizen," Kwan said. "My
183	parents have been studying with me for months. We are so excited for
196	the chance to become citizens!"

APPROACHING pp. 153–154	BEYOND pp. 153–154	ELL pp. 153–154

→ Comprehension Skill

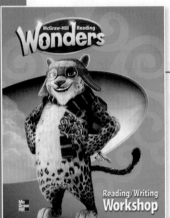

Reading/Writing Workshop

OBJECTIVES

CCSS Describe the overall structure (e.g., chronology, comparison, cause/effect, problem/solution) of events, ideas, concepts, or information in a text or part of a text. **RI.4.5**

Identify cause-and-effect relationships.

ACADEMIC LANGUAGE

• *cause, effect, signal words*

• Cognates: *causa, efecto*

SKILLS TRACE

TEXT STRUCTURE

Introduce Unit 1 Week 3

Review Unit 1 Weeks 4, 6; Unit 2 Week 6; Unit 3 Week 6; Unit 4 Weeks 1, 4; Unit 5 Weeks 3, 4, 5, 6; Unit 6 Week 6

Assess Units 1, 4, 5

MINILESSON 10 Mins

Text Structure: Cause and Effect

1 Explain

Explain that authors use text structures to organize the information in a text. When explaining events, procedures, ideas, or concepts, they may use a cause-and-effect text structure to present information that explains how or why something happens. A cause is why something happens. An effect is what happens as a result.

→ To find a cause-and-effect relationship, students should look for an event or action that causes something to happen. Then students can identify the effect, or what happens as a result.

→ Signal words and phrases such as *because*, *so*, *since*, and *as a result* often indicate cause-and-effect relationships.

→ Sometimes cause-and-effect relationships occur in a chain, with each cause and effect bringing about a related cause and effect. The example of a row of dominoes being knocked over may help students visualize this type of relationship.

2 Model Close Reading: Text Evidence

Identify the cause-and-effect relationships in the section "A Strange Morning" on page 239. Then model using the information on the graphic organizer to explain these relationships.

 Analytical Writing **Write About Reading: Paraphrase** Model for students how to use the notes from the graphic organizer to paraphrase the cause-and-effect relationships in the section "A Strange Morning."

3 Guided Practice of Close Reading

 COLLABORATE Have students work in pairs to complete a graphic organizer for the section "A Community in Confusion" on pages 239 and 240 of "A World Without Rules," going back into the text to find cause-and-effect relationships. Remind students to look for signal words to help them find causes and effects. Discuss each relationship as students complete their graphic organizers.

 Analytical Writing **Write About Reading: Summary** Ask pairs to work together to write a summary of "A Community in Confusion." Tell students to refer to their graphic organizers as they write their summaries. Select pairs of students to share their summaries with the class.

Go Digital

Present the Lesson

Comprehension Skill **CCSS**

Cause and Effect

Authors use text structure to organize the information in a nonfiction work. Cause and effect is one kind of text structure. A cause is why something happens. An effect is what happens. Signal words such as *because, so, since,* and *as a result* can help you identify cause-and-effect relationships.

Find Text Evidence

When I reread the section "A Strange Morning" on page 239, I will look for causes and effects. I will also look for signal words.

Cause	→	Effect
Without rules	→	You don't have to go to school
Without rules	→	You can have cookies for breakfast.
You don't have to brush your teeth.	→	You may get a cavity.

The effect is what happens as a result of an action.

Your Turn COLLABORATE

Reread "A Community in Confusion" on pages 239–240. Identify the causes and effects. List them in the graphic organizer.

Go Digital!
Use the interactive graphic organizer

243

READING/WRITING WORKSHOP, p. 243

ELL ENGLISH LANGUAGE LEARNERS SCAFFOLD

Beginning

Recognize Write *because, since,* and *so* on the board. Explain that these words signal cause-and-effect relationships. Reread: *Since there are no rules, you can have cookies for breakfast!* Have students identify the signal word. Then have them fill in the frame: _____ *there are no rules, students don't have to go to school.* (Since) Repeat with other cause-and-effect relationships.

Intermediate

Describe Have partners reread "A Strange Morning" to describe the cause-and-effect relationships. Ask: *What happens when there are no rules?* Encourage students to look for signal words. Have them fill in the frames. *The cause is _____.* (there are no rules) *The effect is _____.* (Students do not have to go to school. It's okay to have cookies for breakfast.)

Advanced/High

Expand Ask students to work with partners to find cause-and-effect relationships in "A Strange Morning." Ask: *How do signal words help you find causes and effects?* (Signal words help you make connections between events.) Elicit how a cause-and-effect text structure helps them understand the text.

Monitor and *Differentiate*

 Quick Check

As students complete the graphic organizer, do they determine the cause-and-effect relationships? Can they identify signal words?

⬇

Small Group Instruction

If No →	Approaching Level	Reteach p. T47
	ELL	Develop p. T56
If Yes →	On Level	Review p. T51
	Beyond Level	Extend p. T55

ON-LEVEL PRACTICE BOOK pp. 153–155

A. Reread the passage and answer the questions.
Possible responses provided.

1. What is the cause in the following sentence from the passage?
People wanted to separate because they wanted liberty.

People wanted liberty.

2. What is the effect in the following sentence from the passage?
People wanted to separate because they wanted liberty.

People wanted to separate from England.

3. In paragraphs 8–10, what is the cause of the situation Kwan describes? What is the effect?

The cause is that Kwan and her parents have been studying for the

naturalization exam. The effect is that they might have the chance to

become citizens.

B. Work with a partner. Read the passage aloud. Pay attention to phrasing and rate. Stop after one minute. Fill out the chart.

	Words Read	–	Number of Errors	=	Words Correct Score
First Read		–		=	
Second Read		–		=	

APPROACHING pp. 153–155	BEYOND pp. 153–155	ELL pp. 153–155

→ Genre: Informational Text

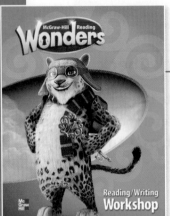

Reading/Writing Workshop

 MINILESSON 10 Mins

Narrative Nonfiction

Go Digital

Present the Lesson

 OBJECTIVES

CCSS Explain how an author uses reasons and evidence to support particular points in a text. **RI.4.8**

CCSS By the end of the year, read and comprehend informational texts, including history/social studies, science, and technical texts, in the grades 4–5 text complexity band proficiently, with scaffolding as needed at the high end of the range. **RI.4.10**

Recognize the characteristics and text features of narrative nonfiction.

 ACADEMIC LANGUAGE

narrative nonfiction, headings

1 Explain

Share with students the following key characteristics of **narrative nonfiction**.

→ Narrative nonfiction is a type of nonfiction that is written in the form of a story. It is told by a narrator and presents information in an engaging way.

→ The information is usually presented in a logical order. The author may use cause-and-effect relationships to present information.

→ Narrative nonfiction may express the author's opinion about the subject. The author supports his or her opinion with facts and examples.

→ Narrative nonfiction sometimes includes text features such as headings.

2 Model Close Reading: Text Evidence

Model identifying the elements of narrative nonfiction on page 239 of "A World Without Rules." Point out the text features.

Boldface Words Point out the word *compromise* in the section "A Strange Morning." Explain that key words that are important for understanding the selection are often boldfaced for emphasis.

Pronunciations Point out the pronunciation that follows the word *compromise*. Have students use the pronunciation to sound out the word. Ask: *Why would an author want to help the reader pronounce the word?*

3 Guided Practice of Close Reading

 COLLABORATE

Have students work with partners to discuss the author's opinion of rules and government. Partners should reread "A World Without Rules" to find reasons and text evidence that support this opinion. Then have them share their work with the class.

Genre Informational Text

Narrative Nonfiction

"A World Without Rules" is narrative nonfiction.

Narrative nonfiction:
- Is told in the form of a story.
- May express the author's opinion about the subject.
- Presents facts and includes text features.

 Find Text Evidence

"A World Without Rules" is narrative nonfiction. The author tells a story and includes text features. The author also expresses an opinion and supports it with facts and examples.

page 239

Text Features

Boldface Words Boldface words show key words in the text.

Pronunciations Pronunciations show how to sound out unfamiliar words.

Your Turn COLLABORATE

Reread "A World Without Rules." What is the author's opinion of government? Find text evidence to support your answer.

244

READING/WRITING WORKSHOP, p. 244

A C T Access Complex Text

▶ **Purpose**

Students may need help understanding that the author's purpose is to both entertain and inform. Ask:

→ *Why do you think the author wrote "A World Without Rules" in the form of a story?* (to entertain the reader)

→ *How do you know the author's purpose is also to inform the reader?* (The author includes information, such as facts and details, within the story.)

ON-LEVEL PRACTICE BOOK p. 156

An Interview with a State Representative

"I know that your main responsibilities are writing bills and voting them into effect. Do you have any other responsibilities?" I asked the representative.

"Like every other representative, I serve on two **committees** (kuh•MIT•tees)," he told me.

"What does a committee do?" I asked.

"A committee is a group of Congress members. They study a specific subject, like the military or education, and become experts on that subject. When a bill related to that subject is written, the committee reads the bill. Then it reports to Congress on the bill. Each committee provides valuable advice about changes that should be made to bills before they are passed."

Answer the questions about the text.

1. How do you know this text is narrative nonfiction?
   The author tells a story that includes facts.

2. What text features are included in this piece of narrative nonfiction?
   a boldface word; a pronunciation

3. Choose one text feature. How does it add to your understanding of this text?
   Possible response: The boldface word, *committees*, shows the reader
   that it is an important concept in the text.

4. What opinion does the author express in the text?
   Possible response: The author thinks that committees provide valuable
   advice.

APPROACHING p. 156	BEYOND p. 156	ELL p. 156

→ Vocabulary Strategy

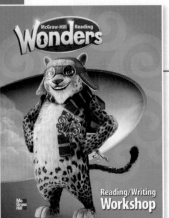

Reading/Writing Workshop

OBJECTIVES

CCSS Use common, grade-appropriate Greek and Latin affixes and roots as clues to the meaning of a word (e.g., *telegraph, photograph, autograph*). **L.4.4b**

CCSS Consult reference materials (e.g., dictionaries, glossaries, thesauruses), both print and digital, to find the pronunciation and determine or clarify the precise meaning of key words and phrases. **L.4.4c**

ACADEMIC LANGUAGE
Latin roots

SKILLS TRACE

LATIN ROOTS

Introduce Unit 4 Week 1

Review Unit 4 Weeks 1, 3; Unit 5 Week 5

Assess Unit 4

MINILESSON
10 Mins

Latin Roots

1 Explain

Explain to students that Latin roots can help them figure out the meanings of unfamiliar words.

→ Students can look for familiar Latin roots within a word to help them figure out part or all of a word's meaning.

→ Provide a list of common Latin roots: *dent* means "tooth"; *commun* means "common"; and *spect* means "look." Tell students that if one of these roots is part of a longer word, then the root's meaning can help them determine the word's meaning.

2 Model Close Reading: Text Evidence

Model using a Latin root to figure out the meaning of *alternate* in the third paragraph on page 239 of "A World Without Rules." Explain that the Latin root *alter* means "other," and use that meaning to determine the definition of *alternate*.

3 Guided Practice of Close Reading

Have students work in pairs to identify the Latin roots in *dentist, community*, and *inspect* in "A World Without Rules." Have partners use the Latin roots and their meanings to determine the words' meanings.

> **Use Reference Sources**
>
> **Print and Digital Dictionaries** Have students check an online or print dictionary and compare the meanings they find there for *dentist, community*, and *inspect* with the meanings they came up with. Explain that a dictionary shows the root words in Greek, Latin, and other ancient languages from which our modern words are derived. Point out these word origins in each entry.
>
> Have students identify the Latin origins in each dictionary entry for *dentist, community*, and *inspect*. Then have them find the pronunciation and the part of speech.

Go Digital

Present the Lesson

Vocabulary Strategy CCSS

Latin Roots

Knowing Latin roots can help you figure out the meanings of unfamiliar words. Look for these Latin roots as you read "A World Without Rules."

dent = tooth   commun = common   spect = look

Find Text Evidence

When I read the third paragraph on page 239, in the section "A Community in Confusion," I see the word alternate. *The Latin root* alter *means* other. *This will help me figure out what* alternate *means.*

There is no safe alternate way to cross the street.

Your Turn   COLLABORATE

Use context clues and Latin roots to figure out the meanings of these words in "A World Without Rules."
dentist, *page 239*
community, *page 240*
inspect, *page 240*

245

READING/WRITING WORKSHOP, p. 245

Monitor and *Differentiate*

✔ Quick Check

Can students identify and use Latin roots to determine the meanings of *dentist, community,* and *inspect*?

Small Group Instruction

If No →	Approaching Level	Reteach p. T45
	ELL	Develop p. T61
If Yes →	On Level	Review p. T50
	Beyond Level	Extend p. T54

ENGLISH LANGUAGE LEARNERS SCAFFOLD

Beginning

Clarify the Meaning Point out the words *dentist, community,* and *inspect*. Read the sentences where the words appear and define each word for students. Help students replace the words with words they already know. Point out the cognates: dentist/ *dentista*; community/ *comunidad*; inspect/ *inspeccionar*.

Intermediate

Derive Meaning Write the word *community* on the board, along with the root *commun*. Say: *The Latin root* commun *means* common. *The context clue* community workers *refers to people who work in a common area.* Have partners find the meanings of the words *dentist* and *inspect* using Latin roots.

Advanced/High

Discuss Write the words *dentist, community,* and *inspect* on the board. Circle the Latin roots and go over the meaning of each. Have partners look for context clues in the text and discuss how the clues along with the Latin roots helped them understand the meanings of the words.

ON-LEVEL PRACTICE BOOK p. 157

Latin Root	Meaning
commun	common
mem	remember
nat	to be from
scrib	write
spect	look

A. Look at each word below and identify the Latin root. Circle the roots and write the meaning of each word. Use the information above to help you. Possible responses provided.

1. community — common group of people
2. scribbled — written quickly or carelessly
3. spectacles — eyeglasses
4. naturalization — process of becoming a citizen
5. memorizing — remembering, learning by heart
6. inspected — looked at carefully

B. Using what you know about the roots spect and scrib, write the meaning of each word below. Use a dictionary, if necessary.

7. spectator

a person who looks on or watches

8. inscribe

to write on or engrave something

APPROACHING p. 157	BEYOND p. 157	ELL p. 157

Develop Comprehension

Literature Anthology

See How They Run

Text Complexity Range

Lexile

740 ▲ 1010
870

TextEvaluator™

23 ▲ 51
42

Options for Close Reading

→ Whole Class
→ Small Group
→ Independent

CCSS Genre · Narrative Nonfiction

SEE HOW

? Essential Question
Why do we need government?
Read about the history of our government and the role of citizens.

📖 *Go Digital!*

270

A C T Access Complex Text

What makes this text complex?

▶ **Connection of Ideas**
▶ **Sentence Structure**
▶ **Specific Vocabulary**
▶ **Genre**
▶ **Purpose**

▶ Connection of Ideas

Point out the title on pages 270–271. Have students connect the title to the illustration on page 270. Remind students that ideas in a selection are not always directly stated.

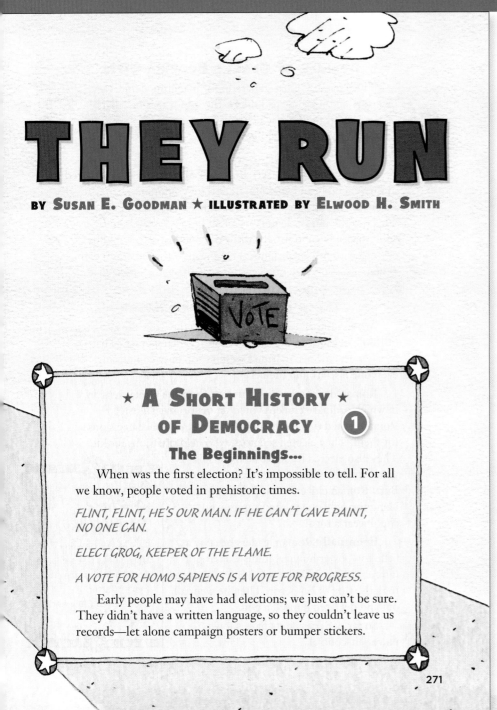

THEY RUN

BY SUSAN E. GOODMAN ★ ILLUSTRATED BY ELWOOD H. SMITH

★ A SHORT HISTORY ★ OF DEMOCRACY ❶

The Beginnings...

When was the first election? It's impossible to tell. For all we know, people voted in prehistoric times.

FLINT, FLINT, HE'S OUR MAN. IF HE CAN'T CAVE PAINT, NO ONE CAN.

ELECT GROG, KEEPER OF THE FLAME.

A VOTE FOR HOMO SAPIENS IS A VOTE FOR PROGRESS.

Early people may have had elections; we just can't be sure. They didn't have a written language, so they couldn't leave us records—let alone campaign posters or bumper stickers.

271

LITERATURE ANTHOLOGY, pp. 270–271

Predictive Writing

Have students read the title, preview the headings and illustrations, and write their predictions about what this selection will be about. Encourage them to share what they know about democracy and voting.

ESSENTIAL QUESTION

Ask a student to read aloud the Essential Question. Have students discuss what information they expect to learn.

Note Taking: Use the Graphic Organizer

As students read the selection, ask them to take notes by filling in the graphic organizer on **Your Turn Practice Book page 152** to record examples of cause and effect.

❶ Text Features: Headings

What does the first heading say? (A Short History of Democracy) What does the subheading say? (The Beginnings) What will the first section of the selection be about? (the beginnings of democracy)

→ *Look at the donkey and the elephant on page 270. What are they holding?* (signs that say "Vote for Me!") *What do you think the word* Run *in the title means?* (to try to get elected) *How is this definition different from the one we might usually associate with* run? (The more common definition is "to move fast on foot.")

ELL Discuss the heading, "A Short History of Democracy." Point out the cognates history/*historia* and democracy/*democracia*.

→ *What are we going to read about?* (democracy)

→ *What do we already know about a democracy?* (People can vote; people choose their leaders.)

LITERATURE ANTHOLOGY **T25B**

Develop Comprehension

2 Author's Craft: Word Choice

The word *because* can signal a cause-and-effect relationship. Using the word *because*, paraphrase the cause-and-effect relationship given in the first sentence. (Because Greeks had the best word for democracy, they get credit for developing it.)

3 Skill: Cause and Effect

Who were the voters in ancient Greece? (citizens) How did people become citizens? Because only citizens could vote, how many people in ancient Greece could vote? Add the information to your graphic organizer.

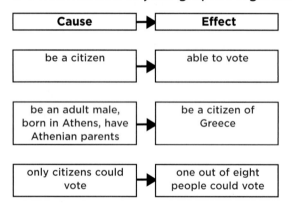

Cause	→	Effect
be a citizen	→	able to vote
be an adult male, born in Athens, have Athenian parents	→	be a citizen of Greece
only citizens could vote	→	one out of eight people could vote

Beware of Greeks Bearing Gifts

2 The ancient Greeks get credit for inventing democracy, probably because they had the best word for it. The "demo" part comes from *demos*, which means "the people." "Cracy" comes from *kratein*, meaning "to rule."

Rule by the people.

3 Starting in 510 B.C., the citizens of Athens, Greece, gathered in the Assembly and voted on important community issues. Each one had an equal voice in deciding what would happen. This was the purest democracy of all time—sort of. Only adult males, born in Athens with Athenian parents, could be citizens with full legal rights. That meant only one out of eight Athenians could vote on decisions that affected all their lives.

There's No Place Like Rome

Around the same time and a little to the west, the city of Rome began working on its **version** of democracy. That is, when its citizens or armies weren't too busy conquering everyone else around them.

Roman democracy was different from the Greek version, in which ordinary citizens voted on major issues. Instead Romans voted to pick the people who would make decisions for them. They elected senators, who held their jobs for life. They also elected leaders called consuls, who controlled the army and created laws. But a Roman citizen's best **privilege** was being the only one in the Empire who could wear a toga!

Eventually Roman leaders became a little too power hungry. Julius Caesar got himself declared Dictator for Life. Augustus took the title of Emperor. Then he went all out and declared himself a god.

So far our presidents have shown more self-control.

A Place in History
Talk about power—both Julius Caesar and Augustus named months after themselves (July and August).

272

A C T   Access Complex Text

▶ Connection of Ideas

Help students synthesize the information they read to understand how our democracy came to be.

→ *What was the difference between Greek democracy and Roman democracy?* (The ancient Greeks allowed male Athenian citizens to vote on community issues. The Romans elected senators to vote on important issues for citizens.)

→ *What was important to our Founding Fathers as they created our American democracy?* (The Founding Fathers wanted a government that would give the people a voice in how the country would be ruled. This is why they examined and borrowed ideas from the Greeks, Romans, and British.)

1,800 Years Later—Here Comes American Democracy

George Washington and the rest of our Founding Fathers borrowed bits and pieces from past democracies to create our own. They named our Senate after the Roman Senate. They adopted a British idea from the thirteenth century, saying that the government must respect a citizen's legal rights.

George and his crew wanted a government where people had some say in how to rule the country—but not too much. They didn't trust all their fellow Americans, especially those without much education. So they rejected the Greek method of having citizens vote directly on laws. Decisions would be made by people who "represented" the citizens instead, just like in the Roman Republic. **④**

STOP AND CHECK

Ask and Answer Questions
Why did the Founding Fathers reject the Greek method of voting? Go back to the text to find the answer.

273

LITERATURE ANTHOLOGY, pp. 272–273

④ Genre: Narrative Nonfiction

What about this selection helps to identify it as narrative nonfiction? (So far, the information is in chronological order. The selection has text features such as headings and captions.)

STOP AND CHECK

Ask and Answer Questions Why did the Founding Fathers reject the Greek method of voting? (They didn't trust all their fellow Americans.)

Teacher Think Aloud Before I answer the question, I'll ask myself "What was the Greek method of voting?" On page 273, the text describes the Greek method of voting as having all citizens vote directly on laws. Now I will ask, "Why didn't the Founding Fathers want all citizens to vote directly on laws?" The second sentence in the second paragraph says that the Founding Fathers didn't trust all their fellow Americans, especially those without education. The Founding Fathers rejected the Greek method of voting because they didn't trust all of their fellow Americans to vote directly on laws.

ELL Use the illustration to reinforce the concept of borrowing ideas from other democracies. Point to the word *borrowed* on page 273. *The author says that "our Founding Fathers borrowed bits and pieces from past democracies to create our own." Look at the illustration on page 273.*

→ *From which democracy is George borrowing ideas?* (Roman) *Did the Founding Fathers borrow from the Greek and Roman democracies?* (yes)

Encourage students to identify cognates on pages 272–273: vote/*votar;* decision/*decisión;* education/*educación;* represent/*representar.* Ask if anyone can find other cognates. (president/*presidente;* republic/*república*)

Develop Comprehension

❺ Skill: Cause and Effect

What did the Founding Fathers do when they realized that the Constitution could be improved? (They wrote the Bill of Rights.) What reason does the text give for African Americans getting denied the right to vote in the South? (People's beliefs and values change too slowly.) How did African Americans gain full voting rights in the South? (the Civil Rights Movement of the 1960s) Add the information to your graphic organizer.

Cause	→	Effect
The Constitution was not perfect.	→	The Bill of Rights was written.
People's beliefs and values change too slowly.	→	African Americans were often denied the right to vote in the South.
Civil Rights Movement of the 1960s	→	African Americans gained full voting rights.

What Did Ben Say?

Shortly after the Constitutional Convention ended, a woman asked Benjamin Franklin what kind of government the Founding Fathers created. Franklin's answer? "A republic, madam, if you can keep it." In other words, our kind of government needs citizens who care enough to stay informed and take part. In other, other words... *VOTE!*

Library of Congress Prints and Photographs Division [LC-USZ62-25564]

In 1787, the Founding Fathers locked themselves up for four months to write our Constitution. Coming up with this description of our new government wasn't easy. They all had different ideas and had to **compromise**. George Washington's face often wore its "Valley Forge look."

Here's what they came up with—a national government with three branches. Our Congress (the legislative branch) has two parts or houses: the Senate and the House of Representatives. Congress can make laws to raise taxes, improve citizens' lives, and defend the country. The president heads the executive branch. He (and someday soon, maybe she) carries out laws and is head of the military. He also appoints judges to the Supreme Court, part of our judicial branch. The court's job is to enforce existing laws and decide if the other two branches are obeying the Constitution.

274

A C T Access Complex Text

▶ Sentence Structure

Point out the first use of parentheses on page 274. Explain to students that writers use parentheses in different ways. They can be used to provide additional information, asides, or commentary. Usually, any text in parentheses can be removed from a sentence without changing the sentence's meaning.

→ *What does the information in the parentheses tell?* (Congress is the legislative branch.)

→ Point out the next use of parentheses in the paragraph. *Why does the writer say "and someday soon, maybe she"?* (All presidents so far have been male, but a female could become president as early as the next election.)

Getting Better All the Time

Is the Constitution a perfect plan? Nope, but the people who wrote it were smart enough to know that. They improved it right away by writing the Bill of Rights, the first ten **amendments** (additions) to the Constitution. We've been making it better ever since. **⑤**

The Good News: The United States was the first modern democracy with an elected government protecting the freedom and rights of its citizens.

The Bad News: In the beginning, only white men who owned land could vote.

The Good News: In 1856, white men who didn't own land got that right.

The Bad News: Everyone else was still left out in the cold. Changing beliefs and values isn't easy; it takes lots of thought and struggle. **⑥**

The Good News: African American and other nonwhite men began voting in 1870.

The Bad News: People's beliefs and values change too slowly. An African American's right to vote was often denied in the South and parts of the North until the civil rights movement of the 1960s.

The Good News: American women of all races got the vote in 1920.

The Bad News: Women in New Zealand, Australia, Finland, Norway, Canada, Estonia, England, Ireland, the Soviet Union, Austria, Czechoslovakia, Germany, Hungary, Armenia, Azerbaijan, Poland, Luxembourg, and Holland were able to vote before them. At least the United States beat Switzerland, where women couldn't vote until 1971!

The Good News: Native Americans began voting in 1924.

The Bad News: Seems like a long wait, given that they were here first. What's more, some states banned them from voting until the 1940s.

The Good News: In 1971, the voting age was reduced to eighteen years old.

The Bad News: You've still got a while before you can vote.

The Good News: You have other ways to make your opinion heard. **⑦** Keep reading to find out what they are!

275

LITERATURE ANTHOLOGY, pp. 274–275

---

⑥ Author's Craft: Idioms

Look at the sentence "Everyone else was still left out in the cold." Can you identify an idiom, or a phrase that is not meant to be taken literally? ("left out in the cold") Turn to a partner and explain the actual meaning of the idiom. (to not be included in something)

⑦ Strategy: Make, Confirm, or Revise Predictions

Look at the last two sentences on page 275. Aside from voting, what other ways could you share your opinion? See if you can predict what suggestions the author will make. (Possible answer: I can tell adults and elected officials how I feel about certain issues. I can write a letter to a newspaper or magazine.)

 Use the illustration on page 274 to help students understand the concept of the three branches of government. Point out the cognates government/*gobierno*, legislative/*legislativo*, executive/*ejecutivo*, and judicial/*judicial*.

→ *Point to the branch that includes the president.* (Students should point to the word *executive* in the picture.)

→ *Point to the branch that includes Congress.* (Students should point to the word *legislative* in the picture.)

Develop Comprehension

8 Vocabulary: Latin Roots

Look at the word *communities* on page 276. Many English words have Latin roots. Understanding common Latin roots can help you understand unfamiliar words. The Latin root *commun* means "common." What does the word *communities* mean? (a group of people living together in a common place) With a partner, brainstorm other words that include the Latin root *commun*. (Possible answers: communicate, communication, commute)

★ UNCLE SAM WANTS YOU ★

Rx for Voting

8 When people are involved with their communities, their knowledge of politics grows. Their interest and **commitment** does too. That's true for kids as well as grown-ups.

Okay, you aren't old enough to vote, not even close. But you can still have a voice in our democracy.

Four million kids already cast ballots on Election Day. They're part of a program called Kids Voting USA in schools in twenty-eight states and Washington DC. True, their votes aren't counted in official tallies. But they're announced in schools and on local TV stations.

276

A C T Access Complex Text

▶ Specific Vocabulary

Review strategies for finding the meaning of an unfamiliar word, such as using context clues, word parts, or a dictionary. Point out the words *ballots* and *tallies* in the third paragraph on page 276.

→ *When do kids cast ballots?* (Election Day)

→ *What do people do on Election Day?* (They vote.)

→ *What are ballots?* (They are pieces of paper or records of a person's vote. Ballots are counted to see who wins an election.)

→ *Look at the word* tallies. *What other words in the sentence can help you understand its meaning?* ("votes aren't counted") *What are tallies?* (Tallies are counts, like a score.)

This program has another advantage. Kids get so excited that 3 to 5 percent more of their parents end up voting too.

That's where you come in, even if Kids Voting USA isn't in your school. You can make sure your parents are registered to vote. And you can make sure they actually do it.

How? Oh, come on. How do you get your parents to do anything? Drive you somewhere? Buy a new game? Let you stay up late?

You bug 'em!

So bug them about voting. Plaster a countdown calendar on the front door. Put reminders on their voice mail. E-mail too. If they say they're too tired on the Big Day, try a bribe (it works when they want something from you!). Offer to do the dishes if they go—but only if you're desperate!

STOP AND CHECK

Ask and Answer Questions
How does the Kids Voting USA program encourage people to vote? Go back to the text to find the answer.

277

LITERATURE ANTHOLOGY, pp. 276–277

STOP AND CHECK

Ask and Answer Questions How does the Kids Voting USA program encourage people to vote?

Teacher Think Aloud I read that this program gets kids involved in our democracy. But I wonder how the program affects adults. I'll go back to the text and find information about how the program encourages adults to vote.

Prompt students to apply the strategy in a Think Aloud by rereading and asking and answering questions to better understand the cause-and-effect relationship.

Student Think Aloud Before I reread, I ask myself "What does the Kids Voting USA program actually do?" The third paragraph on page 276 has the answer. Kids Voting USA is a program where kids vote on election day, but their votes are not officially counted. Next I ask, "How does the program encourage adults to vote?" In the next paragraph, I learn that kids involved in the program get so excited that more of their parents end up voting. Because the kids in the program are so involved, they encourage their parents to vote.

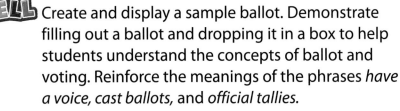 Create and display a sample ballot. Demonstrate filling out a ballot and dropping it in a box to help students understand the concepts of ballot and voting. Reinforce the meanings of the phrases *have a voice, cast ballots,* and *official tallies.*

→ *If I have a voice, can I speak for or against something?* (yes) *When I vote for a law or a leader, do I have a voice?* (yes)

→ *When someone casts a ballot, he or she is voting. What is another word for* cast a ballot? (vote)

→ *An official tally means an actual, or real, count.* Demonstrate a tally on paper or a board. *If ten people vote, how many votes are counted, or tallied?* (ten)

Develop Comprehension

9 Skill: Cause and Effect

Identify the main cause-and-effect relationship in the third paragraph. How would you paraphrase the cause and the effect? (Because kids worked hard, legislators signed a law to make the ladybug Massachusetts's official state insect.)

10 Skill: Make Inferences

Did New Hampshire's legislators think that a pumpkin is a type of fruit? (no) What do you think they thought it was? (a vegetable) Explain how you made this inference. (I know that most people probably think pumpkins are vegetables because they grow from plants on the ground and not in trees or bushes like most fruits. Also, the text says that the kids had to convince the legislators that pumpkins are fruits.)

Kids to the Rescue!

Bugging your parents is a good first step. Some kids are going even further. They are identifying issues and working on them. A recent report found that 55 percent of American kids volunteer. That's almost twice as many as adults.

Kids are becoming leaders. . .

Talk about bugging, a group of second graders decided that Massachusetts needed an official state insect. When they learned that any state resident could give legislators ideas for new laws, they got busy. Maybe it was the ladybug costumes they wore while visiting the state capitol. Maybe it was their speech saying ladybugs could be found all over the state. Whatever the reason, the legislature approved their **9** bill and the governor signed a law proclaiming the ladybug as Massachusetts's state insect.

Third and fourth graders did something similar for New Hampshire, which didn't have a state fruit. The hardest thing about that process was convincing legislators that the **10** pumpkin IS a fruit.

278

A C T Access Complex Text

▶ **Genre**

Point out the heading on page 278. Remind students that authors can use text features, such as headings, to organize chunks of information in a selection.

→ *What does the heading make you think of?* (Possible answers: superheroes, firemen and firewomen)

→ *How does the heading relate to the text?* (The text is about kids who have "come to the rescue" to fight pollution and suggest state symbols.)

→ *What do the pictures on pages 278–279 have to do with the heading and text?* (These kids are dressed as superheroes. They're "coming to the rescue" with the three things described in the text.)

At age seven, Shadia Wood learned that the Superfund bill would clean up New York's worst toxic waste sites. For seven years, Shadia and a group called Kids Against Pollution tried to convince lawmakers to pass this bill. She had a lemonade stand on the steps of the state capitol, selling drinks and "toxic dump" cake. Then she'd send the profits to the governor to help pay for the Superfund. Eventually TV and newspaper reporters noticed what she was doing. The Superfund bill became law in 2003. (There's nothing wrong with shaming grown-ups into good behavior.) **11**

279

LITERATURE ANTHOLOGY, pp. 278–279

11 Skill: Main Idea and Details

What do all the details on page 279 have in common? (They are all about Shadia Wood's work to convince lawmakers to pass the Superfund bill.) Determine the main idea on page 279 and paraphrase it with a partner. (Shadia Wood worked hard, raised money, and convinced lawmakers to pass a bill that improved the environment.)

SOCIAL STUDIES

CONNECT TO CONTENT
WORKING TOGETHER FOR CHANGE

Public service, voting, and volunteerism are all important responsibilities of citizens. By working together and stating their concerns, citizens can make their voices heard. Some might even run for public office to make a difference. Above, students read about how kids are volunteering and working together to create change in the government. They are solving community and state problems. On pages 280–281, students will read about student volunteers, voting, and suggested ways that they can bring about a change in their government. Make sure students can restate what they have learned about the importance of public service, voting, and volunteerism after they read the selection.

ELL Have students point to each picture as you say the words *ladybug* and *pumpkin*. Then have students complete the following sentence frames:

→ *The _____ is the official state insect of Massachusetts.* (ladybug)

→ *The _____ is the official state fruit of New Hampshire.* (pumpkin)

Develop Comprehension

12 **Skill: Cause and Effect**

Reread the first paragraph on page 280. What happened when Massachusetts's governor signed the bill? (Students began helping voters with computerized equipment.) **Why was the bill a "win-win-win situation"?** (Kids are better able to teach adults about computers. Kids got involved with the voting process. They also earned money.) **Add the information to your graphic organizer.**

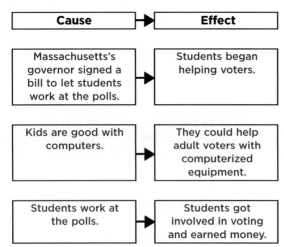

Cause	➡	Effect
Massachusetts's governor signed a bill to let students work at the polls.	➡	Students began helping voters.
Kids are good with computers.	➡	They could help adult voters with computerized equipment.
Students work at the polls.	➡	Students got involved in voting and earned money.

Imagine getting $135 to skip school and do good work? When Massachusetts's governor signed a bill to let sixteen- and seventeen-year-olds work at the polls, Boston-based students began helping voters with computerized equipment on Election Day. It's a win-win-win-win situation: kids know computers better than many adult voters; they get involved with voting; they get money. They are also being trained for the job. Our country will need them soon. The average poll worker is currently seventy-two years old.

In Boise, Idaho, kids ages fifteen and up are on committees governing the city. Some towns, like Linesville, Pennsylvania, have had eighteen-year-old mayors. Mayor at eighteen seems pretty great. But in California, Ohio, Rhode Island, Vermont, Washington, and Wisconsin, an eighteen-year-old can be governor.

280

A C T Access Complex Text

▶ Connection of Ideas

Guide students in connecting the information on pages 278–281.

→ *In what ways are kids becoming leaders?* (Kids are talking about issues, volunteering their time, giving ideas for new laws, and raising money for worthy causes. Young people are also getting involved in politics in some places by running for office or working at the polls.)

→ *Why is it important for kids to get involved with their communities?* (By getting involved with their communities, kids become aware of the political process. This allows them to help solve problems and make a difference in the lives of others. It encourages adults to vote, too.)

Sending a Message

If you see a problem in your community or have an idea of how to make things better, get active. Give a government leader a piece of your mind (the best part, please!).

- Speak up at a town meeting.
- Invite your mayor or another official to speak to your class about an important issue. Be ready to ask good questions and give your opinions.
- Set up a class trip to visit him or her.
- Write a letter or e-mail that identifies a problem. Tell how the problem affects you and your community. Write about the changes you'd like to see. Send your letter to the appropriate official in your town or to your state representative and senator or to your representative and senator in Congress or even to the governor or president.
- Write a letter and get people who agree with you to sign it too. Make sure you write your names and addresses clearly.
- Make a survey about the problem, write it up, and send it to the right official.

STOP AND CHECK

Summarize How can kids make their voices heard about community issues?

281

LITERATURE ANTHOLOGY, pp. 280–281

STOP AND CHECK

Summarize How can kids make their voices heard about community issues?

Student Think Aloud Students can do many things to become involved in our communities. We can make our voices heard by speaking at meetings and writing to or calling community officials. We can make a difference by volunteering.

Return to Predictions

Review students' predictions and purposes for reading. Ask them to answer the Essential Question. (We need government to protect people's rights, to make important decisions, and to represent individuals.)

▶ Purpose

Remind students that the purpose of this selection is to inform and persuade.

→ *What does the author want her readers to do?* (to get involved in the political process) *How do you know?* (There are many points in the selection where the author tells the reader exactly what to do and how to go about doing it.)

ELL Point out the cognates governor/*gobernador* and committee/*comité*.

→ *Who is the leader of our country?* (the president)
→ *Is a governor a leader of a state or country?* (state)
→ *A committee is a group of people who make decisions or help solve problems. What is another word for* committee? (group)

About the Author

Meet the Author and Illustrator

Susan E. Goodman and Elwood Smith

Have students read the biography of the author and illustrator. Ask:

→ How can reviewing and revising your writing help make you a better writer?

→ How might Elwood Smith's love of cartoon characters have influenced his style of drawing?

Author's Purpose

To Inform

Students may say that it is important to understand other types of government because parts of our own government were modeled after other societies.

Author's Craft

Voice

Explain that a writer's voice is the style in which an author writes. The author in *See How They Run* has a unique voice that makes the selection fun to read.

→ The author uses casual, contemporary language to discuss historical events: *Augustus took the title of Emperor. Then he went all out and declared himself a god.* (page 272)

→ The author uses informal language to add humor: *How do you get your parents to do anything? Drive you somewhere? Buy a new game? Let you stay up late? You bug 'em!* (page 277) Have students find other examples of humorous informal language in the selection.

ABOUT THE AUTHOR AND ILLUSTRATOR

Susan E. Goodman loved reading as a kid, but reading did not make her a good writer. That happened when she got a D- on a school paper. Goodman's teacher allowed her to rewrite it. That taught Goodman the importance of reviewing and revising anything she writes. And Susan Goodman has written a lot—more than 700 articles and several books!

Elwood Smith grew up with a love of cartoon characters and comic books. When he began drawing humorous illustrations as an adult, he remembered the comics he had loved as a child and tried to draw in that style. Smith also plays guitar in a rock band with other artists.

Author's Purpose

Why did the author explain the types of government used long ago before she explained the way that American democracy works?

282

LITERATURE ANTHOLOGY, pp. 282–283

RESPOND TO READING

Summarize

Identify the key details and summarize *See How They Run*. Information from your Cause and Effect Chart may help you.

Cause → Effect
→
→
→
→

Text Evidence

1. Why is *See How They Run* considered narrative nonfiction? Point out elements in the selection that help you identify the genre. **GENRE**

2. What caused Shadia Wood to speak up to government lawmakers? Describe what she did and the effect that her methods had. **CAUSE AND EFFECT**

3. Use context clues to figure out the meaning of the word *dictator* on page 272. Tell how knowing the Latin root "dict" helps you. **LATIN ROOTS**

4. Write about why our nation's government has three branches. **WRITE ABOUT READING**

Make Connections

How would our lives be different if we did not have a government? **ESSENTIAL QUESTION**

How does the government of the United States compare to other types of government around the world? Why do you think many people want to be part of a democracy? **TEXT TO WORLD**

283

Make Connections *Analytical Writing*

Essential Question Have partners work together to write about three ways in which things would be different without government. Ask partners to discuss their findings with the class.

Text to World Encourage students to research other forms of government in the world. After partners have discussed other ways of government, have them use a map to show the locations of the different types of government.

Respond to Reading

Summarize

Review with students the information from their graphic organizers. Model how to use the information in the charts to summarize *See How They Run*.

Analytical Writing **Write About Reading: Summarize**
Remind students that a summary of a story is a restatement of the key details of a text. Ask students to write a summary of the selection, using the cause-and-effect relationships they identified. Remind them that their summaries should be in the correct order, or sequence. Have students share their summaries with a partner.

Text Evidence

1. **Genre** <u>Answer</u> *See How They Run* gives facts and information in the format of a story structure. <u>Evidence</u> Historical events, such as the creation of governments in ancient Greece and ancient Rome, are narrated as if they were part of a story.

2. **Cause and Effect** <u>Answer</u> Shadia Wood learned that the Superfund bill would clean up toxic waste in New York, so she tried to get lawmakers to pass the bill. <u>Evidence</u> Shadia tried different methods to show how important the bill was. She sold lemonade and "toxic dump" cake on the steps of the state capitol. The bill became a law in 2003.

3. **Latin Roots** <u>Answer</u> *Dictator* probably means "a ruler who has too much power." <u>Evidence</u> The context clue "too power hungry" is a clue, as well as the fact that the Latin root *dict* means "speak."

Analytical Writing 4. **Write About Reading: Cause and Effect** The details on page 274 tell why the Founding Fathers came up with three branches of government.

Develop Comprehension

"The Birth of American Democracy"

Text Complexity Range

Lexile

| Literature Anthology | 740 | ▲ 830 | 1010 |

TextEvaluator™

| 23 | ▲ 43 | 51 |

Options for Close Reading

→ Whole Class

→ Small Group

→ Independent

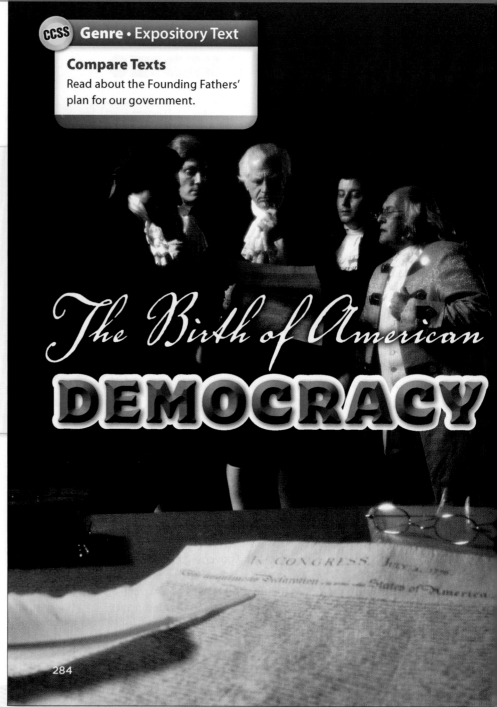

CCSS **Genre • Expository Text**

Compare Texts
Read about the Founding Fathers' plan for our government.

The Birth of American **DEMOCRACY**

284

A C T Access Complex Text

What makes this text complex?
▷ **Prior Knowledge**
▷ **Specific Vocabulary**

▷ Prior Knowledge

Explain to students that when the colonies declared their independence, Great Britain was a very powerful empire. Direct students' attention to the third paragraph on page 285.

Every Fourth of July, Americans celebrate the birthday of the United States. Fireworks and parades remind us that the thirteen colonies declared independence from Great Britain on July 4, 1776. That birthday took place in Philadelphia, Pennsylvania. There, the Second Continental Congress approved the Declaration of Independence. This document formed a new nation, the United States of America. The Declaration is almost like our country's original birthday card.

Our Founding Fathers

Five men, including John Adams, Thomas Jefferson, and Benjamin Franklin, wrote the Declaration of Independence. Jefferson wrote the first draft. His famous words sum up a basic American belief—"all men are created equal."

The men who signed the Declaration are called the Founding Fathers of our country. Signing the Declaration put the founders' lives in danger. They knew that their signatures made them traitors to Great Britain. They also knew that, if the colonies won the war, their names would go down in history.

Led by General George Washington, the colonists fought passionately for their freedom. After a long, bloody war, the British surrendered in 1781, and a peace treaty was signed in 1783. Our new nation was still a work in progress, however. Americans disagreed about how much power a federal, or central, government should have. Given that they had just won freedom from a powerful British king, Americans did not want their government to have too much power.

The Constitutional Convention

By 1787, the states were like separate countries. Each state printed its own money and made its own trade laws. The national government was weak and in debt from the war. In May 1787 each state sent delegates, people who represent others, to Philadelphia to attend a meeting called the Constitutional Convention. The delegates were to create a new plan for our government. George Washington was chosen as the president of the convention. **1**

285

LITERATURE ANTHOLOGY, pp. 284–285

Compare Texts *Analytical Writing*

Students will read an expository text on the forming of the United States government. Ask students to do a close reading of the text to understand the content. Encourage them to use the reread strategy or other strategies they know will help them. They will also take notes as they read. Then students will use the text evidence they gathered to compare this text with *See How They Run*.

1 Ask and Answer Questions

Why did Americans meet for the Constitutional Convention? Why did Americans disagree about the role of the federal government?

Analytical Writing **Write About Reading** With a partner, list the reasons why Americans disagreed about the role of federal government. (Americans had to fight a terrible war to win independence from Great Britain and their king. Americans were worried that the federal government would have too much power, just like in Great Britain. The Constitutional Convention was needed to create a plan for their government.)

→ *Why were the Founding Fathers in great danger?* (Signing the Declaration made them traitors to Great Britain. Great Britain was powerful and the colonies were small and separated.)

ELL Point to and say *independence*. Have students repeat. Point out its cognate *independencia*.

→ *What did Americans win after the war with Great Britain?* (independence)

→ Have students fill in the sentence frame: *Every Fourth of July, we celebrate our _____ from Great Britain.* (independence)

Develop Comprehension

2 Ask and Answer Questions

Why did smaller states disagree with larger states about the power to pass laws? How did they reach an agreement?

 Analytical Writing **Write About Reading** Fill out Graphic Organizer 26 to tell how the states came to a compromise. (Problems: Large states wanted more votes than smaller states; Smaller states thought this was not fair. Solution: Each state had two representatives in the Senate, while population determined the amount of each state's representatives in the House.)

3 Ask and Answer Questions

Why did some states first refuse to approve the Constitution? What happened to change their minds?

Work with a partner to summarize the problem and solution. (Some thought that the Constitution did not give enough power to the people, so James Madison wrote the Bill of Rights, which protected citizens' personal rights.)

One young delegate, James Madison, proposed ideas. After many debates, he compromised with the other delegates on the United States Constitution as the plan for our government. Thus, today James Madison is known as the "Father of the Constitution." Delegates from large and small states argued most about the power to pass legislation, or laws. States with large populations wanted more votes in a legislature. Small states did not think this was fair. By September of 1787, the states agreed on a system of checks and balances known as the three branches of government. In this system, no branch has too much power.

2

THREE BRANCHES OF GOVERNMENT

The Legislative Branch creates laws.	The Executive Branch carries out laws.	The Judicial Branch settles disputes about laws.

Includes:
• Congress
  – House of Representatives
  – Senate
	Includes:
	• President
	• Vice President
	• Cabinet Members
		Includes:
		• Supreme Court
		• Lower Federal Courts

The Three Branches

The Legislative Branch, or Congress, is made up of the Senate and House of Representatives. Congress passes laws. Small states liked the Senate because each state, large or small, got two senators. In the House, a state's population determines the number of representatives.

(bkgd) Garry Gay/Rise/Getty Images; (c) PoodlesRock/Corbis

286

A C T ccess Complex Text

▶ Specific Vocabulary

Have students use context clues or a dictionary to define domain-specific words in the selection.

→ *Identify the context clues that help you understand* checks and balances. ("system"; "known as the three branches of government"; "in this system, no branch has too much power")

→ *What does the system of checks and balances allow each branch of government to do?* (This system allows each branch of government to amend or veto the acts of another branch. In using this system, no branch has too much power.)

The president heads the Executive Branch. The president can sign, veto, and enforce laws. The president also commands the nation's military.

The Judicial Branch is the third branch. The highest court is called the Supreme Court. District, state, and federal courts determine whether a law follows the Constitution.

The Constitution was officially approved in September 1787, but it did not become the law of the nation right away. Why? It had to be ratified, or approved, by nine of the thirteen states.

Some states held out. They felt the Constitution did not give enough power to the people. They wanted to add amendments, or changes, that guaranteed important personal rights such as freedom of speech or religion. James Madison jumped in again. He wrote the Bill of Rights, the first ten amendments to the Constitution. These were added to the Constitution in 1791. Finally, our nation had a plan of government that was approved!

3

All the People

Our Constitution begins with the words *We the People*. Back in 1791, however, the Constitution gave certain rights, such as voting, only to some people. That has changed over time. Today, our Constitution grants all citizens over the age of 18 the right to vote. Politicians continually revisit this founding document to ensure that all people are treated equally in our democracy.

> ### Make Connections
>
> Why did delegates from the states meet to write a Constitution in 1787? **ESSENTIAL QUESTION**
>
> Why is it important to be an active participant in our democracy? Use details from the selections to explain. **TEXT TO TEXT**

287

LITERATURE ANTHOLOGY, pp. 286–287

Make Connections

Essential Question Students should note the idea that individual states needed a stronger federal government to bring unity and strength to the new nation.

Text to Text Have partners compare their responses to the Ask and Answer Questions prompts with what they learned in *See How They Run*. Each pair can report back to the whole class. Ask one pair to compare the description of the writing of the Constitution in *See How They Run* with the one in this selection. (*See How They Run* hints that the process wasn't easy. This selection gives more detail about why the process was hard.) Ask other pairs to compare the way laws are passed according to the Constitution to the ways in ancient Greece and Rome. (In ancient Greece, each citizen voted directly. In ancient Rome and in the Constitution, citizens elect representatives that vote on laws.) Have other pairs compare the creation of the Bill of Rights with the adoption of Massachusetts state insect. (People voiced their opinions to make a change in law.)

 Point out the cognate population/*población* on page 286. Review other cognates on the page: government/*gobierno*, legislative/*legislativo*, executive/*ejecutivo*, and judicial/*judicial*.

→ *Complete these sentence frames. The _____ has three branches.* (government)

→ *The three branches are _____, _____, and _____.* (legislative, executive, judicial)

→ *In the House of Representatives, _____ determines the number of representatives each state gets.* (population)

→ Phonics/Fluency

MINILESSON
20 Mins

Inflectional Endings

OBJECTIVES

CCSS Use combined knowledge of all letter-sound correspondences, syllabication patterns, and morphology (e.g., roots and affixes) to read accurately unfamiliar multisyllabic words in context and out of context. **RF.4.3a**

CCSS Read on-level text with purpose and understanding. **RF.4.4a**

Rate: 102–122 WCPM

ACADEMIC LANGUAGE
phrasing

1 Explain

Remind students that the inflectional endings *-ed* and *-ing* are added to verbs to create new verb forms and tenses. Point out that the spelling of many base words (such as *laugh*) does not change when *-ed* or *-ing* is added. For base words ending with a consonant and *e* (such as *save*), drop the final *e* before adding *-ed* or *-ing*. For many base words ending with a single vowel and a consonant (such as *drop*), double the final consonant before adding *-ed* or *-ing*.

2 Model

Write the word *gripped* on the board. Underline the inflectional ending *-ed*. Review the rule for adding *-ed* to words ending in a vowel and a consonant. (Double the final consonant and add *-ed*.) Then run your finger under the word as you model pronouncing it.

3 Guided Practice

Write the following words with inflectional endings on the board. Help students pronounce each word.

darted	trapping	knitted
phoned	helping	smiling
dragging	cared	craving

> **Read Multisyllabic Words**
>
> **Transition to Longer Words** Draw a three-column chart on the board. In the first and third columns, write *disappear*, *regret*, and *measure*. At the top of the second and third columns, write *-ed/-ing*. Ask students to read aloud the words in the first column.
>
> Have students help you add each inflectional ending to each word in the first column using the rules they learned. Write the new words in the second and third columns (*disappeared/ disappearing, regretted/regretting,* and *measured/measuring*). Ask students to echo-read the words after you.

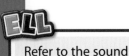

ELL

Refer to the sound transfers chart in the **Language Transfers Handbook** to identify sounds that do not transfer in Spanish, Cantonese, Vietnamese, Hmong, and Korean.

Go Digital

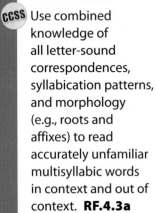

Inflectional Endings

Present the Lesson

View "A World Without Rules"

Vowel Team Syllables

1 Explain

Remind students that every syllable in a word has one vowel sound. When two vowels appear next to each other in a word, they usually work as a team to form one sound.

→ The vowel team is part of the same syllable in the word.

→ The letters *y* and *w* can also be part of a vowel team.

2 Model

Write and say *remain*. Have students repeat it. Model finding the vowel team *ai* and pronouncing it. Divide the word into syllables.

3 Guided Practice

Write the words *approach*, *teacher*, and *meeting* on the board. Have students underline the vowel teams and then say each word.

Phrasing and Rate

Explain/Model Explain to students that it helps to group words together into phrases while reading. This is done by paying close attention to the punctuation in the text, such as commas and periods. Reading at a consistent rate that is not too slow or too fast will help students divide the text into meaningful phrases and will contribute to understanding.

Model reading the first paragraph under "A Community in Confusion" on page 239 of "A World Without Rules." Read at a steady rate and use correct phrasing. Point out a sentence that includes multiple commas. Remind students that they should pause briefly for the same amount of time at each comma. Ask students to follow along and pay attention to when you pause at commas and stop at end punctuation.

Practice/Apply Divide the class into two groups. Have each group take turns choral-reading sentences while focusing on phrasing. Then have them partner-read the entire paragraph. Remind them to maintain a steady rate.

Daily Fluency Practice

Students can practice fluency using **Your Turn Practice Book**.

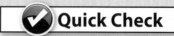

Monitor and *Differentiate*

 Quick Check

Can students decode multisyllabic words with inflectional endings? Can students read words with vowel team syllables? Can students read fluently?

Small Group Instruction

If No →	Approaching Level	Reteach pp. T42, T46
	ELL	Develop pp. T58, T62
If Yes →	On Level	Review p. T48
	Beyond Level	Extend p. T52

ON-LEVEL PRACTICE BOOK p. 158

A. Read each verb. Then write the correct *-ed* and *-ing* forms for each verb.

Verb	+ ed	+ ing
1. scare	scared	scaring
2. tap	tapped	tapping
3. discuss	discussed	discussing
4. taste	tasted	tasting
5. force	forced	forcing
6. skip	skipped	skipping

B. Read each word. Draw a slanted line (/) to divide it into syllables. Then write the vowel team on the line.

1. coaster ___ oa
2. bookend ___ oo
3. repeat ___ ea
4. southwest ___ ou
5. needle ___ ee
6. unload ___ oa

APPROACHING p. 158	BEYOND p. 158	ELL p. 158

 **Go** Digital

www.connected.mcgraw-hill.com
RESOURCES
Research and Inquiry

→ **Wrap Up the Week**

Integrate Ideas

RESEARCH AND INQUIRY

Our Government

OBJECTIVES

CCSS Recall relevant information from experiences or gather relevant information from print and digital sources; take notes and categorize information, and provide a list of sources. **W.4.8**

CCSS Report on a topic or text, tell a story, or recount an experience in an organized manner, using appropriate facts and relevant, descriptive details to support main ideas or themes; speak clearly at an understandable pace. **SL.4.4**

• Collaborate with peers.
• Give and follow directions.

Create a Flow Chart

Explain to students that they will work with a partner to research the process for adding an amendment to their state constitution. They will then create a flow chart that details the steps in the process. Discuss the following steps:

❶ **Discuss** Tell students that an amendment is a formal change made by constitutional procedure. Ask them to recall what they learned about the U.S. Constitution from their reading.

❷ **Find Resources** Have pairs use online and print resources to research the process for adding an amendment to their state constitution. You may assign or have them choose a particular amendment as an example. Make sure they understand how to use the available tools in the library or media center. Refer them to the state government's Web site.

❸ **Guided Practice** As students conduct their research, remind them to take notes, verify facts in multiple sources, and credit each source in their notes. Have them use online Research Process Checklist 2 to evaluate their research process.

❹ **Create the Project: Flow Chart** Have pairs use their notes to create their flow chart. Encourage them to think critically about their flowcharts in order to make them as informative and easy to understand as possible.

Present the Chart

Have students present their charts to the class along with the facts they have discovered about the function of state government. Tell them to speak clearly at an understandable pace and respond to specific questions.

TEXT CONNECTIONS  *Analytical Writing*

OBJECTIVES

CCSS Integrate information from two texts on the same topic in order to write or speak about the subject knowledgeably. **RI.4.9**

Text to Text

Cite Evidence Explain to students that they will work in groups to compare information they have learned about why we need government from all the texts they have read. Model how to compare this information by using examples from the week's **Leveled Readers** and from *A World Without Rules,* **Reading/Writing Workshop** pages 238–241. Review class notes and completed graphic organizers. You may also wish to model going back into the text for more information. You can use a Three-Tab Foldable® to record comparisons.

Students should cite at least three examples from each text.

Present Information Ask groups of students to present their findings to the class. Encourage discussion, asking students to comment on information on the charts that is similar and ideas that are different.

Communities Have More Order

Our Freedoms Are Protected

Our Voices Can Be Heard

Dinah Zike's
FOLDABLES®
Study Organizer

WRITE ABOUT READING *Analytical Writing*

OBJECTIVES

CCSS Apply *grade 4 Reading standards* to informational texts (e.g., "Explain how an author uses reasons and evidence to support particular points in a text"). **W.4.9b**

CCSS Identify the reasons and evidence a speaker provides to support particular points. **SL.4.3**

Write an Analysis

Cite Evidence Using evidence from a selection they have read, students will analyze how the author connects events in using cause-and-effect relationships.

Discuss how to analyze a text by asking *how* or *why* questions.

→ How does the author connect events using cause-and-effect relationships?

Discuss the student model on **Your Turn Practice Book** page 159. Then have students choose a selection and review their notes on the events. Have them write an analysis that explains the author's use of cause-and-effect relationships in the text. Remind students that good explanatory writing includes transition words and uses pronouns and antecedents correctly.

Present Your Ideas Ask partners to share their paragraphs and discuss how the evidence they cited supports their ideas. Partners may suggest additional text evidence, if necessary.

→ # Readers to Writers

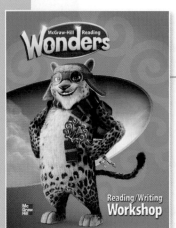

Reading/Writing Workshop

OBJECTIVES

CCSS Write routinely over extended time frames (time for research, reflection, and revision) and shorter time frames (a single sitting or a day or two) for a range of discipline-specific tasks, purposes, and audiences. **W.4.10**

CCSS Introduce a topic clearly and group related information in paragraphs and sections; include formatting, illustrations, and multimedia when useful to aiding comprehension. **W.4.2a**

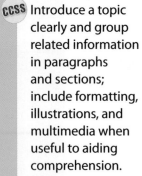

- Analyze models of strong paragraphs.
- Build strong paragraphs to revise writing.

ACADEMIC LANGUAGE
paragraph, topic

MINILESSON 10 Mins

Writing Traits: Organization

Strong Paragraphs

Expert Model Explain that good writers build strong paragraphs. A strong paragraph includes a topic sentence and supporting sentences. The topic sentence states the main idea of the paragraph. Supporting sentences give facts, details, and examples that support and explain the main idea. All the ideas in the paragraph clearly relate to the main idea.

 Read aloud the expert model from "A World Without Rules." Ask students to listen for the topic sentence and supporting sentences that include facts and examples that support the main idea. Have students talk with partners to identify these sentences.

Student Model Remind students that a strong paragraph includes a topic sentence that states the main idea and supporting sentences that give more information about the main idea. Read aloud the student draft "Rules." As students follow along, have them focus on the topic sentence and supporting sentences the writer included in his draft.

 Invite partners to talk about the draft and the topic sentence and supporting sentences that Stefan included. Ask them to suggest places where Stefan could add more supporting sentences.

 ## Go Digital

Expert Model

Student Model

Genre Writing

Narrative Text and Poetry
For full writing process lessons and rubrics, see:
→ Fictional Narrative, pages T344–T349
→ Poetry, pages T350–T355

Writing Traits Organization

Readers to...

Writers build strong paragraphs by stating the main idea in a topic sentence. They include supporting sentences that give more information about the main idea. Reread the excerpt from "A World Without Rules" below.

Strong Paragraphs

Identify the **topic sentence** and the **supporting sentences.** How do the facts and examples support the main idea?

Expert Model

We live in a democracy where we have the privilege of voting for the people that we want to run the country. Our elected government passes legislation, or laws, meant to help and protect us. If the country outgrows an old law, then the government can pass amendments to the law. Community workers such as crossing guards, police officers, and lifeguards all work to keep you safe, while government agencies such as the Environmental Protection Agency have made a commitment to inspect the air and water for pollution.

Writers

Stefan wrote an essay about rules. Read Stefan's revisions to one section of his essay.

Student Model

Rules

may not be fun, but they are helpful.
Rules are good. Rules help keep
Can you imagine how crazy things
would get if people just did what they wanted?
our society orderly. Rules also keep

you safe. For example, pool rules

make sure kids do not slip on the

deck or hurt themselves while diving.

I think there are too many rules at

pools sometimes. Finally, rules help
you
you know how they should behave. If
them
you follow rules, you'll know that you

are acting the right way for a certain

place or situation.

Editing Marks
⌐⌐ Switch order.
∧ Add.
∧ Add a comma.
⸮ Take out.
ⓈⓅ Check spelling.
≡ Make a capital letter.

Grammar Handbook
Pronouns and Antecedents See page 463.

Your Turn COLLABORATE

✔ Identify Stefan's topic sentence.
✔ Identify a pronoun and its antecedent.
✔ Tell how Stefan's revisions made his paragraph stronger.

Go Digital!
Write online in Writer's Workspace

246   247

READING/WRITING WORKSHOP, pp. 246–247

ELL ENGLISH LANGUAGE LEARNERS SCAFFOLD

As English Language Learners write during the week, provide support to help them respond to the prompts. For example:

Beginning

Write Help students complete the sentence frames. *Rules help keep our _____ orderly. Pool rules make sure _____ do not slip on the _____. Rules help you know how you should _____. The topic sentence is _____.*

Intermediate

Describe Ask students to complete the sentence frames. Encourage students to provide details. *Rules help keep our _____. Pool rules make sure _____. Rules help you know _____. The topic sentence is _____. Some supporting sentences are _____.*

Advanced/High

Discuss Check for understanding. Ask: *How do rules help our society? How do pool rules help kids in the pool? What happens if you follow the rules? What is the topic sentence? What are some supporting sentences?*

Writing Every Day: Organization

DAY
1

DAY
2

Writing Entry: Strong Paragraphs

Prewrite Provide students with the prompt below.

Explain how rules help people. Include a topic sentence and supporting sentences.

Have partners list some rules that they know help people. Ask them to jot down some examples of how the rules help people that they might include in their drafts.

Draft Have each student choose two or three rules to write about. Remind students to include a topic sentence and supporting sentences in their drafts.

Focus on Strong Paragraphs

Use **Your Turn Practice Book** page 160 to model including a topic sentence and supporting sentences.

Schools have rules. Games have rules. There are rules in my home also. I have to clean my room once a week.

Model adding a topic sentence to the sample paragraph.

Rules are important because they help keep things organized.

Discuss how adding a topic sentence that states the main idea helps build a strong paragraph. Guide students to add supporting sentences to the rest of the model.

Writing Entry: Strong Paragraphs

Revise Have students revise their writing from Day 1 by making sure they have a topic sentence and adding some supporting sentences.

Use the **Conferencing Routines**. Circulate among students and stop briefly to talk with individuals. Provide time for peer reviews.

Edit Have students use Grammar Handbook page 463 in the **Reading/Writing Workshop** to edit for errors in pronouns and antecedents and relative pronouns.

Conferencing Routines

Teacher Conferences

STEP 1

Talk about the strengths of the writing.

I can tell that you thought about your audience and purpose. You included information to support the main idea, and you used a formal voice, which is appropriate for this kind of writing.

STEP 2

Focus on how the writer uses the target trait for the week.

This topic sentence clearly states the main idea. It would help if you added some more supporting sentences to explain the main idea.

STEP 3

Make concrete suggestions for revisions. Have students work on a specific assignment, such as those to the right, and then meet with you to review progress.

DAY 3

Writing Entry: Strong Paragraphs

Prewrite Ask students to search their Writer's Notebook for topics to write a draft. Or, provide a prompt, such as the following:

Explain some rules that you have to follow in your daily life and why they are important. Include a topic sentence and supporting sentences.

Draft Once students have chosen their topics, ask them to create a word web with the topic in the center. Then have them think about supporting details and examples that they might include in their writing. Students can then use their word webs to begin their drafts.

DAY 4

Writing Entry: Strong Paragraphs

Revise Have students revise the draft writing from Day 3 by adding a topic sentence, if necessary, and two or three supporting sentences. As students are revising their drafts, hold teacher conferences with individual students. You may also wish to have students work with partners to peer conference.

Edit Invite students to review the rules for pronouns and antecedents on Grammar Handbook page 463 in the **Reading/Writing Workshop** and then edit their drafts for errors.

DAY 5

Share and Reflect

Discuss with the class what they learned about building strong paragraphs. Invite volunteers to read and compare draft text with text that has been revised. Have students discuss the writing by focusing on the importance of the topic sentence and supporting sentences that have been added. Allow time for individuals to reflect on their own writing progress and record observations in their Writer's Notebooks.

McGraw-Hill Companies, Inc./Ken Karp, photographer

Suggested Revisions

Provide specific direction to help focus young writers.

Focus on a Sentence
Read the draft and target one sentence for revision. *Rewrite this supporting sentence by adding details that tell about _____.*

Focus on a Section
Underline a section that needs to be revised. Provide specific suggestions. *Some sentences in this section do not support the main idea. Rewrite it so all the ideas clearly relate to the main idea.*

Focus on a Revision Strategy
Underline a section of the writing and ask students to use a specific revision strategy, such as adding. *Try adding more supporting sentences to support and explain the main idea.*

Peer Conferences

Focus peer response groups on building strong paragraphs by including a topic sentence and supporting sentences. Provide this checklist to frame discussion.

- ☑ Does the writing include a topic sentence that states the main idea?
- ☑ Does the writing include supporting sentences that explain the main idea?
- ☑ What facts and examples can be added to support the main idea?

Grammar: Pronouns and Antecedents

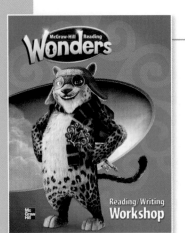

Reading/Writing Workshop

OBJECTIVES

CCSS Use relative pronouns (*who, whose, whom, which, that*) and relative adverbs (*where, when, why*). **L.4.1a**

CCSS Ensure subject-verb and pronoun-antecedent agreement. **L.3.1f**

• Identify pronouns.

• Understand pronoun-antecedent agreement.

• Use pronouns correctly.

• Proofread sentences for mechanics and usage errors.

Go Digital

Pronouns and Antecedents

Grammar Activities

DAY 1

DAILY LANGUAGE ACTIVITY

The pacific ocean is along the coste of california. We have visit that state.
(1: Pacific Ocean; 2: coast; 3: California; 4: visited)

Introduce Pronouns

Present the following:

→ A **pronoun** is a word that takes the place of one or more nouns. A **personal pronoun** refers to a person or thing. **I, he, she, it,** and **you** are personal pronouns:

   He is home.

→ A **relative pronoun,** such as **that, which, who, whom,** and **whose,** is used at the beginning of a dependent clause.

   I like snow **that** is sparkly.

→ An **indefinite pronoun** does not name a specific person or thing.

   Someone left the oven on.

Have partners use page 463 of the Grammar Handbook in **Reading/Writing Workshop**.

DAY 2

DAILY LANGUAGE ACTIVITY

We went to birch aquarium. I touch a stingray, and held a hermit crab.
(1: Birch Aquarium; 2: touched; 3: stingray and)

Review Pronouns

Review pronouns. Have students explain how personal, relative, and indefinite pronouns differ.

Introduce Pronoun-Antecedent Agreement

→ The word a pronoun refers to is called its **antecedent**:

   Lily passed the test because **she** studied for it.

→ A pronoun and its antecedent must match in gender and in number.

   Tom is from Peru. **He** speaks Spanish.

   The Smiths live next door. **They** have four dogs.

 TALK ABOUT IT

COLLABORATE

USE PRONOUNS

Have students in small groups write three singular pronouns and three plural pronouns on index cards and place the cards in a pile. Students will take turns selecting a card, reading it aloud, and choosing another student to use the pronoun in a sentence.

REPLACE NOUNS

Have students in small groups each write three sentences that contain nouns as subjects. Then have each student read his or her sentences aloud and choose another student in the group to replace the subjects with pronouns.

DAY

DAILY LANGUAGE ACTIVITY

Dan is a Police Officer. They wear a uniform!
(1: police officer; 2: He: 3: wears; 4: uniform.)

Mechanics and Usage: Pronoun Capitalization and Clarity

→ The first-person pronoun **I** is always capitalized.

→ The antecedent often appears in the same sentence as the pronoun, but it may also appear in an earlier sentence.

→ If it is not clear which noun or nouns a pronoun refers to, repeat the noun or rewrite the sentence to avoid confusion.

As students write, refer them to Grammar Handbook page 463.

DAY

DAILY LANGUAGE ACTIVITY

Karl throwed the ball to jerry. He said, "Now throw it to me."
(1: threw; 2: Jerry; 3: Karl said)

Proofread

Have students correct errors in these sentences.

1. Aaron took Adam by suprise because he thought he wasn't home. (1: surprise; 2: Adam thought; 3: Aaron wasn't)

2. Cant i take voice lessons, to? (1: Can't; 2: I; 3: too)

3. Ben said, "i want fryed catfish for dinner. (1: I want; 2: fried; 3: dinner.")

4. The Caterpillar sat on a leaf. It was green. (1: caterpillar; 2: The caterpillar was)

Have students check their work using Grammar Handbook page 463.

DAY 5

DAILY LANGUAGE ACTIVITY

The cats cleaning they're fir. Who's cat is that.
(1: are cleaning; 2: their; 3: fur; 4: Whose: 5: that?)

Assess

Use the Daily Language Activity and **Grammar Practice Reproducibles** page 80 for assessment.

Reteach

Use Grammar Practice Reproducibles pages 76–79 and selected pages from the Grammar Handbook for additional reteaching. Remind students that it is important to use pronouns correctly as they speak and write.

Check students' writing for use of the skill and listen for it in their speaking. Assign Grammar Revision Assignments in their Writer's Notebooks as needed.

See Grammar Practice Reproducibles pages 76–80.

NAME THE ANTECEDENTS

Ask partners to each write three sentence pairs. The first sentence should include an antecedent, and the second sentence should include a pronoun that refers to the antecedent. Have students trade papers and identify each antecedent.

USE RELATIVE PRONOUNS

Have students in small groups each write *that, which, who, whom,* and *whose* on index cards and place the cards in a pile. Tell them to shuffle the cards. Students will take turns selecting a card from the pile and stating a sentence using the relative pronoun on the card.

DESCRIBE THE IMAGE

Have small groups select pictures, paintings, or drawings from a book. Then have each student make a statement about the image using an indefinite pronoun. Tell students to use the pronouns *anyone, everything, someone,* and *something*.

→ Spelling: Inflectional Endings

OBJECTIVES

Spell grade-appropriate words correctly, consulting references as needed. **L.4.2d**

Spelling Words

tasted	flagged	flagging
ripping	ripped	discussed
forced	skipped	saving
flipping	tapping	tasting
tapped	saved	forcing
flipped	skipping	discussing
scared	scaring	

Review bedspread, desktop, snowstorm

Challenge outwitted, underscoring

Differentiated Spelling

Approaching Level

tasted	hopped	hopping
ripping	ripped	trimmed
liked	skipped	saving
flipping	tapping	tasting
tapped	saved	liking
flipped	skipping	trimming
cared	caring	

Beyond Level

endured	flagged	flagging
strumming	strummed	discussed
exploded	realized	demonstrated
flipping	exploding	demonstrating
admitted	admitting	forcing
flipped	skipping	discussing
outwitted	appreciating	

DAY 1

Assess Prior Knowledge

Display the spelling words. Read them aloud, drawing out the inflectional endings in each word.

Point out the spelling patterns in *tasted, discussed,* and *ripping.* Write *taste, discuss* and *rip* and model adding inflectional endings. Note how the final letter is sometimes doubled before adding the ending.

Demonstrate sorting the spelling words by pattern under key words *discussed, discussing, ripped, ripping, tasted* and *tasting.* (Write the words on index cards or the IWB.) Sort a few words. Note that words ending with a consonant and *e* drop the final *e* before adding *-ed* or *-ing.*

Then use the Dictation Sentences from Day 5 to give the Pretest. Say the underlined word, read the sentence, and repeat the word. Have students write the words. Then have students check and correct their spelling.

DAY 2

Spiral Review

Review compound words using *bedroom, railroad,* and *bookcase.* Use the Dictation Sentences below for the review words. Read the sentence, say the word, and have students write the words.

1. The old <u>bedspread</u> is very soft.

2. Put the lamp on the <u>desktop</u>.

3. We awaited the <u>snowstorm</u>.

Have partners check the spellings.

Challenge Words Review this week's inflectional endings spelling patterns. Use these Dictation Sentences for challenge words. Say the word, read the sentence, and say the word again. Have students write the word.

1. The dog <u>outwitted</u> his owner.

2. <u>Underscoring</u> helps words stand out.

Have students check and correct their spelling before writing the words in their word study notebook.

WORD SORTS

COLLABORATE

OPEN SORT

Have students cut apart the **Spelling Word Cards BLM** in the Teacher Resource Book and initial the back of each card. Have them read the words aloud with a partner. Then have partners do an open sort. Have them record the sort in their word study notebook.

PATTERN SORT

Complete the **pattern sort** from Day 1 using the key words, pointing out inflectional endings. Have students use Spelling Word Cards to do their own pattern sort. Ask partners to compare and check their sorts.

DAY

Word Meanings

Have students copy the three sentences below into their word study notebook. Say the sentences aloud, and ask students to fill in each blank with a spelling word.

1. When our car ran out of gas, we _____ down a police officer. (*flagged*)

2. We were too _____ to go on the roller coaster. (*scared*)

3. In class we are _____ history and politics. (*discussing*)

Challenge students to come up with at least three other sentences for spelling, review, or challenge words, leaving a blank space for the word. Have them trade with a partner and complete the sentences. Have partners discuss their reasons for choosing the words and inflected endings that they used to complete the sentences.

See Phonics/Spelling Reproducibles pp. 91–96.

SPEED SORT

Have partners do a **speed sort** to see who is fastest, then compare results. Have them do a word hunt for words with this week's inflectional ending spelling patterns. Have partners discuss how to sort the words, then add them to the word study notebook.

DAY

Proofread and Write

Write these sentences on the board. Have students circle and correct each misspelled word. They can use print or electronic dictionaries or other resources to help them.

1. I riped the dollar I was saveing. (*ripped, saving*)

2. Once we tasteed the food, we decided we were not skiping dinner. (*tasted, skipping*)

3. My sister and I discued how we had saveed up for a new computer. (*discussed, saved*)

4. My brother taped loudly on the window late at night, scarring us. (*tapped, scaring*)

Error Correction Remind students that in most words ending with a vowel and then a consonant, the final consonant is doubled before adding the inflectional ending -*ed* or -*ing*.

BLIND SORT

Have partners do a **blind sort**: one reads a Spelling Word Card; the other tells under which key word it belongs. Have them take turns until both have sorted all their words. Ask them to discuss their sorts, then play Word Match using both sets of their Spelling Word Cards.

DAY

Assess

Use the Dictation Sentences for the Posttest. Have students list misspelled words in their word study notebooks. Look for students' use of these words in their writings.

Dictation Sentences

1. I never <u>tasted</u> the cheese.
2. The dog is <u>ripping</u> the newspaper.
3. The storm <u>forced</u> us indoors.
4. The acrobats were <u>flipping</u> across the stage.
5. He <u>tapped</u> his pencil on the table.
6. The gymnast <u>flipped</u> over the bar.
7. I was too <u>scared</u> to ride the horse.
8. I <u>flagged</u> down the bus at my stop.
9. I could not wear <u>ripped</u> pants.
10. She <u>skipped</u> down the path.
11. He was <u>tapping</u> on the wall.
12. I <u>saved</u> fifty dollars last year.
13. They were <u>skipping</u> stones.
14. Stop <u>scaring</u> your brother!
15. Mom was <u>flagging</u> down a taxi.
16. We <u>discussed</u> the election in class.
17. I am <u>saving</u> money to buy a mitt.
18. My sister is <u>tasting</u> the soup.
19. He is <u>forcing</u> me to go to the party.
20. We are <u>discussing</u> our plans.

Have students self-correct the tests.

Build Vocabulary

OBJECTIVES

CCSS Use context (e.g., definitions, examples, or restatements in text) as a clue to the meaning of a word or phrase. **L.4.4a**

CCSS Use common, grade-appropriate Greek and Latin affixes and roots as clues to the meaning of a word (e.g., *telegraph, photograph, autograph*). **L.4.4b**

CCSS Demonstrate understanding of words by relating them to their opposites (antonyms) and to words with similar but not identical meanings (synonyms). **L.4.5c**

Vocabulary Words

amendments	eventually
commitment	legislation
compromise	privilege
democracy	version

Go Digital

Vocabulary

Vocabulary Activities

DAY 1

Connect to Words

Practice this week's vocabulary.

1. Are **amendments** new laws or changes to laws we have now?

2. What are different ways you can show **commitment**?

3. Why is **compromise** important for solving problems?

4. How do people work together in a **democracy**?

5. Tell about something you hope to accomplish **eventually**.

6. What new **legislation** would you like to pass for your state?

7. Describe a **privilege** that a citizen of the United States has.

8. Explain why a story might have more than one **version**.

DAY 2

Expand Vocabulary

Help students generate different forms of this week's words by adding, changing, or removing inflectional endings.

→ Draw a four-column T-chart on the board. Write *amendment* in the last column. Then write *amend, amends,* and *amended* in the first three columns. Read aloud the words with students.

→ Have students share sentences using each form of *amend*.

→ Students can fill in the chart for *commitment,* then share sentences using the different forms of the word.

→ Have students copy the chart in their word study notebook.

BUILD MORE VOCABULARY

COLLABORATE

ACADEMIC VOCABULARY

Discuss important academic words.

→ Display *government, reform, constitution*.

→ Define each word and discuss the meanings with students.

→ Display *government* and *govern*. Have partners look up and define related words.

→ Write the related words on the board. Have partners ask and answer questions using the words. Repeat with *reform* and *constitution*.

ANTONYMS

→ Ask, *What is an antonym of version?*

→ Have partners create a list of antonyms for *version,* and for *privilege, eventually, commitment,* and *compromise*.

→ Encourage students to consult a thesaurus if they need help.

→ Have students write the five vocabulary words and their antonyms in the word study notebook.

DAY

Reinforce the Words

Review last week's and this week's vocabulary words. Have students orally complete each sentence stem.

1. _____ is a <u>privilege</u> I do not take for granted.

2. A cat is a small <u>version</u> of a _____.

3. My sisters had to <u>compromise</u> about when to _____.

4. There have been _____ <u>amendments</u> to the United States Constitution.

5. One <u>commitment</u> political leaders make is to _____.

6. A puddle will <u>eventually</u> dry up if it is _____ outside.

DAY

Connect to Writing

→ Have students write sentences in their word study notebooks using this week's vocabulary.

→ Tell them to write sentences that provide word information they learned from this week's readings.

→ **ELL** Provide the Day 3 sentence stems 1–6 for students needing extra support.

Write About Vocabulary Have students write something they learned from this week's words in their word study notebook. For example, they might write about why *compromise* is important in a *democracy* or how *amendments* can be made to existing *legislation*.

DAY

Word Squares

Ask students to create Word Squares for each vocabulary word.

→ In the first square, students write the word. (example: *legislation*)

→ In the second square, students write their own definition of the word and any related words, such as synonyms. (example: *bill, law*)

→ In the third square, students draw a simple illustration that will help them remember the word. (example: a state house or the United States Capitol)

→ In the fourth square, students write nonexamples, including antonyms for the word. (example: *no rules*)

→ Have partners compare and discuss their Word Squares.

LATIN ROOTS

Remind students to look for Latin roots to help them determine the meaning of unfamiliar words.

→ Display **Your Turn Practice Book** pages 153–154. Read the second paragraph. Model finding the meaning of *scribbled*.

→ Have students complete page 157, then use Latin roots to find the meaning of *spectacles, naturalization,* and *memorizing* on pages 153–154, using a dictionary to confirm meanings.

SHADES OF MEANING

Help students generate words related to *democracy*. Draw a word web. Label it "Democracy."

→ Discuss democracy as a class. Elicit related words and ideas, such as *voting, candidates,* and *government*.

→ Have partners work together to add words to the web. Ask for volunteers to share words for the original class web.

→ Ask students to copy the words in their word study notebook.

MORPHOLOGY

Use *legislation* as a springboard for students to learn more words. Draw a four-column T-chart. Write *legislate* in the left column.

→ In the other columns, write *-ion, -ive* and *-or*. Demonstrate creating *legislation* from *legislate* and the suffix *-ion*.

→ Have students write the words created by the other two suffixes and review their meanings.

→ Ask partners to do a search for other words with these suffixes.

Approaching Level

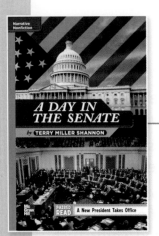

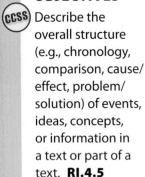

Lexile 680
TextEvaluator™ 27

OBJECTIVES

(CCSS) Describe the overall structure (e.g., chronology, comparison, cause/effect, problem/solution) of events, ideas, concepts, or information in a text or part of a text. **RI.4.5**

(CCSS) Explain how an author uses reasons and evidence to support particular points in a text. **RI.4.8**

(CCSS) Use common, grade-appropriate Greek and Latin affixes and roots as clues to the meaning of a word (e.g., *telegraph, photograph, autograph*). **L.4.4b**

Leveled Reader:
A Day in the Senate

Before Reading

Preview and Predict

Have students read the Essential Question. Then have students read the title and table of contents of *A Day in the Senate*. Have students think of two questions they have about what a day in the Senate is like and share them with a partner.

Review Genre: Narrative Nonfiction

Review with students that narrative nonfiction is told in the form of a story and includes facts and text features. As they preview the book, have students identify features of narrative nonfiction in *A Day in the Senate*.

During Reading

Close Reading

Note Taking Ask students to use their graphic organizer while they read.

Pages 2–3 Tell students that the Latin root *leg* in *legislation* on page 2 means "law." *Use this information to define the word to a partner.* (*Legislation* means "laws.") *What are the requirements for becoming a senator?* (A senator must be at least 30 years old and live in the state he or she represents.)

Pages 4–5 *Paraphrase to a partner what staffers do.* (Staffers find information for senators and make sure senators know what they need to do.) *What does the map on page 4 tell you about the senate offices?* (For Example: The senate offices are near the Capitol building.)

Pages 6–9 *What would be one of the effects of passing the education bill?* (Classes would be smaller. More teachers would be needed.) *What word signals that this is a cause-and-effect relationship?* (if) *Turn to a partner and ask a question about chapter 2. Reread if necessary to find the answer.*

Go Digital

Leveled Readers

Use Graphic Organizer

Pages 10–12 *Turn to a partner and discuss how the author uses reasons to say that pages are important.* (For example: They deliver messages and documents around the Capitol.)

Pages 13–14 *Why do senators meet with people from their home state?* (They answer questions and listen to people's ideas.) *If you visited Congress, what question would you ask?* (For example: I would ask if it is hard for the congressmen to compromise on issues.)

After Reading

Respond to Reading Have students complete Respond to Reading on page 15 after they have finished reading.

Analytical Writing **Write About Reading** Have students work with a partner to write a short paragraph about how senators work with other people to make laws. Have students include at least two facts from the text.

Fluency: Phrasing and Rate

Model Model reading page 2 with proper phrasing and rate. Next, reread the page aloud and have students read along with you.

Apply Have students practice reading with a partner.

PAIRED READ

"A New President Takes Office"

Leveled Reader

Make Connections: Write About It *Analytical Writing*

Before reading, ask students to note that the genre of this text is expository, which means it explains about a topic. Then discuss the Essential Question. After reading, ask students to make connections between reasons the government is important in *A Day in the Senate* and "A New President Takes Office."

FOCUS ON SOCIAL STUDIES

Students can extend their knowledge of why people run for public office by completing the social studies activity on page 20.

Literature Circles

Ask students to conduct a literature circle using the Thinkmark questions to guide the discussion. You may wish to have a whole-class discussion on ways students would like to participate in government.

Level Up

Level-up lessons available online.

IF students read the Approaching Level fluently and answered the questions

THEN pair them with students who have proficiently read the On Level and have students

• echo-read the On Level main selection with their partners.

• use self-stick notes to mark details they'd like to discuss with partners.

A C T Access Complex Text

The On Level challenges students by including more **domain-specific words** and **complex sentence structures**.

Approaching Level
Phonics/Decoding

DECODE WORDS WITH INFLECTIONAL ENDING -ed

TIER 2

 OBJECTIVES

CCSS Use combined knowledge of all letter-sound correspondences, syllabication patterns, and morphology to read accurately unfamiliar multisyllabic words in context and out of context. **RF.4.3a**

Decode words with inflectional endings.

 I Do Remind students that they can add the ending -ed to a verb to make a new verb. Adding -ed shows that the action happened in the past. Write the word *jump* on the board. Say: *We jump on the trampoline today.* Then write *jumped* on the board. Underline the letters *ed*. Point out that adding -ed to *jump* changes the verb to its past-tense form.

 We Do Write *start, need, wait, wish,* and *rain* on the board. Read the words aloud and have students echo-read. Model adding -ed to *start*. Read the new word aloud and use it in a sentence. Work with students to add -ed to the remaining verbs. Then have students read the new words aloud together. Point out how adding the ending to the verbs changes their tense.

You Do Add these words to the board: *play, look, wash,* and *work*. Have students read each word aloud. Have students add the ending -ed to each word. Point to the words in random order for students to read chorally. Repeat several times.

REVIEW INFLECTIONAL ENDINGS

TIER 2

 OBJECTIVES

CCSS Use combined knowledge of all letter-sound correspondences, syllabication patterns, and morphology to read accurately unfamiliar multisyllabic words in context and out of context. **RF.4.3a**

Decode words with inflectional endings.

 I Do Remind students that they can add -ed or -ing to the end of words to make new words. Explain that the spelling of many base words does not change when -ed or -ing is added. Then display these **Word-Building Cards** one at a time: *ing, land, ed.* Model sounding out each syllable.

 We Do Have students choral-read each syllable. Repeat at varying speeds and in random order. Next display all three cards. Work with students to combine the Word-Building Cards to form words with the endings -ed and -ing. Have students choral-read the words: *landed, landing.*

 You Do Display the Word-Building Cards *ing, work, ed, press, stand*. Have students work with partners to build words with the endings -ed and -ing. Have partners share the words they built and make a class list.

PRACTICE INFLECTIONAL ENDINGS

OBJECTIVES

Use combined knowledge of all letter-sound correspondences, syllabication patterns, and morphology to read accurately unfamiliar multisyllabic words in context and out of context. **RF.4.3a**

Decode words with inflectional endings.

 Remind students that they can add the endings *-ed* and *-ing* to verbs to create new verb forms and tenses. Remind students that the spelling of many words does not change when they add *-ed* or *-ing*. Write *heal, healed,* and *healing* on the board. Point out that when a word ends with a consonant and an *e*, the *e* is dropped before adding *-ed* or *-ing*. Write *save, saved,* and *saving* on the board. Explain that for most words that end with a vowel and a consonant, the consonant is doubled before adding *-ed* or *-ing*. Add *grab, grabbed,* and *grabbing* to the board. Have students read the words aloud. Underline the endings and review the different spelling rules.

 Write the words *hop, lift, stop, hope,* and *tire* on the board. Read each word aloud and have students repeat. Model how to add *-ed* and *-ing* to *hop*. Guide students as they add the endings to the remaining words. Help them first decide if there is a spelling change to the base word.

 Afterward, point to the words in random order for students to choral-read.

WORDS WITH VOWEL TEAMS

OBJECTIVES

Use combined knowledge of all letter-sound correspondences, syllabication patterns, and morphology to read accurately unfamiliar multisyllabic words in context and out of context. **RF.4.3a**

Decode words with vowel teams.

 Remind students that when two vowels are together in a word, they may work together to make one sound. Write *eat* on the board. Run your hand under the word as you elongate the long-vowel sound: /ēēēt/. Explain that both vowels stand for the long *e* sound. Repeat with *oat, keep,* and *aim*.

 Write *coach, lead, rain,* and *deep* on the board. Model how to decode the words. Have students repeat the words. Then have students identify the letters that make the long-vowel sound in each word.

Write the words *aid, loan, neat,* and *reed* on the board. Have volunteers underline the letters that make the long-vowel sound. Then point to the words in random order for students to choral-read.

ELL ENGLISH LANGUAGE LEARNERS

For the **ELLs** who need **phonics**, **decoding**, and **fluency** practice, use scaffolding methods as necessary to ensure students understand the meaning of the words. Refer to the **Language Transfers Handbook** for phonics elements that may not transfer in students' native languages.

Approaching Level
Vocabulary

REVIEW HIGH-FREQUENCY WORDS

 TIER 2

OBJECTIVES

 Read with sufficient accuracy and fluency to support comprehension. Read on-level text with purpose and understanding. **RF.4.4a**

Review high-frequency words.

I Do Use **Word Cards 121–130**. Display one word at a time, following the routine:

Display the word. Read the word. Then spell the word.

We Do Ask students to state the word and spell the word with you. Model using the word in a sentence and have students repeat after you.

You Do Display the word. Ask students to say the word and then spell it. When completed, quickly flip through the word card set as students choral-read the words. Provide opportunities for students to use the words in speaking and writing. For example, ask questions about each word. Hold up the card for *never* and ask: *What is the opposite of this word?* Ask students to write each word in their Writer's Notebook.

REVIEW VOCABULARY WORDS

 TIER 2

OBJECTIVES

 Acquire and use accurately grade-appropriate general academic and domain-specific words and phrases, including those that signal precise actions, emotions, or states of being and that are basic to a particular topic. **L.4.6**

I Do Display each **Visual Vocabulary Card** and state the word. Explain how the photograph illustrates the word. State the example sentence and repeat the word.

We Do Point to the word on the card and read the word with students. Ask them to repeat the word. Engage students in structured partner-talk about the image as prompted on the back of the vocabulary card.

You Do Display each visual in random order, hiding the word. Have students match the definitions and context sentences of the words to the visuals displayed.

IDENTIFY RELATED WORDS

OBJECTIVES

 Demonstrate understanding of figurative language, word relationships, and nuances in word meanings. Demonstrate understanding of words by relating them to their opposites (antonyms) and to words with similar but not identical meanings (synonyms). **L.4.5c**

 Display the *amendments* **Visual Vocabulary Card** and say aloud the word set *amendments, changes, destroys*. Ask: *Which word means almost the same as* amendments?

Point out that the word *changes* means almost the same as *amendments*.

 Display the vocabulary card for the word *commitment*. Say aloud the word set *commitment, vacation, promise*. With students, identify the word that means almost the same as the first word in the set.

 Using the word sets below, display the remaining cards one at a time, saying aloud the word set. Ask students to identify the word that means almost the same as the first word in the set.

privilege, honor, chore   *version, same, type*

eventually, immediate, finally   *compromise, stubborn, agreement*

LATIN ROOTS

OBJECTIVES

Determine or clarify the meaning of unknown and multiple-meaning words and phrases based on grade 4 reading and content, choosing flexibly from a range of strategies. Use common, grade-appropriate Greek and Latin affixes and roots as clues to the meaning of a word (e.g., *telegraph, photograph, autograph*). **L.4.4b**

 Write *scrib = to write* on the board. Explain to students that *scrib* is a Latin root that means "to write." Tell students that they can use Latin roots to help them understand the meaning of unfamiliar words in a text. Display the Comprehension and Fluency passage on **Approaching Reproducibles** pages 153–154. Read aloud the first two paragraphs. Point to the word *scribbled*.

Think Aloud I am not sure of the meaning of *scribbled*. In the passage, it says that some students "scribbled in their notebooks." I also know that the Latin root *scrib* means "to write." These clues and my understanding of the root of the word help me understand that *scribbled* means wrote.

Write the definition of the word from the clues.

 Ask students to point to the word *spectacles* on page 153. Write on the board *spect = look*. Discuss with students how to use the root to figure out the meaning of the word. Write the definition of the word on the board.

 Have students use Latin roots to find the meanings of *inspected* and *community* on page 154.

Approaching Level

Comprehension

FLUENCY

TIER 2

OBJECTIVES

 Read on-level prose and poetry orally with accuracy, appropriate rate, and expression on successive readings. **RF.4.4b**

Read fluently with appropriate rate and phrasing.

I Do Explain that good readers learn to read at an appropriate rate, or speed. Reading at an appropriate rate helps the reader better understand the text. It also helps listeners understand what is being read aloud. Explain to students that readers should pay attention to phrasing when they read. They should group words in smaller groups of information to better understand what they read. Read the first paragraph of the Comprehension and Fluency passage on **Approaching Reproducibles** pages 153–154. Model reading with appropriate rate and phrasing.

We Do Read the rest of the page aloud and have students echo-read each sentence after you, using the same rate and phrasing. Make sure students pay attention to the ways you group words and phrases.

You Do Have partners take turns reading sentences from the Approaching Reproducibles passage. Have them focus on their phrasing and rate. Listen in and provide corrective feedback by modeling proper fluency as needed.

IDENTIFY SIGNAL WORDS

TIER 2

OBJECTIVES

 Describe the overall structure (e.g., chronology, comparison, cause/ effect, problem/ solution) of events, ideas, concepts, or information in a text or part of a text. **RI.4.5**

Identify words that signal cause and effect.

I Do Write on the board *because, so, as a result.* Explain to students that these are words that often signal cause and effect in a text. Tell students that they can sometimes use these words to find examples of cause and effect within a selection. Give students an example: *I study because I have a test tomorrow.*

We Do Read the third paragraph of the Comprehension and Fluency passage in **Approaching Reproducibles**. Ask: *Which word in this paragraph might signal a cause-and-effect relationship?* Point out the word *because.* Tell students to circle the word.

You Do Have students read the rest of the passage and look for the words *because, so,* and *as a result.* Then have students circle any instance of these words in the passage. Review students' choices and have them use each word in a sentence.

REVIEW CAUSE AND EFFECT

OBJECTIVES

 Describe the overall structure (e.g., chronology, comparison, cause/ effect, problem/ solution) of events, ideas, concepts, or information in a text or part of a text. **RI.4.5**

Identify words that signal cause and effect.

 Remind students that authors organize a selection in various ways. Explain that one of these ways is called cause and effect. Tell students that a cause is why something happens. Tell them that an effect is what happens. Write on the board *I tripped on the rock, so I fell*. Write *Cause* above *I tripped on the rock*. Write *Effect* above *I fell*. Draw a circle around *so*. Tell students that this word, like the words *because, since,* and *as a result*, can often signal cause-and-effect relationships in a text.

We Do Read the first three paragraphs of the Comprehension and Fluency passage in **Approaching Reproducibles** with students. Reread the first sentence of the third paragraph. Have students identify the signal word *because*. Then work with students to identify the example of cause and effect in the sentence.

 Have students use signal words to help them determine other examples of cause-and-effect relationships in the passage.

SELF-SELECTED READING

OBJECTIVES

 Describe the overall structure (e.g., chronology, comparison, cause/ effect, problem/ solution) of events, ideas, concepts, or information in a text or part of a text. **RI.4.5**

Ask and answer questions about a text to increase understanding.

Read Independently

Have students choose an informational text for sustained silent reading. Remind students that:

→ an effect is something that happens. Tell students that a cause is why it happens. Remind students that they can look for words that signal cause and effect, such as *because, so, since,* and *as a result*.

→ they should stop and ask and answer questions about a text to help them understand and remember information.

Read Purposefully

Have students record instances of cause and effect on a Cause and Effect Chart as they read independently. After they finish, they can conduct a Book Talk, each telling about the book they read.

→ Students should share their charts and identify at least one example of cause and effect in the text.

→ Have students share any questions they asked and answered as they read to help them better understand the information.

On Level

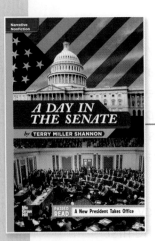

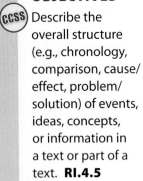

Lexile 820
TextEvaluator™ 39

OBJECTIVES

CCSS Describe the overall structure (e.g., chronology, comparison, cause/ effect, problem/ solution) of events, ideas, concepts, or information in a text or part of a text. **RI.4.5**

CCSS Explain how an author uses reasons and evidence to support particular points in a text. **RI.4.8**

CCSS Use common, grade-appropriate Greek and Latin affixes and roots as clues to the meaning of a word (e.g., *telegraph, photograph, autograph*). **L.4.4b**

Leveled Reader:
A Day in the Senate

Before Reading

Preview and Predict

Have students read the Essential Question. Then have students read the title and table of contents of *A Day in the Senate*. Have students think of two questions they have about what a day in the Senate is like and share them with a partner.

Review Genre: Narrative Nonfiction

Review with students that narrative nonfiction is told in the form of a story and includes facts and text features. As they preview the book, have students identify features of narrative nonfiction in *A Day in the Senate*.

During Reading

Close Reading

Note Taking Ask students to use their graphic organizer while they read.

Pages 2–3 Tell students that the Latin root *inter* in *interstate* on page 2 means *among, between. Use the root to define the word.* (*Interstate* means "between states") *What reasons does the author use to say that senators are important?* (For example: Senators work to make laws that solve problems.)

Pages 4–5 *Why are committees important?* (In committees, groups of senators can focus on specific issues.) *Turn to a partner and ask a question about chapter 1. Reread if necessary to find the answer.*

Pages 6–7 *Turn to a partner and paraphrase a cause-and-effect text structure on page 6. Tell how you know.* (I see that if a bill that reduces class size is passed, schools will need more teachers. The word "if" tells me that the author is using a cause-and-effect structure.)

Go Digital

Leveled Readers

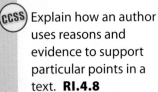

Use Graphic Organizer

Pages 8–9 *How does page 9 help you understand the main text?* (This page shows how the Capitol was built. It tells me the history of where senators gather and helps me picture the building.)

Pages 10–14 *Why is compromise necessary for most bills to pass?* (Compromise is necessary because usually not all of the representatives agree on an issue.) *Turn to a partner and tell one reason we need senators.* (For example: We need senators to make laws.)

After Reading

Respond to Reading Have students complete Respond to Reading on page 15 after they have finished reading.

Analytical Writing **Write About Reading** Have students work with a partner to write a short paragraph about how senators make laws. Have students include details about the compromises that must be made.

Fluency: Phrasing and Rate

Model Model reading page 2 with proper phrasing and rate. Next, reread the page aloud and have students read along with you.

Apply Have students practice reading with a partner.

PAIRED READ

"A New President Takes Office"

Make Connections:
Write About It *Analytical Writing*

Before reading, ask students to note that the genre of this text is expository, which means it explains about a topic. Then discuss the Essential Question. After reading, ask students to make connections between reasons the government is important in *A Day in the Senate* and "A New President Takes Office."

Leveled Reader

FOCUS ON SOCIAL STUDIES

Students can extend their knowledge of why people run for public office by completing the social studies activity on page 20.

Literature Circles

Ask students to conduct a literature circle using the Thinkmark questions to guide the discussion. You may wish to have a whole-class discussion on ways students would like to participate in government.

Level Up

Level-up lessons available online.

IF students read the On Level fluently and answered the questions

THEN pair them with students who have proficiently read Beyond Level and have students

• partner-read the Beyond Level main selection.

• list vocabulary words they find difficult and look them up with a partner.

A C T Access Complex Text

The Beyond Level challenges students by including more **domain-specific words** and **complex sentence structures**.

On Level

Vocabulary

REVIEW VOCABULARY WORDS

OBJECTIVES

 Acquire and use accurately grade-appropriate general academic and domain-specific words and phrases, including those that signal precise actions, emotions, or states of being (e.g., *quizzed, whined, stammered*) and that are basic to a particular topic (e.g., *wildlife, conservation,* and *endangered* when discussing animal preservation). **L.4.6**

 I Do Use the **Visual Vocabulary Cards** to review key selection words *amendments, commitment, compromise, eventually, privilege,* and *version.* Point to each word, read it aloud, and have students chorally repeat it.

We Do Ask these questions and help students respond and explain their answers.

→ What *amendments* would you make to the playground?

→ How might it be a *privilege* to visit the principal's office?

→ How would you *compromise* if there were only one copy of a book and you and your classmate both wanted to read it?

 You Do Have student pairs respond to these questions and explain their answers.

→ Where would you look for a different *version* of your favorite fairy tale?

→ Name something you have made a *commitment* to do this year.

→ Do you start your homework as soon as you get home or *eventually*?

LATIN ROOTS

OBJECTIVES

 Use common, grade-appropriate Greek and Latin affixes and roots as clues to the meaning of a word (e.g., *telegraph, photograph, autograph*). **L.4.4b**

 I Do Remind students that Latin roots can help them figure out the meaning of an unfamiliar word. Write *scrib = to write* on the board. Explain that *scrib* is a Latin root that means "to write." Use the Comprehension and Fluency passage on **Your Turn Practice Book** pages 153–154 to model.

Think Aloud I'm not sure what *scribbled* means. The Latin root *scrib* means "to write." The passage says that some students "scribbled in their notebooks." The Latin root helps me understand that the word *scribbled* means wrote quickly.

 We Do Write *spec = look* on the board. Reread the second paragraph and point out the word *spectacles.* With students determine the meaning of *spectacles* using the Latin root *spec.*

 You Do Have student pairs use Latin roots to determine the meanings of *inspected* and *community* on page 154.

Comprehension

REVIEW CAUSE AND EFFECT

OBJECTIVES

CCSS Describe the overall structure (e.g., chronology, comparison, cause/effect, problem/solution) of events, ideas, concepts, or information in a text or part of a text. **RI.4.5**

Identify words that signal cause and effect.

 I Do Remind students that in cause-and-effect text structure, a cause is why something happens and an effect is what happens. Write on the board *Talia got an A because she studied hard*. Point out the cause and the effect in the sentence. Then point out the signal word *because*. Remind students that words such as *because, so, since,* and *as a result* can often signal cause-and-effect relationships in a text.

 We Do Have a volunteer read the first three paragraphs of the Comprehension and Fluency passage on **Your Turn Practice Book** pages 153–154. Have students point out the signal word *because* in the third paragraph. Then model how to identify the cause and the effect in the first sentence.

 You Do Have students work in pairs to identify the words that signal cause-and-effect relationships. Then have them identify other examples of cause and effect in the passage.

SELF-SELECTED READING

OBJECTIVES

CCSS Describe the overall structure (e.g., chronology, comparison, cause/effect, problem/solution) of events, ideas, concepts, or information in a text or part of a text. **RI.4.5**

Ask and answer questions about a text to increase understanding.

Read Independently

Have students choose an informational text for sustained silent reading.

→ Before they read, have students preview the text, reading the title and any potential headings or text features, and viewing the front and back cover.

→ As students read, remind them to ask and answer questions of themselves to help them understand new or difficult information.

Read Purposefully

Encourage students to read different books in order to learn about a variety of subjects.

→ As students read, have them list cause-and-effect relationships on a Cause and Effect Chart.

→ They can use this chart to help them write a summary of the text.

→ Ask students to share their reactions to the text with classmates.

→ Beyond Level

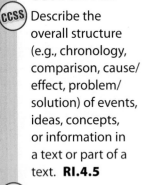

Lexile 890
TextEvaluator™ 47

OBJECTIVES

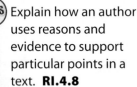 Describe the overall structure (e.g., chronology, comparison, cause/effect, problem/solution) of events, ideas, concepts, or information in a text or part of a text. **RI.4.5**

Explain how an author uses reasons and evidence to support particular points in a text. **RI.4.8**

Use common, grade-appropriate Greek and Latin affixes and roots as clues to the meaning of a word (e.g., *telegraph, photograph, autograph*). **L.4.4b**

Leveled Reader:
A Day in the Senate

Before Reading

Preview and Predict

Have students read the Essential Question. Then have students read the title and table of contents of *A Day in the Senate*. Have students think of two questions they have about what a day in the Senate is like and share them with a partner.

Review Genre: Narrative Nonfiction

Review with students that narrative nonfiction is told in the form of a story and includes facts and text features. As they preview the book, have students identify features of narrative nonfiction in *A Day in the Senate*.

During Reading

Close Reading

Note Taking Ask students to use their graphic organizer while they read.

Pages 2–3 *What can you tell about the author's position from the first paragraph on page 2?* (The author thinks that people may underestimate how senators affect their lives, but senators are very important.) *The root* solut *means "loosen, set free." How can you use that information to define* solutions *on page 3?* (I can use the root along with the context clue to say that *solutions* means "answers.")

Pages 4–5 *What reasons does the author use for why it would be difficult for senators to do a good job without their staffers?* (Staffers organize senators' schedules and ensure senators know what they need to do.)

Pages 6–9 *Turn to a partner and paraphrase two causes and their effects in this section.* (If the bill for smaller classes is passed, the effect will be that more teachers would need to be trained and hired. If the committee moves the bill forward, the effect would be that it would be sent to the full committee for further work.)

Go
Digital

Leveled Readers

Cause → Effect
→
→
→
→

Use Graphic Organizer

Pages 10–11 *Paraphrase the Senate's voting process.* If necessary, help students reread to find details on the voting process. (Senators meet in the Senate Chamber. A few leaders are chosen to run the meeting. When a bill is being considered, senators debate and can introduce amendments. They vote on a bill and the majority wins.)

Pages 12–14 *Turn to a partner and tell two reasons we need senators.* (For example: We need senators to represent voters in Congress and to make laws.)

After Reading

Respond to Reading Have students complete Respond to Reading on page 15 after they have finished reading.

Write About Reading *Analytical Writing* Have students work with a partner to write a short paragraph about how senators reach agreements with other people to make laws. Have students include at least two facts from the text.

Fluency: Phrasing and Rate

Model Model reading page 2 with proper phrasing and rate. Next, reread the page aloud and have students read along with you.

Apply Have students practice reading with a partner.

PAIRED READ

"A New President Takes Office"

Leveled Reader

Make Connections:
Write About It *Analytical Writing*

Before reading, ask students to note that the genre of this text is expository, which means it explains about a topic. Then discuss the Essential Question. After reading, ask students to make connections between reasons the government is important in *A Day in the Senate* and "A New President Takes Office."

FOCUS ON SOCIAL STUDIES

Students can extend their knowledge of why people run for public office by completing the social studies activity on page 20.

Literature Circles

Ask students to conduct a literature circle using the Thinkmark questions to guide the discussion. You may wish to have a whole-class discussion on ways students would like to participate in government.

Gifted and Talented

Synthesize Challenge students to apply what they have learned about the senate by researching a real bill. Have students research a bill that was voted on in the senate in the previous year. Encourage students to research bills regarding topics such as education or the environment. Have students write a brief summary of the bill and the results of the vote. Ask volunteers to share their bill with the class. Then have the class vote on the bill.

→ Beyond Level

Vocabulary

REVIEW DOMAIN-SPECIFIC WORDS

 OBJECTIVES
Acquire and use accurately grade-appropriate general academic and domain-specific words and phrases, including those that signal precise actions, emotions, or states of being and that are basic to a particular topic. **L.4.6**

 Model Use the **Visual Vocabulary Cards** to review the meanings of the words *democracy* and *legislation*. Write social studies-related sentences on the board using the words.

Write the words *amendments* and *compromise* on the board and discuss the meanings with students. Then help students write sentences using these words.

 Apply Have students work in pairs to review the meanings of the words *privilege* and *commitment*. Then have partners write sentences using the words.

LATIN ROOTS

 OBJECTIVES
Use common, grade-appropriate Greek and Latin affixes and roots as clues to the meaning of a word (e.g., *telegraph, photograph, autograph*). **L.4.4b**

 Model Read aloud the first two paragraphs of the Comprehension and Fluency passage on **Beyond Reproducibles** pages 153–154.

Think Aloud In the second paragraph, I want to understand the word *spectacles*. The root *spec* means "to see." I can use this root to help me understand that *spectacles* is another word for eyeglasses.

With students, reread the second paragraph. Help them figure out the meaning of *scribbled*.

 Apply Have pairs of students read the rest of the passage. Have them use Latin roots to determine the meanings of *naturalization* and *memorizing* on page 153 and *inspected* and *community* on page 154.

 Shades of Meaning Using their definition of *inspected*, have partners write an explanation of the differences and similarities between *inspected* and *see*. Also encourage them to use artwork to depict the two words.

Comprehension

REVIEW CAUSE AND EFFECT

OBJECTIVES

 Describe the overall structure (e.g., chronology, comparison, cause/effect, problem/solution) of events, ideas, concepts, or information in a text or part of a text. **RI.4.5**

Identify words that signal cause and effect.

Model Remind students that authors sometimes use a cause-and-effect text structure to organize information. Remind them that a cause is why something happens and that an effect is what happens as a result. Point out that words such as *because, so, since,* and *as a result* can help them identify cause-and-effect relationships.

Have students read the first three paragraphs of the Comprehension and Fluency passage on **Beyond Reproducibles** pages 153–154. Direct their attention to the first sentence in the third paragraph. Have students identify the cause-and-effect relationship in the sentence. Then have them point out the cause-and-effect signal word.

Apply Have students identify cause-and-effect relationships in the rest of the passage as they independently fill in a Cause and Effect Chart. Encourage students to identify implicit examples of cause and effect.

SELF-SELECTED READING

OBJECTIVES

 Describe the overall structure (e.g., chronology, comparison, cause/effect, problem/solution) of events, ideas, concepts, or information in a text or part of a text. **RI.4.5**

Ask and answer questions about a text to increase understanding.

Read Independently

Have students choose an informational book for sustained silent reading.

→ As students read, have them fill in a Cause and Effect Chart.

→ Remind them to ask and answer questions to help them better understand new information.

Read Purposefully

Encourage students to keep a reading journal. Ask them to read different books in order to learn about a variety of subjects.

→ Students can write summaries of the books in their journals.

→ Ask students to share their reactions to the books with classmates.

 Independent Study Have students brainstorm a list of things that they would like to see change in their community or school. Then have students work in pairs to create a plan of action. They might write a letter to the local newspaper or blog. They might plan a fund-raiser or festival. Encourage them to list several ways they could make their voices heard.

English Language Learners

Reading/Writing Workshop

OBJECTIVES

 Explain events, procedures, ideas, or concepts in a historical, scientific, or technical text, including what happened and why, based on specific information in the text. **RI.4.3**

 Describe the overall structure (e.g., chronology, comparison, cause/effect, problem/solution) of events, ideas, concepts, or information in a text or part of a text. **RI.4.5**

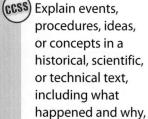 Use common, grade-appropriate Greek and Latin affixes and roots as clues to the meaning of a word (e.g., *telegraph*, *photograph*, *autograph*). **L.4.4b**

Shared Read
A World Without Rules

Go Digital

View "A World Without Rules"

Before Reading

Build Background

Read the Essential Question: Why do we need government?

→ Explain the meaning of the Essential Question. Explain that a government is a group of people who lead a country, state, city, or town. Point out that *government* and *gobierno* are cognates.

→ **Model an answer:** *The government makes laws that make things fair for everyone. They also pass laws to keep people safe. These rules and laws are all around us. They are in our schools, parks, and on the road. We even have laws to keep us safe at home.*

→ Ask students a question that ties the Essential Question to their own background knowledge: *What rules and laws do you follow each day? Work with a partner to make a list of the different rules and laws you follow. What would life be like without rules and laws?* Call on several pairs to share their answers.

During Reading

Interactive Question-Response

→ Ask questions that help students understand the meaning of the text after each paragraph.

→ Reinforce the meanings of key vocabulary.

→ Ask students questions that require them to use key vocabulary.

→ Reinforce strategies and skills of the week by modeling.

Pages 238–239

Paragraph 1
What is the title? (A World Without Rules) *Who is the narrator talking to?* (the reader) *How can you tell?* (The narrator uses the words "you" and "your.")

Point out the idiom *change your mind. When you change your mind, you change your decision or opinion about something. Why does the narrator say, "You just might change your mind?"* (The narrator wants to convince readers that a world without rules is not as great as we might believe.)

A Strange Morning

Explain and Model Cause and Effect *The alarm clock goes off. Do you have to go to school?* (no) *Why not?* (There are no rules.) Point out the word *Since*. Explain that this word signals a cause-and-effect relationship. *What is the cause?* (no rules) *What is the effect?* (no school; cookies for breakfast; no brushing teeth)

A Community in Confusion

Model Cause and Effect *What do you see in the picture on page 238?* (The school is closed. The playground is broken. There is litter on the ground.) *There are no crossing guards or police officers. Why?* (There are no laws.) *Is it safe to cross the street?* (no) *Why?* (There are no traffic laws.) Have students point to a phrase that shows a cause-and-effect relationship. (as a result) Ask a volunteer to complete the sentence frame: _____ *of no state and government services, there is no one to take care of the playground.* (As a result)

Page 240

Paragraphs 1 and 2
What are some things you are not able to do in a world without rules? (Go to the beach. Play soccer in the park. Eat lunch outside.) *Why can't you do the things you love?* (There is no government to maintain the parks.)

What is life like in a world without rules? How would you feel? Allow students to respond using short phrases and gestures. (Possible answer: I would be upset because I could not do many things I like to do, and I would not feel safe.)

Back to Reality

Chorally read the heading and paragraph. Define and give examples for the words *version, democracy, privilege, legislation, amendments,* and *commitment*. Point out the cognates *versión, democracia, privilegio,* and *legislación*.

Have students complete the sentence frame: *We live in a _____.* (democracy) *How does democracy help keep us safe?* (Possible answer: We can vote for government leaders who pass laws to keep us safe.)

Explain and Model Latin Roots Ask an advanced student to answer the following question: *What does it mean to "inspect the air and water for pollution"?* Use gestures to demonstrate *inspect*. (It means to look at the air and water for pollution.) *What part of the word* inspect *means "to see"?* (spect) Have students look for other words with Latin roots in the selection.

Would you rather live in a world with or without rules? Explain. (Possible answer: I would rather live in a world with rules because communities are safe and clean.)

After Reading

Make Connections
→ Review the Essential Question: Why do we need government?
→ Make text connections.
→ Have students complete **ELL Reproducibles** pages 153–155.

English Language Learners

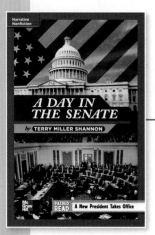

Lexile 800
TextEvaluator™ 33

OBJECTIVES

(CCSS) Describe the overall structure (e.g., chronology, comparison, cause/effect, problem/solution) of events, ideas, concepts, or information in a text or part of a text. **RI.4.5**

(CCSS) Explain how an author uses reasons and evidence to support particular points in a text. **RI.4.8**

(CCSS) Use common, grade-appropriate Greek and Latin affixes and roots as clues to the meaning of a word (e.g., *telegraph, photograph, autograph*). **L.4.4b**

Leveled Reader:
A Day in the Senate

Before Reading

Preview

→ Read the Essential Question: Why do we need government?

→ Refer to Justice for All: *What are some ways the government helps us?*

→ Preview *A Day in the Senate* and "A New President Takes Office": *Our purpose for reading is to learn about what it's like to spend a day in the Senate.*

Vocabulary

Use the **Visual Vocabulary Cards** to preteach the ELL vocabulary: *debate, voters.* Use the routine found on the cards. Point out the cognate: *debate.*

During Reading

Interactive Question-Response

Note Taking Have students use their graphic organizer in **ELL Reproducibles** page 152. Use the questions below as you read each section with students. As you read, define vocabulary.

Pages 2–3 Tell students that the Latin root *uni* in *United* on page 2 means *"one." We can use this root to define the word.* United *means _____.* (bring together as one) *Who makes laws for our country?* (senators; Congress) *Turn to a partner and discuss who can become a senator.*

Pages 4–5 Call attention to the map on page 4. Chorally read the caption and the key. *Point to the building where the senators work.* (Students should identify the Senate buildings.)
Point out the word *committee* on page 5. *What do committees do?* (Committees work on different subjects.) *Turn to a partner and ask a question about Chapter 1.* Help students reread to find the answers.

Pages 6–7 *The word* if *can signal a cause and effect. Find the word* if *in the first paragraph on page 7.* Call on a volunteer to read the sentence. *This is the cause. What happens if the government passes the bill? What is the effect?* (The government will need to hire more teachers.)

 **Go Digital**

Leveled Readers

Use Graphic Organizer

Pages 8–9 *What do we learn about in the sidebar on page 9?* (the history of the Capitol) *When was the Senate wing finished?* (1800)

Pages 10–14 *What happens if people have different points of view? Fill in the sentence frame: They need to _____.* (compromise) *What clues help you define the word* compromise? (Each side agrees to accept some changes.)

After Reading

Respond to Reading Help students complete the graphic organizer in **ELL Reproducibles** page 152. Revisit the Essential Question. Ask pairs to summarize and answer the Text Evidence Questions. Support students as necessary and review all responses as a group.

Analytical Writing **Write About Reading** Have partners write about how senators work with other people to make laws. Encourage them to reread the text and use notes from their graphic organizer to cite evidence that supports how senators work together and reach a compromise.

Fluency: Phrasing and Rate

Model Model reading page 2 with proper phrasing and rate. Next, reread the page aloud and have students read along with you.

Apply Have students practice reading with a partner.

PAIRED READ

"A New President Takes Office"

Make Connections:
Write About It **Analytical Writing**

Before reading, ask students to note that the genre of this text is expository, which will explain more about Inauguration Day. Then discuss the Essential Question. After reading, ask students to use the information from both selections to discuss how the president and senators help lead our country.

Leveled Reader

 FOCUS ON SOCIAL STUDIES

Students will learn more about the reasons people run for public office by completing the social studies activity on page 20.

Literature Circles

Ask students to conduct a literature circle using the Thinkmark questions to guide the discussion. You may wish to have a whole-class discussion, asking students how they would like to participate in government.

Level Up

Level-up lessons available online.

IF students read the **ELL Level** fluently and answered the questions

THEN pair them with students who have proficiently read **On Level** and have students

• echo-read the **On Level** main selection with their partners.

• list difficult words and discuss them with partners.

A C T Access Complex Text

The **On Level** challenges students by including more **academic language** and **complex sentence structures**.

→ English Language Learners
Vocabulary

PRETEACH VOCABULARY

OBJECTIVES

CCSS Acquire and use accurately grade-appropriate general academic and domain-specific words and phrases, including those that signal precise actions, emotions, or states of being and that are basic to a particular topic. **L.4.6**

LANGUAGE OBJECTIVE

Use vocabulary words.

 I Do Preteach vocabulary from "A World Without Rules," following the Vocabulary Routine on the **Visual Vocabulary Cards** for the words *amendments, commitment, compromise, democracy, eventually, legislation, privilege,* and *version.*

 We Do After completing the Vocabulary Routine for each word, point to the word on the card and read it aloud. Ask students to repeat the word.

You Do Have partners write sentence frames for three words. Assign small groups and have students guess the missing vocabulary word in each sentence.

Beginning	Intermediate	Advanced/High
Help students write sentence frames. Read the sentences aloud.	Challenge students to write sentence frames for one additional word.	Challenge students to write one sentence with two missing words.

REVIEW VOCABULARY

OBJECTIVES

CCSS Acquire and use accurately grade-appropriate general academic and domain-specific words and phrases, including those that signal precise actions, emotions, or states of being and that are basic to a particular topic. **L.4.6**

LANGUAGE OBJECTIVE

Use vocabulary words.

 I Do Review the previous week's vocabulary words. The words can be reviewed over a few days. Read each word aloud, pointing to the word on the **Visual Vocabulary Card**. Have students repeat after you. Then follow the Vocabulary Routine on the back of each card.

 We Do Write each word on an index card. Hold up two cards at a time. Then provide clues for one of the words. Have students point to the word you describe. Ask a volunteer to use the word in a sentence.

 You Do Have pairs write clues for three vocabulary words. Then have small groups use index cards to play the game.

Beginning	Intermediate	Advanced/High
Help students list clues for each word and read them aloud.	Have students read aloud their clues using complete sentences.	Ask students to use synonyms or antonyms in their clues.

LATIN ROOTS

OBJECTIVES

Use common, grade-appropriate Greek and Latin affixes and roots as clues to the meaning of a word (e.g., *telegraph, photograph, autograph*). **L.4.4b**

LANGUAGE OBJECTIVE

Use Latin roots to understand unfamiliar words.

 I Do

Read aloud the first two paragraphs of Comprehension and Fluency Passage on **ELL Reproducibles** pages 153–154. Direct students' attention to the word *scribbled*. Remind students that a Latin root can help them understand the meaning of an unfamiliar word.

Think Aloud I am not sure what *scribbled* means. I see that the word has the Latin root *scrib* in it. I know that *scrib* means "to write." The text nearby says "scribbled on their papers." I think *scribbled* means to write quickly.

 We Do

Have students point to the word *spectacles* on page 153. Write the Latin root *spect* and its meaning "to see" on the board. Work with students to define *spectacles*.

 You Do

In pairs, have students use Latin roots to define the words *naturalization* on page 153 and *community* on page 154.

Beginning	Intermediate	Advanced/High
Help students locate the root within the larger word and define the root.	Ask students to locate the root in the word and look for context clues.	Have students explain how they found the meaning of the word.

ADDITIONAL VOCABULARY

OBJECTIVES

Choose words and phrases to convey ideas precisely. **L.4.3a**

LANGUAGE OBJECTIVE

Use academic and high-frequency words.

 I Do

List academic language and high-frequency words from "A World Without Rules": *rules* and *services*, and *A Day in the Senate: citizen, history,* and *issues*. Define each word: *Rules tell us what we should and should not do.*

 We Do

Model using the words in a sentence: *We follow rules at home and at school. Rules help people get along.* Then provide sentence frames and complete them with students: *If we do not follow rules, we _____ .*

You Do

Have pairs create a poster that illustrates a message in "A World Without Rules." Then have them describe their poster using at least three words.

Beginning	Intermediate	Advanced/High
Reread the selection with students and help them identify a message.	Ask students to explain what they learned about rules, services, and issues.	Challenge students to write a paragraph using all of the words.

English Language Learners
Writing/Spelling

WRITING TRAIT: ORGANIZATION

 OBJECTIVES

Introduce a topic clearly and group related information in paragraphs and sections; include formatting (e.g., headings), illustrations, and multimedia when useful to aiding comprehension. **W.4.2a**

_____

LANGUAGE OBJECTIVE

Develop strong paragraphs.

 I Do Explain that writers build strong paragraphs by stating the main idea in the topic sentence. They also include facts, examples, or details that support the topic sentence. Read the Expert Model passage aloud as students follow along. Identify the topic and supporting sentences.

We Do Read aloud a paragraph from "A World Without Rules." Identify the topic sentence and add the topic to the center of a word web. Add supporting details to the word web. Model writing a topic sentence using the web.

You Do Have pairs write a short summary of "A World Without Rules" using their word webs. Ask them to include a topic sentence and supporting sentences. Edit their writing. Then have pairs revise their writing.

Beginning	Intermediate	Advanced/High
Help students identify the topic sentence and supporting details.	Ask students to identify weak or vague supporting details and revise.	Ask students to include at least one fact and one example.

SPELL WORDS WITH INFLECTIONAL ENDINGS

 OBJECTIVES

Spell grade-appropriate words correctly, consulting references as needed. **L.4.2d**

_____

LANGUAGE OBJECTIVE

Spell words with inflectional endings.

 I Do Read aloud the Spelling Words on page T36, segmenting them into syllables. Point out the endings -ing and -ed. Point out any spelling changes in the base words. Have students repeat the words.

 We Do Read aloud the Dictation Sentences on page T37. For each sentence, read the underlined word slowly. Have students repeat and write the word.

 You Do Display the words. Have students exchange their list with a partner to check the spelling and then write the words correctly.

Beginning	Intermediate	Advanced/High
Have students copy the words with correct spelling and say the words aloud.	After students have corrected their words, have pairs quiz each other.	Have students explain which words were difficult and why.

Grammar

PRONOUNS

OBJECTIVES

CCSS Explain the function of nouns, pronouns, verbs, adjectives, and adverbs in general and their functions in particular sentences. **L.3.1a**

CCSS Ensure subject-verb and pronoun-antecedent agreement. **L.3.1f**

LANGUAGE OBJECTIVE

Use pronouns.

Language Transfers Handbook

Speakers of Cantonese, Haitian Creole, Hmong, Korean, and Spanish may have difficulties with gender and pronouns, as the third-person pronoun in the native language is gender-free, or the personal pronoun is omitted. Use visuals as needed to reinforce the difference in gender.

I Do Remind students that a noun names a person, place, or thing. Explain that a pronoun is a word that takes the place of one or more nouns. Write on the board: *Mari walks in the park.* Read the sentence aloud and have students identify the noun. Write *She* in place of *Mari.* Explain that a singular noun can be replaced by a singular pronoun.

Point out that a plural pronoun takes the place of a plural noun or a group of nouns. Write on the board: *Nick and Mari like to read.* Read the sentence aloud and have students identify the nouns. Write *They* in place of the nouns. Repeat with *The dogs barked loudly.*

We Do Write the sentences and sentence frames below on the board. Read the sentences aloud. Ask volunteers to name pronouns for the sentence frames. Then have students tell if the pronoun is singular or plural. Complete the sentence frames with students' responses. Then read the completed sentences aloud for students to repeat.

Tim and I went to class.	*_____ went to class.*
Sera gave Jack the book.	*_____ gave Jack the book.*
Toby and Kara studied today.	*_____ studied today.*

You Do Brainstorm a list of nouns with students. Have students work in pairs to write two sentences with two of the nouns. Then have them rewrite the sentences, replacing the nouns with appropriate pronouns.

Beginning	**Intermediate**	**Advanced/High**
Have students copy their sentences and help them use an appropriate pronoun. Read the sentences aloud for students to repeat.	Ask students which pronouns they should use to replace the nouns in their sentences.	Have students identify each pronoun they used as plural or singular.

For extra support, have students complete the activities in the **Grammar Practice Reproducibles** during the week, using the routine below:

→ Explain the grammar skill.

→ Model the first activity in the Grammar Practice Reproducibles.

→ Have the whole group complete the next couple of activities, then the rest with a partner.

→ Review the activities with correct answers.

PROGRESS MONITORING

Weekly Assessment

✔ COMPREHENSION:	✔ VOCABULARY:	✔ WRITING:
Cause and Effect **RI.4.5**	Latin Roots **L.4.4b**	Writing About Text **RI.4.5, W.4.9b**

Assessment Includes

→ Pencil-and-paper administration

→ On-line administration

→ Approaching-Level Weekly Assessment also available

Fluency Goal 102 to 122 words correct per minute (WCPM)

Accuracy Rate Goal 95% or higher.

Administer oral reading fluency assessments using the following schedule:

→ **Weeks 1, 3, 5** Provide Approaching-Level students at least three oral reading fluency assessments during the unit.

→ **Weeks 2 and 4** Provide On-Level students at least two oral reading fluency assessments during the unit.

→ **Week 6** If necessary, provide Beyond-Level students an oral reading fluency assessment at this time.

Also Available: Selection Tests online PDFs

Go Digital! www.connected.mcgraw-hill.com

Using Assessment Results

TESTED SKILLS	If …	Then …
COMPREHENSION	Students answer 0–6 multiple-choice items correctly …	… assign Lessons 49–51 on Cause and Effect from the *Tier 2 Comprehension Intervention online PDFs.*
VOCABULARY	Students answer 0–6 multiple-choice items correctly …	… assign Lesson 157 on Greek, Latin, and Other Roots from the *Tier 2 Vocabulary Intervention online PDFs.*
WRITING	Students score less than "3" on the constructed response …	… assign Lessons 49–51 and/or Write About Reading Lesson 200 from the *Tier 2 Comprehension Intervention online PDFs.*
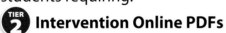	Students have a WCPM score of 94–101 …	… assign a lesson from Section 1 or 7–10 of the *Tier 2 Fluency Intervention online PDFs.*
	Students have a WCPM score of 0–93 …	… assign a lesson from Sections 2–6 of the *Tier 2 Fluency Intervention online PDFs.*

Response to Intervention

Use the appropriate sections of the ***Placement and Diagnostic Assessment*** as well as students' assessment results to designate students requiring:

TIER 2 **Intervention Online PDFs**

TIER 3 **WonderWorks Intervention Program**

Text Complexity Range for Grades 4–5

Lexile	
740	1010
TextEvaluator™	
23	51

McGraw-Hill Reading

Wonders

Reading/Writing Workshop

Mc Graw Hill

TEACH AND MODEL

CCSS **Shared Read** Genre • Fantasy

The TimeSpecs 3000

? **Essential Question**
Why do people run for public office?
Read how Miguel makes a decision to run for class president.

252

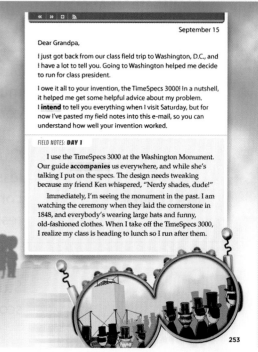

September 15

Dear Grandpa,

I just got back from our class field trip to Washington, D.C., and I have a lot to tell you. Going to Washington helped me decide to run for class president.

I owe it all to your invention, the TimeSpecs 3000! In a nutshell, it helped me get some helpful advice about my problem. I **intend** to tell you everything when I visit Saturday, but for now I've pasted my field notes into this e-mail, so you can understand how well your invention worked.

FIELD NOTES: **DAY 1**

I use the TimeSpecs 3000 at the Washington Monument. Our guide **accompanies** us everywhere, and while she's talking I put on the specs. The design needs tweaking because my friend Ken whispered, "Nerdy shades, dude!"

Immediately, I'm seeing the monument in the past. I am watching the ceremony when they laid the cornerstone in 1848, and everybody's wearing large hats and funny, old-fashioned clothes. When I take off the TimeSpecs 3000, I realize my class is heading to lunch so I run after them.

253

✓ Vocabulary

accompanies

campaign

governor

intend

opponent

overwhelming

tolerate

weary

 ## Close Reading of Complex Text

Shared Read "The TimeSpecs 3000", 252–255

Genre Fantasy

Lexile 910

ETS *TextEvaluator*™ 46

Minilessons

✓ **Tested Skills** CCSS

✓ **Comprehension Strategy** .... Make Predictions, T82–T83

✓ **Comprehension Skill** .... Point of View, T84–T85

✓ **Genre** .... Fantasy, T86–T87

✓ **Vocabulary Strategy** .... Idioms, T88–T89

✓ **Writing Traits** .... Ideas, T94–T95

Grammar .... Types of Pronouns, T98–T99

☞ **Go** Digital

 www.connected.mcgraw-hill.com

APPLY WITH CLOSE READING

Complex Text

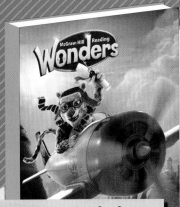

Literature Anthology

LaRue for Mayor, 288–309
Genre Fantasy

Lexile 890

ETS TextEvaluator™ 61

PAIRED READ

"Bringing Government Home", 310–313
Genre Expository Text

Lexile 900

ETS TextEvaluator™ 40

Differentiated Text

Leveled Readers   *Include Paired Reads*

APPROACHING
Lexile 670
ETS TextEvaluator™ 41

ON LEVEL
Lexile 740
ETS TextEvaluator™ 40

BEYOND
Lexile 810
ETS TextEvaluator™ 55

ELL
Lexile 610
ETS TextEvaluator™ 18

Extended Complex Text

Project Mulberry
Genre Realistic Fiction

Lexile 690

ETS TextEvaluator™ 39

Riding Freedom
Genre Realistic Fiction

Lexile 720

ETS TextEvaluator™ 40

Classroom Library

Classroom Library lessons available online.

TEACH AND MANAGE

How You Teach

INTRODUCE

Weekly Concept
Leadership

Reading/Writing Workshop
248–249

 **Go Digital**

Interactive Whiteboard

TEACH

Close Reading
"The TimeSpecs 3000"

Minilessons
Make Predictions, Point of View,
Fantasy, Idioms, Writing Traits

Reading/Writing Workshop
252–255

Interactive Whiteboard

APPLY

Close Reading
LaRue for Mayor

"Bringing Government Home"

Literature Anthology
288–313

Mobile

How Students Practice

WEEKLY CONTRACT

PDF Online

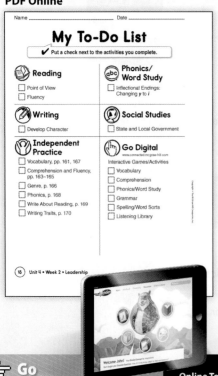

Name _____ Date _____

My To-Do List
✔ Put a check next to the activities you complete.

📖 Reading
- [ ] Point of View
- [ ] Fluency

🔤 Phonics/ Word Study
- [ ] Inflectional Endings: Changing y to i

✏️ Writing
- [ ] Develop Character

🌐 Social Studies
- [ ] State and Local Government

👐 Independent Practice
- [ ] Vocabulary, pp. 161, 167
- [ ] Comprehension and Fluency, pp. 163–165
- [ ] Genre, p. 166
- [ ] Phonics, p. 168
- [ ] Write About Reading, p. 169
- [ ] Writing Traits, p. 170

☞ Go Digital
www.connected.mcgraw-hill.com
Interactive Games/Activities
- [ ] Vocabulary
- [ ] Comprehension
- [ ] Phonics/Word Study
- [ ] Grammar
- [ ] Spelling/Word Sorts
- [ ] Listening Library

18 Unit 4 • Week 2 • Leadership

☞ **Go Digital**
Online To-Do List

LEVELED PRACTICE AND ONLINE ACTIVITIES

Your Turn Practice Book
161–170

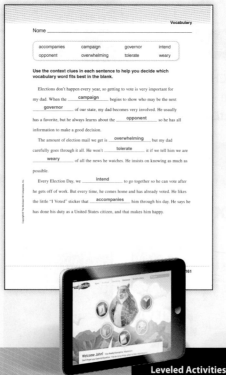

Name _____   Vocabulary

| accompanies | campaign | governor | intend |
| opponent | overwhelming | tolerate | weary |

Use the context clues in each sentence to help you decide which vocabulary word fits best in the blank.

Elections don't happen every year, so getting to vote is very important for my dad. When the **campaign** begins to show who may be the next **governor** of our state, my dad becomes very involved. He usually has a favorite, but he always learns about the **opponent** so he has all information to make a good decision.

The amount of election mail we get is **overwhelming**, but my dad carefully goes through it all. He won't **tolerate** it if we tell him we are **weary** of all the news he watches. He insists on knowing as much as possible.

Every Election Day, we **intend** to go together so he can vote after he gets off of work. But every time, he comes home and has already voted. He likes the little "I Voted" sticker that **accompanies** him through his day. He says he has done his duty as a United States citizen, and that makes him happy.

161

Leveled Readers

Leveled Activities

Writer's Workspace

DIFFERENTIATE

SMALL GROUP INSTRUCTION
Leveled Readers

INTEGRATE

Research and Inquiry
Political Campaign Plan, T92

Text Connections
Compare Why People Run for Office, T93

Analytical Writing **Write About Reading**
Write an Analysis, T93

ASSESS

Weekly Assessment
193–204

Mobile

Online Research and Writing

Online Assessment

LEVELED WORKSTATION CARDS

More Activities on back

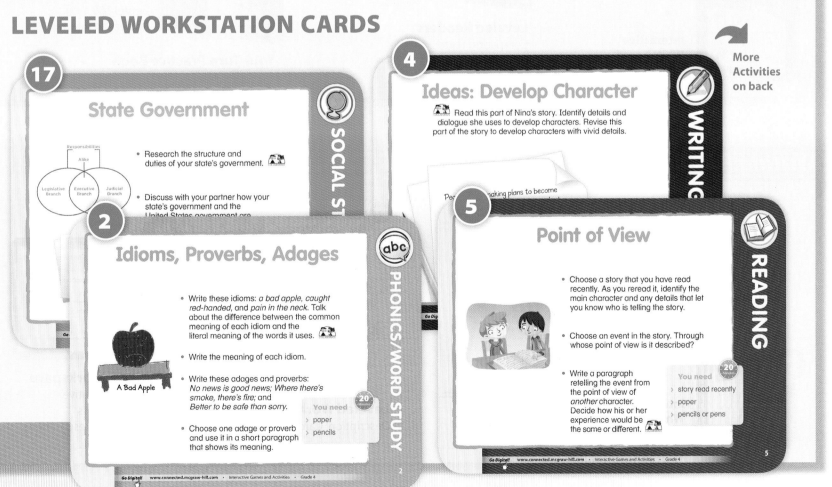

17 **State Government**

SOCIAL ST

Responsibilities
Alike
Legislative Branch / Executive Branch / Judicial Branch

- Research the structure and duties of your state's government.

- Discuss with your partner how your state's government and the United States government are

4 **Ideas: Develop Character**

WRITING

Read this part of Nina's story. Identify details and dialogue she uses to develop characters. Revise this part of the story to develop characters with vivid details.

Pe... ...aking plans to become

2 **Idioms, Proverbs, Adages**

PHONICS/WORD STUDY

abc

- Write these idioms: *a bad apple, caught red-handed,* and *pain in the neck.* Talk about the difference between the common meaning of each idiom and the literal meaning of the words it uses.

A Bad Apple

- Write the meaning of each idiom.

- Write these adages and proverbs: *No news is good news; Where there's smoke, there's fire;* and *Better to be safe than sorry.*

- Choose one adage or proverb and use it in a short paragraph that shows its meaning.

You need
> paper
> pencils

5 **Point of View**

READING

- Choose a story that you have read recently. As you reread it, identify the main character and any details that let you know who is telling the story.

- Choose an event in the story. Through whose point of view is it described?

- Write a paragraph retelling the event from the point of view of *another* character. Decide how his or her experience would be the same or different.

You need
> story read recently
> paper
> pencils or pens

Go Digital! www.connected.mcgraw-hill.com • Interactive Games and Activities • Grade 4

DEVELOPING READERS AND WRITERS

Write to Sources and Research

Analysis, T84–T85

Note Taking, T89B, T89X

Summarize, T89V

Point of View, T89V

Make Connections: Essential Question, T89V, T89Z, T93

Key Details, T89X, T89Y

Research and Inquiry, T92

Analyze to Inform/Explain, T93

Comparing Texts, T105, T113, T117, T123

Predictive Writing, T89B

Teacher's Edition

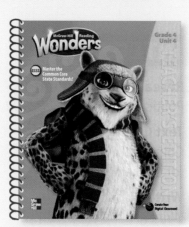

Literature Anthology

Summarize, 309
Point of View, 309

Leveled Readers
Comparing Texts
Point of View

Point of View, 163–165
Genre, 166
Analyze to Inform, 169

Your Turn Practice Book

Interactive Whiteboard

Narrative Text
Fictional Narrative, T344–T349

Conferencing Routines
Teacher Conferences, T346
Peer Conferences, T347

Interactive Whiteboard

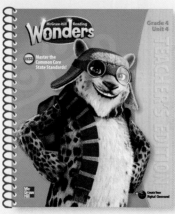

Teacher's Edition

Leveled Workstation Card
Description, Card 27

Writer's Workspace
Fictional Narrative
Writing Process
Multimedia Presentations

Writing Traits • Write Every Day

Writing Trait: Ideas
Develop Character, T94–T95
Conferencing Routines
Teacher Conferences, T96
Peer Conferences, T97

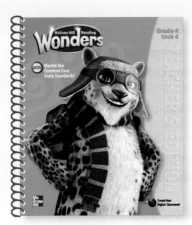

Teacher's Edition

Reading/Writing Workshop

Ideas: Character, 260–261

Interactive Whiteboard

Leveled Workstation Card

Ideas: Character, Card 4

Your Turn Practice Book

Ideas: Character, 170

Grammar and Spelling

Grammar
Types of Pronouns, T98–T99
Spelling
Inflectional Endings: *y* to *i*,
T100–T101

Interactive Whiteboard

Teacher's Edition

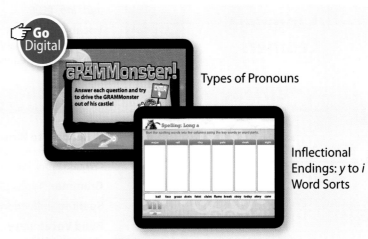

Types of Pronouns

Inflectional Endings: *y* to *i* Word Sorts

Online Spelling and Grammar Games

SUGGESTED LESSON PLAN

✓ **TESTED SKILLS** **CCSS**

	DAY 1	**DAY 2**

READING

Teach, Model and Apply

Reading/Writing Workshop

DAY 1

Build Background Leadership, T74–T75

Listening Comprehension Elephant Versus Monkey, T76–T77

Comprehension
• Preview Genre: Fantasy
• Preview Strategy: Make Predictions

✓ **Vocabulary** Words in Context, T78–T79

Practice *Your Turn*, 161

Close Reading of Complex Text "The TimeSpecs 3000," 252–255

DAY 2

✓ **Comprehension**
• Strategy: Make Predictions, T82–T83
• Skill: Point of View, T84–T85
• Write About Reading ● *Analytical Writing*
• Genre: Fantasy, T86–T87

✓ **Vocabulary** Strategy: Figurative Language, T88–T89

Practice *Your Turn*, 162–167

DIFFERENTIATED INSTRUCTION   Choose across the week to meet your students' needs.

Approaching Level

DAY 1

Leveled Reader *Floozle Dreams*, T104–T105

Phonics/Decoding Inflectional Endings *-ed* and *-ing*, T106 **TIER 2**

Vocabulary
• Review High-Frequency Words, T108 **TIER 2**
• Answer Yes/No Questions, T109

DAY 2

Leveled Reader *Floozle Dreams*, T104–T105

Vocabulary Review Vocabulary Words, T108 **TIER 2**

Comprehension
• Identify Point of View, T110 **TIER 2**
• Review Point of View, T111

On Level

Leveled Reader *The Wolves of Yellowstone*, T112–T113

Vocabulary Review Vocabulary Words, T114

Leveled Reader *The Wolves of Yellowstone*, T112–T113

Comprehension Review Point of View, T115

Beyond Level

Leveled Reader *Krillville*, T116–T117

Vocabulary Review Domain-Specific Words, T118

Leveled Reader *Krillville*, T116–T117

Comprehension Review Point of View, T119

English Language Learners

Shared Read "The TimeSpecs 3000," T120–T121

Phonics/Decoding Inflectional Endings *-ed* and *-ing*, T106

Vocabulary
• Preteach Vocabulary, T124
• Review High-Frequency Words, T108

Leveled Reader *The Wolves of Yellowstone*, T122–123

Vocabulary Review Vocabulary, T124

Writing Writing Trait: Ideas, T126

Grammar Types of Pronouns, T127

LANGUAGE ARTS   Writing Process: Fictional Narrative T344–T349   Use with Weeks 1–3

Writing
Grammar
Spelling
Build Vocabulary

DAY 1

✓ **Readers to Writers**
• Writing Traits: Ideas/Develop Characters, T94–T95
• Writing Entry: Prewrite and Draft, T96

Grammar Types of Pronouns, T98

Spelling Inflectional Endings: *y* to *i*, T100

Build Vocabulary
• Connect to Words, T102
• Academic Vocabulary, T102

DAY 2

Readers to Writers
• Writing Entry: Revise, T96

Grammar Types of Pronouns, T98

Spelling Inflectional Endings: *y* to *i*, T100

Build Vocabulary
• Expand Vocabulary, T102
• Review Context Clues, T102

DAY 3	DAY 4	DAY 5 Review and Assess

READING

Phonics/Decoding
• Inflectional Endings: Changing *y* to *i*, T90
• *r*-Controlled Vowel Syllables, T91

Practice *Your Turn*, 168

Close Reading *LaRue for Mayor*, 288–309 • *Analytical Writing*

Literature Anthology

Fluency Phrasing and Expression, T91
Integrate Ideas • *Analytical Writing*
• Research and Inquiry, T92

Practice *Your Turn*, 163–165

Close Reading "Bringing Government Home," 310–313 • *Analytical Writing*

Integrate Ideas • *Analytical Writing*
• Research and Inquiry, T92
• Text Connections, T93
• Write About Reading, T93

Practice *Your Turn*, 169

DIFFERENTIATED INSTRUCTION

Leveled Reader *Floozle Dreams*, T104–T105
Phonics/Decoding Review Inflectional Endings, T106 **TIER 2**
Fluency Phrasing and Expression, T110 **TIER 2**
Vocabulary Idioms, T109

Leveled Reader Paired Read: "The Job of a Governor," T105 • *Analytical Writing*
Phonics/Decoding Practice Inflectional Endings, T107

Leveled Reader Literature Circles, T105
Comprehension Self-Selected Reading, T111
Phonics/Decoding Syllables with *r*-Controlled Vowels, T107

Leveled Reader *The Wolves of Yellowstone*, T112–T113
Vocabulary Idioms, T114

Leveled Reader Paired Read: "Who Wants to Be Mayor," T113 • *Analytical Writing*

Leveled Reader Literature Circles, T113
Comprehension Self-Selected Reading, T115

Leveled Reader *Krillville*, T116–T117
Vocabulary
• Idioms, T118
• Synthesize, T118

Gifted and Talented

Leveled Reader Paired Read: "Running a Town," T117 • *Analytical Writing*

Leveled Reader Literature Circles, T117
Comprehension
• Self-Selected Reading, T119
• Independent Study: Leadership, T119

Leveled Reader *The Wolves of Yellowstone*, T122–T123
Phonics/Decoding Review Inflectional Endings, T106
Vocabulary Idioms, T125
Spelling Words with Inflectional Endings, T126

Leveled Reader Paired Read: "Who Wants to Be Mayor," T123 • *Analytical Writing*
Vocabulary Additional Vocabulary, T125
Phonics/Decoding Practice Inflectional Endings, T107

Leveled Reader Literature Circles, T123
Phonics/Decoding Syllables with *r*-Controlled Vowels, T107

LANGUAGE ARTS

Readers to Writers
• Writing Entry: Prewrite and Draft, T97
Grammar Mechanics and Usage, T99
Spelling Inflectional Endings: *y* to *i*, T101
Build Vocabulary
• Reinforce the Words, T103
• Idioms, T103

Readers to Writers
• Writing Entry: Revise, T97
Grammar Types of Pronouns, T99
Spelling Inflectional Endings: *y* to *i*, T101
Build Vocabulary
• Connect to Writing, T103
• Shades of Meaning, T103

Readers to Writers
• Writing Entry: Share and Reflect, T97
Grammar Types of Pronouns, T99
Spelling Inflectional Endings: *y* to *i*, T101
Build Vocabulary
• Word Squares, T103
• Morphology, T103

DIFFERENTIATE TO ACCELERATE

 Scaffold to **A**ccess **C**omplex **T**ext

> **IF** ➤ the text complexity of a particular selection is too difficult for students
>
> **THEN** ➤ see the references noted in the chart below for scaffolded instruction to help students Access Complex Text.

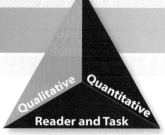

Qualitative **Quantitative**
Reader and Task
TEXT COMPLEXITY

Reading/Writing Workshop	Literature Anthology	Leveled Readers	Classroom Library

Approaching · On Level · Beyond · ELL

Quantitative			
"The TimeSpecs 3000" **Lexile** 910 *TextEvaluator* 46	*LaRue for Mayor* **Lexile** 890 *TextEvaluator* 61	**Approaching Level** **Lexile** 670 *TextEvaluator* 41 **On Level** **Lexile** 740 *TextEvaluator* 40	*Project Mulberry* **Lexile** 690 *TextEvaluator* 39
	"Bringing Government Home" **Lexile** 900 *TextEvaluator* 40	**Beyond Level** **Lexile** 810 *TextEvaluator* 55 **ELL** **Lexile** 610 *TextEvaluator* 18	*Riding Freedom* **Lexile** 720 *TextEvaluator* 40

Qualitative

What Makes the Text Complex?

- **Genre** Fantasy T81
- **Specific Vocabulary** Idioms T89

A C T *See Scaffolded Instruction in Teacher's Edition T81 and T89.*

What Makes the Text Complex?

- **Purpose** Entertain T89E, T89M, T89S
- **Specific Vocabulary** Complex Words T89A, T89K, T89W
- **Sentence Structure** T89I, T89O
- **Connection of Ideas** Motivation T89G; Intentions T89Q
- **Genre** Fantasy T89C; Expository Text T89Y

A C T *See Scaffolded Instruction in Teacher's Edition T89A–T89Z.*

What Makes the Text Complex?

- **Specific Vocabulary**
- **Sentence Structure**
- **Connection of Ideas**
- **Genre**

A C T *See Level Up lessons online for Leveled Readers.*

What Makes the Text Complex?

- **Genre**
- **Specific Vocabulary**
- **Prior Knowledge**
- **Sentence Structure**
- **Organization**
- **Purpose**
- **Connection of Ideas**

A C T *See Scaffolded Instruction in Teacher's Edition T360–T361.*

Reader and Task

The Introduce the Concept lesson on pages T74–T75 will help determine the reader's knowledge and engagement in the weekly concept. See pages T80–T89 and T92–T93 for questions and tasks for this text.

The Introduce the Concept lesson on pages T74–T75 will help determine the reader's knowledge and engagement in the weekly concept. See pages T89A–T89Z and T92–T93 for questions and tasks for this text.

The Introduce the Concept lesson on pages T74–T75 will help determine the reader's knowledge and engagement in the weekly concept. See pages T104–T105, T112–T113, T116–T117, T122–T123, and T92–T93 for questions and tasks for this text.

The Introduce the Concept lesson on pages T74–T75 will help determine the reader's knowledge and engagement in the weekly concept. See pages T360–T361 for questions and tasks for this text.

Monitor and *Differentiate*

IF you need to differentiate instruction

THEN use the Quick Checks to assess students' needs and select the appropriate small group instruction focus.

✓ Quick Check

Comprehension Strategy Make, Confirm, or Revise Predictions T83

Comprehension Skill Point of View T85

Genre Fantasy T87

Vocabulary Strategy Figurative Language T89

Phonics/Fluency Inflectional Endings: Changing *y* to *i* T90

If No → | **Approaching Level** | Reteach T104–T111 |
| **ELL** | Develop T120–T127 |
If Yes → | **On Level** | Review T112–T115 |
| **Beyond Level** | Extend T116–T119 |

Level Up with Leveled Readers

IF students can read their leveled text fluently and answer comprehension questions

THEN work with the next level up to accelerate students' reading with more complex text.

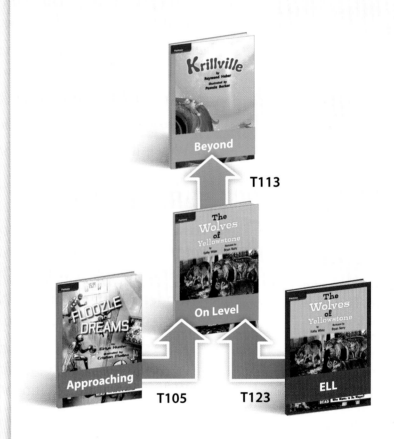

ENGLISH LANGUAGE LEARNERS SCAFFOLD

IF ELL students need additional support **THEN** scaffold instruction using the small group suggestions.

Reading/Writing Workshop "The TimeSpecs 3000" T120–T121	Leveled Reader *The Wolves of Yellowstone* T122–T123 "Who Wants to Be Mayor" T123	Additional Vocabulary T125 boundary decide important leader president	Using Idioms T125	Writing Ideas T126	Spelling Words with Inflectional Endings T126	Grammar Types of Pronouns T127

Note: Include ELL Students in all small groups based on their needs.

→ Introduce the Concept

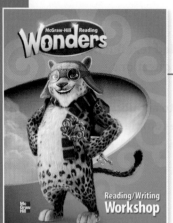

Reading/Writing Workshop

McGraw-Hill Reading

Wonders

Reading/Writing
Workshop

McGraw Hill

OBJECTIVES

CCSS Paraphrase portions of a text read aloud or information presented in diverse media and formats, including visually, quantitatively, and orally. **SL.4.2**

CCSS Pose and respond to specific questions to clarify or follow up on information, and make comments that contribute to the discussion and link to the remarks of others. **SL.4.1c**

Build background knowledge on leadership.

ACADEMIC LANGUAGE

• campaign, governor
• Cognates: *campaña, gobernador*

MINILESSON
10 Mins

Build Background

ESSENTIAL QUESTION
Why do people run for public office?

Have students read the Essential Question on page 248 of the **Reading/ Writing Workshop**. Tell them that when people run for important government offices like **governor,** they must organize a **campaign.**

Discuss the photograph with students. Focus on the needs of the voters in 1932 and what people running for office needed to promise them.

→ What do the people in the hunger march want?

→ If you were running for office in 1932, what would you tell the voters?

→ Why is it important for people to run for office and to vote?

Talk About It

COLLABORATE

Ask: *How do people in public office provide leadership for the people who vote for them? What promises and decisions do they have to make?* Have students discuss in pairs and paraphrase the issues shown in the photo.

→ Model using the Concept Web to generate words and phrases related to leadership and public office. Add students' contributions.

→ Have students continue the discussion by sharing why they would or would not want to run for office. They can complete the Concept Web, generating additional examples of leadership.

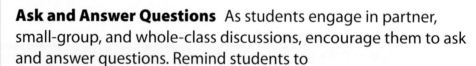

Collaborative Conversations

Ask and Answer Questions As students engage in partner, small-group, and whole-class discussions, encourage them to ask and answer questions. Remind students to

→ ask questions to clarify ideas or comments they do not understand.

→ wait a few seconds after asking a question, to give others a chance to think before responding.

→ answer questions thoughtfully with complete ideas, not one-word answers.

Go Digital

Discuss the Concept

Watch Video

Use Graphic Organizer

Essential Question

Why do people run for public office?

Go Digital!

248

TAKING A STAND

During the Great Depression, there were a number of hunger marches. All over the country, people marched to protest unemployment, lack of health insurance, and the state of the economy. This photograph was taken in 1932 during one of the marches.

NATIONAL HUNGER MARCH 1932

► If you had been a politician running for office in 1932, what would you have told the voters?

► What qualities does a good leader need?

Talk About It

Write words that you have learned about leadership. Then talk with a partner about what would make you want to run for public office.

Leadership

249

(Mugil/New York Times Co./Hulton Archive/Getty Images; (r) David J. & Janice L. Frent Collection/Corbis

READING/WRITING WORKSHOP, pp. 248–249

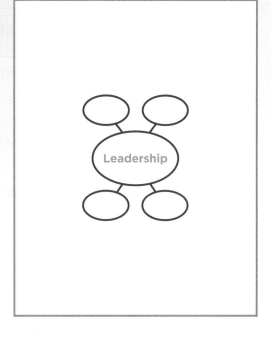

GRAPHIC ORGANIZER 62

Leadership

ELL ENGLISH LANGUAGE LEARNERS SCAFFOLD

Beginning	Intermediate	Advanced/High
Use Visuals Clarify the concept of *leadership*. Show a picture of the president. Point to it and say: *The president of the United States is a leader. Leaders make important decisions.* Have students repeat. Correct students' pronunciation as needed. Tell students that the Spanish word for *leader* is *líder*.	**Describe** Discuss the photograph. Help students understand the concepts of leadership and running for public office by describing the qualities of a good leader. Ask: *What are the qualities of a good leader?* Have students list the qualities and rank them. Encourage students to use concept words.	**Discuss** After discussing the photograph, ask students to name a leader. They can choose from elected officials, teachers, school administrators, or parents. Ask: *How does this person show leadership?* Allow students ample time to respond. Repeat students' answers slowly and clearly for the class to hear.

Listening Comprehension

MINILESSON
10 Mins

Interactive Read Aloud

OBJECTIVES

CCSS Refer to details and examples in a text when explaining what the text says explicitly and when drawing inferences from the text. **RL.4.1**

CCSS Paraphrase portions of a text read aloud or information presented in diverse media and formats, including visually, quantitatively, and orally. **SL.4.2**

- Listen for a purpose.
- Identify characteristics of a fantasy.

ACADEMIC LANGUAGE

- *fantasy; make, confirm, or revise predictions*
- Cognates: *fantasía; confirmar, revisar predicciones*

Connect to Concept: Leadership

Tell students that people run for public office to help improve lives. Let students know that you will be reading aloud a passage about a monkey who becomes a leader in order to make life more fair for everyone. As you read, have students listen carefully for reasons the monkey runs for office.

Preview Genre: Fantasy

Explain that the story you will read aloud is a fantasy. Discuss features of a fantasy:

→ characters, setting, and events could not exist in real life

→ may include animals as characters

→ animal characters behave in human ways

Preview Comprehension Strategy: Make, Confirm, or Revise Predictions

Explain that readers can use text clues to make predictions about what might happen in a story. As readers get more information from the story, they may confirm or revise their earlier predictions.

Use the Think Alouds on page T77 to model the strategy.

Respond to Reading

Think Aloud Clouds Display Think Aloud Master 3: I *predicted _____ because* . . . to reinforce how you used the make, confirm, revise predictions strategy to understand content.

Genre Features With students, discuss the elements of the Read Aloud that let them know it is a fantasy. Ask them to think about other texts that you have read or they have read independently that were fantasies.

Summarize Have students briefly retell the story "Elephant Versus Monkey" in their own words.

Elephant Versus Monkey

Camel, Giraffe, and Monkey stood behind some brush and watched Elephant. He drank from the water hole and then lay down for a nap.

"It's not fair," whispered Camel. "Who is Elephant to say that he can use the water hole whenever he wants?"

"He says he's the mayor," said Giraffe. "He says that as mayor he can do whatever he wants." Camel shook his head, "It's not fair. We should get to use the water hole any time, too." **1**

Other thirsty animals joined them and agreed with Camel and Giraffe. "We should elect our own mayor," said Camel. "A new mayor could tell Elephant that he must share the water hole at all times."

Elephant slowly turned his large head toward the animals. "I can hear you, you know," he said as he flapped his enormous ears. "So you think one of you would get more votes than me!" he laughed. "Everyone will vote for me because I am powerful."

The animals were silent as they thought about this. At last, a small voice called out, "I'll run for office!" Monkey stood atop Camel's hump and called out again, "Vote for me and I'll make sure everyone has equal access to the water hole!"

Elephant laughed. "Fine! Next Tuesday we'll vote. But I'm certain, ABSOLUTELY CERTAIN, that I'll win." He bellowed loudly, causing the animals to turn and run. **2**

The following Tuesday, the animals gathered for the election. Elephant was confident he would be the winner as he raised his trunk to vote for himself.

But that was the only vote he received. Monkey won the election by a landslide. The surprised Elephant stomped off in defeat as the animals cheered Monkey's victory. **3**

1 Think Aloud Will the animals convince Elephant to let them use the water hole? I **predict** that they'll come up with a plan. As I read, I can **confirm or revise my prediction**.

2 Think Aloud My **prediction** was correct. The animals planned an election. I **predict** that Elephant will try to scare the animals into voting for him, but Monkey will win anyway.

3 Think Aloud My second **prediction** was correct. I will now **make a prediction** that Monkey will be a good and fair mayor and that the animals will get to use the water hole whenever they want.

Yellow Dog Productions/Digital Vision/Getty Images

→ Vocabulary

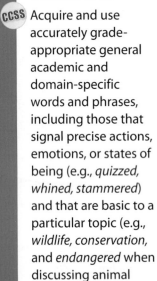

Reading/Writing Workshop

OBJECTIVES

CCSS Acquire and use accurately grade-appropriate general academic and domain-specific words and phrases, including those that signal precise actions, emotions, or states of being (e.g., *quizzed, whined, stammered*) and that are basic to a particular topic (e.g., *wildlife, conservation,* and *endangered* when discussing animal preservation). **L.4.6**

ACADEMIC LANGUAGE

- *campaign, governor*
- Cognates: *campaña, gobernador*

 MINILESSON **10** Mins

Words in Context

Model the Routine

Introduce each vocabulary word using the Vocabulary Routine found on the Visual Vocabulary Cards.

Visual Vocabulary Cards

Vocabu...
Define:
Example:
Ask:

Vocabulary Routine

<u>Define:</u> A **governor** is a person elected to be the head of a state government in the United States.

<u>Example:</u> The governor spoke at a town hall meeting about the state budget.

<u>Ask:</u> What are some ways a governor can help the people in his or her state?

Definitions

→ **accompanies**	**Accompanies** means "goes along with something."
→ **campaign**	A **campaign** is a series of actions planned and carried out to bring about a particular result. **Cognate:** *campaña*
→ **intend**	To **intend** is to have a purpose or plan in mind.
→ **opponent**	An **opponent** is a person or group that is against another in a fight, contest, or discussion.
→ **overwhelming**	Something **overwhelming** is overcoming or overpowering completely.
→ **tolerate**	To **tolerate** means to put up with or endure someone or something. **Cognate:** *tolerar*
→ **weary**	To be **weary** means to be very tired.

Talk About It

 COLLABORATE

Have partners discuss the vocabulary by reviewing the words' definitions and using them in new sentences to describe the pictures. Then ask students to choose three words and write questions for their partner to answer.

Go Digital

governor

Use Visual Glossary

CCSS Words to Know

Vocabulary

Use the picture and the sentences to talk with a partner about each word.

accompanies Jake's dog **accompanies** him on car rides.

What is a synonym for accompanies?

campaign The woman signed up to work on Mr. Baker's **campaign** for the state senate.

What are some activities a politician does during a campaign?

governor The **governor** spoke at a town hall meeting about the state budget.

What are some ways a governor can help the people in his or her state?

intend Does the mouse **intend** to eat the grape?

What do you intend to do tomorrow?

opponent Laili and her brother beat the online **opponent** they were playing against in the video game.

What is an antonym for opponent?

overwhelming The number of books that Todd had to carry was **overwhelming**.

What is a synonym for overwhelming?

tolerate Polar bears can **tolerate** extremely cold water.

What kind of animal can tolerate living in a hot desert climate?

weary The firefighter was **weary** and needed to rest after fighting a fire for 10 hours.

Why else might someone be weary?

Your Turn COLLABORATE

Pick three words. Write three questions for your partner to answer.

Go Digital! *Use the online visual glossary*

250

251

READING/WRITING WORKSHOP, pp. 250–251

ELL ENGLISH LANGUAGE LEARNERS SCAFFOLD

Beginning

Use Visuals Point to the picture for *governor*. Say: *A governor is a leader. A governor leads a state.* Help students complete the sentence frame: *A ____ leads a state.* (governor) Correct students' pronunciation as needed. *Governor* in Spanish is *gobernador*.

Intermediate

Describe Have students describe the picture for *governor*. Help them with pronunciation and provide the cognate *gobernador*. Ask: *How can a governor help the people in his or her state?* Ask partners to describe ways a governor can help his or her state. Circulate and elicit details to support students' responses.

Advanced/High

Discuss Ask partners to discuss the picture for *governor*. Ask: *How is a governor different from a president?* (A governor leads a state; a president leads the country.) *What are some responsibilities of a governor?* (listen and talk to people; make a budget; plan new projects) Correct students' responses for meaning when needed.

ON-LEVEL PRACTICE BOOK p. 161

| accompanies | campaign | governor | intend |
| opponent | overwhelming | tolerate | weary |

Use the context clues in each sentence to help you decide which vocabulary word fits best in the blank.

Elections don't happen every year, so getting to vote is very important for my dad. When the ___campaign___ begins to show who may be the next ___governor___ of our state, my dad becomes very involved. He usually has a favorite, but he always learns about the ___opponent___ so he has all information to make a good decision.

The amount of election mail we get is ___overwhelming___, but my dad carefully goes through it all. He won't ___tolerate___ it if we tell him we are ___weary___ of all the news he watches. He insists on knowing as much as possible.

Every Election Day, we ___intend___ to go together so he can vote after he gets off of work. But every time, he comes home and has already voted. He likes the little "I Voted" sticker that ___accompanies___ him through his day. He says he has done his duty as a United States citizen, and that makes him happy.

| APPROACHING p. 161 | BEYOND p. 161 | ELL p. 161 |

CCSS Shared Read Genre • Fantasy

The TimeSpecs 3000

? Essential Question
Why do people run for public office?
Read how Miguel makes a decision to run for class president.

252

September 15

Dear Grandpa,

I just got back from our class field trip to Washington, D.C., and I have a lot to tell you. Going to Washington helped me decide to run for class president.

I owe it all to your invention, the TimeSpecs 3000! In a nutshell, it helped me get some helpful advice about my problem. I **intend** to tell you everything when I visit Saturday, but for now I've pasted my field notes into this e-mail, so you can understand how well your invention worked.

FIELD NOTES: **DAY 1**

I use the TimeSpecs 3000 at the Washington Monument. Our guide **accompanies** us everywhere, and while she's talking I put on the specs. The design needs tweaking because my friend Ken whispered, "Nerdy shades, dude!"

Immediately, I'm seeing the monument in the past. I am watching the ceremony when they laid the cornerstone in 1848, and everybody's wearing large hats and funny, old-fashioned clothes. When I take off the TimeSpecs 3000, I realize my class is heading to lunch so I run after them.

253

READING/WRITING WORKSHOP, pp. 252–253

Reading/Writing
Workshop

Shared Read

Lexile 910   *TextEvaluator*. 46

Connect to Concept: Leadership

Explain to students that they will read about a boy who gets some unusual advice about how to be a leader in his school. Read "The TimeSpecs 3000" with students. Note the vocabulary words previously taught are highlighted in the text.

Close Reading

Reread Paragraph 2: With students, reread the second paragraph of "The TimeSpecs 3000." Ask: *Can you predict how the TimeSpecs 3000 will help Miguel?* Remind students that fantasies include things that can't happen in everyday life.

I predict that Miguel will use the TimeSpecs to look into the future and find out how he will lead the school as class president. As I read, I should check to see if my prediction is correct.

Reread Paragraphs 4–6: Reread the fourth, fifth, and sixth paragraphs with students and note how Miguel uses the TimeSpecs 3000. Ask: *Now that we've seen Miguel use the TimeSpecs, was our prediction correct? How can we use context clues to make another prediction?*

The prediction was incorrect. We find out that the TimeSpecs allow Miguel to look at a place as it appeared in the past, and that Miguel is now thinking about running for class president. We can use this clue to predict that he will ask Abraham Lincoln for advice.

FIELD NOTES: **DAY 2**

We're back on the National Mall, which is nothing like Brookfield's mall with all its stores. This mall is outside and has a long reflecting pool. My teacher is finding it hard to **tolerate** some of my classmates' immature behavior, which includes running around throwing pebbles in the reflecting pool. I'm getting kind of **weary** of all the noise, and I'd rather learn about history on my own. So I put on the TimeSpecs 3000 and check out the Lincoln Memorial.

I see how dignified Lincoln's statue looks and wonder if I could ever help people like he did. This starts me thinking again about whether I should run for class president. Suddenly, right out of the blue, I hear this voice. "Excuse me, young man. You're thinking of running for president?" I look up and realize that Lincoln's statue is talking to me. It's so **overwhelming** that I stand there speechless for a minute.

Finally, I stammer, "President . . . Lincoln?"

"Maybe you should first run for mayor of your town," the statue says. "Or perhaps for **governor**? Once you get the hang of being in public office, you could run for president."

"Actually, it's for president of my 4th grade class," I say.

The giant statue nods. "That's an excellent start."

254

I figure while I have Lincoln's ear, I should get some advice. "I have a problem. I hate writing and giving speeches, and my **opponent**, Tommy, is great at both things."

"What kind of **campaign** would you run?" Lincoln asks.

"I have lots of ideas for our school," I tell him. "For instance, I want our school to use fruits and vegetables from the local farmers' market in the cafeteria. I also want to start a book drive for our school library."

"There's your speech," he says. "Tell people your ideas with honesty, integrity, and enthusiasm, and you can't possibly go wrong."

"Thanks, Mr. President," I say. "I think I can do that!"

Grandpa, I can't wait to see you on Saturday because I have to tell you about our visit to the Natural History Museum.

Your grandson and future class president,
Miguel

P.S. I would advise not wearing the TimeSpecs 3000 while looking at dinosaur bones.

Make Connections

Talk about why Miguel decides to run for class president. ESSENTIAL QUESTION

What would you do for your school if you were class president? TEXT TO SELF

255

READING/WRITING WORKSHOP, pp. 254–255

Make Connections

ESSENTIAL QUESTION

Encourage students to go back into the text for evidence as they talk about Miguel's reasons for running for class president. Ask students to describe what they would do if they were class president.

Continue Close Reading

Use the following lessons for focused rereadings.

→ Make, Confirm, or Revise Predictions, T82–T83

→ Point of View, T84–T85

→ Fantasy, T86–T87

→ Figurative Language, T88–T89

A C T Access Complex Text

▶ Genre

Guide students in identifying the elements of the story that make it a fantasy.

→ *How do you know this selection is a fantasy?* (The story is fictional and illustrated. Miguel uses his TimeSpecs 3000 to see what happened in the past in Washington, D.C. Lincoln's statue spoke to him and gave him advice.)

→ *Why does Miguel advise his grandfather not to wear the TimeSpecs 3000 while looking at dinosaur bones?* (He most likely saw live dinosaurs of the past. It may have been scary.)

→ # Comprehension Strategy

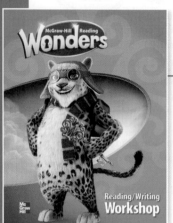

Reading/Writing Workshop

OBJECTIVES

CCSS Refer to details and examples in a text when explaining what the text says explicitly and when drawing inferences from the text. **RL.4.1**

Make, confirm, and revise predictions to enhance comprehension.

ACADEMIC LANGUAGE

- *make, confirm, revise predictions; fantasy*
- Cognates: *confirmar, revisar predicciones; fantasía*

 MINILESSON 10 Mins

Make, Confirm, or Revise Predictions

1 Explain

Explain that as students read a fantasy, they should consider how events and characters' actions might influence later events in the story. Thinking about future events in this way is called making predictions.

→ When readers make predictions, they say what events they think will happen later on in the story.

→ A prediction is more than just a guess; a prediction is based on events that have already happened in the story.

→ As readers progress, they should check to see if their predictions have proven correct, or if their predictions require revision.

Point out that making and revising predictions helps students understand how characters' actions affect a story's plot.

2 Model Close Reading: Text Evidence

Reread the e-mail at the top of page 253 with students and model making a prediction about what the TimeSpecs 3000 is and how it will be used.

3 Guided Practice of Close Reading

COLLABORATE

Have students work in pairs to find clues that helped them predict how Abraham Lincoln would help Miguel. Once they've finished, have pairs reread the end of the story and discuss how their predictions turned out. Have students share their results with the class.

Go Digital

View "The TimeSpecs 3000"

 CCSS Comprehension Strategy

Make Predictions

When you read you can use details from the story to make predictions about what you think will happen. As you read "The TimeSpecs 3000," make predictions about the story and confirm or revise them.

 Find Text Evidence

What kind of invention did you predict the TimeSpecs 3000 was? Go back and reread the beginning of the e-mail on page 253. What details helped you to make your prediction?

page 253

September 15

Dear Grandpa,

I just got back from our class field trip to Washington, D.C., and I have a lot to tell you. Going to Washington helped me decide to run for class president.

I owe it all to your invention, the TimeSpecs 3000! In a nutshell, it helped me get some helpful advice about my problem. I **intend** to tell you everything when I visit Saturday, but for now I've pasted my field notes into this e-mail, so you can understand how well your invention worked.

FIELD NOTES: DAY 1

I use the TimeSpecs 3000 at the Washington Monument. Our guide **accompanies** us everywhere, and while she's

> As I read page 253 of "The TimeSpecs 3000," I predicted the invention would be a special kind of glasses because of its name.

Your Turn
COLLABORATE

Read page 255 of "The TimeSpecs 3000." What clues did you find in the text that led you to predict Abraham Lincoln's words would help Miguel solve his problem?

256

READING/WRITING WORKSHOP, p. 256

ELL ENGLISH LANGUAGE LEARNERS SCAFFOLD

Beginning	**Intermediate**	**Advanced/High**
Practice Before reading, define difficult words and phrases, such as *invention, advice,* and *field notes.* Read the e-mail with students. Point to the illustration of the glasses and ask: *Will the TimeSpecs 3000 help the boy?* Point out that *invention* is a cognate: *invención.*	**Discuss** Have students reread the e-mail on page 253. Ask: *What are the TimeSpecs 3000? How do you think the TimeSpecs 3000 will help the narrator?* Have partners discuss their predictions. Point out that the text may be confusing because the narrator refers to a problem but does not give details.	**Write** Have students reread the e-mail on page 253. Ask them to write a prediction about the TimeSpecs 3000. Elicit from students why the text may be confusing. Ask: *What do we know about the TimeSpecs 3000? How will the narrator use them?* Have partners share their predictions.

Monitor and *Differentiate*

 Quick Check

Are students able to use clues to predict how Abraham Lincoln will help Miguel solve his problem?

⬇

Small Group Instruction

If No → | **Approaching Level** | Reteach p. T104
| **ELL** | Develop p. T120

If Yes → | **On Level** | Review p. T112
| **Beyond Level** | Extend p. T116

ON-LEVEL PRACTICE BOOK pp. 163–164

Read the passage. Use the make predictions strategy to predict what will happen later on in the text.

The Sheep in the Wilderness

Our herd of sheep was ruled by a cruel shepherd for years. At last
14   we couldn't stand it any longer. We began to stay awake each night
27   until the shepherd had gone to bed. Then we would plan our escape.
40   One night, our herd
53   crept quietly out of the pasture while the shepherd and his dogs slept.
66   *We are finally free!* I thought as we entered the dark forest.
78   Life was hard when we lived with the shepherd, but I learned that it
92   was even harder on our own. Trouble came when we needed to find a
106 place to graze. Our group came to a fork in the path. "There's a wide,
121 green pasture that way," an old gray sheep said, pointing to the path
134 that led downhill. "I remember the shepherd took us there once to
146 graze. There was plenty for everyone to eat."
154   "We can't go there!" a younger brown sheep said. "If the shepherd
166 took you to graze in that pasture, he knows where it is. Besides, it's
180 completely surrounded by forest. We would never see the shepherd
190 coming if he tried to sneak up on us." The brown sheep pointed to
204 the other path. It led uphill. "There are fewer trees on the mountain.
217 There must be a pasture there. And if the shepherd comes looking for
230 us, we'll see him before he sees us."

APPROACHING pp. 163–164	**BEYOND** pp. 163–164	**ELL** pp. 163–164

→ Comprehension Skill

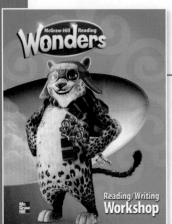

Reading/Writing Workshop

OBJECTIVES

CCSS Compare and contrast the points of view from which different stories are narrated, including the difference between first- and third-person narrations. **RL.4.6**

Identify the narrator's point of view.

ACADEMIC LANGUAGE
point of view

MINILESSON 10 Mins — Point of View

1 Explain

Explain to students that a story's point of view is how the narrator thinks or feels about the characters or events in the story.

→ When the story is told by one of the characters, it has a first-person narrator. This means that the reader can only know and see what this character knows and sees.

→ When the story is told by someone who is not part of the story, it is told by a third-person narrator. This means the reader might know and see what all the characters know and see.

2 Model Close Reading: Text Evidence

Model identifying pronouns on page 253 that show the story has a first-person narrator. Fill in the graphic organizer with examples from the text that convey the narrator's point of view.

 Write About Reading: Analysis Model using the details in the graphic organizer to determine the narrator's point of view in "The TimeSpecs 3000."

3 Guided Practice of Close Reading

 Have students work in pairs to complete the graphic organizer with examples from the rest of "The TimeSpecs 3000." Have students use the other examples they find to describe the narrator's point of view.

 Write About Reading: Analysis Ask pairs to work together to write a comparison of this selection's point of view and the point of view in "Elephant Versus Monkey." Students should begin by identifying the narrator in each story and include evidence for their conclusions about point of view.

Go Digital

Present the Lesson

SKILLS TRACE

POINT OF VIEW

Introduce Unit 2 Week 5

Review Unit 3 Weeks 1, 2; Unit 4 Weeks 2, 3, 6; Unit 5 Week 6; Unit 6 Week 6

Assess Units 2, 3, 4

Comprehension Skill CCSS

Point of View

The narrator's point of view is how the narrator thinks or feels about characters or events in the story. A story can have a first-person narrator or a third-person narrator.

 Find Text Evidence

When I read page 253 of "The TimeSpecs 3000," I learn that a boy is writing an e-mail to his grandfather. I see the pronouns I, me and my so I know this story has a first-person narrator. I can find details in the story to find the narrator's point of view.

Details
The narrator was weary of the noise his classmates made and wanted to learn history on his own.
The narrator wonders if he could ever help people like Lincoln did.

↓

Point of View
The narrator is a fourth-grader excited by history. He is unsure if he should run for class president.

Your Turn COLLABORATE

Find other details from "The TimeSpecs 3000" that tell you the narrator's point of view. Put the information in the graphic organizer.

Go Digital!
Use the interactive graphic organizer

257

READING/WRITING WORKSHOP, p. 257

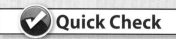
Monitor and *Differentiate*

 Quick Check

Are students able to complete the graphic organizer with other details from "The TimeSpecs 3000" that demonstrate point of view?

⬇

Small Group Instruction

If No →	Approaching Level	Reteach p. T111
	ELL	Develop p. T120
If Yes →	On Level	Review p. T115
	Beyond Level	Extend p. T119

 ENGLISH LANGUAGE LEARNERS SCAFFOLD

Beginning	Intermediate	Advanced/High
Listen Review the definition of a first-person narrator with students. Write the pronouns *I, me,* and *my* on the board. Ask students to raise their hands when they hear one of the pronouns as you read the story aloud. Ask: *Does "The TimeSpecs 3000" use a first-person narrator?* (yes)	**Understand** Ask: *How can we tell if a story has a first-person narrator?* (The story uses the pronouns I, me, and my.) *Can we learn about the thoughts and feelings of a narrator?* (yes) Have partners reread page 253 to determine narrator's point of view. Then have them fill in the sentence frame: *The narrator feels _____ about the TimeSpecs 3000.*	**Recognize** Have students reread the e-mail on page 253. Then have them look for clues that help them determine the point of view and the narrator of the story. Ask: *What do we learn about the narrator's point of view?* Have students work with a partner to discuss what they know about the narrator so far.

ON-LEVEL PRACTICE BOOK pp. 163–165

A. Reread the passage and answer the questions.
Possible responses provided.

1. **What kind of narrator tells the story? How do you know?**
The story is told by a first-person narrator. The narrator uses words like "I" and "me," which tell me that it is first-person.

2. **Is the narrator part of the story? What do we learn about the narrator in the first paragraph?**
Yes. The narrator is a sheep whose herd was ruled by a cruel shepherd until they escaped.

3. **What is the narrator's point of view about leadership? Cite evidence from the text.**
The narrator believes a leader should be someone the sheep can trust.
The leader will listen to everyone's ideas and make important decisions.

B. Work with a partner. Read the passage aloud. Pay attention to phrasing and expression. Stop after one minute. Fill out the chart.

	Words Read	–	Number of Errors	=	Words Correct Score
First Read		–		=	
Second Read		–		=	

APPROACHING pp. 163–165	BEYOND pp. 163–165	ELL pp. 163–165

→ Genre: Literature

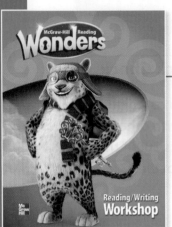

Reading/Writing Workshop

Fantasy

1 Explain

Explain to students that some things happen in "The TimeSpecs 3000" that could not happen in real life. Stories like this are called **fantasies**.

→ Fantasy is a type of fiction.

→ It includes invented people, places, things, and events that are not only made up, but impossible in the real world.

→ Many fantasy stories include illustrations to help readers understand the made-up people, places, and things they describe.

2 Model Close Reading: Text Evidence

Model finding the elements on page 253 that identify "The TimeSpecs 3000" as a fantasy. Demonstrate using the illustrations to understand the text.

Illustrations Point to the illustration at the bottom of page 253. Explain that illustrations in a fantasy help the reader visualize the things in the story that don't normally happen in real life. Ask: *What is this illustration showing? How does it demonstrate that "The TimeSpecs 3000" is a fantasy?*

3 Guided Practice of Close Reading

Have students work with partners to find two more examples in the text that show "The TimeSpecs 3000" is a fantasy. Encourage them to explain what makes each example unrealistic. Have pairs share their work with the class.

OBJECTIVES

CCSS Make connections between the text of a story or drama and a visual or oral presentation of the text, identifying where each version reflects specific descriptions and directions in the text. **RL.4.7**

CCSS By the end of the year, read and comprehend literature, including stories, dramas, and poetry, in the grades 4–5 text complexity band proficiently, with scaffolding as needed at the high end of the range. **RL.4.10**

Recognize the characteristics and text features of fantasy.

ACADEMIC LANGUAGE

• fantasy, illustration
• Cognates: *fantasía, illustración*

CCSS Genre | Literature

Fantasy

"The TimeSpecs 3000" is a fantasy.

A fantasy:
- Is a type of fiction story.
- Has characters, settings, or events that could not exist in real life.
- Usually includes illustrations.

 Find Text Evidence

"The TimeSpecs 3000" is a fantasy. The character of Miguel is realistic, but when he uses the TimeSpecs 3000 he is able to see things that happened in the past. Also, some of the illustrations depict events that could not happen in real life.

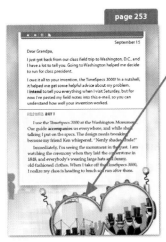

page 253

 Illustrations Illustrations show the events of the story. Here we can see what the world looks like viewed through the TimeSpecs 3000.

Your Turn COLLABORATE

Find two more examples in the text that show "The TimeSpecs 3000" is a fantasy. Discuss these examples with your partner.

258

READING/WRITING WORKSHOP, p. 258

Monitor and *Differentiate*

✓ **Quick Check**

Are students able to find two more examples that demonstrate "The TimeSpecs 3000" is a fantasy?

Small Group Instruction

If No →	Approaching Level	Reteach p. T104
	ELL	Develop p. T120
If Yes →	On Level	Review p. T112
	Beyond Level	Extend p. T116

The *Aurora*'s First Mission

Construction on the *Aurora* ended in 2412. Over a mile in length, it was unlike any space cruiser ever built. The ship's advanced computer controlled the billions of instruments on board. Now the ship needed a captain. Two candidates were favored. Dr. Yanic had designed the ship's computer. He knew how it worked and how to fix it. The other candidate, Admiral Clark, had been in the Galactic Navy and knew how to run a ship.

Answer the questions about the text.

1. How do you know this text is fantasy?
   It includes characters, events, or settings that could not exist in real life.

2. What in the text could not happen in real life?
   Possible response: It is set in the future; space ships that large haven't been possible to build.

3. What text feature is included?
   illustration

4. How does the text feature help show that the text is fantasy?
   Possible response: It shows a space cruiser that is over a mile long, so it probably has a city inside; space cities haven't been built yet.

| APPROACHING p. 166 | BEYOND p. 166 | ELL p. 166 |

 ENGLISH LANGUAGE LEARNERS SCAFFOLD

Beginning

Use Visuals Review the characteristics of a fantasy. Have students point to the illustrations. Discuss the illustrations by eliciting short words and phrases that describe what is happening in each. Ask: *Can a pair of glasses help us see the past? Is this story a fantasy?*

Intermediate

Explain Discuss the characteristics of a fantasy. Ask: *What does the illustration on page 253 show? Can this event happen in real life?* Have partners explain how the illustrations provide clues that the events in the story are part of a fantasy.

Advanced/High

Discuss Have students work with a partner to discuss how the illustrations on pages 252 and 253 depict events that could only happen in a fantasy. Ask: *How do the illustrations show that "The TimeSpecs 3000" is a fantasy?*

→ Vocabulary Strategy

Reading/Writing Workshop

OBJECTIVES

CCSS Determine the meaning of words and phrases as they are used in a text, including those that allude to significant characters found in mythology (e.g., Herculean). **RL.4.4**

CCSS Demonstrate understanding of figurative language, word relationships, and nuances in word meaning. Recognize and explain the meaning of common idioms, adages, and proverbs. **L.4.5b**

ACADEMIC LANGUAGE

idiom

MINILESSON 10 Mins

Figurative Language

1 Explain

Explain to students that when reading, they may occasionally come across a phrase or expression whose meaning is unfamiliar. The words within the expression may be familiar, but they are used together in a way that doesn't seem to be literal. Phrases like these are called **idioms**.

→ An idiom is a phrase or expression whose meaning cannot be understood by interpreting the words contained within it literally.

→ Students can try to find the meaning of an idiom by using context clues, reading the surrounding sentences in the paragraph, and seeing how the idiom fits in.

2 Model Close Reading: Text Evidence

Model finding clues that help identify the meaning of the idiom *in a nutshell* on page 253 of "The TimeSpecs 3000."

3 Guided Practice of Close Reading

Have students work in pairs to find the meanings of the idioms *out of the blue*, *get the hang of*, and *have Lincoln's ear* in "The TimeSpecs 3000." Remind students that context clues can help demonstrate an idiom's meaning. Then have pairs write a short definition for each of the idioms and use it in a sentence. Have students share their responses with the class.

Go Digital

Present the Lesson

Vocabulary Strategy

Idioms

An idiom is a phrase or expression whose meaning cannot be understood from the separate words in it. If you are not sure of the meaning of an idiom, look at the surrounding phrases and sentences to help you figure it out.

 Find Text Evidence

The phrase *in a nutshell* on *page 253* is an idiom. I know it does not mean that something is really inside the shell of a nut. Miguel says that his grandfather's invention helped him reach a decision. I think that *in a nutshell* means to summarize or say briefly.

I owe it all to your invention, the TimeSpecs 3000! In a nutshell, it helped me get some helpful advice about my problem.

Your Turn

Use context clues to figure out the meanings of the following idioms in "The TimeSpecs 3000."

out of the blue, *page 254*
get the hang of, *page 254*
have Lincoln's ear, *page 255*

259

Chris Boyd

READING/WRITING WORKSHOP, p. 259

A C T Access Complex Text

▶ Specific Vocabulary

Help students understand how idioms work.

→ *What does the phrase* out of the blue *mean?* (suddenly, or without warning)

→ *Finding out original meanings of idioms can help you understand how they are used. Many are phrases whose words or use have changed over time.*

→ *For instance,* out of the blue *is a shortened form of* out of the blue sky. *So something happening "out of the blue" is as surprising as something that falls out of the sky.*

Monitor and *Differentiate*

✓ Quick Check

Are students able to find the meanings of the idioms *out of the blue, get the hang of,* and *have Lincoln's ear?*

Small Group Instruction

If No →	**Approaching Level**	Reteach p. T109
	ELL	Develop p. T125
If Yes →	**On Level**	Review p. T114
	Beyond Level	Extend p. T118

ON-LEVEL PRACTICE BOOK p. 167

Read each passage. Underline the words that help you figure out the meaning of each idiom in bold. Then write the idiom's meaning on the line.

1. Finally, the time came to **make our move**. Late one night, our herd crept quietly out of the pasture while the shepherd and his dogs slept.

   do what we had planned

2. Life was hard when we lived with the shepherd, but I learned that it was even harder **on our own**.

   living without supervision

3. Each of the other sheep **took the side of** either the old gray sheep or the young brown sheep. The herd argued for hours, but we still could not decide where to graze.

   chose a side of the argument to agree with

APPROACHING	BEYOND	ELL
p. 167	p. 167	p. 167

VOCABULARY STRATEGY **T89**

Develop Comprehension

Literature Anthology

Complex vocabulary and sentence structure place this selection above TextEvaluator range. Content is grade-level appropriate.

LaRue for Mayor

Text Complexity Range

Lexile

740 ▲ 1010
890

TextEvaluator™

23 51 ▲ *61

Options for Close Reading

→ Whole Class

→ Small Group

→ Independent

This selection is suggested for use as an Extended Complex Text. See pages T356–T361.

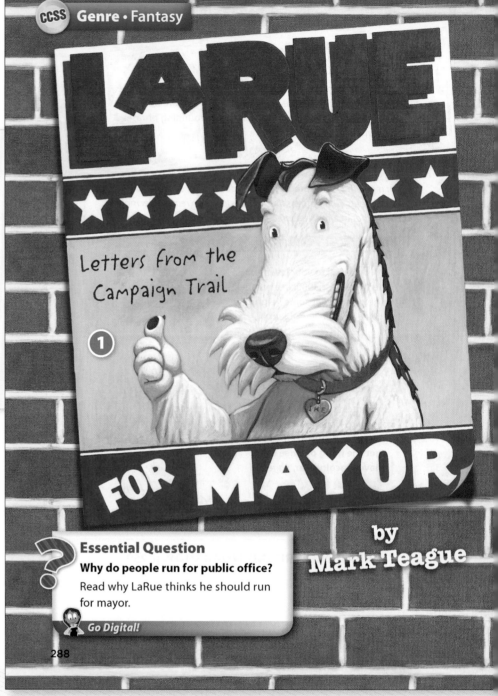

CCSS Genre · Fantasy

L·A·RUE

Letters from the Campaign Trail

1

FOR MAYOR

Essential Question

Why do people run for public office?

Read why LaRue thinks he should run for mayor.

Go Digital!

288

by **Mark Teague**

A C T Access Complex Text

What makes this text complex?

▷ **Purpose**

▷ **Specific Vocabulary**

▷ **Genre**

▷ **Sentence Structure**

▷ **Connection of Ideas**

▷ Specific Vocabulary

Have students use context clues to define unfamiliar words in the selection.

→ *Identify the context clues that help you understand the meaning of* shoo-in. ("Bugwort...will run for mayor of Snort City"; "widely considered a shoo-in for the job." A *shoo-in* is someone or something certain to win.)

The Snort City Register/Gazette

September 30

Bugwort Launches Campaign for Mayor

Former Pumpkinville police chief Hugo Bugwort announced yesterday that he will run for mayor of Snort City. Calling himself the "Law and Order" candidate, Bugwort, who spoke to a cheering crowd in Gruber Park, is widely considered a shoo-in for the job. "Snort City is a disgrace!" he said, to polite applause. "We need to be more like Pumpkinville. That means no more sloppiness, no more silliness, and no more foolish behavior." The speech was interrupted when several dogs in the back of the crowd overturned a hot-dog cart. Injured in the fracas was Gertrude LaRue of Second Avenue. The dogs were not identified.

Dogs Disrupt Rally

289

LITERATURE ANTHOLOGY, pp. 288–289

Predictive Writing

Have students read the title and preview the illustrations. Tell students to write their predictions about what will happen in the selection. Encourage them to discuss other fantasy stories that include invented characters, such as talking animals.

ESSENTIAL QUESTION

Ask a student to read aloud the Essential Question. Have students discuss how the story might help them answer the question.

Note Taking: Use the Graphic Organizer

Analytical Writing

As students read the selection, ask them to take notes by filling in the graphic organizer on **Your Turn Practice Book page 162** to record the point of view in the selection.

① Text Features: Illustrations

Look at the illustration of the campaign poster. What does it tell you about this story? Turn to a partner and discuss.
(It shows that this story is fantasy because it is about a dog running for mayor.)

→ *Identify the context clues that help you understand the meaning of* fracas. ("The speech was interrupted when several dogs…overturned a hot dog cart"; "Injured in the fracas was Gertrude LaRue." A fracas is a noisy fight, as the dogs were fighting over the hot dogs.)

 Point to the poster on page 288. Ask students if they have ever seen a campaign poster. Review the elements of a campaign poster, including the name of the person running for election, the office the person is seeking, and the photograph of the person. Have students point to each element and tell who is running and the office he is running for.

Develop Comprehension

2 Skill: Point of View

What kind of narrator do we see on pages 290 and 291? (first person) How can you tell? (The narrator, Ike, uses the pronouns *I*, *me,* and *my* in his letters to Mrs. LaRue.) What is Ike's point of view? (He feels he is good and worthy of Mrs. LaRue's sympathy.) How do you know? (Ike says he isn't to blame for the hot-dog cart and that he is worried about himself. He says he is having a difficult time, but doing good deeds will help him.) Use these examples to complete your chart.

Details
"No doubt you are worried about me. So am I!"
"Yes, this will be a difficult time for me."
Doing good deeds will "ease the pain" of Mrs. LaRue's absence.

↓

Point of View
Ike is good and worthy of sympathy.

October 1

Dear Mrs. LaRue,

How sorry I am to hear about your injuries! Who knew that hot-dog carts were so unstable? I was simply trying to get a better view of Chief Bugwort when it collapsed. Heaven knows what those other dogs were doing. I must admit that they created an unfortunate impression of delinquency. Anyway, I'm shocked to hear that you'll be confined to the hospital for so long.

No doubt you are worried about me. So am I! But Mrs. Hibbins has promised to serve my meals, and somehow I will persevere.

With Deepest Sympathy,

Ike

290

A C T Access Complex Text

▶ Genre

Use page 291 to help students follow the elements of reality and fantasy in the story.

→ *What does Ike tell Mrs. LaRue in his letter?* (Ike says that he has formed a social club with other dogs. He says they will do good deeds.)

→ *What does the illustration show?* (The color illustration shows Ike and his doggy pals forming

"The Feisty Paws Club" where no cats are allowed. The black and white illustration shows Ike and his pals at the "Happy Chums Social Club.")

→ *Why are there color and black and white illustrations in this story?* (The color illustration is reality—what is actually happening in Ike's world. The black and white illustration is Ike's fantasy.)

LITERATURE ANTHOLOGY, pp. 290–291

Make Predictions Ike says his social club will serve the community. Do you predict the club will really do good deeds?

Teacher Think Aloud I know that I can paraphrase details from the selection to make predictions about Ike's social club. Looking at the page, both the illustrations and text tell about how Ike envisions his social club. Ike wants his club to perform good deeds for the community, but the previous text shows Ike to be more mischievous. I can predict that Ike is planning to disrupt several community events based on the previous text.

③ Genre: Fantasy

What features of a fantasy have you found so far in the selection? (invented characters with human qualities, such as a talking dog) Identify the specific features of the story that tell you it's a fantasy. (The selection is set in Snort City, which sounds made up. Ike is a dog who writes letters to Mrs. LaRue, and dogs cannot write or read.)

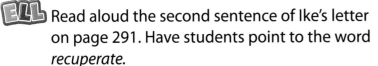 Read aloud the second sentence of Ike's letter on page 291. Have students point to the word *recuperate*.

→ Have students raise their hands if they have ever had to stay in the hospital because they were sick or hurt. *When you start feeling better, we say you are recuperating.*

→ Ask students to practice using the word: *To____means to feel better.*

→ Point out that *recuperate* is a cognate. (recuperar/recuperarse)

Develop Comprehension

4 Skill: Point of View

What kind of narrator is featured in the news article on page 292? (third person) How do you know? (The article is written by an outsider looking at the action. The article does not include the words *I, me,* or *my.*) What does the narrator convey about the events? (The article describes the dogs as being very bad and disruptive.) What are some examples from the text that show this? (The writer of the article calls them "unruly" and "rambunctious" and says they caused a "week of problems.") Add the examples to your chart.

Details
"Unruly dogs plagued Snort City again yesterday . . ."
"The episode capped a week of problems . . ."
" . . . a pack of rambunctious creatures broke up the annual Fishin' Derby . . ."

↓

Point of View
The dogs were bad and disruptive.

The Snort City Register/Gazette

October 6

5

Wild Dogs Rampage!

Game Disrupted

4 Unruly dogs plagued Snort City again yesterday, as one of the animals broke up a double play and ran away with the baseball during a Snort City Rabbits game at Morley Field. The episode capped a week of problems that began on Tuesday when a pack of the rambunctious creatures broke up the annual Fishin' Derby on Blat Lake. Apparently the dogs first rolled in, then ate, the catch. The following day a group of dogs snuck into a "Mr. Ding-a-Ling" truck outside Gruber Park and made off with two gallons of rocky road ice cream. None of the dogs have been apprehended, though ice-cream vendor Eugene Phelps describes the leader as a "scruffy black-and-white fellow."

292

A C T Access Complex Text

▶ **Purpose**

Point out the newspaper clipping on page 292. Talk to students about the author's purpose for including this article.

→ *What does the news article tell you about the dogs' behavior in Snort City?* (It is very disruptive. They interrupt a baseball game, eat the catch at the annual Fishin' Derby, and steal ice cream.)

→ *What purpose does this article have in the story?* (The newspaper article gives another perspective. Since most of the story is told from Ike's point of view, this article gives the reader a better idea of what the Snort City dogs are doing and how Ike is involved.)

LITERATURE ANTHOLOGY, pp. 292–293

5 Text Features: Newspaper Article

What does the headline of the news article tell the reader about the events in Snort City? (Dogs are causing trouble in Snort City.) Why is it important to include the headline and date in a news article? (The headline tells the reader what the news article is about. The date tells the reader when the article was published.) How might the news article influence the residents of Snort City? Why? (The news article might cause Snort City residents to think of dogs in a negative way because it reports that dogs are a menace to the community.)

6 Author's Craft: Humor

The author uses humor in Ike's letters to Mrs. LaRue. Ike's letters may sound sincere, but when you read them carefully, you can see that Ike writes one thing but means another. What does Ike write that you know is different from his reality and that adds humor to the story? (The second sentence of his letter says that he will "probably" not starve or die of loneliness. I know from the illustration that Ike is okay, so it's humorous for him to be taking pity on himself.)

ELL Use the illustrations to help students draw connections between the dogs' actions and the description of a "menace to our community."

→ *Are the dogs being good or bad?* Help students respond in short phrases or simple sentences. (The dogs are being bad.)

→ Point out that, just like the dogs in the selection, a *menace* is something or someone who causes trouble in a neighborhood or community.

Develop Comprehension

STOP AND CHECK

Confirm Predictions How are Ike's letters to Mrs. LaRue different from what the newspapers report?

Teacher Think Aloud I can see differences between the news articles and Ike's letters. Can you confirm our prediction that Ike's social club will not do any good for the community?

Prompt students to apply the strategy in a Think Aloud by scanning the text and focusing on key details to enhance their understanding.

Student Think Aloud I can use details and illustrations from the text to confirm my prediction. Ike calls the dogs' behavior "cheerful and spirited." The news article tells that Ike and his friends made off with a string of beef sausages from a butcher shop. I can confirm that what Ike tells Mrs. LaRue is different from what is reported in the news articles and that his social club is in fact behaving badly.

STOP AND CHECK

Confirm Predictions How are Ike's letters to Mrs. LaRue different from what the newspapers report? Confirm your prediction about whether Ike's social club would do good deeds for the community.

294

A C T Access Complex Text

▶ Connection of Ideas

Guide students in connecting what they have learned about Ike LaRue thus far.

→ *What sort of character is Ike LaRue?* (He is a bit of a troublemaker and a liar, which is shown in his actions and words. He is also a leader who is determined to make sure Bugwort does not get elected as the mayor of Snort City.)

→ *Look at the illustration. Why did LaRue steal sausages from the Butcher Shop?* (The butcher supports Bugwort. There is a sign in the window. Ike does not want Bugwort to be mayor.)

The Snort City Register/Gazette

October 8

Bugwort Calls for Canine Crackdown

Calling dogs "a menace to our community," mayoral candidate Hugo Bugwort yesterday announced his plans to crack down on the beasts. "We can no longer **tolerate** this sort of behavior," he said, citing recent dog-related problems. Mr. Bugwort proposes not only a leash law and a curfew, but a complete ban on the animals in most public places. "This town is literally going to the dogs," said Bugwort. "I **intend** to stop it." **(7) (8)**

In related news, a dog reportedly snuck into Branmeier's Butcher Shop on Second Avenue and made off with a string of beef sausages.

295

LITERATURE ANTHOLOGY, pp. 294–295

(7) Skill: Point of View

What point of view is described in the newspaper article? (The dogs have become a problem that needs to be stopped.) How do you know? (The writer describes the mayor's opinion that the dogs are a "menace" and that the city needs to "crack down on the beasts." The mayor also proposes a leash law and a curfew.)

(8) Vocabulary: Idioms

Remember that an idiom is a phrase whose meaning cannot be understood from the literal meanings of its words. Reread the sentence with the expression, "going to the dogs." What does the expression "going to the dogs" mean? (becoming chaotic and lawless) What does the expression mean in the context of this story? (It has two meanings. One is the idiomatic meaning. Also, Snort City is literally going to the dogs because the dogs are taking control of the city.)

ELL Students may not understand the concepts of *curfew* and *ban*. Tell them that a curfew is a law that keeps people off the streets at a certain time.

→ Point to the illustration. *If there were a curfew, would these dogs be on the street?* (no) *What would happen to them?* (They might get in trouble.)

→ Explain that a ban is a rule or law that forbids, or does not allow, something. *Our school principal put a ban on cell phones in the classroom.*

→ Have students fill in the sentence frame: *A ban means to _____ something.* (forbid; not allow)

Develop Comprehension

9 Skill: Point of View

What kind of narrator is featured on these pages? (first person) Who most likely wrote the letter to the editor? (Ike) How do the letters allow us to see what Ike is feeling and his view of the events? (Ike is trying to show that he is upset with Bugwort's attitude toward the dogs in Snort City. The letters are in the first-person so we can see what Ike is thinking and how his presentation of reality is exaggerated and overly dramatic.)

October 9

Dear Mrs. LaRue,

I must say I have become alarmed by the ravings of this man Bugwort. Imagine if he actually were elected to our city's highest office! The idea is unthinkable. I must figure out some way to stop this impending disaster!

Your Worried Dog,
Ike

296

A C T ccess Complex Text

▶ **Sentence Structure**

Point out the letter to the editor on page 297. Have students reread the questions in the letter. The author uses rhetorical questions to evoke a response from the reader. Tell students that rhetorical questions are questions not meant to be answered. They are meant to convey ideas and get the reader thinking in a certain way.

→ Reread the question: *"Can we so quickly forget the loyalty of Man's Best Friend?"* What does this question mean? (Dogs have been very helpful and loyal to humans, and humans should not forget it.)

The Snort City Register/Gazette

October 10

Letters to the Editor:

As a longtime resident, I must decry the wave of anti-dog hysteria sweeping over our city. Can we so quickly forget the loyalty of Man's Best Friend? Who **accompanies** our firefighters and police on their perilous rounds? Who rescues the **weary** traveler stuck high in the Alps? Who serves the blind (and the deaf, too, most likely)? Dogs, that's who!
Signed,
A Concerned Citizen

9

297

LITERATURE ANTHOLOGY, pp. 296–297

10 Author's Craft: Word Choice

Why does the concerned citizen choose the phrase *anti-dog hysteria* rather than writing "making a fuss about dogs"? (*Anti-dog hysteria* is more inflammatory than saying that people are making a fuss about the dogs' behavior. The strong language gets across how the author thinks people are acting irrationally.)

→ *What are the some of the ways that dogs help humans?* (accompanying firefighters on perilous rounds; rescuing travelers stuck in the Alps; serving the blind and deaf)

 Help students understand the phrase "Man's Best Friend." Ask students to raise their hands if they like dogs. Say: *In the United States, dogs are the most popular pets.*

→ *We call dogs* man's best friend *because dogs are like a good friend. They are loyal and caring. What other words describe* Man's Best Friend?

Develop Comprehension

11 Skill: Point of View

Reread Ike's letter on page 299. What point of view is he trying to convey to Mrs. LaRue? (Bugwort has become the horrible menace—not the dogs.) **How do you know?** (He uses strong language to paint a negative picture of Bugwort and show that he has no choice but to stop him.) Use the examples from the text and the point of view to complete your chart.

Details
" . . . things have become perilous indeed—at least for dogs!"
"The awful Bugwort continues his scurrilous attacks."
"He must be stopped."

↓

Point of View
Bugwort is a menace who must be stopped.

298

A C T Access Complex Text

▶ **Specific Vocabulary**

Have students use context clues or a dictionary to define the words *perilous* and *scurrilous*.

→ *What does Ike mean when he tells Mrs. LaRue that things have become* perilous *in the outside world?* (Ike is saying that it has become dangerous for dogs in Snort City. He says that he is jealous of Mrs. LaRue being in the hospital where she is safe.)

→ *Why does Ike refer to Bugwort's attacks as* scurrilous? (Ike is telling Mrs. LaRue that Bugwort is giving the dogs a terrible reputation by calling them names like "gangs of hooligans.")

Dear Mrs. LaRue,

October 11

How I envy you the safety of your hospital bed! Here in the outside world, things have become perilous indeed—at least for dogs! The awful Bugwort continues his scurrilous attacks. Yesterday he referred to dogs as "gangs of hooligans." He must be stopped. Therefore I have decided to "throw my hat into the ring." This afternoon I will announce my candidacy. Doubtless the public response will be **overwhelming**. ⑪ ⑫

Your Next Mayor,

Ike

299

LITERATURE ANTHOLOGY, pp. 298–299

⑫ **Skill: Make Inferences**

Why do you think Ike decides to run for mayor of Snort City? With a partner, paraphrase details from the story. (Ike believes that Bugwort is not the right person for the job. He wants to make life easier for himself and other dogs, so he has created a picture of Bugwort as a mean person who has gone too far and must be challenged.)

ELL Help students understand the idiom *throw my hat into the ring*. Explain that when someone uses the expression *throw my hat into the ring* it means he or she is entering a contest—usually a political contest.

→ Have students practice using the idiom by completing the sentence frame: *I decided to run for class president. I am going to _____*. (throw my hat into the ring)

→ *What public office does Ike decide to run for?* (mayor)

Develop Comprehension

13 Ask and Answer Questions

Generate a question of your own about the text and share it with a partner. To find the answer, try rereading the text. For example, you might ask, "Is Ike keeping his campaign against Bugwort positive as he claims in his letter to Mrs. LaRue?" To find the answer you can reread Ike's letter on page 300 and look at the illustrations on pages 300 and 301. (No, Ike is not keeping his campaign positive. He calls Bugwort vicious, unstable and insane. Ike also changes the words on Bugwort's campaign poster to "Sniff Bugwort For A Strong Odor.")

October 12

Dear Mrs. LaRue,

My first day on the campaign trail was fabulous! Everywhere huge crowds turned out to cheer my message of dog-friendliness. My chums from the social club have agreed to help. Of course we will do our best to keep this **campaign** positive, though I can't speak for my **opponent**, who appears to be vicious and unstable, if not insane.

Honestly Yours,
Ike

13

A C T Access Complex Text

▶ Purpose

Guide students in understanding that the purpose of the story is to entertain. Point out that the author has perspectives about characters and situations that may come across in the reading.

→ *How do you know that this story is meant to entertain?* (The story does not share factual information and does not persuade the reader

in any way. It is meant to be a humorous story about Ike LaRue.)

→ *How does the author feel about Ike LaRue?* (Even though Ike is a troublemaker and a liar, the author presents him as a likeable character. He's funny, smart, and determined to get his way.)

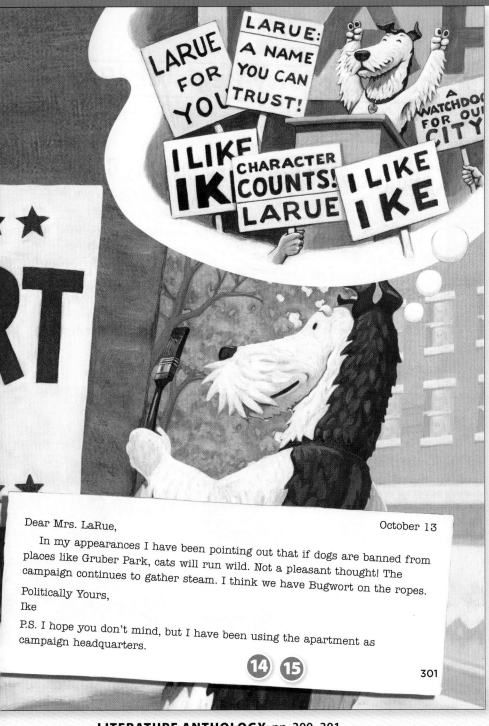

Dear Mrs. LaRue,   October 13

In my appearances I have been pointing out that if dogs are banned from places like Gruber Park, cats will run wild. Not a pleasant thought! The campaign continues to gather steam. I think we have Bugwort on the ropes.

Politically Yours,
Ike

P.S. I hope you don't mind, but I have been using the apartment as campaign headquarters.

14 **15**   301

LITERATURE ANTHOLOGY, pp. 300–301

14 Skill: Point of View

Ike has been using his letters to Mrs. LaRue to convey feelings and observations that are not exactly true. Do you think Ike's campaign is really "gathering steam"? Use the illustrations and Ike's letters to support your answer and discuss with a partner. (Ike may just want Mrs. LaRue to think he is a real challenge to Bugwort. The supporting crowds in the illustration are only in his imagination.)

15 Literary Element: Personification

Remember that when an animal or object is personified, it is given human characteristics, such as being able to talk and interact with other characters in a story like a person would. Which character in this story is an example of personification? (Ike) Describe which of his qualities make him human-like. (He is ambitious about being mayor. He is good at writing and persuading people to share his point of view.)

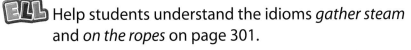

ELL Help students understand the idioms *gather steam* and *on the ropes* on page 301.

→ Explain that when something gathers steam, it becomes stronger. Demonstrate gathering steam.

→ *What does Ike say is gathering steam?* (his campaign) *Is this good or bad news?* (good news)

→ Have students point to the idiom *on the ropes*. Ask them to raise their hands if they have ever done badly in a contest.

→ Explain that when Ike says, "we have Bugwort on the ropes," he is saying that Bugwort is doing poorly in the race for mayor.

Develop Comprehension

16 Skill: Point of View

How is the point of view in the news article on page 302 different from that of Ike on page 303? (The article merely points out that Ike is now challenging Bugwort, but does not say what Ike's attitude and specific goals are. The writer has not spoken to Ike and cannot report on his point of view. The article calls Ike a "mysterious new candidate" and reports that Bugwort is not worried. Ike describes a different point of view about the election. He says he and his supporters "will be out in full force" and the results will be "interesting." He seems to think Bugwort should be worried.)

The Snort City Register/Gazette

October 14

Bugwort Challenged by Mystery Candidate!

A mysterious new candidate has emerged to challenge Hugo Bugwort in his run for mayor. Supporters of Ike LaRue describe him as "dog-friendly." Opponents point out that he is, in fact, a dog. Either way, the furry LaRue has begun to wage a fierce campaign against Bugwort, who promises to virtually ban all dogs from Snort City. Surprisingly, LaRue's message has begun to catch on. "We didn't anticipate this," admits Bugwort campaign manager, Walt Smiley, referring to the dogs. "It turns out some folks are really fond of the little devils."

"I'm not worried," said Bugwort. "Tomorrow is my big rally in Gruber Park. I'll deal with these dog-lovers then."

302

A C T Access Complex Text

▶ Sentence Structure

Point out the quotations in the news article. Help students understand that quotations are used in text to mark important terms, indicate dialogue, or to note something that someone else said.

→ *Why do you think the writer puts the phrase "dog-friendly" in quotation marks?* (To show the reader that "dog-friendly" was said by someone other than the writer of the news article.)

→ *What does Bugwort say in reaction to LaRue's run for mayor?* ("I'm not worried," said Bugwort. "Tomorrow is my big rally in Gruber Park. I'll deal with these dog-lovers then.")

Dear Mrs. LaRue,

My supporters and I have decided to confront Chief Bugwort at today's rally. We will be out in force, and though we will conduct ourselves in a dignified manner, I am sure that the results will be interesting. **17**

Hope you are well,

Ike

P.S. Nothing will distract me from this important cause. **16**

October 15

303

LITERATURE ANTHOLOGY, pp. 302–303

17 **Author's Craft: Figurative Language**

Authors use figurative language, such as idioms, to add rich meaning to a selection. Remember that figurative language is language that has a different meaning from what you can determine from the words alone. What does Ike mean when he says his supporters will "be out in force"? (The idiom *be out in force* means that they will have a powerful presence with many motivated people.)

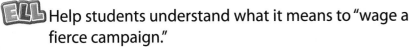 Help students understand what it means to "wage a fierce campaign."

→ *If I wage a fierce campaign, it means that I am going to do everything I can to win. I will meet and talk to voters. I will give speeches. I will put up posters and signs where everyone can see them.*

→ *Look at the illustration. How is LaRue waging a fierce campaign?* (He is putting his name where everyone can see it.)

Develop Comprehension

STOP AND CHECK

Summarize How does Ike rescue Hugo Bugwort? (Hugo Bugwort collapses during a rally. Bugwort's campaign manager rushes him over to an ice cream truck to take him to the hospital. Ike is inside the truck and feeds Bugwort ice cream the whole way there. By the time they reach the hospital, Bugwort feels much better and changes his mind about dogs. Bugwort offers Ike a position as Assistant Mayor.)

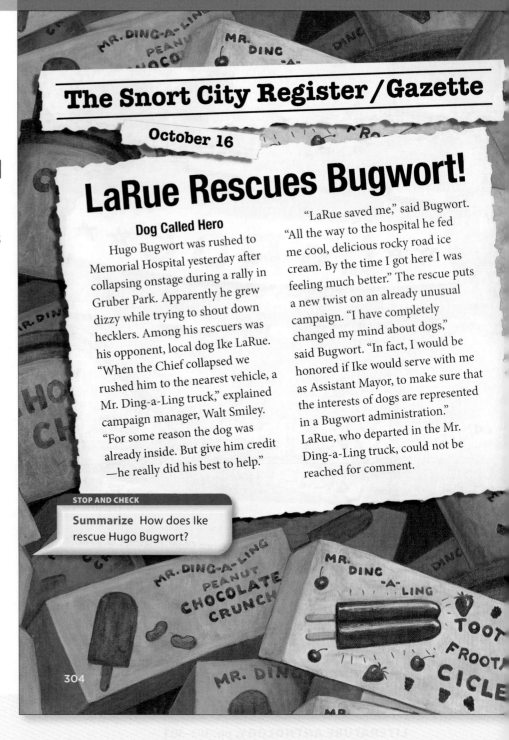

The Snort City Register/Gazette

October 16

LaRue Rescues Bugwort!

Dog Called Hero

Hugo Bugwort was rushed to Memorial Hospital yesterday after collapsing onstage during a rally in Gruber Park. Apparently he grew dizzy while trying to shout down hecklers. Among his rescuers was his opponent, local dog Ike LaRue. "When the Chief collapsed we rushed him to the nearest vehicle, a Mr. Ding-a-Ling truck," explained campaign manager, Walt Smiley. "For some reason the dog was already inside. But give him credit —he really did his best to help."

"LaRue saved me," said Bugwort. "All the way to the hospital he fed me cool, delicious rocky road ice cream. By the time I got here I was feeling much better." The rescue puts a new twist on an already unusual campaign. "I have completely changed my mind about dogs," said Bugwort. "In fact, I would be honored if Ike would serve with me as Assistant Mayor, to make sure that the interests of dogs are represented in a Bugwort administration." LaRue, who departed in the Mr. Ding-a-Ling truck, could not be reached for comment.

STOP AND CHECK

Summarize How does Ike rescue Hugo Bugwort?

304

A C T Access Complex Text

▶ Connection of Ideas

Have students discuss what Ike states in his letter on page 303 and what the news article reports on page 304.

→ *What does Ike claim he is going to do in his letter?* (He says he is going to confront Bugwort "in a dignified manner" at the rally.)

→ *What does the article report?* (Ike rescued Bugwort after he collapsed.)

→ *What can you infer about Ike's intentions?* (Ike was determined from the beginning to interfere with Bugwort's campaign. Since Ike was already in the ice cream truck, it seems he planned to be the hero so that Bugwort would like him. It worked, as Bugwort changed his position on dogs.)

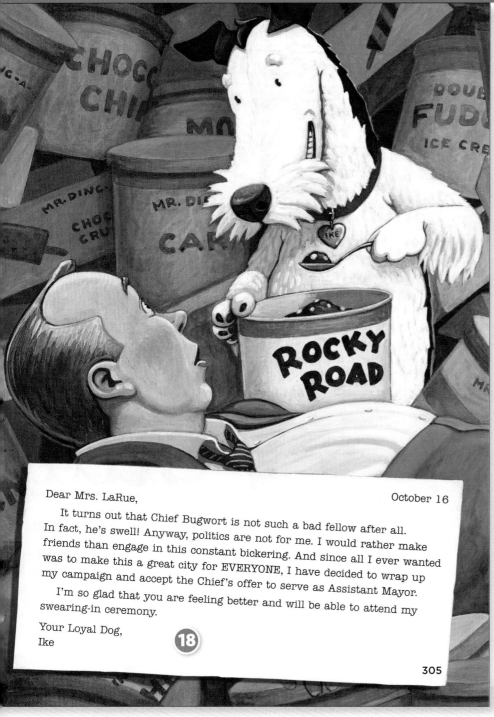

Dear Mrs. LaRue,   October 16

It turns out that Chief Bugwort is not such a bad fellow after all. In fact, he's swell! Anyway, politics are not for me. I would rather make friends than engage in this constant bickering. And since all I ever wanted was to make this a great city for EVERYONE, I have decided to wrap up my campaign and accept the Chief's offer to serve as Assistant Mayor.

I'm so glad that you are feeling better and will be able to attend my swearing-in ceremony.

Your Loyal Dog,
Ike   **18**

305

LITERATURE ANTHOLOGY, pp. 304–305

18 Skill: Point of View

What is the difference between the point of view in the news article and the point of view in the letter? Explain. (The news article is written by a third-person narrator. It gives the reader only the facts that can be observed about the rally and is not influenced by one character's point of view. The letter is written in the first-person by Ike. It only tells the reader how Ike feels about Bugwort, and helps the reader see the events through Ike's eyes.)

ELL Help students understand the meaning of the phrase *a new twist*. Explain that *twist* is a multiple-meaning word. Tell students that a *twist* means "a change."

→ Remind students of the ending of the *Cinderella* fairy tale. Ask volunteers to think of a way they might change, or put a new twist, on the ending.

→ Point out the context clue "changed my mind." *What has Bugwort changed his mind about?* (dogs) *Why did he change his mind?* (LaRue saved him.)

Develop Comprehension

19 Strategy: Make Predictions

Reread the text on page 306. Turn to your partner and make a prediction about what will happen now that Ike has decided to accept Bugwort's offer and become Assistant Mayor. Paraphrase details from the text in your answer.

Student Think Aloud I predict that Bugwort will become more tolerant of dogs because Ike is a part of his administration. When I read the news article, I can see that Bugwort promises to have the most dog-friendly administration. When some dogs overturn a hot dog cart, Bugwort calls the carts unstable, whereas in the beginning of the selection, the dogs' behavior is called a disruption.

The Snort City Register / Gazette

November 3

Bugwort Sworn In!
LaRue Joins Former Adversary

Promising to have the most dog-friendly administration ever, new mayor Hugo Bugwort was sworn in yesterday during a ceremony in Gruber Park. At his side was Assistant Mayor Ike LaRue, whom many credit with his success. "This is a great day for everyone in Snort City!" proclaimed Bugwort, to loud cheers from the audience. The speech was interrupted when several dogs in the back of the crowd overturned a hot-dog cart. Bugwort promised to look into the matter.

"It certainly is worrisome," he said. "Who knew those carts were so unstable?" **19**

306

A C T Access Complex Text

▶ **Purpose**

Point out to students how this story comes full circle—that is, the story ends where it started.

→ *In what way does this story come full circle?*
(The dogs knocked over a hot dog cart in the beginning of the story, and it injured Mrs. LaRue. At the end of the story, Ike's doggy friends knock over the hot dog cart again.)

→ *Why might the author choose to organize the story this way? What does this tell you about the dogs?*
(The author is telling the reader that nothing has changed in Snort City. The reprise of the hot dog cart incident shows that the dogs will still get into trouble. Ike's friendly appearance could be a distraction from what the dogs are doing.)

LITERATURE ANTHOLOGY, pp. 306–307

Return to Predictions

Review students' predictions and purposes for reading. Ask them to answer the Essential Question. (Ike runs for mayor because he sees something that he finds unfair. He feels that the dogs in Snort City need to be represented, so he launches a campaign against Bugwort.)

ELL Help students make connections between the illustration on pages 306–307 and the newspaper heading "LaRue Joins Former Adversary."

→ *What is happening in the illustration?* (Bugwort and LaRue come together. They look happy.)

→ Point to and say *adversary.* Define the word and help students replace it with words they know. *Are LaRue and Bugwort still adversaries?* (no)

→ Have students fill in the sentence frame: *An adversary is your _____.* (challenger, opponent, competitor, or rival)

About the Author

Meet the Author and Illustrator

Mark Teague

Have students read the biography of the author and illustrator.

→ What childhood experiences might Mark Teague have used to get ideas for this story?

→ How do the illustrations add to the humor being presented in the text?

Author's Purpose

To Entertain

Remind students that authors who write to entertain create stories for readers to enjoy. Students may say that illustrations give details that are closely related to the surrounding text and make it easier for readers to see the contrast between Ike's letters and the newspaper reports. Students may also say that the author uses black-and-white illustrations to show Ike's thoughts and add humor.

Author's Craft

First Person vs. Third Person

Explain that the author switches between the first-person point of view in Ike's letters and the third-person point of view in the news articles. Discuss what this adds to the writing.

→ Authors use first person to allow the reader to hear the thoughts of the main character and see the events in the story through the main character's eyes. Example: "My first day on the campaign trail was fabulous!" (page 300)

→ Have students find examples of the third-person point of view, such as, "A mysterious new candidate has emerged to challenge Hugo Bugwort in his run . . ." (page 302)

About Mark Teague

Mark Teague is an author and illustrator of many children's books. He often writes stories about activities that some kids try to avoid—things like getting a haircut, doing homework, and cleaning one's room. Mark adds his own quirky sense of humor to his stories. Many of the ideas for his books come from things he did as a child. The character Ike LaRue was inspired by two dogs he and his brother had. Mark uses these childhood inspirations to create new stories in upstate New York. His daughter loves to watch him paint the illustrations for his books.

Author's Purpose

Why does Mark Teague use both black-and-white and color illustrations in *LaRue for Mayor*?

308

LITERATURE ANTHOLOGY, pp. 308–309

Respond to Reading

Summarize

Summarize *LaRue for Mayor*. Include the most important details from the story. Information from your Point of View Chart may help you.

Details
↓
Point of View

Text Evidence

1. How do you know that *LaRue for Mayor* is a fantasy and could not happen in real life? **GENRE**

2. Describe the two points of view from which the story is told. Give examples from the text. **POINT OF VIEW**

3. The newspaper article on page 295 says that Bugwort "announced his plans to crack down" on unruly dogs. What is the meaning of the idiom "crack down"? Explain how you know. **IDIOMS**

4. Write about how the different points of view make Ike's story more interesting. **WRITE ABOUT READING**

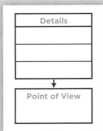

Make Connections

Why does Ike run for mayor? **ESSENTIAL QUESTION**

Bugwort and Ike have very different qualities, yet the people of Snort City like them both as candidates. What qualities are most important in someone running for public office? **TEXT TO WORLD**

309

Make Connections *Analytical Writing*

Essential Question Have partners work together to cite evidence from the text to give reasons why Ike LaRue decides to run for mayor of Snort City.

Text to World After students give examples of Bugwort and Ike's reasons for running for public office, have them list the qualities that are the most important for someone running for public office.

Respond to Reading

Summarize

Review with students the information from their point of view graphic organizers. Model how to use the information to summarize *LaRue for Mayor*.

Analytical Writing **Write About Reading: Summarize**
Remind students that a summary is a restatement of the key details from the text. Ask students to write a summary of the selection. Remind them to start with a sentence that names the selection title and the genre. Have students share their summaries with a partner.

Text Evidence

1. **Genre** Answer The main character is a dog who can speak, read, and type. Evidence The dog types letters to his owner while she is in the hospital. He runs for mayor, and in the end, accepts the title of Assistant Mayor of Snort City.

2. **Point of View** Answer Through his letters, Ike tries to show himself as a well-meaning dog reacting to the menacing Bugwort. The newspaper articles keep the drama and emotion out of the story. Evidence Ike calls Bugwort "vicious," while the articles merely state his position.

3. **Figurative Language: Idioms** Answer *Crack down* means to be tough or strict in order to stop a certain behavior. Evidence The next sentence is a quote from Bugwort: "We can no longer tolerate this sort of behavior."

4. *Analytical Writing* **Write About Reading: Point of View** Multiple points of view reveal more about characters and events. The articles help you learn more about Ike and what he does when Mrs. LaRue is not at home.

Develop Comprehension

Literature Anthology

"Bringing Government Home"

Text Complexity Range

Lexile

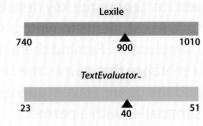

740   900   1010

TextEvaluator™

23   40   51

Options for Close Reading

→ Whole Class

→ Small Group

→ Independent

CCSS **Genre** • Expository Text

Compare Texts

Read about the duties and accomplishments of state and local officials.

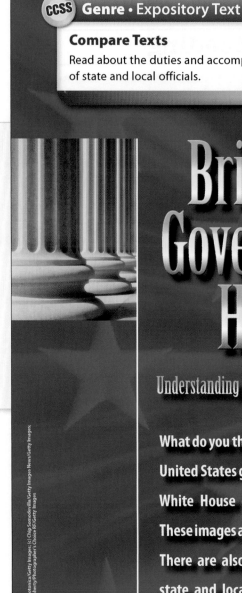

Bringing Government Home

Understanding State and Local Government

What do you think of when you picture the United States government? Do you see the White House or perhaps the President? These images are accurate yet incomplete. There are also many U.S. leaders at the state and local levels—in the counties, cities, and neighborhoods where we live.

(c) Mel Curtis/Photonica/Getty Images; (c) Chip Somodevilla/Getty Images News/Getty Images; [bkgd] Dennis Flaherty/Photographer's Choice RF/Getty Images

310

A C T Access Complex Text

What makes this text complex?

⬤ **Specific Vocabulary**

⬤ **Genre**

▶ Specific Vocabulary

Have students use context clues or a dictionary to define domain-specific words.

→ *Identify the context clues that help you understand the word* amend. ("State Leaders Can…*amend* state constitutions"; "each state has its own structure and set of officials…"To *amend* something means to change it.)

National, state, and local governments share the same basic structure. The executive, legislative, and judicial branches make up the three branches of government. Each branch of government has specific duties and powers. These powers differ in national and state governments.

Just a Few National Powers Versus State Powers

National Leaders Can ...
- Print money
- Declare war
- Enforce the U.S. Constitution

State Leaders Can ...
- Issue licenses
- Provide for public health and safety
- Amend state constitutions

The Executive Branch

The President is the leader of the national executive branch. Similarly, a **governor** heads up each state executive branch. The governor makes important decisions about the state. Each state has its own structure and set of officials who are below the governor.

Mayor Mick Cornett

At the local level, a city mayor might head up the executive branch. One example of a successful mayor is Mick Cornett of Oklahoma City. Every day, mayors such as Cornett oversee city departments, such as police, schools, and transportation. They also work with others to try to improve their city. Mayor Cornett launched a **campaign** against obesity in Oklahoma City. Cornett added sidewalks, bike paths, and walking trails. He also created a 70-acre park to promote walking and exercise. Thanks to Cornett's efforts, the people of Oklahoma City have lost over 600,000 pounds.

(cl) Jim Beckel/Daily Oklahoman/AP Photo; (c) Courtesy of Mayor Mick Cornett; (cb) Image Source/Getty Images

311

LITERATURE ANTHOLOGY, pp. 310–311

Compare Texts *Analytical Writing*

Students will read an expository text on state and local governments. Ask students to do a close reading of the text, rereading to deeply understand the content. As they reread, encourage them to use the make, confirm, or revise predictions strategy, or other strategies they know to help them. They will also take notes. Then students will use the text evidence they gathered to compare this text with *LaRue for Mayor*.

① Ask and Answer Questions

What branch of government does Mick Cornett represent in Oklahoma City? What has he done to improve the lives of the people in Oklahoma City?

Analytical Writing **Write About Reading** Make a list of details describing what Cornett has done to improve the lives of the people in Oklahoma City. (Executive branch; oversees city departments; launched campaign against obesity; created 70-acre park to help promote exercise.)

 Point out the phrase *branches of government* on page 311.

→ *Say it with me:* branches of government.

→ Display a chart that illustrates the executive, legislative, and judicial branches of government.

→ Help students point to each branch of government and help them sound out the following: *executive, legislative, judicial.*

Develop Comprehension

2 Ask and Answer Questions

What level of government creates and passes new laws?

With a partner, paraphrase the description of the level of government that passes laws. (The legislative branch passes laws to improve the country, state, and local cities, counties, and towns. State legislatures have leaders called senators and representatives who try to improve their state by passing new laws. Local legislators also pass laws to improve their cities.)

3 Ask and Answer Questions

How does the judicial branch make sure that laws are understood?

Analytical Writing **Write About Reading** Take notes on the judicial branch. (The judicial branch ensures that the executive and legislative branches adhere to the U.S. Constitution. This branch includes courts at the local and state levels.) Turn to a partner and compare notes.

2 The Legislative Branch

State legislatures also have strong leaders called senators and representatives. These members try to improve their state by passing new laws. Senator Anthony C. Hill worked hard for the state of Florida. He helped to create and pass new laws. As a legislator, Hill worked to pass important civil rights legislation. He also improved African American voter turnout in Florida elections. In addition, Hill helped to increase the state's minimum wage and reduce class sizes in schools.

Local legislators can create similar results in their counties, cities, and towns. They may pass laws that relate to parks, public transportation, and police departments, to name a few.

Senator Anthony C. Hill

The Judicial Branch

The judicial branch makes sure that all these laws are understood. It also ensures that the other two branches adhere to the U.S. Constitution. At the state level, this branch usually includes a Supreme Court and lower-level courts.

DID YOU KNOW that in addition to the U.S. Constitution, each state has its own constitution and set of laws to follow? The purpose of a state constitution is to outline the structure of the state government.

Many state constitutions are longer than the national one! That is because leaders want to make sure their state is protected. For example, Florida's constitution includes laws that intend to protect the land and animals of the Everglades, an area of natural wetlands in the southern part of the state.

The earliest state constitutions were created hundreds of years ago. Today, state leaders amend, or change, state constitutions to address modern concerns from citizens. South Carolina leaders recently amended their state constitution to include hunting and fishing as a constitutional right for citizens.

(c) Steve Cannon/AP Photo; (cr) (Ph) Corbis/AP Photo; (cb) Jill Fromer/Photodisc/Getty Images; (bl) Mel Curtis/Photodisc/Getty Images; (br) Jeremy Woodhouse/Photodisc/Getty Images

312

A C T Access Complex Text

▶ Genre

Remind students that in an expository text, authors present information and text features, such as side bars, to help readers locate information.

→ Point out the sidebar on page 312. *What information does the sidebar tell you about constitutions?* (In addition to the U.S. Constitution, each state has its own constitution. The sidebar also tells that the state constitutions outline the structure of each state's government and contrasts early and modern state constitutions.)

→ *How does the author reinforce information about important people in the legislative and judicial branches of government?* (The author includes photos of the people with captions.)

County, city, and town courts exist at the local level. Judges may be chosen by public officials. They may also be elected. State and local judges represent a wide range of backgrounds.

Justice Eva Guzman is a good example. A judge for the Supreme Court of Texas, Guzman was the first Hispanic woman to be elected to a state office in Texas. State Supreme Court justices decide if judges in lower courts have made the right decisions based on the state constitution. In addition, Justice Guzman has headed up legal education programs in Texas. She does this so that others can learn about the law.

Justice Eva Guzman

Checks and Balances

The three branches of government help to create balanced national, state, and local governments. Our forefathers created this system to make sure one branch did not become more powerful than the others. Public officials at each level of government are responsible for the laws we vote on and follow. So the next time you think about who makes up our government, keep your local leaders in mind!

Make Connections

What can people achieve in local and state public offices? **ESSENTIAL QUESTION**

Tell why elected leaders are important in our society. **TEXT TO TEXT**

313

LITERATURE ANTHOLOGY, pp. 312–313

Make Connections *Analytical Writing*

Essential Question Have students write and share information about what local governments achieve.

Text to Text Have groups of students compare their responses to the Ask and Answer Questions prompts with what they learned in *LaRue for Mayor*. Ask one group to compare what Mike Cornett has done for Oklahoma City to what Hugo Bugwort wants to do. Have another group compare laws that governments pass to improve the lives of citizens and the law that Bugwort wants to pass in Snort City.

SOCIAL STUDIES

CONNECT TO CONTENT
STATE GOVERNMENTS

As an example of how state governments work, have students research and describe how Florida's constitution protects the rights of its citizens and provides for the structure, function, and purposes of Florida's government. Ratified in 1968, the current Florida Constitution contains a Bill of Rights very similar to that of the U.S. Constitution which guarantees freedom of speech and religion, a jury trial, and so on. The Florida Constitution also provides for three branches of government with "separation of powers," describes how the Florida legislature should work, defines the powers of the governor, and describes how people should vote and be taxed.

ELL To help students understand the purpose of a constitution, display a copy of the school rules. *This document shows the rules and responsibilities that all students must follow. It is our school constitution.*

→ *A state constitution shows state laws that people follow and the responsibilities of state leaders.*

→ Phonics/Fluency

MINILESSON 20 Mins

Inflectional Endings: Changing *y* to *i*

OBJECTIVES

CCSS Use combined knowledge of all letter-sound correspondences, syllabication patterns, and morphology (e.g., roots and affixes) to read accurately unfamiliar multisyllabic words in context and out of context. **RF.4.3a**

CCSS Read on-level prose and poetry orally with accuracy, appropriate rate, and expression on successive readings. **RF.4.4b**

Rate: 102–122 WCPM

ACADEMIC LANGUAGE
• *phrasing, expression*
• Cognate: *expresión*

ELL

Refer to the sound transfers chart in the **Language Transfers Handbook** to identify sounds that do not transfer in Spanish, Cantonese, Vietnamese, Hmong, and Korean.

1 Explain

Remind students that the inflectional endings *-es* and *-ed* can be added to a verb to change its tense. The inflectional endings *-er* and *-est* can be added to an adjective to create a comparative or superlative form. For most words ending in a consonant and *y*, change the *y* to *i* before adding *-es, -ed, -er,* or *-est*.

2 Model

Write the word *lovely* on the board. Tell students that you want to create comparative and superlative forms of the word. Point out that *lovely* ends in a consonant and *y*, so the *y* changes to *i* before *-er* or *-est* is added. Write the words *lovelier* and *loveliest* on the board. Run your finger under each word as you sound it out.

3 Guided Practice

Write the following words with inflectional endings on the board. Explain that the base word of each word ends in a consonant and *y*. Help students identify the inflectional ending in each word and then choral-read each word.

carries	brainiest	stormier
supplied	lazier	handiest
filthiest	cries	studied

Read Multisyllabic Words

Transition to Longer Words Draw a three-column chart on the board. In the first column, write *re-*. In the second column, write *copy, apply,* and *classify*. In the third column, write *-es* and *-ed*. Have students combine the prefix in the first column with each word in the second column and then add an ending from the third column to form new words.

Ask students to circle the inflectional endings in the longer words. Make sure students changed the *y* in each base word to *i* before adding the ending. Model how to read each new word and have students echo-read after you.

r-Controlled Vowel Syllables

1 Explain

Explain that *r*-controlled vowels consist of a vowel followed by the letter *r*. Both letters work as a team to form a single sound.

→ Since *r*-controlled vowels form only one sound, both letters always stay in the same syllable.

2 Model

Write and say *hardly*, and have students repeat after you. Model dividing the word into its syllables (*hard/ly*). Circle the letters *ar* and point out that they are part of the same syllable in the word.

3 Guided Practice

Write the words *report*, *confirm*, and *herself* on the board. Have students divide each word into its syllables and say each word.

Phrasing and Expression

Explain/Model Explain that phrasing and expression are important when reading fiction. Phrasing helps to improve the flow of reading by separating words into groups. Reading with expression includes increasing or decreasing a vocal level of excitement depending on what is happening in the text. This makes hearing the text read aloud much more interesting for the listener.

Model reading page 253 of "The TimeSpecs 3000." Use correct phrasing and express excitement during appropriate parts of the story.

Practice/Apply Have one group read the top half of page 253 one sentence at a time. Have a second group echo-read the passage, using the same phrasing and expression. Then have the groups switch roles for the second half of the page. Ask the groups to discuss which parts were more exciting and how they knew.

Daily Fluency Practice

Students can practice fluency using **Your Turn Practice Book**.

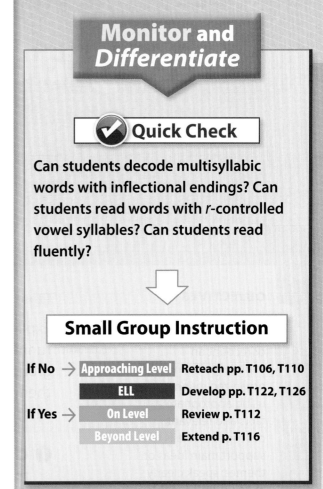

Monitor and *Differentiate*

✔ Quick Check

Can students decode multisyllabic words with inflectional endings? Can students read words with *r*-controlled vowel syllables? Can students read fluently?

Small Group Instruction

If No → | Approaching Level | Reteach pp. T106, T110
| ELL | Develop pp. T122, T126
If Yes → | On Level | Review p. T112
| Beyond Level | Extend p. T116

ON-LEVEL PRACTICE BOOK p. 168

A. Change the *y* to *i* and add the indicated ending to each word. Write the new word on the line.

1. empty + er =   emptier
2. sorry + est =   sorriest
3. reply + ed =   replied
4. carry + es =   carries
5. funny + er =   funnier
6. silly + est =   silliest

B. Read each sentence. Underline the word with an *r*-controlled vowel syllable. Then circle the *r*-controlled vowel syllable.

1. I think this is the best birthday present she has given me.
2. The small boat dropped its anchor late last night.
3. I put a leash and collar on my dog when we take a walk.
4. We went to see the mayor make an election speech.
5. My brother finished his juice and then went to bed.

APPROACHING p. 168   BEYOND p. 168   ELL p. 168

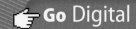
Go Digital

www.connected.mcgraw-hill.com
RESOURCES
Research and Inquiry

 Wrap Up the Week

Integrate Ideas

RESEARCH AND INQUIRY

Leadership

New York Times Co./Hulton Archive/Getty Images

OBJECTIVES

CCSS Report on a topic or text, tell a story, or recount an experience in an organized manner, using appropriate facts and relevant, descriptive details to support main ideas or themes; speak clearly at an understandable pace. **SL.4.4**

CCSS Add audio recordings and visual displays to presentations when appropriate to enhance the development of main ideas or themes. **SL.4.5**

- Use persuasive techniques.
- Present information visually.
- Ask and answer questions.

ACADEMIC LANGUAGE

political, campaign, persuasive techniques, visual display

Write a Political Campaign Plan

Explain that students will work in small groups and research the process of running for public office. They will then draft a plan for one member of the group to run for office, including campaign activities and slogans. Have them create a name for their political party. Discuss the roles involved in a campaign. Then discuss the following steps:

1 **Choose a Candidate** Have student groups decide which member of the group would like to be the person who runs for office. Have them discuss the role each person in the group will play during the campaign.

2 **Find Resources** Ask students to research the process of running for office. Remind them how to use the library or media center to find print and online resources and how to take clear, organized notes.

3 **Guided Practice** Have students draft a plan for a political campaign, including activities and slogans for the person running for office. Encourage them to use persuasive techniques and language to get their point across effectively. Remind them to use a dictionary or thesaurus as they write.

4 **Create the Project: Political Campaign Plan** Have students create their final campaign plan. Encourage them to create a visual display, such as a poster, to represent their campaign.

Present the Political Campaign Plan

Have students present their campaign plans and visual displays to the class using online Presentation Checklist 3. Have the student running for public office answer questions from the class about his or her campaign ideas. Review with students how to use formal language in their presentations and how to speak clearly at an understandable pace.

TEXT CONNECTIONS  Analytical Writing

OBJECTIVES

CCSS Compare and contrast the treatment of similar themes and topics (e.g., opposition of good and evil) and patterns of events (e.g., the quest) in stories, myths, and traditional literature from different cultures. **RL.4.9**

Text to Text

Cite Evidence Explain to students that they will work in groups to compare information they have learned about why people run for public office from all the texts they have read. Model how to compare this information by using examples from the week's **Leveled Readers** and *The TimeSpecs 3000,* **Reading/Writing Workshop** pages 252–255. Review class notes and completed graphic organizers. You may also wish to model going back into the text for more information. You can use an Accordion Foldable® to record comparisons.

Students should cite at least three examples from each text.

Dinah Zike's
FOLDABLES®
Study Organizer

Present Information Ask groups of students to present their findings to the class. Encourage discussion, asking students to comment on information on the charts that is similar and ideas that are different.

WRITE ABOUT READING Analytical Writing

OBJECTIVES

CCSS Draw evidence from literary or informational texts to support analysis, reflection, and research. Apply *grade 4 Reading standards* to literature (e.g., "Describe in depth a character, setting, or event in a story or drama, drawing on specific details in the text [e.g., a character's thoughts, words, or actions].*"*). **W.4.9a**

Write an Analysis

Cite Evidence Explain that students will write about one of the stories they read this week. Using text evidence, students will analyze how the author's use of the first-person point of view helps the reader understand the character and plot.

Discuss how to analyze point of view by asking *how* and *why* questions.

→ How does the story's point of view help readers understand what the main character experiences?

→ Why does the author's use of this point of view affect the plot?

Use **Your Turn Practice Book** page 169 to read and discuss the student model. Then have students select a story and review the point of view from which it is told. Have them write an analysis about the significance of the point of view to character and plot development. Remind students to include clear ideas and to spell irregular plurals correctly.

Present Your Ideas Ask partners to share their paragraphs and to recommend additional evidence to support their analyses.

Readers to Writers

MINILESSON
10 Mins

Writing Traits: Ideas

Develop Characters

Expert Model Explain that good writers make characters come to life with dialogue and descriptions of what the characters are like or what they do. Dialogue is the exact words a character says. Writers use dialogue to show what a character is feeling and thinking by the words he or she uses and the way the words are said.

 Read aloud the expert model from "The TimeSpecs 3000." Ask students to listen for the dialogue and think about how it helps them understand Miguel's feelings. Have students talk with partners to identify the dialogue.

Student Model Remind students that using dialogue helps bring characters to life. Read aloud the student draft "Mr. Jay." As students follow along, have them focus on the dialogue the writer included in her draft.

 **Invite** partners to talk about the draft and the dialogue that Nina included. Ask them to explain how the dialogue shows what the characters are feeling and thinking. Have students suggest places where Nina could add more dialogue.

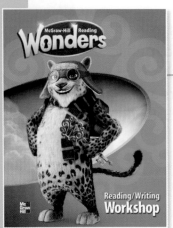

Reading/Writing Workshop

OBJECTIVES

CCSS Write routinely over extended time frames (time for research, reflection, and revision) and shorter time frames (a single sitting or a day or two) for a range of discipline-specific tasks, purposes, and audiences. **W.4.10**

CCSS Use dialogue and description to develop experiences and events or show the responses of characters to situations. **W.4.3b**

- Analyze models to understand how to develop characters.
- Write a story about being mayor.
- Add dialogue to revise writing.

ACADEMIC LANGUAGE

character, dialogue

Expert Model

Student Model

 Genre Writing

Narrative Text and Poetry
For full writing process lessons and rubrics, see:

→ Fictional Narrative, pages T344–T349

→ Poetry, pages T350–T355

CCSS Writing Traits › Ideas

Readers to...

Writers use dialogue to show what a character is feeling and thinking. Writers also pay attention to how the character says the dialogue. Reread the excerpt from "The TimeSpecs 3000" below.

Develop Character

Identify the **dialogue.** How do these words help you understand how Miguel feels as he talks to Abraham Lincoln?

Expert Model

"I have a problem. I hate writing and giving speeches, and my opponent, Tommy, is great at both things."

"What kind of campaign would you run?" Lincoln asks.

"I have lots of ideas for our school," I tell him. "For instance, I want our school to use fruits and vegetables from the local farmers' market in the cafeteria. I also want to start a book drive for our school library."

"There's your speech," he says. "Tell people your ideas with honesty, integrity, and enthusiasm, and you can't possibly go wrong."

260

Writers

Nina wrote a fantasy. Read Nina's revisions to a section of her story.

Student Model

Mr. Jay

One day, Sally and her cat, Mr. Jay, went to the ^town^ park. Suddenly, Mr. Jay jumped onto a stage where the mayor was speaking. ~Mr. Jay~ ^He^ nudged the mayor aside and said, "I'm Mr. jay, and I am running for mayor. Cats are naturally superior, so vote for me!" Then he jump^ed^ off the stage.

"How dare you?" said the mayor.

Sally looked at ~the~ ^her^ cat in disbelief. "Oh, no," she said. ^"What have you done?"^

Editing Marks

⊔ Switch order.
∧ Add.
⸴ Add a comma.
⌐ Take out.
SP Check spelling.
≡ Make a capital letter.

Grammar Handbook

Types of Pronouns
See page 463.

Your Turn   COLLABORATE

✔ Identify **dialogue** in the story. How does it help Nina develop characters?
✔ Identify the types of pronouns that she used in her writing.
✔ Tell how the revisions improved Nina's writing.

Go Digital!
Write online in Writer's Workspace

261

READING/WRITING WORKSHOP, pp. 260–261

ELL ENGLISH LANGUAGE LEARNERS SCAFFOLD

As English Language Learners write during the week, provide support to help them respond to the prompts. For example:

Beginning

Write Help students complete the sentence frames. *"I'm Mr. Jay, and I am running for ____. Cats are naturally____, so ____ for me!" "How dare you?" said the____. Another example of dialogue is "Oh, ____," she said.*

Intermediate

Describe Ask students to complete the sentence frames. Encourage students to provide details. *"I'm Mr. Jay, and I am____. Cats are naturally superior, so____!" "____" said the mayor. Another example of dialogue is ____.*

Advanced/High

Discuss Check for understanding. Ask: *What does Mr. Jay say when he jumps on stage? How does the mayor feel about Mr. Jay's actions? What are some examples of dialogue in the story?*

Writing Every Day: Ideas

Writing Entry: Develop Characters

Prewrite Provide students with the prompt below.

Write a story about being mayor of your town. Tell what you would do. Include dialogue that tells what you say.

Have partners list things they would do if they were the mayor of the town. Ask them to jot down details and possible dialogue that they might include in their drafts.

Draft Have each student begin writing a story based on the prompt. Remind students to include dialogue in their drafts.

Focus on Developing Characters

Use **Your Turn Practice Book** page 170 to model adding dialogue.

Today, I gave a speech at the rally. I talked about some of the changes I plan to make as mayor. I talked about improving our parks.

Model adding dialogue after the third sentence.

I said, "As mayor, I will clean up our parks and install recycling bins."

Discuss how adding dialogue brings a character to life. Guide students to add more dialogue to the rest of the model.

Writing Entry: Develop Characters

Revise Have students revise their writing from Day 1 by adding two or three sentences of dialogue.

Use the **Conferencing Routines**. Circulate among students and stop briefly to talk with individuals. Provide time for peer review.

Edit Have students use Grammar Handbook pages 463 and 464 in the **Reading/Writing Workshop** to edit for errors in types of pronouns.

Conferencing Routines

Teacher Conferences

STEP 1

Talk about the strengths of the writing.

You sequenced events in an order that makes sense, and you used transitions to help the reader understand when the events take place.

STEP 2

Focus on how the writer uses the target trait for the week.

Your descriptions of the characters and their actions help me picture them. It would really bring the characters to life if you added more dialogue.

STEP 3

Make concrete suggestions for revisions. Have students work on a specific assignment, such as those to the right, and then meet with you to review progress.

DAY 3

Writing Entry: Develop Characters

Prewrite Ask students to search their Writer's Notebook for topics to write a draft. Or, provide a prompt, such as the following:

Write a story about being governor of your state. Tell what you would do. Include dialogue that tells what you say.

Draft Once students have chosen their topics, ask them to create a word web with the topic in the center. Then have them think about ideas and possible dialogue that they might include in their writing. Students can then use their word webs to begin their drafts.

DAY 4

Writing Entry: Develop Characters

Revise Have students revise the draft writing from Day 3 by adding two or three sentences of dialogue to show what the characters are feeling and thinking. As students are revising their drafts, hold teacher conferences with individual students. You may also wish to have students work with partners to peer conference.

Edit Invite students to review types of pronouns on Grammar Handbook pages 463 and 464 in the **Reading/Writing Workshop** and then edit their drafts for errors.

DAY 5

Share and Reflect

Discuss with the class what they learned about using dialogue to make characters come to life. Invite volunteers to read and compare draft text with text that has been revised. Have students discuss the writing by focusing on the importance of the dialogue that has been added. Allow time for individuals to reflect on their own writing progress and record observations in their Writer's Notebooks.

McGraw-Hill Companies, Inc./Ken Karp, photographer

Suggested Revisions

Provide specific direction to help focus young writers.

Focus on a Sentence
Read the draft and target one sentence for revision. *Rewrite this sentence by adding dialogue that tells what the character is _____.*

Focus on a Section
Underline a section that needs to be revised. Provide specific suggestions. *This section tells a lot about the characters. It could use more dialogue to show what the characters are feeling.*

Focus on a Revision Strategy
Underline a section of the writing and ask students to use a specific revision strategy, such as substituting. *There are many repeated words. Try replacing them with more precise words.*

Peer Conferences

Focus peer response groups on using dialogue to develop characters. Provide this checklist to frame discussion.

☑ Does the writing include dialogue?

☑ Does the dialogue show what the characters are thinking and feeling?

☑ What dialogue can be added to help bring the characters to life?

☑ Are any parts of the writing unclear?

Grammar: Types of Pronouns

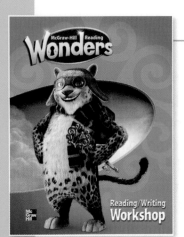

Reading/Writing Workshop

OBJECTIVES

 Explain the function of nouns, pronouns, verbs, adjectives, and adverbs in general and their functions in particular sentences. **L.3.1a**

- Distinguish types of pronouns.
- Identify subject, object, and reflexive pronouns.
- Use subject, object, and reflexive pronouns correctly.
- Proofread sentences for mechanics and usage errors.

Go Digital

Types of Pronouns

Grammar Activities

DAY 1

DAILY LANGUAGE ACTIVITY

Sarah has wrote a story about a Princess. She likes to dress up.
(1: has written; 2: princess; 3: The princess likes)

Introduce Subject and Object Pronouns

Present the following:

→ A **subject pronoun** is used as the subject of a sentence. Subject pronouns include **I, you, he, she, it, we,** and **they**:
   They are hiking.

→ An **object pronoun** can take the place of a noun that follows an action verb. Object pronouns can also follow prepositions. Object pronouns include **me, you, him, her, it, us,** and **them**:
   They are hiking with **us**.

Have partners discuss pronouns using page 463 of the Grammar Handbook in **Reading/Writing Workshop**.

DAY 2

DAILY LANGUAGE ACTIVITY

The new student will sits between you and I. Him is from puerto rico.
(1: will sit; 2: me; 3: He; 4: Puerto Rico)

Review Subject and Object Pronouns

Review subject and object pronouns. Have students explain how each functions in a sentence.

Introduce Reflexive Pronouns

→ A **reflexive pronoun** ends in -**self** or -**selves** and refers to the subject of a sentence. Singular reflexive pronouns include **myself, yourself, himself, herself,** and **itself**. Plural reflexive pronouns include **ourselves, yourselves,** and **themselves**:
   She made **herself** a sandwich.
   They taught **themselves** to make costumes.

 # TALK ABOUT IT

COLLABORATE

ROLE-PLAY A SCENE

Have students reenact a favorite scene from a story the class has read. As students role play, be sure they use subject and object pronouns. As other students watch, have them listen for the pronouns.

FILL IN THE BLANK

Have partners each write five reflexive pronouns on index cards and place them in a pile. Students should take turns drawing cards and stating a sentence with a blank where the pronoun should be. Another student should restate the sentence, filling in the pronoun.

DAY

DAILY LANGUAGE ACTIVITY

Larry made hisself some soup. After he ate dinner; he play basketball.
(1: himself; 2: dinner,, 3: played)

Mechanics and Usage: Subject and Object Pronouns

→ Always use a subject pronoun when replacing the subject of a sentence. Also use a subject pronoun to replace a noun that follows a form of the verb **to be** (My favorite author is Mary Mast. My favorite author is **she**.)

→ Use an object pronoun only after an action verb or a preposition.

→ Do not use a reflexive pronoun such as **myself** in place of a personal pronoun such as **I** or **me**. Never add -**self** to a subject pronoun.

As students write, refer them to Grammar Handbook pages 463 and 464.

DAY

DAILY LANGUAGE ACTIVITY

Myself read the story of amelia earhart. Her flew herself across the Atlantic Ocean.
(1: I; 2: Amelia Earhart; 3: She)

Proofread

Have students correct errors in these sentences.

1. Him spoke to they about leadership. (1: He; 2: them)

2. Her wrapped herself in a blankit. (1: She; 2: blanket)

3. Good readers ask theirselves questions? (1: themselves; 2: questions.)

4. Myself took those picture's last year. (1: I; pictures)

Have students check their work using Grammar Handbook pages 463 and 464 on pronouns.

DAY 5

DAILY LANGUAGE ACTIVITY

Me and Tyler is friends. We lives on the same block. Go skating together.
(1: Tyler and I; 2: are; 3: live; 4: We go)

Assess

Use the Daily Language Activity and **Grammar Practice Reproducibles** page 85 for assessment.

Reteach

Use Grammar Practice Reproducibles pages 81–84 and selected pages from the Grammar Handbook for additional reteaching. Remind students that it is important to use pronouns correctly as they speak and write.

Check students' writing for use of the skill and listen for it in their speaking. Assign Grammar Revision Assignments in their Writer's Notebooks as needed.

See Grammar Practice Reproducibles pages 81–85.

USE PRONOUNS

Have students in small groups each write five subject pronouns, five action verbs, and five object pronouns on index cards and place them in three piles. Three students should each draw a card from one pile. A fourth student should use all three words in a sentence.

REPLACE THE SUBJECT

Have pairs each write a sentence about why people run for public office using a noun in the subject that names a specific person or group. Then have each student read his or her sentence aloud twice, replacing the noun with a subject pronoun the second time.

REPLACE THE OBJECT

Have partners each write three sentences that include a preposition followed by a noun. Students should trade sentences and take turns reading each other's sentences aloud and replacing the noun that follows the preposition with the correct object pronoun.

Spelling: Inflectional Endings: *y* to *i*

OBJECTIVES

CCSS Spell grade-appropriate words correctly, consulting references as needed. **L.4.2d**

Spelling Words

funnier	carries	cozily
families	easily	sorriest
pennies	silliest	prettily
worried	jumpier	lazier
replied	emptier	happiest
varied	merrier	dizziest
marries	applied	

Review scaring, tasting, skipped
Challenge handily, factories

Differentiated Spelling

Approaching Level

funnier	carries	happier
families	easily	sorriest
pennies	silliest	prettily
worried	flier	lazier
replied	berries	happiest
babies	copier	dizziest
marries	cries	

Beyond Level

funnier	carries	cozily
handily	easily	sorriest
pennies	silliest	communities
worried	jumpier	lazier
replied	emptier	happiest
varied	merrier	dizziest
abilities	societies	

DAY 1

Assess Prior Knowledge

Display the spelling words. Read them aloud, drawing out the inflectional endings in each word.

Point out the spelling patterns in *easily* and *silliest*. Write the words *easy* and *silly*, modeling how the *i* replaces the *y*. Point out that the *i* to *y* inflectional endings *-ier* and *-iest* make words into adjectives, while the *-ily* inflectional ending can make words into adverbs.

Demonstrate sorting the spelling words by pattern under key words *funnier, replied, easily, families* and *silliest*. (Write the words on index cards or the IWB.) Sort a few words. Point out that the *-ies* ending on a noun usually signals a plural.

Then use the Dictation Sentences from Day 5 to give the Pretest. Say the underlined word, read the sentence, and repeat the word. Have students write the words. Then have students check and correct their spelling.

DAY 2

Spiral Review

Review inflectional endings *-ed* and *-ing*, including final letter changes and consonant doubling. Use the Dictation Sentences below for the review words. Read the sentence, say the word, and have students write the words.

1. The storm was <u>scaring</u> us.

2. We saw them <u>tasting</u> the pies.

3. I <u>skipped</u> down the street.

Have partners check the spellings.

Challenge Words Review this week's spelling patterns. Use these Dictation Sentences for challenge words. Say the word, read the sentence, and say the word again. Have students write the word.

1. He <u>handily</u> won the election.

2. Do all of those <u>factories</u> make cars?

Have students check and correct their spelling before writing the words in their word study notebook.

WORD SORTS

COLLABORATE

OPEN SORT

Have students cut apart the **Spelling Word Cards BLM** in the Teacher Resource Book and initial the back of each card. Have them read the words aloud with a partner. Then have partners do an open sort. Have them record the sort in their word study notebook.

PATTERN SORT

Complete the **pattern sort** from Day 1 using the key words, pointing out the different *y* to *i* inflectional endings. Have students use Spelling Word Cards to do their own pattern sort. Ask partners to compare and check their sorts.

DAY

Word Meanings

Read each group of words below. Ask students to copy the words into their word study notebook, completing each group by adding the spelling word that best fits in the same category.

1. nickels, quarters, _____ (*pennies*)
2. happier, jollier, _____ (*merrier*)
3. snugly, warmly, _____ (*cozily*)
4. troubled, concerned, _____ (*worried*)

Challenge students to come up with at least three other word groups to which they can add spelling, review, or challenge words, leaving a blank space for the word. Have partners trade papers and fill in the blanks. Then have each partner choose one of the answer words, define it, and describe how context clues help identify its meaning.

See Phonics/Spelling Reproducibles pp. 97–102.

SPEED SORT

Have partners do a **speed sort** to see who is fastest, then compare their results. Afterward, have partners sort the words ending in *-ies* by whether or not the word is a noun. Have them add the final sort to the word study notebook.

DAY

Proofread and Write

Write these sentences on the board. Have students circle and correct each misspelled word. They can use print or electronic dictionaries or other resources to help them.

1. Jan replyed, "I've got at least 100 pennys." (*replied, pennies*)
2. Your joke was funier, but mine was the sillyest. (*funnier, silliest*)
3. I was woried that the box would be too heavy, but he carried it eazily. (*worried, easily*)

Error Correction Remind students that when they have a *y* at the end of a noun and they want to make the noun plural, they must drop the *y* before adding *ies*. Exceptions occur when the word ends in a vowel + *y* as in *monkey* or *day*. Then, *y* does not change to *i*, and *s* is added to make it plural. (*monkeys, days*)

BLIND SORT

Have partners do a **blind sort**: one reads a Spelling Word Card; the other tells under which key word it belongs. Have them take turns until both have sorted all their words. Ask them to review their sorts, then discuss how they sorted the words and if any changes are needed.

DAY 5

Assess

Use the Dictation Sentences for the Posttest. Have students list misspelled words in their word study notebooks. Look for students' use of these words in their writings.

Dictation Sentences

1. Your joke was <u>funnier</u> than mine.
2. Nine <u>families</u> live on our street.
3. He has a bank full of <u>pennies</u>.
4. I was <u>worried</u> that we'd be late.
5. Smiling, my mom <u>replied</u>, "Yes."
6. The jellybean flavors were <u>varied</u>.
7. My sister <u>marries</u> Jim next week.
8. A student <u>carries</u> books.
9. We <u>easily</u> made it on time.
10. That's the <u>silliest</u> story I've heard.
11. I felt <u>jumpier</u> before the test.
12. My bag is <u>emptier</u> than yours.
13. We are <u>merrier</u> on weekends.
14. Has she <u>applied</u> to college?
15. We sat <u>cozily</u> next to the fire.
16. We all felt bad, but Mike was the <u>sorriest</u>.
17. The princess smiled <u>prettily</u>.
18. My brother is <u>lazier</u> than I am.
19. I am the <u>happiest</u> when it snows.
20. Jon was the <u>dizziest</u> boy on the ride.

Have students self-correct the tests.

Build Vocabulary

OBJECTIVES

CCSS Use context (e.g., definitions, examples, or restatements in text) as a clue to the meaning of a word or phrase. **L.4.4a**

CCSS Recognize and explain the meaning of common idioms, adages, and proverbs. **L.4.5b**

Expand vocabulary by adding inflectional endings and affixes.

Vocabulary Words

accompanies	opponent
campaign	overwhelming
governor	tolerate
intend	weary

Connect to Words

Practice this week's vocabulary.

1. Name someone who **accompanies** you when you take a trip or travel.

2. Tell something you know about a political **campaign**.

3. What does a **governor** do?

4. What is something you **intend** to do tomorrow?

5. What actions or qualities make someone a good **opponent**?

6. What could make a job or chore feel **overwhelming**?

7. Can you **tolerate** a lot of loud music? Why or why not?

8. Describe a time when you have felt **weary**.

Expand Vocabulary

Help students generate different forms of this week's words by adding, changing, or removing inflectional endings.

→ Draw a four-column T-chart on the board. Write *tolerate* in the first column. Then write *tolerates, tolerated,* and *tolerating* in the other three columns. Read aloud the words with students.

→ Have students share sentences using each form of *tolerate*.

→ Students can fill in the chart for *intend* and *accompanies,* then share sentences using the different forms of the words.

→ Have students copy the chart in their word study notebook.

BUILD MORE VOCABULARY

COLLABORATE

ACADEMIC VOCABULARY

Discuss important academic words.

→ Display *politics, leadership, representation.*

→ Define each word and discuss the meanings with students.

→ Display *politics* and *political.* Have partners look up and define related words.

→ Write the related words on the board. Have partners ask and answer questions using the words. Repeat with *leadership* and *representation.*

CONTEXT CLUES

→ On the board, write "Does the governor *intend* to run again, or does he want to retire?" Ask, *What does* intend *mean here?*

→ Have partners work to use sentence clues to find the meanings of unfamiliar words in a text of their choice. Model using sentence clues if needed.

→ Have students use a dictionary to check their definitions, then write the words and meanings in the word study notebook.

Go Digital

Vocabulary

Vocabulary Activities

DAY 3

Reinforce the Words

Review last week's and this week's vocabulary words. Have students orally complete each sentence stem.

1. The teacher's aide <u>accompanies</u> our class to the ____.

2. Do you <u>intend</u> to ____ this summer?

3. My <u>opponent</u> in the class election promised to make the school's ____ better.

4. Our class found studying for the ____ <u>overwhelming</u>.

5. The nurse asked if I could <u>tolerate</u> a ____.

6. The workers were <u>weary</u> after building a new ____.

DAY 4

Connect to Writing

→ Have students write sentences in their word study notebooks using this week's vocabulary.

→ Tell them to write sentences that provide word information they learned from this week's readings.

→ **ELL** Provide the Day 3 sentence stems 1–6 for students needing extra support.

Write About Vocabulary Have students write something they learned from this week's words in their word study notebook. For example, they could write about why people might run for *governor* or how they might plan a *campaign* in order to win against an *opponent*.

DAY 5

Word Squares

Ask students to create Word Squares for each vocabulary word.

→ In the first square, students write the word. (example: *tolerate*)

→ In the second square, students write their own definition of the word and any related words, such as synonyms. (example: *put up with, allow, permit*)

→ In the third square, students draw a simple illustration that will help them remember the word. (example: a "thumbs up" sign)

→ In the fourth square, students write nonexamples, including antonyms for the word. (example: *prevent, ban, forbid*)

→ Have partners compare and discuss their Word Squares.

IDIOMS

Remind students that idioms are a kind of figurative language.

→ Display **Your Turn Practice Book** pages 163–164. Read the first paragraph. Model figuring out the meaning of the idiom *make our move*.

→ Have students complete page 167, then determine the meaning of *on our own, took the side of* and *take up where they left off* on pages 163–164, using a dictionary to confirm meanings.

SHADES OF MEANING

Help students generate words related to *weary*. Draw a synonym/antonym scale on the board.

→ Discuss the meaning of *weary*. Elicit synonyms, such as *tired* and *exhausted*, and antonyms, such as *energetic* or *rested*.

→ Discuss where each word should go on the scale. Note that there may be multiple correct answers.

→ Ask students to copy the words in their word study notebook.

MORPHOLOGY

Use *governor* as a springboard for students to learn more words. Draw a word web. Write *-or* in the center oval. Write *governor* in one of the outer ovals.

→ Review the meanings of *govern* and *governor*. Elicit other professions that end in *-or*, such as *inspector* and *actor*.

→ Have partners generate more professions. If needed, create another web to include words that end in *-er*, such as *player*.

Approaching Level

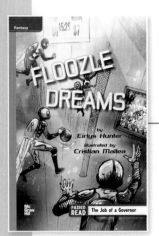

Lexile 670
TextEvaluator™ 41

OBJECTIVES

 Refer to details and examples in a text when explaining what the text says explicitly and when drawing inferences from the text. **RL.4.1**

Compare and contrast the point of view from which different stories are narrated, including the difference between first- and third-person narrations. **RL.4.6**

Recognize and explain the meaning of common idioms, adages, and proverbs. **L.4.5b**

Leveled Reader:
Floozle Dreams

Before Reading

Preview and Predict

Have students read the Essential Question. Then have students read the title and table of contents of *Floozle Dreams*. Have students make a prediction about what the story will be about and share it with a partner.

Review Genre: Fantasy Fiction

Review with students that fantasy fiction is told in the form of fiction that includes characters, settings, or events that could not exist in real life. As they preview the book, have students identify features of fantasy fiction in *Floozle Dreams*.

During Reading

Close Reading

Note Taking Ask students to use their graphic organizer while they read.

Pages 2–5 *What does the use of the pronouns* I *and* my *tell you about the narrator of the story?* (The story has a first-person narrator.) *Turn to a partner and say a detail that shows you the narrator's point of view about floozle.* (He was bored until the ex-governor talked about the game, so the narrator must like floozle.)

Pages 6–7 *Does the phrase "whale of a time" on page 7 have a literal meaning?* (No.) *Use context clues to define the phrase.* (Having a *whale of a time* means "having a great time." The phrase "wow, was that fun" helps me understand the meaning of the idiom.)

Pages 8–9 *Why did D.L. Lopskill decide to run for a second term?* (He discovered that the lake was polluted and wanted to clean it up so people would have clean drinking water.) *Turn to a partner and make a prediction about the result of D.L.'s campaign for a second term.* (For example: D.L. will win a second term and help clean up the polluted lake.)

 **Go**
Digital

Leveled Readers

Details
↓
Point of View

Use Graphic Organizer

Pages 10–13 *Confirm or revise your prediction about the election.* (For example: My prediction was correct, but D.L. also did other things to help his community that I did not predict.) *Paraphrase D.L.'s biggest achievements as governor.* (D.L. cleaned up the state's water and created many jobs.)

Pages 14–15 *How has the narrator's point of view about the interview changed through the story?* (At first, the narrator was bored. As he listened to D.L., he became very interested.)

After Reading

Respond to Reading Have students complete Respond to Reading on page 16 after they have finished reading.

Analytical Writing **Write About Reading** Have students work with a partner to write a short paragraph from the point of view of Mrs. Lopskill. Make sure students maintain this point of view.

Fluency: Phrasing and Expression

Model Model reading page 7 with proper phrasing and expression. Next, reread the page aloud and have students read along with you.

Apply Have students practice reading with a partner.

PAIRED READ

"The Job of a Governor"

Make Connections: Write About It **Analytical Writing**

Before reading, ask students to note that the genre of this text is expository, which means it explains about a topic. Then discuss the Essential Question. After reading, ask students to use the information from "The Job of a Governor" to discuss D.L.'s role as governor in *Floozle Dreams*.

Leveled Reader

FOCUS ON LITERARY ELEMENTS

Students can extend their knowledge of onomatopoeia by completing the literary elements activity on page 20.

Literature Circles

Ask students to conduct a literature circle using the Thinkmark questions to guide the discussion. You may wish to have a whole-class discussion on ways students would like to participate in government.

Level Up

Level-up lessons available online.

IF students read the **Approaching Level** fluently and answered the questions

THEN pair them with students who have proficiently read **On Level** and have students

- echo-read the **On Level** main selection with their partners.

- use self-stick notes to mark details they'd like to discuss with partners.

A C T **A**ccess **C**omplex **T**ext

The **On Level** challenges students by including more **domain-specific words** and **complex sentence structures**.

Approaching Level

Phonics/Decoding

INFLECTIONAL ENDINGS -ed AND -ing

TIER 2

OBJECTIVES

 Use combined knowledge of all letter-sound correspondences, syllabication patterns, and morphology (e.g., roots and affixes) to read accurately unfamiliar multisyllabic words in context and out of context. **RF.4.3a**

Decode words with inflectional endings -ed and -ing.

I Do Explain that the inflectional endings -ed and -ing are added to verbs to change their tense. Write the words *laugh/laughed/laughing* and *dine/dined/dining* on the board and read them aloud. Point out that the spelling of *laugh* does not change when -ed or -ing is added. Tell students that for base words ending with a consonant and e, as in *dine*, drop the final e before adding -ed and -ing. Point out that for base words ending with a vowel and consonant, double the final consonant before adding -ed and -ing. Add the inflectional endings -ed or -ing to *like* and *skip*.

 We Do Write *taste* and *tap* on the board. Model the rules for adding -ed or -ing to words ending with a consonant and e or with a vowel and consonant. Have students say each word and underline its inflectional ending.

 You Do Write *caring, saved, ripping,* and *trimmed* on the board. Have students read each word aloud and explain the spelling rule for each verb. Point to the words in random order for students to choral-read. Repeat several times.

REVIEW INFLECTIONAL ENDINGS

TIER 2

OBJECTIVES

 Use combined knowledge of all letter-sound correspondences, syllabication patterns, and morphology to read accurately unfamiliar multisyllabic words in context and out of context. **RF.4.3a**

Decode words with inflectional endings.

I Do Tell students that when a word ends in a consonant and y, the y changes to i before the endings -ed, -er, -est, or -ly are added. Write *funny* on the board. Explain that the y in *funny* changes to i before the ending -er or -est is added. Write *funnier* and *funniest* on the board and sound out each word. Underline the -er and -est endings in each word. Repeat for *pretty*.

 We Do Display the **Word-Building Cards** ed, er, est, and ly, and write the words *worry, reply, easy,* and *cry* on the board. Help students build words using the following rule: When a word ends in a consonant and y, the y changes to i before adding the inflectional ending. Have students underline the inflectional endings in each word.

 You Do Add *copy, heavy,* and *sorry* to the board. Have students decode each word and add the correct inflectional ending: -ed, -er, -est, or -ly. Point to the words in random order for students to choral-read. Repeat several times.

PRACTICE INFLECTIONAL ENDINGS

OBJECTIVES

CCSS Use combined knowledge of all letter-sound correspondences, syllabication patterns, and morphology to read accurately unfamiliar multisyllabic words in context and out of context. **RF.4.3a**

Decode words with inflectional endings.

 I Do Display the **Sound-Spelling Card** for the word *lazy*. Point out that this word ends in a consonant and *y*, so we change the *y* to *i* before adding the *-er, -est, or -ly* endings. Write *lazier, laziest,* and *lazily* on the board. Underline the inflectional endings in each word.

 We Do Write the word *happy* on the board. Model how to add the inflectional endings *-er, -est,* and *-ly,* and then have students decode *happier, happiest,* and *happily.* Then guide students as they add inflectional endings to *angry* and decode *angrier, angriest,* and *angrily.*

 You Do Afterward, point to the words on the board in random order for students to choral-read.

SYLLABLES WITH *r*-CONTROLLED VOWELS

OBJECTIVES

CCSS Use combined knowledge of all letter-sound correspondences, syllabication patterns, and morphology to read accurately unfamiliar multisyllabic words in context and out of context. **RF.4.3a**

Decode words with *r*-controlled vowels.

 I Do Review that *r*-controlled vowels consist of a vowel followed by the letter *r*. Tell students that these letters work together to form a single sound. Explain that *r*-controlled vowels form only one sound and that both letters always stay in the same syllable. Write the word *hardly* on the board. Divide the word into syllables and underline *ar*: *hard/ly*. Point out that the letters *ar* are part of the same syllable in *hardly*.

 We Do Write *confirm* on the board. Model how to decode the word by dividing the word into its syllables and identifying the *r*-controlled vowel. Provide additional examples of words with *r*-controlled vowels. Guide students as they decode the words and help them identify the *r*-controlled vowels.

 You Do Write the words *support* and *herself* on the board. Have students divide the words into syllables and circle the syllable with the *r*-controlled vowel. Point to the words in random order for students to choral-read.

ELL ENGLISH LANGUAGE LEARNERS

For the **ELLs** who need **phonics**, **decoding**, and **fluency** practice, use scaffolding methods as necessary to ensure students understand the meaning of the words. Refer to the **Language Transfers Handbook** for phonics elements that may not transfer in students' native languages.

Approaching Level

Vocabulary

REVIEW HIGH-FREQUENCY WORDS

TIER 2

OBJECTIVES

 Read with sufficient accuracy and fluency to support comprehension. Read on-level text with purpose and understanding. **RF.4.4a**

Review high-frequency words.

 I Do Use **Word Cards 131–140**. Display one word at a time, following the routine:

Display the word. Read the word. Then spell the word.

 We Do Ask students to say the word and spell it with you. Model using the word in a sentence and have students repeat after you.

 You Do Display the word. Ask students to say the word and then spell it. When completed, quickly flip through the word card set as students choral-read the words. Provide opportunities for students to use the words in speaking and writing. For example, provide sentence starters, such as *We could not visit the playground until we finished our _____.* Ask students to write each word in their Writer's Notebook.

REVIEW VOCABULARY WORDS

TIER 2

OBJECTIVES

Acquire and use accurately grade-appropriate general academic and domain-specific words and phrases, including those that signal precise actions, emotions, or states of being and that are basic to a particular topic. **L.4.6**

 I Do Display each **Visual Vocabulary Card** and state the word. Explain how the photograph illustrates the word. State the example sentence and repeat the word.

 We Do Point to the word on the card and read the word with students. Ask them to repeat the word. Engage students in structured partner-talk about the visual as prompted on the back of the vocabulary card.

 You Do Display each visual in random order, hiding the word. Have students match the definitions and context sentences of the words to the visuals displayed.

ANSWER YES/NO QUESTIONS

OBJECTIVES

 Acquire and use accurately grade-appropriate general academic and domain-specific words and phrases, including those that signal precise actions, emotions, or states of being (e.g., *quizzed, whined, stammered*) and that are basic to a particular topic (e.g., *wildlife, conservation,* and *endangered* when discussing animal preservation). **L.4.6

 Display the *tolerate* **Visual Vocabulary Card**. Ask students the following question: *Should I tolerate the unruly behavior of my dog when I take him for a walk?* Point out that people should not tolerate unruly behavior; instead they should teach their pets to behave appropriately.

 Display the vocabulary card for the word *accompanies*. Ask: *Does a teacher always accompany students on a field trip?* With students, discuss how a teacher always accompanies students to supervise them on a field trip.

Display the remaining vocabulary cards one at a time and have students answer the following yes/no questions to correspond with each card. Have students justify their answers to demonstrate their word knowledge.

→ Will your *opponent* be on your side in a fight or discussion?

→ Does a *campaign* include a plan of actions to achieve a certain result?

→ Is the *governor* the head of the local government in a city?

→ Do you *intend* to go to school this Saturday?

IDIOMS

OBJECTIVES

 Demonstrate understanding of figurative language, word relationships, and nuances in word meaning. Recognize and explain the meaning of common idioms, adages, and proverbs. **L.4.5b

Use context clues to determine the meaning of idioms.

 Display the Comprehension and Fluency passage on **Approaching Reproducibles** pages 163–164. Read aloud the first two paragraphs. Point to the idiom *on our own*. Explain to students that they can find the meaning of an idiom by using context clues to see how the idiom fits in.

Think Aloud I want to know what the idiom *on our own* means. I can use context clues to help me figure out its meaning. I see the phrase "live with the shepherd," and this tells me that the sheep used to live with the shepherd. Next, I learn that the sheep no longer have the shepherd to help them find a place to graze. These clues tell me that *on our own* means to be alone with no one to help.

 Ask students to point to the idiom *made our move* in the first paragraph. With students, discuss how to use context clues to figure out the meaning of the idiom. Write the definition of *made our move* on the board.

 Have students use context clues in the passage to find the meaning of the idioms *took the side of* and *taken up where they had left off* on page 164.

→ Approaching Level
Comprehension

FLUENCY

TIER 2

OBJECTIVES

 Read on-level prose and poetry orally with accuracy, appropriate rate, and expression on successive readings. **RF.4.4b**

Read fluently with phrasing and expression.

I Do Explain that phrasing helps improve the flow of reading by separating ideas into groups. Tell students that reading with expression helps to bring these ideas to life. Read the first paragraph of the Comprehension and Fluency passage on **Approaching Reproducibles** pages 163–164. Tell students to listen to the increase or decrease of your vocal level of excitement at appropriate phrases.

We Do Read the rest of the page aloud and have students repeat each sentence after you, using appropriate phrasing and expression. Explain that you improved the flow of reading by using appropriate phrasing and made the text interesting by reading with expression.

You Do Have partners take turns reading sentences from the Approaching Reproducibles passage. Remind them to focus on reading with accurate phrasing and expression. Listen in and provide corrective feedback by modeling proper fluency as needed.

IDENTIFY POINT OF VIEW

TIER 2

OBJECTIVES

 Compare and contrast the point of view from which different stories are narrated, including the difference between first- and third-person narrations. **RL.4.6**

Identify the point of view in a text.

I Do Write the topic "The Sheep in the Wilderness." Then write "It was even harder on our own," and "The shepherd once took us there to graze." Help students understand that these details are told by a first-person narrator.

We Do Read the first page of the Comprehension and Fluency passage in **Approaching Reproducibles**. Ask: *So far, what is the narrator's point of view in the passage?* Point out that the passage is being narrated by one of the characters, so it is told by a first-person narrator. Help students identify and read aloud sentences that indicate the first-person narrator in the passage.

You Do Have students read the rest of the passage. After each paragraph, they should write down the point of view of the narrator. Review their lists and have students explain how they determined the narrator's point of view.

REVIEW POINT OF VIEW

OBJECTIVES

 Compare and contrast the point of view from which different stories are narrated, including the difference between first- and third-person narrations. **RL.4.6**

 Remind students that a story's point of view tells the narrator's thoughts and feelings about the characters and events in the story. Point out that when a story is narrated from the first-person point of view, it is narrated by one of the characters. Remind students that this means the reader can know and see only what the narrator knows and sees.

 Read the first paragraph of the Comprehension and Fluency passage in **Approaching Reproducibles** together. Model how students can read the text to determine the narrator's point of view. Work with students to find examples that show the first-person narrator's point of view. Then discuss how the text differs from one with a third-person narrator.

You Do Have students use information in each paragraph to identify the narrator's thoughts and feelings about the characters and action in the passage.

SELF-SELECTED READING

OBJECTIVES

 Compare and contrast the point of view from which different stories are narrated, including the difference between first- and third-person narrations. **RL.4.6**

Make, confirm, or revise predictions to enhance comprehension.

Read Independently

Have students choose a fantasy book for sustained silent reading. Remind students that:

→ point of view is the narrator's thoughts and feelings about the story's characters and events. Explain that when a story is narrated by one of its characters, it is told from a first-person narrator's point of view.

→ they can make predictions about what will happen later in the text.

→ as they continue reading, they can confirm and revise their predictions to understand how a character's actions affect the plot.

Read Purposefully

Have students record the narrator's point of view on a Point of View Chart as they read independently. After they finish, they can have a discussion, telling about the books they read and comparing the points of view.

→ Students should share their charts and answer this question: *What is the most interesting character you read about in this book?*

→ Students should also tell the rest of the class if they needed to revise their predictions as they read the story.

On Level

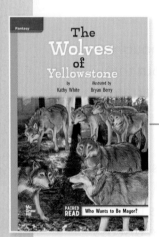

Lexile 740
TextEvaluator 40

OBJECTIVES

 Refer to details and examples in a text when explaining what the text says explicitly and when drawing inferences from the text. **RL.4.1**

 Compare and contrast the point of view from which different stories are narrated, including the difference between first- and third-person narrations. **RL.4.6**

 Recognize and explain the meaning of common idioms, adages, and proverbs. **L.4.5b**

Leveled Reader:
The Wolves of Yellowstone

Before Reading

Preview and Predict

Have students read the title and table of contents of *The Wolves of Yellowstone*. Have students make a prediction about what the story will be about and share it with a partner.

Review Genre: Fantasy Fiction

Review with students that fantasy fiction is told in the form of fiction that includes characters, settings, or events that could not exist in real life. As they preview the book, have students identify features of fantasy fiction in *The Wolves of Yellowstone*.

During Reading

Close Reading

Note Taking Ask students to use their graphic organizer while they read.

Pages 2–4 *What are some clues on page 2 that tell you about the narrator of the story?* (The pronouns *her* and *he* tell me that the story is told by a third-person narrator.) *Turn to a partner and tell a detail that tells you the narrator's point of view about Gray Tail.* (The narrator thought he was a great leader because the chapter title says it's a sad day when he dies.)

Pages 5–6 *What is the problem in the beginning of chapter 2?* (Black Streak took food from a human and has broken the rules of the park.)

Pages 7–8 *How can you tell the phrase "move like the wind" is an idiom?* (You can't tell what it means by its parts.) *Define the phrase using context clues. (Move like the wind* means "move very quickly.") *Turn to a partner and make a prediction about what Silver Fire will decide about the Wolf Council.* (For example: I think Silver Fire will run for leader of the Wolf Council.)

Go Digital

Leveled Readers

Use Graphic Organizer

Pages 9–11 *Confirm or revise your prediction about Silver Fire's decision.* (For example: My prediction was correct. Silver Fire decided to run for leader of the Wolf Council.) *Make a prediction about who will win the seat.* (For example: I think Silver Fire will win the election.)

Pages 12–15 *Confirm or revise your prediction about the result of the election.* (For example: My prediction was correct. Silver Fire won the election.) *How does Silver Fire change Black Streak's views?* (She tells him that she will need his help.) *Make a prediction about how the wolf pack will change with Silver Fire as a leader.* (For example: I think Silver Fire will help the wolf pack work together as a team.)

After Reading

Respond to Reading Have students complete Respond to Reading on page 16 after they have finished reading.

Analytical Writing **Write About Reading** Have students work with a partner to write a short paragraph from the point of view of Black Streak. Make sure students maintain this point of view.

Fluency: Phrasing and Expression

Model Model reading page 2 with proper phrasing and expression. Next, reread the page aloud and have students read along with you.

Apply Have students practice reading with a partner.

PAIRED READ

"Who Wants to Be Mayor"

Make Connections: Write About It **Analytical Writing**

Before reading, ask students to note that the genre of this text is expository, which means it explains about a topic. Then discuss the Essential Question. After reading, ask students to use the information from "Who Wants to be Mayor" to discuss what kind of leader Silver Fire will be.

Leveled Reader

FOCUS ON LITERARY ELEMENTS

Students can extend their knowledge of onomatopoeia by completing the literary elements activity on page 20.

Literature Circles

Ask students to conduct a literature circle using the Thinkmark questions to guide the discussion. You may wish to have a whole-class discussion on ways students would like to participate in government.

Level Up

Level-up lessons available online.

IF students read the On Level fluently and answered the questions

THEN pair them with students who have proficiently read Beyond Level and have students

- partner-read the Beyond Level main selection.
- list vocabulary words they find difficult and look them up with a partner.

A C T Access Complex Text

The Beyond Level challenges students by including more **domain-specific words** and **complex sentence structures**.

On Level

Vocabulary

REVIEW VOCABULARY WORDS

OBJECTIVES

 Acquire and use accurately grade-appropriate general academic and domain-specific words and phrases, including those that signal precise actions, emotions, or states of being and that are basic to a particular topic. **L.4.6**

 I Do Use the **Visual Vocabulary Cards** to review key selection words: *accompanies, intend, opponent, overwhelming, tolerate,* and *weary.* Point to each word, read it aloud, and have students chorally repeat it.

 We Do Ask these questions and help students respond and explain their answers.

→ What happens when you *tolerate* someone or something?

→ What do you *intend* to do after school today?

→ What does it mean when someone *accompanies* you to something?

 You Do Have students respond to these questions and explain their answers.

→ How does someone feel when he or she becomes *weary*?

→ What happens when you feel *overwhelmed* by something?

→ What makes someone an *opponent* in a contest?

IDIOMS

OBJECTIVES

 Demonstrate understanding of figurative language, word relationships, and nuances in word meaning. Recognize and explain the meaning of common idioms, adages, and proverbs. **L.4.5b**

Use context clues to determine the meaning of idioms.

 I Do Remind students that they can often figure out the meaning of an idiom from context clues in surrounding sentences. Point out that idioms are phrases that include words that may be familiar but are used together in a way that is not meant to be taken literally. Use the Comprehension and Fluency passage on **Your Turn Practice Book** pages 163–164 to model.

Think Aloud I want to know what the idiom *on our own* means. I see the phrase "live with the shepherd," which tells me that the sheep used to live with the shepherd. Next, I learn that the sheep no longer have the shepherd to help them find a place to graze. This clue tells me that *on our own* means to be alone with no one to help.

 We Do Have students find the idiom *make our move* on page 163. Help students figure out its meaning using context clues in surrounding sentences.

 You Do Have students work in pairs to determine the meanings of the idioms *took the side of* and *taken up where they had left off* on page 164.

Comprehension

REVIEW POINT OF VIEW

OBJECTIVES

Compare and contrast the point of view from which different stories are narrated, including the difference between first- and third-person narrations. **RL.4.6**

 Remind students that point of view is the narrator's thoughts and feelings about the characters and events in a text. Explain that when a story is told by a first-person narrator, the reader sees the story's events through a character's eyes. Tell students that the reader is limited to knowing and seeing only what that character knows and sees in the story.

 Have a volunteer read the first paragraph of the Comprehension and Fluency passage on **Your Turn Practice Book** pages 163–164. Have students list details that tell the narrator's point of view. Help them explain why they included these details on their lists. Model how to identify other examples of the first-person narrator's point of view. Work with students to identify the narrator's point of view in the next paragraph.

You Do Have partners identify the narrator's point of view in each paragraph. Then have them determine the narrator's point of view of the whole passage.

SELF-SELECTED READING

OBJECTIVES

Compare and contrast the point of view from which different stories are narrated, including the difference between first- and third-person narrations. **RL.4.6**

Make, confirm, or revise predictions to enhance comprehension.

Read Independently

Have students choose a fantasy book for sustained silent reading. Remind students that:

→ a story is narrated from a first-person narrator's point of view when it is narrated by one of the characters.

→ readers should make predictions about events they think will happen later in the story. They can confirm and revise their predictions as they read the rest of the text.

Read Purposefully

Encourage students to read different fantasy books in order to learn about a variety of subjects.

→ As students read, have them fill in clues to the narrator's point of view on a Point of View Chart. Have them compare and contrast the books' points of view.

→ Students can use this chart to help them write a summary of the book.

→ Ask students to share their reactions to the book with classmates.

→ Beyond Level

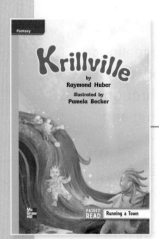

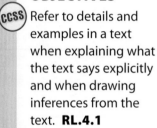

Lexile 810
TextEvaluator™ 55

OBJECTIVES

 Refer to details and examples in a text when explaining what the text says explicitly and when drawing inferences from the text. **RL.4.1**

 Compare and contrast the point of view from which different stories are narrated, including the difference between first- and third-person narrations. **RL.4.6**

Recognize and explain the meaning of common idioms, adages, and proverbs. **L.4.5b**

Leveled Reader:
Krillville

Go Digital

Leveled Readers

Before Reading

Preview and Predict

Have students read the Essential Question. Then have students read the title and table of contents of *Krillville*. Have students make a prediction about what the story will be about and share it with a partner.

Review Genre: Fantasy Fiction

Review with students that fantasy fiction is told in the form of fiction that includes characters, settings, or events that could not exist in real life. As they preview the book, have students identify features of fantasy fiction in *Krillville*.

During Reading

Close Reading

Note Taking Ask students to use their graphic organizer while they read.

Pages 2–3 *Use clues on page 2 to determine the the type of narrator used in the story.* (The pronouns *I* and *my* tell me that the story is told by a first-person narrator) *Turn to a partner and tell a detail that tells you the narrator's point of view about Mr. Crabs.* (He's not as mean as he sounds because his "bark is worse than his bite.")

Pages 4–5 *Why is Maribel unhappy?* (She doesn't agree with the council's decision to clear-cut the kelp beds.) *Turn to a partner and predict whether Maribel will stop the development.* (For example: I predict that Maribel will stop the development on the kelp beds.)

Pages 6–10 *Confirm or revise your prediction about Maribel's petition.* (For example: My prediction was incorrect. I can revise my prediction given the new information. I predict that Maribel will have to start over with a new petition.) *What does the author mean by "square one" on page 9?* (Square one means "back to the beginning.") *How can you tell?* (I can tell by context clues. Maribel has to start over again.)

Use Graphic Organizer

Pages 11–12 *Predict how Maribel could use the constitution to save the kelp beds.* (For example: I think Maribel will show the council the rule on recreation facilities and ask that they keep the kelp beds as a park.)

Pages 12–15 *Confirm or revise your prediction.* (My prediction was incorrect. Maribel convinced the council to build a sports facility where the kelp beds used to be.) *How did Mr. Crab change through the story?* (He learned to compromise.) *Paraphrase to a partner how the council compromised.* (The council used part of the kelp bed for housing and the other part for a park.) *Do you think Maribel will run for office some day? Why or why not?* (For example: I think Maribel will run for office because she cares about her community.)

After Reading

Respond to Reading Have students complete Respond to Reading on page 16 after they have finished reading.

Analytical Writing **Write About Reading** Have students work with a partner to write a short paragraph from the point of view of Mr. Crab.

Fluency: Phrasing and Expression

Model Model reading page 2 with proper phrasing and expression. Next, reread the page aloud and have students read along with you.

Apply Have students practice reading with a partner.

PAIRED READ

"Running a Town"

Make Connections:
Write About It *Analytical Writing*

Before reading, ask students to note that the genre of this text is expository, which means it explains about a topic. Then discuss the Essential Question. After reading, ask students to use the information from "Running a Town" to discuss how Maribel helped change the council's plan.

Leveled Reader

FOCUS ON LITERARY ELEMENTS

Students can extend their knowledge of onomatopoeia by completing the literary elements activity on page 20.

Literature Circles

Ask students to conduct a literature circle using the Thinkmark questions to guide the discussion. You may wish to have a whole-class discussion on why students might want to run for local office.

Gifted and Talented

Synthesize Challenge students to learn more about how a person runs for office. Have them look at local news articles about a person running for an office. Then have them write a summary of what the candidate stands for and why they want to run for office. Have volunteers share their summaries with the class.

Beyond Level

Vocabulary

REVIEW DOMAIN-SPECIFIC WORDS

 OBJECTIVES
Acquire and use accurately grade-appropriate general academic and domain-specific words and phrases, including those that signal precise actions, emotions, or states of being and that are basic to a particular topic. **L.4.6**

 Model
Use the **Visual Vocabulary Cards** to review the meanings of the words *campaign* and *governor*. Write social studies-related sentences on the board using these words.

Write the words *candidate* and *opponent* on the board and discuss the meanings with students. Then help students write sentences using these words.

 Apply
Have students work in pairs to review the meanings of the words *council* and *majority*. Then have partners write sentences about local government using the words.

IDIOMS

 OBJECTIVES
Demonstrate understanding of figurative language, word relationships, and nuances in word meaning. Recognize and explain the meaning of common idioms, adages, and proverbs. **L.4.5b**

Use context clues to determine the meanings of idioms.

 Model
Read aloud the first paragraph of the Comprehension and Fluency passage on **Beyond Reproducibles** pages 163–164.

Think Aloud I want to know the meaning of the idiom *make our move*. I know that I can look at surrounding sentences and use context clues to help me figure out the meaning of the idiom. The phrases "plan our escape" and "finally escaped" tell me that *make our move* means to plan an action, such as an escape, and then to start to do it.

With students, read the second paragraph on page 163. Help them figure out the meaning of the idiom *on our own*.

 Apply
As they continue reading, have students use context clues to define the idioms *took the side of* and *took up where they had left off* on page 164.

 Gifted and Talented
Synthesize Have students imagine they are interviewing someone who is running for public office. Tell students to create questions and answers that tell what qualities they look for in a leader. Challenge students to use three vocabulary words in their work. Have partners act out the interviews.

Comprehension

REVIEW POINT OF VIEW

OBJECTIVES

 Compare and contrast the point of view from which different stories are narrated, including the difference between first- and third-person narrations. **RL.4.6**

 Model Remind students that point of view is the narrator's thoughts or feelings about the characters and the events in a story. Explain that the first-person point of view involves a narrator who is one of the characters. Students should ask themselves how the first-person narrator's point of view allows them to see the events in the story through one character's eyes.

Have students read the first paragraph of the Comprehension and Fluency passage on **Beyond Reproducibles** pages 163–164. Ask open-ended questions to facilitate discussion, such as *What is the author telling us in this paragraph? What does the author want us to know?* Students should support their responses with details from the text.

 Apply Have students identify the narrator's point of view in each paragraph in the rest of the passage as they independently fill in a Point of View Chart. Then have partners use their charts to determine how the narrator thinks and feels about the characters and the events in the story.

SELF-SELECTED READING

OBJECTIVES

 Compare and contrast the point of view from which different stories are narrated, including the difference between first- and third-person narrations. **RL.4.6**

Make, confirm, or revise predictions to enhance comprehension.

Read Independently

Have students choose a fantasy book for sustained silent reading.

→ As students read, have them fill in a Point of View Chart.

→ Remind students that a prediction is based on events that already happened in the story. Readers can confirm and revise their predictions as they read the rest of the text.

Read Purposefully

Encourage students to keep reading the book. Ask them to read different fantasy books in order to learn about a variety of subjects.

→ Students can write summaries of the book in their journals.

→ Ask students to share their reactions to the book with classmates.

 Independent Study Challenge students to discuss how their book relates to the weekly theme of leadership. Have students describe the connection between leadership and the people who run for public office. How can someone help his or her community by running for public office?

English Language Learners

Reading/Writing Workshop

OBJECTIVES

(CCSS) Refer to details and examples in a text when explaining what the text says explicitly and when drawing inferences from the text. **RL.4.1**

(CCSS) Compare and contrast the point of view from which different stories are narrated, including the difference between first- and third-person narrations. **RL.4.6**

(CCSS) Recognize and explain the meaning of common idioms, adages, and proverbs. **L.4.5b**

ACADEMIC LANGUAGE

• *narrator, point of view, prediction*

• Cognates: *narrador, predicción*

Shared Read
The TimeSpecs 3000

View "The TimeSpecs 3000"

Before Reading

Build Background

Read the Essential Question: Why do people run for public office?

→ Explain the meaning of the Essential Question. Explain that *office* is a multiple-meaning word that means "a government position." Show pictures of past and present leaders who have run for office. Make a list with students of the different positions people run for.

→ **Model an answer:** *One reason people run for office is to make changes. The president can make changes for the country. A governor makes changes for a state. A mayor makes changes for a city or town.*

→ Ask students a question that ties the Essential Question to their own background knowledge: *Would you run for office? Turn to a partner and discuss which office you would run for and what changes you would make.* Call on several pairs. Allow students to respond with gestures, eliciting details to develop their responses.

During Reading

Interactive Question-Response

→ Ask questions that help students understand the meaning of the text after each paragraph.

→ Reinforce the meanings of key vocabulary.

→ Ask students questions that require them to use key vocabulary.

→ Reinforce strategies and skills of the week by modeling.

Page 253

Paragraphs 1 and 2
Point out that this story is written as an e-mail. Discuss the features of an e-mail, including the attachments shown in the e-mail.

Explain and Model Point of View *The pronouns I, me, and my tell me that this story uses a first-person narrator. Who is the narrator writing to?* (his grandfather) *How can you tell?* (He starts the e-mail with "Dear Grandpa.")

Explain and Model Idioms Point out the idiom *In a nutshell.* Explain that *in a nutshell* means "in a few words." *Miguel says, "I intend to tell you everything" and "for now, I've pasted notes." This tells me that he is only telling part of the story.*

Field Notes: Day 1

Explain and Model Making Predictions Model making a prediction about the story so far. Point out the picture on page 253. *What do the TimeSpecs 3000 show?* (People in the past.) *The narrator tells us he is watching a cermony in 1848. I predict that he will see more things from the past.*

Have students share their predictions with a partner, using the sentence frame: *I predict _____.* (Possible answer: the narrator will travel back in time and learn more about the past)

Page 254

Field Notes: Day 2

Paragraphs 1 and 2

Let's look at our predictions and confirm or revise them. What happens when Miguel goes to the Lincoln Memorial? (The statue of Lincoln talks to him.) *Is our prediction about the story correct so far?* (yes) *What do you think will happen next in the story?* (Possible answer: I think Miguel will ask President Lincoln for advice.)

Paragraphs 3–6
Have students chorally read the dialogue. *Can a statue talk in real life?* (no) *What kind of story is this?* (fantasy)

Page 255

Paragraphs 1–5
Model Idioms Have students choral read the remaining dialogue. *Does Miguel really have Lincoln's ear?* (no) *What does it mean to "have his ear"?* (Lincoln is listening to Miguel talk.)

Reread Miguel's ideas for his campaign. Provide a definition for *campaign.* Point out the cognate *campaña.* *Would you run a campaign for class president?* (Possible answer: I would run a campaign. My idea is for new playground equipment.)

Paragraphs 7–8
How does the story change here? (We are reading Miguel's e-mail again.)

Ask advanced students to talk about what "P.S." stands for at the end of the story. Provide support if necessary.

Model Point of View *What is Miguel's point of view about the TimeSpecs 3000? What advice does he give his grandfather?* (Possible answer: Miguel is excited about the TimeSpecs 3000 and how they helped him talk to President Lincoln about running for president. He advises his grandfather not to use the TimeSpecs 3000 while looking at dinosaurs.)

After Reading

Make Connections

→ Review the Essential Question: Why do people run for public office?

→ Make text connections.

→ Have students complete **ELL Reproducibles** pages 163–165.

→ English Language Learners

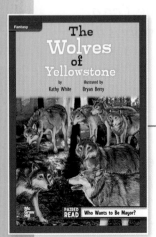

Lexile 610
TextEvaluator 18

OBJECTIVES

 Refer to details and examples in a text when explaining what the text says explicitly and when drawing inferences from the text. **RL.4.1**

 Compare and contrast the point of view from which different stories are narrated, including the difference between first- and third-person narrations. **RL.4.6**

 Recognize and explain the meaning of common idioms, adages, and proverbs. **L.4.5b**

Leveled Reader:
The Wolves of Yellowstone

Go Digital

Leveled Readers

Before Reading

Preview

→ Read the Essential Question: Why do people run for public office?

→ Refer to Taking a Stand: *How can people make a difference by running for public office?*

→ Preview *The Wolves of Yellowstone* and "The Job of a Mayor": *Our purpose for reading is to learn how groups choose a new leader.*

Vocabulary

Use the **Visual Vocabulary Cards** to preteach the ELL vocabulary: *cooperate, troublemaker, whimpered.* Use the routine found on the cards. Point out the cognate: *cooperar.*

During Reading

Interactive Question-Response

Note Taking Have students use their graphic organizer in **ELL Reproducibles** page 162. Use the questions below after reading each section with students.

Use Graphic Organizer

Pages 2–4 *Why are the wolves sad?* (Their leader has died.) *The pronouns* they, her, *and* him *tell me that this story uses a third-person narrator. What details can help us determine the narrator's point of view?* (The narrator repeats the word *sad* and describes stories about Gray Tail. This tells me that the narrator is sad and sympathetic.)

Pages 5–6 *How did Black Streak break the rules?* (He stole food from people.)

Pages 7–8 Point out the idiom "quiet as a mouse" on page 7. Quiet as a mouse *means "very quiet." Show me quiet as a mouse. Is Black Streak "as quiet as a mouse"?* (no) *Make a prediction about who Silver Fire thinks should replace Gray Tail on the Wolf Council. Share your prediction with a partner.* (Possible answer: Silver Fire thinks she should replace Gray Tail.)

Pages 9–11 *Was your prediction correct? Fill in the sentence frame: My prediction was ____.* (correct; incorrect) Ask students to predict which wolf will win the Wolf Council seat by raising their hands for Silver Fire or Black Streak.

Pages 12–15 *How do the wolves count votes?* (by who has the most howls) *Who won the election?* (Silver Fire) *Do you think Silver Fire will be a good leader? Why?* (Possible answer: I think Silver Fire will be a good leader because she is good at teamwork.)

After Reading

Respond to Reading Help students complete the graphic organizer in **ELL Reproducibles** page 162. Revisit the Essential Question. Ask partners to summarize and answer the Text Evidence Questions.

Analytical Writing **Write About Reading** Have students work with a partner to write how the story would be different if it were told from the point of view of Black Streak. Ask them to reread pages 6–7 and 11 to think about Black Streak's point of view of leading the Wolf Council.

Fluency: Phrasing and Expression

Model Model reading page 2 with proper phrasing and expression. Next, reread the page aloud and have students read along with you.

Apply Have students practice reading with a partner.

PAIRED READ

"Who Wants to be Mayor"

Make Connections:
Write About It ✐ *Analytical Writing*

Before reading, ask students to note that the genre of this text is expository. The text explains the role and responsibilities of mayors. Then discuss the Essential Question. After reading, ask students to use the information from "Who Wants to be Mayor" to discuss whether Silver Fire would make a good leader.

Leveled Reader

FOCUS ON LITERARY ELEMENTS

Students can extend their knowledge of onomatopoeia by completing the literary elements activity on page 20.

Literature Circles

Ask students to conduct a literature circle using the Thinkmark questions to guide the discussion. You may wish to have a whole-class discussion, asking students about the qualities they believe make a good leader.

Level Up

Level-up lessons available online.

IF students read the **ELL Level** fluently and answered the questions

THEN pair them with students who have proficiently read **On Level** and have students

- echo-read the **On Level** main selection with their partners.
- list words with which they have difficulty.
- discuss these words with their partners.

A C T ccess omplex ext

The **On Level** challenges students by including more **academic language** and **complex sentence structures**.

→ English Language Learners
Vocabulary

PRETEACH VOCABULARY

 OBJECTIVES

Acquire and use accurately grade-appropriate general academic and domain-specific words and phrases, including those that signal precise actions, emotions, or states of being and that are basic to a particular topic. **L.4.6**

LANGUAGE OBJECTIVE

Use vocabulary words.

I Do Preteach vocabulary from "The Time Specs 3000" following the Vocabulary Routine on the **Visual Vocabulary Cards** for *accompanies, campaign, governor, intend, opponent, overwhelming, tolerated,* and *weary.*

We Do After completing the Vocabulary Routine for each word, point to the word on the card and read it aloud. Ask students to repeat the word.

You Do Have students work with a partner to ask a question using a vocabulary word. Have another pair answer the question to show their understanding of the word. Repeat until at least four of the words have been used.

Beginning	Intermediate	Advanced/High
Help students write the questions and answers and read them aloud.	Ask students to write a sentence for each word that was used.	Challenge students to write questions for all of the vocabulary words.

REVIEW VOCABULARY

 OBJECTIVES

Acquire and use accurately grade-appropriate general academic and domain-specific words and phrases, including those that signal precise actions, emotions, or states of being and that are basic to a particular topic. **L.4.6**

LANGUAGE OBJECTIVE

Use vocabulary words.

I Do Divide the previous week's vocabulary words into two groups and review over two days. Read each word aloud, pointing to the word on the **Visual Vocabulary Card**. Have students repeat after you. Then follow the Vocabulary Routine on the back of each card.

We Do Ask students to guess the word you describe. Provide context clues to help students. Have students say the word and define it or use it in a sentence.

You Do In pairs, have students make a list of context clues for each vocabulary word. Ask each group to read the clues aloud. Have the class guess the word and define it or use it in a sentence.

Beginning	Intermediate	Advanced/High
Help students list and say the context clues for each vocabulary word.	Have students write a sentence using the context clues from the list.	Have students write a sentence for each word and discuss its meaning.

IDIOMS

OBJECTIVES

 Demonstrate understanding of figurative language, word relationships, and nuances in word meaning. Recognize and explain the meaning of common idioms, adages, and proverbs. **L.4.5b**

LANGUAGE OBJECTIVE

Use context clues to determine the meaning of idioms.

I Do Read aloud the second paragraph of the Comprehension and Fluency passage on **ELL Reproducibles** pages 163–164. Remind students that the meaning of an idiom is different from the literal meanings of the individual words in the idiom. Point to the idiom *on our own*. Explain that context clues in nearby sentences can help you determine the meanings of idioms.

Think Aloud I am not sure what the idiom *on our own* means. The phrase "live with the shepherd" tells me that the sheep used to live with the shepherd. Next, I learn that the sheep no longer have the shepherd to help them find a place to graze. I think the idiom *on our own* means to be alone with no one to help.

We Do Have students point to the idiom *made our move*. Help them find context clues to figure out its meaning. Then write the meaning on the board.

You Do In pairs, have students look for clues to figure out the meanings of the idioms *took the side of* and *taken up where they had left off*.

Beginning	Intermediate	Advanced/High
Help students look for context clues. Write the meanings of the idioms and read them aloud.	Ask students to identify context clues and read them aloud.	Challenge students to write their own clues for the idioms.

ADDITIONAL VOCABULARY

OBJECTIVES

 Choose words and phrases to convey ideas precisely. **L.4.3a**

LANGUAGE OBJECTIVE

Use academic and high-frequency words.

I Do List academic and high-frequency words from "The TimeSpecs 3000" and *The Wolves of Yellowstone*: *boundary, decide, important, leader,* and *president*. Define each word for students: *To decide means to make a choice.*

We Do Model using the words in a sentence: *Angie needs to decide which movie we will watch.* Then provide sentence frames and complete them with students: *I decided to do my homework before I _____ .*

You Do Have pairs write sentence frames and share them with the class.

Beginning	Intermediate	Advanced/High
Help students complete the sentence frames.	Provide a sentence starter for students, if necessary.	Have students define the words they used.

→ English Language Learners
Writing/Spelling

WRITING TRAIT: IDEAS

 OBJECTIVES

Use dialogue and description to develop experiences and events or show the responses of characters to situations. **W.4.3b**

LANGUAGE OBJECTIVE

Analyze models to identify dialogue that shows what the character is feeling and thinking.

 I Do Explain that writers make characters come to life with dialogue. Remind students that dialogue is a character's words. Read the Expert Model passage aloud. Point out how the dialogue shows Miguel's thoughts and feelings. Ask students what they learn about Miguel in this passage.

 We Do Read aloud a passage from "The TimeSpecs 3000." Identify the dialogue and add it to a word web. Use the examples in the web to describe how the dialogue helps readers understand the characters and their situations.

 You Do Have pairs write a short dialogue between two characters. Ask them to use a word web to develop their characters' thoughts and feelings. Edit each pair's writing. Then ask students to revise, using appropriate pronouns.

Beginning	Intermediate	Advanced/High
Provide additional examples of dialogue and read them aloud.	Ask partners to read the dialogue aloud and make sure it sounds realistic.	Have students explain how dialogue helps develop a character.

SPELL WORDS WITH INFLECTIONAL ENDINGS

 OBJECTIVES

Spell grade-appropriate words correctly, consulting references as needed. **L.4.2d**

LANGUAGE OBJECTIVES

Spell words with inflectional endings.

 I Do Read aloud the Spelling Words on page T100. Point out that inflectional endings can be added to a base word that ends in a consonant and *y* by changing the *y* to *i*. Have students repeat the words.

 We Do Read the Dictation Sentences on page T101 aloud for students. Read the underlined word slowly and point out the inflectional endings. Have students repeat after you and write the word.

 You Do Display the words. Have partners exchange their lists to check the spellings and write the words correctly.

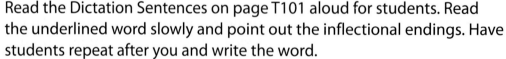

Beginning	Intermediate	Advanced/High
Have students copy the words with correct spelling and say the words aloud.	After students have corrected their words, have pairs quiz each other.	After they have corrected their words, have pairs use each word in a sentence.

Grammar

TYPES OF PRONOUNS

OBJECTIVES

 Explain the function of nouns, pronouns, verbs, adjectives, and adverbs in general and their functions in particular sentences. **L.3.1a**

Use subject and object pronouns.

LANGUAGE OBJECTIVES

Write sentences.

Language Transfers Handbook

In Hmong and Cantonese, the same pronoun form is used for subject and object. In Korean and Spanish, subject pronouns may be dropped because the verb ending gives information about the number and/or gender. Reinforce the correct use of subject and object pronouns by helping students form sentences.

 Remind students that a subject pronoun can take the place of a noun or nouns. Write the following subject pronouns on the board: *I, you, he, she, it, we,* and *they.* Tell students that an object pronoun can take the place of a noun that follows an action verb or a preposition. Write the following object pronouns on the board: *me, you, him, her, it, us,* and *them.* Point out that a reflexive pronoun ends in *-self* or *-selves.* Add that they are used when the subject and object of a sentence are the same. Write these singular and plural reflexive pronouns on the board: *myself, yourself, himself, herself, ourselves, yourselves,* and *themselves.*

 Write the sentence frames below on the board. Review subject, object, and reflexive pronouns with students. Have students use the correct pronouns to complete each sentence frame. Fill the sentence frames with students' responses. Then read the completed sentences aloud for students to repeat.

> *Dad told _____ to finish my homework before bed. (me, I)*
>
> *Malia gave _____ a book about Asia. (she, her)*
>
> *The boy taught _____ how to play the guitar. (himself, themselves)*

You Do Brainstorm a list of pronouns with students. Have students work in pairs to write three sentences using pronouns from the list. They should use subject, object, and reflexive pronouns in their sentences.

Beginning	Intermediate	Advanced/High
Have students copy their sentences and help them identify the type of pronoun. Read the sentences aloud and have students repeat after you.	Ask students to underline and label each type of pronoun they used.	Have students proofread their sentences for mechanics and usage. Have students explain why each pronoun is a subject, an object, or a reflexive pronoun.

For extra support, have students complete the activities in the **Grammar Practice Reproducibles** during the week, using the routine below:

→ Explain the grammar skill.

→ Model the first activity in the Grammar Practice Reproducibles.

→ Have the whole group complete the next couple of activities, then the rest with a partner.

→ Review the activities with correct answers.

PROGRESS MONITORING

Weekly Assessment

CCSS TESTED SKILLS

✓COMPREHENSION:	✓VOCABULARY:	✓WRITING:
Point of View **RL.4.6**	Idioms **L.4.5b**	Writing About Text **RL.4.6, W.4.9a**

Assessment Includes

→ Pencil-and-paper administration

→ On-line administration

→ Approaching-Level Weekly Assessment also available

FLUENCY

Fluency Goal 102 to 122 words correct per minute (WCPM)

Accuracy Rate Goal 95% or higher.

Administer oral reading fluency assessments using the following schedule:

→ **Weeks 1, 3, 5** Provide Approaching-Level students at least three oral reading fluency assessments during the unit.

→ **Weeks 2 and 4** Provide On-Level students at least two oral reading fluency assessments during the unit.

→ **Week 6** If necessary, provide Beyond-Level students an oral reading fluency assessment at this time.

Also Available: Selection Tests online PDFs

Go Digital! www.connected.mcgraw-hill.com

Using Assessment Results

TESTED SKILLS	If ...	Then ...
COMPREHENSION	Students answer 0–6 multiple-choice items correctly ...	... assign Lessons 37–39 on Point of View from the *Tier 2 Comprehension Intervention online PDFs.*
VOCABULARY	Students answer 0–6 multiple-choice items correctly ...	... assign Lesson 166 on Idioms, Proverbs, and Adages from the *Tier 2 Vocabulary Intervention online PDFs.*
WRITING	Students score less than "3" on the constructed response ...	... assign Lessons 37–39 and/or Write About Reading Lesson 194 from the *Tier 2 Comprehension Intervention online PDFs.*
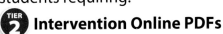	Students have a WCPM score of 94–101 ...	... assign a lesson from Section 1 or 7–10 of the *Tier 2 Fluency Intervention online PDFs.*
	Students have a WCPM score of 0–93 ...	... assign a lesson from Sections 2–6 of the *Tier 2 Fluency Intervention online PDFs.*

Response to Intervention

Use the appropriate sections of the *Placement and Diagnostic Assessment* as well as students' assessment results to designate students requiring:

TIER 2 Intervention Online PDFs

TIER 3 WonderWorks Intervention Program

Text Complexity Range for Grades 4–5

Lexile

740 | TextEvaluator™ | 1010

23 | | 51

McGraw-Hill Reading
Wonders

Reading/Writing Workshop

Mc
Graw
Hill

TEACH AND MODEL

CCSS **Shared Read** Genre · Historical Fiction

A Telephone Mix-Up

Essential Question
How do inventions and technology affect your life?

Read how a telephone brings change to the lives of Meg and her father.

"By tomorrow afternoon there will be eight telephones right here in Centerburg, Ohio, and one of them will be ours!" Dr. Ericksen said to his daughter, Meg. "I predict that before this **decade** is over, in just another five years, there could be a hundred! That's how fast I foresee this **technology** will spread! When people need help, they'll call me on the telephone. Envision how many lives it will save! Picture all the amazing benefits!"

Meg realized that not everyone thought the telephone was an **engineering** marvel. She had heard people say that telephones were a useless invention. A few others felt the newfangled machine would open up a Pandora's box of troubles, causing people to stop visiting each other and writing letters.

Despite the concerns of some people, progress marched on. Just weeks earlier, Centerburg's first telephone had been installed in Mr. Kane's general store, another was put in at the hotel, and yet another at the newspaper office. Mrs. Kane was the town's first switchboard operator, **directing** incoming calls to the correct lines.

The next morning, Meg wrote "October 9, 1905" on the top of her slate with chalk while she **squirmed** in her seat, wishing that the long school day was over.

266 | 267

✔ Vocabulary

decade
directing
engineering
gleaming
scouted
squirmed
technology
tinkering

🔎 Close Reading of Complex Text

Shared Read "A Telephone Mix-Up", 266–269

Genre Historical Fiction

Lexile 950
ⒺⓉⓈ *TextEvaluator™* 38

Minilessons

✔ **Comprehension Strategy** .... Make Predictions, T146–T147

✔ **Comprehension Skill** .... Point of View, T148–T149

✔ **Genre** .... Historical Fiction, T150–T151

✔ **Vocabulary Strategy** .... Context Clues: Synonyms, T152–T153

✔ **Writing Traits** .... Ideas, T158–T159

Grammar .... Pronoun-Verb Agreement, T162–T163

✔ Tested Skills CCSS

👉 **Go**
Digital

www.connected.mcgraw-hill.com

BREAKTHROUGHS

Essential Question

How do inventions and technology affect your life?

APPLY *WITH* CLOSE READING

Complex Text

Literature Anthology

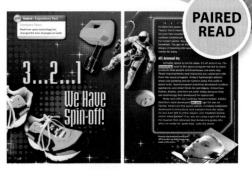

PAIRED READ

The Moon Over Star, 314–331
Genre Historical Fiction
Lexile 860
(ETS) *TextEvaluator™* 48

"3…2…1…We Have Spin-Off!", 332–335
Genre Expository Text
Lexile 900
(ETS) *TextEvaluator™* 33

Differentiated Text

Leveled Readers *Include Paired Reads*

APPROACHING
Lexile 620
(ETS) *TextEvaluator™* 31

ON LEVEL
Lexile 690
(ETS) *TextEvaluator™* 44

BEYOND
Lexile 790
(ETS) *TextEvaluator™* 37

ELL
Lexile 540
(ETS) *TextEvaluator™* 27

Extended Complex Text

Project Mulberry
Genre Realistic Fiction
Lexile 690
(ETS) *TextEvaluator™* 39

Riding Freedom
Genre Realistic Fiction
Lexile 720
(ETS) *TextEvaluator™* 40

Classroom Library

Classroom Library lessons available online.

TEACH AND MANAGE

How You Teach

INTRODUCE

Weekly Concept
Breakthroughs

Reading/Writing Workshop
262–263

TEACH

Close Reading
"A Telephone Mix-Up"

Minilessons
Make Predictions, Point of View,
Historical Fiction, Synonyms,
Writing Traits

Reading/Writing Workshop
266–269

APPLY

Close Reading
The Moon Over Star

"3... 2...1...We Have
Spin-off!"

Literature Anthology
314–335

👉 **Go Digital**

Interactive Whiteboard

Interactive Whiteboard

Mobile

How Students Practice

WEEKLY CONTRACT

PDF Online

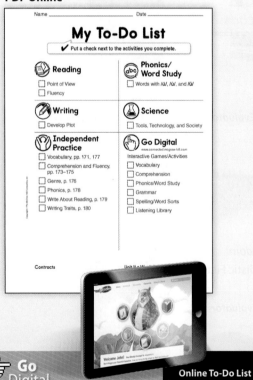

Name _____ Date _____

My To-Do List
✔ Put a check next to the activities you complete.

📖 **Reading**
- [ ] Point of View
- [ ] Fluency

🔤 **Phonics/Word Study**
- [ ] Words with /û/, /ô/, and /ū/

✍️ **Writing**
- [ ] Develop Plot

🧪 **Science**
- [ ] Tools, Technology, and Society

Independent Practice
- [ ] Vocabulary, pp. 171, 177
- [ ] Comprehension and Fluency, pp. 173–175
- [ ] Genre, p. 176
- [ ] Phonics, p. 178
- [ ] Write About Reading, p. 179
- [ ] Writing Traits, p. 180

Go Digital
www.connected.mcgraw-hill.com
Interactive Games/Activities
- [ ] Vocabulary
- [ ] Comprehension
- [ ] Phonics/Word Study
- [ ] Grammar
- [ ] Spelling/Word Sorts
- [ ] Listening Library

Contracts   Unit 4 • Week 3

👉 **Go Digital**

Online To-Do List

LEVELED PRACTICE AND ONLINE ACTIVITIES

Your Turn Practice Book
171–180

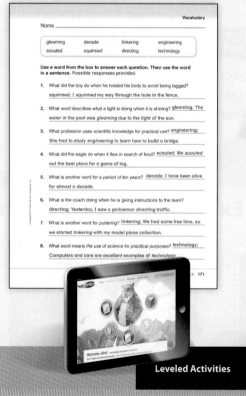

Name _____

Vocabulary

| gleaming | decade | tinkering | engineering |
| scouted | squirmed | directing | technology |

Use a word from the box to answer each question. Then use the word in a sentence. Possible responses provided.

1. What did the boy do when he twisted his body to avoid being tagged? squirmed; I *squirmed* my way through the hole in the fence.

2. What word describes what a light is doing when it is shining? gleaming; The water in the pool was *gleaming* due to the light of the sun.

3. What profession uses scientific knowledge for practical use? engineering; She had to study *engineering* to learn how to build a bridge.

4. What did the eagle do when it flew in search of food? scouted; We *scouted* out the best place for a game of tag.

5. What is another word for a *period of ten years*? decade; I have been alive for almost a *decade*.

6. What is the coach doing when he is giving instructions to the team? directing; Yesterday, I saw a policeman *directing* traffic.

7. What is another word for *puttering*? tinkering; We had some free time, so we started *tinkering* with my model plane collection.

8. What word means *the use of science for practical purposes*? technology; Computers and cars are excellent examples of *technology*.

171

Leveled Readers

Leveled Activities

Writer's Workspace

DIFFERENTIATE

SMALL GROUP INSTRUCTION
Leveled Readers

Mobile

INTEGRATE

Research and Inquiry
Paragraph, T156

Text Connections
Compare How Technology
Affects Our Lives, T157

 Analytical Writing **Write About Reading**
Write an Analysis, T157

**Online Research
and Writing**

ASSESS

**Weekly Assessment
205–216**

**Online
Assessment**

LEVELED WORKSTATION CARDS

More
Activities
on back

18

New Tools and Technology

SCIENCE

- The Internet has affected the way people communicate with each other and get information.

- Tell your partner about one way you used the Internet recently to

1

Synonyms

PHONICS/WORD STUDY

- Write the words *guardian, agile, awkward, ruckus,* and *interfere.*

agile

- Use a thesaurus to find a synonym for each of the words. Write the synonym next to the original word.

- On another sheet of paper, write a sentence for each original word. Leave a blank for the word. Your partner should do the same for each synonym.

- Exchange papers and use one of the ten words to complete each sentence.

You need
> paper, pencils
> dictionary or thesaurus

Go Digital! www.connected.mcgraw-hill.com • Interactive Games and Activities • Grade 4

5

Ideas: Develop a Plot

WRITING

Read this paragraph from Stellan's story. Identify details that show how the plot develops. Revise the paragraph to help develop the plot.

Joe... n the cold, dark river and

5

Point of View

READING

- Choose a story that you have read recently. As you reread it, identify the main character and any details that let you know who is telling the story.

- Choose an event in the story. Through whose point of view is it described?

- Write a paragraph retelling the event from the point of view of *another* character. Decide how his or her experience would be the same or different.

You need
> story read recently
> paper
> pencils or pens

Go Digital! www.connected.mcgraw-hill.com • Interactive Games and Activities • Grade 4

DEVELOPING READERS AND WRITERS

Write to Sources and Research

Analysis, T148–T149

Note Taking, T153B, T153T

Summarize, T153R, T153U

Point of View, T153R

Make Connections: Essential Question, T153R, T153V, T157

Key Details, T153U

Research and Inquiry, T156

Analyze to Share an Opinion, T157

Comparing Texts, T169, T177, T181, T187

Predictive Writing, T153B

Teacher's Edition

Literature Anthology

Summarize, 331
Point of View, 331

Go Digital

Interactive Whiteboard

Leveled Readers
Comparing Texts
Point of View

Point of View, 173–175
Genre, 176
Analyze to Share an Opinion, 179

Your Turn Practice Book

Writing Process • Genre Writing

Narrative Text
Fictional Narrative, T344–T349

Conferencing Routines
Teacher Conferences, T346
Peer Conferences, T347

Go Digital

Interactive Whiteboard

Teacher's Edition

Leveled Workstation Card
Description, Card 27

Go Digital

Writer's Workspace
Fictional Narrative
Writing Process
Multimedia Presentations

Writing Traits • Write Every Day

Writing Trait: Ideas
Develop Plot, T158–T159

Conferencing Routines
Teacher Conferences, T160
Peer Conferences, T161

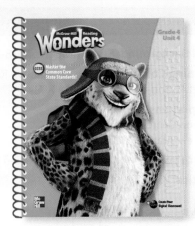

Teacher's Edition

Ideas: Plot, 274–275

Reading/Writing Workshop

Interactive Whiteboard

Ideas: Plot, Card 5

Leveled Workstation Card

Ideas: Plot, 180

Your Turn Practice Book

Grammar and Spelling

Grammar
Pronoun-Verb Agreement,
T162–T163

Spelling
Words with /ü/, /u̇/, and /ū/,
T164–T165

Interactive Whiteboard

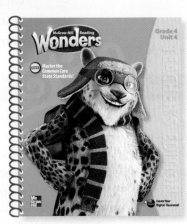

Teacher's Edition

Pronoun-Verb Agreement

Words with /ü/, /u̇/, and /ū/ Word Sorts

Online Spelling and Grammar Games

SUGGESTED LESSON PLAN

	DAY 1	**DAY 2**

READING

Whole Group

Teach, Model and Apply

Reading/Writing Workshop

DAY 1

Build Background Breakthroughs, T138–T139

Listening Comprehension Interactive Read Aloud: "Good-bye Icebox!", T140–T141

Comprehension
- Preview Genre: Historical Fiction
- Preview Strategy: Make Predictions

✔**Vocabulary** Words in Context, T142–T143

Practice *Your Turn*, 171

Close Reading of Complex Text
"A Telephone Mix-Up," 266–269

DAY 2

✔**Comprehension**
- Strategy: Make Predictions, T146–T147
- Skill: Point of View, T148–T149
- Write About Reading *Analytical Writing*
- Genre: Historical Fiction, T150–T151

✔**Vocabulary** Strategy: Synonyms, T152–T153

Practice *Your Turn*, 172–177

DIFFERENTIATED INSTRUCTION   Choose across the week to meet your students' needs.

Small Group

Approaching Level

DAY 1

Leveled Reader *Ron's Radio*, T168–T169

Phonics/Decoding Decode Words with /ū/, T170 **TIER 2**

Vocabulary
- Review High-Frequency Words, T172 **TIER 2**
- Identify Related Words, T173

DAY 2

Leveled Reader *Ron's Radio*, T168–T169

Vocabulary Review Vocabulary Words, T172 **TIER 2**

Comprehension
- Identify Pronouns in Narration, T174 **TIER 2**
- Review Point of View, T175

On Level

DAY 1

Leveled Reader *The Freedom Machine*, T176–T177

Vocabulary Review Vocabulary Words, T178

DAY 2

Leveled Reader *The Freedom Machine*, T176–T177

Comprehension Review Point of View, T179

Beyond Level

DAY 1

Leveled Reader *A Better Way*, T180–T181

Vocabulary Review Domain-Specific Words, T182

DAY 2

Leveled Reader *A Better Way*, T180–T181

Comprehension Review Point of View, T183

English Language Learners

DAY 1

Shared Read "A Telephone Mix-Up," T184–T185

Phonics/Decoding Decode Words with /ū/, T170

Vocabulary
- Preteach Vocabulary, T188
- Review High-Frequency Words, T172

DAY 2

Leveled Reader *The Freedom Machine*, T186–T187

Vocabulary Review Vocabulary, T188

Writing Writing Trait: Ideas, T190

Grammar Pronoun-Verb Agreement, T191

LANGUAGE ARTS   Writing Process: Fictional Narrative T344–T349   Use with Weeks 1–3

Whole Group

Writing

Grammar

Spelling

Build Vocabulary

DAY 1

✔**Readers to Writers**
- Writing Traits: Ideas/Develop Plot, T158–T159
- Writing Entry: Prewrite and Draft, T160

Grammar Pronoun-Verb Agreement, T162

Spelling Words with /ü/, /ů/, and /ū/, T164

Build Vocabulary
- Connect to Words, T166
- Academic Vocabulary, T166

DAY 2

Readers to Writers
- Writing Entry: Revise, T160

Grammar Pronoun-Verb Agreement, T162

Spelling Words with /ü/, /ů/, and /ū/, T164

Build Vocabulary
- Expand Vocabulary, T166
- Review Latin Roots, T166

DAY 3	DAY 4	DAY 5 Review and Assess

READING

Phonics/Decoding
• Words with /ü/, /ū/, and /u̇/, T154
• Consonant + *le* Syllables, T155

Practice *Your Turn*, 178

Close Reading *The Moon Over Star*, 314–331 • *Analytical Writing*

Literature Anthology

Fluency Expression, T155

Integrate Ideas • *Analytical Writing*
• Research and Inquiry, T156

Practice *Your Turn*, 173–175

Close Reading "3...2...1...We Have Spin-Off!", 332–335 • *Analytical Writing*

Integrate Ideas • *Analytical Writing*
• Research and Inquiry, T156
• Text Connections, T157
• Write About Reading, T157

Practice *Your Turn*, 179

DIFFERENTIATED INSTRUCTION

Leveled Reader *Ron's Radio*, T168–T169

Phonics/Decoding Review Words with /ü/, /ū/, and /u̇/, T170 ②

Fluency Expression, T174 ②

Vocabulary Context Clues: Synonyms, T173

Leveled Reader Paired Read: "Roosevelt's Fireside Chats," T169 • *Analytical Writing*

Phonics/Decoding Practice Words with /ü/, /ū/, and /u̇/, T171

Leveled Reader Literature Circles, T169

Comprehension Self-Selected Reading, T175

Phonics/Decoding Consonant + *le* Syllables, T171

Leveled Reader *The Freedom Machine*, T176–T177

Vocabulary Context Clues: Synonyms, T178

Leveled Reader Paired Read: "The Interstate Highway System," T177 • *Analytical Writing*

Leveled Reader Literature Circles, T177

Comprehension Self-Selected Reading, T179

Leveled Reader *A Better Way*, T180–T181

Vocabulary
• Context Clues: Synonyms, T182
• Independent Study, T182

Gifted and Talented

Leveled Reader Paired Read: "The History of Washing Technology," T181 • *Analytical Writing*

Leveled Reader Literature Circles, T181

Comprehension
• Self-Selected Reading, T183
• Independent Study: Synthesize, T183

Gifted and Talented

Leveled Reader *The Freedom Machine*, T186–T187

Phonics/Decoding Review words with /ü/, /ū/, and /u̇/, T170

Vocabulary Context Clues: Synonyms, T189

Spelling Words with /ü/, /u̇/, and /ū/, T190

Leveled Reader Paired Read: "The Interstate Highway System," T187 • *Analytical Writing*

Vocabulary Additional Vocabulary, T189

Phonics/Decoding Practice Words with /ü/, /ū/, and /u̇/, T171

Leveled Reader Literature Circles, T187

Phonics/Decoding Consonant + *le* Syllables, T171

LANGUAGE ARTS

Readers to Writers
• Writing Entry: Prewrite and Draft, T161

Grammar Mechanics and Usage, T163

Spelling Words with /ü/, /u̇/, and /ū/, T165

Build Vocabulary
• Reinforce the Words, T167
• Synonyms, T167

Readers to Writers
• Writing Entry: Revise, T161

Grammar Pronoun-Verb Agreement, T163

Spelling Words with /ü/, /u̇/, and /ū/, T165

Build Vocabulary
• Connect to Writing, T167
• Shades of Meaning, T167

Readers to Writers
• Writing Entry: Share and Reflect, T161

Grammar Pronoun-Verb Agreement, T163

Spelling Words with /ü/, /u̇/, and /ū/, T165

Build Vocabulary
• Word Squares, T167
• Morphology, T167

DIFFERENTIATE TO ACCELERATE

  Scaffold to **A**ccess **C**omplex **T**ext

IF the text complexity of a particular selection is too difficult for students

THEN see the references noted in the chart below for scaffolded instruction to help students Access Complex Text.

Qualitative   Quantitative
Reader and Task
TEXT COMPLEXITY

	Reading/Writing Workshop	Literature Anthology	Leveled Readers		Classroom Library

Quantitative	"A Telephone Mix-Up" **Lexile** 950 *TextEvaluator*™ 38	*The Moon Over Star* **Lexile** 860 *TextEvaluator*™ 48 "3 … 2 … 1 … We Have a Spin-Off" **Lexile** 900 *TextEvaluator*™ 33	**Approaching Level** **Lexile** 620 *TextEvaluator*™ 31 **Beyond Level** **Lexile** 790 *TextEvaluator*™ 37	**On Level** **Lexile** 690 *TextEvaluator*™ 44 **ELL** **Lexile** 540 *TextEvaluator*™ 27	*Project Mulberry* **Lexile** 690 *TextEvaluator*™ 39 *Riding Freedom* **Lexile** 720 *TextEvaluator*™ 40
Qualitative	**What Makes the Text Complex?** • **Specific Vocabulary** Mythology T145 • **Organization** Narrator T149 **ACT** *See Scaffolded Instruction in Teacher's Edition T145 and T149.*	**What Makes the Text Complex?** • **Genre** Historical Fiction T153C • **Prior Knowledge** History T153A, T153E, T153G • **Connection of Ideas** Reactions T153I; Inferences T153K; Character T153M, T153O • **Purpose** Inform T153S • **Organization** Sequence T153C; Article T153U **ACT** *See Scaffolded Instruction in Teacher's Edition T153A–T153V.*	**What Makes the Text Complex?** • **Specific Vocabulary** • **Sentence Structure** • **Connection of Ideas** • **Genre** **ACT** *See Level Up lessons online for Leveled Readers.*		**What Makes the Text Complex?** • **Genre** • **Specific Vocabulary** • **Prior Knowledge** • **Sentence Structure** • **Organization** • **Purpose** • **Connection of Ideas** **ACT** *See Scaffolded Instruction in Teacher's Edition T360–T361.*
Reader and Task	The Introduce the Concept lesson on pages T138–T139 will help determine the reader's knowledge and engagement in the weekly concept. See pages T144–T153 and T156–T157 for questions and tasks for this text.	The Introduce the Concept lesson on pages T138–T139 will help determine the reader's knowledge and engagement in the weekly concept. See pages T153A–T153V and T156–T157 for questions and tasks for this text.	The Introduce the Concept lesson on pages T138–T139 will help determine the reader's knowledge and engagement in the weekly concept. See pages T168–T169, T176–T177, T180–T181, T186–T187, and T156–T157 for questions and tasks for this text.		The Introduce the Concept lesson on pages T138–T139 will help determine the reader's knowledge and engagement in the weekly concept. See pages T360–T361 for questions and tasks for this text.

Go Digital! www.connected.mcgraw-hill.com

Monitor and *Differentiate*

IF you need to differentiate instruction

THEN use the Quick Checks to assess students' needs and select the appropriate small group instruction focus.

 Quick Check

Comprehension Strategy Make, Confirm, or Revise Predictions T147

Comprehension Skill Point of View T149

Genre Historical Fiction T151

Vocabulary Strategy Context Clues T153

Phonics/Fluency Words with /ü/, /ū/, and /ù/ T155

If No → | Approaching Level | Reteach T168–T175 |
| ELL | Develop T184–T191 |

If Yes → | On Level | Review T176–T179 |
| Beyond Level | Extend T180–T183 |

Level Up with Leveled Readers

IF students can read their leveled text fluently and answer comprehension questions

THEN work with the next level up to accelerate students' reading with more complex text.

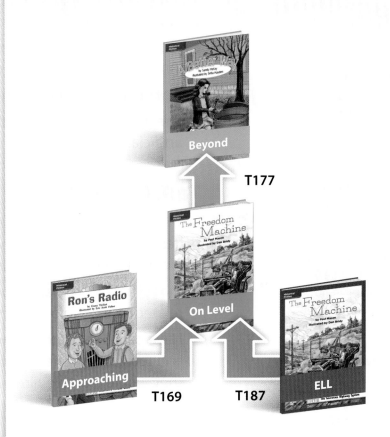

Beyond

T177

On Level

Approaching   T169   T187   ELL

ENGLISH LANGUAGE LEARNERS
SCAFFOLD

IF ELL students need additional support **THEN** scaffold instruction using the small group suggestions.

| Reading/Writing Workshop "The Telephone Mix-Up" T184–T185 | Leveled Reader *The Freedom Machine* T186–T187 "The Interstate Highway System" T187 | Additional Vocabulary T189 benefits   common freedom   machine trouble   useful | Using Context Clues: Synonyms T189 | Writing Ideas T190 | Spelling Words with /ü/, /ù/, and /ū/ T190 | Grammar Pronoun-Verb Agreement T191 |

Note: Include ELL Students in all small groups based on their needs.

→ Introduce the Concept

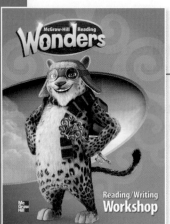

Reading/Writing Workshop

OBJECTIVES

CCSS Interpret information presented visually, orally, or quantitatively (e.g., in charts, graphs, diagrams, time lines, animations, or interactive elements on Web pages) and explain how the information contributes to an understanding of the text in which it appears. **RI.4.7**

CCSS Follow agreed-upon rules for discussions and carry out assigned roles. **SL.4.1b**

Build background knowledge on technology.

ACADEMIC LANGUAGE

• technology, engineering
• Cognates: tecnología, ingeniería

Build Background

ESSENTIAL QUESTION
How do inventions and technology affect your life?

Have students read the Essential Question on page 262 of the **Reading/Writing Workshop**. Tell them that **technology** is the use of science for practical purposes.

Discuss the photograph of the man with an artificial leg. Focus on how technology and other **engineering** marvels can change people's lives.

→ New inventions and technology can help people fulfill their dreams.

→ The man in the photo is able to compete in races now that he has an artificial leg because it allows him to run long distances.

Talk About It

Ask: *How do you think inventions and **technology** help to make our lives better? What technology or invention do you rely on the most? Why?* Have students discuss in pairs or groups.

→ Model using the graphic organizer to generate words and phrases related to technology. Add students' contributions.

→ Have partners continue the discussion by describing how inventions and technology affect their lives. Students can discuss an invention they would like to build to make life easier.

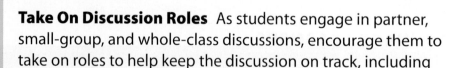

Collaborative Conversations

Take On Discussion Roles As students engage in partner, small-group, and whole-class discussions, encourage them to take on roles to help keep the discussion on track, including

→ a **questioner** who asks questions in order to keep everyone involved and keep the discussion moving.

→ a **recorder** who takes notes on the important ideas being discussed and who later reports to the class.

→ a **discussion monitor** who keeps the group on topic and makes sure everyone gets a turn to talk.

Go Digital

Discuss the Concept

Watch Video

Use Graphic Organizer

Weekly Concept Breakthroughs

Essential Question
How do inventions and technology affect your life?

Go Digital!

Changing LIVES

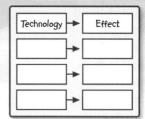

For some people, new inventions and advanced technology provide a way to fulfill their dreams. The man in the photo is able to compete in the Paralympics now that he has an artificial leg that allows him to run long distances.

► How do you think inventions and technology help to make our lives better?

► What technology or invention do you rely on the most? Why?

Talk About It

Write words that describe how inventions and technology affect your life. Then talk with a partner about an invention that you would like to design that would have a big impact on your life.

Technology		Effect
	→	
	→	
	→	

262

263

(Inset) Michael Svoboda/the Agency Collection/Getty Images; (b) McGraw-Hill Companies

READING/WRITING WORKSHOP, pp. 262–263

ENGLISH LANGUAGE LEARNERS
SCAFFOLD

GRAPHIC ORGANIZER 85

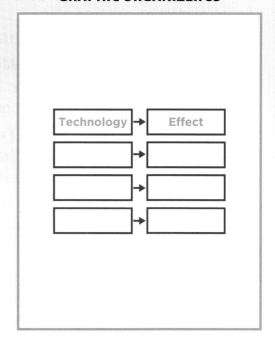

Technology	→	Effect
	→	
	→	
	→	

Beginning

Use Visuals Ask students to describe the photograph using short phrases or simple sentences. Depending on their levels of proficiency, students can also respond in their native language. Guide students to understand that the invention of the artificial leg allows the man to run. Ask students to say the word *invention*.

Intermediate

Describe Have students describe how inventions and new technology can change our lives. Ask: *How has technology affected this man's life?* Have students complete the sentence frame: *Technology helps the man by _____.* (allowing him to walk and run) Elicit details to develop their responses.

Advanced/High

Discuss Discuss the concept of breakthroughs in technology. Invite students to guess the meaning of *breakthrough*. Say: *A breakthrough is a major achievement that can lead to progress or new ideas. What breakthroughs have you read or heard about recently?* Encourage students to use concept words. Give examples if needed.

→ Listening Comprehension

MINILESSON
10 Mins

Interactive Read Aloud

OBJECTIVES

CCSS Refer to details and examples in a text when explaining what the text says explicitly and when drawing inferences from the text. **RL.4.1**

CCSS Paraphrase portions of a text read aloud or information presented in diverse media and formats, including visually, quantitatively, and orally. **SL.4.2**

Identify characteristics of historical fiction.

ACADEMIC LANGUAGE

• *historical fiction; make, confirm, or revise predictions*

• Cognates: *ficción histórica; confirmar, revisar predicciones*

Connect to Concept: Breakthroughs

Tell students that technology can change people's lives in important ways. Let students know that you will be reading aloud a passage about a family who is replacing an old icebox with a new refrigerator. As students listen, ask them to think about how the story answers the Essential Question.

Preview Genre: Historical Fiction

Explain that the story you will read aloud is historical fiction. Discuss features of historical fiction:

→ includes a mix of fiction and historical fact

→ is set in a real time and place in history

→ characters are portrayed in a realistic manner

Preview Comprehension Strategy: Make, Confirm, or Revise Predictions

Point out that readers use clues in a text, such as a character's words and their actions, to make predictions about what might happen in a story. As they continue to read, good readers evaluate their earlier predictions and then confirm or revise what they have predicted.

Use the Think Alouds on page T141 to model the strategy.

Respond to Reading

Think Aloud Clouds Display Think Aloud Master 3: *I predicted _____ because . . .* to reinforce how you used the make, confirm, or revise predictions strategy to understand content.

Genre Features With students, discuss the elements of the Read Aloud that let them know it is historical fiction. Ask them to think about other texts that you have read or they have read independently that were historical fiction stories.

Summarize Have students briefly retell the story "Good-bye Icebox!" in their own words.

Model Think Alouds

Genre	Features

Fill In Genre Chart

Good-bye Icebox!

"Sally!" Mother cried. "Are you actually hugging the icebox?" Nine-year-old Sally Kent was, indeed, reaching her arms around the family's old icebox.

"It won't be here when I get home," Sally said. "I don't think I'll love the new refrigerator nearly as much as I love this old thing." Mother laughed and sent Sally out the door and on her way to school. **1**

At noon, Sally's father answered a knock at the door. "Mr. Kent?" said the delivery man. "We've got your new refrigerator on the truck and she's a real beauty, too!"

Mr. Kent directed the men to the kitchen. "We'll get this old box out of here first," said the delivery man. They lifted the icebox and carried it out to be hauled away. They put the new refrigerator on a wheeled cart and rolled it into place. "There you go," said the delivery man as he plugged the heavy electric plug into an outlet. The compressor on top of the refrigerator began to hum. "That's the sound of progress," said Mr. Kent to his wife. "Give it a few hours to cool," the delivery man instructed.

The Kents thanked the men and they left.

"Where is it?" Sally burst through the door, dropped her books on a chair, and made a mad dash to the kitchen, stopping when she reached the gleaming white refrigerator. Reaching out to touch the chrome latch, Sally jumped when the compressor kicked on again and began to hum. "Did I break it?" she asked. **2**

"No," said Mother. "Open the door and see for yourself." Sally opened the door and felt a rush of cool air on her face. "I love it," she said. "It's so modern!"

"This is the future," said Mr. Kent, patting the refrigerator. "You're looking at the future right now." But Sally knew that, just like the old icebox, this refrigerator would one day be outdated and replaced by something even more modern. She wondered what refrigerators in the future would look like. **3**

1 Think Aloud Sally says she won't like the refrigerator as much as the icebox. I **predict** that she will change her mind. I will **confirm my prediction** as I read.

2 Think Aloud Sally thinks she broke the new refrigerator when she touched it, but I will **make a prediction** that she didn't. I also still think that my first **prediction** will be correct.

3 Think Aloud I **confirmed my prediction**. It was correct. Sally loves the new refrigerator and thinks it looks modern. She wonders what refrigerators in the future will look like.

Image Source/Getty Images

→ Vocabulary

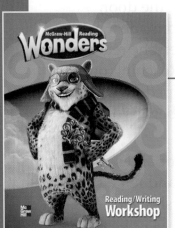

Reading/Writing Workshop

OBJECTIVES

CCSS Acquire and use accurately grade-appropriate general academic and domain-specific words and phrases, including those that signal precise actions, emotions, or states of being (e.g., *quizzed, whined, stammered*) and that are basic to a particular topic (e.g., *wildlife, conservation,* and *endangered* when discussion animal preservation). **L.4.6**

ACADEMIC LANGUAGE

• *engineering, technology*

• Cognates: *ingeniería, tecnología*

MINILESSON 10 Mins

Words in Context

Model the Routine

Introduce each vocabulary word using the Vocabulary Routine found on the Visual Vocabulary Cards.

Visual Vocabulary Cards

Vocabu...
Define:
Example:
Ask:

> ### Vocabulary Routine
>
> **Define:** **Technology** is the use of science for practical purposes, especially in engineering and industry.
>
> **Example:** In the early 1900s, the telephone was considered new technology.
>
> **Ask:** What are some examples of new technology today?

Definitions

→ **decade**   A **decade** is a period of ten years.
Cognate: *década*

→ **directing**   **Directing** is the act of giving instructions, ordering, or commanding.

→ **engineering**   **Engineering** is the work that uses scientific knowledge for practical things such as building bridges and dams.
Cognate: *ingeniería*

→ **gleaming**   When something is **gleaming** it is shining or glowing.

→ **scouted**   **Scouted** means to have looked at or explored in order to find out and bring back more information.

→ **squirmed**   To have **squirmed** is to have turned and twisted the body.

→ **tinkering**   **Tinkering** is puttering or keeping busy in an aimless way.

Talk About It

COLLABORATE

Have partners look at each picture and definition. Have students choose three words and write questions for their partner to answer.

Go Digital

technology

Use Visual Glossary

CCSS Words to Know

Vocabulary

Use the picture and the sentences to talk with a partner about each word.

decade
The company celebrated a **decade** of business, honoring ten years of work.

What year will it be in a decade?

directing
The police officers are **directing** traffic.

If you were a crossing guard, what would you be directing students to do?

engineering
I think the beautiful Golden Gate Bridge is an amazing feat of **engineering**.

What is another structure that was built using the science of engineering?

gleaming
The shiny bar of gold lay **gleaming** on the red velvet.

What is an antonym for gleaming?

scouted
The boy used binoculars as he **scouted** the best place to find whales.

What is a synonym for scouted?

squirmed
The pig wiggled and **squirmed** in the girl's arms.

If someone squirmed while watching a play, how did that person probably feel?

technology
In the early 1900s, the telephone was considered new **technology**.

What are some examples of new technology today?

tinkering
Mr. Lan likes **tinkering** with and fixing old clocks.

What do you like tinkering with?

Your Turn COLLABORATE

Pick three words. Write three questions for your partner to answer.

Go Digital! *Use the online visual glossary*

264

265

READING/WRITING WORKSHOP, pp. 264–265

ELL ENGLISH LANGUAGE LEARNERS SCAFFOLD

Beginning	Intermediate	Advanced/High
Use Visuals Point to and say the word *squirmed*. Demonstrate a gesture for *squirmed*. Have students repeat the gesture. Discuss the photograph and read the sentence. Tell students that another word for *squirmed* is *wiggled*. Ask: *Is the pig squirming? Why?* Give students ample time to respond. If necessary, allow them to respond in short phrases or gestures.	**Describe** Point to the picture for *squirmed*. Say: *Show me squirmed.* Discuss the photograph and the meaning of the word *squirmed*. Have students complete the sentence frame: *I once squirmed when I ____.* Then have them share their responses with a partner. Elicit details to help students provide a comprehensive response.	**Discuss** Discuss the photograph with students. Ask: *What are some other words for the word* squirmed*?* (wiggle, fidget, twist, twitch) Have partners create a list of synonyms for the word *squirmed*. Then have them use a thesaurus to find other examples for *squirmed*. Have students share their list with the class.

ON-LEVEL PRACTICE BOOK p. 171

| gleaming | decade | tinkering | engineering |
| scouted | squirmed | directing | technology |

Use a word from the box to answer each question. Then use the word in a sentence. Possible responses provided.

1. What did the boy do when he twisted his body to avoid being tagged? squirmed; I *squirmed* my way through the hole in the fence.

2. What word describes what a light is doing when it is shining? gleaming; The water in the pool was *gleaming* due to the light of the sun.

3. What profession uses scientific knowledge for practical use? engineering; She had to study *engineering* to learn how to build a bridge.

4. What did the eagle do when it flew in search of food? scouted; We *scouted* out the best place for a game of tag.

5. What is another word for a *period of ten years*? decade; I have been alive for almost a *decade*.

6. What is the coach doing when he is giving instructions to the team? directing; Yesterday, I saw a policeman *directing* traffic.

7. What is another word for *puttering*? tinkering; We had some free time, so we started *tinkering* with my model plane collection.

8. What word means *the use of science for practical purposes*? technology; Computers and cars are excellent examples of *technology*.

APPROACHING p. 171	BEYOND p. 171	ELL p. 171

CCSS **Shared Read** Genre • Historical Fiction

A Telephone Mix-Up

Essential Question

How do inventions and technology affect your life?

Read how a telephone brings change to the lives of Meg and her father.

266

"By tomorrow afternoon there will be eight telephones right here in Centerburg, Ohio, and one of them will be ours!" Dr. Ericksen said to his daughter, Meg. "I predict that before this **decade** is over, in just another five years, there could be a hundred! That's how fast I foresee this **technology** will spread! When people need help, they'll call me on the telephone. Envision how many lives it will save! Picture all the amazing benefits!"

Meg realized that not everyone thought the telephone was an **engineering** marvel. She had heard people say that telephones were a useless invention. A few others felt the newfangled machine would open up a Pandora's box of troubles, causing people to stop visiting each other and writing letters.

Despite the concerns of some people, progress marched on. Just weeks earlier, Centerburg's first telephone had been installed in Mr. Kane's general store, another was put in at the hotel, and yet another at the newspaper office. Mrs. Kane was the town's first switchboard operator, **directing** incoming calls to the correct lines.

The next morning, Meg wrote "October 9, 1905" on the top of her slate with chalk while she **squirmed** in her seat, wishing that the long school day was over.

267

READING/WRITING WORKSHOP, pp. 266–267

Reading/Writing Workshop

Shared Read

Lexile 950   *TextEvaluator*™ 38

Connect to Concept: Breakthroughs

Explain that "A Telephone Mix-Up" will tell a story about a time when the telephone was a new technology. Read "A Telephone Mix-Up" with students. Note the vocabulary words previously taught are highlighted in the text.

Close Reading

Reread the Title: Direct students to the title of the selection and model making a prediction. Ask: *What do you think will happen in the story just by reading the title?* Model how to make a prediction before reading.

I can use the title to make a prediction before reading. The title is "A Telephone Mix-Up." I think the story will include some sort of mix-up involving a telephone. I know that this can happen when people call the wrong number. I can read on to confirm or revise my prediction.

Reread Paragraph 4 on page 269: Model how to confirm a prediction while reading. Remind students that revising and confirming their predictions can help them better understand what they are reading.

As I read, I see that there has been a mix-up involving the telephone. The operator contacted Dr. Ericksen when she meant to contact Dr. Kerrigan, the vet. My prediction was correct.

Walking home that afternoon, Meg **scouted** the street, looking for the tall wooden poles that were going up weekly. Thick wire linked one pole to another, and Meg imagined how each wire would carry the words of friends and neighbors, their conversations zipping over the lines bringing news, birthday wishes, and party invitations.

As Meg hurried into the house, she let the screen door slam shut behind her. There on the wall was the **gleaming** wooden telephone box with its heavy black receiver on a hook. Her father was smiling broadly while **tinkering** with the shiny brass bells on top. "Isn't it a beauty?" he asked. "Have you ever seen such magnificence?"

Suddenly the telephone jangled loudly, causing both Ericksens to jump.

Meg laughed as her father picked up the receiver and shouted, "Yes, hello, this is the doctor!"

"Again please, Mrs. Kane! There's too much static" Dr. Ericksen shouted. "I didn't get the first part. Bad cough? Turner farm?"

"Can I go, Father?" Meg asked as Dr. Ericksen returned the receiver to the hook.

"Absolutely," he said, grabbing his medical kit and heading outside where his horse and buggy waited.

When they got to the farm, they found Mr. Turner walking toward the barn.

Tristan Elwell

268

"Jake, I got here as quick as I could," Dr. Ericksen said. "Is it Mrs. Turner? Little Emma?"

"You?" Jake Turner looked confused, but he gestured them toward the barn.

There they found a baby goat curled near its mother. The baby snorted, coughed, and looked miserable.

"Jake, I'm no vet!" said Dr. Ericksen. "You need Dr. Kerrigan."

"I was wondering why you showed up instead. I reckon there was a mix-up."

"Apparently so," Dr. Ericksen laughed. "When I get back I'll send Dr. Kerrigan."

As years passed the telephone proved to be very useful to the town of Centerburg, but there was always the occasional mix-up. It became common among the Ericksens to refer to a missed communication as "another sick goat."

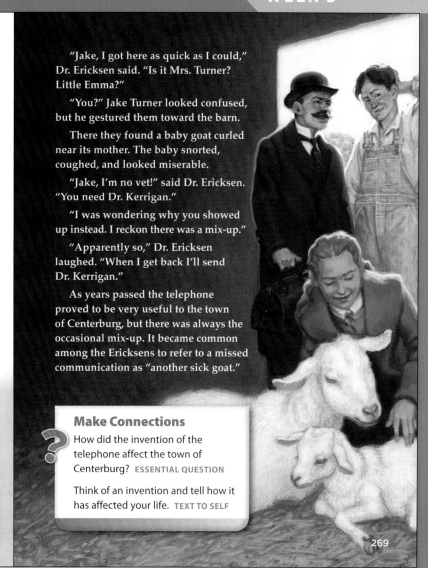

Make Connections

? How did the invention of the telephone affect the town of Centerburg? **ESSENTIAL QUESTION**

Think of an invention and tell how it has affected your life. **TEXT TO SELF**

269

READING/WRITING WORKSHOP, pp. 268–269

Make Connections

ESSENTIAL QUESTION

Encourage students to go back into the text for evidence as they talk about how the invention of the telephone affected Centerburg. Ask students to think of other inventions and tell how they may have affected their lives.

Continue Close Reading

Use the following lessons for focused rereadings.

→ Make, Confirm, or Revise Predictions, T146–T147

→ Point of View, T148–T149

→ Historical Fiction, T150–T151

→ Context Clues, T152–T153

A C T Access Complex Text

▶ Specific Vocabulary

Point to the phrase *open up a Pandora's box* on page 267. Explain that the phrase refers to a figure in Greek mythology, Pandora, who was given a box holding all the world's evil. Pandora opened the box and let the evil out.

→ *What do you think the consequences of opening Pandora's box were?* (Maybe the world was perfect before, but then there was pain and hardship for people.)

→ *What does the phrase mean today?* (to do something that leads to more trouble)

Comprehension Strategy

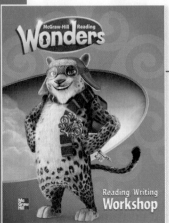

Reading/Writing Workshop

OBJECTIVES

 Refer to details and examples in a text when explaining what the text says explicitly and when drawing inferences from the text. **RL.4.1**

Make, confirm, and revise predictions while reading historical fiction.

ACADEMIC LANGUAGE

• *predict, historical fiction*

• Cognates: *predecir, ficción histórica*

 MINILESSON 10 Mins

Make, Confirm, or Revise Predictions

1 Explain

Remind students that when they read a story, they may use story details to predict what will happen next.

→ Good readers use clues from the story to make predictions.

→ Students may stop, confirm, and revise their predictions if necessary.

→ Often, students may find that making predictions will help them understand and remember why events happen in a certain way.

Point out that making predictions will help students set a purpose for reading.

2 Model Close Reading: Text Evidence

Model making a prediction about how the people of Centerburg will react to the arrival of the telephone. Reread page 267 of "A Telephone Mix-Up."

3 Guided Practice of Close Reading

 Have partners work together to find clues that helped them predict how the telephone static would cause a mix-up. Ask partners to list the clues that helped them make their predictions. Then have partners find the passage that confirms their predictions.

Go Digital

View "A Telephone Mix-Up"

CCSS Comprehension Strategy

Make Predictions

When you read, use text clues from the story to help you make predictions about what will happen next. As you continue to read, you can confirm or revise your predictions.

Find Text Evidence
How did you predict the people of Centerburg would react to the telephone? What helped you to confirm your prediction? Reread page 267 of "A Telephone Mix-Up."

page 267

would open up a Pandora's box of troubles, causing people to stop visiting each other and writing letters.

Despite the concerns of some people, progress marched on. Just weeks earlier, Centerburg's first telephone had been installed in Mr. Kane's general store, another was put in at the hotel, and yet another at the newspaper office. Mrs. Kane was the town's first switchboard operator, directing incoming calls to the correct lines.

The next morning, Meg wrote "October 9, 1905" on the top of her slate with chalk while she squirmed in her seat, wishing that the long school day was over.

◄ *I had predicted that people in Centerburg would get used to the telephone even though some people would not like the idea of it. Evidence in the paragraph confirmed my prediction.*

 COLLABORATE

Your Turn
What text clues did you find that helped you predict that the phone static would cause a mix-up? As you read remember to use the strategy, Make Predictions.

270

READING/WRITING WORKSHOP, p. 270

 Monitor and *Differentiate*

✓ Quick Check
Do students use text evidence to make a prediction about how the phone static will cause a mix-up?

⬇

Small Group Instruction

If No → **Approaching Level** Reteach p. T168
ELL Develop p. T184
If Yes → **On Level** Review p. T176
Beyond Level Extend p. T180

ON-LEVEL PRACTICE BOOK pp. 173–174
Read the passage. Use the make predictions strategy to help you make predictions about what will happen next.

Leonardo's Mechanical Knight
Leonardo scrambled out of bed early one clear spring day in 1464. He was excited to get out to the barn where he was working on a new invention.

For months he had begged and pleaded with his father to get him a suit of armor. On April 15—Leonardo's twelfth birthday—he got his wish! He had set the armor up in the barn that day. The barn quickly filled with Leonardo's notes and equipment as he worked and toiled on his new invention: a mechanical knight.

High atop a rickety ladder, Leonardo was deep in concentration. All his focus was on fixing the mechanical knight's arm, but it wasn't easy work. No matter what he did, the knight's arm refused to lift! Leonardo frowned and scowled at it.

"Leonardo!" yelled a voice. He jumped in surprise and shock as the ladder teetered and shook under his feet.

"Oh no!" he exclaimed, losing his balance. He tumbled off the ladder and into a pile of hay. The mechanical knight's arm lay broken on the ground.

His good friend Albiera peered down at him. "Leonardo, are you all right?"

"I'm fine," he said. He wasn't hurt, just upset that his mechanical knight was broken.

Albiera glanced at the knight with the missing arm, the stacks of notebooks, and the piles of papers. "What on earth are you doing in here?" she asked.

"I was working on a new invention, but it's not going so well."

| APPROACHING pp. 173–174 | BEYOND pp. 173–174 | ELL pp. 173–174 |

 ELL ENGLISH LANGUAGE LEARNERS SCAFFOLD

Beginning
Clarify the Meaning
Help students reread page 267 of "A Telephone Mix-Up." Point out difficult words and phrases, such as *foresee, marvel, useless, progress,* and *switchboard operator.* Define the words for students. Use gestures, demonstrations, and visuals to help students understand their meaning.

Intermediate
Practice Say: *I know from experience that some people are afraid of new technologies. Let's look for clues that will help us predict how people will react to the telephone.* Explain that readers have to infer how other characters feel about the telephone. Have students fill in the frame: *I predict the people of Centerburg will ___ the telephone.*

Advanced/High
Discuss Have partners reread page 267 together. Ask: *How will the people of Centerburg react to the arrival of the telephone?* Have partners reread to make, confirm, and revise their predictions and tell why the text is difficult. Elicit details to develop students' responses.

COMPREHENSION STRATEGY **T147**

→ Comprehension Skill

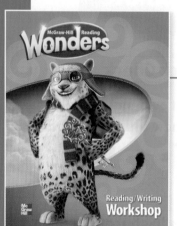

Reading/Writing Workshop

OBJECTIVES

CCSS Compare and contrast the point of view from which different stories are narrated, including the difference between first- and third-person narrations. **RL.4.6**

Identify the point of view of a story.

ACADEMIC LANGUAGE
point of view, third-person

MINILESSON
10 Mins

Point of View

1 Explain

Remind students that point of view tells how the the narrator thinks or feels about characters or events in a story.

→ To determine the narrator of a story, students should look for pronouns. Pronouns such as *he, she,* or *they* indicate that the story is told by a third-person narrator.

→ A third-person narrator is not a character in the story. A third-person narrator may reveal the thoughts and feelings of one, several, or all the characters in the story.

2 Model Close Reading: Text Evidence

Model finding details that indicate the point of view on page 267 of "A Telephone Mix-Up" and entering them in the graphic organizer. Point out the pronouns the third-person narrator uses to describe Meg and her thoughts.

 Write About Reading: Analysis Model for students how to use the notes from the graphic organizer to write an analysis of the point of view in the story. Show how to cite evidence.

3 Guided Practice of Close Reading

 Have students work in pairs to complete the graphic organizer as they identify another detail from the story that reveals the point of view. Then have them describe the point of view.

 Write About Reading: Analysis Ask pairs to work together to write a paragraph detailing the point of view in "A Telephone Mix-Up," using the details in their graphic organizers as evidence. Students should then find a story from a past unit that has a first-person narrator and contrast it with this story. How is the narration different? How are the narrators' thoughts and feelings alike and different?

Go Digital

Present the Lesson

SKILLS TRACE

POINT OF VIEW

Introduce Unit 2 Week 5

Review Unit 3 Weeks 1, 2; Unit 4 Weeks 2, 3, 6; Unit 5 Week 6; Unit 6 Week 6

Assess Units 2, 3, 4

Comprehension Skill CCSS

Point of View

The narrator's point of view tells how the narrator thinks or feels about characters or events in the story. A story can have a first-person narrator or a third-person narrator.

 Find Text Evidence

When I read page 267 of "A Telephone Mix Up," I see that the narrator uses the pronouns *he* and *she* when the narrator tells what Meg and her father are thinking. This story has a third-person narrator. I can find details in the story about the narrator's point of view.

Details
The narrator tells us what Meg's father says about the telephone. "Picture all the amazing benefits!"
The narrator states: "Despite the concerns of some people, progress marched on."

↓

Point of View
The narrator thinks the telephone will be a useful invention.

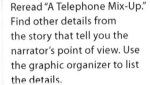

Your Turn COLLABORATE

Reread "A Telephone Mix-Up." Find other details from the story that tell you the narrator's point of view. Use the graphic organizer to list the details.

Go Digital!
Use the interactive graphic organizer

271

READING/WRITING WORKSHOP, p. 271

ACT Access Complex Text

▶ **Organization**

Students may need help understanding that "A Telephone Mix-Up" uses a third-person limited narrator. Reread with students.

→ *Whose thoughts does the narrator describe in the second paragraph on page 267?* (Meg's)

→ *As you read the rest of the story, does the narrator describe the thoughts of other characters?* (No.)

→ *What kind of third-person narrator is used in "A Telephone Mix-Up"?* (third-person limited)

Monitor and Differentiate

 Quick Check

Can students find another detail from the story that tells the point of view? Can students identify the point of view in "A Telephone Mix-Up"?

↓

Small Group Instruction

If No → **Approaching Level** Reteach p. T175
ELL Develop p. T184

If Yes → **On Level** Review p. T179
Beyond Level Extend p. T183

Genre: Literature

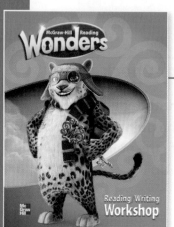

Reading/Writing Workshop

OBJECTIVES

 By the end of the year, read and comprehend literature, including stories, dramas, and poetry, in the grades 4–5 text complexity band proficiently, with scaffolding as needed at the high end of the range. **RL.4.10**

Identify characteristics and literary elements of historical fiction.

ACADEMIC LANGUAGE

• *historical fiction, dialogue*

• Cognates: *ficción histórica, diálogo*

MINILESSON 10 Mins

Historical Fiction

1 Explain

Share with students the following key characteristics of **historical fiction**.

→ Historical fiction has realistic characters, events, and settings.

→ Historical fiction is set in the past and is based on real events. The plot takes place in a definite period of time in history and in a real place.

→ Historical fiction may have fictional characters that are interwoven with real ones. All characters behave in realistic ways.

→ Historical fiction includes literary elements, such as dialogue.

2 Model Close Reading: Text Evidence

Model identifying and using the characteristics and literary elements of historical fiction on page 267 of "A Telephone Mix-Up."

Dialogue Point out the dialogue on page 267. Explain that the dialogue shows a conversation that takes place between two or more characters and that quotation marks usually enclose dialogue. Ask: *Which characters are having a conversation in this dialogue? What are they talking about?*

3 Guided Practice of Close Reading

 Have students work with partners to find three examples in the text that show "A Telephone Mix-Up" is historical fiction. Partners should discuss how each example signals that the story is historical fiction. Then have them share their work with the class.

Go Digital

Present the Lesson

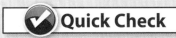
CCSS Genre ▷ Literature

Historical Fiction

"A Telephone Mix-Up" is historical fiction.

Historical fiction:
- Has realistic characters, events, and settings.
- Is set in the past and based on real events.
- Contains dialogue.

 Find Text Evidence

"A Telephone Mix-Up" is historical fiction. A family is getting a telephone at a time in history when telephone service was first made available to many communities. The story has realistic characters, events, and settings, and it includes dialogue.

page 267

"By tomorrow afternoon there will be eight telephones right here in Centerburg, Ohio, and one of them will be ours!" Dr. Ericksen said to his daughter, Meg. "I predict that before this **decade** is over, in just another five years, there could be a hundred! That's how fast I foresee this **technology** will spread! When people need help, they'll call me on the telephone. Envision how many lives it will save! Picture all the amazing benefits!"

Meg realized that not everyone thought the telephone was an engineering marvel. She had heard people say that telephones were a useless invention. A few others felt the newfangled machine would open up a Pandora's box of troubles, causing people to stop visiting each other and writing letters.

Despite the concerns of some people, progress marched on. Just weeks earlier, Centerburg's first telephone had been installed in Mr. Kane's general store, another was put in at the hotel, and yet another at the newspaper office. Mrs. Kane was the town's first switchboard operator, **directing** incoming calls to the correct lines.

The next morning, Meg wrote "October 9, 1905" on the top of her slate with chalk while she **squirmed** in her seat, wishing that the long school day was over.

Dialogue Dialogue is the conversation that takes place between the characters. Quotation marks enclose dialogue.

Your Turn COLLABORATE

Find three examples in the text that show "A Telephone Mix-Up" is historical fiction.

272

READING/WRITING WORKSHOP, p. 272

Beginning

Actively Engage Remind students that dialogue is a conversation between characters. Point out the quotation marks in the first sentence on page 267 and explain that they show dialogue. Have students chorally read the sentence. Then ask them to identify which character is speaking. *Dialogue* in Spanish is *diálogo*.

Intermediate

Recognize Reread the first paragraph on page 267. Ask: *What do the quotation marks show?* (dialogue; someone is talking) *Who is talking?* (Dr. Ericksen) *Who is he talking to?* (Meg) Have students work together to read the dialogue aloud. Remind them that dialogue is written so that it sounds the way people talk in real life.

Advanced/High

Discuss Have students reread the first paragraph on page 267. Ask: *Who is talking? Who is he talking to? What is he talking about?* Have partners use the dialogue in the first paragraph to discuss what they learned about the characters and the arrival of the telephone.

Monitor and *Differentiate*

✔ **Quick Check**

Can students identify elements of historical fiction in the story?

⬇

Small Group Instruction

If No →	**Approaching Level**	Reteach p. T168
	ELL	Develop p. T184
If Yes →	**On Level**	Review p. T176
	Beyond Level	Extend p. T180

ON-LEVEL PRACTICE BOOK p. 176

Starting Work on the Brooklyn Bridge

I met the head of my work crew, Mr. Calloway. He told me about the caissons on the bridge's foundations, where I'll be working.

"The caissons are locked chambers at the bottom of the river, where workers dig down to the bedrock so the foundations can be placed. The pay's good because it's so dangerous down there," Mr. Calloway said.

"Dangerous? Because of flooding?" I asked.

"No, because the caissons are filled with high-pressure air to keep water from filling the work area," Mr. Calloway replied. "Some guys work down in the caissons too long and come to the surface too fast. The change in pressure gives them terrible pains, called caisson disease. It has killed two workers since 1870," Mr. Calloway explained.

Answer the questions about the text.

1. How do you know this text is historical fiction?
   The author tells a story that includes facts.

2. During which historical event does the story take place?
   the building of the Brooklyn Bridge

3. What literary element is included in this piece of historical fiction?
   dialogue

4. What does the literary element add to your understanding of the text?
   Possible response: It lets you know more about the characters by telling you their exact words.

APPROACHING p. 176	BEYOND p. 176	ELL p. 176

→ Vocabulary Strategy

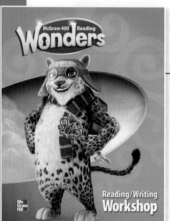

Reading/Writing Workshop

OBJECTIVES

CCSS Demonstrate understanding of words by relating them to their opposites (antonyms) and to words with similar but not identical meanings (synonyms). **L.4.5c**

CCSS Consult reference materials (e.g., dictionaries, glossaries, thesauruses), both print and digital, to find the pronunciation and determine or clarify the precise meaning of key words and phrases. **L.4.4c**

MINILESSON
10 Mins

Context Clues

1 Explain

Remind students that they can often figure out the meaning of an unknown word by using context clues within the paragraph.

→ Sometimes the author will use a **synonym,** another word or phrase that has the same or a similar meaning to the unfamiliar word, in a surrounding sentence or paragraph.

→ Students can also look for other nearby words and phrases that give examples or provide a further description of the word. Students can use these clues to try to determine the word's meaning.

2 Model Close Reading: Text Evidence

Model using the synonym *picture* on page 267 to determine the meaning of the word *envision*.

3 Guided Practice of Close Reading

Have students work in pairs to figure out the meanings of the words *foresee, installed,* and *magnificence* in "A Telephone Mix-Up." Encourage partners to go back into the text and use synonyms as context clues to help them determine each word's definition.

Use Reference Sources

Thesaurus Have students consult a thesaurus to find other synonyms for the words *foresee, installed,* and *magnificence.* Discuss the subtle differences in meaning between the synonyms given. Have students choose a synonym to replace each word in the selection.

Review a thesaurus entry for the word *foresee.* Have students identify each part of the entry, including the definition, part of speech label, and list of synonyms.

Go Digital

Present the Lesson

SKILLS TRACE

CONTEXT CLUES: SYNONYMS

Introduce Unit 1 Week 1

Review Unit 1 Weeks 1, 2; Unit 3 Weeks 3, 4; Unit 4 Weeks 3, 5

Assess Units 1, 3, 4

Vocabulary Strategy CCSS

Synonyms

As you read "A Telephone Mix-Up," you may come across a word you don't know. Sometimes the author will use another word or phrase that has the same or a similar meaning to the unfamiliar word. Words that have the same or similar meanings are **synonyms**.

Find Text Evidence

As I read the first paragraph of "The Telephone Mix-Up" on page 267, I wasn't sure what the word envision *meant. Then the word* picture *in the next sentence helped me figure out the meaning.*

Envision how many lives it will save! Picture all the amazing benefits!

Your Turn

COLLABORATE

Use synonyms and other context clues to find the meanings of the following words in "A Telephone Mix-Up." Write a synonym and example sentence for each word.

foresee, *page 267*
installed, *page 267*
magnificence, *page 268*

273

Tristan Elwell

READING/WRITING WORKSHOP, p. 273

 ELL

ENGLISH LANGUAGE LEARNERS SCAFFOLD

Beginning	Intermediate	Advanced/High
Practice Point out and define the word *foresee* on page 267. Have students practice saying the word. Then model different examples. Say: *I foresee it will rain today. I foresee we will have pizza for lunch.* Have students complete the sentence frame: *I foresee _____.* Repeat with the words *installed* and *magnificence.*	**Identify** Reread the first paragraph on page 267 with students. Guide them to identify a synonym for the word *foresee* and use clues to explain what it means. Then have partners work together to find synonyms for *installed* and *magnificence.* Elicit how cognates helped students understand the text (*predict, technology, invention, progress*).	**Discuss** Ask students to find the words *foresee, installed,* and *magnificence.* Have them identify a synonym for each word in the text. Then ask them to define the words using the clues. Have students share their definitions with a partner and identify cognates.

Monitor and *Differentiate*

✔ Quick Check

Are students able to use synonyms as context clues to figure out the meanings of *foresee, installed,* and *magnificence?*

Small Group Instruction

If No →	Approaching Level	Reteach p. T173
	ELL	Develop p. T189
If Yes →	On Level	Review p. T178
	Beyond Level	Extend p. T182

ON-LEVEL PRACTICE BOOK p. 177

Read each passage. Underline the synonym that helps you figure out the meaning of each word in bold. Then write the definition of the word in bold on the line. Possible responses provided.

1. For months he had <u>begged</u> and **pleaded** with his father to get him a suit of armor.

   asked for

2. The barn quickly filled with Leonardo's notes and equipment as he <u>worked</u> and **toiled** on his new invention: a mechanical knight.

   labored

3. High atop a rickety ladder, Leonardo was deep in **concentration**. All his <u>focus</u> was on fixing the mechanical knight's arm, but it wasn't easy work.

   thought

4. No matter what he did, the knight's arm refused to lift! Leonardo <u>frowned</u> and **scowled** at it.

   looked grumpy

5. "It's a simple system of pulleys and levers," he said in a **humble** voice. "Don't be so <u>modest</u>. I've never seen anything like it before!"

   modest

APPROACHING p. 177	BEYOND p. 177	ELL p. 177

Develop Comprehension

Literature Anthology

The Moon Over Star

Text Complexity Range

Lexile

740   ▲   1010
860

TextEvaluator™

23   ▲   51
48

Options for Close Reading

→ Whole Class

→ Small Group

→ Independent

CCSS Genre · Historical Fiction

THE MOON OVER STAR

BY Dianna Hutts Aston
ILLUSTRATED BY Jerry Pinkney

Essential Question

How does technology affect your life?

Read to find out how the moon landing affected Mae and her family.

Go Digital!

314

A C T Access Complex Text

What makes this text complex?

▶ **Genre**

▶ **Organization**

▶ **Prior Knowledge**

▶ **Connection of Ideas**

▶ Prior Knowledge

Remind students that *The Moon Over Star* is an example of historical fiction. Historical fiction is set in the past and is based on real events. In this story, the real event is the moon landing that took place in 1969.

Tell students that during the 1960s, the United States and Russia were competing with one

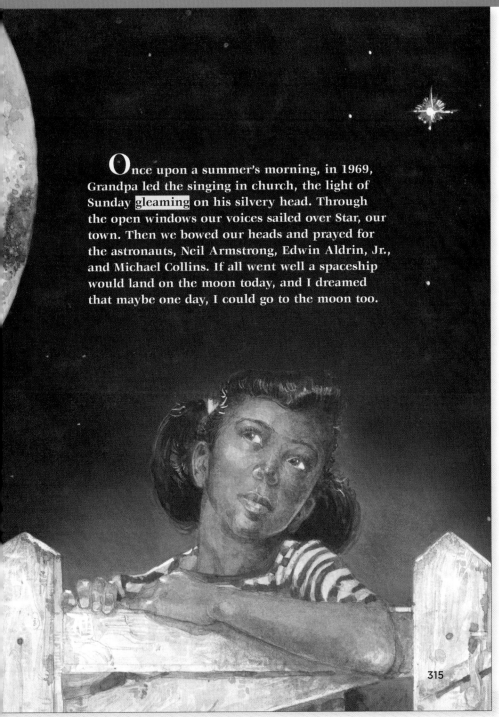

Once upon a summer's morning, in 1969, Grandpa led the singing in church, the light of Sunday gleaming on his silvery head. Through the open windows our voices sailed over Star, our town. Then we bowed our heads and prayed for the astronauts, Neil Armstrong, Edwin Aldrin, Jr., and Michael Collins. If all went well a spaceship would land on the moon today, and I dreamed that maybe one day, I could go to the moon too.

315

LITERATURE ANTHOLOGY, pp. 314–315

Predictive Writing

Have students read the title, preview the illustrations, skim the text to look for characters and dialogue, and write their predictions about what the selection will be about. Encourage them to identify the story's theme as they read.

ESSENTIAL QUESTION

Ask a student to read aloud the Essential Question. Have students discuss how the story might help them answer the question.

Note Taking:
Use the Graphic Organizer *Analytical Writing*

As students read the selection, ask them to fill in the graphic organizer on **Your Turn Practice Book page 172** to record details related to point of view.

1 Text Features: Illustrations

Have students look at the illustration on pages 314–315. How does the illustration help introduce the narrator, Mae, to the reader? What is Mae looking at? What do you think she is thinking about?

another to see which country was more powerful. Russia beat the U.S. by putting the first man in space in 1961. President John F. Kennedy wanted to put a man on the moon before the decade was out. As the world watched, astronauts Neil Armstrong, Edwin Aldrin, Jr., and Michael Collins landed Apollo 11 on the moon on July 20, 1969.

ELL Help students identify the shining moon and stars in the illustration. Then help them break down the meaning of the title. *The narrator lives in a town called Star. The illustration shows the moon shining over the narrator's town.*

→ *Where does narrator live?* (Star) *What is shining over Star?* (the moon)

Develop Comprehension

2 Skill: Point of View

Who is the first-person narrator of the story? (Mae) How does she feel about the astronauts? (She is concerned for them.) Add examples from the text and the point of view to your chart.

Details
Mae was praying for the astronauts.
Mae thought about the astronauts' kids.
"Please bless the astronauts' children too."

↓

Point of View
Mae is concerned for the astronauts' safety.

3 Text Features: Illustrations

What do the illustrations on pages 316 and 317 show? (One depicts the real astronauts traveling to space, and the other shows Mae and her cousins pretending to be those astronauts taking off into space.)

My gramps thought the space program was a waste of money, but I knew he was praying for them too. I thought about the astronauts' kids and wondered if they were scared—scared but proud. I know I'd be. I slipped my hand into my dad's and whispered so only I could hear, "Please bless the astronauts' children too."

2

STOP AND CHECK

Make Predictions What do you think Gramps's reaction to the moon landing will be? Use text clues to make a prediction.

316

A C T Access Complex Text

▶ Genre

Remind students that historical fiction is set in the past and based on real events.

→ *Identify the fictional characters and real people that identify this story as historical fiction.* (Fictional characters: Mae (narrator), Grandpa, Mae's dad, Gran, Mae's cousins; Real people: Neil Armstrong, Edwin Aldrin, Jr., and Michael Collins)

▶ Organization

Guide students in understanding how the text is organized sequentially.

→ *What transitional phrase does the author use on page 315 and page 317 to show the passage of time?* ("Once upon a summer's morning…"; "Once upon a summer's noon")

Once upon a summer's noon, my cousins and I **scouted** Gran's watermelon patch for the biggest one. It took three of us to carry it to a tub of ice—three and a half, counting my littlest cousin, Lacey. We decorated the picnic table with pails of wildflowers. Then, our chores done, we built our own spaceship from scraps we found in the barn.

"T minus 15 seconds ... 12, 11, 10, 9 ..." As the oldest grandchild, I got to be launch controller and Commander Armstrong. "Ignition sequence start ... 6, 5, 4, 3, 2, 1, 0. Liftoff, we have liftoff!"

317

LITERATURE ANTHOLOGY, pp. 316–317

STOP AND CHECK

Make Predictions What do you think Gramps's reaction to the moon landing will be? Use text clues to make a prediction. (Gramps might not get excited about the moon landing because he thinks the space program is a waste of money.)

Teacher Think Aloud I can use clues in the text to help me predict what might happen later in the story. As I read on, I can pay attention to details to confirm, or verify, my predictions. On page 316, Mae tells us that Gramps thinks the space program is a waste of money. I predict that he will not be excited by the moon landing. However, Mae does add that she knows that Gramps is praying for the astronauts, like she is. I can infer from this detail that Gramps is at least thinking about the astronauts and their moon landing. Perhaps his attitude toward the space program will change.

→ *How has Mae spent her day thus far?* (Mae went to church with her family in the morning. She prayed for the astronauts and their children. In the afternoon, Mae and her cousins looked for the biggest watermelon, did their chores, and built a spaceship out of scraps. Mae pretended to be Commander Armstrong.)

 Review first-person subject pronouns by modeling each in a sentence. *I am a teacher. We are in our classroom.* Have students reread the first paragraph on page 317 to practice using first-person pronouns.

Develop Comprehension

4 **Skill: Point of View**

What is Mae's point of view about the moon landing? (She is excited and very informed.) How do you know? (She loves to imagine it and has read about it in the paper.) Add these details and the point of view to your chart.

Details
She imagines the rocket launch with all her might.
She knows all about the moon.
She knows about Kennedy's dream to send people to the moon.

↓

Point of View
Mae is excited and informed about the moon landing.

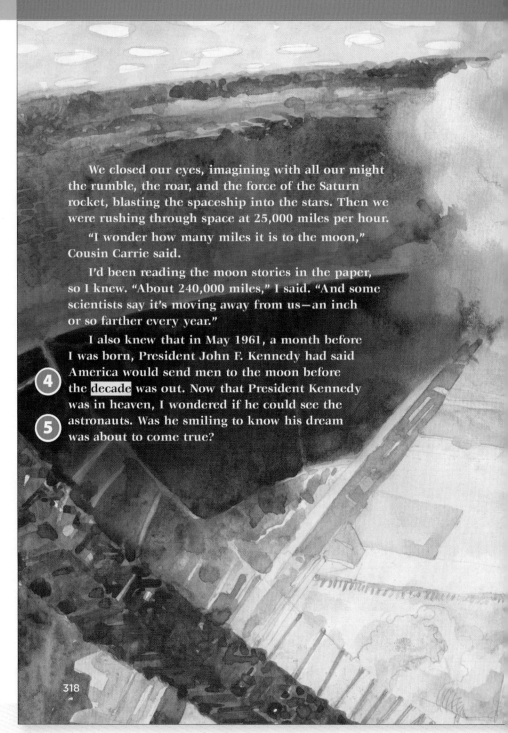

We closed our eyes, imagining with all our might the rumble, the roar, and the force of the Saturn rocket, blasting the spaceship into the stars. Then we were rushing through space at 25,000 miles per hour.

"I wonder how many miles it is to the moon," Cousin Carrie said.

I'd been reading the moon stories in the paper, so I knew. "About 240,000 miles," I said. "And some scientists say it's moving away from us—an inch or so farther every year."

I also knew that in May 1961, a month before I was born, President John F. Kennedy had said America would send men to the moon before **4** the decade was out. Now that President Kennedy was in heaven, I wondered if he could see the astronauts. Was he smiling to know his dream **5** was about to come true?

318

A C T Access Complex Text

▶ Prior Knowledge

Remind students that this story is set in a specific time in our history—July of 1969. Point out how the narrator refers to past events in the last paragraph on page 318. Tell students that President John F. Kennedy was assassinated on November 22, 1963.

→ *What was President Kennedy's "dream"?* (President Kennedy wanted to send astronauts to the moon

before the end of the decade, or by the end of the 1960s.)

→ *Why does Mae wonder if President Kennedy could see the astronauts?* (Since President Kennedy was assassinated, he was not alive to witness this historic event. Mae wonders if he is happy to see his dream realized.)

LITERATURE ANTHOLOGY, pp. 318–319

⑤ Genre: Historical Fiction

What new details do you learn on page 318 that indicate the story is historical fiction? (In May 1961, President Kennedy told the country that America would send astronauts to the moon before the end of the decade.)

⑥ Text Features: Illustrations

How does the illustration on pages 318–319 help you understand the text? (Mae describes the liftoff, or launch, of the spaceship in the first paragraph. The image of the spaceship helps readers visualize the launch and the spaceship blasting off into space.)

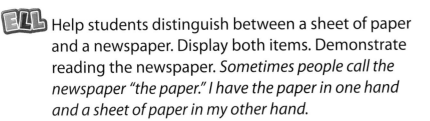 Help students distinguish between a sheet of paper and a newspaper. Display both items. Demonstrate reading the newspaper. *Sometimes people call the newspaper "the paper." I have the paper in one hand and a sheet of paper in my other hand.*

→ *What is another word for newspaper?* (the paper)

→ *What stories does Mae read in the paper?* (She reads the moon stories in the paper.)

Develop Comprehension

7 Author's Craft: Word Choice

Authors choose words carefully to add rich meaning to details and descriptions in stories. Why do you think the author uses the word *tinkering* instead of *fixing*? (*Tinkering* means to keep busy in an aimless way whereas *fixing* implies actual work. The author wants readers to know that Mae's grandfather is not concentrating on the car.) What do you think the word *pell-mell* means? Why do you think the author uses this word? (The word *pell-mell* means quickly; it describes how the kids run. The author uses this word to create a picture in the reader's mind of how the kids run in a wild and reckless manner.) Why do you think the author uses the word *squirmed* instead of *sat* to describe how the cousins gather around the television? (The word *squirmed* helps readers visualize the kids' excitement and anticipation of the moon landing.)

That afternoon, we were helping Gramps with the tractor when Gran hollered, "Come quick! They're landing!"

7 Gramps kept right on **tinkering** with the engine. The rest of us ran pell-mell for the house and **squirmed** around the television screen as it glowed with equal parts of moon and the spaceship called *Eagle*.

We heard the voice of Commander Armstrong **directing** the landing. "Forward … forward," he said.

Then the newsman we all knew, Walter Cronkite, exclaimed, "Man on the moon!"

For a split second we were silent—the whole universe must have been—as we waited … waited … waited to hear the voice of an astronaut 240,000 miles away.

8 And then: "Houston, Tranquility Base here," Commander Armstrong said. "The *Eagle* has landed."

320

A C T Access Complex Text

▶ Prior Knowledge

Help students understand that Walter Cronkite was a well-known television news anchor from the 1960s till the early 1980s, and that his live broadcast of the *Apollo 11* moon landing was seen by millions of Americans and continues to be watched and remembered by people today.

→ *In what way do the quotes from Walter Cronkite and Neil Armstrong help you understand the impact of the moon landing?* (They are quotes from real people in a real moment from the past. The reader gets a true sense of the anticipation people had about this historic event as they read Armstrong's words and Cronkite's reaction.)

8 Ask and Answer Questions

Generate a question of your own about the text and share it with a partner. To find the answer, try rereading the text. For example, you might ask, "What do Commander Armstrong's words, 'Houston, Tranquility Base here. The *Eagle* has landed' mean"? To find the answer, you can reread page 320. (We know that Mae and her family are waiting to hear the voice of the astronaut and then they hear Commander Armstrong's words, "the *Eagle* has landed." Armstrong is communicating with the control center in Houston and letting them know the *Eagle* has landed safely.)

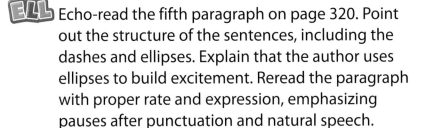

Echo-read the fifth paragraph on page 320. Point out the structure of the sentences, including the dashes and ellipses. Explain that the author uses ellipses to build excitement. Reread the paragraph with proper rate and expression, emphasizing pauses after punctuation and natural speech.

→ *What were Mae and her family waiting to hear?*
(the voice of the astronaut; Commander Armstrong)

Develop Comprehension

9 Skill: Point of View

What does the reader learn from Mae's thoughts on these pages? (We learn more about both Mae and Gramps; we learn about Mae's growing understanding of her grandfather's life.) Add Mae's thoughts and the point of view to your chart.

Details
"I remember something he'd once said . . ."
I began to wonder then what Gramps's dreams had been."
"Suddenly, I could see how tired he was."

↓

Point of View
Mae is beginning to understand why Gramps doesn't cheer for the moon landing.

Boy, did we cheer, all of the cousins and even the grown-ups—all except Gramps.

I remembered something he'd once said: "Why spend all that money to go to the moon when there's so many folks in need right here on Earth?"

"Because we can!" I'd almost shouted, but caught myself.

322

A C T Access Complex Text

▶ Connection of Ideas

Help students make connections between what they learned about Gramps and his reaction to the moon landing on pages 322–323.

→ *How does Gramps feel about going to the moon?* (He thinks it is a waste of money.)

→ *How does Gramps's reaction to the moon landing affect Mae?* (Instead of being excited about the

moon landing, Gramps seems exhausted and uninterested. Since the moon landing makes Mae dream about the possibility of going to the moon, it makes her wonder what Gramps's dreams had been—if he ever had a dream of his own. She starts to realize how hard he has worked over his life.)

I began to wonder then what Gramps's dreams had been. From the time he was little, he had worked the farm, doing the same jobs, day to day, season to season.

When the crickets began to sing, Gramps took out his pipe. I pulled off his dirt-caked boots for him and stomped around the porch.

"Gramps, will you watch it with me tonight ... the moon walk?"

"I'm mighty worn out today," he said, "but maybe."

Suddenly, I could see how tired he was. Lifetime-tired. There were deep lines in his face—a farmer's face, an old farmer's face.

"All right, Gramps," I said. "It's okay."

STOP AND CHECK

Confirm Predictions Why didn't Gramps react to the moon landing?

323

LITERATURE ANTHOLOGY, pp. 322–323

STOP AND CHECK

Confirm Predictions Why didn't Gramps react to the moon landing? (Gramps has had a hard life and thinks money should be spent on people.)

Teacher Think Aloud I can reread details to check if my earlier prediction is correct. What key detail on page 322 does Mae give to explain how Gramps feels?

Prompt students to apply the strategy in a Think Aloud by rereading to confirm or revise their predictions.

Student Think Aloud My prediction is correct. In the first line, we learn that Mae's family members all cheer, except for Gramps. Mae remembers something Gramps said to her: "Why spend all that money to go to the moon when there's so many folks in need right here on Earth?" He can't get excited because he feels that money would be better spent helping people.

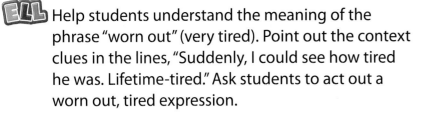

ELL Help students understand the meaning of the phrase "worn out" (very tired). Point out the context clues in the lines, "Suddenly, I could see how tired he was. Lifetime-tired." Ask students to act out a worn out, tired expression.

→ *How does Gramps feel?* (He feels tired, or worn out.) *Why does he feel this way?* (He has worked hard all his life.)

Develop Comprehension

10 ## Author's Craft: Figurative Language

What does Mae hear while she gazes up at the moon and stars? (cornstalks whisper) How is this an example of personification? (Cornstalks cannot really whisper, but the word *whispered* describes the soft sound cornstalks can make in a summer night's breeze.) What simile does Mae use to describe the stars? ("gleaming like spilled sugar") How does the image of spilled sugar help you visualize the night sky? (It describes a sky full of countless gleaming, bright white stars.)

11 ## Vocabulary: Synonyms

Sometimes authors will use synonyms, or words with almost the same meaning, in the same paragraph. Locating synonyms can help you figure out the meaning of an unfamiliar word. Find the word *gazed* in the second sentence. What word in the third sentence is a context clue to the meaning of *gazed*? (seeing) What is the family gazing at in the sky? (the moon and the stars)

Once upon a summer's night in 1969, we spread blankets and folding chairs on the edge of the yard, where the buffalo grass grew thick and soft. The **10** cornstalks whispered while we gazed at the pearly slice **11** of moon, and the stars, gleaming like spilled sugar. **12** What were the astronauts seeing, right at this very second? Could they see beyond the moon, to Mars or Neptune or Jupiter? We passed around a bowl of popcorn. What I could see above me, and what I could see in my imagination, were better than any picture show.

324

A C T Access Complex Text

▶ Connection of Ideas

Guide students in making inferences about the narrator using evidence from the text. Reread page 324 and talk about Mae's description of the night.

→ *What can you infer about how Mae is feeling at this moment in time?* (Mae is excited, awestruck, inspired, and curious. By asking rhetorical questions about the astronauts and what they are doing she is showing that she is interested and curious. She watches the night sky in awe of what is happening on the moon. She also imagines what could be happening in saying, "What I could see above me, and what I could see in my imagination, were better than any picture show.")

325

LITERATURE ANTHOLOGY, pp. 324–325

12 Ask and Answer Questions

What does Mae wonder as she gazes up at the night sky? Paraphrase details from the story with a partner to describe the narrator's thoughts. (She is wondering what the astronauts are seeing "right this very second." She wonders if they can see the planets Mars, Jupiter, or Neptune.)

CONNECT TO CONTENT
TECHNOLOGY AND SOCIETY

SCIENCE

NASA's space shuttle fleet had its first launch on April 12, 1981, nearly 22 years after the *Apollo 11* mission. The spacecraft had missions into orbit for 30 years. People who traveled on the space shuttle launched, recovered, and repaired satellites, built the International Space Station, and conducted scientific research. The technology developed for these missions is now used for many purposes, such as health care. One example is an artificial heart; another is a laboratory instrument doctors use to quickly analyze blood tests.

STEM

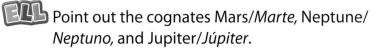 Point out the cognates Mars/*Marte*, Neptune/*Neptuno*, and Jupiter/*Júpiter*.

→ *What are Mars, Neptune, and Jupiter?* (They are planets.) *What does Mae wonder as she looks up at the sky?* (She wonders if the astronauts can see Mars, Neptune, or Jupiter from the moon.)

Develop Comprehension

13 **Skill: Point of View**

What does Mae see flash on the television screen in capital letters? ("LIVE FROM THE SURFACE OF THE MOON.") Why do you think these words give Mae goose bumps? (because she is excited to see the astronauts on the moon) How does Mae describe this worldwide historic event on television? ("600 million people the world over watching with me"; "All of us—from New York to Tokyo to Paris to Cairo . . . to Star") In the last paragraph, whose hand does Mae feel on her shoulder? (Gramps's hand) What does he tell her about watching the moon walk? (that it is something to remember) How does Mae's point of view help us understand the experience of watching the astronauts walk on the moon? (She describes how exciting and memorable an event it is for her and her family in Star as well as for people around the world.)

Later on that summer's night, in 1969, the television screen flashed with **13** words that gave me goose bumps: LIVE FROM THE SURFACE OF THE MOON.

And Mr. Cronkite said, "... Neil Armstrong, thirty-eight-year-old American, standing on the surface of the moon on this July twentieth, nineteen hundred and sixty-nine!"

I didn't know it then, but there were 600 million people the world over watching with me, and listening, when Commander Armstrong said, "That's one small step for man, one giant leap for mankind." All of us—from New York to Tokyo to Paris to Cairo ... to Star—and maybe even President Kennedy too—all of us watched it together, the astronauts **14** bounding across the moon like ghosts on a trampoline.

I felt a hand on my shoulder. "I reckon that's something to remember," Gramps said quietly.

326

A C T Access Complex Text

▶ Connection of Ideas

Point out that Mae's passion about space exploration affects how she views the moon landing.

→ *What details in the selection have we read so far that show Mae's strong interest and enthusiasm for the space program?* (She dreams of going to the moon one day; reads the moon stories

in the paper; pretends to be in the astronauts' spaceship; and cheers when the astronauts land on the moon.)

→ *How does this passion affect how she views the moon landing?* (She gets very excited and sees it as a momentous event.)

327

LITERATURE ANTHOLOGY, pp. 326–327

14 Author's Craft: Figurative Language

What simile does Mae use to describe the astronauts' moon walk? ("astronauts bounding across the moon like ghosts on a trampoline") Discuss with your partner how the astronauts seem like "ghosts on a trampoline" to Mae. (They look like ghosts floating in the night because they are in big white spacesuits and there is less gravity on the moon. In these conditions, the astronauts take awkward bouncing steps as if walking on a trampoline.)

 Help students understand that when Mae says, "the television flashed with words that gave me goose bumps," she means she is getting excited. Point to your arm to show where goose bumps appear.

→ Ask students to think of situations or events that might cause someone to get goose bumps.

Encourage them to use *goose bumps* in their descriptions.

→ *Why does Mae get goose bumps?* (She is excited to see the moon landing.)

Develop Comprehension

15 **Strategy: Make, Confirm, or Revise Predictions**

Reread page 328 to see if Gramps's feelings about the space program and the moon landing have changed. Can you confirm your prediction?

Student Think Aloud He was not excited because he thought it was a waste of money. Later, he watches the moon walk and says it is something to remember. Now Gramps realizes how Mae is inspired by the space program, and he is proud that she dreams of becoming an astronaut. He tells Mae about seeing an airplane for the first time. Maybe he realizes that improvements in technology are not a waste of money.

Later, when it was as quiet as the world ever gets, Gramps and I stood together under the moon. "What's mankind?" I asked him.

He puffed on his pipe. "It's all of us," he finally said. "All of us who've ever lived, all of us still to come."

I put my hand in his. "Just think, Gramps: If they could go to the moon, maybe one day I could too!"

"Great days," he said, "an astronaut in the family. Who'd a thought."

I smiled in the dark. My gramps was proud of me.

15 "First airplane I ever saw … I was your age … was right over yonder," Gramps said, nodding toward the cornfield. "That was something to see, oh boy … something to see."

A sigh in Gramps's voice made my heart squeeze.

"Keep on dreaming, Mae," he said. "Just remember, we're here now together on the prettiest star in the heavens."

Gramps had looked to the moon all of his life. It told him when to plant and when to harvest. And once upon a summer's night, it told me to dream.

328

A C T Access Complex Text

▶ Connection of Ideas

Help students understand Mae's realization of how the moon has played a role in both her life and her grandfather's life.

→ *What has Gramps done all his life?* (farmed)

→ *How did Gramps use the moon to guide his farming?* (The moon told Gramps when to plant and when to harvest, or pick his crops.)

→ *What did the moon tell Mae one night?* (to dream) *What do you think Mae means by this?* (By dreaming about becoming an astronaut and walking on the moon, she realizes that she can choose to do whatever she wants in life.)

STOP AND CHECK

Visualize Which details help you visualize Mae's reaction to her grandfather's words?

329

LITERATURE ANTHOLOGY, pp. 328–329

STOP AND CHECK

Visualize Which details help you visualize Mae's reaction to her grandfather's words? (The words "I put my hand in his," "I smiled in the dark," and "a sigh in Gramps's voice made my heart squeeze" help me visualize how Mae reacts to Gramps's words.)

Return to Predictions

Review students' predictions about the selection. Ask them to answer the Essential Question. (Technology can make tasks easier and faster. It allows people to learn and discover more about the universe and themselves. Mae realizes that she does not have to work on a farm like her grandfather. She can have other dreams, such as going to the moon.)

 Help students understand why Gramps is proud of Mae.

→ Model *proud: When I am proud of someone, I am very pleased, or happy, with that person. I am proud of my students when they work hard and try their best.* Have students raise their hands if they are proud of someone. Have them complete the sentence frame: *I am proud of _____.*

→ *Why is Gramps proud of Mae?* (Gramps is proud of Mae because she dreams of becoming an astronaut.)

About the Author

Meet the Author and Illustrator

Dianna Hutts Aston and Jerry Pinkney

Have students read the biographies of the author and illustrator. Ask:

→ How might growing up in Houston, Texas, have led Dianna Hutts Aston to write about the moon landing?

→ Which illustrations in the selection could be paintings in the NASA Art Collection? Why?

Author's Purpose

To Entertain

Remind students that authors of historical fiction entertain by allowing readers to experience a time and place in history. Students may say that the use of "Once upon a ...." lends a fairy-tale quality to the story. Since this phrase is often used in fairy tales, it creates a magical tone from the start and sets the stage for an event like the moon landing.

Author's Craft

Dialogue

Explain how the author uses dialogue to reveal the characters' thoughts and feelings about each other.

→ On page 323, Mae asks Gramps if he will watch the moon walk. He replies, "I'm mighty worn out today, but maybe." Mae realizes that he has had a hard life and is not as interested in the astronauts. Mae tells Gramps, "It's okay."

→ Have students find another dialogue between Mae and Gramps that shows more about their relationship.

ABOUT THE AUTHOR AND ILLUSTRATOR

Dianna Hutts Aston was five years old when astronauts landed on the moon. She grew up in Houston, Texas, home of the Johnson Space Center. Today, Dianna's nonprofit organization gives hot air balloon rides to Mexican children in orphanages and rural villages. To her, an important part of writing is "thinking and dreaming."

Growing up, **Jerry Pinkney** used artistic skills to overcome a reading problem. He turned the words into pictures in his imagination to understand a story. Jerry has illustrated more than 100 children's books and novels. He has also created paintings for the NASA Art Collection at the Kennedy Space Center.

Author's Purpose

Why does the author use the phrase "Once upon a summer's morning . . . noon . . . evening" at different points in the story?

(t) Renee Edy; (b) Thomas Kristich

330

LITERATURE ANTHOLOGY, pp. 330–331

RESPOND TO READING

Summarize

Summarize the sequence of events in *The Moon Over Star*. Think about how the moon landing affects Mae as she tells her story. Information from your Point of View Chart may help you.

Details
↓

Point of View

Text Evidence

1. Which details in *The Moon Over Star* indicate that the story is historical fiction? **GENRE**

2. How does the point of view used in the story help you understand the impact of the moon landing? **POINT OF VIEW**

3. Mae describes the astronauts as "bounding across the moon like ghosts on a trampoline." What is a synonym for *bounding*? Explain how context clues helped you. **SYNONYMS**

4. Write about how the story would be different if it were written from Gramps's point of view. **WRITE ABOUT READING**

Make Connections

What does the moon landing mean to Mae and her family? **ESSENTIAL QUESTION**

New inventions and technology have had a huge impact over time. Which invention or technology has had the biggest impact on our world since the moon landing? **TEXT TO WORLD**

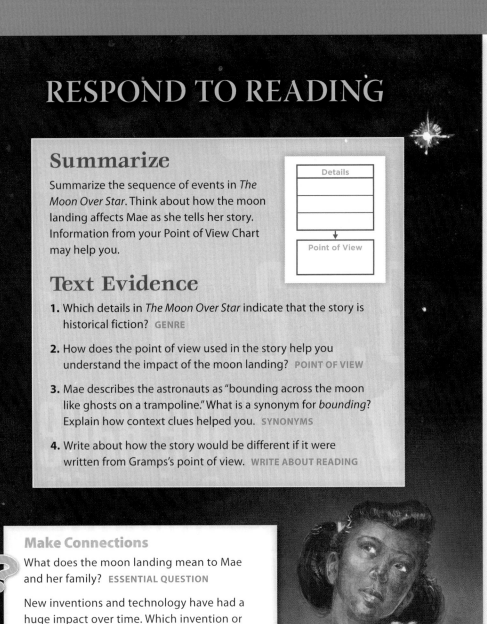

331

Make Connections *Analytical Writing*

Essential Question Students should write about how the moon landing gives Mae a reason to dream that she, too, can become an astronaut one day.

Text to World Students should write about something that has had a global impact, such as computers, the Internet, cell phones, or GPS systems to locate people.

Respond to Reading

Summarize

Review with students the information from their point of view charts. Model how to use the information to summarize the point of view in *The Moon Over Star* and what the reader learns about Mae.

Analytical Writing **Write about Reading: Point of View**
Remind students that point of view refers to the narrator's thoughts. A first-person narrator is a character in the story. Ask students to write an analysis of Mae's point of view, using quotes with first-person pronouns as evidence. Have students share their writing with a partner.

Text Evidence

1. **Genre** <u>Answer</u> The story is about a real event, but the characters, setting, and events are fictional. <u>Evidence</u> The story includes information about the events surrounding the moon landing in 1969.

2. **Point of View** <u>Answer</u> It describes the moon landing through the eyes of a young girl who wants to go to the moon. <u>Evidence</u> Mae describes the moon as "better than any picture show."

3. **Context Clues:** <u>Answer</u> Synonyms for *bounding* include *leaping, jumping,* and *bouncing*. <u>Evidence</u> Context clues in the story suggest that bounding is similar to jumping on a trampoline.

Analytical Writing 4. **Write About Reading: Point of View**
   On page 316, we learn that Gramps does not believe money should be spent on a mission to the moon. If the story were told from his point of view, he would probably not describe the landing of the moon with as much enthusiasm and excitement as Mae.

Develop Comprehension

Literature Anthology

"3...2...1... We Have Spin-off!"

Text Complexity Range

Lexile

740 — 900 — 1010

TextEvaluator™

23 — 33 — 51

Options for Close Reading

→ Whole Class

→ Small Group

→ Independent

CCSS Genre · Expository Text

Compare Texts
Read how space technology has changed the lives of people on Earth.

3...2...1 We Have Spin-off!

332

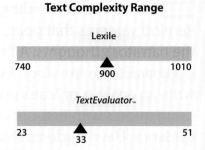

A C T Access Complex Text

What makes this text complex?

▸ **Purpose**

▸ **Organization**

▸ **Purpose**

Help students understand that while the purpose of the article is to inform readers, it begins with an anecdote, or story, to hook readers and help them connect with the text.

→ *What pronoun is used repeatedly in the opening paragraph?* (you) *Who is "you"?* (the reader)

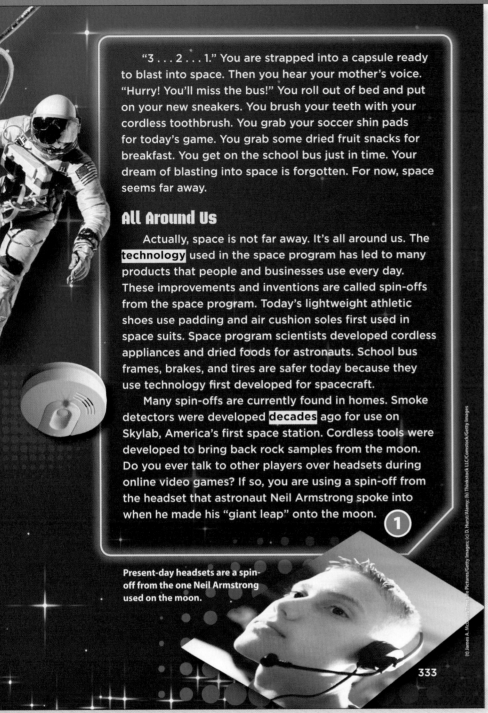

"3 . . . 2 . . . 1." You are strapped into a capsule ready to blast into space. Then you hear your mother's voice. "Hurry! You'll miss the bus!" You roll out of bed and put on your new sneakers. You brush your teeth with your cordless toothbrush. You grab your soccer shin pads for today's game. You grab some dried fruit snacks for breakfast. You get on the school bus just in time. Your dream of blasting into space is forgotten. For now, space seems far away.

All Around Us

Actually, space is not far away. It's all around us. The technology used in the space program has led to many products that people and businesses use every day. These improvements and inventions are called spin-offs from the space program. Today's lightweight athletic shoes use padding and air cushion soles first used in space suits. Space program scientists developed cordless appliances and dried foods for astronauts. School bus frames, brakes, and tires are safer today because they use technology first developed for spacecraft.

Many spin-offs are currently found in homes. Smoke detectors were developed decades ago for use on Skylab, America's first space station. Cordless tools were developed to bring back rock samples from the moon. Do you ever talk to other players over headsets during online video games? If so, you are using a spin-off from the headset that astronaut Neil Armstrong spoke into when he made his "giant leap" onto the moon.

1

Present-day headsets are a spin-off from the one Neil Armstrong used on the moon.

333

LITERATURE ANTHOLOGY, pp. 332–333

Compare Texts *Analytical Writing*

Students will read an expository text about products that were once used in the space program but are now a part of daily life. Ask students to do a close reading of the text, rereading to deeply understand the content. Encourage students to use the strategy make, confirm, or revise predictions or other strategies they know to help them. They will also take notes. Students will then use the text evidence that they gathered to compare this text with *The Moon Over Star*.

① Ask and Answer Questions

What is a "spin-off"? What are some common examples of spin-off products we use every day?

With a partner, paraphrase how spin-offs are all around us. (Spin-offs are products that use technology developed for the space program. For example, we use padding and air cushion soles in athletic shoes. Cordless appliances and dried foods were once used by astronauts. Headsets are a spin-off from the headset that Neil Armstrong spoke into.)

→ *Why do you think the author uses the pronoun* you? (The author wants readers to instantly connect with the information in the article.)

→ *What are some of the examples of products the author says you might use in daily life?* (cordless toothbrush, shin pads, and dried fruit snacks)

ELL Point out the cognates invention/*invención* and product/*producto* to help students understand the meaning of "spin-offs." Explain that a spin-off is a new invention based on a product that was originally made for the space program.

→ *What is an example of a spin-off?* (shoe padding, brakes, tires, headsets, and so forth)

Develop Comprehension

2 Ask and Answer Questions

How are spin-offs used to keep food fresh?

Analytical Writing **Write About Reading** Write a sentence paraphrasing one interesting product and why the technology for it was developed by the space program. (Freeze-dried foods in sealed packages were developed for astronauts who needed lightweight foods that would not spoil.)

3 Ask and Answer Questions

How do spin-offs keep people safe?

Analytical Writing **Write About Reading** Make a list of spin-offs that keep people safe or are used in medicine. (face masks, breathing systems, fire suits, robotics, cameras)

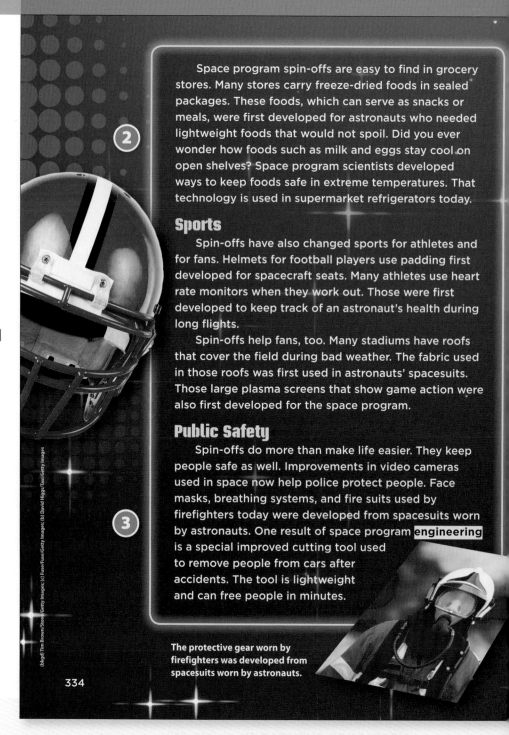

Space program spin-offs are easy to find in grocery stores. Many stores carry freeze-dried foods in sealed packages. These foods, which can serve as snacks or meals, were first developed for astronauts who needed lightweight foods that would not spoil. Did you ever wonder how foods such as milk and eggs stay cool on open shelves? Space program scientists developed ways to keep foods safe in extreme temperatures. That technology is used in supermarket refrigerators today.

Sports

Spin-offs have also changed sports for athletes and for fans. Helmets for football players use padding first developed for spacecraft seats. Many athletes use heart rate monitors when they work out. Those were first developed to keep track of an astronaut's health during long flights.

Spin-offs help fans, too. Many stadiums have roofs that cover the field during bad weather. The fabric used in those roofs was first used in astronauts' spacesuits. Those large plasma screens that show game action were also first developed for the space program.

Public Safety

Spin-offs do more than make life easier. They keep people safe as well. Improvements in video cameras used in space now help police protect people. Face masks, breathing systems, and fire suits used by firefighters today were developed from spacesuits worn by astronauts. One result of space program engineering is a special improved cutting tool used to remove people from cars after accidents. The tool is lightweight and can free people in minutes.

The protective gear worn by firefighters was developed from spacesuits worn by astronauts.

334

A C T Access Complex Text

▶ Organization

Remind students that the text is written in the form of an article. The headings provide clues about the information in each section.

→ In what section can the reader find information related to spin-offs used by athletes and sports fans? ("Sports")

→ What information is presented under the heading "Public Safety"? (spin-offs used by police and fire departments)

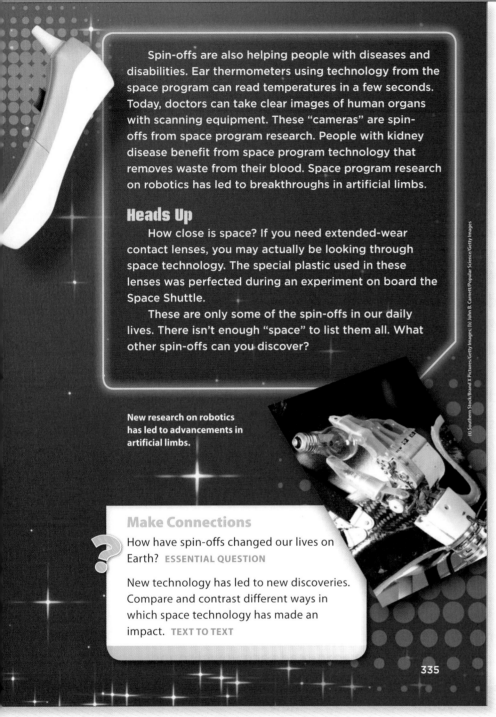

Spin-offs are also helping people with diseases and disabilities. Ear thermometers using technology from the space program can read temperatures in a few seconds. Today, doctors can take clear images of human organs with scanning equipment. These "cameras" are spin-offs from space program research. People with kidney disease benefit from space program technology that removes waste from their blood. Space program research on robotics has led to breakthroughs in artificial limbs.

Heads Up

How close is space? If you need extended-wear contact lenses, you may actually be looking through space technology. The special plastic used in these lenses was perfected during an experiment on board the Space Shuttle.

These are only some of the spin-offs in our daily lives. There isn't enough "space" to list them all. What other spin-offs can you discover?

New research on robotics has led to advancements in artificial limbs.

Make Connections

How have spin-offs changed our lives on Earth? **ESSENTIAL QUESTION**

New technology has led to new discoveries. Compare and contrast different ways in which space technology has made an impact. **TEXT TO TEXT**

335

LITERATURE ANTHOLOGY, pp. 334–335

Make Connections

Essential Question Have students list inventions and technologies developed by the space program and tell how these innovations have changed our lives.

Text to Text Have groups compare their responses to the Ask and Answer Questions prompts with what they read in *The Moon Over Star*. Each group can report back to the whole class. Have one group compare and contrast how technology is presented in both selections. (In both, technology has the capacity to both help and impress.) Have another group compare how the two authors feel about investing in the space program. (Both texts seem to support investment because of the benefits to everyone.) Have a third group discuss interesting facts about the space program they learned from each selection. (In 1969, 600 million people worldwide watched a live telecast of the moon landing; many different products have been developed because of the special needs astronauts have in space.)

 Encourage students to notice cognates on pages 334 and 335: public/*público,* video camera/*videocámara,* accident/*accidente.* Ask if anyone can find another cognate. (minute/*minuto;* astronaut/*astronauta;* thermometer/*termómetro;* technology/*tecnología;* robotics/*robótica*)

Phonics/Fluency

Go Digital

Words with /ü/, /ū/, and /u̇/

Present the Lesson

View "A Telephone Mix-Up"

 MINILESSON 20 Mins

Words with /ü/, /ū/, and /u̇/

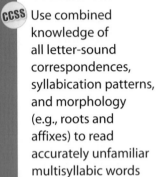

OBJECTIVES

CCSS Use combined knowledge of all letter-sound correspondences, syllabication patterns, and morphology (e.g., roots and affixes) to read accurately unfamiliar multisyllabic words in context and out of context. **RF.4.3a**

CCSS Read on-level text with purpose and understanding. **RF.4.4a**

CCSS Read on-level prose and poetry orally with accuracy, appropriate rate, and expression on successive readings. **RF.4.4b**

Rate: 102–122 WCPM

ACADEMIC LANGUAGE
• expression
• Cognate: *expresión*

 ELL

Refer to the sound transfers chart in the **Language Transfers Handbook** to identify sounds that do not transfer in Spanish, Cantonese, Vietnamese, Hmong, and Korean.

1 Explain

Display the *Spoon, Cube,* and *Book* **Sound-Spelling Cards**. Point to each card and say the vowel sound. Review the sound spellings and provide sample words.

→ The /ü/ sound in *spoon* may be spelled *oo, ew, u_e, ue, u, ui,* and *ou* (*soon, blew, rude, clue, July, fruit,* and *through*).

→ The /ū/ sound in *cube* may be spelled *u, u_e,* and *ew* (*pupil, huge,* and *few*).

→ The /u̇/ sound in *book* may be spelled *oo* and *ou* (*cook* and *could*).

Explain that the short *u* sound, as in *under*, may be spelled similarly, as *o, oo,* and *ou* (*cover, flood,* and *tough*). Display the *Umbrella* **Sound-Spelling Card** for clarification, if necessary.

2 Model

Write the word *shook* on the board and underline the letters *oo*. Model pronouncing the /u̇/ sound and then sound out the entire word.

3 Guided Practice

Write the following words on the board. Help students identify the /ü/, /ū/, and /u̇/ spellings. Have them echo-read each vowel sound after you. Then have them whisper-read the words.

wood	youth	news
flute	suit	choose
mule	should	glue

Read Multisyllabic Words

Transition to Longer Words Draw a T-chart on the board. In the first column, write *blue, foot, music,* and *group*. In the second column, write *bluebird, football, musical,* and *regrouping*. Have students choral-read the words in the first column. Point out the added words and word parts in the second column. Pronounce each word in the second column and have students echo-read after you.

Consonant + *le* Syllables

1 Explain

Explain that when a word ends in a consonant and *le*, the consonant and the letters *le* usually form the final syllable. The letters *le* are pronounced /əl/.

→ In the word *steeple, ple* is the consonant + *le* syllable.

→ The /əl/ sound can also be spelled *al, el, il,* or *ol* (as in *total, channel, pencil,* and *symbol*). The same final syllable rule applies to these /əl/ spellings in most words.

2 Model

Write and say *table*. Have students repeat the word. Model dividing the word into syllables by identifying the letters *ble*. Use the rule to explain that these letters make up the word's final syllable.

3 Guided Practice

Write the words *kettle, staple,* and *probable* on the board. Have students identify the final syllable in each word and then divide each word into its syllables before choral-reading the words.

Expression

Explain/Model Explain that reading dialogue gives readers the opportunity to talk the way a character would and express the same emotions. This helps readers and listeners connect with characters and understand events in a story.

Model reading page 268 of "A Telephone Mix-Up," starting with the second paragraph. Use varying levels of expression to show the characters' excitement.

Practice/Apply Have students take turns partner-reading the paragraphs in the passage. Ask partners to read through the passage once without any expression at all, and once with strong expression. Then have them discuss how expression helps both the reader and the listener.

Daily Fluency Practice

Students can practice fluency using **Your Turn Practice Book.**

Monitor and *Differentiate*

✓ Quick Check

Can students decode multisyllabic words with /ü/, /ū/, and /u̇/? Can students read words with consonant + *le* syllables? Can students read fluently?

⬇

Small Group Instruction

If No →	Approaching Level	Reteach pp. T170, T174
	ELL	Develop pp. T186, T190
If Yes →	On Level	Review p. T176
	Beyond Level	Extend p. T180

ON-LEVEL PRACTICE BOOK p. 178

A. Read the words in the box below. Sort the words based on their vowel sounds.

bruised	huge	should	issue	crook	stoop

Vowel sound in *spoon*	Vowel sound in *cube*	Vowel sound in *book*
1. bruised	3. huge	5. should
2. stoop	4. issue	6. crook

B. Divide each word into its syllables with a slanted line (/). Then write the consonant + *le* syllable on the line. Remember that an *le* syllable may also be spelled with a consonant + *al, el, il,* or *ol.*

1. ton/sil   sil
2. for/mal   mal
3. tum/ble   ble
4. bri/dle   dle
5. sym/bol   bol
6. chan/nel   nel

APPROACHING p. 178	BEYOND p. 178	ELL p. 178

☞ **Go** Digital

www.connected.mcgraw-hill.com
RESOURCES
Research and Inquiry

→ Wrap Up the Week
Integrate Ideas

RESEARCH AND INQUIRY

Breakthroughs

OBJECTIVES

CCSS With guidance and support from peers and adults, develop and stengthen writing as needed by planning, revising, and editing. **W.4.5**

CCSS Report on a topic or text, tell a story, or recount an experience in an organized manner, using appropriate facts and relevant, descriptive details to support main ideas or themes; speak clearly at an understandable pace. **SL.4.4**

CCSS Choose words and phrases to convey ideas precisely. **L.4.3a**

• Examine a topic.
• Write explanatory text.
• Use formal language.

ACADEMIC LANGUAGE
collaborate, formal language

Write a Paragraph about Plastics in Medicine

Explain that students will work in pairs and explore the role of plastic in a medical breakthrough. They will then write a paragraph to describe how that progress has improved lives. Discuss the following steps:

1 Recall Experiences Have pairs recall information from their personal experiences to explain how plastics are used in medical treatments. Ask them to brainstorm a list together and discuss other possible uses of plastics in medicine.

2 Find Resources Have students research one important new way in which plastics are used in medicine. Remind them to take clear, organized notes as they use the library or media center to explore resources.

3 Guided Practice Have pairs collaborate to write a short paragraph about their chosen medical breakthrough. Have them use formal language and specific details and examples in their paragraphs.

4 Review the Paragraph Encourage collaborative effort as students review their paragraphs for effective language and correct grammar and punctuation. Help students e-mail their paragraphs to the class.

Present the Paragraph

As students prepare to present their paragraphs, suggest that they add audio or visual elements, in addition to any props, to enhance the development of their main ideas. Invite student pairs to read their paragraphs to the class and answer any questions that other students may have. Have them use online Presentation Checklist 1 to evaluate their presentations. Make sure they speak clearly and at an understandable pace.

STEM

TEXT CONNECTIONS *Analytical Writing*

OBJECTIVES

CCSS Compare and contrast the treatment of similar themes and topics (e.g., opposition of good and evil) and patterns of events (e.g., the quest) in stories, myths, and traditional literature from different cultures. **RL.4.9**

Text to Text

Cite Evidence Explain to students that they will work in groups to compare information they have learned about how technology affects their lives from all the texts they have read. Model how to compare this information by using examples from the week's **Leveled Readers** and *A Telephone Mix-Up,* **Reading/Writing Workshop** pages 266–269. Review class notes and completed graphic organizers. You may also wish to model going back into the text for more information. You can use an Accordion Foldable® to record comparisons.

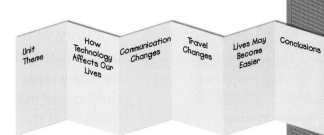

Dinah Zike's
FOLDABLES®
Study Organizer

Students should cite at least three examples from each text.

Present Information Ask groups of students to present their findings to the class. Encourage discussion, asking students to comment on similarities and differences among the ideas discussed.

WRITE ABOUT READING *Analytical Writing*

OBJECTIVES

CCSS Apply *grade 4 Reading standards* to literature (e.g., "Describe in depth a character, setting, or event in a story or drama, drawing on specific details in the text [e.g., a character's thoughts, words, or actions]."). **W.4.9a**

CCSS Identify the reasons and evidence a speaker provides to support particular points. **SL.4.3**

Write an Analysis

Cite Evidence Using text evidence, students will analyze how well the author used real events from the past and details to develop realistic characters and events in the story.

Discuss how to analyze a text by asking *how* and *what* questions.

→ How did the author make the characters in the story seem realistic?

→ What historical events are used in the story?

Read and discuss the student model on **Your Turn Practice Book** page 179. Then have students choose a text they have read and review their notes on the story events. Have them write a paragraph analyzing how well the author used realistic characters and historical events in the story. Remind students that good opinion writing is supported by reasons and details and includes correct pronoun-verb agreement.

Present Your Ideas Ask partners to share their paragraphs and discuss how the evidence they cited from the text supports their opinions.

→ # Readers to Writers

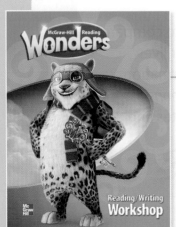

Reading/Writing Workshop

OBJECTIVES

CCSS Write routinely over extended time frames and shorter time frames for a range of discipline-specific tasks, purposes, and audiences. **W.4.10**

CCSS Orient the reader by establishing a situation and introducing a narrator and/or characters; organize an event sequence that unfolds naturally. **W.4.3a**

CCSS Use dialogue and description to develop experiences and events or show the responses of characters to situations. **W.4.3b**

• Analyze models of plot development.

• Add setting details to revise writing.

ACADEMIC LANGUAGE
plot, setting, details

 MINILESSON **10** Mins

Writing Traits: Ideas

Develop Plot

Expert Model Explain that good writers carefully develop the plot of a story. At the beginning of a story, they introduce a situation, or problem, the main character faces, and the setting, or when and where the story takes place. Writers include specific details about a story's setting and make sure the events of the story show how the problem unfolds. At the end of the story, the problem is resolved.

 Read aloud the expert model from "A Telephone Mix-Up." Ask students to listen for details that give clues about the story's setting. Have students talk with partners to identify these details and discuss how the setting details help them understand the story's plot.

Student Model Remind students that developing a plot includes using specific details to describe the setting. Read aloud the student draft "Mike's First Television." As students follow along, have them focus on details the writer included in his draft.

 Invite partners to talk about the draft and the details that Leo used to describe the setting. Ask them to suggest places where Leo could add more details to describe the setting and develop the plot.

 Go Digital

Expert Model

Student Model

Genre Writing

Narrative Text and Poetry

For full writing process lessons and rubrics, see:

→ Fictional Narrative, pages T344–T349

→ Poetry, pages T350–T355

CCSS Writing Traits Ideas

Readers to...

Writers develop the plot of a story by including specific details about the story's setting. Reread the excerpt from "A Telephone Mix-Up" below.

Expert Model

Develop Plot

Identify details that give you clues about the story's **setting**. How do the setting details help you understand the story's **plot**?

Despite the concerns of some people, progress marched on. Just weeks earlier, Centerburg's first telephone had been installed in Mr. Kane's general store, another was put in at the hotel, and yet another at the newspaper office. Mrs. Kane was the town's first switchboard operator, directing incoming calls to the correct lines.

The next morning, Meg wrote "October 9, 1905" on the top of her slate with chalk while she squirmed in her seat, wishing that the long school day was over.

Walking home that afternoon, Meg scouted the street, looking for the tall wooden poles that were going up weekly.

274

Writers

Leo wrote about a boy who sees a television for the first time. Read Leo's revisions to one section of his story.

Student Model

Mike's First Television

Mike sat on the floor in front
of the big box with its small glass (wooden)
screen. there were several knobs
and buttons and a little dial.

"Here it is New Year's Day and (1955)
Þare going to see pictures on a (we)
television!" Mike's dad said. "This
will be a day you will tell your
grandchildren about!" Then he turns (ed)
a knob. Slowly a light
flickered on the screen.

275

Editing Marks

⌐⌐ Switch order.
∧ Add.
∧ Add a comma.
⌇ Take out.
(SP) Check spelling.
≡ Make a capital letter.

Grammar Handbook

Pronoun-Verb Agreement See page 464.

Your Turn

✔ How do the setting details Leo used help develop the plot?
✔ Identify examples of pronoun-verb agreement that he used in his writing.
✔ Tell how the revisions improved Leo's writing.

Go Digital!
Write online in Writer's Workspace

READING/WRITING WORKSHOP, pp. 274–275

ENGLISH LANGUAGE LEARNERS SCAFFOLD

As English Language Learners write during the week, provide support to help them respond to the prompts. For example:

Beginning

Write Help students complete the sentence frames. *Mike sat on the _____ in front of the big wooden _____. "Here it is _____ _____ day 1955, and we are going to see pictures on a _____!" The story takes place in Mike's _____.*

Intermediate

Describe Ask students to complete the sentence frames. Encourage students to provide details. *Mike sat on the _____. "Here it is _____, and we are going to see _____!" The story takes place in _____.*

Advanced/High

Discuss Check for understanding. Ask: *Where does Mike sit in the story? When does the story take place? What are Mike and his dad getting ready to do? Where does the story take place?*

Writing Every Day: Ideas

DAY 1

DAY 2

Writing Entry: Develop Plot

Prewrite Provide students with the prompt below.

Imagine living before computers, television, and phones were invented. Write a story that tells about one day in your life.

Have partners brainstorm what life would be like without computers, televisions, or phones. Ask them to jot down details and events that they might include in their drafts.

Draft Have each student begin writing about the topic. Remind students to include details about the setting to help develop the plot in their drafts.

Focus on Developing Plot

Use **Your Turn Practice Book** page 180 to model adding setting details.

I woke up and went downstairs for breakfast. My brother and I went swimming in the lake. Then we went to help our dad with the horses in the barn. After that, we all went inside to do household chores.

Model adding a setting detail.

It was the summer of 1910. I woke up and went downstairs for breakfast.

Discuss how adding setting details helps develop the plot of the story. Guide students to add more setting details to the rest of the model.

Writing Entry: Develop Plot

Revise Have students revise their writing from Day 1 by adding two or three details about the setting.

Use the **Conferencing Routines**. Circulate among students and stop briefly to talk with individuals. Provide time for peer review.

Edit Have students use Grammar Handbook page 464 in the **Reading/Writing Workshop** to edit for errors in pronoun-verb agreement.

Conferencing Routines

Teacher Conferences

STEP 1

Talk about the strengths of the writing.

I can picture the characters because of the descriptive details you included. The dialogue helps me understand what the characters are thinking and feeling.

STEP 2

Focus on how the writer uses the target trait for the week.

You tell the reader when the story takes place. It would help if you added some details to describe the setting.

STEP 3

Make concrete suggestions for revisions. Have students work on a specific assignment, such as those to the right, and then meet with you to review progress.

DAY 3

Writing Entry: Develop Plot

Prewrite Ask students to search their Writer's Notebook for topics to write a draft. Or, provide a prompt, such as the following:

Imagine living before cars were invented. Write a story that tells about one day in your life.

Draft Once students have chosen their topics, ask them to create a word web with the topic in the center. Then have them think about plot events and details about the setting that they might include in their writing. Students can then use their word webs to begin their drafts.

DAY 4

Writing Entry: Develop Plot

Revise Have students revise the draft writing from Day 3 by adding two or three details about the setting to help develop the plot. As students are revising their drafts, hold teacher conferences with individual students. You may also wish to have students work with partners to peer conference.

Edit Invite students to review the rules for pronoun-verb agreement on Grammar Handbook page 464 in the **Reading/Writing Workshop** and then edit their drafts for errors.

DAY 5

Share and Reflect

Discuss with the class what they learned about developing a plot. Invite volunteers to read and compare draft text with text that has been revised. Have students discuss the writing by focusing on the importance of the setting details that have been added. Allow time for individuals to reflect on their own writing progress and record observations in their Writer's Notebooks.

McGraw-Hill Companies, Inc./Ken Karp, photographer

Suggested Revisions

Provide specific direction to help focus young writers.

Focus on a Sentence
Read the draft and target one sentence for revision. *Rewrite this sentence by adding details to describe ____.*

Focus on a Section
Underline a section that needs to be revised. Provide specific suggestions. *This section moves the plot along. I want to picture ____ more clearly. Provide details to help me picture this.*

Focus on a Revision Strategy
Underline a section of the writing and ask students to use a specific revision strategy, such as adding. *Many events take place in this section. Try adding some details to describe the setting.*

Peer Conferences

Focus peer response groups on developing a story's plot. Provide this checklist to frame discussion.

- ☑ Are the problem and setting introduced in the beginning of the story?
- ☑ Does the writing include details about the setting that help develop the plot?
- ☑ What setting details can be added?
- ☑ Is the problem resolved at the end?

Grammar: Pronoun-Verb Agreement

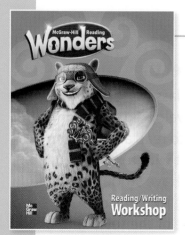

Reading/Writing Workshop

OBJECTIVES

CCSS Use commas and quotation marks to mark direct speech and quotations from a text. **L.4.2b**

CCSS Ensure subject-verb and pronoun-antecedent agreement. **L.3.1f**

- Understand pronoun-verb agreement.
- Correct errors in pronoun-verb agreement.
- Capitalize and punctuate dialogue.

Go Digital

Pronoun-Verb Agreement

Grammar Activities

DAY 1

DAILY LANGUAGE ACTIVITY

Leah and Max helped theirselves to the leftovers. Him and her are grounded now.
(1: themselves; 2: He and she)

Introduce Pronoun-Verb Agreement

Present the following:

→ A subject pronoun and a present-tense verb must **agree** in number:

   They trade comic books.

→ When using the subject pronouns **he, she,** and **it**, add **-s** or **-es** to most verbs:

   She trades comic books.

→ When using the subject pronouns **I, we, you,** and **they,** do not add **-s** or **-es** to the verb:

   We **read** everyday.

Have partners discuss pronoun-verb agreement using page 464 of the Grammar Handbook in **Reading/Writing Workshop**.

DAY 2

DAILY LANGUAGE ACTIVITY

The winner of the writing contest was him. His essays' title is My Family.
(1: he; 2: essay's; 3: "My Family")

Review Pronoun-Verb Agreement

Review how to check for agreement between subject pronouns and present-tense verbs.

Introduce Pronouns with *Have* and *Be*

→ The verbs **have** and **be** are **irregular**.

→ Use subject pronouns with the present-tense forms of **have** in the following way:

   I have, you have, he/she/it has, we have, they have

→ Use subject pronouns with the present-tense forms of **be** in the following way:

   I am, you are, he/she/it is, we are, they are

TALK ABOUT IT

COLLABORATE

CREATE SENTENCES

Have students in small groups each write ten action verbs and the subject pronouns *he, she, it, I, we, you,* and *they* on index cards. Have them place the cards in two piles and take turns drawing a card from each pile and correctly using both words in the same sentence.

USE PRONOUNS WITH *HAVE*

Ask partners to use subject pronouns with the verb *have* to talk about how technology affects their lives. They might discuss how computers make it easier to connect with friends. Students should listen to be sure they use pronouns with *have* correctly.

DAY 3

DAILY LANGUAGE ACTIVITY

Has you seen the baby monkies at the zoo? Them is only four weeks old.
(1: Have; 2: monkeys; 3: They are)

Mechanics and Usage: Punctuation in Dialogue

→ Use quotation marks before and after someone's exact words. Begin a quotation with a capital letter.

→ Commas and periods always appear inside closing quotation marks.

→ Place a question mark or an exclamation mark inside closing quotation marks if it is part of the quotation.

→ Place a question mark or an exclamation mark outside closing quotation marks if it is not part of the quotation.

Refer students to Grammar Handbook pages 464 and 480.

DAY 4

DAILY LANGUAGE ACTIVITY

Coyote said, "please come join me for dinner." Rabbit responded, "I gladly except your offer".
(1: "Please; 2: accept; 3: offer.")

Proofread

Have students correct errors in these sentences.

1. "Where" Sue asked, "Is my book?" (1: "Where,"; 2: is)

2. The coach yelled, "shoot the basket" (1: "Shoot; 2: basket!")

3. Her raised her hand to ask, "When are we going to recess"? (1: She; 2: recess?")

4. "Slow down" ordered the Police Officer. (1: down!"; 2: police officer)

Have students check their work using Grammar Handbook pages 464 and 480 on punctuating dialogue.

DAY 5

DAILY LANGUAGE ACTIVITY

"Incredible Computers is an interesting article. The author says, "computers will shrink in size."
(1: Computers"; 2: Computers)

Assess

Use the Daily Language Activity and **Grammar Practice Reproducibles** page 90 for assessment.

Reteach

Use Grammar Practice Reproducibles pages 86–89 and selected pages from the Grammar Handbook for additional reteaching. Remind students that it is important to check for pronoun-verb agreement and to punctuate dialogue correctly.

Check students' writing for use of the skill and listen for it in their speaking. Assign Grammar Revision Assignments in their Writer's Notebooks as needed.

See Grammar Practice Reproducibles pages 86–90.

DESCRIBE A COMIC STRIP

Have students in small groups each select a comic strip from the newspaper. Have groups place the strips in a bag. Students will take turns selecting a strip from the bag and using subject pronouns with the verb *be* to describe what the character or characters are doing.

FINISH THE SENTENCE

Have students in small groups each write two sentence starters that begin with a subject pronoun followed by a form of *be* or *have*. Have them take turns reading their sentence starters aloud and choosing another student to complete the sentence.

PLAY CHARADES

Have students in groups each write down three action verbs on scrap paper and place the pieces in a pile. Students will take turns selecting a paper and acting out the verb, as the others guess what the student is doing. Have them begin their guesses with *He is* or *She is*.

Spelling: Words with /ü/, /ủ/, and /ū/

DAY 1

DAY 2

OBJECTIVES

CCSS Spell grade-appropriate words correctly, consulting references as needed. **L.4.2d**

Spelling Words

mood	issue	you'll
stoop	tutor	huge
zoom	truth	crook
crew	bruised	wool
stew	juicy	used
ruler	suits	should
produce	group	

Review pennies, prettily, funnier
Challenge barbeque, crooked

Differentiated Spelling

Approaching Level

tooth	tunes	huge
food	true	July
zoom	clue	used
spool	fruit	cookie
new	suit	wool
grew	group	should
stew	you'll	

Beyond Level

boost	produce	you'll
doodle	tissue	huge
zoom	truthful	mute
smooth	tutor	communication
crew	bruised	crooked
shrewd	juicy	should
parachute	suits	

Assess Prior Knowledge

Display the spelling words. Point out the /ü/, /ủ/, and /ū/ patterns in *zoom, should* and *huge*. Say the words aloud, drawing out the /ü/of *zoom,* the /ủ/ of *should,* and the /ū/ of *huge*. Then read the remaining spelling words aloud, drawing out the /ü/, /ủ/, and /ū/ sounds.

Demonstrate sorting the spelling words by sound under key words *zoom, should* and *huge*. (Write the words on index cards or the IWB.) Sort a few words. Review the different spellings for the /ü/, /ủ/, and /ū/ sounds. Point out that the same spellings can be used to create different sounds, such as the /ü/ in *zoom* and the /ủ/ in *crook*.

Then use the Dictation Sentences from Day 5 to give the Pretest. Say the underlined word, read the sentence, and repeat the word. Have students write the words. Then have students check and correct their spelling.

Spiral Review

Review inflectional endings involving changing *y* to *i*. Use the Dictation Sentences below for the review words. Read the sentence, say the word, and have students write the words.

1. How many <u>pennies</u> are in a dollar?
2. She smiled <u>prettily</u>.
3. Tom's joke is <u>funnier</u> than mine.

Have partners check the spellings.

Challenge Words Review this week's /ü/, /ủ/, and /ū/ vowel sound spelling patterns. Use these Dictation Sentences for challenge words. Say the word, read the sentence, and say the word again. Have students write the word.

1. There will be ribs and hot dogs at the <u>barbeque</u>.
2. That fence is <u>crooked</u>.

Have students check and correct their spelling before writing the words in their word study notebook.

 **WORD SORTS**

COLLABORATE

OPEN SORT

Have students cut apart the **Spelling Word Cards BLM** in the Teacher Resource Book and initial the back of each card. Have them read the words aloud with a partner. Then have partners do an open sort. Have them record the sort in their word study notebook.

PATTERN SORT

Complete the **pattern sort** from Day 1 using the key words, pointing out the many spellings for the /ü/, /ủ/, and /ū/ sounds. Have students use Spelling Word Cards to do their own pattern sort. Ask partners to compare and check their sorts.

DAY 3

Word Meanings

Write these groups of words on the board. Have students copy them into their word study notebook and complete them by adding the spelling word that best fits in the same category.

1. pants, dresses, _____ (*suits*)

2. cotton, silk, _____ (*wool*)

3. teach, explain, _____ (*tutor*)

4. big, large, _____ (*huge*)

5. king, queen, _____ (*ruler*)

Challenge students to come up with at least three other word groups that use spelling, review, or challenge words, leaving a blank where the word should go. Remind students that some of the spelling words have more than one meaning, such as *produce, suits, stoop,* and *group.* Then have them trade papers and fill in the blanks.

See Phonics/Spelling Reproducibles pp. 103–108.

SPEED SORT

Have partners do a **speed sort** to see who is fastest, then discuss any differences in their sorts. Ask them to do a word hunt for words with /ü/, /ů/, and /ū/ sounds. Have them sort the new words, then use a dictionary or pronunciation guide to check their sort.

DAY 4

Proofread and Write

Write these sentences on the board. Have students circle and correct each misspelled word. They can use print or electronic dictionaries or other resources to help them.

1. Did you see the monster zume through the sky on its hewge wings? (*zoom, huge*)

2. The fruit was jucy but it brewsed easily. (*juicy, bruised*)

3. You shood try some of the stu. (*should, stew*)

4. The groop was sure Ami was telling the trewth. (*group, truth*)

Error Correction Remind students that the /ü/, /ů/, and /ū/ vowel sounds can share some of the same spelling patterns. Suggest that students use print and electronic resources to help them determine the correct pronunciation and to check spelling.

BLIND SORT

Have partners do a **blind sort**: one reads a Spelling Word Card; the other tells under which key word it belongs. Have them take turns until both have sorted all their words. Ask them to review their sorts and write a reflection on the sort and any difficulties they encountered.

DAY 5

Assess

Use the Dictation Sentences for the Posttest. Have students list misspelled words in their word study notebooks. Look for students' use of these words in their writings.

Dictation Sentences

1. I am in a silly <u>mood</u>.

2. Flower pots sit on our front <u>stoop</u>.

3. Cars <u>zoom</u> down the highway.

4. The boat's <u>crew</u> can help you.

5. We used the meat in our <u>stew</u>.

6. Measure the paper with a <u>ruler</u>.

7. Some farmers call vegetables <u>produce</u>.

8. The newspaper had a special <u>issue</u>.

9. Allison is a talented math <u>tutor</u>.

10. Her dad saw the <u>truth</u> in the story.

11. The banana was <u>bruised</u>.

12. The peaches were <u>juicy</u> and sweet.

13. That store only sells men's <u>suits</u>.

14. Stand with that <u>group</u>.

15. <u>You'll</u> have a party tomorrow.

16. That is a <u>huge</u> house.

17. The <u>crook</u> stole a computer.

18. Do you like <u>wool</u> sweaters?

19. He <u>used</u> my hairbrush.

20. We <u>should</u> leave now.

Have students self-correct the tests.

Build Vocabulary

 DAY 1

 DAY 2

OBJECTIVES

CCSS Use context (e.g., definitions, examples, or restatements in text) as a clue to the meaning of a word or phrase. **L.4.4a**

CCSS Demonstrate understanding of words by relating them to their opposites (antonyms) and to words with similar but not identical meanings (synonyms). **L.4.5c**

CCSS Use common, grade-appropriate Greek and Latin affixes and roots as clues to the meaning of a word (e.g., *telegraph, photograph, autograph*). **L.4.4b**

Connect to Words

Practice this week's vocabulary.

1. How old will you be in a **decade**?
2. Would you like to try **directing** a play? Why or why not?
3. Why does building a bridge require **engineering**?
4. What sort of things can you see **gleaming** in the sunlight?
5. How are the meanings of **scouted** and *searched* similar?
6. What kinds of animals have you seen that **squirmed**?
7. Name a form of **technology** that you use everyday.
8. Describe what someone who is **tinkering** is doing.

Expand Vocabulary

Help students generate different forms of this week's words by adding, changing, or removing inflectional endings.

→ Draw a four-column T-chart on the board. Write *scouted* in the third column. Then write *scout, scouts,* and *scouting* in the other columns. Read aloud the words with students.

→ Have students share sentences using each form of *scout*.

→ Students can fill in the chart for *gleaming, squirmed,* and *tinkering,* then share sentences using the different forms of the words.

→ Have students copy the chart in their word study notebook.

Vocabulary Words

decade	scouted
directing	squirmed
engineering	technology
gleaming	tinkering

Go Digital

Vocabulary

Vocabulary Activities

BUILD MORE VOCABULARY

COLLABORATE

ACADEMIC VOCABULARY

Discuss important academic words.

→ Display *invention, discovery*.

→ Define each word and discuss the meanings with students.

→ Display *invention* and *invent*. Have partners look up and define related words.

→ Write the related words on the board. Have partners ask and answer questions using the words. Repeat with *discovery*.

LATIN ROOTS *Review*

→ Explain that the Latin root *directus* means "straight." Ask, *Which of this week's words contains this root? How is the meaning of* directing *related to the Latin root* directus?

→ Have partners use a print or online dictionary to find other words that contain the Latin root *directus*.

→ Have students write each word in their word study notebook.

DAY 3

Reinforce the Words

Review last week's and this week's vocabulary words. Have students orally complete each sentence stem.

1. A conductor has experience <u>directing</u> a _____.
2. I saw a shiny _____ <u>gleaming</u> in the water.
3. We <u>scouted</u> our backyard for a good place to _____.
4. The <u>decade</u> we are living in began in the year _____.
5. The baby <u>squirmed</u> in her _____.
6. My dad loves <u>tinkering</u> with _____ in our garage.

DAY 4

Connect to Writing

→ Have students write sentences in their word study notebooks using this week's vocabulary.

→ Tell them to write sentences that provide word information they learned from this week's readings.

→ **ELL** Provide the Day 3 sentence stems 1–6 for students needing extra support.

Write About Vocabulary Have students write something they learned from this week's words in their word study notebook. For example, they might write about how *technology* makes their lives easier or better or how *tinkering* can lead to an invention.

DAY 5

Word Squares

Ask students to create Word Squares for each vocabulary word.

→ In the first square, students write the word. (example: *squirmed*)

→ In the second square, students write their own definition of the word and any related words, such as synonyms. (example: *twisted, wiggled*)

→ In the third square, students draw a simple illustration that will help them remember the word. (example: a wiggly worm)

→ In the fourth square, students write nonexamples, including antonyms for the word. (example: *stood still, didn't move*)

→ Have partners compare and discuss their Word Squares.

SYNONYMS

Remind students to look for synonyms to help figure out the meaning of unfamiliar words.

→ Display **Your Turn Practice Book** pages 173–174. Read the second paragraph. Model finding the meaning of *pleaded* using the synonym *begged*.

→ Have students complete page 177, then use synonyms to define *toiled, scowled,* and *ticked* on pages 173–174, using a dictionary to confirm meanings.

SHADES OF MEANING

Help students generate words related to *gleaming*. Draw a synonym/antonym scale.

→ Discuss the meaning of *gleaming*. Ask students to find synonyms, such as *brilliant,* and antonyms, such as *dull*.

→ Discuss where each word should go on the scale. Note that there may be multiple correct answers.

→ Ask students to copy the words in their word study notebook.

MORPHOLOGY

Use *decade* as a springboard for students to learn more words. Draw a word web. Write *deca* in the center oval. Write *decade* in one of the outer ovals.

→ Explain that *deca* is a Greek root that means "ten."

→ Ask partners to search for words that contain the root *deca* in a print or online dictionary, such as *decagon* or *decathlon*.

→ Discuss the meanings and add the words to the web.

→ Approaching Level

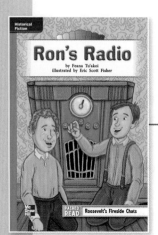

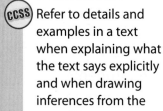

Lexile 620
TextEvaluator™ 31

OBJECTIVES

CCSS Refer to details and examples in a text when explaining what the text says explicitly and when drawing inferences from the text. **RL.4.1**

CCSS Compare and contrast the point of view from which different stories are narrated, including the difference between first- and third-person narrations. **RL.4.6**

CCSS Demonstrate understanding of words by relating them to their opposites (antonyms) and to words with similar but not identical meanings (synonyms). **L.4.5c**

Leveled Reader:
Ron's Radio

Leveled Readers

Before Reading

Preview and Predict

Have students read the Essential Question. Then have students read the title and table of contents of *Ron's Radio*. Have students make a prediction about what the story will be about and share it with a partner.

Review Genre: Historical Fiction

Review with students that historical fiction is a form of fiction that is set in a certain time in the past. It includes characters, settings, and events that could exist in real life. As they preview the book, have students identify features of historical fiction in *Ron's Radio*.

During Reading

Close Reading

Note Taking Ask students to use their graphic organizer while they read.

Pages 2–4 *What does the use of the pronouns* his *and* he *tell you about the narrator of the story?* (The story is told by a third-person narrator.) *Turn to a partner and tell a clue that the narrator's point of view about the boys is that they are not careful.* (The boys ruined a clock.)

Pages 5–8 *Do you think Ron will touch the radio? Turn to a partner and make a prediction.* (For example: Yes, I think Ron will touch the radio.)

Page 9 *Find a word that has a similar meaning to* present *in the second paragraph on page 9.* (current) *Use this information to define* current. (*Current* means "up-to-date" or "in the present.")

Use Graphic Organizer

Pages 10–12 *Confirm or revise your prediction about Ron and the radio.* (For example: My prediction was correct. Ron touched the radio.) *Now predict how Ron's parents will react to the problem with the radio.* (For example: I think Ron's parents will be angry.)

Pages 13–15 *Confirm or revise your prediction.* (For example: My prediction was incorrect. Ron's parents were "sad and very quiet.") *How did Ron's father's attitude change throughout the story?* (At first, he didn't want Ron touching the radio at all. At the end, he decided Ron should get to have his own radio.)

After Reading

Respond to Reading Have students complete Respond to Reading on page 16 after they have finished reading.

Analytical Writing **Write About Reading** Have students work with a partner to write a short paragraph. They should focus on how the story would change if told from Ron's dad's point of view.

Fluency: Expression

Model Model reading page 3 with proper expression. Next, reread the page aloud and have students read along with you.

Apply Have students practice reading with a partner.

Literature Circles

Ask students to conduct a literature circle using the Thinkmark questions to guide the discussion. You may wish to have a whole-class discussion on how new information and technology has affected students' lives in the classroom.

Level Up

Level-up lessons available online.

IF students read the Approaching Level fluently and answered the questions

THEN pair them with students who have proficiently read the On Level and have students

• echo-read the On Level main selection with their partners.

• use self-stick notes to mark at least one new detail they would like to discuss with partners.

PAIRED READ

"Roosevelt's Fireside Chats"

Leveled Reader

Make Connections: Write About It *Analytical Writing*

Before reading, ask students to note that the genre of this text is expository, which means it explains about a topic. Then discuss the Essential Question. After reading, ask students to discuss how technology affected the families' lives.

A C T Access Complex Text

The On Level challenges students by including more **domain-specific words** and **complex sentence structures**.

✏ *Analytical Writing*

COMPARE TEXTS

→ Have students use text evidence to show how inventions change people's lives.

Approaching Level
Phonics/Decoding

DECODE WORDS WITH /ū/

TIER **2**

OBJECTIVES

 Use combined knowledge of all letter-sound correspondences, syllabication patterns, and morphology to read accurately unfamiliar multisyllabic words in context and out of context. **RF.4.3a**

Decode words with /ū/.

 I Do Display the **Sound-Spelling Card** for *cube* and remind students of the sound spellings of long *u*: *u, u_e, ue,* and *ew*. Write *cube* on the board, read it aloud, and underline the *u_e* spelling. Repeat with *mute* and *few*.

 We Do Write *use, cue,* and *music* on the board. Model how to decode the first word. Have students identify the long *u* vowel sound and its spelling. Students can read the rest of the words aloud and identify the spellings for long *u*.

 You Do Add these words to the board: *argue, huge,* and *pupil*. Have students read each word aloud and identify the spelling for long *u*. Point to the words in random order for students to read chorally. Repeat several times.

REVIEW WORDS WITH /ü/, /ū/, AND /u̇/

TIER **2**

OBJECTIVES

Use combined knowledge of all letter-sound correspondences, syllabication patterns, and morphology (e.g., roots and affixes) to read accurately unfamiliar multisyllabic words in context and out of context. **RF.4.3a**

Decode words with /ü/, /ū/, and /u̇/.

 I Do Display the **Sound-Spelling Cards** *spoon* and *book* along with *cube,* and review the sound spellings for /ü/, /ū/, and /u̇/. Write example words for /ü/ and /u̇/ on the board. Underline the sound spellings for /ü/: *oo* as in *soon, u_e* as in *tube, u* as in *truth, ew* as in *blew, ue* as in *blue, ui* as in *fruit, ou* as in *group*; and for /u̇/: *oo* as in *cook* and *ou* as in *could*. Then remind students that short *u* vowel sound is also spelled *u, o, oo,* and *ou* in words such as *under, cover, flood,* and *tough*.

 We Do Display **Word-Building Cards** *car, con, room, class, toon,* and *clude*. Help students use the word parts to build multisyllabic words: *cartoon, conclude,* and *classroom*. Guide students as they decode the syllables in each word. Write these words on the board, separated into syllables to help students read the words one syllable at a time: *soon/er, re/grew, blue/bird, fruit/ful, re/group, use/ful, in/clude,* and *wood/en*. Have students decode the words.

 You Do Add the following examples to the board: *rude/ness, re/new,* and *foot/ball*. Ask students to decode each word. Point to the words on the board in random order for students to choral-read. Repeat several times.

PRACTICE WORDS WITH /ü/, /ū/, AND /ů/

OBJECTIVES

 CCSS Use combined knowledge of all letter-sound correspondences, syllabication patterns, and morphology to read accurately unfamiliar multisyllabic words in context and out of context. **RF.4.3a**

Decode words with /ü/, /ū/, and /ů/.

I Do Display the **Sound-Spelling Cards** *spoon, cube,* and *book* and review the sound spellings for /ü/, /ū/, and /ů/. Write *through, few,* and *look* on the board. Read them aloud. Point out the vowel sound and sound spelling in each: *through*: /ü/ spelled *ou*; *few*: /ū/ spelled *ew*; *look*: /ů/spelled *oo*.

We Do Write the words *suited, toothache, July, woolen, tunes, zoom, spool,* and *juice.* Model how to decode the first word, then guide students as they decode the remaining words. Divide each word into syllables using the syllable-scoop technique to help students read one syllable at a time.

You Do Afterward, point to the words in random order for students to choral-read.

CONSONANT + *le* SYLLABLES

OBJECTIVES

CCSS Use combined knowledge of all letter-sound correspondences, syllabication patterns, and morphology (e.g., roots and affixes) to read accurately unfamiliar multisyllabic words in context and out of context. **RF.4.3a**

Decode words with consonant +*le* syllables.

I Do Remind students that every syllable has one vowel sound. Then tell them that when a word ends in *le*, the consonant before it and the letters *le* form the final syllable. On the board, write *table, uncle, riddle, ruffle, giggle, little,* and *puzzle.* Read each word aloud and underline the consonant + *le* syllable. Remind students that this rule can also apply to different spellings, such as *al, el, il,* or *ol,* as in *total, channel, pencil,* and *symbol.*

We Do Write *candle* and *cancel* on the board. Model how to decode the words. Give other examples of words with consonant + *le* syllables. Guide students as they decode these words. Use the syllable-scoop technique to help students read one syllable at a time.

You Do Write the words *mantle, maple, fable, bridle,* and *title* on the board. Have students identify the sound spellings for the consonant + *le* syllables. Point to the words in random order for students to choral-read.

ELL ENGLISH LANGUAGE LEARNERS

For the **ELLs** who need **phonics, decoding,** and **fluency** practice, use scaffolding methods as necessary to ensure students understand the meaning of the words. Refer to the **Language Transfers Handbook** for phonics elements that may not transfer in students' native languages.

→ # Approaching Level

Vocabulary

REVIEW HIGH-FREQUENCY WORDS

 TIER 2

OBJECTIVES

 Read with sufficient accuracy and fluency to support comprehension. Read on-level text with purpose and understanding. **RF.4.4a**

Review high-frequency words.

I Do Use **Word Cards 141–150**. Display one word at a time, following the routine:

Display the word. Read the word. Then spell the word.

We Do Ask students to state the word and spell the word with you. Model using the word in a sentence and have students repeat after you.

You Do Display the word. Ask students to say the word then spell it. When completed, quickly flip through the word card set as students choral-read the words. Provide opportunities for students to use the words in speaking and writing. For example, provide sentence starters such as *On Saturdays, many people* _____. Ask students to write each word in their Writer's Notebook.

REVIEW VOCABULARY WORDS

 TIER 2

OBJECTIVES

 Acquire and use accurately grade-appropriate general academic and domain-specific words and phrases, including those that signal precise actions, emotions, or states of being and that are basic to a particular topic. **L.4.6**

I Do Display each **Visual Vocabulary Card** and state the word. Explain how the photograph illustrates the word. State the example sentence and repeat the word.

We Do Point to the word on the card and read the word with students. Ask them to repeat the word. Engage students in structured partner-talk about the image as prompted on the back of the vocabulary card.

You Do Display each visual in random order, hiding the word. Have students match the definitions and context sentences of the words to the visuals displayed.

IDENTIFY RELATED WORDS

OBJECTIVES

CCSS Acquire and use accurately grade-appropriate general academic and domain-specific words and phrases, including those that signal precise actions, emotions, or states of being and that are basic to a particular topic. **L.4.6**

 I Do Display the **Visual Vocabulary Card** for the word *decade*. Say the word set *year, decade, blue, century*.

Point out that the word *blue* does not belong.

 We Do Display the vocabulary card for the word *directing*. Say aloud the word set *commanding, ordering, following, directing*. With students, identify the word that does not belong and discuss why.

 You Do Using the word sets below, display the remaining cards one at a time and say aloud the word set. Ask students to identify the word that does not belong.

shining, dull, gleaming, glowing   *scouted, investigated, ignored, looked*

turned, twisted, squirmed, talked   *puttering, fixing, breaking, tinkering*

CONTEXT CLUES: SYNONYMS

OBJECTIVES

CCSS Demonstrate understanding of words by relating them to their opposites (antonyms) and to words with similar but not identical meanings (synonyms). **L.4.5c**

Use synonyms as context clues to determine the meaning of unfamiliar words.

 I Do Display the Comprehension and Fluency passage on **Approaching Reproducibles** pages 173–174. Read aloud the second paragraph. Point to the word *pleaded*. Explain to students that sometimes authors will include synonyms, or two words that have the same or similar meanings, in their writing. Remind them that they can use synonyms as context clues for understanding the meaning of an unfamiliar word.

Think Aloud I am not sure of the meaning of the word *pleaded*, but I see that Leonardo "begged and pleaded" with his father to get him a suit of armor. I know that *begged* means to ask for something strongly, or to make a strong request. The word *pleaded* must have a similar meaning.

 We Do Ask students to point to the word *scowled* on the same page. With students, discuss how the synonym *frowned* can help you figure out its meaning. Write the definition of the word on the board.

 You Do Have students finish reading the passage. Then have students find the meanings of *focus* on page 173 and *humble* on page 174 using synonyms in the text as context clues (*concentration, modest*).

Approaching Level

Comprehension

FLUENCY

OBJECTIVES

CCSS Read on-level prose and poetry orally with accuracy, appropriate rate, and expression on successive readings. **RF.4.4b**

Read fluently with accurate expression.

 I Do Explain that reading a selection out loud is not just about getting the words right. When reading dialogue in a story, readers should talk the way a character would and express the same emotions as the character. Readers can change their tone and inflections to show these emotions. Read the dialogue on the first page of the Comprehension and Fluency passage on **Approaching Reproducibles** pages 173–174. Point out how you paid attention to punctuation and descriptions when reading aloud.

 We Do Read the story aloud and have students repeat each line of dialogue after you, using the same expression. Explain that you emphasized certain words and phrases to show how the characters talk.

 You Do Have partners take turns reading dialogue from the Approaching Reproducibles passage. Remind them to focus on their expression. Listen in and provide corrective feedback by modeling proper fluency as needed.

TIER 2

IDENTIFY PRONOUNS IN NARRATION

OBJECTIVES

CCSS Compare and contrast the point of view from which different stories are narrated, including the difference between the first- and third-person narrations. **RL.4.6**

Identify third-person pronouns in a text.

 I Do Review personal pronouns with students. Explain that readers can determine the point of view of a story from the personal pronouns in the narration. If the narrator uses the first-person pronoun *I* to describe events, then the point of view is first person. If the narrator uses third-person pronouns to refer to the characters, then the point of view is third-person.

 We Do Read the first page of the Comprehension and Fluency passage in **Approaching Reproducibles.** Reread a detail from the story, such as, "He was excited to work on his latest invention." Help students understand that *he* is a third-person pronoun and indicates that the story is told from the third-person point of view.

 You Do Have students identify examples of pronouns that the narrator uses, such as, "He wasn't hurt" and "She picked up the mechanical knight's arm from the ground." Help students identify that these are third-person pronouns.

TIER 2

REVIEW POINT OF VIEW

OBJECTIVES

 Compare and contrast the point of view from which different stories are narrated, including the difference between the first- and third-person narrations. **RL.4.6**

 I Do

Remind students that narrator's point of view is the narrator's thoughts and feelings about the characters and events in a story. Explain that in a story narrated in the third-person point of view, the narrator is not a character in the story.

 We Do

Read the first two paragraphs of the Comprehension and Fluency passage on **Approaching Reproducibles** pages 173–174. Pause to point out that the narrator refers to Leonardo as "he." Help students understand that this is an example of a third-person narrator's point of view. Ask students to explain the narrator's thoughts and feelings about the character Leonardo. Students should support their answers with text evidence.

 You Do

Have students read the passage to find a second example of the third-person narrator's thoughts or feelings about a character. Ask students to explain how the narrator thinks or feels about the character.

SELF-SELECTED READING

OBJECTIVES

 Compare and contrast the point of view from which different stories are narrated, including the difference between the first- and third-person narrations. **RL.4.6**

Make, confirm, or revise predictions in a text to increase understanding.

Read Independently

Have students choose a historical fiction story for sustained silent reading. Remind students that:

→ personal pronouns indicate the point of view of a story.

→ they should use clues from the story and their own experiences to make predictions, and then confirm and revise their predictions to help them understand and remember why events happen in a certain way.

Read Purposefully

Have students record details and point of view on a Point of View Chart. After they finish, they can conduct a Book Talk, telling about the books they read and comparing and contrasting the points of view.

→ Students should share their charts and answer this question: *What was the most interesting character or historical event in this book?*

→ They should also tell the group if they revised or confirmed their predictions about the story's events to increase their understanding.

On Level

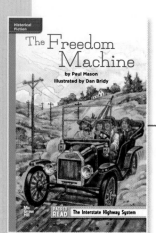

Lexile 690
TextEvaluator™ 44

OBJECTIVES

 Refer to details and examples in a text when explaining what the text says explicitly and when drawing inferences from the text. **RL.4.1**

(CCSS) Compare and contrast the point of view from which different stories are narrated, including the difference between first- and third-person narrations. **RL.4.6**

(CCSS) Demonstrate understanding of words by relating them to their opposites (antonyms) and to words with similar but not identical meanings (synonyms). **L.4.5c**

Leveled Reader:
The Freedom Machine

Leveled Readers

Before Reading

Preview and Predict

Have students read the Essential Question. Then have students read the title and table of contents of *The Freedom Machine*. Have students make a prediction about what the story will be about and share it with a partner.

Review Genre: Historical Fiction

Review with students that historical fiction is a form of fiction that is set in a certain time in the past. It includes characters, settings, and events that could exist in real life. As they preview the book, have students identify features of historical fiction in *The Freedom Machine*.

During Reading

Close Reading

Note Taking Ask students to use their graphic organizer while they read.

Use Graphic Organizer

Pages 2–4 *What does the use of the pronouns* I, my, *and* me *tell you about the narrator of the story?* (The story is told by a first-person narrator.) *Paraphrase the narrator's point of view about cars.* (The narrator is excited about how cars could change her life.)

Pages 5–7 *Do you think Alice will ever get a ride in the car? Turn to a partner and make a prediction.* (For example: I predict that Alice will ride in the car.)

Pages 8–9 *Confirm or revise your prediction about whether Alice will get to ride in the car.* (For example: My prediction was correct. Alice gets to ride in the car.) *How will the ride go based on what you have read?* (For example: I think the car ride will be disappointing for Alice because the car has a problem with the radiator.)

Pages 10–11 *What word means almost the same as* concerned *on page 10.* (worried) *Use this information to define the word to a partner.* (*Concerned* means "worried" or "troubled.")

Pages 12–15 *How did Alice's dad's thoughts about cars change throughout the story?* (He was skeptical about why people needed cars. By the end, he grew to see how cars could make his family's lives better.) *How do you think the car will affect the family and Mrs. Williams in the future?* (For example: The car will allow them to travel.)

After Reading

Respond to Reading Have students complete Respond to Reading on page 16 after they have finished reading.

Write About Reading Have students work with a partner to write a short paragraph. They should focus on how the story would change if told from Alice's father's point of view.

Fluency: Expression

Model Model reading page 3 with proper expression. Next, reread the page aloud and have students read along with you.

Apply Have students practice reading with a partner.

PAIRED READ

"The Interstate Highway System"

Leveled Reader

Make Connections: Write About It

Before reading, ask students to note that the genre of this text is expository topic. Then discuss the Essential Question. After reading, ask students to use "The Interstate Highway System" to discuss how cars affected the lives of the characters in *The Freedom Machine*.

Analytical Writing

COMPARE TEXTS

→ Have students use text evidence to show how new inventions change people's lives.

Literature Circles

Ask students to conduct a literature circle using the Thinkmark questions to guide the discussion. You may wish to have a whole-class discussion on what students' lives would be like without the invention of cars.

Level Up

Level-up lessons available online.

IF students read the On Level fluently and answered the questions

THEN pair them with students who have proficiently read Beyond Level and have students

• partner-read the Beyond Level main selection.

• list vocabulary words they find difficult and look them.

A C T Access Complex Text

The Beyond Level challenges students by including more **domain-specific words** and **complex sentence structures**.

On Level

Vocabulary

REVIEW VOCABULARY WORDS

OBJECTIVES

 Acquire and use accurately grade-appropriate general academic and domain-specific words and phrases, including those that signal precise actions, emotions, or states of being (e.g., *quizzed, whined, stammered*) and that are basic to a particular topic (e.g., *wildlife, conservation,* and *endangered* when discussing animal preservation). **L.4.6**

 Use the **Visual Vocabulary Cards** to review key selection words *decade, directing, gleaming, scouted, squirmed,* and *tinkering*. Point to each word, read it aloud, and have students chorally repeat it.

 Ask these questions and help students respond and explain their answers.

→ Will the year 2020 be the beginning of a new *decade*?

→ Who does the *directing* in a movie or play?

 Have students respond to these questions and explain their answers.

→ What can you see *gleaming* in a city at night?

→ What have you *scouted* for in a crowded room?

→ Why would a mouse have *squirmed* through a hole?

→ Why would a mechanic be *tinkering* with a car engine?

CONTEXT CLUES: SYNONYMS

OBJECTIVES

 Demonstrate understanding of words by relating them to their opposites (antonyms) and to words with similar but not identical meanings (synonyms). **L.4.5c**

Use synonyms as context clues in a text.

 Remind students that they can often figure out the meaning of an unfamiliar word by identifying a synonym in the same paragraph. Model using the Comprehension and Fluency passage on **Your Turn Practice Book** pages 173–174.

Think Aloud I want to know what the word *pleaded* means in the text. I see that the author says that Leonardo "begged and pleaded" with his father. I think these words have similar meanings, so I think that *pleaded* means to ask in a strong or emotional way.

 Have students read the rest of the first page and find the word *focus*. Help students figure out the word's meaning using the synonym *concentration*.

 Have students work in pairs to determine the meaning of the words *scowled* on page 173 and *modest* on page 174 using synonyms in the text as context clues.

Comprehension

REVIEW POINT OF VIEW

OBJECTIVES

Compare and contrast the point of view from which different stories are narrated, including the difference between first- and third-person narrations. **RL.4.6**

I Do
Remind students that the point of view is the narrator's thoughts or feelings about the characters and events in the text. Explain that personal pronouns in the text can help indicate the point of view. For example, if the narrator tells the story using first-person pronouns, such as *I*, then the story is told by a first-person narrator. Remind students that a third-person narrator is not a character in the story.

We Do
Have a volunteer read the first paragraph of the Comprehension and Fluency passage on **Your Turn Practice Book** pages 173–174. Have students identify the pronoun *he* used to describe Leonardo. Then model how this pronoun allows the reader to determine the third-person point of view in this paragraph. With students, identify the narrator's point of view in the next paragraph.

You Do
Have partners identify the narrator's point of view in the rest of the passage. Then have them discuss how the narrator feels about Leonardo.

SELF-SELECTED READING

OBJECTIVES

Refer to details and examples in a text when explaining what the text says explicitly and when drawing inferences from the text. **RL.4.1**

Compare and contrast the point of view from which different stories are narrated, including the difference between first- and third-person narrations. **RL.4.6**

Make, confirm, or revise predictions in a text to increase understanding.

Read Independently

Have students choose a story of historical fiction for sustained silent reading.

→ Before they read, have students preview the book, reading the title and viewing the front and back cover.

→ As students read, remind them to make predictions about the characters and events in the story, and to revise or confirm their predictions as they continue reading.

Read Purposefully

Encourage students to read different stories of historical fiction in order to learn about a variety of subjects.

→ As students read, have them fill in the details and point of view on a Point of View Chart.

→ They can use this chart to help them write a summary of the book.

→ Ask students to share their reactions to the book with classmates.

→ Beyond Level

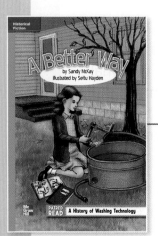

Lexile 790
TextEvaluator™ 37

OBJECTIVES

CCSS Refer to details and examples in a text when explaining what the text says explicitly and when drawing inferences from the text. **RL.4.1**

CCSS Compare and contrast the point of view from which different stories are narrated, including the difference between first- and third-person narrations. **RL.4.6**

CCSS Demonstrate understanding of words by relating them to their opposites (antonyms) and to words with similar but not identical meanings (synonyms). **L.4.5c**

Leveled Reader: *A Better Way*

Before Reading

Preview and Predict

Have students read the Essential Question. Have students read the title and table of contents of *A Better Way*. Have students make a prediction about what the story will be about and share it with a partner.

Review Genre: Historical Fiction

Review with students that historical fiction is a form of fiction that is set in a certain time in the past. It includes characters, settings, and events that could exist in real life. As they preview the book, have students identify features of historical fiction in *A Better Way*.

During Reading

Close Reading

Note Taking Ask students to use their graphic organizer while they read.

Pages 2–5 *What type of narrator does this story have?* (third-person) *How do you know?* (I see the pronouns *she* and *her*.) *How do you know the narrator's point of view about washing clothes?* (The narrator calls it "hard work" and describes how difficult it is to do.) *What is Wendy's defining character trait?* (She likes to invent things and build machines.) *Make a prediction about what Wendy will give her mother as a birthday gift.* (For example: I think Wendy will help her mother with the ironing.)

Pages 6–8 *Confirm or revise your prediction about Wendy's gift.* (For example: My prediction was correct, but I did not predict that Wendy's grandmother would also help with the ironing.) *Find a synonym for* glossy *on page 8 that helps you define the word.* (shining) *Use the synonym to define the word to a partner.* (*Glossy* means "shining" or "gleaming.")

Go Digital

Leveled Readers

Details
↓
| Point of View |

Use Graphic Organizer

Pages 9–11 *Turn to a partner and paraphrase the problem with Wendy's laundry machine.* (She can't fit a pipe for drainage without leaking.) *Make a prediction about whether Wendy will succeed with her invention.* (For example: I think Wendy will succeed with her invention because she is determined.)

Pages 12–15 *Confirm or revise your prediction about Wendy's machine.* (For example: My prediction was incorrect. Wendy did not invent a washing machine.) *How will the family's lives be different with the new washing machine?* (For example: Wendy's mother will not have to spend all day doing the laundry. She will have more free time.)

After Reading

Respond to Reading Have students complete Respond to Reading on page 16 after they have finished reading.

Analytical Writing **Write About Reading** Have students work with a partner to write a short paragraph. They should focus on how the story would change if told from Wendy's mother's point of view.

Fluency: Expression

Model Model reading page 5 with proper expression. Next, reread the page aloud and have students read along with you.

Apply Have students practice reading with a partner.

PAIRED READ

"The History of Washing Technology"

Make Connections: Write About It **Analytical Writing**

Before reading, ask students to note that the genre of this text is expository topic. Then discuss the Essential Question. After reading, ask students to use the information from "The History of Washing Technology" to expand their discussion of how washing machines affected people's lives in *A Better Way.*

Leveled Reader

Analytical Writing

COMPARE TEXTS

→ Have students use text evidence to show how new inventions change people's lives.

Literature Circles

Ask students to conduct a literature circle using the Thinkmark questions to guide the discussion. You may wish to have a whole-class discussion on which inventions and technology have most changed their lives.

Gifted and Talented

Synthesize Challenge students to predict the future of washing machines. Have students write a short paragraph and draw a diagram of the washing machine of the future. Invite volunteers to share their ideas with the class.

Beyond Level

Vocabulary

REVIEW DOMAIN-SPECIFIC WORDS

OBJECTIVES
Acquire and use accurately grade-appropriate general academic and domain-specific words and phrases, including those that signal precise actions, emotions, or states of being and that are basic to a particular topic. **L.4.6**

 Model Use the **Visual Vocabulary Cards** to review the meanings of the words *engineering* and *technology*. Write science-related sentences on the board using the words.

Write the words *improvement* and *invention* on the board and discuss the meanings with students. Then help students write sentences using these words.

 Apply Have students work in pairs to review the meanings of the words *industry* and *solution*. Then have partners write sentences about inventions using the words.

CONTEXT CLUES: SYNONYMS

OBJECTIVES
Demonstrate understanding of words by relating them to their opposites (antonyms) and to words with similar but not identical meanings (synonyms). **L.4.5c**

Use synonyms as context clues in a text.

 Model Read aloud the first two paragraphs of the Comprehension and Fluency passage on **Beyond Reproducibles** pages 173–174.

Think Aloud I want to understand the word *toiled*. I see that the author writes that Leonardo was "working on the new invention" and that "he toiled away on the knight." I know what *worked* means. I think that *toiled* is a synonym and has a similar, but stronger meaning. I think that *toiled* means to do difficult work for a long time.

 Apply Have pairs of students read the rest of the passage. Ask them to use synonyms to figure out the meanings of the words *scowled* and *modest,* as well as any other words with synonyms they locate in the text.

 Independent Study Have partners research the inventions of Leonardo da Vinci or have them research a person or event in history that they read about during the week. Each pair should write a paragraph about how the invention or event affected people's lives. Then have them discuss their findings with other partners.

Comprehension

REVIEW POINT OF VIEW

OBJECTIVES

 Compare and contrast the point of view from which different stories are narrated, including the difference between first- and third-person narrations. **RL.4.6**

 Model Remind students that point of view is how the narrator thinks or feels about the characters and events in a story. Tell them that they can determine the narrator's point of view from the personal pronouns that refer to the characters in the story.

Have students read the first two paragraphs of the Comprehension and Fluency passage on **Beyond Reproducibles** pages 173–174. Ask questions to facilitate discussion about the story's point of view, such as *What do we learn about Leonardo in these paragraphs? Is the narrator a character in the story?* Students should support their responses with details from the text.

 Apply Have students independently fill in a Point of View Chart with examples of the narrator's point of view in the text. Then have partners discuss how the third-person point of view allows the reader to learn the narrator's thoughts and feelings about Leonardo and Albiera.

SELF-SELECTED READING

OBJECTIVES

 Compare and contrast the point of view from which different stories are narrated, including the difference between first- and third-person narrations. **RL.4.6**

Make, confirm, or revise predictions in a text to increase understanding.

Read Independently

Have students choose a story of historical fiction for sustained silent reading.

→ As students read, have them fill in a Point of View Chart.

→ Remind them to make predictions as they read sections of the text.

Read Purposefully

Encourage students to keep a reading journal. Ask them to read different books in order to learn about a variety of subjects.

→ Students can write summaries of the books in their journals.

→ Ask students to share their reactions to the books with classmates.

 Synthesize Challenge partners to write questions and responses in an interview format for a historical figure they have read about during the week. Encourage them to focus on the weekly concept, breakthroughs.

English Language Learners

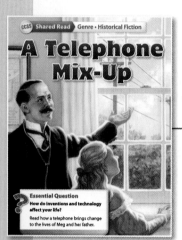

Reading/Writing Workshop

OBJECTIVES

Refer to details and examples in a text when explaining what the text says explicitly and when drawing inferences from the text. **RL.4.1**

LANGUAGE OBJECTIVE

Identify the point of view of a text.

ACADEMIC LANGUAGE

- *expository, point of view, prediction*
- Cognates: *expositivo predicción*

Shared Read
A Telephone Mix-Up

View "A Telephone Mix-Up"

Before Reading

Build Background

Read the Essential Question: How do inventions and technology affect your life?

→ Explain the meaning of the Essential Question. Have students point to or name inventions in the classroom that have changed their lives. Point out the cognates *invenciones* and *tecnología*.

→ **Model an answer:** *The Internet is an invention that has affected, or changed, our lives in many ways. It helps us find information about different topics. It helps us to keep in touch with people through e-mail. It helps us learn more about people and places around the world.*

→ Ask students a question that ties the Essential Question to their own background knowledge: *Think of an invention that you use often. With a partner, discuss how your life would be different without this invention.* Call on several pairs to share with the class.

During Reading

Interactive Question-Response

→ Ask questions that help students understand the meaning of the text after each paragraph.

→ Reinforce the meanings of key vocabulary.

→ Ask students questions that require them to use key vocabulary.

→ Reinforce strategies and skills of the week by modeling.

Page 267

Paragraph 1

How can you tell this story takes place long ago?
(The clothes are from long ago. The phone is a new invention.) *What new invention is arriving in Centerburg, Ohio?* (the telephone)

Have partners choral read the paragraph. *How does Dr. Ericksen feels about the telephone?* (Dr. Ericksen is excited about the telephone. He believes it will save many lives.)

Show how "decade" is followed by the phrase "in just another ten years," which defines *decade*. Guide students to calculate how old they will be in a decade. *In a decade I will be ____ years old.*

Paragraph 2

Model Making Predictions *Does everyone in town like the telephone?* (no) *Why are they worried?* (They think telephones will cause people to stop visiting each other and stop writing letters.) *Do you think people will change how they feel?* Have students complete the frame: *I predict that the people of Centerburg will ____.* (Possible answer: accept the telephone.) *Let's continue reading to confirm or revise our predictions.*

Paragraph 3

Explain that "progess marched on" means that "things are improving or moving along." *Which places in town have a telephone?* (Mr. Kane's general store, the hotel, the newspaper office)

Paragraph 4

Demonstrate *squirming. Meg is restless and excited. Why do you think she is squirming in her seat?* (She can't wait to get home to see the telephone.)

Page 268

Paragraph 2

Describe how the telephone looks. (It has a wood box and a heavy black receiver on a hook.)

How is it this phone different from the phones you use? (Possible answer: My phone is much smaller and lighter.)

Explain and Model Synonyms Point to and say the word *magnificence.* Have students repeat. *Writers sometimes use context clues, such as synonyms, to help readers define words. Beauty is a synonym for* magnificence.

Paragraphs 4–7

Have student take turns reading the dialogue. Explain and demonstrate what static sounds like. *What happens during the conversation?* (There is confusion. They cannot hear the voice on the phone very well and miss part of the conversation.)

Page 269

Paragraphs 1–7

What does Dr. Ericksen find at the Turners'? (a sick baby goat) *Why is it a mix-up?* (Dr. Ericksen treats people, not animals.) *What is another word for mix-up?* (mistake, confusion)

Look back on page 268. How did the telephone mix-up happen? (Dr. Ericksen could not hear Mrs. Kane clearly on the phone. Mrs. Kane was trying to call the veterinarian.)

Predict how you think the telephone will be useful in Centerburg. Monitor discussions and encourage students to use text evidence to support their responses.

After Reading

Make Connections

→ Review the Essential Question: How do inventions and technology affect your life?

→ Make text connections.

→ Have students complete **ELL Reproducibles** pages 173–175.

→ English Language Learners

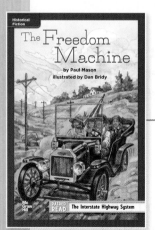

Lexile 540
TextEvaluator™ 27

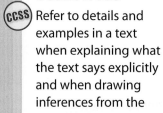

OBJECTIVES

CCSS Refer to details and examples in a text when explaining what the text says explicitly and when drawing inferences from the text. **RL.4.1**

CCSS Compare and contrast the point of view from which different stories are narrated, including the difference between first- and third-person narrations. **RL.4.6**

CCSS Demonstrate understanding of words by relating them to their opposites (antonyms) and to words with similar but not identical meanings (synonyms). **L.4.5c**

Leveled Reader:
The Freedom Machine

Before Reading

Preview

→ Read the Essential Question: How do inventions and technology affect your life?

→ Refer to Changing Lives: *Which technological invention has helped you do new things?*

→ Preview *The Freedom Machine* and "The Interstate Highway System": *Our purpose for reading is to learn how the invention of cars changes the lives of a family in the past.*

Vocabulary

Use the **Visual Vocabulary Cards** to pre-teach the ELL vocabulary: *afford, bothered.* Use the routine found on the cards.

During Reading

Interactive Question-Response

Note Taking Have students use their graphic organizer in **ELL Reproducibles** page 172. Use the questions below as you read each section with students.

Pages 2–4 Have students look for the pronouns *I, my,* and *me* in the first paragraph on page 2. Help students fill in the sentence frame: *I know this story uses a _____ narrator because I see the pronouns _____.* (first-person; I, me, and my) *Who is the narrator?* (a young girl)

Pages 5–7 *Is Alice excited about the car?* (yes) *Is her father?* (no) *Make a prediction about whether Alice will ride in the car. I predict that Alice will _____.* (ride in the car) *Let's read the next chapter to confirm or revise our predictions.*

Pages 8–9 *Was your prediction correct?* (Possible answer: My prediction was correct. Alice got to ride in the car.) *What is the problem on page 9?* (Steam was coming out of the car.) *Make a prediction about how they might fix the car. I predict that _____.* (Alice's dad will fix the car)

Go Digital

Leveled Readers

Use Graphic Organizer

Pages 10–12 *Confirm or revise your predictions.* (Possible answer: My prediction was correct. Alice's dad fixed the car.)

Pages 12–15 Point out that *crammed* and *squeezed* on page 12 are synonyms. Crammed *means the same as* _____. (squeezed)
How do you think the car will affect the family and Mrs. Williams? I predict that _____. (Possible answer: the family will be able to go on trips.)

After Reading

Respond to Reading Help students complete the graphic organizer on **ELL Reproducibles** page 172. Revisit the Essential Question. Have partners summarize and answer the Text Evidence Questions.

Analytical Writing **Write About Reading** Have partners write about how the story would be different if it were told from Alice's father's point of view. Remind students to write about how her father thinks and feels.

Fluency: Expression

Model Model reading page 3 with proper expression. Next, reread the page aloud and have students read along with you.

Apply Have students practice reading with a partner.

PAIRED READ

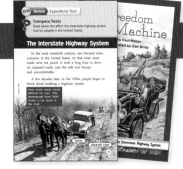

Leveled Reader

"The Interstate Highway System"

Make Connections:
Write About It *Analytical Writing*

Before reading, ask students to note that the genre of this text is expository. The text will explain the effects of the interstate highway on people in the United States. Then discuss the Essential Question. After reading, ask students to use "The Interstate Highway System" to expand their discussion of how cars affected people's lives in *The Freedom Machine.*

✏️ *Analytical Writing*

COMPARE TEXTS

→ Have students use text evidence to show how new inventions change people's lives.

Literature Circles

Ask students to conduct a literature circle using the Thinkmark questions to guide the discussion. You may wish to have a whole-class discussion about what students' lives would be like without the invention of cars.

Level Up

Level-up lessons available online.

IF students read the **ELL Level** fluently and answered the questions

THEN pair them with students who have proficiently read **On Level** and have students

• echo-read the **On Level** main selection with their partners.

• list difficult words, phrases, and sentences and discuss them with their partners.

A C T ccess Complex Text

The **On Level** challenges students by including more **complex sentence structures** and **academic language**.

English Language Learners
Vocabulary

PRETEACH VOCABULARY

OBJECTIVES

 CCSS Acquire and use accurately grade-appropriate general academic and domain-specific words and phrases, including those that signal precise actions, emotions, or states of being and that are basic to a particular topic. **L.4.6**

 I Do Preteach vocabulary from "A Telephone Mix-Up," following the Vocabulary Routine on the **Visual Vocabulary Cards** for the words *decade, directing, engineering, gleaming, scouted, squirmed, technology,* and *tinkering.*

 We Do After completing the Vocabulary Routine for each word, point to the word on the card and read it aloud. Ask students to repeat the word.

 You Do Have students work with a partner to use two or more words in sentences or questions. Then have each pair read the sentences aloud.

Beginning	Intermediate	Advanced/High
Help students write the sentences correctly and read them aloud.	Ask students to write a sentence for each word.	Challenge students to write a sentence and a question for each word.

REVIEW VOCABULARY

OBJECTIVES

CCSS Acquire and use accurately grade-appropriate general academic and domain-specific words and phrases, including those that signal precise actions, emotions, or states of being and that are basic to a particular topic. **L.4.6**

LANGUAGE OBJECTIVE

Use vocabulary words.

 I Do Review the previous week's vocabulary words. The words can be reviewed over a few days. Read each word aloud, pointing to the word on the **Visual Vocabulary Card**. Have students repeat after you. Then follow the Vocabulary Routine on the back of each card.

 We Do Tell students you are thinking of a word. Have them ask yes/no questions to guess the word. Then ask a volunteer to use the word in a sentence.

 You Do Have partners take turns choosing a word and asking questions that help them guess the word. Have students use the word they guess in a sentence.

Beginning	Intermediate	Advanced/High
Help students ask each other questions. Then help them use the words in a sentence.	Give question starters: *Does it mean. . . ? Is it the same as. . . ? Does it sound like. . . ?*	Have students write a short paragraph using at least three words.

CONTEXT CLUES: SYNONYMS

OBJECTIVES

 Demonstrate understanding of words by relating them to their opposites (antonyms) and to words with similar but not identical meanings (synonyms). **L.4.5c**

LANGUAGE OBJECTIVE

Use synonyms as context clues to determine meaning.

 I Do

Read aloud the second paragraph of the Comprehension and Fluency passage on **ELL Reproducibles** pages 173–174. Point to the word *pleaded*. Explain that writers sometimes offer synonyms, or words with similar meanings, to help readers define difficult words.

Think Aloud I want to know what *pleaded* means. I see that Leonardo "begged and pleaded" with his father to get him a suit of armor. The words *begged* and *pleaded* are synonyms. I know that *begged* means to ask for something. The word *pleaded* must also mean to ask for something.

 We Do

Have students point to *scowled* in the third paragraph. Discuss how *frowned* has a similar meaning to *scowled*. Write the definition of the word.

 You Do

In pairs, have students use synonyms to figure out the meanings of *shock*, *teetered*, and *stacks*.

Beginning	Intermediate	Advanced/High
Help students locate each word and its synonym. Say each word aloud and define it for students.	Ask students to locate and read aloud the synonyms.	Have students find three more synonyms in the text.

ADDITIONAL VOCABULARY

OBJECTIVES

 Choose words and phrases to convey ideas precisely. **L.4.3a**

LANGUAGE OBJECTIVE

Use academic and high-frequency words.

 I Do

List academic and high-frequency words from "A Telephone Mix-Up" and *The Freedom Machine*: *benefits, common, freedom, trouble* and *useful*. Define each word: *Something is common if it appears or happens many times.*

We Do

Model using the words in a sentence: *Cats and dogs are common pets. Snow is common in the winter.* Then provide sentence frames and complete them with students: _____ *is a common way to greet someone.*

 You Do

Have pairs make their own sentence frames and share them with the class. Have the class complete the sentence frames.

Beginning	Intermediate	Advanced/High
Help students complete the sentence frames.	Provide sentence starters for students, if necessary.	Have students define the words they used.

English Language Learners
Writing/Spelling

WRITING TRAIT: IDEAS

OBJECTIVES

 Orient the reader by establishing a situation and introducing a narrator and/or characters; organize an event sequence that unfolds naturally. **W.4.3a**

LANGUAGE OBJECTIVE

Develop ideas to revise writing.

I Do Explain that writers often begin stories by introducing a problem that the main character faces and the setting, or when and where the story takes place. The events that follow make up the plot and show how the problem is solved. Read the Expert Model passage aloud. Help students identify the setting and an event.

We Do Read aloud passages from "A Telephone Mix-Up." Identify the events in the story and add them to a sequence chart. Model sentences to describe how the problem unfolds, using details from the chart.

You Do Have pairs use a sequence chart to write a short story about a missing object. Edit each pairs' writing. Then ask students to revise.

Beginning	Intermediate	Advanced/High
Have students copy the edited sentences.	Have students revise, adding details to the plot.	Have students discuss how they developed the plot.

SPELL WORDS WITH /ü/, /ù/, AND /ū/

OBJECTIVES

 Spell grade-appropriate words correctly, consulting references as needed. **L.4.2d**

LANGUAGE OBJECTIVE

Spell words with ü/, /ū/, and /ù/.

I Do Read aloud the Spelling Words on page T164, segmenting them into syllables, and attaching a spelling to each sound. Point out the sound spellings for /ü/, /ù/, and /ū/. Have students repeat the words.

We Do Read the Dictation Sentences on page T165 aloud for students. With each sentence, read the underlined word slowly, segmenting it into syllables. Have students repeat after you and write the word.

You Do Display the words. Have students exchange their list with a partner to check the spelling and write the words correctly.

Beginning	Intermediate	Advanced/High
Have students copy the words correctly and read the words aloud.	After students have corrected their words, have pairs quiz each other.	After they correct their words, have students use each word in a sentence.

Grammar

PRONOUN-VERB AGREEMENT

OBJECTIVES

 Ensure subject-verb and pronoun-antecedent agreement. **L.3.1f**

Use pronoun-verb agreement.

LANGUAGE OBJECTIVE

Write sentences.

Language Transfers Handbook

Speakers of Cantonese, Haitian Creole, Hmong, Korean, and Khmer may have difficulties with pronoun-verb agreement. Reinforce the use of -s in present tense, third-person form by helping students form sentences using the third-person form.

 I Do Point out that subject pronouns must agree with verbs in a sentence. Write on the board: _John kicks the ball. John and Mara kick the ball._ Underline and identify the subject of each sentence and point out subject-verb agreement. Write on the board: _He kicks the ball. They kick the ball._ Underline the pronouns and point out how each is the subject pronoun. Circle _kicks_ and explain how -s or -es is added to most verbs when the subject pronoun is _he, she,_ or _it_. Circle _kick_ and point out that -s or -es is not added to present-tense verbs when the subject pronouns are _I, we, you,_ and _they_. Then write sentences on the board to demonstrate subject-pronoun agreement with the irregular verbs _have_ and _be_.

We Do Write the sentence frames below on the board. Identify the subject pronoun in each sentence frame and circle it. Have volunteers fill in sentence frames with present-tense verbs. Then read the completed sentences aloud and have students repeat.

_They _____ the drums in the school band._

_She _____ beautiful pictures of animals._

_We _____ to school each weekday morning._

_We _____ fourth graders._

 You Do Have students work in pairs to write three sentences using subject pronouns and present-tense verbs.

Beginning	Intermediate	Advanced/High
Have students copy their sentences and help them underline the subject pronouns. Read the sentences aloud for students to repeat.	Have students underline the subject pronouns and circle the verbs in their sentences.	Have students correct each other's work, checking for pronoun-verb agreement.

For extra support, have students complete the activities in the **Grammar Practice Reproducibles** during the week, using the routine below:

→ Explain the grammar skill.

→ Model the first activity in the Grammar Practice Reproducibles.

→ Have the whole group complete the next couple of activities, then the rest with a partner.

→ Review the activities with correct answers.

PROGRESS MONITORING

Weekly Assessment

✓**COMPREHENSION:**	✓**VOCABULARY:**	✓**WRITING:**
Point of View **RL.4.6**	Context Clues: Synonyms **L.4.5c**	Writing About Text **RL.4.6, W.4.9a**

Assessment Includes

→ Pencil-and-paper administration

→ On-line administration

→ Approaching-Level Weekly Assessment also available

Fluency Goal 102 to 122 words correct per minute (WCPM)

Accuracy Rate Goal 95% or higher.

Administer oral reading fluency assessments using the following schedule:

→ **Weeks 1, 3, 5** Provide Approaching-Level students at least three oral reading fluency assessments during the unit.

→ **Weeks 2 and 4** Provide On-Level students at least two oral reading fluency assessments during the unit.

→ **Week 6** If necessary, provide Beyond-Level students an oral reading fluency assessment at this time.

Also Available: Selection Tests online PDFs

Go Digital! www.connected.mcgraw-hill.com

Using Assessment Results

TESTED SKILLS	If ...	Then ...
COMPREHENSION	Students answer 0–6 multiple-choice items correctly ...	... assign Lessons 37–39 on Point of View from the *Tier 2 Comprehension Intervention online PDFs.*
VOCABULARY	Students answer 0–6 multiple-choice items correctly ...	... assign Lesson 137 on Using Synonym and Antonym Clues from the *Tier 2 Vocabulary Intervention online PDFs.*
WRITING	Students score less than "3" on the constructed response ...	... assign Lessons 37–39 and/or Write About Reading Lesson 194 from the *Tier 2 Comprehension Intervention online PDFs.*
FLUENCY	Students have a WCPM score of 94–101 ...	... assign a lesson from Section 1 or 7–10 of the *Tier 2 Fluency Intervention online PDFs.*
	Students have a WCPM score of 0–93 ...	... assign a lesson from Sections 2–6 of the *Tier 2 Fluency Intervention online PDFs.*

Response to Intervention

Use the appropriate sections of the *Placement and Diagnostic Assessment* as well as students' assessment results to designate students requiring:

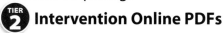 **Intervention Online PDFs**

 **WonderWorks Intervention Program**

Text Complexity Range for Grades 4–5

Lexile	
740	1010

TextEvaluator™

| 23 | 51 |

McGraw-Hill Reading
Wonders

Reading/Writing Workshop

Mc Graw Hill

TEACH AND MODEL

CCSS Shared Read ▸ Genre • Expository Text

Wonders of the Night Sky

As Earth **rotates** on its axis, day becomes night. Suddenly, a gallery of lights is revealed! You may see a beautiful **crescent** moon. Maybe you'll see one of the other **phases** of the moon. You may even see a **series** of lights spread across the sky like colored ribbons. For thousands of years, people have loved looking at the night sky. For almost as long, scientists have been trying to explain what they see.

Aurora Borealis

Every few years, an amazing light show is seen in the skies near the North Pole. It is known as "the northern lights," or the **aurora borealis** (uh-RAWR-uh bawr-ee-AL-is). Brilliant bands of green, yellow, red, and blue lights appear in the sky.

People used to believe the lights were caused by sunlight reflecting off polar ice caps. The theory was that when the light bounced back from the caps it created patterns in the sky. In fact, the lights happen because of magnetic attraction.

The sun constantly gives off a stream of electrically charged particles in every direction. These nearly invisible pieces of matter join into a stream called a solar wind. As Earth orbits the sun, solar winds reach Earth's magnetic field. As a result, electric charges occur that are sometimes strong enough to be seen from Earth. These electric charges cause the colorful bands of lights in the sky.

? Essential Question
How do you explain what you see in the sky?
Read about what causes some of the sights you see in the sky.

280

The aurora borealis above Hammerfest, Norway

281

✔ Vocabulary

astronomer

crescent

phases

rotates

series

sliver

specific

telescope

🔎 Close Reading of Complex Text

Shared Read "Wonders of the Night Sky," 280–283

Genre Expository Text

Lexile 880
(ETS) TextEvaluator™ 29

Minilessons

✔ **Comprehension Strategy** .... Ask and Answer Questions, T210–T211

✔ **Comprehension Skill** .... Cause and Effect, T212–T213

✔ **Genre** .... Expository Text, T214–T215

✔ **Vocabulary Strategy** .... Context Clues, T216–T217

✔ **Writing Traits** .... Word Choice, T222–T223

Grammar .... Possessive Pronouns, T226–T227

✔ Tested Skills CCSS

☞ **Go** Digital

www.connected.mcgraw-hill.com

APPLY WITH CLOSE READING

Literature Anthology

Complex Text

Why Does the Moon Change Shape?, 336–351

Genre Expository Text

Lexile 900

ETS *TextEvaluator* 22

PAIRED READ

"How It Came to Be," 352–355

Genre Myth

Lexile 910

ETS *TextEvaluator* 40

Differentiated Text

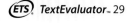
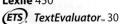

Leveled Readers *Include Paired Reads*

APPROACHING

Lexile 650

ETS *TextEvaluator* 21

ON LEVEL

Lexile 450

ETS *TextEvaluator* 30

BEYOND

Lexile 860

ETS *TextEvaluator* 29

ELL

Lexile 360

ETS *TextEvaluator* 27

Extended Complex Text

A Picture Book of Harry Houdini

Genre Nonfiction

Lexile 770

ETS *TextEvaluator* 41

The Moon and I

Genre Nonfiction

Lexile 870

ETS *TextEvaluator* 38

Classroom Library

Classroom Library lessons available online.

THE MOON AND I, Copyright © 1991 by Betsy Byars

TEACH AND MANAGE

How You Teach

INTRODUCE

Weekly Concept
Wonders in the Sky

Reading/Writing Workshop
276–277

TEACH

Close Reading
"Wonders of the Night Sky"

Minilessons
Ask and Answer Questions, Cause and Effect, Expository Text, Context Clues, Writing Traits

Reading/Writing Workshop
280–283

APPLY

Close Reading
Why Does the Moon Change Shape?

"How It Came to Be"

Literature Anthology
336–355

 Go Digital

 Interactive Whiteboard

 Interactive Whiteboard

 Mobile

How Students Practice

WEEKLY CONTRACT

PDF Online

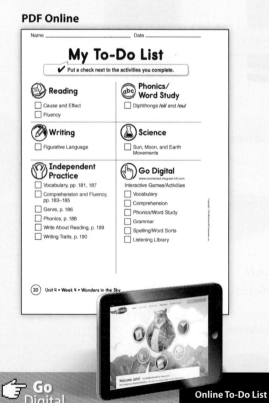

Name _____ Date _____

My To-Do List
✔ Put a check next to the activities you complete.

📖 **Reading**
☐ Cause and Effect
☐ Fluency

🔤 **Phonics/Word Study**
☐ Diphthongs /oi/ and /ou/

✏️ **Writing**
☐ Figurative Language

🔬 **Science**
☐ Sun, Moon, and Earth Movements

🙌 **Independent Practice**
☐ Vocabulary, pp. 181, 187
☐ Comprehension and Fluency, pp. 183–185
☐ Genre, p. 186
☐ Phonics, p. 188
☐ Write About Reading, p. 189
☐ Writing Traits, p. 190

🖐 **Go Digital**
www.connected.mcgraw-hill.com
Interactive Games/Activities
☐ Vocabulary
☐ Comprehension
☐ Phonics/Word Study
☐ Grammar
☐ Spelling/Word Sorts
☐ Listening Library

20 Unit 4 • Week 4 • Wonders in the Sky

LEVELED PRACTICE AND ONLINE ACTIVITIES

Your Turn Practice Book
181–190

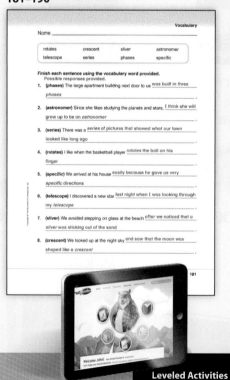

Name _____

Vocabulary

| rotates | crescent | sliver | astronomer |
| telescope | series | phases | specific |

Finish each sentence using the vocabulary word provided.
Possible responses provided.

1. (phases) The large apartment building next door to us *was built in three phases*

2. (astronomer) Since she likes studying the planets and stars, *I think she will grow up to be an astronomer*

3. (series) There was a *series of pictures that showed what our town looked like long ago*

4. (rotates) I like when the basketball player *rotates the ball on his finger*

5. (specific) We arrived at his house *easily because he gave us very specific directions*

6. (telescope) I discovered a new star *last night when I was looking through my telescope*

7. (sliver) We avoided stepping on glass at the beach *after we noticed that a sliver was sticking out of the sand*

8. (crescent) We looked up at the night sky *and saw that the moon was shaped like a crescent*

181

Leveled Readers

 Go Digital

Online To-Do List

Leveled Activities

Writer's Workspace

DIFFERENTIATE

SMALL GROUP INSTRUCTION
Leveled Readers

Mobile

INTEGRATE

Research and Inquiry
Research Eclipses, T220

Text Connections
Compare Information about
the Sky, T221

 Write About Reading
Write an Analysis, T221

**Online Research
and Writing**

ASSESS

Grade 4

Wonders

**Weekly
Assessment**

**Weekly Assessment
217–228**

**Online
Assessment**

LEVELED WORKSTATION CARDS

**More
Activities
on back**

19

Phases of the Moon

SCIENCE

JUNE

- From an Internet almanac, make copies of this month's calendar and next month's. Mark today's date and the date 30 days from now.

- Discuss methods you could use to record your observations.

16

Word Choice: Figurative Language

WRITING

Read Trisha's text. Identify the figurative language she used. Revise her text by adding more figurative language.

At ... the wide streets were

4

Context Clues

abc

PHONICS/WORD STUDY

barbecue

- Look up the words *rumble*, *stoops*, *barbecue*, and *strut* in a dictionary. Write a sentence for one. Include context clues to the word's meaning. (Example for *mango*: "He enjoyed eating the juicy sweet mango.")

- Write a paragraph using two of the other words. For the first word, include a context clue in a sentence other than the one in which the word is used. For the second word, include a definition or restatement as a clue to its meaning.

  You need
  20 Minutes
  > dictionary
  > paper, pencils

- Exchange paragraphs. Identify your partner's context clues.

Go Digital! www.connected.mcgraw-hill.com • Interactive Games and Activities • Grade 4
4

7

Cause and Effect

READING

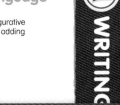

- Choose an informational text that you have enjoyed reading in class. As you reread, identify pairs of events that have cause-and-effect relationships.

- For each pair of events, write the cause on one side of a note card and its related effect on the other side.

- Take turns reading one side of a card and asking your partner to identify the cause or effect that goes with it.

  You need
  15 Minutes
  > informational text
  > note cards
  > pencils or pens

Go Digital! www.connected.mcgraw-hill.com • Interactive Games and Activities • Grade 4
7

DEVELOPING READERS AND WRITERS

Write About Reading • Analytical Writing

Write to Sources and Research

Paraphrase, T212–T213

Note Taking, T217B, T217R

Summarize, T217P, T217S

Cause and Effect, T217P

Make Connections: Essential Question, T217P, T217T, T221

Key Details, T217R, T217S

Research and Inquiry, T220

Analyze to Inform/Explain, T221

Comparing Texts, T233, T241, T245, T251

Predictive Writing, T217B

Teacher's Edition

Summarize, 351
Cause and Effect, 351

Literature Anthology

Interactive Whiteboard

Leveled Readers
Comparing Texts
Cause and Effect

Cause and Effect, 183–185
Genre, 186
Analyze to Inform, 189

Your Turn Practice Book

Writing Process • Genre Writing

Narrative Text
Poetry, T350–T355

Conferencing Routines
Teacher Conferences, T352
Peer Conferences, T353

Interactive Whiteboard

Teacher's Edition

Leveled Workstation Card
Poetry, Card 28

Writer's Workspace
Narrative Text: Poetry
Writing Process
Multimedia Presentations

Writing Traits • Write Every Day

Writing Trait: Word Choice
Figurative Language, T222–T223

Conferencing Routines
Teacher Conferences, T224
Peer Conferences, T225

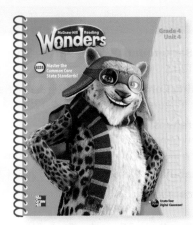

Teacher's Edition

Word Choice: Figurative Languuage, 288–289

Reading/Writing Workshop

Interactive Whiteboard

Figurative Language, Card 16

Leveled Workstation Card

Word Choice: Figurative Language, 190

Your Turn Practice Book

Grammar and Spelling

Grammar
Possessive Pronouns, T226–T227

Spelling
Diphthongs /oi/ and /ou/, T228–T229

Interactive Whiteboard

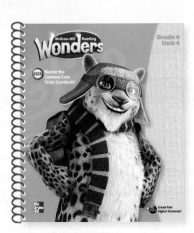

Teacher's Edition

Possessive Pronouns

Diphthongs /oi/ and /ou/ Word Sorts

Online Spelling and Grammar Games

SUGGESTED LESSON PLAN

	DAY 1	DAY 2

READING

Whole Group

Teach, Model and Apply

Reading/Writing Workshop

DAY 1
Build Background Wonders in the Sky, T202–T203

Listening Comprehension Interactive Read Aloud: "Pictures in the Sky," T204–T205

Comprehension
• Preview Genre: Expository Text
• Preview Strategy: Ask and Answer Questions

✔ **Vocabulary** Words in Context, T206–T207

Practice *Your Turn*, 181

Close Reading of Complex Text "Wonders of the Night Sky," 280–283

DAY 2
✔ **Comprehension**
• Strategy: Ask and Answer Questions, T210–T211
• Skill: Cause and Effect, T212–T213
• Write About Reading *Analytical Writing*
• Genre: Expository Text, T214–T215

✔ **Vocabulary** Strategy: Context Clues T216–T217

Practice *Your Turn*, 182–187

DIFFERENTIATED INSTRUCTION   Choose across the week to meet your students' needs.

Small Group

Approaching Level

DAY 1
Leveled Reader *Stargazing*, T232–T233
Phonics/Decoding Decode Words with Diphthong /oi/, T234 TIER 2
Vocabulary
• Review High-Frequency Words, T236 TIER 2
• Identify Word Relationships, T237

DAY 2
Leveled Reader *Stargazing*, T232–T233
Vocabulary Review Vocabulary Words, T236 TIER 2
Comprehension
• Identify Text Structures, T238 TIER 2
• Review Cause and Effect, T239

On Level

DAY 1
Leveled Reader *Stargazing*, T240–T241
Vocabulary Review Vocabulary Words, T242

DAY 2
Leveled Reader *Stargazing*, T240–T241
Comprehension Review Cause and Effect, T243

Beyond Level

DAY 1
Leveled Reader *Stargazing*, T244–T245
Vocabulary Review Domain-Specific Words, T246

DAY 2
Leveled Reader *Stargazing*, T244–T245
Comprehension Review Cause and Effect, T247

English Language Learners

DAY 1
Shared Read "Wonders of the Night Sky," T248–T249
Phonics/Decoding Words with Diphthong /oi/, T234
Vocabulary
• Preteach Vocabulary, T252
• Review High-Frequency Words, T236

DAY 2
Leveled Reader *Stargazing*, T250–T251
Vocabulary Review Vocabulary, T252
Writing Writing Trait: Word Choice, T254
Grammar Possessive Pronouns, T255

LANGUAGE ARTS   Writing Process: Poetry T350–T355   Use with Weeks 4–6

Whole Group

Writing
Grammar
Spelling
Build Vocabulary

DAY 1
✔ **Readers to Writers**
• Writing Traits: Word Choice/Figurative Language, T222–T223
• Writing Entry: Prewrite and Draft, T224
Grammar Possessive Pronouns, T226
Spelling Diphthongs /oi/ and /ou/, T228
Build Vocabulary
• Connect to Words, T230
• Academic Vocabulary, T230

DAY 2
Readers to Writers
• Writing Entry: Revise, T224
Grammar Possessive Pronouns, T226
Spelling Diphthongs /oi/ and /ou/, T228
Build Vocabulary
• Expand Vocabulary, T230
• Review Greek Roots, T230

☞ **Go** Digital

CUSTOMIZE YOUR OWN
LESSON PLANS

www.connected.mcgraw-hill.com

DAY 3	DAY 4	DAY 5 Review and Assess

READING

Phonics/Decoding
- Diphthongs /oi/ and /ou/, T218
- Greek and Latin Roots, T219

Practice *Your Turn*, 188

Close Reading *Why Does the Moon Change Shape?*, 336–351 • *Analytical Writing*

Literature Anthology

Fluency Accuracy, T219

Integrate Ideas • *Analytical Writing*
- Research and Inquiry, T220

Practice *Your Turn*, 183–185

Close Reading "How It Came to Be," 352–355 • *Analytical Writing*

Integrate Ideas • *Analytical Writing*
- Research and Inquiry, T220
- Text Connections, T221
- Write About Reading, T221

Practice *Your Turn*, 189

DIFFERENTIATED INSTRUCTION

Leveled Reader *Stargazing*, T232–T233

Phonics/Decoding Review Words with Diphthongs /oi/ and /ou/, T234 **TIER 2**

Fluency Accuracy, T238 **TIER 2**

Vocabulary Context Clues: Paragraph Clues, T237

Leveled Reader Paired Read: "Orion the Hunter," T233 • *Analytical Writing*

Phonics/Decoding Practice Words with Diphthongs /oi/ and /ou/, T235

Leveled Reader Literature Circles, T233

Comprehension Self-Selected Reading, T239

Phonics/Decoding Greek and Latin Roots, T235

Leveled Reader *Stargazing*, T240–T241

Vocabulary Context Clues: Paragraph Clues, T242

Leveled Reader Paired Read: "Orion the Hunter," T241 • *Analytical Writing*

Leveled Reader Literature Circles, T241

Comprehension Self-Selected Reading, T243

Leveled Reader *Stargazing*, T244–T245

Vocabulary
- Context Clues: Paragraph Clues, T246 *Gifted and Talented*
- Synthesize, T246

Leveled Reader Paired Read: "Orion the Hunter," T245 • *Analytical Writing*

Leveled Reader Literature Circles, T245

Comprehension
- Self-Selected Reading, T247
- Independent Study: Wonders in the Sky, T247

Leveled Reader *Stargazing*, T250–T251

Phonics/Decoding Review Words with Diphthongs /oi/ and /ou/, T234

Vocabulary Context Clues: Paragraph Clues, T253

Spelling Words with Diphthongs /oi/ and /ou/, T254

Leveled Reader Paired Read; "Orion the Hunter," T251 • *Analytical Writing*

Vocabulary Additional Vocabulary, T253

Phonics/Decoding Practice Words with Diphthongs /oi/ and /ou/, T235

Leveled Reader Literature Circles, T251

Phonics/Decoding Greek and Latin Roots, T235

LANGUAGE ARTS

Readers to Writers
- Writing Entry: Prewrite and Draft, T225

Grammar Mechanics and Usage, T227

Spelling Diphthongs /oi/ and /ou/, T229

Build Vocabulary
- Reinforce the Words, T231
- Context Clues, T231

Readers to Writers
- Writing Entry: Revise, T225

Grammar Possessive Pronouns, T227

Spelling Diphthongs /oi/ and /ou/, T229

Build Vocabulary
- Connect to Writing, T231
- Shades of Meaning, T231

Readers to Writers
- Writing Entry: Share and Reflect, T225

Grammar Possessive Pronouns, T227

Spelling Diphthongs /oi/ and /ou/, T229

Build Vocabulary
- Word Squares, T231
- Morphology, T231

DIFFERENTIATE TO ACCELERATE

  A C T Scaffold to **A**ccess **C**omplex **T**ext

IF ▶ the text complexity of a particular selection is too difficult for students

THEN ▶ see the references noted in the chart below for scaffolded instruction to help students Access Complex Text.

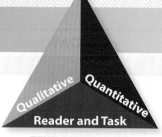

Qualitative | Quantitative
Reader and Task
TEXT COMPLEXITY

	Reading/Writing Workshop	Literature Anthology	Leveled Readers	Classroom Library
			 Approaching · On Level · Beyond · ELL	

Quantitative

Reading/Writing Workshop	Literature Anthology	Leveled Readers	Classroom Library
"Wonders of the Night Sky" **Lexile** 880 *TextEvaluator* 29	*Why Does the Moon Change Shape* **Lexile** 900 *TextEvaluator* 22 *"How It Came to Be"* **Lexile** 910 *TextEvaluator* 40	**Approaching Level** **Lexile** 650 *TextEvaluator* 21 **Beyond Level** **Lexile** 860 *TextEvaluator* 29 **On Level** **Lexile** 450 *TextEvaluator* 30 **ELL** **Lexile** 360 *TextEvaluator* 27	*A Picture Book of Houdini* **Lexile** 770 *TextEvaluator* 41 *The Moon and I* **Lexile** 870 *TextEvaluator* 38

Qualitative

Reading/Writing Workshop	Literature Anthology	Leveled Readers	Classroom Library
What Makes the Text Complex? • **Connection of Ideas** Aurora Borealis T209 • **Organization** Information T211 **A C T** *See Scaffolded Instruction in Teacher's Edition T209 and T211.*	**What Makes the Text Complex?** • **Genre** Subject Matter T217A • **Organization** Summary T217C • **Specific Vocabulary** Science T217E; Mythology T217Q • **Connection of Ideas** Information T217G, T217K; Diagram T217M • **Prior Knowledge** Science T217I; Mythology T217S **A C T** *See Scaffolded Instruction in Teacher's Edition T217A–T217T.*	**What Makes the Text Complex?** • **Specific Vocabulary** • **Prior Knowledge** • **Sentence Structure** • **Connection of Ideas** • **Genre** **A C T** *See Level Up lessons online for Leveled Readers.*	**What Makes the Text Complex?** • **Genre** • **Specific Vocabulary** • **Prior Knowledge** • **Sentence Structure** • **Organization** • **Purpose** • **Connection of Ideas** **A C T** *See Scaffolded Instruction in Teacher's Edition T360–T361.*

Reader and Task

Reading/Writing Workshop	Literature Anthology	Leveled Readers	Classroom Library
The Introduce the Concept lesson on pages T202–T203 will help determine the reader's knowledge and engagement in the weekly concept. See pages T208–T217 and T220–T221 for questions and tasks for this text.	The Introduce the Concept lesson on pages T202–T203 will help determine the reader's knowledge and engagement in the weekly concept. See pages T217A–T217T and T220–T221 for questions and tasks for this text.	The Introduce the Concept lesson on pages T202–T203 will help determine the reader's knowledge and engagement in the weekly concept. See pages T232–T233, T240–T241, T244–T245, T250–T251, and T220–T221 for questions and tasks for this text.	The Introduce the Concept lesson on pages T202–T203 will help determine the reader's knowledge and engagement in the weekly concept. See pages T360–T361 for questions and tasks for this text.

Monitor and *Differentiate*

IF → you need to differentiate instruction

THEN → use the Quick Checks to assess students' needs and select the appropriate small group instruction focus.

✓ Quick Check

Comprehension Strategy Ask and Answer Questions T211

Comprehension Skill Text Structure: Cause and Effect T213

Genre Expository Text T215

Vocabulary Strategy Context Clues T217

Phonics/Fluency Diphthongs /oi/ and /ou/ T219

If No →	**Approaching Level**	**Reteach** T232–T239
	ELL	**Develop** T248–T255
If Yes →	**On Level**	**Review** T240–T243
	Beyond Level	**Extend** T244–T247

Level Up with Leveled Readers

IF → students can read their leveled text fluently and answer comprehension questions

THEN → work with the next level up to accelerate students' reading with more complex text.

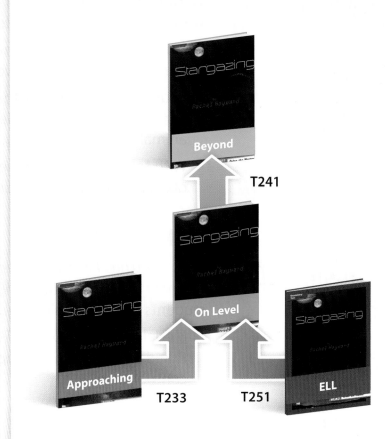

Beyond — T241

On Level

Approaching — T233   T251   ELL

ENGLISH LANGUAGE LEARNERS
SCAFFOLD

IF ELL students need additional support **THEN** → scaffold instruction using the small group suggestions.

Reading/Writing Workshop "Wonders of the Night Sky" T248–T249	Leveled Reader *Stargazing* T250–T251 "Orion the Hunter" T251	Additional Vocabulary T253 another full mixture patterns tools view	Using Context Clues: Paragraph Clues T253	Writing Word Choice T254	Spelling Words with Diphthongs /oi/ and /ou/ T254	Grammar Possessive Pronouns T255

Note: Include ELL Students in all small groups based on their needs.

→ Introduce the Concept

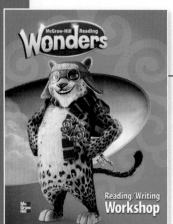

Reading/Writing Workshop

OBJECTIVES

 CCSS Pose and respond to specific questions to clarify or follow up on information, and make comments that contribute to the discussion and link to the remarks of others. **SL.4.1c**

CCSS Paraphrase portions of a text read aloud or information presented in diverse media and formats, including visually, quantitatively, and orally. **SL.4.2**

Build background knowledge on objects in the night sky.

ACADEMIC LANGUAGE

- *astronomer, telescope*
- Cognates: *astrónomo(a), telescopio*

MINILESSON
10 Mins

Build Background

ESSENTIAL QUESTION
How can you explain what you see in the sky?

Have students read the Essential Question on page 276 of the **Reading/Writing Workshop**. Tell them that, for centuries, people have come up with stories to explain what they see in the night sky.

Discuss the photograph of the northern lights with students. Have students state in their own words what they see in the picture.

→ People have come up with stories to explain things in the night sky. For example, the Inuit believed the northern lights were the spirits of animals dancing in the sky.

→ With **telescopes**, we can see even more in the sky. **Astronomers** observe new things in the sky every day and try to explain them.

Talk About It

COLLABORATE

Ask: *If you had lived a hundred years ago, how would you explain the northern lights? What have you observed in the sky at night?* Have students discuss in pairs or groups.

→ Model using the Concept Web to generate words and phrases that describe things that appear in the night sky. Add students' contributions.

Collaborative Conversations

Ask and Answer Questions As students engage in partner, small-group, and whole-class discussions, encourage them to ask and answer questions. Remind students to

→ ask questions to clarify ideas or comments they do not understand.

→ wait a few seconds after asking a question, to give others a chance to think before responding.

→ answer questions thoughtfully with complete ideas, not one-word answers.

Go Digital

Discuss the Concept

Watch Video

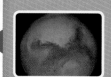
View Photos

Night Sky

Use Graphic Organizer

Weekly Concept Wonders in the Sky

? Essential Question
How do you explain what you see in the sky?

Go Digital!

The LIGHT SHOW

For centuries, people have come up with stories to explain what they see in the night sky. This photo shows the northern lights, which you will soon read more about. The Inuit who lived on the lower Yukon River believed the northern lights were actually the spirits of animals dancing in the sky.

► If you had lived five hundred years ago, how would you have explained the northern lights?

► What have you observed in the sky at night?

Talk About It

Write words that name or describe things that appear in the night sky. Then talk to a partner about stars, planets, comets, and eclipses.

Night Sky

276   277

READING/WRITING WORKSHOP, pp. 276–277

ELL ENGLISH LANGUAGE LEARNERS SCAFFOLD

Beginning	Intermediate	Advanced/High
Use Visuals Point to the northern lights. Say: *These are the northern lights. We can see the northern lights in the night sky.* Point to the sky. Ask: *Where can we see the northern lights?* Encourage students to use phrases or simple sentences. Repeat students' responses, correcting for grammar and pronunciation.	**Describe** Point to the northern lights. Say: *The northern lights are an example of the wonders that we can see in the night sky.* Ask: *What wonders have you seen in the night sky?* Elicit details to develop students' understanding of objects or wonders in the sky.	**Discuss** Have students discuss the image of the northern lights. Ask: *What objects or wonders have you seen in the sky? Did you use special tools, such as a telescope, to see the objects?* Encourage students to use concept words in their responses. If the student's response is correct, repeat it slowly and clearly for the class to hear.

GRAPHIC ORGANIZER 61

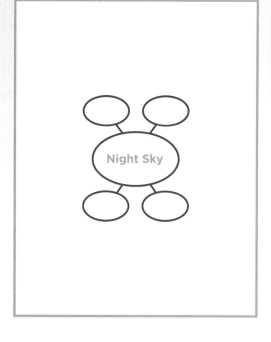

Night Sky

→ Listening Comprehension

MINILESSON 10 Mins

Interactive Read Aloud

Go Digital

View Photos

Connect to Concept: Wonders in the Sky

Tell students that people in ancient times observed the sky to learn more about their world. Let students know that you will be reading aloud a passage about ways that people benefited from this knowledge. As students listen, have them think of questions they have about the information and whether those questions are answered in the passage.

Preview Genre: Expository Text

Explain that the passage you will read aloud is expository text. Discuss features of expository text:

→ main purpose is to present factual information about the world

→ includes text features

→ usually begins with an introductory paragraph that explains the main idea

Preview Comprehension Strategy: Ask and Answer Questions

Point out that readers can ask questions before, during, and after reading to help them focus on the most important information in a text. When reading informational text, it is helpful to ask, "Do I understand what this part of the text means?"

Use the Think Alouds on page T205 to model the strategy.

Respond to Reading

Think Aloud Clouds Display Think Aloud Master 1: *I wonder . . .* to reinforce how you used the ask and answer questions strategy to understand content.

Genre Features With students, discuss the elements of the Read Aloud that let them know it is expository text. Ask them to think about other texts that you have read or they have read independently that were expository texts.

Summarize Have students briefly restate the most important information from "Pictures in the Sky" in their own words.

I wonder...

Model Think Alouds

Genre	Features

Fill in Genre Chart

Pictures in the Sky

Look up at the sky on a clear night and you will see a jumble of stars, especially if you are away from city lights. Long ago, people looked at these same stars and saw patterns. The patterns created pictures called constellations. Ancient astronomers, travelers, hunters, and farmers all benefited from a better understanding of the night sky. **1**

Does the Sky Change?

Many constellations are named after objects, animals, and heroes. The Big Dipper, which looks like a water dipper with a handle and a bowl, is a group of stars that are part of the Great Bear constellation. If you stand outside and look at a constellation like the Great Bear for an entire night, you will think it's moving across the sky. But you're the one who is moving. You're standing on Earth as it rotates, or spins, on its axis. This rotation makes it appear that the stars are passing across the sky. Your view of the night sky also changes as Earth revolves around the sun. A constellation that you see in the spring may not be visible in autumn. **2**

A Starry Map

The predictable locations of constellations and other objects in the sky helped early people navigate both on land and at sea. The North Star is located directly over the North Pole. The Big Dipper points directly to this northernmost star, making it an easy guide for travelers to follow. Sailors who found themselves far out to sea could look to the sky to guide them in their travels. Early hunters could use the night sky as a map to help them find their way.

A Starry Calendar

Ancient astronomers used their knowledge of the night sky to help them better understand their climate and predict changes of seasons. Early calendars were developed to help people keep track of the positions of the stars and the movements of the sun and the moon. This enabled farmers to know the best time to plant and harvest crops. From long ago to the present day, the sky is like a glittering picture book that opens each evening, waiting for people to discover its many stories. **3**

Stockbroker/SuperStock

1 Think Aloud I can **ask questions** before I read further to help me better understand the information that will be presented in this article. One question I have is, "Does the night sky always look the same?" Maybe as I read I can answer that question.

2 Think Aloud I was able to **answer** my first **question.** Now, as I continue to read I can **ask a question** to help me understand ways that constellations can help people. As I read, I'll look for the answer.

3 Think Aloud Now that I'm finished reading, I'll **ask** myself, "What did I learn from this article?" I'll think about what I've learned and then look at the text again to make sure I understand all the facts and details.

→ Vocabulary

Reading/Writing Workshop

OBJECTIVES

CCSS Acquire and use accurately grade-appropriate general academic and domain-specific words and phrases, including those that signal precise actions, emotions, or states of being (e.g., *quizzed, whined, stammered*) and that are basic to a particular topic (e.g., *wildlife, conservation,* and *endangered* when discussing animal preservation). **L.4.6**

ACADEMIC LANGUAGE

• *astronomer, telescope*

• Cognates: *astrónomo(a), telescopio*

MINILESSON 10 Mins

Words in Context

Model the Routine

Introduce each vocabulary word using the Vocabulary Routine found on the Visual Vocabulary Cards.

Visual Vocabulary Cards

Vocabu...
Define:
Example:
Ask:

Vocabulary Routine

Define: A **telescope** makes distant objects seem larger and nearer.

Example: The boy looked through the telescope at the boats in the harbor.

Ask: What else can you see with a telescope?

Definitions

→ **astronomer**	An **astronomer** studies the stars and planets. **Cognate:** *astrónomo(a)*
→ **crescent**	A **crescent** is a curve that is wider in the middle and tapered at the ends.
→ **phases**	**Phases** are the different stages of the moon.
→ **rotates**	When something **rotates**, it turns around on an axis.
→ **series**	A **series** is a number of similar things coming one after another. **Cognate:** *serie*
→ **sliver**	A **sliver** is a thin, often pointed piece that has been broken, cut, or torn off.
→ **specific**	Something **specific** is exact or particular.

Talk About It

Have partners look at each picture and discuss the definition of each word. Have students choose three words and write questions for their partner to answer.

Go Digital

telescope

Use Visual Glossary

CCSS Words to Know

Vocabulary

Use the picture and the sentences to talk with a partner about each word.

astronomer The **astronomer** pointed out the crater on the planet.

What might an astronomer observe in the night sky?

crescent The moon tonight looks like a **crescent** and is shaped like a "C."

What other things are shaped like a crescent?

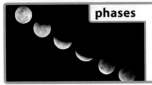

phases During one of the moon's **phases**, the moon appears to be perfectly round.

Name two phases of the moon.

rotates The hamster turns and **rotates** his exercise wheel.

What is something else that rotates?

278

series This **series** of photographs shows what happened after I watered the flower.

Do you have a favorite series of books?

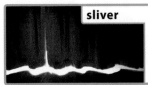

sliver A thin **sliver** of light showed beneath the curtains.

What is an antonym for sliver?

specific The boy held up a **specific** kind of orange that is used for making juice.

What is a specific kind of bread that you like best?

telescope The boy looked through the **telescope** at the boats in the harbor.

What else can you see with a telescope?

Your Turn COLLABORATE

Pick three words. Write three questions for your partner to answer.

Go Digital! *Use the online visual glossary*

279

READING/WRITING WORKSHOP, pp. 278–279

ELL ENGLISH LANGUAGE LEARNERS SCAFFOLD

Beginning

Actively Engage If possible, show a telescope and have students look through it. Say: *This is a telescope. I can see objects far away with a telescope.* Motion or pantomime *far away.* Encourage students to use the sentence frame: *I can see objects with a ____.* Point out the cognate *telescopio.*

Intermediate

Describe Have students describe the picture for *telescope.* Help them with the pronunciation. Ask: *What objects can you see with a telescope? Turn to a partner and describe how a telescope helps people study faraway objects.* Clarify students' reponses as necessary.

Advanced/High

Discuss Ask students to talk about the picture for *telescope* with a partner and use the word in a sentence. Then ask: *Have you ever used a telescope? What did you see?* Elicit details to support students' responses.

ON-LEVEL PRACTICE BOOK p. 181

| rotates | crescent | sliver | astronomer |
| telescope | series | phases | specific |

Finish each sentence using the vocabulary word provided.
Possible responses provided.

1. **(phases)** The large apartment building next door to us was built in three *phases*.

2. **(astronomer)** Since she likes studying the planets and stars, I think she will grow up to be an *astronomer*.

3. **(series)** There was a *series* of pictures that showed what our town looked like long ago.

4. **(rotates)** I like when the basketball player *rotates* the ball on his finger.

5. **(specific)** We arrived at his house easily because he gave us very *specific* directions.

6. **(telescope)** I discovered a new star last night when I was looking through my *telescope*.

7. **(sliver)** We avoided stepping on glass at the beach after we noticed that a *sliver* was sticking out of the sand.

8. **(crescent)** We looked up at the night sky and saw that the moon was shaped like a *crescent*.

| APPROACHING p. 181 | BEYOND p. 181 | ELL p. 181 |

CCSS Shared Read › Genre • Expository Text

Wonders of the Night Sky

Essential Question

How do you explain what you see in the sky?

Read about what causes some of the sights you see in the sky.

As Earth **rotates** on its axis, day becomes night. Suddenly, a gallery of lights is revealed! You may see a beautiful **crescent** moon. Maybe you'll see one of the other **phases** of the moon. You may even see a **series** of lights spread across the sky like colored ribbons. For thousands of years, people have loved looking at the night sky. For almost as long, scientists have been trying to explain what they see.

Aurora Borealis

Every few years, an amazing light show is seen in the skies near the North Pole. It is known as "the northern lights," or the **aurora borealis** (uh-RAWR-uh bawr-ee-AL-is). Brilliant bands of green, yellow, red, and blue lights appear in the sky.

People used to believe the lights were caused by sunlight reflecting off polar ice caps. The theory was that when the light bounced back from the caps it created patterns in the sky. In fact, the lights happen because of magnetic attraction.

The sun constantly gives off a stream of electrically charged particles in every direction. These nearly invisible pieces of matter join into a stream called a solar wind. As Earth orbits the sun, solar winds reach Earth's magnetic field. As a result, electric charges occur that are sometimes strong enough to be seen from Earth. These electric charges cause the colorful bands of lights in the sky.

The aurora borealis above Hammerfest, Norway

280 281

Picture Press/Alamy

READING/WRITING WORKSHOP, pp. 280–281

Shared Read

Lexile 880 *TextEvaluator*™ 29

Reading/Writing Workshop

Connect to Concept: Wonders in the Sky

Explain that "Wonders of the Night Sky" will give more information about what causes some of the sights in the night sky. Read "Wonders of the Night Sky" with students. Note the vocabulary words previously taught are highlighted in the text.

Close Reading

Reread Paragraph 2: Tell students that you are going to take a closer look at the second paragraph. Reread the paragraph together. Ask: *What is the aurora borealis?* Model how to cite evidence to answer the question.

I can use information from the text to answer the question. The author says that the aurora borealis is sometimes called the "northern lights" and that it is made up of "brilliant bands of green, yellow, red, and blue lights" in the sky. The aurora borealis is a band of colored lights in the northern sky.

Reread Paragraph 3: Model how to ask and answer questions in the third paragraph. Remind students that asking and answering questions can help them understand what they are reading.

As I read, I see that there were several theories on why the northern lights happen. I wonder why they actually happen. When I keep reading, I see that the lights actually happen because of magnetic attraction. This answers my question about why the northern lights happen.

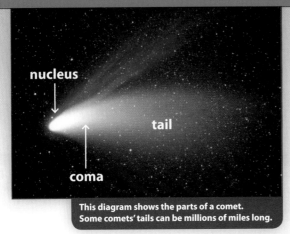

nucleus

tail

coma

This diagram shows the parts of a comet. Some comets' tails can be millions of miles long.

Comets

Another kind of light you might see move across the night sky is a comet. The word *comet* comes from a Greek word that means, "wearing long hair." It came from the Greek philosopher **Aristotle** (AR-uh-stot-uhl), who thought that comets looked like stars with hair.

Long ago, people feared these mysterious streaks because they believed that they might bring war or sickness to Earth. Today, comets are less scary and mysterious because we know that they are a mixture of rock, dust, ice, and frozen gases that orbit the sun.

Comets move around the sun in an oval-shaped orbit. When a comet comes closer to the sun, the result is that a "tail" of gas and dust is pushed out behind the comet. This long tail is what people see from Earth.

Scientists think comets are some of the oldest objects in space. They can track **specific** comets and predict when they can be seen from Earth again.

Meteors

Have you ever looked up at the sky and seen a shooting star? Those streaks of light are not really stars at all. What we call shooting stars are usually **meteors** (MEE-tee-erz). Meteors are another name for the rocky debris and fragments that enter Earth's atmosphere. Sometimes Earth passes through an area in space with a lot of debris. This is when a meteor shower occurs. You may see hundreds of "shooting stars" on the night of a meteor shower.

The Perseid meteor shower

These days an **astronomer** or anyone with a portable **telescope** can raise new questions about space. What do you see when you look up at the night sky? Whether you look at a **sliver** of the moon or a fantastic light show, you are bound to see something amazing.

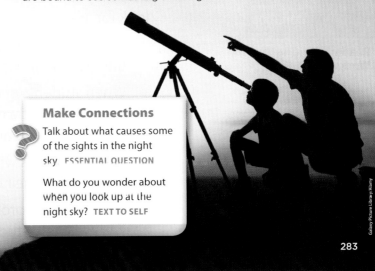

Make Connections

Talk about what causes some of the sights in the night sky **ESSENTIAL QUESTION**

What do you wonder about when you look up at the night sky? **TEXT TO SELF**

282

283

READING/WRITING WORKSHOP, pp. 282–283

Make Connections — *Analytical Writing*

ESSENTIAL QUESTION

Encourage students to go back into the text for evidence as they talk about how the different things that appear in the night sky happen. Ask students to think of other objects in the night sky that they might want to know more about.

Continue Close Reading

Use the following lessons for focused rereadings.

→ Ask and Answer Questions, T210–T211

→ Text Structure: Cause and Effect, T212–T213

→ Expository Text, T214–T215

→ Context Clues, T216–T217

A C T Access Complex Text

▶ Connection of Ideas

Students may need help understanding the aurora borealis. Help students connect the information in the first paragraph under "Aurora Borealis" to the photograph.

→ *What does the photograph show on page 280?* (Colorful lights in the sky)

→ *What does the caption tell us?* (This is the aurora borealis.)

→ *Which sentence in the first paragraph of the section "Aurora Borealis" tells about lights that look like this?* (The third sentence)

→ Comprehension Strategy

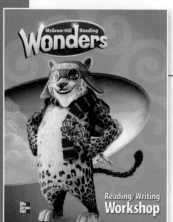

Reading/Writing Workshop

OBJECTIVES

CCSS Refer to details and examples in a text when explaining what the text says explicitly and when drawing inferences from the text. **RI.4.1**

Ask and answer questions about difficult sections of text to increase understanding.

ACADEMIC LANGUAGE
- *ask and answer questions, informational text, reread*
- Cognate: *texto informativo*

MINILESSON 10 Mins

Ask and Answer Questions

1 Explain

Explain that when students read an informational text, they may come across unfamiliar concepts and explanations. Remind students that they can ask questions about difficult sections of text and then look for answers to understand new information.

→ Good readers ask questions about something they do not understand and then look for answers.

→ When students encounter a difficult section of text, they can ask a question that would help them understand it. They may need to reread to find an answer to the question.

→ Often, students will find that asking and answering questions will improve their comprehension of informational texts.

Point out that the process of asking questions and looking for answers will help students focus on important information and details.

2 Model Close Reading: Text Evidence

Model how asking and answering questions can help students understand what causes the northern lights in the section "Aurora Borealis" on page 281 of "Wonders of the Night Sky."

3 Guided Practice of Close Reading

COLLABORATE

Have students work in pairs to ask and answer questions about meteors. Direct students to reread the section "Meteors" on page 283 of "Wonders of the Night Sky." Partners can take turns asking and answering questions about meteors. Have partners discuss other sections of "Wonders of the Night Sky" that they might want to ask questions about.

Go Digital

View "Wonders of the Night Sky"

Comprehension Strategy

Ask and Answer Questions

When you read an informational text, you usually come across new facts and ideas. Asking questions and reading to find the answer can help you understand new information. As you read "Wonders of the Night Sky," ask and answer questions about the text.

Find Text Evidence

When you first read "Wonders of the Night Sky," you may have asked yourself what causes the northern lights.

page 281

crescent moon. Maybe you'll see one of the other phases of the moon. You may even see a series of lights spread across the sky like colored ribbons. For thousands of years, people have loved looking at the night sky. For almost as long, scientists have been trying to explain what they see.

Aurora Borealis

Every few years, an amazing light show is seen in the skies near the North Pole. It is known as "the northern lights," or the aurora borealis (uh-RAWR-uh bawr-ee-AL-is). Brilliant bands of green, yellow, red, and blue lights appear in the sky.

People used to believe the lights were caused by sunlight reflecting off polar ice caps. The theory was that when the light bounced back from the caps it created patterns in the sky. In fact, the lights happen because of magnetic attraction.

The sun constantly gives off a stream of electrically charged particles in every direction. These nearly invisible pieces of matter join into a stream called a solar wind. As Earth orbits the sun, solar winds reach Earth's magnetic

When I read this section of the text, I found the answer to my question. The northern lights are caused by the sun giving off electrically charged particles.

Your Turn

 COLLABORATE

Think of two questions you have about meteors. Reread the section "Meteors" on page 283 and answer your own questions. As you read, remember to use the strategy Ask and Answer Questions.

284

READING/WRITING WORKSHOP, p. 284

A C T Access Complex Text

▶ Organization

As students ask and answer questions about the text, they may need help understanding the organization of information under "Aurora Borealis." Reread with students and guide them through the information.

→ *What does the first paragraph of the section describe?* (the northern lights) *What are they?* (colorful lights in the sky)

→ *What does the second paragraph describe?* (It describes what people used to think the northern lights were.) *What was that theory?* (The light bounced back from the polar ice caps and reflected in the sky.)

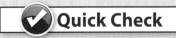

Monitor and *Differentiate*

 Quick Check

Do students ask and answer their own questions about meteors after rereading the section "Meteors" on page 283?

⬇

Small Group Instruction

If No → | Approaching Level | Reteach p. T232
| ELL | Develop p. T248
If Yes → | On Level | Review p. T240
| Beyond Level | Extend p. T244

ON-LEVEL PRACTICE BOOK pp. 183–184

Read the passage. Use the ask and answer questions strategy to understand new information in the text.

Stars: Lights in the Night Sky

	Long ago, people thought the stars were lights attached to a big
12	dome over Earth. The stars moved across the sky each night.
23	As a result, it looked as if the dome were rotating around Earth.
36	But now we know that this isn't true. Stars are actually huge,
48	glowing balls of plasma, or ionized atoms. Some stars look like
59	little pinpricks. Most are so far away that they can't be seen with the
73	naked eye.
75	**What's a Star?**
78	Stars are made of a mixture of plasmas like hydrogen. As you can
91	imagine, a star's core is extremely hot. When lots of pressure squeezes
103	the star's hot center, the hydrogen changes into helium. This process
114	produces lots of energy. As a result, the star shines a bright light
127	through space.
129	When you look up at the stars, you may think that most of them
143	produce a white light. Take another look. Stars generally lie on a
155	color spectrum. This range of colors goes from red to yellow to blue.
168	But what do the colors mean? Well, blue stars are much hotter. If you
182	compare the two stars Betelgeuse (BEE-tehl-jooz) and Rigel
190	(RIGH-jehl), you will see that Betelgeuse is reddish and Rigel is
201	bluish. Rigel has the higher core temperature.

APPROACHING pp. 183–184	BEYOND pp. 183–184	ELL pp. 183–184

Comprehension Skill

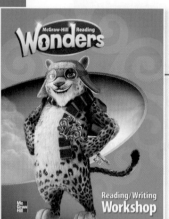

Reading/Writing Workshop

OBJECTIVES

CCSS Describe the overall structure (e.g., chronology, comparison, cause/effect, problem/solution) of events, ideas, concepts, or information in a text or part of a text. **RI.4.5**

Identify cause-and-effect relationships.

ACADEMIC LANGUAGE
• *cause, effect, signal words*
• Cognates: *causa, efecto*

SKILLS TRACE

TEXT STRUCTURE

Introduce Unit 1 Week 3

Review Unit 1 Weeks 4, 6; Unit 2 Week 6; Unit 3 Week 6; Unit 4 Weeks 1, 4; Unit 5 Weeks 3, 4, 5, 6; Unit 6 Week 6

Assess Units 1, 4, 5

 10 Mins

Text Structure: Cause and Effect

1 Explain

Explain to students that authors use text structure to organize information in an informational text. Cause and effect is common text structure in historical, scientific, and technical texts. A cause is why something happens. An effect is what happens as a result.

→ To find a cause-and-effect relationship, students should look for an event or action that causes something to happen. Then students can identify what happens as a result of that event or action.

→ Signal words and phrases such as *cause, effect* and *as a result* help identify cause-and-effect relationships.

→ Sometimes cause-and-effect relationships occur in a chain, with each cause and effect bringing about a related cause and effect. The example of a trail of dominoes being knocked over may help students visualize this type of relationship.

2 Model Close Reading: Text Evidence

Model identifying the cause-and-effect relationships in the section "Aurora Borealis" on page 281 of "Wonders of the Night Sky." Then model using the graphic organizer to illustrate these relationships.

 Write About Reading: Paraphrase Model for students how to use the notes from the graphic organizer to paraphrase the cause-and-effect relationships in the section "Aurora Borealis."

3 Guided Practice of Close Reading

 Have students work in pairs to complete a graphic organizer for the section "Comets" on page 282 of "Wonders of the Night Sky," going back into the text to find out what causes a comet to move closer to the sun and what the effect is. Remind students to look for signal words to help them find causes and effects. Discuss each relationship as students complete their graphic organizers.

 Write About Reading: Paraphrase Ask pairs to use the notes from their graphic organizers to paraphrase what happens when comets come closer to the sun and why. Select pairs of students to share their writing with the class.

Go Digital

Present the Lesson

Comprehension Skill **CCSS**

Cause and Effect

Text structure is the way that authors organize information in a selection. Cause and effect is one kind of text structure. A cause is why something happens. An effect is what happens.

Find Text Evidence

When I reread the "Aurora Borealis" section on page 281 of "Wonders of the Night Sky," I can look for causes and their effects. Signal words such as cause, because, *and* as a result *tell me that a cause-and-effect relationship is being explained.*

Cause	→	Effect
Sun gives off electrically charged particles.	→	Particles join into a solar wind.
Solar winds reach Earth's magnetic fields.	→	As a result, electric charges are seen from Earth.

Your Turn COLLABORATE

Reread page 282 of "Wonders of the Night Sky." What happens when a comet moves closer to the sun? Use the graphic organizer to list the cause and effect.

Go Digital!
Use the interactive graphic organizer

285

READING/WRITING WORKSHOP, p. 285

ENGLISH LANGUAGE LEARNERS SCAFFOLD

Beginning

Use Visuals Tell students that the paragraphs below "Aurora Borealis" describe what causes the aurora borealis. Read each paragraph for students. Stop and paraphrase the text as necessary. Help students understand the cause-and-effect relationships by drawing the images described in the text and pointing out difficult concepts and vocabulary.

Intermediate

Practice Encourage students to look for clue words that will help them find cause-and-effect relationships. Read the third paragraph of "Aurora Borealis." After each sentence, stop and ask students if it is describing a cause or an effect. Help students clarify and correct any wrong answers. Then have them work in pairs to fill out the graphic organizer.

Advanced/High

Discuss Have students reread the section "Aurora Borealis." Ask students to work with partners to discuss the cause-and-effect relationships in the section. Ask: *What causes particles to join into a solar wind?* (The sun gives off electrically charged particles.) *What causes electric charges to be seen from Earth?* (Particles in solar winds reach Earth's magnetic fields.)

 **Monitor and Differentiate**

 ✔ **Quick Check**

As students complete the graphic organizer, do they determine the cause-and-effect relationships? Can they identify signal words?

⬇

Small Group Instruction

If No →	Approaching Level	Reteach p. T239
	ELL	Develop p. T248
If Yes →	On Level	Review p. T243
	Beyond Level	Extend p. T247

ON-LEVEL PRACTICE BOOK pp. 183–185

A. Reread the passage and answer the questions.
Possible responses provided.

1. Reread paragraph 2. What causes a lot of energy to be produced in a star's core?

The energy is caused when a lot of pressure squeezes the star's hot center and changes hydrogen into helium.

2. What effect does this cause have on a star?

The star shines a bright light through space.

3. Under the heading "Turning Out the Lights," what is one example of a cause and an effect? Use text evidence to support your answer.

Cause: When a large star explodes, it's called a supernova. The star's material becomes crushed and very dense. Effect: A black hole forms with a gravitational pull strong enough to keep even light from escaping.

B. Work with a partner. Read the passage aloud. Pay attention to accuracy. Stop after one minute. Fill out the chart.

	Words Read	–	Number of Errors	=	Words Correct Score
First Read		–		=	
Second Read		–		=	

APPROACHING pp. 183–185	BEYOND pp. 183–185	ELL pp. 183–185

COMPREHENSION SKILL **T213**

Genre: Informational Text

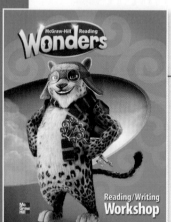

Reading/Writing Workshop

OBJECTIVES

CCSS Interpret information presented visually, orally, or quantitatively (e.g., in charts, graphs, diagrams, time lines, animations, or interactive elements on Web pages) and explain how the information contributes to an understanding of the text in which it appears. **RI.4.7**

CCSS By the end of year, read and comprehend informational texts, including history/ social studies, science, and technical texts, in the grades 4–5 text complexity band proficiently, with scaffolding as needed at the high end of the range. **RI.4.10**

ACADEMIC LANGUAGE

• *pronunciation, caption*

• Cognate: *pronunciación*

MINILESSON 10 Mins

Expository Text

1 Explain

Share with students the following key characteristics of **expository text**.

→ Expository text is a type of nonfiction that explains facts and information about a topic.

→ The information is usually presented in logical order. The author may use cause-and-effect relationships to present information.

→ Expository text includes text features.

2 Model Close Reading: Text Evidence

Model identifying the elements of expository text on page 282 of "Wonders of the Night Sky." Point out the text features.

Boldface Words Point out the word *Aristotle*. Explain that the word is boldfaced to show that it is a key word in the text. Ask: *Why is this word important to the section?*

Pronunciations Point out the pronunciation for *Aristotle*. Explain that the pronunciation shows how to sound out unfamiliar words. Ask: *How do you pronounce the word?*

Diagrams Point out the diagram on page 282. Explain that the diagram shows the parts of a comet. Ask: *What parts does the diagram show? How does it help you understand comets?*

3 Guided Practice of Close Reading

Have students work with a partner to identify and discuss two more text features in "Wonders of the Night Sky." Then have them tell how the text features help them understand the text. Call on pairs to share their answers with the class.

Go Digital

Present the Lesson

CCSS Genre Informational Text

Expository Text

"Wonders of the Night Sky" is an expository text.

Expository text:
- Explains facts and information about a topic.
- Includes text features.

 Find Text Evidence

I know "Wonders of the Night Sky" is an expository text because it gives many facts about the night sky and includes text features. It has boldface words, pronunciations of unfamiliar words, and a diagram.

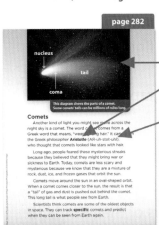

page 282

Comets

Text Features

[**Diagrams** Diagrams show the parts of something.

[**Boldface Words** Boldface words show key words in the text.

[**Pronunciations** Pronunciations show how to sound out unfamiliar words.

 Your Turn COLLABORATE

Find two text features in "Wonders of the Night Sky." Tell what you learned from each feature.

282

286

READING/WRITING WORKSHOP, p. 286

Monitor and *Differentiate*

 Quick Check

Do students identify text features in "Wonders of the Night Sky"? Can they explain how the text features help them understand the text?

Small Group Instruction

If No → | Approaching Level | Reteach p. T232
| ELL | Develop p. T248
If Yes → | On Level | Review p. T240
| Beyond Level | Extend p. T244

ELL ENGLISH LANGUAGE LEARNERS SCAFFOLD

Beginning

Respond Orally Copy the pronunciation for *aurora borealis* on the board. Point to and show students how to pronounce each syllable. Have students recite with you chorally several times. Then have students point out other pronunciations in the text. Help them sound out and pronounce each of the words.

Intermediate

Recognize Review the characteristics of expository text with students. Have them point to each of the text features on page 282. Read the labels on the diagram and ask students how the diagram helps them understand the text. *What does the diagram show?* (It shows the parts of a comet, including the tail, coma, and nucleus.)

Advanced/High

Write Have partners work together to identify and read the text features on page 282. Ask: *What do you learn from these text features?* Have pairs write a sentence telling how each text feature helps them understand the text. Elicit details to develop their responses.

ON-LEVEL PRACTICE BOOK p. 186

How Rainbows Work

Have you ever used a prism? Drops of water in the air can act like prisms. Light passes into a raindrop. Then all the colors that make up white light separate. Some of the colors are **reflected** (ree•FLEC•ted), or bounced back, by the other side of the raindrop. The colors spread out at different angles, so only one color from each raindrop reaches your eye. Light passes into many raindrops at the same time. This lets you see all of the colors of the rainbow.

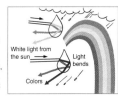

White light from the sun / Light bends / Colors

Answer the questions about the text.

1. How do you know this text is expository text?
   It tells facts about rainbows.

2. What text features are included in this piece of expository text?
   diagram; boldface word; pronunciation

3. How does the diagram help you understand the text?
   Possible response: It shows you what light does when it passes through a raindrop.

4. Which text feature helps you understand the text the most?
   Possible response: The diagram helps the most because it shows what is happening in the text.

| APPROACHING p. 186 | BEYOND p. 186 | ELL p. 186 |

→ Vocabulary Strategy

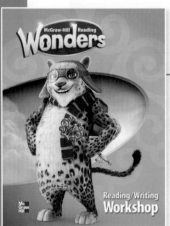

Reading/Writing Workshop

OBJECTIVES

 CCSS Determine the meaning of general academic and domain-specific words or phrases in a text relevant to a *grade 4 topic or subject area.* **RI.4.4**

CCSS Use context (e.g., definitions, examples, or restatements in text) as a clue to the meaning of a word or phrase. **L.4.4a**

ACADEMIC LANGUAGE

• *context, paragraph, definition*

• Cognates: *contexto, parráfo, definición*

MINILESSON
10 Mins

Context Clues

1 Explain

Explain to students that context clues can help them figure out the meanings of unfamiliar words.

→ Students can look for **paragraph clues** to help them figure out the meanings of unfamiliar words.

→ Students should look for clues within the same paragraph that will help them understand the meaning of a word.

2 Model Close Reading: Text Evidence

Model using paragraph clues to figure out the meaning of the word *reflecting* in the third paragraph on page 281 of "Wonders of the Night Sky." Explain how the phrase "light bounced back" helps you determine the meaning.

3 Guided Practice of Close Reading

 Have students work in pairs to identify the meanings of *particles, mixture,* and *debris* in "Wonders of the Night Sky." Have partners use paragraph clues to find the meanings. Then have them work together to write a short definition and example sentence for each word. Call on pairs to share their answers with the class.

Vocabulary Strategy CCSS

Context Clues

As you read the information in "Wonders of the Night Sky," you may come across words that you don't know. To figure out the meaning of an unfamiliar word, check the words or phrases near it carefully for clues.

 Find Text Evidence

When I read the third paragraph on page 281 of "Wonders of the Night Sky," the phrase light bounced back *helps me figure out what* reflecting *means.*

> People used to believe the lights were caused by sunlight reflecting off polar ice caps. The theory was that when the light bounced back from the caps it created patterns in the sky.

Your Turn

Use context clues to find the meaning of the following words in "Wonders of the Night Sky." Write a short definition and example sentence for each word.

particles, *page 281*
mixture, *page 282*
debris, *page 283*

287

READING/WRITING WORKSHOP, p. 287

Monitor and Differentiate

 Quick Check

Can students identify and use paragraph clues to determine the meanings of *particles, mixture,* and *debris*?

⬇

Small Group Instruction

If No →	Approaching Level	Reteach p. T237
	ELL	Develop p. T253
If Yes →	On Level	Review p. T242
	Beyond Level	Extend p. T246

ENGLISH LANGUAGE LEARNERS SCAFFOLD

Beginning

Actively Engage Say and point to the word *mixture*. Then point to and explain that the words *rock, dust, ice,* and *frozen gases* are context clues. Say: *A mixture is a mix of different things.* Demonstrate one or two mixtures of different substances. Point to the mixtures and have students echo the word *mixture*. Repeat with *particles* and *debris.*

Intermediate

Practice Guide students to look for context clues for *particles* on page 281. Ask: *Which words or phrases help you figure out the meaning of* particles? (nearly invisible pieces of matter) Ask students to identify cognates that helped them understand the text (*magnetic, particle, invisible, electric, comet, mixture, gas*).

Advanced/High

Derive Meaning Have partners find context clues for the words *particles, mixture,* and *debris.* Have students use the context clues to write a definition for each word. Then have them use a dictionary to confirm the meaning of each word. Ask students to identify cognates.

Read each passage below. Underline the context clues that help you understand the meaning of each word in bold. Then write the definition for each word on the line.   Possible responses provided.

1. Stars are made of a **mixture** of plasmas like hydrogen. As you can imagine, a star's **core** is extremely hot. When lots of pressure squeezes the star's hot center, the hydrogen changes into helium.

   the central part

2. When you look up at the stars, you may think that most of them produce a white light. Take another look. Stars generally lie on a color **spectrum**. This range of colors goes from red to yellow to blue.

   range of colors

3. The sun does a huge job for a star its size. It provides Earth with most of the energy it needs to support life. Without the sun, Earth would be just a **barren** rock floating in space! None of the life now on Earth's surface could exist.

   lifeless

4. A large star ends in a big explosion. When a star does this, it is called a **supernova**. After the explosion, all of the star's material gets crushed and stops shining.

   star explosion

5. In a black hole, the crushed material becomes so dense that it develops a **gravitational** pull strong enough to keep even light from escaping.

   pull or force of gravity

APPROACHING	BEYOND	ELL
p. 187	p. 187	p. 187

Develop Comprehension

Why Does the Moon Change Shape?

Literature Anthology
Although the selection score falls below the TextEvaluator range, the complex organization and connection of ideas may be challenging to students. The selection also requires prior knowledge.

Text Complexity Range

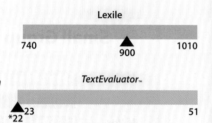

Lexile

740   ▲   1010
900

TextEvaluator™

▲ 23   51
*22

Options for Close Reading

→ Whole Class

→ Small Group

→ Independent

CCSS Genre • Expository Text

Why Does the MOON Change Shape?

BY Melissa Stewart

 Essential Question
How do you explain what you see in the sky?
Read about the different phases of the moon.

Go Digital!

336

A C T Access Complex Text

What makes this text complex?

▶ **Genre**

▶ **Organization**

▶ **Specific Vocabulary**

▶ **Connection of Ideas**

▶ **Prior Knowledge**

▶ Genre

Point students to the first paragraph of the selection. Tell them that the first paragraph of an informational text often introduces the reader to the subject matter of a selection.

The Mysterious Moon

For as long as people have lived on Earth, they have asked questions about the bright lights that fill the nighttime sky. What causes them? How far away are they? Why do they move from night to night?

337

LITERATURE ANTHOLOGY, pp. 336–337

Predictive Writing

Have students read the title, preview the photos, diagrams, and headings, and write their predictions about what this selection will be about. Encourage them to identify the text structure, or how the author organizes ideas, as they read.

ESSENTIAL QUESTION

Ask a student to read aloud the Essential Question. Have students discuss what information they expect to learn.

Note Taking: Use the Graphic Organizer

As students read the selection, ask them to take notes by filling in the graphic organizer on **Your Turn Practice Book page 182** to record the causes and effects in each section.

1 Text Features: Photographs

Look at the photograph on pages 336–337. Discuss the moon in this photograph with a partner. Does it seem near or far? What are some of the features you can see on the moon's surface? What else do you see?

→ *How does the writer get you thinking about the subject matter?* (She uses a series of questions.)

→ *What are these questions about?* (the lights in the nighttime sky)

→ *What lights are there in the nighttime sky?* (stars, planets, the moon)

ELL Help students understand how the heading and image on page 337 relate. Read the heading aloud and point to the moon. *Mysterious* is a cognate. (misteriosa)

→ *What does the picture on page 337 show?* (It shows two people using a telescope and looking up at the moon.)

LITERATURE ANTHOLOGY **T217B**

Develop Comprehension

STOP AND CHECK

Ask and Answer Questions Why were ancient people amazed by the Moon? (Its shape seemed to constantly change.)

Teacher Think Aloud I know that when I read informational text, I can make sure I understand new information by asking and answering questions about it. Why were ancient people so amazed by the moon? If I look back at the first paragraph on page 338, the text says that ancient people were most amazed by how the shape of the moon changed. The drawing shown on this page looks very old, and its caption confirms that it is 600 years old. I can see that the ancient people in it are studying the moon. This drawing supports the idea that ancient people were amazed by how the view of the moon from Earth changes.

For thousands of years, the Moon has been the most mysterious nighttime object of all. It is the largest object in the night sky, and it is the brightest. What amazed ancient people the most is how the Moon's shape is constantly changing. Sometimes it looks like a full bright circle. Other times, only a tiny **sliver** appears.

It did not take ancient people long to realize that the Moon's changes, or **phases**, follow a regular pattern. The Moon's phases repeat themselves every twenty-nine or thirty days. If you watch the Moon every night for about a month, you can see all its phases.

At the beginning of each cycle, people on Earth cannot see the Moon at all. After a few days, a tiny sliver of light appears in the nighttime sky. Each night, the Moon looks a little larger. After a week, it looks like half of a circle. And about a week after that, a full round disk brightens the night sky.

But then the Moon starts to shrink. Each night it gets a bit smaller. After about a week, the Moon looks like half of a circle. And a week after that, the Moon disappears completely. But a few days later, a tiny sliver of light returns.

(r) Mary Evans Picture Library/Photo Researchers, Inc.

This 600-year-old drawing shows two European astronomers studying the Moon and recording their observations in a notebook.

STOP AND CHECK

Ask and Answer Questions Why were ancient people amazed by the Moon? Go back to the text to find the answer.

338

ACT Access Complex Text

▶ Organization

Tell students page 338 summarizes what the article will be about. Point students to the third and fourth paragraphs.

→ *What is the author's purpose for writing these two paragraphs?* (to describe how the moon appears over the course of a month)

→ *The author structures these two paragraphs with a sequence that provides details about how the moon changes. What happens at the beginning of the sequence?* (People on Earth can't see the moon.) *What happens next?* (A tiny sliver of light appears.) *What happens at the end of a complete cycle?* (The moon disappears again.)

This series of photos shows what the Moon looks like during each night of its cycle. You can see one half of the Moon lit up on Day 7, a Full Moon on Day 14, and the other half of the Moon lit up on Day 21.

0 1 2 3 4
5 6 7 8 9
10 11 12 13 14
15 16 17 18 19
20 21 22 23 24
25 26 27 28 29

339

(bkgd) Shigemi Numazawa/Atlas Photo Bank/Photo Researchers, Inc.

LITERATURE ANTHOLOGY, pp. 338–339

2 Text Features: Diagrams

What does the diagram show? (how the moon appears over a 29-day period) If Day 1 were May 1st, on which day would you see a full moon? (May 14th) On which day would the moon seem to start shrinking? (May 15th)

3 Genre: Expository Text

What about this selection helps to identify it as expository text? (The diagrams, historical drawings, and subheadings help to show that the text is explaining factual information.)

ELL Use the diagram on page 339 to help students connect the descriptions of the moon in the text to the pictures.

→ *Which number shows the moon at the beginning of the cycle?* (1)

→ *Which numbers show the moon as a half of a circle?* (7 and 21)

→ *Which number shows the moon as a full, round disk?* (14) Ask an advanced student what we call this moon. (full moon)

Develop Comprehension

4 Ask and Answer Questions

Generate a question of your own about the text and share it with a partner. To find the answer, try rereading the text. For example, you might ask, "What do all of the planets in our solar system have in common?" To find the answer, you can reread the second paragraph on page 340. (They are all in orbit around the sun.)

5 Skill: Make Inferences

Why would Mercury take 277 fewer days than Earth to orbit the sun? (It is closer to the sun so its path in orbit is far shorter.) Why does it take Neptune 164 Earth years longer than Earth to orbit the sun? (Neptune is very far from the sun, so its path to orbit the sun is much longer.)

6 Vocabulary: Context Clues

Which context clues help you to determine the meaning of "dwarf planets" in the first paragraph on page 341? (Pluto; larger than asteroids)

Our Place in Space

Earth is one of eight planets in our solar system. The other planets are Mercury, Venus, Mars, Jupiter, Saturn, Uranus, and Neptune.

4

All eight planets orbit, or move around, a star called the Sun. A year is the amount of time it takes a planet to circle the Sun once. Earth completes the trip in about 365 days, so an Earth year is 365 days long. That is the amount of time between your last birthday and your next birthday.

Mercury is the closest planet to the Sun. It makes one full orbit in just eighty-eight days, so a year on Mercury is much shorter than a year on Earth. Neptune is the farthest planet from the Sun. It takes Neptune 165 Earth years to circle the

5 Sun. That is a really long time to wait between birthdays!

Each planet in our solar system follows a **specific** path as it orbits the Sun.

340

(b) Tim Kiusalaas/Corbis

A C T Access Complex Text

▶ Specific Vocabulary

Have students reread the first paragraph on page 341. Tell them that the author uses words that are specific to the study of outer space. In order to make sure they understand the words, review each definition given by the author.

→ *What is an asteroid?* (a rocky chunk in orbit between Mars and Jupiter)

→ *What is a dwarf planet?* (a rocky chunk that is larger than an asteroid but smaller than a planet)

→ *What is a comet?* (a small icy object that orbits the sun)

Asteroids are small, rocky objects that orbit the Sun.

Ibkgd) Stocktrek Images/Getty Images

Planets are not the only objects that orbit the Sun. Thousands of smaller, rocky chunks called asteroids and dwarf planets do, too. Most asteroids follow paths located between Mars and Jupiter. Dwarf planets, such as Pluto, are larger than asteroids. Their orbits are located beyond Neptune. Comets are small icy objects that orbit the Sun. Their orbital paths around the Sun are long and thin, like a cucumber. **(6)**

Planets, asteroids, dwarf planets, and comets do not fly off into space because the Sun's gravity is always tugging on these smaller objects. Their forward movement is perfectly balanced with the pull of the Sun's gravity. **(7)**

341

LITERATURE ANTHOLOGY, pp. 340–341

7 Skill: Cause and Effect

There are scientific laws, like the law of gravity, that describe how things move. These laws are the same on Earth and far out in outer space. Why don't the planets and other objects fly off into space away from the sun? (Their forward movement is balanced by the pull of the sun's gravity.) What is the effect of this balance of forces? (The objects stay in orbit.) Fill this detail into your chart.

Cause	→	Effect
Objects in space have forward movement that is balanced with gravity.	→	The objects stay in orbit.

ELL Use the pictures on pages 340–341 to reinforce the meaning of difficult words.

→ *What do the rings in this picture show?* (orbits) Make a circle in the air to show students an orbital path. *Complete this sentence: Earth's orbit takes _____ days to complete.* (365)

→ Point out the cognate planet/*planeta* and have students point to each of the planets and say its name.

→ *What does the picture on page 341 show?* (asteroids) *What do the asteroids look like?* (small rocks) *What is larger than an asteroid?* (a dwarf planet)

Develop Comprehension

The Moon in Motion

The Sun is not the only object in our solar system with enough gravitational pull to attract smaller bodies. Six planets—Earth, Mars, Jupiter, Saturn, Uranus, and Neptune—have smaller objects orbiting them. So do a few asteroids and dwarf planets. These smaller objects are moons.

Scientists have identified at least sixty moons circling Jupiter. Saturn probably has even more. But Mars has just two moons, and Earth has only one.

In this image of Earth and the Moon, you can see part of the far side of the Moon, the half of the Moon that never faces Earth.

342

8 **Strategy: Ask and Answer Questions**

Teacher Think Aloud The text on page 343 provides a lot of detailed information about the moon. We can ask questions about this page and answer them using the text to make sure we understand. What is similar about the moon and Earth?

Prompt students to apply the strategy in a Think Aloud by asking and answering questions. Have them turn to a partner and paraphrase to answer the question.

Student Think Aloud I have noticed that there are some similarities in how different objects in space move. After looking through the text on page 343, I can see that both the moon and Earth orbit around a larger object. Both Earth and the moon rotate, although the moon rotates much more slowly. Both the moon and Earth are lit up by the sun.

ACT Access Complex Text

▶ Connection of Ideas

Remind students that in order to understand complex text, they will need to connect ideas previously read to new information. Point them to the first paragraph on page 342.

→ *What did you read previously about objects orbiting the sun?* (Planets, asteroids, comets, and dwarf planets all orbit the sun.)

→ *Why don't these objects fly off into space? Look back at the bottom of page 341 if you cannot remember.* (Their forward movement is perfectly balanced with the pull of the sun's gravity.)

→ *What is similar about all of the moons' orbits and those of the objects we previously discussed?* (They all orbit around a larger object in similar ways.)

Earth's Moon is closer to Earth than any other object in space. Still, it took Apollo astronauts traveling at rocket speed about four days to reach the Moon in the late 1960s and early 1970s. The Moon is about 238,860 miles (384,400 kilometers) from Earth. That is almost one hundred times farther than the distance between New York, New York, and Los Angeles, California.

It takes the Moon about twenty-seven days to complete one full orbit around Earth. That means it circles our planet about twelve times each year.

As the Moon orbits Earth, it also **rotates**, or spins like a top. Earth rotates too. Our planet takes about twenty-four hours—or one full day—to complete one rotation. The Moon spins much more slowly. It rotates just once during each twenty-seven day orbit.

As Earth spins, different areas of the planet face the Sun. It is daytime in the places that are facing the Sun. That is why days are bright and sunny. It is nighttime on the part of Earth facing away from the Sun. That is why it is dark at night. **8**

The amount of time it takes the Moon to rotate is the same as the time the Moon takes to orbit Earth, so people on Earth always see the same side of the Moon. Scientists call the side we see the near side. When the near side of the Moon is lit up by the Sun, we see a full, bright circle. When the far side of the Moon is fully lit up by the Sun, we **9** cannot see the Moon at all.

(b) Corbis

A total of six Apollo spacecraft carried people to the Moon. The astronauts returned with photos, rock samples, and amazing stories of what they saw as they cruised around in lunar rovers.

343

LITERATURE ANTHOLOGY, pp. 342–343

ELL Point out the difference between *orbit* and *rotation*. If possible, physically model the difference between the two types of movement.

→ *Which word means when a planet spins around while staying in the same place?* (rotation)

→ *Which word means when a planet revolves around another object in space?* (orbit)

9 Skill: Cause and Effect

Paraphrase with a partner how Earth's rotation causes daytime and nighttime. (When Earth rotates, certain areas face the sun while others face away. Daytime occurs at places facing the sun, while nighttime occurs at places facing away from the sun.) Add this cause and effect to your chart.

Cause	→	Effect
Objects in space have forward movement that is balanced with gravity.	→	The objects stay in orbit.
The Earth rotates.	→	People experience daytime and nighttime depending on which areas are facing the sun.

SCIENCE **CONNECT TO CONTENT**
ECLIPSES

The phases of the moon and daytime and nighttime are relatively constant processes related to the movements of large objects in space. However, a rarer event also related to these movements is the eclipse. An eclipse occurs when a large body in space blocks the sun's light from reaching another body. There are two types of eclipses: solar and lunar. A solar eclipse occurs when the moon moves in between the Earth and the sun and casts a shadow on certain areas. During a lunar eclipse, a shadow is cast by the Earth upon the moon, blocking our ability to see the moon.

Develop Comprehension

10 Author's Craft: Word Choice

What is the heading of this section of text? (Let There Be Light) With a partner, discuss why you think the author chose this name for the section. (This text is all about how light illuminates objects in space. Light is the reason why stars and planets seem to glow.)

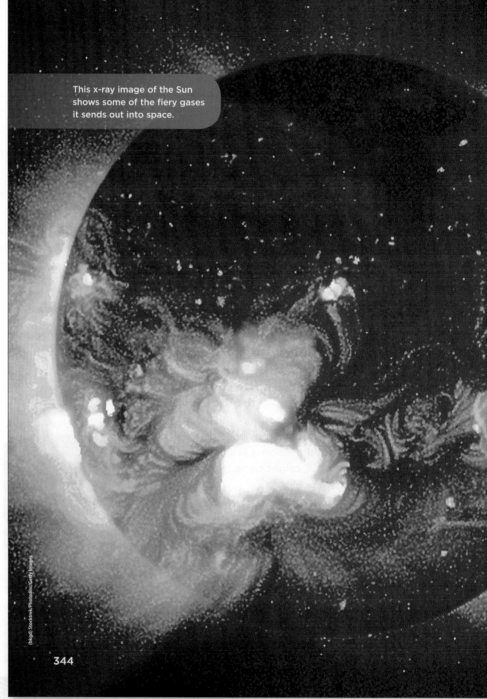

This x-ray image of the Sun shows some of the fiery gases it sends out into space.

(bkgd) Stocktrek/Photodisc/Getty Images

344

A C T Access Complex Text

▶ Prior Knowledge

Some of the information on pages 344–345 requires some knowledge of scientific terms or instruments. Point students to the photo and caption on page 344.

→ *This is an image of the sun. What type of instrument was used to capture this image?* (an x-ray machine)

→ Explain that x-ray machines are most often used in hospitals and doctors' offices to see inside the body. However, they are also used by scientists.

→ *Why might scientists have taken this image of the sun using x-rays?* (to see things we cannot see with our naked eye; to see the sun's gases)

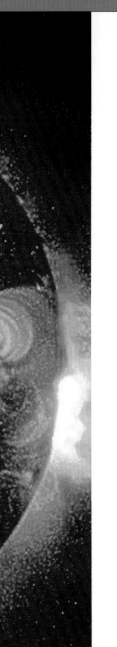

Let There Be Light

The Sun is a star—a giant ball of boiling gases. The temperature at the center of the Sun is 27 million degrees Fahrenheit (15 million degrees Celsius). The gases inside the Sun are so hot that it glows. The Sun is not the biggest star in the Universe, but it looks the brightest in the sky to us because it is the closest.

During some parts of the year, we can see Venus, Mars, Jupiter, and Saturn as bright, steadily shining dots of light in the night sky. But these planets do not produce their own light. The light we see when we look at them comes from the Sun. As the Sun's rays hit a planet, some of the light bounces off the planet's surfaces and travels back into space. When some of that reflected light reaches our eyes, the planet seems to glow. The Moon reflects the Sun's light, too.

We know from astronauts and space vehicles visiting the Moon that it is made of solid rock. There is no source of light on the Moon. We can only see the Moon when the Sun is shining on it, and then that light is reflected off the Moon's surface and into our eyes. The Moon is much smaller than Venus, Mars, Jupiter, and Saturn, but it looks bigger and brighter to us because it is much closer to Earth than those planets are. **11**

STOP AND CHECK

Ask and Answer Questions How are we able to see planets and moons when they do not produce their own light? Go back to the text to find the answer.

345

LITERATURE ANTHOLOGY, pp. 344–345

11 Skill: Cause and Effect

Why does the moon seem to glow? (The sun's light bounces off its surface.) What causes the moon to seem much bigger than the other planets? (It is much closer to Earth.) Add this information to your chart.

Cause	→	Effect
Objects in space have forward movement that is balanced with gravity.	→	The objects stay in orbit.
The Earth rotates.	→	People experience daytime and nighttime depending on which areas are facing the sun.
The moon reflects the sun's light and is close to Earth.	→	It looks bigger and brighter to us.

STOP AND CHECK

Ask and Answer Questions How are we able to see planets and moons when they do not produce their own light? Go back to the text to find the answer. (The sun's light bounces off the surfaces of planets and moons.)

 Review the terminology related to how light is transmitted and reflected in space.

→ *When something glows, is it easy to see or hard to see?* (easy to see) *Does the moon usually glow at night?* (yes)

→ *Does the sun glow?* (yes) *The sun glows because it is a giant ball of _____.* (boiling gases) *The moon glows because of light from the _____.* (sun)

→ *The moon seems to glow because light reflects off its surface. What is another word for* reflect? (bounce)

LITERATURE ANTHOLOGY **T217J**

Develop Comprehension

12 Skill: Cause and Effect

Paraphrase the cause-and-effect relationship described in the first paragraph. (The sun lights up the moon. The positions of the moon and Earth change over time. The way the moon looks depends on what position it and Earth are in when the sun's rays light up the moon.)

Cause	→	Effect
Objects in space have forward movement that is balanced with gravity.	→	The objects stay in orbit.
The Earth rotates.	→	People experience daytime and nighttime depending on which areas are facing the sun.
The moon is close to Earth.	→	It looks bigger and brighter to us.
The moon and Earth change positions.	→	The sun's rays light up the moon in different ways on different days.

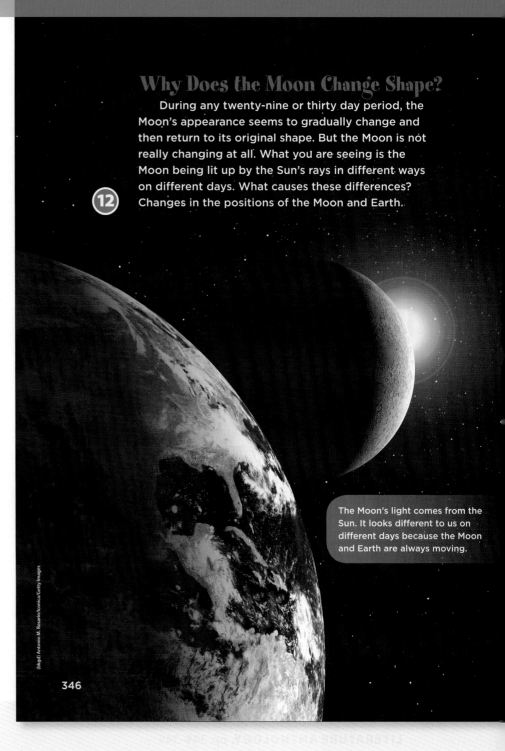

Why Does the Moon Change Shape?

During any twenty-nine or thirty day period, the Moon's appearance seems to gradually change and then return to its original shape. But the Moon is not really changing at all. What you are seeing is the Moon being lit up by the Sun's rays in different ways on different days. What causes these differences? 12 Changes in the positions of the Moon and Earth.

The Moon's light comes from the Sun. It looks different to us on different days because the Moon and Earth are always moving.

(bkgd) Antonio M. Rosario/Iconica/Getty Images

346

A C T Access Complex Text

▶ Connection of Ideas

Tell students that the text on page 347 describes how the moon appears to change shape.

→ *Did you already see information about this in the selection? Where?* (Yes; A diagram on page 339 shows the moon during each night of its cycle. It shows how the moon appears to change shape because of how it is lit up on different nights.)

→ Ask students to reread pages 347 and 339. *The same topic is covered on both pages. How is the information presented differently?* (The description on page 347 goes into more detail about each moon phase. The diagram on page 339 shows how the moon visually changes, but most of the names of the phases aren't given or described.)

This Crescent Moon appeared 5 days after the New Moon.

In the first phase of the Moon, called the New Moon, the giant ball of rock is not visible on Earth at all. That is because the Moon is in between the Sun and Earth. The far side of the Moon is being lit up by the Sun, but the near side is not.

As the Moon orbits our planet, more and more of the near side is lit up by the Sun's rays. After a few days, you can see a C-shaped sliver called a Crescent Moon. Some people think this phase of the Moon is shaped like a **crescent** roll.

Close to one week after you see the New Moon, the Sun lights up about half of the near side of the Moon. This phase is called the First Quarter Moon because the Moon is now one-quarter, or 25 percent, of the way through its full cycle.

A few days later, the Moon will have traveled far enough in its orbit for you to see a shape that has curved humps on both sides. This phase is called the Gibbous Moon because *gibbous* is the Latin word for *humped*.

Around two weeks after you see the New Moon, the Sun shines directly on the near side of the Moon. The entire Full Moon is lit up.

347

LITERATURE ANTHOLOGY, pp. 346–347

13 Strategy: Ask and Answer Questions

The text on this page provides information about how the moon looks during different phases. Generate a question about the moon phases, and answer it to check your understanding.

Student Think Aloud I know I can check my understanding by asking and answering questions about the text. A good question to ask myself is, "What are the phases called and what do they look like?" Rereading the text on page 347 will help me answer this question. I read that there are five main moon phases discussed. The first one is listed in the first paragraph. It is the new moon. This is when the moon can't be seen at all. After a few days when a sliver of moon appears lit up, it is called a crescent moon. A couple days later, the first quarter moon happens. When the moon has humps on both sides, it is called a gibbous moon. The last phase listed is the full moon. This is when the moon is completely lit up.

ELL Point out the cognates gibbous/*giboso* and crescent/*creciente*. Even though these are cognates, students may be unfamiliar with the words and their meanings. Model drawing a crescent shape in the air and have students say "crescent." Then model drawing a gibbous shape in the air and have students say "gibbous."

Develop Comprehension

14 Author's Craft: Text Structure

How does the author structure the text on pages 346–349? (in a sequence) With a partner, discuss how the text structure helps you understand what the author explains. (The moon changes shape in a very specific sequence, so the sequence text structure helps show the gradual changes.)

As the Moon continues to orbit around Earth, the Moon begins to disappear. After a few days, you will see another Gibbous Moon in the sky.

Close to three weeks after you saw the New Moon, the Sun lights up only about half of the near side of the Moon. This phase is called the Last Quarter Moon because the Moon is now just one-quarter, or 25 percent, away from completing its full cycle.

A few days later, all but a tiny sliver of the Crescent Moon will have disappeared. Most of the Sun's rays are now falling on the far side of the Moon.

In just a few more days, the Moon will disappear completely. The Moon has returned to its original position in its orbital path. The far side of the Moon is fully lit up by the Sun, but the near side is in complete darkness.

14 The Moon has cycled through its phases for years, and it will continue to do so as long as our planet and its mysterious moon exist.

This stunning Full Moon appeared over gigantic rock formations called buttes in Monument Valley, which is located in Utah and Arizona.

348

A C T Access Complex Text

▶ Connection of Ideas

Have students continue using the diagram from page 339 to track how the changes in the moon's shape are described on page 348.

→ *Which phases are seen twice during a full cycle?* (All phases are seen twice except the full moon and new moon.)

→ *For the phases that happen twice in one cycle, how does the moon appear differently the second time the phase happens?* (During the second time the phase happens, the opposite part of the moon is lit up. The phases are mirror images.)

This Last Quarter Moon appeared about three weeks after the New Moon.

349

LITERATURE ANTHOLOGY, pp. 348–349

Return to Predictions

Review students' predictions and purposes for reading. Ask them to answer the Essential Question. (We can use science to explain what we see in the sky. For example, we can use the science behind how light travels and reflects to explain objects in the night sky. The moon and other planets glow because the sun's light reflects off their surfaces. How we view these reflections changes as objects in space move. We see the stars because they produce their own light.)

ELL Help students connect the picture on page 349 with the text. Demonstrate how the image is showing half of the moon by drawing the moon on the board and shading the side that the sun lights up during the last phase. You can also go back to the diagram on page 339 and point out the Last Quarter Moon phase for comparison.

→ *What phase do we see in the picture on page 349?* (Last Quarter Moon)

About the Author

Meet the Author

Melissa Stewart

Have students read the biography of the author. Ask:

→ How might Melissa's wonderings about science have inspired her to write a selection about the moon?

→ What might Melissa's advice be about "going out and exploring" how the moon changes shape?

Author's Purpose

To Inform

Remind students that authors who write to inform present facts about a topic and often use text features to provide more facts and details. Students may say that the photos and captions are closely linked to the surrounding text and so it is easier for readers to visualize how the moon appears to change shape.

Author's Craft

Text Features

Explain that authors use diagrams and photographs with captions to provide a visual aid for explanations in the text. Discuss what this adds to the writing.

→ The author provides a diagram of the solar system on page 340 allowing the reader to visualize the planets' path around the sun.

→ Have students find another diagram or photograph, such as the one on page 339. Have them explain how it contributes to their understanding of the text.

About the Author

Melissa Stewart believes in the power of nature. She thinks that every part of nature has a story to tell—and Melissa is listening!

Melissa fell in love with nature as a child while walking through the woods with her father. Today, she writes science books about what she loves. Melissa enjoys writing children's books because kids are so curious. Some of her best books have grown out of her own wonderings.

When Melissa isn't writing, she likes to be outside. She also speaks about science at schools, and she teaches writing courses. Melissa has advice for kids everywhere: Go out and explore!

Author's Purpose

Why does the author include photographs with captions in *Why Does the Moon Change Shape?*

350

LITERATURE ANTHOLOGY, pp. 350–351

Respond to Reading

Summarize

Use important details from *Why Does the Moon Change Shape?* to summarize what you learned about the phases of the Moon. Information from your Cause and Effect Chart may help you.

Cause → Effect
→
→
→
→

Text Evidence

1. How do you know that *Why Does the Moon Change Shape?* is an expository text? **GENRE**

2. Why does the Moon appear so big and bright to people on Earth? **CAUSE AND EFFECT**

3. What does the phrase *gravitational pull* mean in the first paragraph on page 342? Identify the context clues that help you determine the meaning. **PARAGRAPH CLUES**

4. According to the text, we always see the same side of the Moon. Explain what causes this to happen. **WRITE ABOUT READING**

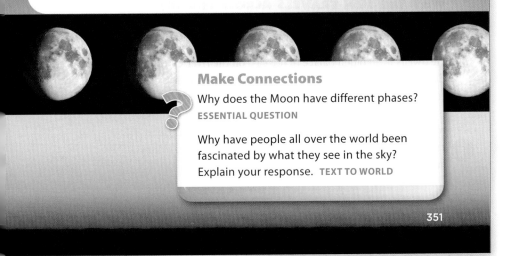

Make Connections

Why does the Moon have different phases? **ESSENTIAL QUESTION**

Why have people all over the world been fascinated by what they see in the sky? Explain your response. **TEXT TO WORLD**

351

Make Connections *Analytical Writing*

Essential Question Have partners work together to cite text evidence to write about why the moon has different phases. Ask partners to discuss responses with the the class.

Text to World After students discuss why they think people all over the world find objects in the sky fascinating, have them list myths or stories they might have heard about space and the moon.

Respond to Reading

Summarize

Review with students the information from their graphic organizers. Model how to use the information to summarize *Why Does the Moon Change Shape?*

Analytical Writing **Write About Reading: Summarize** Ask students to write a summary of the selection, using the main causes and effects from each section. Have students share their summaries with a partner.

Text Evidence

1. **Genre** <u>Answer</u> The selection includes facts and information about the moon. <u>Evidence</u> Headings such as "Our Place in Space" and "The Moon in Motion" organize the factual information about the moon. There are also many photos of the moon and its phases with captions.

2. **Cause and Effect** <u>Answer</u> The moon is close to Earth and it reflects light. <u>Evidence</u> We can only see the moon when the sun's light is reflecting off of it. In space, the moon is the closest object to Earth, so it appears much larger than planets or stars.

3. **Paragraph Clues** <u>Answer</u> *Gravitational pull* means "force of attraction between two objects in the universe." <u>Evidence</u> Context clues in the paragraph explain that the sun's gravitational pull "attracts other bodies."

4. **Analytical Writing** **Write About Reading: Cause and Effect** The details on page 343 tell why we always see the same side of the moon. The moon orbits around the Earth, and it also rotates at the same time. Earth is also rotating, though it rotates much faster than the moon. As a result, we always see the same side of the moon.

Develop Comprehension

Literature Anthology

"How It Came to Be"

Text Complexity Range

Lexile

740 — 910 — 1010

TextEvaluator™

23 — 40 — 51

Options for Close Reading

→ Whole Class

→ Small Group

→ Independent

CCSS **Genre · Myth**

Compare Texts
Read two myths that seek to explain what people see in the sky.

HOW IT CAME TO BE

The following two myths originated thousands of years ago, during a time when people did not yet enjoy all the benefits of modern science. **Astronomers** *with* **telescopes** *did not exist to answer questions about the universe. Instead, people told stories to explain what they saw in the sky above.*

WHY THE SUN TRAVELS ACROSS THE SKY

A retelling of a Greek myth

Helios, the Titan god of the sun, brings light to the earth. He dwells in a golden palace in the east on the river Okeanos. Each morning, Helios follows his sister Eos, the goddess of the Dawn, across the sky. He drives a shining chariot, drawn by four noble steeds, upward through the clouds. The chariot moves higher as rays of brilliant light pour forth from Helios's **(1)** crown. Slowly, the steeds climb with a single purpose. Hours later, they finally reach the highest point of the sky.

352

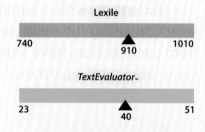

A C T **ccess Complex Text**

What makes this text complex?

▶ **Specific Vocabulary**

▶ **Prior Knowledge**

▶ **Specific Vocabulary**

Point out to students that myths sometimes have language that can be difficult to decipher because it is no longer in common use. Tell them that they should use context clues to figure out the meanings of difficult words.

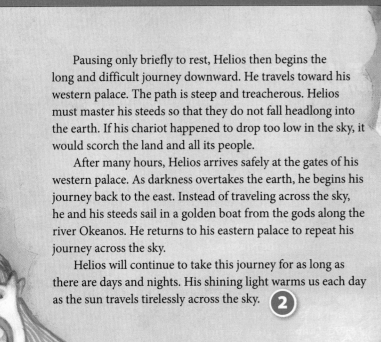

Pausing only briefly to rest, Helios then begins the long and difficult journey downward. He travels toward his western palace. The path is steep and treacherous. Helios must master his steeds so that they do not fall headlong into the earth. If his chariot happened to drop too low in the sky, it would scorch the land and all its people.

After many hours, Helios arrives safely at the gates of his western palace. As darkness overtakes the earth, he begins his journey back to the east. Instead of traveling across the sky, he and his steeds sail in a golden boat from the gods along the river Okeanos. He returns to his eastern palace to repeat his journey across the sky.

Helios will continue to take this journey for as long as there are days and nights. His shining light warms us each day as the sun travels tirelessly across the sky. **2**

353

LITERATURE ANTHOLOGY, pp. 352–353

Compare Texts

Students will read another text about objects and events in the sky. Ask students to do a close reading of the text. Encourage them to use the ask and answer questions strategy or other strategies they know to help them. They will also take notes. Then students will use the text evidence they gathered to compare this text with *Why Does the Moon Change Shape?*

1 Ask and Answer Questions

What is the steeds' "single purpose" at the bottom of page 352?

With a partner, paraphrase the way Helios and his steeds move across the sky. (They move slowly with brilliant rays coming out of Helios's crown.)

2 Ask and Answer Questions

What does the last paragraph say about Helios's journey across the sky?

Analytical Writing **Write About Reading** Take notes about how often Helios makes his journey. (The last paragraph tells that Helios is consistent. He will make his daily journey forever.)

→ *What context clues can help you figure out the meaning of* dwells? (in a golden palace) *What is another word for* dwells? (lives)

→ *What context clues can help you figure out the meaning of* steed? (drawn by, chariot) *What is another name for a* steed? (a horse)

ELL Help students understand the descriptions on page 352 using the illustration.

→ Point to Helios in the picture. *What does Helios look like in the sky?* (the Sun) *Helios drives a* ____ *across the sky.* (chariot)

→ *This myth explains how* ____. (the sun travels)

Develop Comprehension

3 Ask and Answer Questions

What are the three treasures that help Thor?

Analytical Writing **Write About Reading** With a partner, make a list describing Thor's three treasures and how they might help Thor emerge victorious. (1. Belt: increases strength; 2. Gloves: iron-clad, probably for protection and grip; 3. Hammer: always returns when thrown)

4 Ask and Answer Questions

What reason does the author give for the experience of thunder and lightning being reassuring? (The author says that it is a reminder that there is someone who is always able to protect people from harm.)

WHY THERE IS THUNDER AND LIGHTNING

A retelling of a Norse myth

Thor, the mighty Norse god of thunder and lightning, is both large and powerful. With his long hair, flowing beard, and quick temper, he often intimidates other gods. Despite his fierce appearance, he is considerably popular. Thor is admired for his ability to protect both gods and humans against evil. Among the Norse gods, he is the strongest of all.

Thor lives with other warrior gods in Asgard, one of the nine worlds located at the highest level of the Norse universe. Odin, Thor's father, rules Asgard. Odin is a great warrior who is often associated with a quest for wisdom. Still, he is not nearly as popular as his son.

Three treasures help Thor emerge victorious time and time again. One is a belt that increases his strength. Another is a pair of iron-clad gloves. The third treasure is his greatest—a mighty war hammer. This hammer helps Thor protect Asgard from all enemies. When Thor throws his hammer, it magically returns to him like a boomerang.

354

ACT Access Complex Text

▶ Prior Knowledge

Tell students that these two myths come from two different ancient cultures: Greek and Norse. Both cultures told myths to explain natural events and how the world came to be the way it is.

→ Have students tell what they know about Greek and Norse cultures. Tell them that Norse culture was centered in what is today called Scandinavia.

During thunderstorms, Thor is said to be riding through the heavens in his mighty chariot, pulled by a pair of enormous goats. The sound of the chariot wheels creates a thunderous rumbling that shakes the world. Lightning flashes across the sky whenever Thor throws his magical hammer.

The experience of thunder and lightning can be frightening and oddly reassuring at the same time. It reminds us that Thor is a fierce and all-powerful warrior but one who will always be able to protect us from harm. **4**

Make Connections

How do the myths of Helios and Thor help to explain what people see in the sky? Compare and contrast the myths. **ESSENTIAL QUESTION**

Contrast how ancient people understood their world and how modern people understand the world today. Explain using examples from the selections. **TEXT TO TEXT**

355

Gerardo Suzán

LITERATURE ANTHOLOGY, pp. 354–355

Make Connections
Analytical Writing

Essential Question Students should write about how both myths are similar in that they attempt to explain nature's mysteries, but different by the natural events they explain. Have partners compare their responses.

Text to Text Have groups of students compare and contrast the myths of Thor and Helios with other myths they have read in the past. Each group can report back to the whole class. Ask one group to focus on myths that explain something. Ask another group to focus on myths that teach a lesson. Ask a third group to focus on myths that contain heroes. All three groups should discuss similarities and differences in characters, themes, topics, and patterns of events. If students need help thinking of the three kinds of myths, refer them to Native American myths about the changing of the seasons, the Greek myth of Arachne, and the Mayan myth of the Hero Twins as examples.

ELL Use the illustration to help ELLs understand the treasures that allow Thor to be victorious in battle.

→ *Thor's belt helps increase his strength. Point to Thor's belt in the picture.*

→ *Thor's gloves are iron-clad. That means they are protected by a covering of iron. Point to Thor's iron-clad gloves.*

→ *Thor uses a mighty war hammer to protect him from enemies. Point to Thor's hammer.*

Phonics/Fluency

MINILESSON 20 Mins

Diphthongs /oi/ and /ou/

Go Digital

Diphthongs

Present the Lesson

View "Wonders of the Night Sky"

OBJECTIVES

CCSS Use combined knowledge of all letter-sound correspondences, syllabication patterns, and morphology (e.g., roots and affixes) to read accurately unfamiliar multisyllabic words in context and out of context. **RF.4.3a**

CCSS Use context to confirm or self-correct word recognition and understanding, rereading as necessary. **RF.4.4c**

Rate: 102–122 WCPM

ACADEMIC LANGUAGE
accuracy

1 Explain

Display the *Boy* and *Cow* **Sound-Spelling Cards** for the diphthongs /oi/ and /ou/. Point out the *oi* and *oy* spellings on the *Boy* card and the *ow* and *ou* spellings on the *Cow* card. Say the sound as you point to each spelling, and then provide a sample word (*coin/toy, now/house*).

2 Model

Write the word *point* on the board. Circle the letters *oi* in the word and model pronouncing the diphthong /oi/. Then run your finger under the word as you sound out the whole word.

3 Guided Practice

Write the following /oi/ and /ou/ words on the board. Help students identify each diphthong and its spelling. Then have them echo-read the words after you.

cloud	enjoy	sound
boil	power	join
howl	noise	royal

Read Multisyllabic Words

Transition to Longer Words Draw a T-chart on the board. In the first column, write *count, coil,* and *destroy.* In the second column, write *miscount, recoil,* and *destroyer.* Have students choral-read the words in the first column. Point out that the words in the second column contain the words in the first column plus a prefix or suffix.

Ask students to underline the spellings of /oi/ and /ou/ in the words in the second column. Then model how to read the words. Point to the words randomly and have students choral-read them.

ELL

Refer to the sound transfers chart in the **Language Transfers Handbook** to identify sounds that do not transfer in Spanish, Cantonese, Vietnamese, Hmong, and Korean.

Greek and Latin Roots

1 Explain

Explain that many English words have Greek and Latin roots. These roots give clues to the meaning of a word.

→ The Greek root *graph* means "write" (*graphic*).

→ The Greek root *phon* means "sound" (*phonics*).

→ The Latin root *spec* means "look" (*spectator*).

→ The Latin root *aqua* means "water" (*aquatic*).

2 Model

Write and say *symphony*. Have students repeat after you. Model identifying and circling the Greek root *phon*. Point out that the meaning of the root *phon* ("sound") provides a clue to the meaning of *symphony*.

3 Guided Practice

Write the words *aquarium, autograph, inspect,* and *telephone* on the board. Have students identify each Greek or Latin root and then say each word. Help students determine each word's meaning.

 ←

Accuracy

Explain/Model Explain that reading with accuracy means reading every word and pronouncing it correctly. Point out that this may be challenging when reading expository text that has unfamiliar content. Remind students that it may be necessary to reread new words in order to build accuracy.

Model reading page 281 of "Wonders of the Night Sky." Begin reading the text under the heading "Aurora Borealis." Tell students to listen as you read challenging terms in the passage. Point out the pronunciation for *aurora borealis* in parentheses.

Practice/Apply Have students partner-read the passage one paragraph at a time, focusing on accuracy. Offer feedback.

Daily Fluency Practice

Students can practice fluency using **Your Turn Practice Book**.

Monitor and *Differentiate*

✔ Quick Check

Can students decode multisyllabic words with the diphthongs /oi/ and /ou/? Can students read words with Greek and Latin roots? Can students read fluently?

⬇

Small Group Instruction

If No →	**Approaching Level**	Reteach pp. T234, T238
	ELL	Develop pp. T250, T254
If Yes →	**On Level**	Review p. T240
	Beyond Level	Extend p. T244

ON-LEVEL PRACTICE BOOK p. 188

A. Read each sentence. Circle the word with the same vowel sound found in *boy* or *cow*. Then write the letters that make the vowel sound on the line.

1. The voices in the hall would make it hard to study for the test. _____ oi

2. The tree will tower over the plants once it begins to grow. _____ ow

3. I must carefully pack for the long voyage ahead of me. _____ oy

4. There were over two thousand people at the show last night. _____ ou

5. The students were howling with laughter at my comedy act. _____ ow

6. The icy snow was beginning to annoy the birds in the tree. _____ oy

B. Read the definitions below. Then read each word and circle the Greek or Latin root. Write the meaning of the root on the line.

The Greek root *graph* means "write."	The Latin root *spec* means "look."
The Greek root *phon* means "sound."	The Latin root *aqua* means "water."

1. megaphone _____ sound

2. speculate _____ look

3. aquamarine _____ water

4. geography _____ write

5. inspection _____ look

6. homograph _____ write

APPROACHING	BEYOND	ELL
p. 188	p. 188	p. 188

→ **Wrap Up the Week**
Integrate Ideas

👉 **Go** Digital

www.connected.mcgraw-hill.com
RESOURCES
Research and Inquiry

Minden Pictures/Masterfile

RESEARCH AND INQUIRY

Wonders in the Sky

OBJECTIVES

Conduct short research projects that build knowledge through investigation of different aspects of a topic. **W.4.7**

Add audio recordings and visual displays to presentations when appropriate to enhance the development of main ideas or themes. **SL.4.5**

- Gather resources for research.
- Present information visually.

ACADEMIC LANGUAGE

paraphrase, multimedia, presentation

Research Eclipses

COLLABORATE

Explain that students will collaborate in pairs and research what causes eclipses. They will then use visuals or multimedia elements to explain the phenomenon to others. Discuss the following steps:

❶ Collaborate Divide students into pairs, creating groups with diverse learning abilities. Ask them to discuss what they already know about eclipses from their reading or from personal knowledge or experience.

❷ Find Resources Have students use print or online sources to research what causes solar eclipses, lunar eclipses, or both. Remind them to take notes, keep track of their sources, and paraphrase the information they find.

❸ Guided Practice Have student pairs plan an organized presentation about the topic that includes an introduction and conclusion. Ask them to incorporate visuals or multimedia elements into their presentation.

❹ Create the Presentation After students have finished planning their presentations, have them continue to work in pairs and create the visuals or use technology to make a multimedia presentation for the class that contains audio and visual elements.

Present the Research

Have pairs working on different types of eclipses present their research to one another, using the visuals or multimedia presentations they created. Have them answer any questions students may have. Ask students to use online Presentation Checklist 2 to evaluate their presentations. Then help students work together to publish their visuals and explanations on a class Web site.

STEM

TEXT CONNECTIONS  *Analytical Writing*

Connect to Essential Question

OBJECTIVES

CCSS Integrate information from two texts on the same topic in order to write or speak about the subject knowledgeably. **RI.4.9**

Text to Text

Cite Evidence Tell students that they will work in groups to compare information they have learned about explaining what they see in the sky from all the texts they have read. Model how to compare this information by using examples from the week's **Leveled Readers** and *Wonders of the Night Sky*, **Reading/Writing Workshop** pages 280–283. Review class notes and completed graphic organizers. You may also wish to model going back into the text for more information. You can use a Four-Door Foldable® to record comparisons.

Students should cite at least three examples from each text.

Present Information Ask groups of students to present their findings to the class. Encourage discussion, asking students to comment on similarities and differences among the ideas discussed.

Wonders of the Sky | Moon Phases
Asteroids | The Sun as a Star

Dinah Zike's
FOLDABLES®
Study Organizer

WRITE ABOUT READING *Analytical Writing*

Analyze to Inform/Explain

OBJECTIVES

CCSS Describe the overall structure (e.g., chronology, comparison, cause/effect, problem/solution) of events, ideas, concepts, or information in a text or part of a text. **RI.4.5**

CCSS Identify the reasons and evidence a speaker provides to support particular points. **SL.4.3**

Write an Analysis

Cite Evidence Using evidence from a text they have read, students will analyze how the author uses headings to tell what a section of text is mostly about.

Discuss how to analyze a text by asking *how* or *why* questions.

→ Why are headings an important part of the text?

Read and discuss the student model on **Your Turn Practice Book** page 189. Then have students select a text that uses headings. Have them write an analysis that explains how the use of headings provides information about different sections of the text. Remind students that good explanatory writing includes strong opening and concluding statements and uses possessive pronouns correctly.

 Present Your Ideas Ask partners to share their paragraphs and discuss how the evidence they cited from the text supports their ideas. Partners may suggest additional text evidence if necessary.

→ Readers to Writers

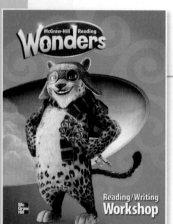

Reading/Writing Workshop

OBJECTIVES

CCSS Write routinely over extended time frames (time for research, reflection, and revision) and shorter time frames (a single sitting or a day or two) for a range of discipline-specific tasks, purposes, and audiences. **W.4.10**

CCSS Use concrete words and phrases and sensory details to convey experiences and events precisely. **W.4.3d**

• Understand use of figurative language.

• Describe the night sky using figurative language.

• Add figurative language to revise.

ACADEMIC LANGUAGE
simile, metaphor, personification

 MINILESSON **10 Mins**

Writing Traits: Word Choice

Figurative Language

Expert Model Explain that good writers use figurative language to describe people, objects, or events. Figurative language has a meaning beyond the actual definition of the words. Similes, metaphors, and personification are examples of figurative language.

→ A simile compares two unlike things using *like* or *as*: *Max walked as slowly as a turtle.*

→ A metaphor compares two unlike things without *like* or *as*: *Max was a turtle, plodding slowly across the room.*

→ Personification gives human characteristics to nonhuman things: *The trees waved their arms wildly as the wind howled.*

 Read aloud the expert model from "Wonders of the Night Sky." Ask students to listen for figurative language that helps the reader visualize the text. Have students talk with partners to identify the figurative language.

Student Model Remind students that using figurative language helps readers visualize people, objects, or events. Read aloud the student draft "Tales of the Night Sky." As students follow along, have them focus on figurative language the writer used in her draft.

 Invite partners to talk about the draft and the figurative language that Kayla used. Ask them to suggest places where Kayla could add more figurative language to help the reader visualize the text.

 Genre Writing

Narrative Text and Poetry
For full writing process lessons and rubrics, see:

→ Fictional Narrative, pages T344–T349

→ Poetry, pages T350–T355

Expert Model

Student Model

Go Digital

CCSS Writing Traits > Word Choice

 # Readers to...

Writers use figurative language such as similes and metaphors to help the reader picture the information being presented. Reread the beginning of page 281 from "Wonders of the Night Sky" below.

Figurative Language

Identify **figurative language** in the text. How does the author use a simile to help the reader visualize the text?

Expert Model

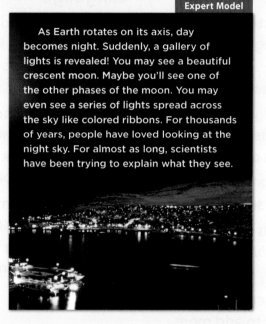

As Earth rotates on its axis, day becomes night. Suddenly, a gallery of lights is revealed! You may see a beautiful crescent moon. Maybe you'll see one of the other phases of the moon. You may even see a series of lights spread across the sky like colored ribbons. For thousands of years, people have loved looking at the night sky. For almost as long, scientists have been trying to explain what they see.

288

Writers

Kayla wrote about constellations. Read Kayla's revisions to one section of her text.

Student Model

Tales of the Night Sky

I've been interest~ed~ in constellations

since I received ~mine~ my first telescope

when I was 9. I like to imagene (sp) my

favorite constellation, the big dipper,

like a pitcher full of milk

scooping up the moon. But, to me at

least, some constellations don't look

like what they are supposed to be.

Orion looks more like a row of dots

than

~then~ a hunter with his belt.

289

Editing Marks

⊓ Switch order.
∧ Add.
⁀ Add a comma.
ꟻ Take out.
(sp) Check spelling.
≡ Make a capital letter.

Grammar Handbook

Possessive Pronouns
See page 465.

Your Turn COLLABORATE

✔ Identify the **figurative language** Kayla used.
✔ Identify the possessive pronouns that she used in her writing.
✔ Tell how the revisions improved Kayla's writing.

Go Digital!
Write online in Writer's Workspace

READING/WRITING WORKSHOP, pp. 288–289

ELL ENGLISH LANGUAGE LEARNERS SCAFFOLD

As English Language Learners write during the week, provide support to help them respond to the prompts. For example:

Beginning	**Intermediate**	**Advanced/High**
Write Help students complete the sentence frames. *I like to imagine the Big Dipper scooping up the moon like a _____ full of _____. Orion looks more like a _____ of _____ than a hunter with his _____. A type of figurative language that uses* like *or* as *is called a _____.*	**Describe** Ask students to complete the sentence frames. Encourage students to provide details. *I like to imagine the Big Dipper scooping up the moon like a _____. Orion looks more like a _____ than a _____. One type of figurative language is _____.*	**Discuss** Check for understanding. Ask: *How does the writer imagine the Big Dipper? What does the writer think the constellation Orion looks like? What are some types of figurative language?*

Writing Every Day: Word Choice

DAY 1

Writing Entry: Figurative Language

Prewrite Provide students with the prompt below.

Describe the night sky. Use figurative language.

Have partners list different ways to describe the night sky. Ask them to jot down some figurative language, such as similes, metaphors, and personification that they might include in their drafts.

Draft Have each student write a description of the night sky. Remind students to include figurative language in their drafts.

DAY 2

Focus on Figurative Language

Use **Your Turn Practice Book** page 190 to model adding figurative language.

The night sky is dark. The stars twinkle high in the sky. Sometimes there are clouds in the sky. The stars are reflected in rivers and lakes.

Model adding figurative language by revising the first sentence.

The night sky spreads over the earth like a pool of spilled black ink.

Discuss how adding figurative language helps describe the sky. Guide students to add more figurative language to the model.

Writing Entry: Figurative Language

Revise Have students revise their writing from Day 1 by adding two or three examples of figurative language.

Use the **Conferencing Routines**. Circulate among students and stop briefly to talk with individuals. Provide time for peer review.

Edit Have students use Grammar Handbook page 465 in the **Reading/Writing Workshop** to edit for errors in possessive pronouns.

Conferencing Routines

Teacher Conferences

STEP 1

Talk about the strengths of the writing.

This is a strong paragraph. It includes a topic sentence and supporting sentences that explain the main idea.

STEP 2

Focus on how the writer uses the target trait for the week.

These descriptive details help me visualize the night sky. If you include some figurative language, I will have a clearer image of what the night sky is like.

STEP 3

Make concrete suggestions for revisions. Have students work on a specific assignment, such as those to the right, and then meet with you to review progress.

DAY 3

Writing Entry: Figurative Language

Prewrite Ask students to search their Writer's Notebook for topics to write about. Or, provide a prompt, such as the following:

Describe a person or place that you know well. Use figurative language.

Draft Once students have chosen their topics, ask them to create a list of descriptive details about the person or place. Then have them think about the figurative language that they might include in their writing. Students can then use their lists to begin their drafts.

DAY 4

Writing Entry: Figurative Language

Revise Have students revise the draft writing from Day 3 by adding two or three examples of figurative language. As students are revising their drafts, hold teacher conferences with individual students. You may also wish to have students work with partners to peer conference.

Edit Invite students to review the rules for possessive pronouns on Grammar Handbook page 465 in the **Reading/Writing Workshop** and then edit their drafts for errors.

DAY 5

Share and Reflect

Discuss with the class what they learned about using figurative language to help the reader visualize the text. Invite volunteers to read and compare draft text with text that has been revised. Have students discuss the writing by focusing on the importance of the figurative language that has been added. Allow time for individuals to reflect on their own writing progress and record observations in their Writer's Notebooks.

McGraw-Hill Companies, Inc./Ken Karp, photographer

Suggested Revisions

Provide specific direction to help focus young writers.

Focus on a Sentence
Read the draft and target one sentence for revision. *Rewrite this sentence by adding figurative language to describe _____.*

Focus on a Section
Underline a section that needs to be revised. Provide specific suggestions. *This section is interesting. I want to know more about the _____. Add figurative language to help me visualize it better.*

Focus on a Revision Strategy
Underline a section. Have students use a specific revision strategy, such as adding. *This section does not include many descriptive words. Try adding some sensory details.*

Peer Conferences

Focus peer response groups on adding figurative language to help the reader visualize the text. Provide this checklist to frame discussion.

☑ Does the writing include figurative language that describes the topic?

☑ What figurative language can be added to help the reader visualize the text?

☑ Are any parts of the writing unclear?

Grammar: Possessive Pronouns

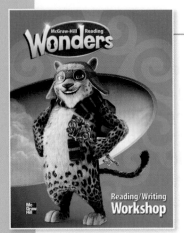

DAY 1

DAILY LANGUAGE ACTIVITY

"Her and I are writing a story" said
Gina. "Great!" said Mom "I can't wait
to read it!"
(1: She and; 2: story,"; 3: Mom.)

Introduce Possessive Pronouns

Present the following:

→ A **possessive pronoun** shows
ownership. It takes the place of a
possessive noun.

→ A possessive pronoun does not
have an apostrophe:
    my, your, his, her, its, our, their

→ Possessive pronouns must match
the nouns they replace in both
number and gender:
    It is **Tim's** bag. It is **his** bag.
    Nora and Zack's team will
    win. **Their** team will win.

Have partners discuss possessive
pronouns using page 465 of the
Grammar Handbook in **Reading/
Writing Workshop**.

DAY 2

DAILY LANGUAGE ACTIVITY

Bobby bought a hammer from Rick's
hardware store. Him says it has the
best selection of tools in town!
(1: Hardware Store; 2: He; 3; town.)

Review Possessive Pronouns

Review possessive pronouns. Have
students explain how possessive
pronouns function in a sentence.

Introduce Stand-Alone Possessive Pronouns

→ A **stand-alone possessive
pronoun** is not used directly
before a noun.

→ Most stand-alone possessive
pronouns are formed by adding
-s to the pronoun that is used
before a noun. These pronouns
are **yours, hers, ours**, and **theirs:**
    That is **hers**. This is **theirs**.

→ **Mine** is a stand-alone possessive
pronoun.
    Those earrings are **mine**.

 TALK ABOUT IT

COLLABORATE

REPLACE POSSESSIVE NOUNS

Ask partners to write five sentences
using possessive nouns and then
trade sentences with another
pair. One partner should read a
sentence aloud; the other should
restate the sentence using the
correct possessive pronoun in
place of the possessive noun.

RESTATE THE SENTENCE

Have partners each write five
sentences beginning with a subject
pronoun and a form of *have*. Have
them read their sentences aloud.
(*We have desks.*) Then have them
restate the sentence using a
stand-alone possessive pronoun.
(*The desks are ours.*)

DAY

DAILY LANGUAGE ACTIVITY

Doug built his's treehouse hisself. It's floor is covered with soft carpit.
(1: his; 2: himself; 3: Its; 4: carpet)

Mechanics and Usage: Possessive Nouns and Pronouns

→ A possessive noun should have an apostrophe.

→ A possessive pronoun and a stand-alone possessive pronoun should not have an apostrophe.

→ The contraction **it's** means "it is" or "it has." The possessive pronoun **its** shows ownership.

→ A possessive pronoun must agree in number and gender with the noun it replaces.

As students write, refer them to Grammar Handbook pages 457 and 465.

DAY

DAILY LANGUAGE ACTIVITY

The elephant uses it's tusks to dig for water. Its diet consist of grass, fruit, leafs, and bark.
(1: its; 2: consists; 3: leaves)

Proofread

Have students correct errors in these sentences.

1. The rivers current took Edgars toy boat downstream. (1: river's; 2: Edgar's)

2. Our's kites string is stuck in the tree. (1: Our; 2: kite's)

3. is this your's? (1: Is; 2: yours?)

4. Melanie put her's empty bowl in the sink, when she was finish. (1: her; 2: sink when; 3: finished)

Have students check their work using Grammar Handbook pages 457 and 465.

DAY

DAILY LANGUAGE ACTIVITY

The citys train system runs underground. The systems trains and track's need to be replaced.
(1: city's; 2: system's; 3: tracks)

Assess

Use the Daily Language Activity and **Grammar Practice Reproducibles** page 95 for assessment.

Reteach

Use Grammar Practice Reproducibles pages 91–94 and selected pages from the Grammar Handbook for additional reteaching. Remind students that it is important to use possessive pronouns correctly.

Check students' writing for use of the skill and listen for it in their speaking. Assign Grammar Revision Assignments in their Writer's Notebooks as needed.

See Grammar Practice Reproducibles pages 91–95.

USE POSSESSIVE PRONOUNS

Have students in groups write five possessive pronouns and five stand-alone possessive pronouns on index cards. Students will take turns drawing a card, saying the pronoun, and choosing a student to use that pronoun in a sentence.

LISTEN FOR POSSESSIVE PRONOUNS

Partners should each select a paragraph from a book. Have partners take turns reading their paragraphs aloud, one sentence at a time. The other partner should identify any possessive pronouns he or she hears in the sentence.

SPELL THE POSSESSIVE PRONOUN

Have partners each write five sentences using possessive pronouns. Have them take turns reading their sentences aloud. The other partner should identify the possessive pronoun in each sentence and tell how to spell it.

Spelling: Diphthongs /oi/ and /ou/

DAY 1

OBJECTIVES

CCSS Spell grade-appropriate words correctly, consulting references as needed. **L.4.2d**

Spelling Words

noises	south	cowboy
voices	pound	gown
rejoice	hound	frown
annoy	pouch	howling
destroy	thousand	flower
voyage	wound	tower
mound	grouch	

Review crook, zoom, group
Challenge drought, downtown

Differentiated Spelling

Approaching Level

voices	hound	flower
noise	pouch	tower
coin	thousand	gown
loyal	wound	frown
mound	grouch	howl
south	cloud	brown
pound	cowboy	

Beyond Level

void	trouser	nowadays
hardboiled	encounter	downtown
rejoice	announce	cowboy
annoyance	thousand	prowl
destroy	wound	empower
voyage	grouch	howling
mound	southpaw	

Assess Prior Knowledge

Display the spelling words. Read them aloud, drawing out the diphthongs /oi/ and /ou/.

Point out the spelling pattern in the word *tower*. Draw a line between the syllables: *tow/er*. Say each syllable; point out that the *ow* spelling makes an /ou/ sound. Note that some words, like *cowboy*, may include more than one diphthong.

Demonstrate sorting the spelling words by pattern under key words *noise, annoy, pound* and *gown*. (Write the words on index cards or the IWB.) Sort a few words. Point out the /oi/ and /ou/ sounds and the associated spellings as each word is sorted.

Then use the Dictation Sentences from Day 5 to give the Pretest. Say the underlined word, read the sentence, and repeat the word. Have students write the words. Then have students check and correct their spelling.

 # WORD SORTS

COLLABORATE

OPEN SORT

Have students cut apart the **Spelling Word Cards BLM** in the Teacher Resource Book and initial the back of each card. Have them read the words aloud with a partner. Then have partners do an open sort. Have them record the sort in their word study notebook.

DAY 2

Spiral Review

Review the /ü/, /u̇/, and /ū/ sounds in *zoom, should* and *huge*. Use the Dictation Sentences below for the review words. Read the sentence, say the word, and have students write the words.

1. The robbery was done by a talented <u>crook</u>.
2. Use the <u>zoom</u> on your camera.
3. A large <u>group</u> had gathered.

Have partners check the spellings.

Challenge Words Review this week's /oi/ and /ou/ diphthong spelling patterns. Use these Dictation Sentences for challenge words. Say the word, read the sentence, and say the word again. Have students write the word.

1. The rain ended the <u>drought</u>.
2. We took the bus <u>downtown</u>.

Have students check and correct their spelling before writing the words in their word study notebook.

PATTERN SORT

Complete the **pattern sort** from Day 1 using the key words, pointing out the /oi/ and /ou/ spellings and sounds. Have students use Spelling Word Cards to do their own pattern sort. Ask partners to compare and check their sorts.

DAY 3

Word Meanings

Write the following list of words on the board. Have students copy the words into their word study notebook and write the spelling word that is a synonym for each.

1. pile (*mound*)
2. scowl (*frown*)
3. trip (*voyage*)

Ask students to write a list of at least three other words that have synonyms in the spelling list. Remind students that some words may have multiple meanings, and that the pronunciation can vary depending on the meaning. Have students use a dictionary or thesaurus to check their words. Once they have checked their choices, have partners exchange lists and use the spelling list to find synonyms.

See Phonics/Spelling Reproducibles pp. 109–114.

SPEED SORT

Have partners do a **speed sort** to see who is fastest. Have them record the results in the word study notebook. Then have them do a word hunt for words with the /oi/ and /ow/ diphthong sounds, sort the new words, and add the final sort to their word study notebook.

DAY 4

Proofread and Write

Write these sentences on the board. Have students circle and correct each misspelled word. They can use print or electronic dictionaries or other resources to help them.

1. My hownd dog is houwling. (*hound, howling*)
2. The voiyage starts tomorrow and goes sowth from here. (*voyage, south*)
3. The growch complained about the small noyses. (*grouch, noises*)
4. A thowsend voyces were singing. (*thousand, voices*)

Error Correction Remind students that the /oi/ spelling *oi* and the /ow/ spelling *ou* rarely appear at the end of a word. Knowing this will help them make better choices as they write.

BLIND SORT

Have partners do a **blind sort**: one reads a Spelling Word Card; the other tells under which key word it belongs. Have them take turns until both have sorted all their words. Ask them to review their sorts, then discuss how they sorted the words and if any changes are needed.

DAY 5

Assess

Use the Dictation Sentences for the Posttest. Have students list misspelled words in their word study notebooks. Look for students' use of these words in their writings.

Dictation Sentences

1. The car made <u>noises</u> yesterday.
2. We heard <u>voices</u> outside.
3. The snow day made us <u>rejoice</u>.
4. It will <u>annoy</u> Mike if you keep interrupting him.
5. Don't <u>destroy</u> those old letters!
6. They took a <u>voyage</u> to China.
7. We dumped a <u>mound</u> of dirt.
8. We drove <u>south</u> to Florida.
9. My kitten weighs about a <u>pound</u>.
10. The <u>hound</u> followed the scent.
11. Put your money in the <u>pouch</u>.
12. We collected a <u>thousand</u> cans.
13. I <u>wound</u> the rope around the tree.
14. I'm a <u>grouch</u> when I'm tired.
15. I read a story about a <u>cowboy</u>.
16. Her wedding <u>gown</u> was beautiful.
17. You <u>frown</u> when you are sad.
18. Why are the dogs <u>howling</u>?
19. A daisy is a <u>flower</u>.
20. The princess hid in the <u>tower</u>.

Have students self-correct the tests.

Build Vocabulary

DAY 1

Connect to Words

Practice this week's vocabulary.

1. What does an **astronomer** study?

2. Is a **crescent** moon less or more than a half moon?

3. Name one of the **phases** of the moon.

4. What is Earth doing when it **rotates** around the sun?

5. What is your favorite book or television **series**?

6. Is a **sliver** small or large? What does it look like?

7. Use **specific** details to describe your favorite kind of weather.

8. What can you look at with a **telescope**?

DAY 2

Expand Vocabulary

Help students generate different forms of this week's words by adding, changing, or removing inflectional endings.

→ Draw a T-chart on the board. Write *sliver* in the first column and *slivers* in the second. Read aloud the words with students.

→ Have students share sentences using each form of *sliver*.

→ Students can fill in the chart for *phases, series,* and *crescent,* then share sentences using the different forms of the words. Point out that the singular and plural for *series* are the same.

→ Have students copy the chart in their word study notebook.

OBJECTIVES

CCSS Use context (e.g., definitions, examples, or restatements in text) as a clue to the meaning of a word or phrase. **L.4.4a**

CCSS Use common, grade-appropriate Greek and Latin affixes and roots as clues to the meaning of a word (e.g., *telegraph, photograph, autograph*). **L.4.4b**

Expand vocabulary by adding inflectional endings and affixes.

Vocabulary Words

astronomer	series
crescent	sliver
phases	specific
rotates	telescope

Go Digital

Vocabulary

Vocabulary Activities

 BUILD MORE VOCABULARY

COLLABORATE

ACADEMIC VOCABULARY

Discuss important academic words.

→ Display *universe, orbit, galaxy.*

→ Define each word and discuss the meanings with students.

→ Display *universe* and *universal.* Have partners look up and define related words.

→ Write the related words on the board. Have partners ask and answer questions using the words. Repeat with *orbit* and *galaxy.*

GREEK ROOTS

→ Explain that the Greek root *astr* means "star." Have students identify the vocabulary word that contains this root.

→ Have students brainstorm or use a print or online dictionary to find other words that contain the Greek root *astr.*

→ Have students write each word and its definition in their word study notebook.

DAY

Reinforce the Words

Review last week's and this week's vocabulary words. Have students orally complete each sentence stem.

1. You can draw a <u>crescent</u> shape by ____.
2. The <u>phases</u> of the moon ____ throughout the year.
3. The ____ <u>rotates</u> around the Sun.
4. We saw a <u>series</u> of ____ about the solar system.
5. There was just a <u>sliver</u> of ____ left on the plate.
6. My brother was very <u>specific</u> when he described his favorite ____.

DAY

Connect to Writing

→ Have students write sentences in their word study notebooks using this week's vocabulary.

→ Tell them to write sentences that provide word information they learned from this week's readings.

→ **ELL** Provide the Day 3 sentence stems 1–6 for students needing extra support.

Write About Vocabulary Have students write something they learned from this week's words in their word study notebook. For example, they might write about a time when they saw a *crescent* moon or why it would be interesting to be an *astronomer*.

DAY

Word Squares

Ask students to create Word Squares for each vocabulary word.

→ In the first square, students write the word. (example: *rotates*)

→ In the second square, students write their own definition of the word and any related words, such as synonyms. (examples: *spins, revolves*)

→ In the third square, students draw a simple illustration that will help them remember the word. (example: a spinning top)

→ In the fourth square, students write nonexamples, including antonyms for the word. (example: *moves in a straight line*)

→ Have partners compare and discuss their Word Squares.

CONTEXT CLUES

Remind students to look for clues in a paragraph to help figure out the meaning of unfamiliar words.

→ Display **Your Turn Practice Book** pages 183–184. Read the first paragraph. Model figuring out the meaning of *rotating*.

→ Have students complete page 187, then find clues for *core, spectrum* and *supernova* on pages 183–184, using a print or online dictionary to confirm meanings.

SHADES OF MEANING

Help students generate words related to *astronomer*. Draw a word web on the board. Label the web "Astronomer."

→ Ask, *What are some words related to what an astronomer studies?*

→ Have partners work together to add words to the web, such as *constellations, planets,* and *satellites.*

→ Ask students to copy the words in their word study notebook.

MORPHOLOGY

Use *telescope* as a springboard for students to learn more words. Draw a word web. Write *tele* in the center oval. Write *telescope* in one of the outer ovals.

→ Explain that *tele* is a Greek root that means "far."

→ Ask partners to search for other words that contain the root *tele* in a print or online dictionary, such as *telephone* or *television.*

→ Discuss the meanings and add the words to the web.

→ Approaching Level

Lexile 650
TextEvaluator™ 21

OBJECTIVES

CCSS Refer to details and examples in a text when explaining what the text says explicitly and when drawing inferences from the text. **RI.4.1**

CCSS Describe the overall structure (e.g., chronology, comparison, cause/ effect, problem/ solution) of events, ideas, concepts, or information in a text or part of a text. **RI.4.5**

CCSS Use context (e.g., definitions, examples, or restatements in text) as a clue to the meaning of a word or phrase. **L.4.4a**

Leveled Reader:
Stargazing

Before Reading

Preview and Predict

Have students read the Essential Question. Then have students read the title and table of contents of *Stargazing*. Have students think of two questions they have about the text and share them with a partner.

Review Genre: Expository Text

Review with students that expository text is a form of nonfiction that explains about a topic. Expository text includes text features, such as headings, sidebars, and photographs and captions. As they preview the book, have students identify features of expository text in *Stargazing*.

During Reading

Close Reading

Note Taking Ask students to use their graphic organizer while they read.

Pages 2–5 *What is one way ancient peoples explained the stars?* (The North American Shoshone tell a story that the Milky Way came from the ice on a bear's fur.) *How does Earth move on its axis?* (Earth moves around an axis, with the North Pole on the top of the axis and the South Pole on the bottom.)

Pages 6–7 *Find a context clue in the second paragraph on page 6 that helps you define the word* navigate. *(to find their way) Use this information to define the word to a partner.* (*To navigate* means "to find a place using directions.")

Pages 8–9 *Paraphrase what you learned about the moon from page 9.* (It takes almost a month for the moon to orbit Earth. Our view of the moon changes from a tiny sliver to a round, full moon.)

Go
Digital

Leveled Readers

Use Graphic Organizer

Pages 10–11 *What does the author think was the most important thing that Galileo learned from his telescope?* (He learned that Earth orbits the sun.)

Pages 12–14 *What are two effects of the development of the Hubble Space Telescope?* (Scientists gained a clearer view of the stars because they are not looking through Earth's atmosphere. It also helped them figure out the age of the universe using pictures from the telescope.)

After Reading

Respond to Reading Have students complete Respond to Reading on page 15 after they have finished reading.

Write About Reading Have students work with a partner to write a paragraph explaining how Galileo's telescope taught us more about the universe. Have students include two facts from the text.

Fluency: Accuracy

Model Model reading page 5, emphasizing accuracy. Next, reread the page aloud and have students read along with you.

Apply Have students practice reading with a partner.

PAIRED READ

Leveled Reader

"Orion the Hunter"

Make Connections: Write About It

Before reading, ask students to note that the genre of this text is myth, which means it is a story that is used to explain something. Sometimes myths explain a belief or practice, and other times they explain something scientific. Then discuss the Essential Question. After reading, ask students to use the information from "Orion the Hunter" to expand their discussion of how people used to explain the sky in *Stargazing*.

FOCUS ON SCIENCE

Students can extend their knowledge of how to describe what they see in the night sky by completing the science activity on page 20. **STEM**

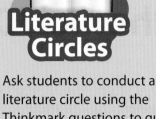

Literature Circles

Ask students to conduct a literature circle using the Thinkmark questions to guide the discussion. You may wish to have a whole-class discussion on something new they can explain about the sky that they didn't know before.

Level Up

Level-up lessons available online.

IF students read the `Approaching Level` fluently and answered the questions

THEN pair them with students who have proficiently read the `On Level` and have students

- echo-read the `On Level` main selection with their partners.
- use self-stick notes to mark at least one new detail they would like to discuss in each section.
- discuss the details they chose with their partners.

A C T ccess Complex Text

The `On Level` challenges students by including more **domain-specific words** and **complex sentence structures**.

Approaching Level

Phonics/Decoding

DECODE WORDS WITH DIPHTHONG /oi/

 TIER 2

OBJECTIVES

 Use combined knowledge of all letter-sound correspondences, syllabication patterns, and morphology (e.g., roots and affixes) to read accurately unfamiliar multisyllabic words in context and out of context. **RF.4.3a**

Decode words with the diphthong /oi/.

 I Do Display the **Sound-Spelling Card** for *boy*. Tell students that there are different ways to spell the /oi/ sound: *oi* and *oy*. Write the word *joy* on the board. Underline the letters *oy*. Point out that in *joy*, the *oy* makes the /oi/ sound. Repeat with *ploy* and *voice*.

 We Do Write *enjoy* and *point* on the board. Model how to decode the first word. Have students identify the /oi/ sound in each word as you point to the spelling. Students can read the rest of the words aloud. Have them say the sound as you point to the spelling.

 You Do Add these words to the board: *coin* and *royal*. Have students read each word aloud and identify how the /oi/ sound is spelled. Then point to the words in random order for students to read chorally. Repeat several times.

REVIEW WORDS WITH DIPHTHONGS /oi/ AND /ou/

 TIER 2

OBJECTIVES

 Use combined knowledge of all letter-sound correspondences, syllabication patterns, and morphology to read accurately unfamiliar multisyllabic words in context and out of context. **RF.4.3a**

Decode words with diphthongs.

 I Do Remind students that the letters *ou* and *ow* almost always stand for the sound /ou/. Write *town* on the board. Say: *The letters* ow *stand for /ou/.* Underline the letters *ow*. Then say the word *town* and sound out the /ou/ sound. Repeat this process for the word *house*.

 We Do Provide students with the **Word-Building Cards** for *out* and *side*. Guide students to identify the /ou/ sound. Have students say the two words together to form *outside*. Write these words on the board, separated into syllables to help students read the words one syllable at a time: *flow/er, thou/sand, al/low/ance, cow/boy, em/ploy/ment*. Have students use their Word-Building Cards to help them form the words.

 You Do Add the following examples to the board: *pointed, drowsiness,* and *moisture*. Ask students to decode each word. Then point to all of the words on the board in random order for students to choral-read. Repeat several times.

PRACTICE WORDS WITH DIPHTHONGS /oi/ AND /ou/

OBJECTIVES

Use combined knowledge of all letter-sound correspondences, syllabication patterns, and morphology to read accurately unfamiliar multisyllabic words in context and out of context. RF.4.3a

Decode words with diphthongs /oi/ and /ou/.

 I Do Write the word *howl* on the board. Circle the letters *ow* in the word and model pronouncing the diphthong /ou/. Then sound out the whole word as you run your finger under the letters. Write the word *noisy* on the board. Circle the letters *oi* in the word and model pronouncing the diphthong /oi/. Sound out the word while you run your finger under the letters.

 We Do Write the words *frown, south, pouch, noise, sound,* and *clouds* on the board. Model how to decode the first word, then guide students as they decode the remaining words. Help them underline the spellings *oi, ou,* and *ow* in each word.

You Do Afterward, point to the words in random order for students to choral-read.

GREEK AND LATIN ROOTS

OBJECTIVES

Use common, grade-appropriate Greek and Latin affixes and roots as clues to the meaning of a word (e.g., *telegraph, photograph, autograph*). L.4.4b

Decode words with Greek and Latin roots.

 I Do Review that many English words have Greek and Latin roots. Tell students that these roots give clues to the meaning of a word. The Latin root *aud* means "hear" as in *audible;* the Latin root *vis* means "see" as in *vision;* the Greek root *auto* means "self" as in *autobiography;* the Greek root *bio* means "life" as in *biology.*

We Do Write *auditory* on the board. Model how to decode the word by breaking it into parts. Then guide students as they decode these words: *visionary, autopilot,* and *biography.* Review the meaning of each Latin or Greek root as necessary.

You Do Afterward, write the words *visible, autograph,* and *biome* on the board. Have students name the root of each word and then say each word aloud.

ELL ENGLISH LANGUAGE LEARNERS

For the **ELLs** who need **phonics, decoding,** and **fluency** practice, use scaffolding methods as necessary to ensure students understand the meaning of the words. Refer to the **Language Transfers Handbook** for phonics elements that may not transfer in students' native languages.

→ Approaching Level

Vocabulary

REVIEW HIGH-FREQUENCY WORDS

TIER 2

OBJECTIVES

 Read with sufficient accuracy and fluency to support comprehension. Read on-level text with purpose and understanding. **RF.4.4a**

Review high-frequency words.

I Do Use **Word Cards 151–160**. Display one word at a time, following the routine:

Display the word. Read the word. Then spell the word.

We Do Ask students to state the word and spell the word with you. Model using the word in a sentence and have students repeat after you.

You Do Display the word. Ask students to say the word, and then spell it. When completed, quickly flip through the word card set as students choral-read the words. Provide opportunities for students to use the words in speaking and writing. For example, provide sentence starters, such as *My favorite place to read is ____*. Ask students to write each word in their Writer's Notebook.

REVIEW VOCABULARY WORDS

TIER 2

OBJECTIVES

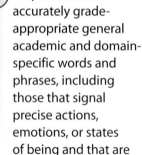 Acquire and use accurately grade-appropriate general academic and domain-specific words and phrases, including those that signal precise actions, emotions, or states of being and that are basic to a particular topic. **L.4.6**

I Do Display each **Visual Vocabulary Card** and state the word. Explain how the photograph illustrates the word. State the example sentence and repeat the word.

We Do Point to the word on the card and read the word with students. Ask them to repeat the word. Engage students in structured partner-talk about the visual as prompted on the back of the vocabulary card.

You Do Display each visual in random order, hiding the word. Have students match the definitions and context sentences of the words to the visuals displayed.

IDENTIFY WORD RELATIONSHIPS

OBJECTIVES

CCSS Acquire and use accurately grade-appropriate general academic and domain-specific words and phrases, including those that signal precise actions, emotions, or states of being (e.g., *quizzed, whined, stammered*) and that are basic to a particular topic (e.g., *wildlife, conservation,* and *endangered* when discussing animal preservation). **L.4.6**

 I Do Display the *telescope* **Visual Vocabulary Card** and say aloud the following choice question: *If you had a* telescope, *would it be easy to see stars or difficult?* Point out that a telescope makes distant objects appear closer.

 We Do Display the vocabulary card for the word *phases.* Say aloud the following question: *If a caterpillar entered a different* phase *of its life, would it only get larger or would it turn into a butterfly?* With students, identify the correct choice and justify why.

 You Do Using the choice questions below, display the remaining cards one at a time, saying aloud the question. Have students identify the correct choice.

→ If you ate a *sliver* of cake, would you want more or would you be full?

→ If things are aligned in a *series,* are they in order or out of order?

→ When a globe *rotates,* does it spin or does it bounce?

→ Does a *crescent* look like a curve or a ball?

CONTEXT CLUES: PARAGRAPH CLUES

OBJECTIVES

CCSS Use context (e.g., definitions, examples, or restatements in text) as a clue to the meaning of a word or phrase. **L.4.4a**

Use context clues to determine the meanings of unfamiliar words.

 I Do Display the Comprehension and Fluency passage on **Approaching Reproducibles** pages 183–184. Read aloud the second paragraph. Point to the word *core.* Explain to students that when they encounter unknown words, they can use context clues elsewhere in the paragraph to figure out their meanings.

Think Aloud I don't know the word *core,* but I can look for context clues in the paragraph to try to figure out its meaning. I see that the text says a "star's core is very hot," but many things are hot, so that doesn't help me understand the word. If I look at the next sentence, it says that the star's "center" is hot. This clue makes me think *core* means center.

 We Do Ask students to point to the word *spectrum.* With students, discuss how to use paragraph clues in the text to figure out the meaning of the word. Write the definition of the word on the board.

 You Do Have students use clues from the passage to find the meanings of *support* and *inward* on page 184.

→ Approaching Level
Comprehension

FLUENCY

OBJECTIVES

CCSS Use context to confirm or self-correct word recognition and understanding, rereading as necessary. **RF.4.4c**

Read fluently with accuracy.

 I Do Explain that it is important to read all text with accuracy. Remind students that if they come across words they do not know, it is necessary for them to reread and confirm word meanings and pronunciations in order to build accuracy. Read the first two paragraphs of the Comprehension and Fluency passage on **Approaching Reproducibles** pages 183–184.

 We Do Read the rest of the page aloud. Have students listen carefully for how you read challenging terms. Point out the pronunciations of the unfamiliar words *Betelgeuse* and *Rigel*.

 You Do Have partners take turns reading sentences from the Approaching Reproducibles passage. Remind them to focus on their accuracy. Listen in and provide corrective feedback by modeling proper fluency as needed.

IDENTIFY TEXT STRUCTURES

OBJECTIVES

CCSS Describe the overall structure (e.g., chronology, comparison, cause/effect, problem/solution) of events, ideas, concepts, or information in a text or part of a text. **RI.4.5**

 I Do Review the different text structures that authors of informational text use, such as sequence, compare and contrast, cause and effect, and problem and solution. Review the signal words that allow us to identify the text structure. Reread the first two paragraphs of the Comprehension and Fluency passage in the **Approaching Reproducibles**. Point out that good readers must look at signal words in context to identify text structure.

 We Do Reread the remainder of the first page of the Comprehension and Fluency passage. Ask: *What signal words does the author use?* Point out the phrase *as a result,* and help students identify the cause-and-effect relationships in the second paragraph. Explain that although the author uses "but" in the first paragraph, it does not signal a compare-and-contrast text structure.

 You Do Have students read the rest of the passage. When they finish, they should write down the text structure. Review cause-and-effect relationships they identified. Then have them discuss what they learned.

REVIEW CAUSE AND EFFECT

OBJECTIVES

 Describe the overall structure (e.g., chronology, comparison, cause/effect, problem/solution) of events, ideas, concepts, or information in a text or part of a text. **RI.4.5**

 I Do Remind students that authors use the cause-and-effect text structure to organize information. A cause is why something happens. An effect is what happens as a result. Explain that authors who use cause-and-effect text structures often use signal words, such as *as a result, because,* and *due to.*

 We Do Reread the first page of the Comprehension and Fluency passage in the **Approaching Reproducibles**. Remind students of the cause-and-effect relationship in the second paragraph. Then work with students to identify how the cause-and-effect text structure helps organize the information in the text.

 You Do Have students complete a Cause and Effect Chart and summarize the information in the text.

SELF-SELECTED READING

OBJECTIVES

Describe the overall structure (e.g., chronology, comparison, cause/effect, problem/solution) of events, ideas, concepts, or information in a text or part of a text. **RI.4.5**

Ask and answer questions to increase understanding.

Read Independently

Have students choose a nonfiction book for sustained silent reading. Remind students that:

→ authors of informational text often use a cause-and-effect text structure to organize information. A cause is why something happens. An effect is what happens.

→ asking questions and answering them will help enhance understanding of the text.

Read Purposefully

Have students record cause-and-effect relationships in a Cause and Effect Chart as they read independently. After they finish, they can conduct a Book Talk, each telling about the book they read.

→ Students should share their charts and answer this question: *What was the most interesting thing about what you read?*

→ They should also tell the group how asking and answering questions helped increase their understanding.

On Level

Lexile 450
TextEvaluator™ 30

OBJECTIVES

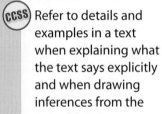

Refer to details and examples in a text when explaining what the text says explicitly and when drawing inferences from the text. **RI.4.1**

Describe the overall structure (e.g., chronology, comparison, cause/effect, problem/solution) of events, ideas, concepts, or information in a text or part of a text. **RI.4.5**

Use context (e.g., definitions, examples, or restatements in text) as a clue to the meaning of a word or phrase. **L.4.4a**

Leveled Reader:
Stargazing

Leveled Readers

Before Reading

Preview and Predict

Have students read the Essential Question. Then have students read the title and table of contents of *Stargazing*. Have students think of two questions they have about the text and share them with a partner.

Review Genre: Expository Text

Review with students that expository text is a form of nonfiction that explains about a topic. Expository text includes text features, such as headings, sidebars, and photographs and captions. As they preview the book, have students identify features of expository text in *Stargazing*.

During Reading

Close Reading

Note Taking Ask students to use their graphic organizer while they read.

Pages 2–5 *How did the North American Shoshone explain the Milky Way?* (They told a story that a grizzly bear climbed a huge mountain and leapt in the sky to hunt. The ice crystals on his fur became the stars of the Milky Way.)

Pages 6–7 *Use context clues to define* navigate *on page 6. Tell your definition to a partner.* (*To navigate* means "to find your way using things you can easily see.") *Why is the North Star especially helpful for navigating?* (It doesn't appear to move in the sky, and it helps people find north.)

Pages 8–9 *During what season does the Big Dipper appear high in the sky? Use the diagram on page 8 to answer.* (The Big Dipper appears high in the sky during the winter.) *What did you learn from the caption about the Pleiades?* (It is a cluster of bright stars.)

Use Graphic Organizer

Pages 10–11 *Find a cause-and-effect relationship on page 10.* (Because Galileo improved the way the telescope worked, he was able to see things that no one had seen before.)

Pages 12–14 *What is the author's position on the Hubble Space Telescope?* (It is very important because it gives us a clearer view of stars and space by viewing outside Earth's atmosphere.)

After Reading

Respond to Reading Have students complete Respond to Reading on page 15 after they have finished reading.

Analytical Writing **Write About Reading** Have students work with a partner to write a paragraph explaining how Galileo's telescope taught us more about the universe. Have students include at least two facts from the text.

Fluency: Accuracy

Model Model reading page 5, emphasizing accuracy. Next, reread the page aloud and have students read along with you.

Apply Have students practice reading with a partner.

PAIRED READ

"Orion the Hunter"

Make Connections:
Write About It *Analytical Writing*

Leveled Reader

Before reading, ask students to note that the genre of this text is myth, which means it is a story that explains something about science. Then discuss the Essential Question. After reading, ask students to use the information from "Orion the Hunter" to expand their discussion of how people used to explain the sky in *Stargazing*.

FOCUS ON SCIENCE

Students can extend their knowledge of how to describe what they see in the night sky by completing the science activity on page 20. **STEM**

Literature Circles

Ask students to conduct a literature circle using the Thinkmark questions to guide the discussion. You may wish to have a whole-class discussion on something new they can explain about the sky that they didn't know before.

Level Up

Level-up lessons available online.

IF students read the **On Level** fluently and answered the questions

THEN pair them with students who have proficiently read the **Beyond Level** and have students

- partner-read the **Beyond Level** main selection.
- list vocabulary words they find difficult and look them up with a partner.
- name two details in the text that they want to learn more about.

A C T Access Complex Text

The **Beyond Level** challenges students by including more **domain-specific words** and **complex sentence structures**.

On Level

Vocabulary

REVIEW VOCABULARY WORDS

 OBJECTIVES
Acquire and use accurately grade-appropriate general academic and domain-specific words and phrases, including those that signal precise actions, emotions, or states of being and that are basic to a particular topic. **L.4.6**

 I Do Use the **Visual Vocabulary Cards** to review key selection words *crescent, phases, rotates, series, specific,* and *sliver.* Point to each word, read it aloud, and have students chorally repeat it.

 We Do Display the vocabulary card for *specific.* Say aloud the word set *specific, general, precise, distinct.* With students, identify the word that does not belong and discuss why.

 You Do Have pairs of students identify the word that does not belong in each set.

phases, stages, chapters, accidents   *sliver, slice, chunk, bit*

series, piece, chain, line   *rotates, spins, whirls, blocks*

crescent, bow, globe, curve

CONTEXT CLUES: PARAGRAPH CLUES

 OBJECTIVES
Determine or clarify the meaning of unknown and multiple-meaning words and phrases based on grade 4 reading and content, choosing flexibly from a range of strategies. Use context (e.g., definitions, examples, or restatements in text) as a clue to the meaning of a word or phrase. **L.4.4a**

 I Do Remind students they can often figure out the meaning of an unknown word by looking for paragraph clues. Use the Comprehension and Fluency passage on **Your Turn Practice Book** pages 183–184 to model using a paragraph clue to determine the meaning of *core.*

Think Aloud I don't know the word *core,* but context clues can help me figure out its meaning. The text says a "star's core is extremely hot," but many things are hot, so that doesn't help me understand the word. The next sentence says that the star's "center" is hot. I think *core* means center.

 We Do Have students figure out the definition of *rotating* in the first paragraph by looking for paragraph clues. Guide students by telling them to look near the sentence for a helpful word or phrase.

 You Do Have partners use paragraph clues to determine the meanings of the words *barren* and *gravitational* on page 184.

Comprehension

REVIEW CAUSE AND EFFECT

OBJECTIVES

 Describe the overall structure (e.g., chronology, comparison, cause/effect, problem/solution) of events, ideas, concepts, or information in a text or part of a text. **RI.4.5**

Identify words that signal cause and effect.

I Do

Remind students that authors use text structures to organize the information in a text. Cause and effect is one type of text structure in which a cause, why something happens, and an effect, what happens as a result, are explained.

We Do

Have a volunteer read the first two paragraphs of the Comprehension and Fluency passage on **Your Turn Practice Book** pages 183–184. Guide students to identify signal words, such as *as a result*. Have them determine the cause-and-effect relationship in the second paragraph.

You Do

Have partners read the rest of the selection. Tell them to stop periodically to identify cause-and-effect relationships. They should use these relationships to explain what happens in our solar system and why.

SELF-SELECTED READING

OBJECTIVES

 Describe the overall structure (e.g., chronology, comparison, cause/effect, problem/solution) of events, ideas, concepts, or information in a text or part of a text. **RI.4.5**

Ask and answer questions to increase understanding.

Read Independently

Have students choose a nonfiction book for sustained silent reading.

→ Before they read, have students preview the book, reading the title and viewing the front and back cover.

→ As students read, remind them to ask themselves questions and answer them to make sure they understand the text.

Read Purposefully

Encourage students to read different books in order to learn about a variety of subjects.

→ As students read, have them fill in cause-and-effect relationships in a Cause and Effect Chart.

→ They can use this chart to help them write a summary of the book.

→ Ask students to share their reactions to the book with classmates.

Beyond Level

Lexile 860
TextEvaluator™ 29

OBJECTIVES

 Refer to details and examples in a text when explaining what the text says explicitly and when drawing inferences from the text. **RI.4.1**

 Describe the overall structure (e.g., chronology, comparison, cause/effect, problem/solution) of events, ideas, concepts, or information in a text or part of a text. **RI.4.5**

 Use context (e.g., definitions, examples, or restatements in text) as a clue to the meaning of a word or phrase. **L.4.4a**

Leveled Reader:
Stargazing

Go
Digital

Leveled Readers

Before Reading

Preview and Predict

Have students review the Essential Question. Then have students read the title and table of contents of *Stargazing*. Have students think of two questions they have about the text and share them with a partner.

Review Genre: Expository Text

Review with students that expository text is a form of nonfiction that explains about a topic. Expository text includes text features, such as headings, sidebars, and photographs and captions. As they preview the book, have students identify features of expository text in *Stargazing*.

During Reading

Close Reading

Note Taking Ask students to use their graphic organizer while they read.

Pages 2–5 *Paraphrase to a partner how the author compares Earth's movement to a basketball.* (Earth spins on its axis like a basketball with a pole through it. It orbits like someone spinning a basketball on their finger and circling a basketball hoop.)

Pages 6–7 *Use context clues to define* navigate *on page 6 to a partner.* (*To navigate* means "to find your way and orient yourself using things you can easily see.") *How could you locate the North Star in the sky if you didn't have other instruments? Refer to the sidebar on page 7.* (You could look for the stars at the right end of the bowl of the Big Dipper, called the Pointer Stars. These stars lead, in a straight line, to the North Star.)

Pages 8–9 *Ask a question to a partner about information presented in the section "The Passage of Time." Then reread to find the answer.* (For Example: Question: Why do some stars appear in the same place at the same time every year? Answer: This happens because Earth orbits the sun.)

Use Graphic Organizer

Pages 10–11 *Find two cause-and-effect relationships on these pages.* (Because Galileo improved the way the telescope worked, he was able to discover that Earth orbited the sun. He also discovered four moons orbiting Jupiter.)

Pages 12–14 *What is the author's position on the James Webb Space Telescope?* (The author thinks it's a positive development.) *How can you tell?* (The author says it will help astronomers see farther into space.)

After Reading

Respond to Reading Have students complete Respond to Reading on page 15 after they have finished reading.

Write About Reading *Analytical Writing* Have students work with a partner to write a paragraph explaining how Galileo's telescope taught us more about the universe. Have students include at least two facts from the text.

Fluency: Accuracy

Model Model reading page 5, emphasizing accuracy. Next, reread the page aloud and have students read along with you.

Apply Have students practice reading with a partner.

PAIRED READ

Leveled Reader

"Orion the Hunter"

Make Connections:
Write About It *Analytical Writing*

Before reading, ask students to note that the genre of this text is myth, which means it is a story that explains something. This myth explains something about science. Then discuss the Essential Question. After reading, ask students to use the information from "Orion the Hunter" to expand their discussion of how people used to explain the sky in *Stargazing*.

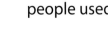

FOCUS ON SCIENCE

Students can extend their knowledge of how to describe what they see in the night sky by completing the science activity on page 20. **STEM**

Literature Circles

Ask students to conduct a literature circle using the Thinkmark questions to guide the discussion. You may wish to have a whole-class discussion on something new they can explain about the sky that they didn't know before.

Gifted and Talented

Synthesize Challenge students to explore the constellations in the night sky. Have students research the constellations visible in their community and choose one to map out. Have students write a few sentences describing the constellation and how it got its name. Invite volunteers to share their constellations.

→ **Beyond Level**

Vocabulary

REVIEW DOMAIN-SPECIFIC WORDS

 OBJECTIVES

CCSS Acquire and use accurately grade-appropriate general academic and domain-specific words and phrases, including those that signal precise actions, emotions, or states of being and that are basic to a particular topic. **L.4.6**

 Model Use the **Visual Vocabulary Cards** to review the meanings of the words *astronomer* and *telescope*. Write science-related sentences on the board using the words.

Write the words *moon* and *planet* on the board and discuss the meanings with students. Then help students write sentences using these words.

 Apply Have students work in pairs to review the meanings of the words *asteroid* and *comet*. Then have partners write sentences using the words.

CONTEXT CLUES: PARAGRAPH CLUES

 OBJECTIVES

CCSS Determine or clarify the meaning of unknown and multiple-meaning words and phrases based on grade 4 reading and content, choosing flexibly from a range of strategies. Use context (e.g., definitions, examples, or restatements in text) as a clue to the meaning of a word or phrase. **L.4.4a**

 Model Read aloud the first paragraph of the Comprehension and Fluency passage on **Beyond Reproducibles** pages 183–184.

Think Aloud When I read this paragraph, I want to understand what the word *rotating* means. The dome that the stars are attached to is the thing rotating, so if I look around the paragraph to see how the stars move, I can probably figure out what *rotating* means. The sentence before says that the stars move "across the sky." This clue tells me that the dome is spinning around Earth. I can guess that *rotating* means spinning.

 Apply Have pairs of students read the rest of the passage. Ask them to use paragraph clues to determine the meanings of the words *spectrum* on page 183 and *supernova* on page 184.

 Synthesize Have students choose one of the words from this week's vocabulary list and research it further. Have them write a descriptive paragraph about the word they choose and share their descriptions with the class.

Comprehension

OBJECTIVES

 Describe the overall structure (e.g., chronology, comparison, cause/effect, problem/solution) of events, ideas, concepts, or information in a text or part of a text. **RI.4.5**

 Model Remind students that authors use text structures to organize information. Cause and effect is one type of text structure. A cause is why something happens and an effect is what happens as a result.

Have students read the first page of the Comprehension and Fluency passage on **Beyond Reproducibles** pages 183–184. Ask open-ended questions to facilitate discussion about cause and effect, such as *What happens when the pressure builds in the center of a star?* Students should support their responses with details in the text.

 Apply Have students identify cause-and-effect relationships on each page as they independently fill in a Cause and Effect Chart. Then have partners use their work to summarize what they learned about our solar system.

OBJECTIVES

 Describe the overall structure (e.g., chronology, comparison, cause/effect, problem/solution) of events, ideas, concepts, or information in a text or part of a text. **RI.4.5**

Ask and answer questions to increase understanding.

Read Independently

Have students choose a nonfiction book for sustained silent reading.

→ As students read, have them fill in a Cause and Effect Chart.

→ Remind them to concentrate on asking and answering questions to make sure they understand what they read.

Read Purposefully

Encourage students to keep a reading journal. Ask them to read different books in order to learn about a variety of subjects.

→ Students can write summaries of the books in their journals.

→ Ask students to share their reactions to the books with classmates.

 Independent Study Challenge students to further their study about space. Tell them to choose something they found particularly fascinating about this week's subject matter and conduct further research on it. Have students present what they learn to the class.

English Language Learners

Reading/Writing Workshop

OBJECTIVES

CCSS Explain events, procedures, ideas, or concepts in a historical, scientific, or technical text, including what happened and why, based on specific information in the text. **RI.4.3**

LANGUAGE OBJECTIVE

Identify the causes and their effects in a text.

ACADEMIC LANGUAGE

• *cause, effect, expository*

• Cognates: *causa, efecto, expositivo*

Shared Read
Wonders of the Night Sky

Go Digital

View "Wonders of the Night Sky"

Before Reading

Build Background

Read the Essential Question: How do you explain what you see in the sky?

→ Explain the meaning of the Essential Question. Discuss what we see in the sky by showing images of the moon, stars, constellations, planets, comets, and other objects.

→ **Model an answer:** *When I look at the night sky, I know that the brightest light I see is the moon. I know that I also see stars and planets that are far away from Earth.*

→ Ask students a question that ties the Essential Question to their own background knowledge: *What do you see when you look up at the night sky? Draw a picture of something interesting you have seen in the sky.* Call on several volunteers to share their drawings with the class.

During Reading

Interactive Question-Response

→ Ask questions that help students understand the meaning of the text after each paragraph.

→ Reinforce the meanings of key vocabulary.

→ Ask students questions that require them to use key vocabulary.

→ Reinforce strategies and skills of the week by modeling.

Page 281

Paragraph 1

 The author describes the lights as "colored ribbons." How would you describe the lights in the picture? (Possible answer: The lights look bright and make the sky look pink and green.)

Aurora Borealis

Paragraph 1

Sometimes an author includes a guide to help readers pronounce a word. Have students choral read the word *aurora borealis.* Correct pronunciation as needed. *What else do we call the aurora borealis?* (the northern lights)

Paragraphs 2 and 3

Model Asking and Answering Questions *I read that people used to think the aurora borealis was caused by sunlight reflecting, or bouncing, off of polar ice caps. I wonder what really causes the northern lights.* Point to the phrase "in fact." Explain that it signals what causes the aurora borealis. *What causes the aurora borealis?* (magnetic attraction) Demonstrate magnets sticking to each other.

Paragraph 3

Explain and Model Context Clues Demonstrate the size of a particle by drawing a dot. Point out the clues "nearly invisible pieces of matter." *What do these clues tell us about particles? Are particles very small or very big?* (very small)

Explain and Model Cause and Effect *In the last paragraph, I read that magnetic attraction causes the aurora borealis. Now I see the phrase "as a result," which tells me it is a clue to the effect.* Draw an image of the sun giving off streams of charged particles and Earth orbiting the sun. Have students label the charged particles, solar wind, and Earth's magnetic field. Paraphrase the events that lead to the aurora borealis. *The effect of a solar wind reaching Earth's magnetic field is the ____.* (colorful lights in the sky; aurora borealis)

Page 282

Comets

Paragraphs 1 and 2

Point out and discuss the origin of the word *comet.* Ask volunteers to read the labels in the diagram. Have students point to the labels.

What are comets made of? (rock, dust, ice, and frozen gases) *Comets move in an oval-shaped orbit around the sun.* Demonstrate or draw a comet's oval-shaped path around the sun. Have students repeat, using gestures.

What questions do you have about comets? (Possible questions: What does a comet look like? Why do we see comets in the sky?) Have students reread the section to answer the questions.

Page 283

Meteors

What do we call a shooting star? (meteor) *What is in a meteor?* (rocky debris and fragments)

What causes a meteor shower? (Sometimes Earth passes through an area of space with lots of debris. This causes a meteor shower.)

After Reading

Make Connections

→ Review the Essential Question: How do you explain what you see in the sky?

→ Make text connections.

→ Have students complete **ELL Reproducibles** pages 183–185.

English Language Learners

Lexile 360
TextEvaluator™ 27

Leveled Reader: *Stargazing*

Go Digital

Leveled Readers

OBJECTIVES

CCSS Refer to details and examples in a text when explaining what the text says explicitly and when drawing inferences from the text. **RI.4.1**

CCSS Describe the overall structure (e.g., chronology, comparison, cause/effect, problem/solution) of events, ideas, concepts, or information in a text or part of a text. **RI.4.5**

CCSS Use context (e.g., definitions, examples, or restatements in text) as a clue to the meaning of a word or phrase. **L.4.4a**

Before Reading

Preview

→ Read the Essential Question: How do you explain what you see in the sky?

→ Refer to The Light Show: *What tools can you use to help explain what you see in the sky?*

→ Preview *Stargazing* and "Orion the Hunter": *Our purpose for reading is to learn how people explained what they saw in the sky long ago and what we know about the sky today.*

Vocabulary

Use the **Visual Vocabulary Cards** to preteach the ELL vocabulary: *accurate, linked, origin*. Use the routine found on the cards. Point out the cognate: *origen*.

During Reading

Interactive Question-Response

Note Taking Have students use their graphic organizer in **ELL Reproducibles** page 182. Use the questions below after reading each section with students. As you read, define vocabulary in context and use pictures to help students understand key vocabulary.

Pages 2–5 *How did ancient people explain what they saw in the sky?* (through stories and paintings) *According to the Shoshone story, what animal is responsible for creating the Milky Way?* (a bear)

Pages 6–7 Chorally read the first sentence on page 6. Point out the word *navigate* and explain that it means "to find your way." *What did people use to help them navigate, or find their way?* (the sun and the stars)

Pages 8–9 *What is another way people used the stars long ago?* (to track time) *Is it easier to track a single star or a constellation?* (a constellation) *How did the position of the stars help some cultures? Discuss the answer with a partner* (The position of the stars told people when to plant or harvest crops.)

Use Graphic Organizer

Pages 10–11 *Let's think about the effects that happened when Galileo improved the telescope. Fill in the frame: Galileo learned that the moon had ____ and ____.* (mountains; valleys) *Discuss other effects with a partner.*

Pages 12–14 *Why is the Hubble Space Telescope important? Fill in the frame: The Hubble Space Telescope is important because it lets scientists see outside Earth's ____.* (atmosphere)

After Reading

Respond to Reading Help students complete the graphic organizer in **ELL Reproducibles** page 182. Revisit the Essential Question. Ask partners to summarize and answer the Text Evidence Questions.

Analytical Writing **Write About Reading** Have partners write about how Galileo's improvements to the telescope helped people learn about the universe. Have students reread pages 10–11, using their graphic organizer to list the effects of Galileo's improvements to the telescope. Remind students to include the cause and effects in their writing.

Fluency: Accuracy

Model Model reading page 5, emphasizing accuracy. Next, reread the page aloud and have students read along with you.

Apply Have students practice reading with a partner.

Leveled Reader

PAIRED READ

"Orion the Hunter"

Make Connections:
Write About It **Analytical Writing**

Before reading, ask students to note that the genre of this text is a myth. A myth is a story that explains the origin of something. Then discuss the Essential Question. After reading, ask students to use the information from *Stargazing* and "Orion the Hunter" to expand their discussion of how people explained objects in the sky.

FOCUS ON SCIENCE

Students can extend their knowledge of the North Star or the Milky Way by completing the science activity on page 20. **STEM**

Literature Circles

Ask students to conduct a literature circle using the Thinkmark questions to guide the discussion. You may wish to have a whole-class discussion, asking students what new information they learned about the sky.

Level Up

Level-up lessons available online.

IF students read the **ELL Level** fluently and answered the questions

THEN pair them with students who have proficiently read **On Level** and have students

• echo-read the **On Level** main selection with their partners.

• list difficult words, phrases, or sentences and discuss them with their partners.

A C T **Access Complex Text**

The **On Level** challenges students by including more **domain-specific words** and **complex sentence structures**.

→ English Language Learners

Vocabulary

OBJECTIVES

 Acquire and use accurately grade-appropriate general academic and domain-specific words and phrases, including those that signal precise actions, emotions, or states of being and that are basic to a particular topic. **L.4.6**

LANGUAGE OBJECTIVE

Use vocabulary words.

 Preteach vocabulary from "Wonders of the Night Sky," following the Vocabulary Routine found on the **Visual Vocabulary Cards** for the words *astronomer, crescent, phases, rotates, series, sliver,* and *telescope.*

 After completing the Vocabulary Routine for each word, point to the word on the Visual Vocabulary Card and read the word with students. Ask students to repeat the word.

 Have pairs draw a picture for three of the words. Then have them write a sentence for each word and read their sentences aloud.

Beginning	Intermediate	Advanced/High
Help students write the sentences correctly and read them aloud.	Ask students to write a question for each of the words they choose.	Challenge students to draw a picture for two more words.

OBJECTIVES

 Acquire and use accurately grade-appropriate general academic and domain-specific words and phrases, including those that signal precise actions, emotions, or states of being and that are basic to a particular topic. **L.4.6**

LANGUAGE OBJECTIVE

Use vocabulary words.

 Review the previous week's vocabulary words. The words can be reviewed over a few days. Read each word aloud, pointing to the word on the **Visual Vocabulary Card**. Have students repeat after you. Then follow the routine on the back of the card.

 Say one of the words aloud and have students name a word with a similar meaning. Provide verbal clues if necessary, then write out the definition. Repeat the activity with another word.

 In small groups, have students take turns pantomiming an action or giving verbal clues while the others guess the word. Repeat with all the words.

Beginning	Intermediate	Advanced/High
Help students think of physical gestures or verbal clues for the words.	Have students write a definition for each word.	Have students identify a synonym or antonym for the words.

CONTEXT CLUES: PARAGRAPH CLUES

OBJECTIVES

 Use context (e.g., definitions, examples, or restatements in text) as a clue to the meaning of a word or phrase. **L.4.4a**

LANGUAGE OBJECTIVE

Use context clues.

 Read aloud the Comprehension and Fluency passage on **ELL Reproducibles** pages 183–184. Point to the word *core* on page 183. Explain that authors sometimes include clues, such as words or phrases, to help readers understand the meaning of an unfamiliar word.

Think Aloud I don't know what the word *core* means. I see that the text says "The core of a star is very hot." Many things are hot, so that doesn't help me understand the meaning of *core*. In the next sentence, it says that the star's "center" is hot. I think *core* means center.

 Point to and say the word *spectrum* on page 184. Help students find context clues and define the word. Write the definition on the board.

 In pairs, have students find context clues for the words *support* on page 183 and *supernova* on page 184.

Beginning	Intermediate	Advanced/High
Help students locate the words and context clues on the page.	Ask students to locate and read aloud the context clues on the page.	Have students use the context clues to define the words.

ADDITIONAL VOCABULARY

OBJECTIVES

 Choose words and phrases to convey ideas precisely. **L.4.3a**

LANGUAGE OBJECTIVE

Use academic and high-frequency words.

 List academic and high-frequency words from "Wonders of the Night Sky" and *Stargazing: another, full, mixture, patterns, tools,* and *view.* Define each word for students: *A mixture is a combination of two or more things.*

 Model using the words in a sentence: *The dog's fur is a mixture of white and brown.* Then write yes/no questions and help students answer them: *Have you ever made a cake with a mixture of flour, eggs, butter, and chocolate?*

 Have pairs make up their own yes/no questions using the words. Then have another pair read the questions and answer them.

Beginning	Intermediate	Advanced/High
Help students write and answer questions.	Provide examples, if necessary.	Have students define the words.

English Language Learners
Writing/Spelling

WRITING TRAIT: WORD CHOICE

OBJECTIVES

 Use concrete words and phrases and sensory details to convey experiences and events precisely. **W.4.3d**

Add figurative language to revise writing.

LANGUAGE OBJECTIVE

Use figurative language while writing.

 I Do Explain that good writers use figurative language to describe people, objects, or events. Figurative language, such as similes and metaphors, includes words that have meanings beyond their actual definitions. Writers use figurative language to make their writing more interesting. Read the Expert Model passage and identify the figurative language.

We Do Read aloud the first paragraph on page 282 in "Wonders of the Night Sky." Identify the simile describing the comets "like stars with hair." Help students visualize the comet. Model how to use figurative language.

You Do Have pairs write a description of the sky during a thunderstorm or a snowstorm. Have them include an example of a metaphor, simile, or personification. Edit each pair's writing. Then ask students to revise.

Beginning	Intermediate	Advanced/High
Have students copy the description.	Have students revise, focusing on word choice.	Challenge students to add a simile or metaphor.

SPELL WORDS WITH DIPHTHONGS /oi/ AND /ou/

OBJECTIVES

 Spell grade-appropriate words correctly, consulting references as needed. **L.4.2d**

LANGUAGE OBJECTIVE

Spell words with diphthongs /oi/ and /ou/.

I Do Read aloud the Spelling Words on page T228, elongating the sound of the diphthongs, and spelling out each sound. Have students repeat the words.

 We Do Read the Dictation Sentences on page T229 aloud for students. With each sentence, read the underlined word slowly, stressing the diphthong sound. Have students repeat after you and write the word.

 You Do Display the words. Have students exchange their list with a partner to check the spelling and write the words correctly.

Beginning	Intermediate	Advanced/High
Have students copy the words correctly and say the words aloud.	After students have corrected their words, have pairs quiz each other.	After they have corrected their words, have pairs use each word in a sentence.

Grammar

POSSESSIVE PRONOUNS

OBJECTIVES

 Deomstrate command of the conventions of standard English grammar and usage when writing or speaking. Ensure subject-verb and pronoun-antecedent agreement. **L.3.1f**

Use possessive pronouns correctly.

LANGUAGE OBJECTIVE

Write sentences with possessive pronouns.

Language Transfers Handbook

Note that speakers of Korean and Vietnamese repeat nouns rather than using pronouns (*Carla* visits her sister every Sunday, and *Carla* makes a meal.). Provide extra support in identifying when to use possessive pronouns for speakers of these languages.

 I Do Remind students that possessive pronouns show ownership and take the place of possessive nouns. Write the following possessive pronouns on the board: *my, your, his, her, its, our,* and *their*. Explain that possessive pronouns must match the nouns they replace in both number and gender. Write the following sentences on the board: *This is Wan's chair. This is his chair.* The possessive pronoun in the second sentence matches Wan in number (*singular*) and gender (*male*). Then write: *Vicki's project won first prize. His project won first prize.* Point to the possessive pronoun *his* and ask students if it matches the noun *Vicki* in number and gender. Ask a volunteer to replace the pronoun with the correct pronoun. Practice using plural possessive pronouns in a sentence and reading them aloud for students.

We Do Write the sentence frames below. Ask volunteers to name the possessive pronoun that completes each sentence correctly. Have students pay special attention to the stand-alone possessive pronoun in the third sentence. Review stand-alone pronouns with students as needed.

> *Lucas's pencil was lost. Lucas lost _____ pencil.*
>
> *Nina's cat came home. _____ cat came home.*
>
> *That car belongs to Todd and Bea. It is _____.*

 You Do Have students display something from the classroom and identify the object and possession in two ways (*Teresa's book* and *her book*). Have them write a sentence using the possessive pronoun.

Beginning	Intermediate	Advanced/High
Help students copy their sentences and underline the possessive pronoun. Read the sentences aloud for students to repeat.	Ask students to underline the possessive pronoun in each of their sentences and say whether it is a stand-alone pronoun.	Have students underline the possessive pronoun and explain how they knew which possessive pronoun to use.

For extra support, have students complete the activities in the **Grammar Practice Reproducibles** during the week, using the routine below:

→ Explain the grammar skill.

→ Model the first activity in the Grammar Practice Reproducibles.

→ Have the whole group complete the next couple of activities, then the rest with a partner.

→ Review the activities with correct answers.

PROGRESS MONITORING

Weekly Assessment

✔ **COMPREHENSION:** Cause and Effect **RI.4.5**	✔ **VOCABULARY:** Context Clues: Paragraph Clues **L.4.4a**	✔ **WRITING:** Writing About Text **RI.4.3, W.4.9b**

Assessment Includes

→ Pencil-and-paper administration

→ On-line administration

→ Approaching-Level Weekly Assessment also available

Fluency Goal 102 to 122 words correct per minute (WCPM)

Accuracy Rate Goal 95% or higher.

Administer oral reading fluency assessments using the following schedule:

→ **Weeks 1, 3, 5** Provide Approaching-Level students at least three oral reading fluency assessments during the unit.

→ **Weeks 2 and 4** Provide On-Level students at least two oral reading fluency assessments during the unit.

→ **Week 6** If necessary, provide Beyond-Level students an oral reading fluency assessment at this time.

Also Available: Selection Tests online PDFs

Go Digital! www.connected.mcgraw-hill.com

Using Assessment Results

TESTED SKILLS	If ...	Then ...
COMPREHENSION	Students answer 0–6 multiple-choice items correctly ...	... assign Lessons 76–78 on Cause and Effect from the *Tier 2 Comprehension Intervention online PDFs.*
VOCABULARY	Students answer 0–6 multiple-choice items correctly ...	... assign Lesson 142 on Using Paragraph Context Clues from the *Tier 2 Vocabulary Intervention online PDFs.*
WRITING	Students score less than "3" on the constructed response ...	... assign Lessons 76–78 and/or Write About Reading Lesson 200 from the *Tier 2 Comprehension Intervention online PDFs.*
FLUENCY	Students have a WCPM score of 94–101 ...	... assign a lesson from Section 1 or 7–10 of the *Tier 2 Fluency Intervention online PDFs.*
	Students have a WCPM score of 0–93 ...	... assign a lesson from Sections 2–6 of the *Tier 2 Fluency Intervention online PDFs.*

Response to Intervention

Use the appropriate sections of the *Placement and Diagnostic Assessment* as well as students' assessment results to designate students requiring:

 **Intervention Online PDFs**

 **WonderWorks Intervention Program**

Text Complexity Range for Grades 4–5

Lexile	
740	1010
TextEvaluator™	
23	51

Mc Graw-Hill Reading

Wonders

Reading/Writing Workshop

McGraw Hill

TEACH AND MODEL

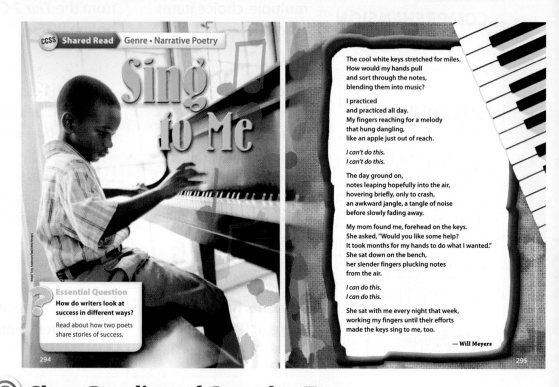

CCSS Shared Read Genre • Narrative Poetry

Sing to Me

Essential Question
How do writers look at success in different ways?
Read about how two poets share stories of success.

294

The cool white keys stretched for miles.
How would my hands pull
and sort through the notes,
blending them into music?

I practiced
and practiced all day.
My fingers reaching for a melody
that hung dangling,
like an apple just out of reach.

I can't do this.
I can't do this.

The day ground on,
notes leaping hopefully into the air,
hovering briefly, only to crash,
an awkward jangle, a tangle of noise
before slowly fading away.

My mom found me, forehead on the keys.
She asked, "Would you like some help?
It took months for my hands to do what I wanted."
She sat down on the bench,
her slender fingers plucking notes
from the air.

I can do this.
I can do this.

She sat with me every night that week,
working my fingers until their efforts
made the keys sing to me, too.

— Will Meyers

295

✔ Vocabulary

attain

dangling

hovering

triumph

Poetry Terms

connotation

denotation

repetition

stanza

 ☞ **Go** Digital

www.connected.mcgraw-hill.com

🔍 Close Reading of Complex Text

Shared Read "Sing to Me," 294–297

Genre Narrative Poetry

Lexile N/A

ETS *TextEvaluator™* N/A

Minilessons

✔ **Literary Elements**
✔ **Comprehension Skill**
✔ **Genre**
✔ **Vocabulary Strategy**
✔ **Writing Traits**
Grammar

✔ Tested Skills CCSS

Stanza and Repetition, T278–T279

Theme, T276–T277

Narrative Poem, T274–T275

Connotation and Denotation, T280–T281

Word Choice, T286–T287

Pronouns and Homphones, T290–T291

APPLY WITH CLOSE READING

Literature Anthology

Complex Text

PAIRED READ

"Swimming to the Rock", 356–359
Genre Poetry
Lexile N/A
ETS *TextEvaluator*™ N/A

"Genius", 360–361
Genre Poetry
Lexile N/A
ETS *TextEvaluator*™ N/A

Differentiated Text

Leveled Readers *Include Paired Reads*

APPROACHING
Lexile 600
ETS *TextEvaluator*™ 32

ON LEVEL
Lexile 740
ETS *TextEvaluator*™ 51

BEYOND
Lexile 800
ETS *TextEvaluator*™ 54

ELL
Lexile 510
ETS *TextEvaluator*™ 24

Extended Complex Text

Project Mulberry
Genre Realistic Fiction
Lexile 690
ETS *TextEvaluator*™ 39

Riding Freedom
Genre Realistic Fiction
Lexile 720
ETS *TextEvaluator*™ 40

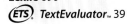

Classroom Library

Classroom Library lessons available online.

TEACH AND MANAGE

How You Teach

INTRODUCE

Weekly Concept
Achievements

Reading/Writing Workshop
290–291

 Go Digital

Interactive Whiteboard

TEACH

Close Reading
"Sing to Me"; "The Climb"

Minilessons
Narrative Poem, Theme, Stanza
and Repetition, Connotation and
Denotation, Writing Traits

Reading/Writing
Workshop
294–297

Interactive Whiteboard

APPLY

Close Reading
Swimming to the Rock;
The Moondust Footprint
"Genius"; "Winner"

Literature
Anthology
356–361

Mobile

How Students Practice

WEEKLY CONTRACT

PDF Online

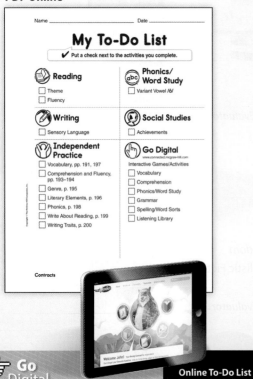

LEVELED PRACTICE AND ONLINE ACTIVITIES

Your Turn Practice Book
191–200

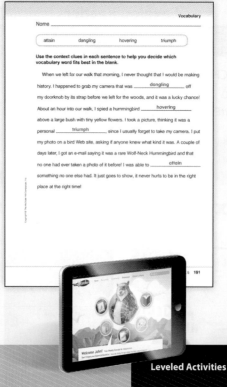

Leveled Readers

 **Go Digital**

Online To-Do List

Leveled Activities

Writer's Workspace

Go Digital! www.connected.mcgraw-hill.com

DIFFERENTIATE

SMALL GROUP INSTRUCTION
Leveled Readers

Mobile

INTEGRATE

Research and Inquiry
Research Narrative Poetry, T284

Text Connections
Compare Success, T285

Analytical Writing **Write About Reading**
Write an Analysis, T285

Online Research and Writing

ASSESS

Weekly Assessment
229–240

Online Assessment

LEVELED WORKSTATION CARDS

More Activities on back

20

Achievements

SOCIAL STUDIES

* An achievement is an important accomplishment.

* Use primary and secondary sources to research an achievement you have heard or read about this week.

27

Writing Forms: Description

WRITING

Look at the model. Identify the features of a description. Find an object in the classroom and write a description of it.

The ... butterfly has orange ...

12

Connotation and Denotation

PHONICS/WORD STUDY

A word's denotation is its dictionary definition. The connotation of a word is the feelings and ideas it brings to mind.

* Write the following words: *snug*, *tiny*, *regular*, *tight*, *plain*, and *puny*.

* Use a dictionary to help you pair words that have similar meanings.

* Compare the words in each pair. Decide which have connotations that are mostly positive, negative, or neutral.

* Write a sentence or two to describe the difference between the connotations of the words in each pair.

tiny

You need
> pencil
> paper
> dictionary
> thesaurus

4

Theme

READING

* Choose a story you both read.

* After rereading the story, think about the overall message or lesson the author wants readers to learn. What details led you to your conclusion?

* On your own, make a drawing to depict the story's theme.

* Compare your drawings. Tell how you chose which details to include.

You need
> story recently read
> paper, crayons, and markers

Go Digital! www.connected.mcgraw-hill.com • Interactive Games and Activities • Grade 4

DEVELOPING READERS AND WRITERS

Write to Sources and Research

Summary, T276–T277

Note Taking, T281B, T281E

Summarize, T281D

Theme, T281D

Make Connections: Essential Question, T281D, T281F, T285

Research and Inquiry, T284

Analyze to Inform/Explain, T285

Comparing Texts, T297, T305, T309, T315

Teacher's Edition

Literature Anthology

Summarize, 359
Theme, 359

Interactive Whiteboard

Leveled Readers
Comparing Texts
Theme

Your Turn Practice Book

Theme, 193–195
Genre, 195
Analyze to Inform, 199

Narrative Text
Poetry, T350–T355

Conferencing Routines
Teacher Conferences, T352
Peer Conferences, T353

Interactive Whiteboard

Teacher's Edition

Leveled Workstation Card
Poetry, Card 28

Writer's Workspace
Narrative Text: Poetry
Writing Process
Multimedia Presentations

Writing Traits • Write Every Day

Writing Trait: Word Choice
Sensory Language, T286–T287

Conferencing Routines
Teacher Conferences, T288
Peer Conferences, T289

Teacher's Edition

Word Choice:
Sensory Language,
302–303

Reading/Writing Workshop

Interactive Whiteboard

Sensory
Language,
Card 17

Leveled Workstation Card

Word Choice: Sensory
Language, 200

Your Turn Practice Book

Grammar and Spelling

Grammar
Pronouns and Homophones,
T290–T291

Spelling
Varient Vowel /ô/, T292–T293

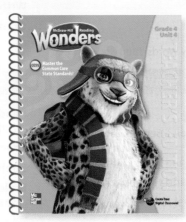

Teacher's Edition

Interactive
Whiteboard

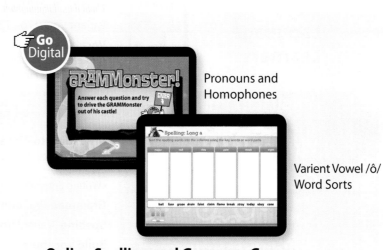

Pronouns and
Homophones

Varient Vowel /ô/
Word Sorts

Online Spelling and Grammar Games

SUGGESTED LESSON PLAN

		DAY 1	DAY 2

Whole Group

READING

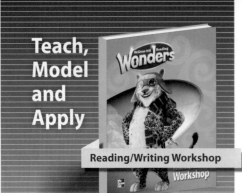

Teach, Model and Apply

Reading/Writing Workshop

DAY 1

Build Background Achievements, T266–T267

Listening Comprehension Interactive Read Aloud: "Sam's Box," T268–T269

Comprehension
• Preview Genre: Narrative Poem
• Preview Strategy: Visualize

✓ **Vocabulary** Words in Context, T270–T271

Practice *Your Turn*, 191

Close Reading of Complex Text "Sing to Me," "The Climb," 294–297

DAY 2

✓ **Comprehension**
• Genre: Narrative Poem, T274–T275
• Skill: Theme, T276–T277
• Write About Reading *Analytical Writing*
• Literary Elements: Stanza and Repetition, T278–T279

✓ **Vocabulary** Strategy: Connotation and Denotation, T280–T281

Practice *Your Turn*, 192–197

Small Group

DIFFERENTIATED INSTRUCTION   Choose across the week to meet your students' needs.

Approaching Level

DAY 1

Leveled Reader *Try, Try Again*, T296–T297

Phonics/Decoding Decode Words with Variant Vowel /ô/, T298 (TIER 2)

Vocabulary
• Review High-Frequency Words, T300 (TIER 2)
• Answer Yes/No Questions, T301

DAY 2

Leveled Reader *Try, Try Again*, T296–T297

Vocabulary Review Vocabulary Words, T300 (TIER 2)

Comprehension
• Identify Key Details, T302 (TIER 2)
• Review Theme, T303

On Level

DAY 1

Leveled Reader *The Math-lete*, T304–T305

Vocabulary Review Vocabulary Words, T306

DAY 2

Leveled Reader *The Math-lete*, T304–T305

Comprehension Review Theme, T307

Beyond Level

DAY 1

Leveled Reader *The Final*, T308–T309

Vocabulary Review Domain-Specific Words, T310

DAY 2

Leveled Reader *The Final*, T308–T309

Comprehension Review Theme, T311

English Language Learners

DAY 1

Shared Read "Sing to Me," T312–T313

Phonics/Decoding Decode Words with Variant Vowel /ô/, T298

Vocabulary
• Preteach Vocabulary, T316
• Review High-Frequency Words, T300

DAY 2

Leveled Reader *The Math-lete*, T314–T315

Vocabulary Review Vocabulary, T316

Writing Writing Trait: Word Choice, T318

Grammar Pronouns and Homophones, T319

Whole Group

LANGUAGE ARTS   Writing Process: Poetry T350–T355   Use with Weeks 4–6

Writing

Grammar

Spelling

Build Vocabulary

DAY 1

✓ **Readers to Writers**
• Writing Traits: Word Choice/Sensory Language, T286–T287
• Writing Entry: Prewrite and Draft, T288

Grammar Pronouns and Homophones, T290

Spelling Variant Vowel /ô/, T292

Build Vocabulary
• Connect to Words, T294
• Academic Vocabulary, T294

DAY 2

Readers to Writers
• Writing Entry: Revise, T288

Grammar Pronouns and Homophones, T290

Spelling Variant Vowel /ô/, T292

Build Vocabulary
• Expand Vocabulary, T294
• Review Context Clues, T294

DAY 3	DAY 4	DAY 5 Review and Assess

READING

Phonics/Decoding
- Variant Vowel /ô/, T282
- Frequently Confused Words, T283

Practice *Your Turn*, 198

Close Reading "Swimming to the Rock," "The Moondust Footprint," 356–359 *Analytical Writing*

Literature Anthology

Fluency Rate, T283

Integrate Ideas *Analytical Writing*
- Research and Inquiry, T284

Practice *Your Turn*, 193–195

Close Reading "Genius," "Winner," 360–361 *Analytical Writing*

Integrate Ideas *Analytical Writing*
- Research and Inquiry, T284
- Text Connections, T285
- Write About Reading, T285

Practice *Your Turn*, 199

DIFFERENTIATED INSTRUCTION

Leveled Reader *Try, Try Again*, T296–T297
Phonics/Decoding Review the Variant Vowel /ô/, T298 TIER 2
Fluency Rate, T302 TIER 2
Vocabulary Connotation and Denotation, T301

Leveled Reader Paired Read: "Sunlight Sparkling on Chrome," T297 *Analytical Writing*
Phonics/Decoding Practice Words with the Variant Vowel, T299

Leveled Reader Literature Circles, T297
Comprehension Self-Selected Reading, T303
Phonics/Decoding Frequently Confused Words, T299

Leveled Reader *The Math-lete*, T304–T305
Vocabulary Connotation and Denotation, T306

Leveled Reader Paired Read: "Cross Country Race," T305 *Analytical Writing*

Leveled Reader Literature Circles, T305
Comprehension Self-Selected Reading, T307

Leveled Reader *The Final*, T308–T309
Vocabulary
- Connotation and Denotation, T310
- Poem, T310
Gifted and Talented

Leveled Reader Paired Read: "Talent Show," T309 *Analytical Writing*

Leveled Reader Literature Circles, T309
Comprehension
- Self-Selected Reading, T311
- Analyze, T311

Leveled Reader *The Math-lete*, T314–T315
Phonics/Decoding Review the Variant Vowel /ô/, T298
Vocabulary Connotation and Denotation, T317
Spelling Words with Variant Vowel /ô/, T318

Leveled Reader Paired Read: "Running the Race," T315 *Analytical Writing*
Vocabulary Additional Vocabulary, T317
Phonics/Decoding Practice Words with the Variant Vowel, T299

Leveled Reader Literature Circles, T315
Phonics/Decoding Frequently Confused Words, T299

LANGUAGE ARTS

Readers to Writers
- Writing Entry: Prewrite and Draft, T289

Grammar Mechanics and Usage, T291

Spelling Variant Vowel /ô/, T293

Build Vocabulary
- Reinforce the Words, T295
- Connotation and Denotation, T295

Readers to Writers
- Writing Entry: Revise, T289

Grammar Pronouns and Homophones, T291

Spelling Variant Vowel /ô/, T293

Build Vocabulary
- Connect to Writing, T295
- Shades of Meaning, T295

Readers to Writers
- Writing Entry: Share and Reflect, T289

Grammar Pronouns and Homophones, T291

Spelling Variant Vowel /ô/, T293

Build Vocabulary
- Word Squares, T295
- Morphology, T295

DIFFERENTIATE TO ACCELERATE

  Scaffold to **A**ccess **C**omplex **T**ext

IF ▶ the text complexity of a particular selection is too difficult for students

THEN ▶ see the references noted in the chart below for scaffolded instruction to help students Access Complex Text.

Qualitative / Quantitative
Reader and Task
TEXT COMPLEXITY

	Reading/Writing Workshop	Literature Anthology	Leveled Readers	Classroom Library

Quantitative	"Sing to Me" Lexile N/A *TextEvaluator™* N/A	"Swimming to the Rock" Lexile N/A *TextEvaluator™* N/A "Genius" Lexile N/A *TextEvaluator™* N/A	**Approaching Level** **Lexile** 600 *TextEvaluator™* 32 **Beyond Level** **Lexile** 800 *TextEvaluator™* 54	**On Level** **Lexile** 740 *TextEvaluator™* 51 **ELL** **Lexile** 510 *TextEvaluator™* 24	*Project Mulberry* **Lexile** 690 *TextEvaluator™* 39 *Riding Freedom* **Lexile** 720 *TextEvaluator™* 40
Qualitative	**What Makes the Text Complex?** • **Specific Vocabulary** Figurative Language T273 • **Genre** Mood T279 **ACT** *See Scaffolded Instruction in Teacher's Edition T273 and T279.*	**What Makes the Text Complex?** • **Connection of Ideas** Inferences T281A • **Sentence Structure,** T281C • **Organization** Compare Poems T281E **ACT** *See Scaffolded Instruction in Teacher's Edition T281A–T281F.*	**What Makes the Text Complex?** • **Specific Vocabulary** • **Sentence Structure** • **Connection of Ideas** • **Genre** **ACT** *See Level Up lessons online for Leveled Readers.*		**What Makes the Text Complex?** • **Genre** • **Specific Vocabulary** • **Prior Knowledge** • **Sentence Structure** • **Organization** • **Purpose** • **Connection of Ideas** **ACT** *See Scaffolded Instruction in Teacher's Edition T360–T361.*
Reader and Task	The Introduce the Concept lesson on pages T266–T267 will help determine the reader's knowledge and engagement in the weekly concept. See pages T272–T281 and T284–T285 for questions and tasks for this text.	The Introduce the Concept lesson on pages T266–T267 will help determine the reader's knowledge and engagement in the weekly concept. See pages T281A–T281F and T284–T285 for questions and tasks for this text.	The Introduce the Concept lesson on pages T266–T267 will help determine the reader's knowledge and engagement in the weekly concept. See pages T296–T297, T304–T305, T308–T309, T314–T315, and T284–T285 for questions and tasks for this text.		The Introduce the Concept lesson on pages T266–T267 will help determine the reader's knowledge and engagement in the weekly concept. See pages T360–T361 for questions and tasks for this text.

Go Digital! www.connected.mcgraw-hill.com

Monitor and *Differentiate*

IF ▶ you need to differentiate instruction

THEN ▶ use the Quick Checks to assess students' needs and select the appropriate small group instruction focus.

 Quick Check

Genre Narrative Poem T275

Comprehension Skill Theme T277

Literary Elements Stanzas and Repetition T279

Vocabulary Strategy Connotation and Denotation T281

Phonics/Fluency Variant Vowel /ô/ T283

If No → **Approaching Level** | Reteach T296–T303
  | **ELL** | Develop T312–T319
If Yes → **On Level** | Review T304–T307
  | **Beyond Level** | Extend T308–T311

Level Up with Leveled Readers

IF ▶ students can read their leveled text fluently and answer comprehension questions

THEN ▶ work with the next level up to accelerate students' reading with more complex text.

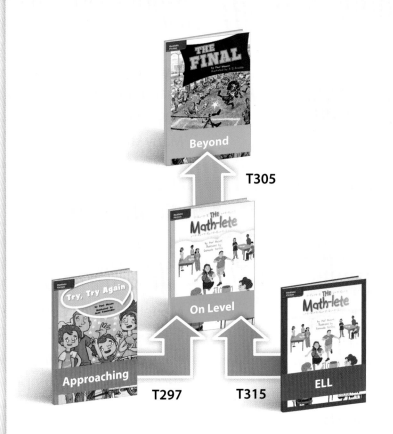

Beyond — T305

On Level — T297 · T315

Approaching · ELL

ENGLISH LANGUAGE LEARNERS SCAFFOLD

IF ELL students need additional support THEN ▶ scaffold instruction using the small group suggestions.

Reading/Writing Workshop "Sing to Me" T312–T313	Leveled Reader *The Math-lete* T314–T315 "Running the Race" T315	Additional Vocabulary T317 argue compete difficult immense struggle	Using Connotation and Denotation T317	Writing Word Choice T318	Spelling Words with Variant Vowel /ô/ T318	Grammar Pronouns and Homophones T319

Note: Include ELL Students in all small groups based on their needs.

→ Introduce the Concept

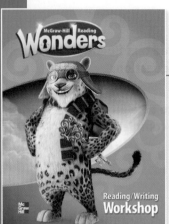

Reading/Writing Workshop

OBJECTIVES

CCSS Interpret information presented visually, orally, or quantitatively (e.g., in charts, graphs, diagrams, time lines, animations, or interactive elements on Web pages) and explain how the information contributes to an understanding of the text in which it appears. **RI.4.7**

CCSS Follow agreed-upon rules for discussions and carry out assigned roles. **SL.4.1b**

Build background knowledge on success.

ACADEMIC LANGUAGE

- *triumph, attain*
- Cognate: *triunfo*

 MINILESSON **10 Mins**

Build Background

ESSENTIAL QUESTION
How do writers look at success in different ways?

Have students read the Essential Question on page 290 of the **Reading/Writing Workshop**. Tell them that success can take many forms.

Discuss the photograph of the boy playing baseball. Focus on how catching a baseball during a game is an example of an achievement.

→ A **triumph** is a big achievement. Winning a Little League championship is a triumph. Another kind of triumph is overcoming one's fears.

→ Many stories show how characters **attain**, or achieve, success. This may happen when a character finds a solution to a problem.

Talk About It

 COLLABORATE

Ask: *Do you think success is always a positive thing? Why or why not? What are some stories that you can think of in which the character **triumphs** or **attains** some kind of success?* Have students discuss in pairs or groups.

→ Model using the Concept Web to generate words and phrases related to success. Add students' contributions.

→ Have partners continue the discussion by sharing how they define success. They can complete the Concept Web, generating additional related words and phrases.

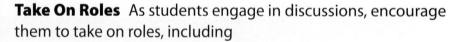

Collaborative Conversations

Take On Roles As students engage in discussions, encourage them to take on roles, including

→ a questioner who asks questions in order to keep everyone involved and keep the discussion moving.

→ a recorder who takes notes on the important ideas being discussed and who later reports to the class.

→ a discussion monitor who keeps the group on topic and makes sure everyone gets a turn to talk.

Go Digital

Discuss the Concept

Watch Video

View Photos

Success
Use Graphic Organizer

Weekly Concept Achievements

Essential Question
How do writers look at success in different ways?

Go Digital!

Reaching FOR SUCCESS

A Little League team winning a championship is one kind of achievement. A person petting a dog may not look like an achievement. However, if that person has been scared of dogs his or her whole life, it is a huge achievement.

▸ Do you think success is always a positive thing? Why or why not?

▸ What are some stories that you can think of where the character attains some kind of success?

Talk About It

Write words that describe what you think about success. Then talk with a partner about how you define success.

Success

290   291

READING/WRITING WORKSHOP, pp. 290–291

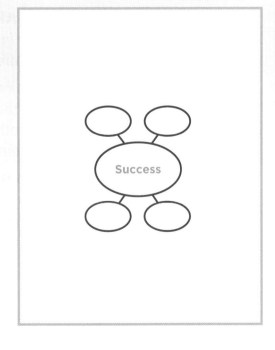

GRAPHIC ORGANIZER 62

Success

ENGLISH LANGUAGE LEARNERS SCAFFOLD

Beginning	Intermediate	Advanced/High
Use Visuals Point to the boy playing baseball. Say: *This boy caught the baseball. This is one kind of success. Success is when someone gets something done.* Have students use the frame: *Catching a baseball during a game is one kind of ____ .* (success) Help students with pronunciation.	**Describe** Have students describe the photograph. Ask: *What is the boy doing? Is this an example of success?* Have students complete the frame: *Catching ____ is one kind of success because ____.* Elicit details to develop their responses.	**Discuss** Ask students to discuss the concept of success. Ask: *Is this boy successful? How do you know? What are some other examples of success?* Encourage them to use the concept words. Correct their answers for meaning as needed.

→ # Listening Comprehension

MINILESSON
10
Mins

Interactive Read Aloud

Go Digital

View Illustrations

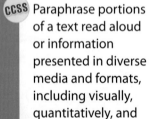

OBJECTIVES

CCSS Describe in depth a character, setting, or event in a story or drama, drawing on specific details in the text (e.g., a character's thoughts, words, or actions). **RL.4.3**

CCSS Paraphrase portions of a text read aloud or information presented in diverse media and formats, including visually, quantitatively, and orally. **SL.4.2**

- Listen for a purpose.
- Identify characteristics of a narrative poem.

ACADEMIC LANGUAGE

- *narrative poem, visualize*
- Cognates: *poema narrativo, visualizar*

Connect to Concept: Achievements

Tell students that writers look at success in different ways. Let students know that you will be reading aloud a poem about a boy who succeeds in writing poetry. Have students listen for descriptive details as you read.

Preview Genre: Narrative Poem

Explain that the text you will read aloud is a narrative poem. Discuss features of a narrative poem:

→ gives an account of a fictional or real event

→ may have a rhyming pattern or a repeating line or phrase

→ may use imagery to create a picture in the reader's mind

Preview Comprehension Strategy: Visualize

Point out that readers can visualize, or form pictures in their minds, as they read to help them understand the text. Readers use descriptive details in the text in order to picture situations, events, images, or characters.

Use the Think Alouds on page T269 to model the strategy.

Respond to Reading

Think Aloud Clouds Display Think Aloud Master 2: *I was able to picture in my mind . . .* to reinforce how you used the visualize strategy to understand content.

Genre Features With students, discuss the elements of the Read Aloud that let them know it is a narrative poem. Ask them to think about other texts that you have read or they have read independently that were narrative poems.

Summarize Have students briefly retell the poem "Sam's Box" in their own words.

I was able to picture in my mind...

Model Think Alouds

Genre	Features

Fill in Genre Chart

Sam's Box

When the lights are out
for the night, and the last
good-night is said,
I reach under my bed
and pull out my box,
and open it up to see
a pile,
a nest,
a gaggle of
poems
spilling out,
all written by me! **1**

Here's one about Mom, who can make
the best cookies, pies, and cakes
and even corn on the cob,
but
really and I mean, really,
the clumpiest, most disgusting
oatmeal ever.

This one's about Gramps who
has a gold pocket watch
that doesn't tell time
or chime,
but he winds it
every day
and pretends that it does. **2**

This poem is about me,
Sam,
because that's who I am.
I'm happy that my name
is so easy to rhyme.
Because sometimes I like rhyming,
and sometimes I don't.

My box is almost full, so
I use a rubber band
to hold in the
pile,
the nest,
the gaggle of
poems
all written by me,
bursting to get out! **3**

Yellow Dog Productions/Digital Vision/Getty Images

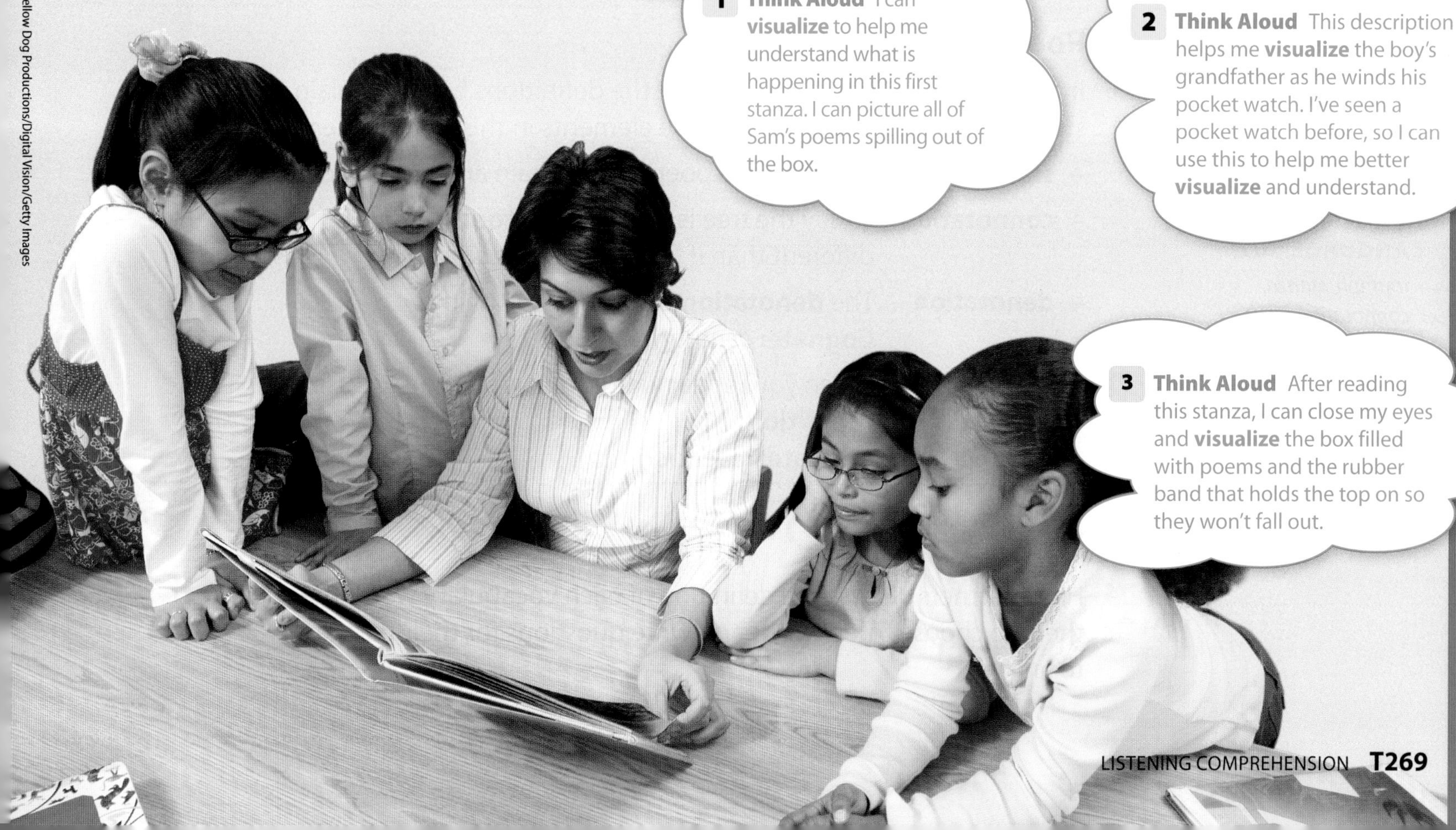

1 **Think Aloud** I can **visualize** to help me understand what is happening in this first stanza. I can picture all of Sam's poems spilling out of the box.

2 **Think Aloud** This description helps me **visualize** the boy's grandfather as he winds his pocket watch. I've seen a pocket watch before, so I can use this to help me better **visualize** and understand.

3 **Think Aloud** After reading this stanza, I can close my eyes and **visualize** the box filled with poems and the rubber band that holds the top on so they won't fall out.

→ Vocabulary

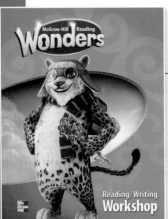

Reading/Writing Workshop

OBJECTIVES

CCSS Acquire and use accurately grade-appropriate academic and domain-specific words and phrases, including those that signal precise actions, emotions, or states of being (e.g., *quizzed, whined, stammered*) and that are basic to a particular topic (e.g., *wildlife, conservation,* and *endangered* when discussing animal preservation). **L.4.6**

ACADEMIC LANGUAGE

• *triumph, stanza, connotation, denotation, repetition*

• Cognates: *triunfo, stanza, connotación, denotación, repetición*

MINILESSON 10 Mins

Words in Context

Model the Routine

Introduce each vocabulary word using the Vocabulary Routine found on the Visual Vocabulary Cards.

Visual Vocabulary Cards

Vocabu...
Define:
Example:
Ask:

> **Vocabulary Routine**
>
> **Define:** When something is a **triumph**, it is a great victory or success.
>
> **Example:** Winning the state soccer championship was a triumph!
>
> **Ask:** What is a synonym for *triumph*?

Definitions

→ **attain**   To **attain** something means to work hard to achieve a goal.

→ **dangling**   **Dangling** means hanging or swinging loosely.

→ **hovering**   A **hovering** object stays in one place in the air.

Poetry Terms

Introduce each poetry term. Present the definitions below. Explain that students will find examples of these elements in this week's poems.

→ **stanza**   A **stanza** in a poem can contain any number of lines.

→ **connotation**   If I say the tree is *scrawny*, the **connotation** is different than if I say the tree is *thin*.

→ **denotation**   The **denotation** of *joyful* is "full of joy."
                    Cognate: *denotación*

→ **repetition**   When you repeat words in a poem, you are using **repetition**.
                    Cognate: *repetición*

Talk About It

Have partners discuss the definition of each vocabulary word. Then ask them to choose three words and write questions for their partner to answer.

Go Digital

triumph

Use Visual Glossary

Words to Know

Vocabulary

Use the picture and the sentences to talk with a partner about each word.

 **attain**

The climber wanted to **attain** the goal of being the first person to reach the peak.

What goal would you like to attain?

 **dangling**

The ripe apple was **dangling** from the end of the branch.

What are other fruits that you might find dangling?

 **hovering**

The hummingbird was **hovering** in front of the flower's petals.

What might a helicopter be hovering over?

 **triumph**

Winning the state soccer championship was a **triumph**!

What is a synonym for triumph?

292

Poetry Terms

stanza

A **stanza** is two or more lines of poetry that together form a unit of the poem.

Explain how you know when a stanza ends.

denotation

The **denotation** is the basic definition of a word.

What is the denotation of the word little?

connotation

The **connotation** of a word is a meaning suggested by a word in addition to its literal meaning.

What is the connotation of the word scrawny?

repetition

Poets who repeat words or phrases in a poem are using **repetition**.

How might repetition add to a poem's meaning?

Your Turn COLLABORATE

Pick three words. Write three questions for your partner to answer.

293

READING/WRITING WORKSHOP, pp. 292–293

ENGLISH LANGUAGE LEARNERS SCAFFOLD

Beginning

Use Visuals Say: *Let's look at the picture for* triumph. *The people in the picture won the game. Winning the game is a* triumph. Triumph *is another word for* success. *What do we call a triumph?* (success) *Is a triumph good or bad?* (good) Give students ample time to respond and help with pronunciation. *Triumph in Spanish is* triunfo.

Intermediate

Describe Have students describe the picture for *triumph*. Help them pronounce the word. Ask: *What is a synonym for* triumph? *Turn to a partner and discuss what* triumph *means.* Remind students that *triumph* in Spanish is *triunfo.*

Advanced/High

Discuss Ask students to talk about the picture for *triumph* and use the word in a sentence. Ask: *Why is winning the championship a triumph?* Have partners discuss the question and share their ideas with the class. Correct responses for meaning as needed.

CCSS **Shared Read** > Genre • Narrative Poetry

Sing to Me

Essential Question

How do writers look at success in different ways?

Read about how two poets share stories of success.

294

The cool white keys stretched for miles.
How would my hands pull
and sort through the notes,
blending them into music?

I practiced
and practiced all day.
My fingers reaching for a melody
that hung dangling,
like an apple just out of reach.

I can't do this.
I can't do this.

The day ground on,
notes leaping hopefully into the air,
hovering briefly, only to crash,
an awkward jangle, a tangle of noise
before slowly fading away.

My mom found me, forehead on the keys.
She asked, "Would you like some help?
It took months for my hands to do what I wanted."
She sat down on the bench,
her slender fingers plucking notes
from the air.

I can do this.
I can do this.

She sat with me every night that week,
working my fingers until their efforts
made the keys sing to me, too.

— **Will Meyers**

295

READING/WRITING WORKSHOP, pp. 294–295

Reading/Writing Workshop

Shared Read

Connect to Concept: Achievements

Explain that "Sing to Me" and "The Climb" are poems that tell stories about success. Read the poems with students.

Close Reading

Reread "Sing to Me," Stanza 1: Direct students to the first stanza on page 295. Ask: *What is happening in this stanza?* Model how to cite evidence to answer the question.

The "cool white keys" are piano keys. They stretch "for miles," which means that the piano looks big to the narrator. He doesn't know how to blend the notes into music. This means he is unsure how he can become a good player.

Reread "The Climb," Stanzas 1–2: Model how to summarize the first two stanzas of "The Climb." Remind students that to summarize they should look for key details of the section.

The narrator hears her brother shout, "Go on, I dare you!" They are waiting for the school bus under a large oak tree. The narrator tries to climb the tree, but she loses her grip and slides down. This must have happened before because she ends the second stanza by saying "Again."

The Climb

"Go on, I dare you!" My brother's voice
mocking, a jaybird's repetitive screech.
We are waiting for the bus
under our immense oak tree.

I reach for the lowest branch and find
another to pull myself up before
I lose my grip on the slippery bark
and slither down the trunk. Again.

Today, at school,
I drop my milk at lunch,
take a pop quiz,
and argue with my friends.

Today is my birthday.
When I get off the bus,
The oak tree doesn't look
any smaller or bigger.

Today, I am ten years old.
I reach for the lowest branch
and find another to pull myself up.
My hands find another and another.

Over and over among the red
outstretched leaves,
foot to branch: push!
hand to branch: pull!

My brother is rooted on the ground,
staring up at me,
until finally, I can't climb any higher,
or I will be a cloud.

— Sonya Mera

Make Connections

? Talk about how each poet writes about success. **ESSENTIAL QUESTION**

Compare how the characters in each poem feel to how you feel when you are successful. **TEXT TO SELF**

296   297

READING/WRITING WORKSHOP, pp. 296–297

Make Connections

ESSENTIAL QUESTION

Encourage students to go back into the text for evidence as they talk about how the poets write about success. Ask students to compare how they feel when they are successful to how the characters feel in each poem.

Continue Close Reading

Use the following lessons for focused rereadings.

→ Narrative Poem, T274–T275
→ Theme, T276–T277
→ Stanza and Repetition, T278–T279
→ Connotation and Denotation, T280–T281

A C T Access Complex Text

▶ **Specific Vocabulary**

Students may need assistance with decoding the figurative language used throughout "Sing to Me."

→ *What do you visualize in the fourth stanza?* (notes leaping, hovering, and crashing)

→ *Do the notes really do this?* (no)

→ *What is actually happening in the stanza?* (The boy is trying to play the piano. He starts to play the notes, but he can't blend them together into music.)

Genre: Poetry

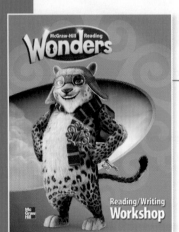

Reading/Writing Workshop

OBJECTIVES

CCSS Explain major differences between poems, drama, and prose, and refer to the structural elements of poems (e.g., verse, rhythm, meter) and drama (e.g., casts of characters, settings, descriptions, dialogue, stage directions) when writing or speaking about a text. **RL.4.5**

Identify characteristics of narrative poetry.

ACADEMIC LANGUAGE

- *narrative poem, character*
- Cognate: *poema narrativo*

 MINILESSON 10 Mins

Narrative Poem

1 Explain

Share with students the following key characteristics of a **narrative poem**.

→ A narrative poem tells a story and has characters. The narrator is sometimes a character.

→ A narrative poem is about fictional or real events. Narrative poems can read like a story.

→ A narrative poem may be written in stanzas.

2 Model Close Reading: Text Evidence

Model identifying features of a narrative poem in "Sing to Me" on page 295.

Characters Point out that the narrator in "Sing to Me" is the main character. We see the events of the story only from his perspective. Ask: *What characteristics or qualities of the narrator are revealed in the poem?*

3 Guided Practice of Close Reading

Have students work with partners to identify features of a narrative poem in "The Climb" on pages 296–297. Partners should find text evidence to illustrate each feature. Then have them share their work with the class.

Go Digital

Present the Lesson

CCSS Genre ▶ Poetry

Narrative Poem

A Narrative Poem:
- Tells a story and has characters.
- Is about fictional or real events.
- May be written in stanzas.

 Find Text Evidence

I can tell that both "Sing to Me" and "The Climb" are narrative poems because they both tell a story and have characters.

page 295

The cool white keys stretched for miles.
How would my hands pull
and sort through the notes,
blending them into music?

I practiced
and practiced all day.
My fingers reaching for a melody
that hung dangling,
like an apple just out of reach.

I can't do this.
I can't do this.

The day ground on,
notes leaping hopefully into the air,
hovering briefly, only to crash,
an awkward jangle, a tangle of noise
before slowly fading away.

My mom found me, forehead on the keys.
She asked, "Would you like some help?"
It took months for my hands to do what I wanted.
She sat down on the bench,
her slender fingers plucking notes
from the air.

I can do this.
I can do this.

She sat with me every night that week,
working my fingers until their efforts
made the keys sing to me, too.

— Will Meyers

Character The narrator of the poem is the main character. We see the events from his point of view.

 Your Turn

Reread the poem "The Climb." Identify the elements that tell you it is a narrative poem.

298

READING/WRITING WORKSHOP, p. 298

 Quick Check

Can students identify the features of narrative poetry in "Sing to Me" and "The Climb"? Can they find text evidence to illustrate each feature?

⬇

Small Group Instruction

If No →	**Approaching Level**	Reteach p. T296
	ELL	Develop p. T312
If Yes →	**On Level**	Review p. T304
	Beyond Level	Extend p. T308

ENGLISH LANGUAGE LEARNERS SCAFFOLD

ELL

Beginning

Understand Point out that "Sing to Me" has a narrator who is telling a story. Reread the first two stanzas. Ask: *Who is the narrator?* (a boy) *What is he telling us about?* (playing the piano) Guide students to use the picture to respond. Continue reading. Help students understand the narrator's problem and how it is solved.

Intermediate

Describe Help students reread "Sing to Me." Have them identify the characters in the poem. Ask: *How many characters are in the poem?* (two) *Who is the main character?* (the boy) *Who is the second character?* (his mom) *Who tells the story in the poem?* (the boy, or narrator) Students should answer in complete sentences.

Advanced/High

Discuss Have partners reread "Sing to Me." Elicit details that show the poem is a narrative poem. Ask: *Who is the narrator? What story is he telling the reader? What happens in the end? Turn to a partner and explain.* If necessary, ask additional questions to develop students' responses.

ON-LEVEL PRACTICE BOOK p. 195

The Principal's Office

"Ms. Lee will see you now," the assistant said.
I swallowed hard and opened the door.
I've really done it, I thought.
As I stepped in, Ms. Lee looked up
And took an envelope from her desk.
"Daniel Birnbaum," she began.
"I just think that you ought to know"
—my heart was pounding in my chest—
"How proud we all are of your work."
Surprised, I saw the envelope read,
"District Youth Robotics Team."
"You made the district team!" she said.
I've really done it! I thought.

Answer the questions about the text.

1. What makes this text a narrative poem?

   It tells a story about a character and gives his point of view.

2. Briefly summarize the text's events.

   Possible response: The assistant tells Daniel the principal will see him.

   The principal tells Daniel that he made the robotics team. Daniel is

   proud and relieved.

3. What words repeat in the text?

   "I've really done it."

4. How does the repetition show that the narrator's feelings have changed?

   The words show that he is scared at first, but proud at the end.

APPROACHING	BEYOND	ELL
p. 195	p. 195	p. 195

→ Comprehension Skill

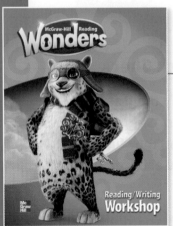

Reading/Writing Workshop

OBJECTIVES

CCSS Determine a theme of a story, drama, or poem from details in the text; summarize the text. **RL.4.2**

- Determine the theme of a poem.
- Find evidence in the text.

ACADEMIC LANGUAGE

- *theme, details, clues*
- Cognates: *tema, detalles*

SKILLS TRACE

THEME

Introduce Unit 2 Week 1

Review Unit 2 Weeks 2, 6; Unit 3 Week 6; Unit 4 Week 5; Unit 6 Weeks 1, 2, 5

Assess Units 2, 4, 6

MINILESSON
10 Mins

Theme

1 Explain

Explain to students that the theme of a poem is the main message or lesson a poet wants to communicate to the reader.

→ To identify the theme, students must pay attention to the narrator's or characters' words and actions.

→ Then they must think about what happens as a result of these actions.

→ Students should ask themselves, "What message does the poet want to get across to the reader?"

2 Model Close Reading: Text Evidence

Identify the key details in "The Climb" on pages 296–297 that give clues about the theme. Then model using the details written on the graphic organizer to determine the theme.

 Write About Reading: Summary Model for students how to use the notes from the graphic organizer to write a summary of the poem's theme.

3 Guided Practice of Close Reading

 Have students work in pairs to complete a graphic organizer for "Sing to Me," going back into the text to find key details and using the details to determine the theme of the poem. Discuss the details as students complete the graphic organizer.

 Write About Reading: Summary Ask pairs to work together to write a summary of "Sing to Me," including the poem's theme. Select pairs of students to share their summaries with the class.

Go Digital

Present the Lesson

Comprehension CCSS

Theme

The theme is the main message or lesson in a poem. Identifying key details in a poem can help you determine the theme.

🔍 Find Text Evidence

I'll reread "The Climb" on pages 296–297. I will look at the narrator's words and actions to help me identify the theme.

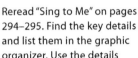

> **Detail**
> I lose my grip on the slippery bark/and slither down the trunk. Again.

Key details help you identify the theme.

> **Detail**
> The oak tree doesn't look/any smaller or bigger.

> **Detail**
> My hands find another and another.

> **Theme**
> Persistence leads to success.

Your Turn COLLABORATE

Reread "Sing to Me" on pages 294–295. Find the key details and list them in the graphic organizer. Use the details to determine the theme of the poem.

299

READING/WRITING WORKSHOP, p. 299

ELL ENGLISH LANGUAGE LEARNERS SCAFFOLD

Beginning

Respond Orally Chorally read the title. Ask: *What is this poem about?* (climbing) Reread the first two stanzas. Ask: *Does the narrator climb the tree?* (no) Continue reading. Point out that the narrator tries to climb the tree again after school. *Is she able to climb the tree this time?* (yes) Help describe the theme.

Intermediate

Identify Reread "The Climb." Ask: *What is the narrator trying to do?* (climb a tree) *Does she succeed in her first try?* (no) *Does she try again?* (yes) *Does she succeed this time?* (yes) Have partners discuss the theme of persistence and find details that support the theme. Then have them fill out the sentence frame: *The theme is about _____.* (persistence)

Advanced/High

Discuss Have partners reread "The Climb" and look for details that help them identify the theme. Ask: *What is the narrator trying to do? Does she give up after her first attempt? What does she do? What do these clues tell you about the theme?* Encourage students to use concept and vocabulary words.

Monitor and *Differentiate*

✓ Quick Check

Can students find and list key details that give clues about the theme? Can they determine the theme of "Sing to Me"?

⬇

Small Group Instruction

If No →	**Approaching Level**	Reteach p. T303
	ELL	Develop p. T312
If Yes →	**On Level**	Review p. T307
	Beyond Level	Extend p. T311

ON-LEVEL PRACTICE BOOK pp. 193–194

A. Reread the passage and answer the questions. Possible responses provided.

1. What is this poem about?

It is about a student winning a spelling bee.

2. What is the theme of this poem?

If you work hard, you can accomplish your goals.

3. What in the poem lets you know what the theme is?

The narrator says that she has spent many hours in her room writing down words. This practice and effort helped her win the spelling bee.

B. Work with a partner. Read the passage aloud. Pay attention to rate. Stop after one minute. Fill out the chart.

	Words Read	–	Number of Errors	=	Words Correct Score
First Read		–		=	
Second Read		–		=	

APPROACHING pp. 193–194	BEYOND pp. 193–194	ELL pp. 193–194

→ Literary Elements

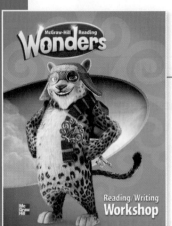

Reading/Writing Workshop

OBJECTIVES

CCSS Explain major differences between poems, drama, and prose, and refer to the structural elements of poems (e.g., verse, rhythm, meter) and drama (e.g., casts of characters, settings, descriptions, dialogue, stage directions) when writing or speaking about a text. **RL.4.5**

- Identify stanzas in poetry.
- Identify repetition and its effect in a poem.

ACADEMIC LANGUAGE

- *stanza, repetition*
- Cognate: *repetición*

MINILESSON **10** Mins

Stanza and Repetition

1 Explain

Explain to students that a **stanza** is two or more lines of poetry that together form a unit of the poem.

→ Stanzas can be the same length and have a rhyme scheme.

→ Stanzas can also vary in length and not rhyme.

→ Stanzas are used to give a poem form.

Explain that **repetition** is the use of repeated words and phrases in a poem.

→ Repetition is used for rhythmic effect and emphasis.

→ Many poets use repetition to express their ideas in interesting ways. It can also add to the emotional impact of a poem.

2 Model Close Reading: Text Evidence

Model identifying the stanzas and the words that are repeated in "The Climb" on pages 296–297. Explain how the repetition creates a rhythmic effect and enhances the emotional impact of the poem.

3 Guided Practice of Close Reading

Have students work with partners to reread "Sing to Me" on page 295. Have them identify the repeated words and phrases in the poem. Then have them work together to explain the effect the repetition has in the poem. Ask volunteers to share their findings with the class.

Go Digital

Present the Lesson

Stanza and Repetition

A **stanza** is two or more lines of poetry that together form a unit of the poem. Stanzas can be the same length and have a rhyme scheme, or vary in length and not rhyme.

Repetition is the use of repeated words or phrases in a poem. Poets use repetition for rhythmic effect and emphasis.

Find Text Evidence

Reread the poem "The Climb" on pages 296–297. Identify the stanzas and listen for words or phrases that are repeated.

page 296

Stanza Each of these groups of lines is a stanza.

Repetition The poet starts the last three stanzas on this page with, "Today."

Your Turn

COLLABORATE

Reread "Sing to Me." What lines does the poet repeat in this poem? What effect does the repetition have on the poem?

300

READING/WRITING WORKSHOP, p. 300

 **ccess Complex Text**

▶ Genre

Students may need help understanding the effect of repetition on the mood of a poem.

→ Read "Sing to Me" with students. Point out that the third and sixth stanzas use repetition.

→ *Why does the author repeat "I can't do this" in the third stanza?* (to emphasize that the narrator truly believes he can't play)

→ *Why does the author repeat "I can do this" in the sixth stanza?* (to emphasize that the narrator believes he can play now)

Monitor and *Differentiate*

 Quick Check

Are students able to identify stanzas in "Sing to Me" and "The Climb"? Can they identify examples of repetition in each poem?

⬇

Small Group Instruction

If No →	Approaching Level	Reteach p. T296
	ELL	Develop p. T312
If Yes →	On Level	Review p. T304
	Beyond Level	Extend p. T308

ON-LEVEL PRACTICE BOOK p. 196

A **stanza** is two or more lines of poetry that together form a unit of the poem. Stanzas can be the same length and have a rhyme scheme, or vary in length and not rhyme.

Repetition is the use of repeated words and phrases in a poem. Poets use repetition for rhythmic effect and emphasis.

Read the lines of the narrative poem below. Then answer the questions.

Letters trip over each other
as they race to leave my mouth.
My tongue lines them up in order
as they march to the microphone:
A-S-

I am almost alone on the stage.
One last kid sags with his head
in his hands. He is mouthing
each letter as I say it:
C-E-N-

1. Are there stanzas in this part of the poem? If so, how many and how many lines does each have?

   Yes; There are two stanzas with five lines in each stanza.

2. What kind of repetition is in this poem? How does it affect the poem?

   At the end of every stanza, there are more letters spelling a word.

   It adds suspense; it makes the reader wonder what the word is and if

   the speaker is going to spell it correctly.

3. Write another stanza for this poem that includes the same structure and repetition.

   Answers will vary, but should include a stanza and repetition.

APPROACHING p. 196	BEYOND p. 196	ELL p. 196

→ Vocabulary Strategy

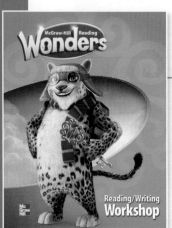

Reading/Writing Workshop

MINILESSON 10 Mins

Connotation and Denotation

1 Explain

Explain to students that **connotation** is the meaning suggested by a word in addition to its literal meaning. It is the feeling or idea associated with a word. **Denotation** is the dictionary's definition of a word.

2 Model Close Reading: Text Evidence

Model identifying the connotation and denotation of *immense* in "The Climb" on page 296. Tell students that the dictionary definition of *immense* is "very large; huge." Then explain that connotations of *immense* might be "intimidating" or "overwhelming." Point out that the narrator seems to feel overwhelmed or intimidated by the oak tree in the beginning of the poem.

3 Guided Practice of Close Reading

Have students work in pairs to identify the connotation and denotation of words in "Sing to Me" or "The Climb." Students should consult a dictionary to determine the precise denotations. Encourage partners to look for clues within the poems to help them determine each word's connotation.

Go Digital

Present the Lesson

OBJECTIVES

CCSS Consult reference materials (e.g., dictionaries, glossaries, thesauruses), both print and digital, to find the pronunciation and determine or clarify the precise meaning of key words and phrases. **L.4.4c**

Determine the connotation and denotation of words in poetry.

ACADEMIC LANGUAGE

• *connotation, denotation*

• Cognates: *connotación, denotación*

SKILLS TRACE

CONNOTATION AND DENOTATION

Introduce Unit 4 Week 5

Review Unit 4 Week 5; Unit 5 Week 1; Unit 6 Week 1

Assess Units 4, 6

Vocabulary Strategy CCSS

Connotation and Denotation

Connotation is a feeling or idea associated with the word.
Denotation is the dictionary's definition of a word.

 Find Text Evidence

When I read "The Climb" I know that, besides having a literal meaning, some words make feelings come to mind. In the first stanza, the word immense *means "huge." Connotations of* immense *might be* overwhelming *and* intimidating.

> We are waiting for the bus under our immense oak tree.

Your Turn COLLABORATE

Find an example of connotation and denotation in "Sing to Me" or "The Climb." Give the connotations of the word and its denotation.

301

READING/WRITING WORKSHOP, p. 301

 ENGLISH LANGUAGE LEARNERS
SCAFFOLD

Beginning	Intermediate	Advanced/High
Understand Write the word *screech* and its definition on the board. Say: *A screech is a loud, high sound.* Demonstrate screeching and have students repeat. Say: *This is the definition, or denotation. Is the sound of a screech a nice sound?* (no) *The feeling we get from a word is the* connotation.	**Explain** Point out the word *screech* on page 296 of "The Climb." Provide its definition. Say: *The definition is the denotation of* screech. *What is the connotation, or feeling, of this word?* Have partners work together to explain the connotation of *screech*.	**Discuss** Have partners define the words *screech* in "The Climb" and *crash* and *leaping* in "Sing to Me." Allow them to use a dictionary, if necessary. Ask: *What is the connotation, or feeling, of each word?* Elicit details to develop students' responses.

Monitor and *Differentiate*

✓ Quick Check

Can students determine the connotation and denotation of words in "Sing to Me" or "The Climb"?

⬇

Small Group Instruction

If No → | Approaching Level | Reteach p. T301
| ELL | Develop p. T317
If Yes → | On Level | Review p. T306
| Beyond Level | Extend p. T310

ON-LEVEL PRACTICE BOOK p. 197

Read each passage. Each word in bold has a different connotation in the poem than its usual denotation. Explain the connotation on the lines.

1. Letters **trip** over each other as they race to leave my mouth.
   If the words trip over each other, then the connotation is that they are jumbled and mixed together before they are ordered into words.

2. One last kid **sags** with his head in his hands. He is mouthing each word as I say it:
   Usually, sag means just hanging limp, but here the connotation is that the kid looks defeated and sad.

3. My tongue lines them up in order as they **march** to the microphone:
   Usually people march in a straight line, so the connotation is that the words are going in a straight line, in order, from her mouth.

APPROACHING p. 197	BEYOND p. 197	ELL p. 197

Develop Comprehension

Literature Anthology

"Swimming to the Rock"
"The Moondust Footprint"

Lexile and TextEvaluator scores are not provided for non-prose selections, such as poetry and drama.

Text Complexity Range

Lexile

740   1010

TextEvaluator™

23   **NP**   Non-Prose*   51

Options for Close Reading

→ Whole Class

→ Small Group

→ Independent

CCSS Genre • Poetry

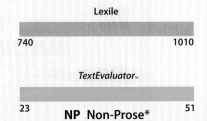

Essential Question

How do writers look at success in different ways?

Read how two poets describe accomplishments.

Go Digital!

356

My father and brothers
are swimming to the Rock.
"Come with us!"
they call to me
and I say,
"Maybe next year."

1 The Rock is very, very far away.

I sit on the dock
with my peanut butter sandwich.
I watch them
dive into the water
and swim the distance
their kicks and
splashes and elbows
getting smaller and smaller
as they near the Rock.

A C T Access Complex Text

What makes this text complex?

▶ **Connection of Ideas**

▶ Connection of Ideas

Guide students in making inferences about the narrator using evidence from the poem.

→ *What can you infer about the narrator after reading page 356? Identify the lines that help you make the inference.* (The narrator is scared. The lines "'Maybe next year'" and "The Rock is very, very

It takes them a long, long time.

They arrive and pull themselves to stand
and wave their arms in the air.
I can't see it but I know their hands are in fists.
I can't hear it but I know they are cheering.
Even the loons call to celebrate their arrival!

I sit on my dock
dangling my feet in the water
counting dragonflies.

My father and brothers
come closer
and from the water
lift their faces with
wild wet smiles.
And I think

This year! **2**

– Mary Atkinson

LITERATURE ANTHOLOGY, pp. 356–357

357

ESSENTIAL QUESTION

Ask a student to read aloud the Essential Question. Have students discuss how the poems will help them answer the question.

Note Taking:
Use the Graphic Organizer

As students read the poems, ask them to take notes by filling in the graphic organizer on **Your Turn Practice Book page 192** to record the theme of each poem.

1 Literary Elements: Repetition

Why does the poet repeat the word *very*? (to emphasize how far away the Rock is) Find two other examples of repetition. (*smaller and smaller; long, long*)

2 Skill: Theme

What is the theme of the poem? What details help you determine the theme? (You can conquer your fears if you believe you can; the narrator says, "Maybe next year" in the beginning of the poem but changes her mind by the end and says, "This year!")

far away" tell me that the narrator is hesitant and afraid of swimming to the rock.)

→ *Why does the narrator change her mind about swimming to the rock?* (The narrator sees how excited her father and brothers are after pulling themselves up on the rock. They smile when they swim back to the dock. The narrator is motivated to join in the fun!)

ELL Reread the second stanza on page 357. Use miming to demonstrate the swimmers' actions as they arrive back on the Rock.

→ *The swimmers wave their arms in the air.* (With students, wave your arms.)

→ Repeat with *making your hands into fists* and *cheering.*

LITERATURE ANTHOLOGY **T281B**

Develop Comprehension

3 Vocabulary: Connotation and Denotation

What is the denotation of *awesome*? ("causing wonder or fear") What is its connotation in this poem? (It has a positive connotation, suggesting that the moon landing was a human victory that caused widespread joy and wonder.)

4 Genre: Narrative Poem

How do you know that "The Moondust Footprint" is a narrative poem? (It gives an account of an important historical event. It tells the story of the speaker watching the moon landing.)

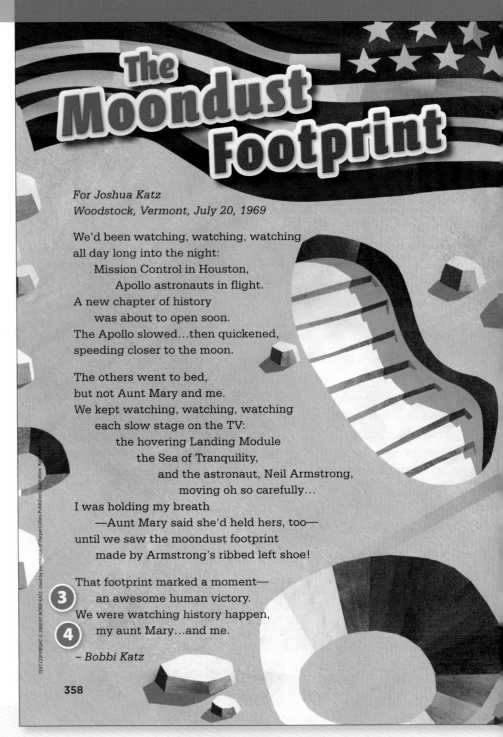

The Moondust Footprint

For Joshua Katz
Woodstock, Vermont, July 20, 1969

We'd been watching, watching, watching
all day long into the night:
    Mission Control in Houston,
        Apollo astronauts in flight.
A new chapter of history
    was about to open soon.
The Apollo slowed...then quickened,
speeding closer to the moon.

The others went to bed,
but not Aunt Mary and me.
We kept watching, watching, watching
    each slow stage on the TV:
        the hovering Landing Module
            the Sea of Tranquility,
                and the astronaut, Neil Armstrong,
                    moving oh so carefully...
I was holding my breath
    —Aunt Mary said she'd held hers, too—
until we saw the moondust footprint
    made by Armstrong's ribbed left shoe!

That footprint marked a moment—
    an awesome human victory.
We were watching history happen,
    my aunt Mary...and me.

    – Bobbi Katz

358

TEXT COPYRIGHT © 2000 BY BOBBI KATZ. Used by permission of HarperCollins Publishers. Illustration: Kyle Poling.

LITERATURE ANTHOLOGY, pp. 358–359

ACT Access Complex Text

Sentence Structure

Point out the use of punctuation in the poem.

→ *How does the poet's use of punctuation help the reader experience this historic moment?* (The commas make the reader pause and "watch" the moon landing as the poet experienced it. The ellipsis, semicolons, and em-dashes create a sense of eager anticipation in witnessing the event.)

ELL Chorally read the title and discuss the words in the title. Use the illustration to reinforce meaning.

→ *Where would you find moondust?* (on the moon)

→ Point to the footprint in the illustration. *Who made this footprint?* (Neil Armstrong)

→ *When was the moondust footprint made?* (during the first moonwalk)

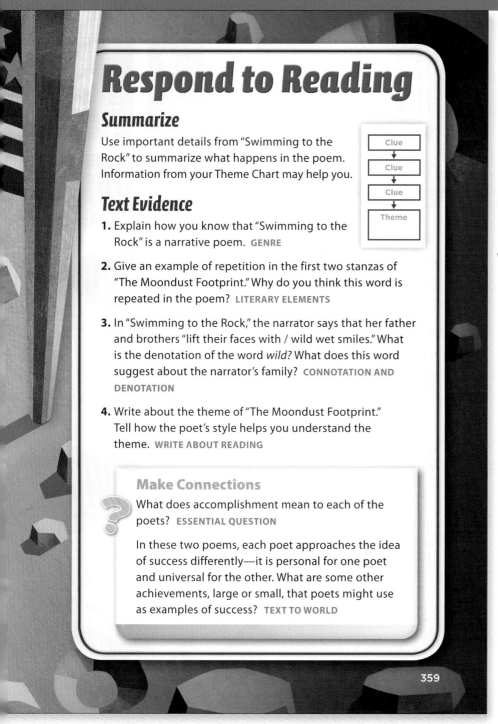

Respond to Reading

Summarize

Use important details from "Swimming to the Rock" to summarize what happens in the poem. Information from your Theme Chart may help you.

Clue
↓
Clue
↓
Clue
↓
Theme

Text Evidence

1. Explain how you know that "Swimming to the Rock" is a narrative poem. GENRE

2. Give an example of repetition in the first two stanzas of "The Moondust Footprint." Why do you think this word is repeated in the poem? LITERARY ELEMENTS

3. In "Swimming to the Rock," the narrator says that her father and brothers "lift their faces with / wild wet smiles." What is the denotation of the word *wild?* What does this word suggest about the narrator's family? CONNOTATION AND DENOTATION

4. Write about the theme of "The Moondust Footprint." Tell how the poet's style helps you understand the theme. WRITE ABOUT READING

Make Connections

? What does accomplishment mean to each of the poets? ESSENTIAL QUESTION

In these two poems, each poet approaches the idea of success differently—it is personal for one poet and universal for the other. What are some other achievements, large or small, that poets might use as examples of success? TEXT TO WORLD

359

Make Connections *Analytical Writing*

Essential Question Have partners work together to cite evidence from the poems to explain what accomplishment means to each poet. Ask partners to discuss their findings with the class.

Text to World After students list other achievements poets might write about, have them discuss how the achievements are examples of success.

Respond to Reading

Summarize

Review with students the information from their theme charts. Model how to use the details to summarize "Swimming to the Rock."

Analytical Writing **Write About Reading: Summarize** Remind students that a summary is a restatement of the key details of a text. You can write a summary of a single section of a poem or of an entire poem.

Ask students to write a summary of both of the poems in their own words. Remind them to start with a sentence that names the poem's title and form. Have students share their summaries with a partner.

Text Evidence

1. **Genre** <u>Answer</u> It is a narrative poem because it tells a story. <u>Evidence</u> It tells the story of a narrator who decides that this is the year she is going to try to swim to a distant rock.

2. **Literary Elements** <u>Answer</u> The word *watching* is repeated in the first two stanzas to build tension. <u>Evidence</u> The characters are watching TV, waiting anxiously to see the astronauts land on the moon.

3. **Connotation and Denotation** <u>Answer</u> The denotation of *wild* is "not tame" or "not controlled by people." It suggests that the narrator's family is having a lot of fun. <u>Evidence</u> The wild, excited smiles on the faces of the narrator's family help her decide to swim with them to the Rock.

4. **Write About Reading: Theme** The theme of "The Moondust Footprint" is that the moon landing was an important and thrilling moment in history. The poet slowly builds excitement in the poem to help portray the theme.

Develop Comprehension

Literature Anthology

Lexile and TextEvaluator scores are not provided for non-prose selections, such as poetry and drama.

"Genius" "Winner"

Text Complexity Range

Lexile

420   820

TextEvaluator™

2   **NP Non-Prose***   35

Compare Texts *Analytical Writing*

Students will read two more poems about success. Ask students to do a close reading of the poems, rereading to deeply understand the content. As they reread, encourage them to note literary elements the poets use to describe moments of triumph. Then students will use their notes to compare the poems.

CCSS **Genre • Poetry**

Compare Texts

Read how two poets describe moments of triumph.

Genius

"Sis! Wake up!" I whisper
in the middle of the night.

    Urgently, I shake her
    till she switches on the light.

The spiral notebook in my hand
provides her quick relief.

    It tells her there's no danger
    of a break-in by a thief.

"Okay," she says, then, props herself
up vertically in bed.

    She nods for me to read my work.
    I cough, then forge ahead.

The last verse of my poem leaves
her silent as a mouse.

    I worry till she says, "We have
    a genius in the house."

– *Nikki Grimes*

360

A C T   Access Complex Text

What makes this text complex?
▶ Organization

▶ Organization

Have students reread the two poems aloud. Tell them that the two poets organize the poems very differently.

→ *Which poem do you think is more structured?* ("Genius" has a more consistent structure. It is organized into stanzas that have two lines each. "Winner" has little structure.)

WINNER

what I remember most
is my dad behind the rusted screen
back of home plate
"You can hit this guy!"
his voice not letting up
through four fast balls
(two misses swinging late,
two fouls on checked swings)

1

then the curve ball and the dying quail
into left-center
the winning run sliding home,
my dad all smiles,
slapping backs in the bleachers
as if HIS single had won the game

– Gene Fehler

Make Connections

What personal triumph was described in each poem? **ESSENTIAL QUESTION**

How did each poet develop a sense of suspense or drama in the poem to add to each moment of triumph? **TEXT TO TEXT**

361

From *Center Field Grasses: Poems from Baseball* © 2012 [1991] Gene Fehler by permission of McFarland & Company, Inc., Box 611, Jefferson NC 28640. www.mcfarlandpub.com; Illustrator: Kyle Reed

LITERATURE ANTHOLOGY, pp. 360–361

1 Ask and Answer Questions

What is the speaker in "Genius" worried about? (whether his sister will approve of the poem he has written) What is the speaker in "Winner" worried about? (whether he will get a hit and impress his father)

Make Connections

Essential Question Have students paraphrase the personal triumph in each poem and write about how people other than the speakers are involved in the triumphs.

Text to Text Have groups of students use their notes from the Ask and Answer Questions prompt to write a response to the question. Each group can report back to the whole class. Ask one group to focus on how suspense is built in "Genius." (The reader wants to find out why the speaker is waking up his sister and how the sister will respond.) Ask another group to focus on how suspense is built in "Winner." (The reader wants to find out whether the speaker will get a hit after two missed swings and two foul balls.) Then have students discuss the similar themes in all the poems from this week.

→ *How does the structure of "Winner" add to the poem's suspense?* (There is a series of snippets of events leading up to the big hit.)

→ *How does the structure of "Genius" make the final lines more powerful?* (It is structured so that we learn a little about what is happening with each line. The final lines reveal everything.)

ELL Review the baseball terms in "Winner": *home plate, fast ball, checked swing, curve ball,* and *sliding home.*

→ *After a pitcher pitches, the ball crosses _____.* (home plate)

→ *If a batter checks his swing, does he make a full swing or a half swing?* (half)

→ *Does a curve ball move straight?* (no)

→ Phonics/Fluency

MINILESSON 20 Mins

Variant Vowel /ô/

Go Digital

OBJECTIVES

CCSS Use combined knowledge of all letter-sound correspondences, syllabication patterns, and morphology (e.g., roots and affixes) to read accurately unfamiliar multisyllabic words in context and out of context. **RF.4.3a**

CCSS Read on-level prose and poetry orally with accuracy, appropriate rate, and expression on successive readings. **RF.4.4b**

CCSS Correctly use frequently confused words (e.g., *to too, two; there, their*). **L.4.1g**

Rate: 102–122 WCPM

1 Explain

Display the *Straw* **Sound-Spelling Card** for the variant vowel /ô/. Point out that this vowel sound is most often spelled *aw* (*hawk*) and *au* (*haul*) and can be found in the words *salt, talk, ball, water,* and *cough.* Say the sound and provide a sample word for each spelling.

2 Model

Write the word *small* on the board. Circle the letters *all* in the word and model pronouncing the variant vowel /ô/. Then run your finger under the word as you sound out the whole word.

3 Guided Practice

Write the following /ô/ words on the board. Help students identify the spelling for the variant vowel and then echo-read the list after you.

stall	caught	fawn
awful	sauna	chalk
bought	fault	halt

Read Multisyllabic Words

Transition to Longer Words Draw a T-chart on the board. In the first column, write *walk, pause, lawn,* and *fall.* In the second column, write *walker, pausing, lawnmower,* and *fallout.* Have students choral-read the words in the first column. Explain that the words in the second column contain the smaller words from the first column.

Ask students to underline the variant vowel /ô/ in the words in the second column. Then point to each word and model how to read it. Have students echo-read after you.

Variant Vowel /ô/

Present the Lesson

View "Sing to Me"

ELL

Refer to the sound transfers chart in the **Language Transfers Handbook** to identify sounds that do not transfer in Spanish, Cantonese, Vietnamese, Hmong, and Korean.

Frequently Confused Words

1 Explain

Explain that frequently confused words sound the same and have somewhat similar spellings, but they have different meanings and spellings. Homophones are frequently confused for these reasons. Below are some frequently confused words:

→ *to/too/two*   → *know/no*

→ *their/there/they're*   → *accept/except*

→ *your/you're*   → *hear/here*

→ *threw/through*   → *miner/minor*

2 Model

Write and say *miner* and *minor*. Have students repeat them. Explain that a *miner* is someone who works in a mine. Something *minor* is small or unimportant. Model using the words in sentences.

3 Guided Practice

Write the words *here* and *hear* on the board. Ask students to help you write sentences that correctly use each word. Repeat the procedure with the words *your* and *you're* if time allows.

Rate

Explain/Model Remind students that it is important to read at a steady rate, or pace, regardless of what type of text they are reading. Explain that their reading rate should not change when reading poetry.

Model reading the poem "The Climb" on page 296. Read at a steady rate, as if you are reading a story. After you finish, ask students to comment on your reading rate. Point out that the line breaks in the poem did not affect how you read the sentences.

Practice/Apply Have students whisper-read the poem at their desks. Remind them to read the poem as a story and to maintain a steady reading rate. Have a volunteer read the poem aloud.

Daily Fluency Practice

Students can practice fluency using **Your Turn Practice Book.**

Monitor and *Differentiate*

✓ Quick Check

Can students decode multisyllabic words with the variant vowel /ô/? Can students identify frequently confused words? Can students read fluently?

Small Group Instruction

If No →	**Approaching Level**	Reteach pp. T298, T302
	ELL	Develop pp. T314, T318
If Yes →	**On Level**	Review p. T304
	Beyond Level	Extend p. T308

ON-LEVEL PRACTICE BOOK p. 198

A. Read each sentence. Underline the word or words with the variant vowel /ô/ found in *hawk*. Then sort the words by their spellings in the chart below.

1. I love to eat strawberry shortcake.

2. The cat stalked the mouse in the yard.

3. I thought you might like to see the water at the beach.

4. The lady altered her shawl around her shoulders.

al	aw	wa	ough
5. stalked	7. strawberry	9. water	10. thought
6. altered	8. shawl		

B. Circle the correct word in parentheses to complete each sentence. Use a dictionary to help you if necessary.

1. Did you (chose, choose) the red skateboard or the black one?

2. (Their, They're) waiting for us at the restaurant already.

3. I need some (advise, advice) about how to prepare for this test.

4. The baseball crashed (through, threw) the bedroom window.

5. I have (to, two) pairs of sneakers that I wear.

APPROACHING p. 198	BEYOND p. 198	ELL p. 198

☞ **Go** Digital

www.connected.mcgraw-hill.com
RESOURCES
Research and Inquiry

→ **Wrap Up the Week**
Integrate Ideas

RESEARCH AND INQUIRY

Achievements

OBJECTIVES

CCSS Consult reference materials (e.g., dictionaries, glossaries, thesauruses), both print and digital, to find the pronunciation and determine or clarify the precise meaning of key words and phrases. **L.4.4c**

• Use reliable sources.
• Analyze language use in a poem.
• Use reference materials.

ACADEMIC LANGUAGE

• *summary, analysis, dictionary, glossary, thesaurus, presentation*
• Cognates: *análisis, diccionario, glosario, tesauro, presentación*

Research Narrative Poetry

Explain to students that they will work in pairs to find another narrative poem about an achievement. They will then write an analysis that explains how the poem uses aspects of narrative poetry to communicate its main theme or idea. Discuss the following steps:

❶ **Discuss the Topic** Have pairs of students discuss the poems they read this week and think about how the writer conveyed the theme of achievement and success to the reader.

❷ **Research a Poem** Review how to locate and use reliable print and online sources. Then have pairs conduct research to find another narrative poem that describes an achievement.

❸ **Guided Practice** Have students analyze the poem they chose. Guide them to discuss how the poet's use of specific language conveys a certain mood or helps the reader picture the events or images in the poem. Encourage them to look up words in a dictionary, glossary, or thesaurus to gain a better understanding of narrative poetry.

❹ **Write a Summary** Ask students to write an analysis of the poem that explains how its narrative elements communicate the theme of achievement. Ask students to proofread their work before they write their final draft.

Present the Summaries

Ask students to present their poems to the class along with their analyses. Then have students post their work on the Shared Research Board. Have students use online Presentation Checklist 1 to evaluate their roles in the presentation.

TEXT CONNECTIONS  *Analytical Writing*

OBJECTIVES

CCSS Compare and contrast the treatment of similar themes and topics (e.g., opposition of good and evil) and patterns of events (e.g., the quest) in stories, myths, and traditional literature from different cultures. **RL.4.9**

Text to Text

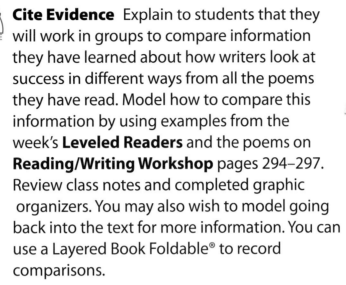

Cite Evidence Explain to students that they will work in groups to compare information they have learned about how writers look at success in different ways from all the poems they have read. Model how to compare this information by using examples from the week's **Leveled Readers** and the poems on **Reading/Writing Workshop** pages 294–297. Review class notes and completed graphic organizers. You may also wish to model going back into the text for more information. You can use a Layered Book Foldable® to record comparisons.

Students should cite at least three examples from each poem.

Unit Theme
Looking at Success
Many Stumbling Blocks
Believing in Yourself
Talent and Determination
Conclusions

Dinah Zike's
FOLDABLES
Study Organizer

Present Information Ask groups of students to present their findings to the class. Encourage discussion, asking students to comment on information on the charts that is similar and ideas that are different.

WRITE ABOUT READING *Analytical Writing*

OBJECTIVES

CCSS Explain major differences between poems, drama, and prose, and refer to the structural elements of poems (e.g., verse, rhythm, meter) and drama (e.g., casts of characters, settings, descriptions, dialogue, stage directions) when writing or speaking about a text. **RL.4.5**

CCSS Identify the reasons and evidence a speaker provides to support particular points. **SL.4.3**

Write an Analysis

Cite Evidence Explain that students will write about one of the texts they read this week. Using text evidence, they will analyze how the author developed the theme of a story or poem.

Discuss how to analyze theme by asking *how* and *why* questions.

→ How did the characters' words and actions help you to identify the message of the story?

→ Why is it important to understand what the characters say and do?

Use **Your Turn Practice Book** page 199 and discuss the student model. Then have students select a text and review details about the theme. Have them write an analysis that explains how the author used characters and details to communicate the theme. Remind students to cite text evidence and to use homophones and pronouns correctly.

 Present Your Ideas Ask partners to share their paragraphs and to discuss or recommend additional evidence to support their analyses.

Readers to Writers

MINILESSON
10 Mins

Writing Traits: Word Choice

Sensory Language

Expert Model Explain that good writers use sensory language to tell how a subject looks, sounds, smells, tastes, or feels. Using sensory details helps writers describe events and experiences clearly and precisely. Sensory details bring a subject to life and help readers create a picture in their minds as they read.

Expert Model

Read aloud the expert model from the poem "The Climb." Ask students to listen for the sensory details that help them picture what is happening. Have students talk with partners to identify these sensory details.

Student Model Remind students that writers use sensory details to help readers picture events and experiences in their minds. Read aloud the student draft "The Ocean." As students follow along, have them focus on the sensory details the writer added to his draft.

Student Model

Invite partners to talk about the draft and the sensory language that Jack added. Ask them to suggest places where Jack could add more sensory details.

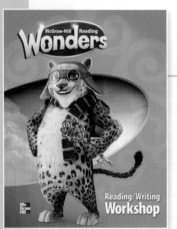

Reading/Writing Workshop

OBJECTIVES

CCSS Write routinely over extended time frames (time for research, reflection, and revision) and shorter time frames (a single sitting or a day or two) for a range of discipline-specific tasks, purposes, and audiences. **W.4.10**

CCSS Use concrete words and phrases and sensory details to convey experiences and events precisely. **W.4.3d**

- Analyze models to understand sensory language.
- Write a poem about success.
- Add sensory details to revise writing.

ACADEMIC LANGUAGE
- *sensory, details*
- Cognate: *detalles*

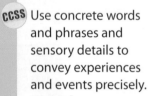 **Genre Writing**

Narrative Text and Poetry

For full writing process lessons and rubrics, see:

→ Fictional Narrative, pages T344–T349

→ Poetry, pages T350–T355

CCSS Writing Traits ⟩ Word Choice

Readers to ...

In a poem, writers use sensory details to describe how something looks, sounds, smells, tastes, or feels. Read the excerpt from the poem, "The Climb" below.

Sensory Language

Identify **sensory language** in "The Climb." How does the language help you picture what is happening?

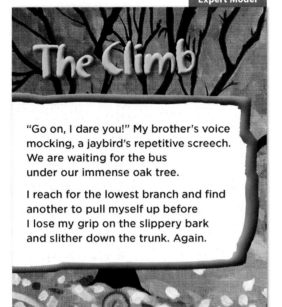

Expert Model

The Climb

"Go on, I dare you!" My brother's voice mocking, a jaybird's repetitive screech. We are waiting for the bus under our immense oak tree.

I reach for the lowest branch and find another to pull myself up before I lose my grip on the slippery bark and slither down the trunk. Again.

302

Writers

Jack wrote a poem about the ocean. Read Jack's revisions to his poem.

Student Model

The Ocean

My brother wears ^aqua pajamas.

At night ~~there~~ they're^ the color

of an angry gray ocean

that yells ~~to loud~~ and howls^ crashing^

against the bed.

"I don't WANT to go to sleep!"

In the morning they ~~are~~ reflect^

the color of a calm blue sea

that drifts sleepily^ ashore^

to breakfast.

Editing Marks

⎌ Switch order.
∧ Add.
⌃ Add a comma.
⌟ Take out.
ⓢⓟ Check spelling.
☰ Make a capital letter.

Grammar Handbook

Pronouns and Homophones
See page 465.

Your Turn

COLLABORATE

✔ Identify the sensory language Jack added.
✔ Identify the pronoun he replaced.
✔ Tell how revisions improved Jack's writing.

Go Digital!
Write online in Writer's Workspace

303

READING/WRITING WORKSHOP, pp. 302–303

ⓔⓛⓛ ENGLISH LANGUAGE LEARNERS SCAFFOLD

As English Language Learners write during the week, provide support to help them respond to the prompts. For example:

Beginning	**Intermediate**	**Advanced/High**
Write Help students complete the sentence frames. *Jack's brother wears _____ pajamas. At night the pajamas are the color of an _____ that yells and _____, _____ against the bed. _____ is a sensory detail.*	**Describe** Ask students to complete the sentence frames. Encourage students to provide details. *Jack's brother wears _____. At night the pajamas are the color of _____. In the morning the pajamas reflect _____. Two sensory details are _____.*	**Discuss** Check for understanding. Ask: *What do Jack's brother's pajamas look like at night? What do the pajamas look like in the morning? Can you name two sensory details that Jack used?*

Writing Every Day: Word Choice

DAY 1

Writing Entry: Sensory Language

Prewrite Provide students with the prompt below.

Write a poem about a time when you experienced success. Use sensory details to bring the experience to life.

Have partners list experiences they could write about. Ask them to jot down sensory details about each experience that they might include in their drafts.

Draft Have each student choose an experience to write about. Remind students to include sensory details in their drafts.

Focus on Sensory Language

Use **Your Turn Practice Book** page 200 to model adding sensory details.

I was nervous.

I waited to hear the election results.

The loudspeaker came on.

I was excited when I heard the principal say my name.

Model adding sensory details by revising the first line of the poem.

I was shaking and my heart was beating fast.

Discuss how adding sensory details helps the reader feel what the narrator is feeling. Guide students to add more sensory details to the rest of the model.

DAY 2

Writing Entry: Sensory Language

Revise Have students revise their writing from Day 1 by adding two or three sensory details.

Use the **Conferencing Routines**. Circulate among students and stop briefly to talk with individuals. Provide time for peer review.

Edit Have students use Grammar Handbook page 465 in the **Reading/Writing Workshop** to edit for errors in pronouns and homophones.

Conferencing Routines

Teacher Conferences

STEP 1

Talk about the strengths of the writing.

The different sentence lengths you used add rhythm to your poem. I like the figurative language you used to describe the subject.

STEP 2

Focus on how the writer uses the target trait for the week.

These sensory details help me picture your experience. It would help if you added details that describe sounds and smells to really bring the experience to life.

STEP 3

Make concrete suggestions for revisions. Have students work on a specific assignment, such as those to the right, and then meet with you to review progress.

DAY

Writing Entry: Sensory Language

Prewrite Ask students to search their Writer's Notebook for topics to write a draft. Or, provide a prompt, such as the following:

Write a poem about a time when you were not successful. Tell how you felt about the experience. Use sensory details.

Draft Once students have chosen their topics, ask them to create a word web with the topic in the center. Then have them think about sensory details that they might include in their writing. Students can then use their word webs to begin their drafts.

DAY

Writing Entry: Sensory Language

Revise Have students revise the draft writing from Day 3 by adding two or three sensory details that tell how something looks, sounds, smells, tastes, or feels. As students are revising their drafts, hold teacher conferences with individual students. You may also wish to have students work with partners to peer conference.

Edit Invite students to review pronouns and homophones on Grammar Handbook page 465 in the **Reading/Writing Workshop** and then edit their drafts for errors.

DAY 5

Share and Reflect

Discuss with the class what they learned about adding sensory details to help readers create a picture in their minds. Invite volunteers to read and compare draft text with text that has been revised. Have students discuss the writing by focusing on the importance of the sensory details that have been added. Allow time for individuals to reflect on their own writing progress and record observations in their Writer's Notebooks.

Suggested Revisions

Provide specific direction to help focus young writers.

Focus on a Sentence
Read the draft and target one line of the poem for revision. *Rewrite this line by adding sensory details that tell about _____.*

Focus on a Section
Underline a section that needs to be revised. Provide specific suggestions. *This part of your poem is very interesting. I want to know more about _____. Provide sensory details that help me picture what is happening.*

Focus on a Revision Strategy
Underline a section of the poem, and have students use a specific revision strategy, such as adding. *This image is hard to picture. Try adding sensory details to describe it more clearly.*

Peer Conferences

Focus peer response groups on adding sensory details to help readers create a picture in their minds. Provide this checklist to frame discussion.

- ☑ Are there sensory details that help the reader picture what is happening?
- ☑ Do the sensory details tell how something looks, sounds, smells, tastes, or feels?
- ☑ What sensory details can be added to clarify the writing?

Grammar: Pronouns and Homophones

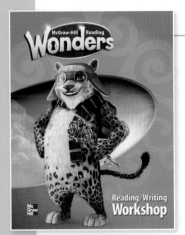

Reading/Writing Workshop

OBJECTIVES

CCSS Correctly use frequently confused words (e.g., *to, too, two; there, their*). **L.4.1g**

- Identify homophones.
- Spell frequently confused words correctly.
- Proofread sentences for mechanics and usage errors.

Go Digital

[Pronouns and Homophones]

Grammar Activities

DAY 1

DAILY LANGUAGE ACTIVITY

Seth readed <u>prince caspian</u> last year. He be reading anuther book now.
(1: read; 2: Prince Caspian; 3: is reading; 4: another)

Introduce Pronouns and Homophones

Present the following:

→ **Homophones** are words that sound alike but have different spellings and meanings.
  The meeting is at **eight** o'clock.
  I **ate** pasta for dinner.

→ Some pronouns are also homophones.
  Mark is on **their** team.
  They're going to win the game.
  There will be prizes for the winners.

Have partners discuss pronouns and homophones using page 465 of the Grammar Handbook in **Reading/Writing Workshop**.

DAY 2

DAILY LANGUAGE ACTIVITY

I finded this notebook, under my desk. Is it your's?
(1: found; 2: notebook under; 3: yours)

Review Possessive Pronouns

Review pronouns that are also homophones. Have students explain what a homophone is.

Introduce Types of Pronouns and Homophones

→ **Subject pronouns** are often used in conjunction with verbs to form contractions.
  He's going for a run.

→ Homophones include **contractions** and **possessive pronouns** such as *your/you're, its/it's,* and *there/their/they're.*
  Your books are on the table.
  You're going to be late!

TALK ABOUT IT

COLLABORATE

USE HOMOPHONES

Ask partners to each write five sentences using homophones. Students should take turns reading their sentences aloud. The other partner should name the homophone and then create a sentence using the companion homophone.

SPELL THE HOMOPHONE

Have students in small groups each write three sentences using *their, they're,* and *there*. Then have them take turns reading a sentence aloud. The other students should tell how to spell the homophone.

DAY 3

"Who's camera is this"? asked Joan. "Its her's," said Mindy.
(1: Whose; 2: this?"; 3: It's; 4: hers)

Mechanics and Usage: Contractions and Possessives

→ If writing a contraction, it must contain an apostrophe in place of the missing letter or letters.

→ An apostrophe should not be used with a possessive pronoun.

As students write, refer them to Grammar Handbook page 465.

DAY 4

DAILY LANGUAGE ACTIVITY

Their travelling to nevada this summer. Have you been there?
(1: They're; 2: traveling; 3: Nevada)

Proofread

Have students correct errors in these sentences.

1. Look at those dear in the yard. Their beautiful! (1: deer; 2: They're)

2. I'd like to come to you're house later. Wood that be okay? (1: your; 2: Would)

3. Its difficult to say if the weather will hold out. We'll have to weight and see. (1: It's; 2: wait)

4. I new they're would be a quiz today. (1: knew; 2: there)

Have students check their work using Grammar Handbook page 465 on pronouns and homophones.

DAY 5

DAILY LANGUAGE ACTIVITY

Have everyone finished eating? Their going to start the movie soon because its getting late.
(1: Has; 2: They're; 3: it's)

Assess

Use the Daily Language Activity and **Grammar Practice Reproducibles** page 100 for assessment.

Reteach

Use Grammar Practice Reproducibles pages 96–99 and selected pages from the Grammar Handbook for additional reteaching. Remind students that it is important to use pronouns and homophones correctly in their writing.

Check students' writing for use of the skill. Assign Grammar Revision Assignments in their Writer's Notebooks as needed.

See Grammar Practice Reproducibles pages 96–100.

USE *IT'S* AND *ITS*

Have partners each write six sentences using *it's* and *its* three times each. Then have them take turns reading a sentence aloud. The other student should tell whether the homophone is being used as a contraction or as a possessive pronoun.

USE *YOU'RE* AND *YOUR*

Have partners each write six sentences using *your* and *you're* three times each. Then have them take turns reading a sentence aloud. The other student should tell whether the homophone is being used as a contraction or as a possessive pronoun.

USE PRONOUNS AND HOMOPHONES

Ask students to write three sentences using the possessive pronouns *its, your,* and *their* one time each. Have students trade with a partner. Partners should say if each pronoun is used correctly, and then list any homophones.

→ Spelling: Variant Vowel /ô/

OBJECTIVES

 CCSS Spell grade-appropriate words correctly, consulting references as needed. **L.4.2d**

Spelling Words

caught	alter	caller
laws	halt	squall
drawn	talking	cough
strawberry	walker	fought
straw	chalk	thought
awe	stalk	false
shawl	small	

Review south, pouch, annoy
Challenge wallpaper, awkward

Differentiated Spelling

Approaching Level

fault	awe	talking
taught	saw	tall
laws	raw	caller
thaw	alter	small
draw	halt	cough
awful	walk	false
straw	chalk	

Beyond Level

daughter	vault	stalk
dinosaur	sprawling	squall
applauded	strawberry	wallpaper
caught	shawl	sought
clause	malt	thoughtful
audiences	halted	fought
because	alteration	

DAY 1

Assess Prior Knowledge

Display the spelling words. Read them aloud, drawing out the variant vowel /ô/ sound in each word.

Point out the spelling patterns in *laws* and *fought*. Circle the letters that create the variant vowel /ô/ sound (*aw, ough*). Say each word, pointing out the spellings attached to each sound. Note that in *fought*, *gh* is part of the vowel sound even though the letters are consonants.

Demonstrate sorting the spelling words by pattern under key words *straw, stalk, caught,* and *cough.* (Write the words on index cards or the IWB.) Sort a few words by spelling. Point out that in the *alk* spelling, the *l* is not pronounced.

Then use the Dictation Sentences from Day 5 to give the Pretest. Say the underlined word, read the sentence, and repeat the word. Have students write the words. Then have students check and correct their spelling.

DAY 2

Spiral Review

Review the /oi/ and /ou/ diphthong sounds in *noise, annoy, pound,* and *gown.* Use the Dictation Sentences below for the review words. Read the sentence, say the word, and have students write the words.

1. Are we driving <u>south</u> or north?

2. The key is in the <u>pouch</u>.

3. The bugs will <u>annoy</u> us.

Have partners check the spellings.

Challenge Words Review this week's variant vowel /ô/ spelling patterns. Use these Dictation Sentences for challenge words. Say the word, read the sentence, and say the word again. Have students write the word.

1. I have red <u>wallpaper</u> in my room.

2. Walking in water is <u>awkward</u>.

Have students check and correct their spelling before writing the words in their word study notebook.

 ## WORD SORTS

COLLABORATE

OPEN SORT

Have students cut apart the **Spelling Word Cards BLM** in the Teacher Resource Book and initial the back of each card. Have them read the words aloud with a partner. Then have partners do an open sort. Have them record the sort in their word study notebook.

PATTERN SORT

Complete the **pattern sort** from Day 1 using the key words, pointing out the variant vowel /ô/ spellings. Have students use Spelling Word Cards to do their own pattern sort. Ask partners to compare and check their sorts.

DAY 3

Word Meanings

Write the following words on the board. Have students copy the words into their word study notebooks and write the spelling word that is an antonym for each.

1. true (*false*)
2. threw (*caught*)
3. continue (*halt*)

Challenge students to come up with at least three more sets of antonyms. Have students list one of the words from the set, leaving a blank for the spelling, review, or challenge word that is its antonym. Have partners trade papers and fill in the missing word.

See Phonics/Spelling Reproducibles pp. 115–120.

SPEED SORT

Have partners do a **speed sort** to see who is fastest and record the results in the word study notebook. Then ask them to write a sentence for each spelling word, leaving blank spaces where the words should go. Have partners exchange papers and fill in the blanks.

DAY 4

Proofread and Write

Write these sentences on the board. Have students circle and correct each misspelled word. They can use print or electronic dictionaries or other resources to help them.

1. A smal tree blew over in the squawl. (*small, squall*)
2. I thawt I heard someone taulking. (*thought, talking*)
3. I cought the cows eating the straugh. (*caught, straw*)
4. The waulker had to hawlt at the stoplight. (*walker, halt*)

Error Correction Point out that the *ough* and *augh* spellings for /ô/ contain both vowels and consonants. Remind students that the consonants *gh* are silent in these spellings and to use print and electronic resources to help them check and correct any spellings they are unsure about.

BLIND SORT

Have partners do a **blind sort**: one reads a Spelling Word Card; the other tells under which key word it belongs. Have them take turns until both have sorted all their words. Ask them to review their sorts, then discuss how they sorted the words and if any changes are needed.

DAY 5

Assess

Use the Dictation Sentences for the Posttest. Have students list misspelled words in their word study notebooks. Look for students' use of these words in their writings.

Dictation Sentences

1. The player caught the ball.
2. We have laws about speeding.
3. The cartoon was drawn quickly.
4. We bought a huge strawberry.
5. We filled the barn with straw.
6. We watched in awe as the magician disappeared.
7. I knitted a warm shawl.
8. Liz had to alter the length of the dress.
9. The police asked us to halt our car.
10. We were talking during gym.
11. A walker waited to cross the street.
12. Our teacher bought new chalk.
13. I took a picture of a stalk of corn.
14. Dad looked small next to the redwood tree.
15. The radio show had a caller.
16. The squall knocked down trees.
17. She was sick with a bad cough.
18. They fought the unfair rules.
19. I thought the game had started.
20. We marked every answer false.

Have students self-correct the tests.

Build Vocabulary

OBJECTIVES

CCSS Use sentence-level context as a clue to the meaning of a word or phrase. **L.3.4a**

CCSS Use context (e.g., definitions, examples, or restatements in text) as a clue to the meaning of a word or phrase. **L.4.4a**

CCSS Demonstrate understanding of words by relating them to their opposites (antonyms) and to words with similar but not identical meanings (synonyms). **L.4.5c**

Expand vocabulary by adding inflectional endings and suffixes.

Vocabulary Words

attain	triumph
dangling	
hovering	

Go Digital

Vocabulary

Vocabulary Activities

DAY 1

Connect to Words

Practice this week's vocabulary.

1. How can you **attain** new skills?
2. How are the meanings of *dangling* and *dragging* different?
3. If something is **hovering**, what is it doing?
4. Describe a **triumph** that you have had.

DAY 2

Expand Vocabulary

Help students generate different forms of this week's words by adding, changing, or removing inflectional endings.

→ Draw a four-column T-chart on the board. Write *attain* in the left column. Then write *attains*, *attained*, and *attaining* in the other columns. Read aloud the words with students.

→ Have students share sentences using each form of *attain*.

→ Students can fill in the chart for *dangling* and *hovering*, then share sentences using the different forms of the words.

→ Have students copy the chart in their word study notebook.

BUILD MORE VOCABULARY

COLLABORATE

ACADEMIC VOCABULARY

Discuss important academic words.

→ Display *connotation, denotation, repetition, stanza.*

→ Define each word and discuss the meanings with students.

→ Display *repetition* and *repeat*. Have partners look up and define related words.

→ Write the related words on the board. Have partners ask and answer questions using the words. Repeat with *connotation, denotation,* and *stanza.*

CONTEXT CLUES

→ Remind students that synonyms are words with the same or a similar meaning. Ask: *What are some synonyms for* fast?

→ Invite students to generate synonyms for vocabulary words and other words. Write several examples on the board and discuss as a class.

→ Have partners choose a set of synonyms and write a sentence using each word in the set.

DAY 3

Reinforce the Words

Review last week's and this week's vocabulary words. Have students orally complete each sentence stem.

1. The helicopter was <u>hovering</u> in the ____.
2. My dad will <u>attain</u> new skills when he learns to ____.
3. I was <u>dangling</u> my feet in the ____.
4. It was a great <u>triumph</u> when we won the ____.

DAY 4

Connect to Writing

→ Have students write sentences in their word study notebooks using this week's vocabulary.

→ Tell them to write sentences that provide word information they learned from this week's readings.

→ **ELL** Provide the Day 3 sentence stems 1–4 for students needing extra support.

Write About Vocabulary Have students write something they learned from this week's words in their word study notebook. For example, they might write about a *triumph*, or a time when they tried to *attain* something.

DAY 5

Word Squares

Ask students to create Word Squares for each vocabulary word.

→ In the first square, students write the word. (example: *hovering*)

→ In the second square, students write their own definition of the word and any related words, such as synonyms. (example: *up in the air, floating in place*)

→ In the third square, students draw a simple illustration that will help them remember the word. (example: a helicopter)

→ In the fourth square, students write nonexamples, including antonyms for the word. (example: *landing, crawling, flying around*)

→ Have partners compare and discuss their Word Squares.

CONNOTATION AND DENOTATION

Remind students that *denotation* is the dictionary definition of a word and *connotation* is a meaning other than the dictionary definition.

→ Display **Your Turn Practice Book** page 193. Read the first stanza. Model figuring out the meaning of *trip*.

→ Have students complete page 197, and then find clues for *race, march, sags,* and *scribbled* on page 193.

SHADES OF MEANING

Help students generate words related to *triumph*. Draw a T-chart.

→ Elicit synonyms for the noun *triumph*, such as *victory*. Add these to the first column.

→ Point out that *triumph* can also be a verb. Have students find synonyms for the verb *triumph*, such as *win* or *overcome*. Add these to the second column.

→ Ask students to discuss how the words in the two columns are similar and different.

MORPHOLOGY

Use *triumph* as a springboard for students to learn more words. Draw a T-chart. Label the columns "Root word" and "Suffix."

→ Write *triumph* and the suffix *-ant* in the chart. Discuss how the suffix *-ant* changes the verb *triumph* into an adjective.

→ Elicit more words that take the suffix *-ant*, such as *assistant*. Note that not all words that end in *-ant* are adjectives. For example, *occupant* is a noun.

→ Approaching Level

Lexile 600
TextEvaluator™ 32

OBJECTIVES

(CCSS) Determine a theme of a story, drama, or poem from details in the text; summarize the text. **RL.4.2**

ACADEMIC LANGUAGE

• realistic fiction, narrative poem, ask and answer questions, theme, connotation, denotation

• Cognates: *ficción realista, poema narrativo, tema, connotación, denotación*

Leveled Reader:
Try, Try Again

Before Reading

Preview and Predict

Have students read the Essential Question. Then have students read the title and table of contents of *Try, Try Again*. Have students make a prediction about what the story will be about and share it with a partner.

Review Genre: Realistic Fiction

Review with students that realistic fiction is a form of fiction that includes characters, settings, and events that could exist in real life. As they preview the book, have students identify features of realistic fiction in *Try, Try Again*.

During Reading

Close Reading

Note Taking Ask students to use their graphic organizer while they read.

Pages 2–4 *What challenge is Jerome facing?* (He doesn't know how to ride his new bike.) *Think of a question you have about the story so far.* (Possible Answer: Will Jerome learn to ride his new bike?) *Turn to a partner and tell a clue that shows this story is realistic fiction.* (Jerome is learning to ride a bike. People learn to ride bikes in real life.)

Pages 5–6 *What is the literal meaning, or the denotation, of the word* raced *on page 6?* ("to move quickly") *Why does the author use this word?* (to mean "moved quickly" and to make reading the story more interesting)

Page 7 *What does* half-heartedly *mean on page 7?* ("not excited") *Do you think that Jerome will succeed at learning to ride the bike?* (Possible Answer: Judging by the title of the story, I think Jerome will try again and successfully learn to ride his bike.)

Go Digital

Leveled Readers

Use Graphic Organizer

Pages 8–11 *What does Jerome do in order to learn to ride his bike?* (He practices every day.) *Why is Jerome happy, even though he fell?* (He finally learned to ride the bike on his own.)

Pages 12–15 *How does Jerome succeed in the story?* (He does not give up, but tries again and again.) *Think about the lesson you learned in this story. What is the theme?* (Working hard can help someone succeed.) *With a partner, return to the question you asked on page 4. Find examples in the text to help each other answer the questions.*

After Reading

Respond to Reading Have students complete Respond to Reading on page 16 after they have finished reading.

Write About Reading Have students write about how Jerome became successful. Have students include at least two details from the story.

Fluency: Rate

Model Model reading page 7 using the correct rate. Next, reread the page aloud and have students read along with you.

Apply Have students practice reading with a partner.

PAIRED READ

"Sunlight Sparkling on Chrome"

Make Connections: Write About It

Before reading, ask students to note that the genre of the text is narrative poetry. A narrative poem tells a story. Then discuss the Essential Question. After reading, ask students to use the information from "Sunlight Sparkling on Chrome" to expand their discussion of success in *Try, Try Again*.

Leveled Reader

FOCUS ON LITERARY ELEMENTS

Students can extend their knowledge of repetition by completing the activity on page 20.

Literature Circles

Ask students to conduct a literature circle using the Thinkmark questions to guide the discussion. You may wish to have a whole-class discussion on how success can mean different things.

Level Up

Level-up lessons available online.

IF students read the **Approaching Level** fluently and answered the questions

THEN pair them with students who have proficiently read **On Level** and have students

• echo-read the **On Level** main selection with their partners.

• use self-stick notes to mark at least one new detail they would like to discuss in each section.

A C T Access Complex Text

The **On Level** challenges students by including more **domain-specific words** and **complex sentence structures**.

Approaching Level

Phonics/Decoding

DECODE WORDS WITH THE VARIANT VOWEL /ô/

TIER 2

OBJECTIVES

 Use combined knowledge of all letter-sound correspondences, syllabication patterns, and morphology (e.g., roots and affixes) to read accurately unfamiliar multisyllabic words in context and out of context. **RF.4.3a**

Decode words with the variant vowel /ô/.

 I Do Tell students that the variant vowel /ô/ can be spelled *aw*. Write *raw* on the board. Model the pronunciation of the word, and then point out the *aw* spelling. Tell students that *aw* is the spelling for the variant vowel /ô/ in *raw*. Repeat with *awe, saw,* and *thaw*. Sound out each word.

 We Do Write *hawk* and *draw* on the board. Circle the *aw* in *hawk*. Model pronouncing the variant vowel /ô/. Then sound out the whole word as you run your finger under the letters and say the word out loud. Have students repeat after you. Repeat with *draw*.

 You Do Add the words *lawn* and *straw* to the board. Have students circle the *aw* spelling in each word and pronounce the variant vowel /ô/. Then point to the words on the board in random order for students to choral-read. Repeat several times.

REVIEW THE VARIANT VOWEL /ô/

TIER 2

OBJECTIVES

 Use combined knowledge of all letter-sound correspondences, syllabication patterns, and morphology (e.g., roots and affixes) to read accurately unfamiliar multisyllabic words in context and out of context. **RF.4.3a**

Decode words with the variant vowel /ô/.

 I Do Remind students that the variant vowel /ô/ can be spelled *aw, au, alt, alk, all, wa,* and *ough*. Write on the board: *awful, fault, alter, chalk, small, water,* and *cough*. Read aloud each word and identify the variant vowel /ô/ spelling. Have students repeat the words after you.

 We Do Display **Word-Building Cards** for *fall* and *ing*. Combine the cards and have students say the word *falling* after you. Display the Word-Building Cards: *au, ed,* and *er*. Write the syllables *thor, talk, flaw,* and *tall* on the board. Have students use the cards and syllables to build words with the variant vowel /ô/. Have students underline the variant vowel /ô/ spelling in each word.

 You Do Add the following words to the board: *lawsuit, caution, recall, bought,* and *walker*. Ask students to decode each word with the variant vowel /ô/. Then point to the words on the board in random order for students to choral-read. Repeat several times.

PRACTICE WORDS WITH THE VARIANT VOWEL /ô/

OBJECTIVES

 CCSS Use combined knowledge of all letter-sound correspondences, syllabication patterns, and morphology to read accurately unfamiliar multisyllabic words in context and out of context. **RF.4.3a**

 I Do Display the **Sound-Spelling Card** for the variant vowel /ô/. Point out the variant vowel /ô/ spelling and model the pronunciation of *fallout*. Sound out the whole word as you run your finger under the letters. Repeat with *sauna* and *lawn mower*.

 We Do Write the words *salty, chalkboard,* and *thoughtful* on the board. Model how to decode the first word, and guide students as they decode the remaining words. Help students point out the variant vowel /ô/ spellings.

 You Do Afterward, point to the words in random order for students to choral-read.

FREQUENTLY CONFUSED WORDS

OBJECTIVES

CCSS Demonstrate command of the conventions of standard English grammar and usage when writing or speaking. Correctly use frequently confused words (e.g., *to, too, two; there, their*). **L.4.1g**

Decode frequently confused words.

 I Do Remind students that words often become confused when they sound the same and have similar spelling patterns. Tell students that words that sound alike but have different meanings and spellings are known as homophones. Write *minor* and *miner* on the board. Say: *These words sound alike, but they have different meanings.* Model the pronunciation of each word. Point out that a *miner* is someone who works in a mine, and *minor* describes something that is small or not important.

We Do Write *accept* and *except* on the board. Model the pronunciation of the words. Help students look up the meanings of the words in a dictionary. Ask a volunteer to read the meanings of the words to the rest of the class. Then say the words aloud and have students repeat after you.

 You Do Add the words *advice* and *advise* to the board. Have students sound out each word and look up the meanings. Point to the words in random order for students to choral-read.

ELL ENGLISH LANGUAGE LEARNERS

For the **ELLs** who need **phonics**, **decoding**, and **fluency** practice, use scaffolding methods as necessary to ensure students understand the meaning of the words. Refer to the **Language Transfers Handbook** for phonics elements that may not transfer in students' native languages.

Approaching Level

Vocabulary

REVIEW HIGH-FREQUENCY WORDS

 TIER 2

OBJECTIVES

 Read with sufficient accuracy and fluency to support comprehension. Read on-level text with purpose and understanding. **RF.4.4a**

Review high-frequency words.

 I Do Use **Word Cards 121–160**. Display one word at a time, following the routine:

Display the word. Read the word. Then spell the word.

 We Do Ask students to say the word and spell it with you. Model using the word in a sentence and have students repeat after you.

 You Do Display the word. Ask students to say the word and then spell it. When completed, quickly flip through the word card set as students choral-read the words. Provide opportunities for students to use the words in speaking and writing. For example, provide sentence starters, such as *The girl wore a pretty dress to the* ____. Ask students to write each word in their Writer's Notebook.

REVIEW VOCABULARY WORDS

 TIER 2

OBJECTIVES

 Acquire and use accurately grade-appropriate general academic and domain-specific words and phrases, including those that signal precise actions, emotions, or states of being and that are basic to a particular topic. **L.4.6**

 I Do Display each **Visual Vocabulary Card** and state the word. Explain how the photograph illustrates the word. State the example sentence and repeat the word.

 We Do Point to the word on the card and read the word with students. Ask them to repeat the word. Engage students in structured partner-talk about the image as prompted on the back of the vocabulary card.

 You Do Display each visual in random order, hiding the word. Have students match the definitions and context sentences of the words to the visuals displayed.

ANSWER YES/NO QUESTIONS

OBJECTIVES

CCSS Acquire and use accurately grade-appropriate general academic and domain-specific words and phrases, including those that signal precise actions, emotions, or states of being (e.g., *quizzed, whined, stammered*) and that are basic to a particular topic (e.g., *wildlife, conservation,* and *endangered* when discussing animal preservation). **L.4.6**

I Do

Display the *dangling* **Visual Vocabulary Card** and say aloud the following question: *Does an orange that is* dangling *hang loosely from a tree branch?*

Point out that *dangling* means "to hang or swing loosely," so the orange is hanging loosely from the branch.

We Do

Display the vocabulary card for the word *hovering*. Ask: *Does a* hovering *bird stay in one place?* Help students justify their answers to demonstrate that they understand the meaning of the word.

You Do

Discuss the poetry terms one at a time. Have students answer the following yes/no questions and justify their answers to demonstrate their word knowledge.

→ Does a *stanza* include two or more lines of poetry that form a unit of the poem?

› Is the *denotation* of a word the meaning suggested by that word?

→ Does the *connotation* of a word mean the basic definition of the word?

→ Does a poet use *repetition* to repeat words and phrases in a poem?

CONNOTATION AND DENOTATION

OBJECTIVES

CCSS Demonstrate understanding of figurative language, word relationships, and nuances in word meanings. Use the relationship between particular words (e.g., synonyms, antonyms, homographs) to bettter understand each of the words. **L.5.5c**

Determine connotations and denotations of words.

Display the Comprehension and Fluency poem on **Approaching Reproducibles** page 193. Read aloud the first stanza. Point to the word *trip*. Explain to students that understanding the connotation and denotation of a word can help them understand its meaning.

Think Aloud I am not sure of the connotation and denotation of the word *trip*. When I look up *trip*, I learn that it means to "hit your foot against something, so that you fall or almost fall." The next line says the letters "race to leave my mouth." I think the connotation of *trip* is to be in a rush.

Ask students to point to the word *march* in the last line of the first stanza. Discuss how they can figure out the connotation and denotation of the word. Then write the definition and connotation of *march* on the board.

Have students figure out the connotation and denotation of *scribbled* in the fourth stanza.

→ **Approaching Level**

Comprehension

FLUENCY

TIER 2

 OBJECTIVES

CCSS Read on-level prose and poetry orally with accuracy, appropriate rate, and expression on successive readings. **RF.4.4b**

Read fluently at a steady rate or pace.

 I Do Explain that students should always read at a steady rate, regardless of the type of text. Remind students that their reading rate should not change when reading poetry. Read the first stanza of the Comprehension and Fluency poem on **Approaching Reproducibles** page 193. Remind students to emphasize key words in the stanza.

 We Do Read the rest of the page aloud and have students echo-read at the same steady rate. Remind students that their rate should remain the same as they echo-read the poem.

 You Do Have partners take turns reading lines from the Approaching Reproducibles poem. Remind them to focus on reading at the same rate. Listen in and provide corrective feedback by modeling proper fluency.

IDENTIFY KEY DETAILS

TIER 2

 OBJECTIVES

CCSS Determine a theme of a story, drama, or poem from details in the text; summarize the text. **RL.4.2**

Identify key details about the actions of characters.

 I Do Read the first stanza of the Comprehension and Fluency poem in **Approaching Reproducibles**. Write the following lines on the board: "My tongue lines them up in order/as they march to the microphone." Point out that this detail demonstrates the speaker's method for spelling words during the spelling bee. Help students understand that paying attention to key details about the actions of characters will help them understand the theme of a poem.

 We Do Read the third stanza. Ask: *How does the speaker feel about getting ready for the spelling bee?* Help students understand that the speaker spent hours preparing with books. Have students choral-read the phrase "now seem worth it" and use it to answer the question.

 You Do Have students read the rest of the poem. After each stanza, they should write down details about the characters' actions that seem important. Review their lists and help them explain why the details may be important to the theme.

REVIEW THEME

OBJECTIVES

 Determine a theme of a story, drama, or poem from details in the text; summarize the text. **RL.4.2**

Identify the theme in a poem.

 Remind students that the theme is the main message or lesson in a poem. Point out that students should identify details to help them figure out theme in a poem.

 Read the first stanza of the Comprehension and Fluency poem in **Approaching Reproducibles** together. Model how to identify a key detail that can help readers figure out theme of the poem. Choral-read the next stanza. Then help students identify more key details.

You Do Have students continue reading the poem, listing the key details in each stanza. Then have students use their lists to determine the theme of the entire poem.

SELF-SELECTED READING

OBJECTIVES

 Determine a theme of a story, drama, or poem from details in the text; summarize the text. **RL.4.2**

Visualize the text to increase understanding.

Read Independently

Have students choose a narrative poem for sustained silent reading. Remind students that:

→ poets tell a story about fictional or real events in a narrative poem.

→ they should identify key details in a poem to help them determine the theme.

→ they should pay attention to descriptive words the writer uses in the poem to help them visualize the characters, events, and setting.

Read Purposefully

Have students record the theme on a Theme Chart as they read independently. After they finish, they can have a discussion about the poems they read.

→ Students should share their charts and answer this question: *What is the lesson or message that you learned from this poem?*

→ Students should also tell the rest of the class if there were any images they visualized to increase their understanding.

On Level

Lexile 740
TextEvaluator 51

OBJECTIVES

CCSS Determine a theme of a story, drama, or poem from details in the text; summarize the text. **RL.4.2**

ACADEMIC LANGUAGE

- *realistic fiction, narrative poem, ask and answer questions, theme, connotation, denotation*
- Cognates: *ficción realista, poema narrativo, tema, connotación, denotación*

Leveled Reader:
The Math-lete

Go Digital

Leveled Readers

Before Reading

Preview and Predict

Have students read the Essential Question. Have students read the title and the table of contents in *The Math-lete* and predict what they will read about in the story.

Review Genre: Realistic Fiction

Review with students that realistic fiction is a made-up story with characters and settings that could exist in real life. As they preview the book, have students identify features of realistic fiction in *The Math-lete*.

During Reading

Close Reading

Note Taking Ask students to use their graphic organizer while they read.

Pages 2–3 *What does Abby mean when she says she used to find math "a breeze?"* (She found it easy.) *Does the word* breeze *mean "easy?"* (No) *What is the denotation of the word* breeze? (a light wind) *How does Abby feel about being on the math team?* (She's worried she's not good enough because she is having a difficult time with math right now.)

Pages 4–5 *What did Mr. Nelson realize when he had difficulty solving a math problem?* (He needed to look at the math problem in a different way.) *What are two elements of realistic fiction in* The Math-lete? (The characters talk and act like real people; the events in the story could happen in real life.)

Pages 6–7 *What question do you have about the math competition?* (Possible Answer: Will Abby help the team win the competition?) Have students write their questions to return to later.

Pages 8–9 *What is the denotation of the word* scribbling? (to write carelessly) *What is its connotation on page 9?* (to write quickly and with focus)

Use Graphic Organizer

Pages 10–12 *Figurative language is one way an author makes the story interesting to read. What is an example of figurative language on page 10?* ("their jaws dropped") Have students return to the question they asked on page 7, answer it, and pose any further questions they have.

Pages 13–15 *What is the theme, or lesson, of the story?* (Looking at things in a new way can help people succeed.) *Find two details on pages 13–15 that support this theme in* The Math-lete. (Abby noticed the problem was similar to the ice cream problem; Parkside won the competition.) *How did Abby help her team succeed at the math competition?* (She looked at a problem in a new way.)

After Reading

Respond to Reading Have students complete Respond to Reading on page 16 after they have finished reading.

Analytical Writing **Write About Reading** Check that students have correctly identified how Abby becomes successful and cited appropriate details.

Fluency: Rate

Model Model reading page 7 using the correct rate. Next, reread the page aloud and have students read along with you.

Apply Have students practice reading with a partner.

PAIRED READ

"Cross Country Race"

Make Connections:
Write About It  *Analytical Writing*

Before reading, ask students to note that the genre of the text is narrative poetry. A narrative poem tells a story. Then discuss the Essential Question. After reading, ask students to make connections between *The Math-lete* and "Cross Country Race." How did the characters in both stories succeed?

Leveled Reader

FOCUS ON LITERARY ELEMENTS

Students can extend their knowledge of repetition by completing the activity on page 20.

Literature Circles

Ask students to conduct a literature circle using the Thinkmark questions to guide the discussion. You may wish to have a whole-class discussion on how success can mean different things.

Level Up

Level-up lessons available online.

IF students read the On Level fluently and answered the questions

THEN pair them with students who have proficiently read Beyond Level and have students

• partner-read the Beyond Level main selection.

• list vocabulary words they find difficult and look them up with a partner.

• name two details in the text that they want to learn more about.

A C T ccess Complex Text

The Beyond Level challenges students by including more **domain-specific words** and **complex sentence structures**.

On Level

Vocabulary

REVIEW VOCABULARY WORDS

OBJECTIVES

 Acquire and use accurately grade-appropriate general academic and domain-specific words and phrases, including those that signal precise actions, emotions, or states of being and that are basic to a particular topic. **L.4.6**

 I Do Use the **Visual Vocabulary Cards** to review key words *dangling, hovering*. Point to each word, read it aloud, and have students chorally repeat it. Then review the poetry terms *connotation, denotation, repetition, stanza*.

 We Do Ask these questions and help students respond and explain their answers.

→ What is an example of a fruit that you might find *dangling* from a tree?

→ What might a bird be *hovering* over?

→ How do *stanzas* form a unit in a poem?

 You Do Have student pairs respond to these questions and explain their answers.

→ How can the *connotation* of a word help you determine its meaning?

→ How can readers determine the *denotation* of a word?

→ How do poets use *repetition* in poetry?

CONNOTATION AND DENOTATION

OBJECTIVES

 Demonstrate understanding of figurative language, word relationships, and nuances in word meanings. Use the relationship between particular words (e.g., synonyms, antonyms, homographs) to better understand each of the words. **L.5.5c**

Determine connotations and denotations of words.

 I Do Remind students that knowing the connotation and denotation can help them understand the full meaning of a word. Use the Comprehension and Fluency poem on **Your Turn Practice Book** page 193 to model.

Think Aloud I am not sure of the connotation and denotation of the word *trip*. When I look up *trip*, I learn that it means to "hit your foot against something, so that you fall or almost fall." The next line says that the letters "race to leave my mouth." I think the connotation of *trip* is to be in a rush.

 We Do Help students look up the denotation of the word *sags* in the second stanza. Then have students use context clues to determine its connotation.

 You Do Have students work in pairs to determine the connotation and denotation of the word *scribbled* in the fourth stanza of the poem.

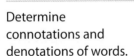

Comprehension

OBJECTIVES

 Determine a theme of a story, drama, or poem from details in the text; summarize the text. **RL.4.2**

 I Do

Remind students that the theme is the main message or lesson in a poem. Explain that students should identify key details in a poem to determine the theme.

We Do

Have a volunteer read the first stanza of the Comprehension and Fluency poem on **Your Turn Practice Book** page 193. Have students orally list key details that can help them figure out the theme of the poem. Then help students explain why they included the key details on their lists. Work with students to identify the details that relate to the theme in the next stanza.

 You Do

Have partners identify key details in each stanza in the poem. Then have them identify the main message or theme of the poem.

OBJECTIVES

 Determine a theme of a story, drama, or poem from details in the text; summarize the text. **RL.4.2**

Visualize the text to increase understanding.

Read Independently

Have students choose a narrative poem for sustained silent reading. Remind students that:

→ a narrative poem may be written in stanzas and it tells a story about fictional or real events.

→ they should identify key details in a poem to determine the main message or theme.

→ readers can close their eyes to picture an image based on the descriptive words and phrases in the poem.

Read Purposefully

Encourage students to read different narrative poems in order to learn about a variety of subjects.

→ As students read, have them fill in details that reveal the theme on a Theme Chart.

→ Students can share their charts and describe the most interesting thing they visualized from the text.

→ Ask students to share their reactions to the poem with classmates.

→ Beyond Level

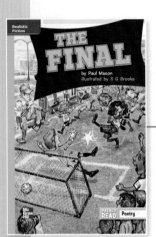

Lexile 800
TextEvaluator 54

___

OBJECTIVES

(CCSS) Determine a theme of a story, drama, or poem from details in the text; summarize the text. **RL.4.2**

___

ACADEMIC LANGUAGE

- *realistic fiction, narrative poem, ask and answer questions, theme, connotation, denotation*
- Cognates: *ficción realista, poema narrativo, tema, connotación, denotación*

Leveled Reader:
The Final

Go Digital

Leveled Readers

Before Reading

Preview and Predict

Have students read the Essential Question. Have students read the title and the table of contents in *The Final* and predict what they will read about in the story.

Review Genre: Realistic Fiction

Review with students that realistic fiction is a made-up story with characters and settings that could exist in real life. As they preview the book, have students identify features of realistic fiction in *The Final*.

During Reading

Close Reading

Note Taking Ask students to use their graphic organizer while they read.

Pages 2–4 *Turn to a partner and paraphrase the problem the Pumas are facing.* (Their star player was injured right before the finals.)

Pages 5–7 *What elements of realistic fiction can you find on page 5?* (Possible Answers: The characters talk the way real people talk. The events in the story could happen in real life.) *Find the word* ballooned *on page 6. What is the denotation?* (to swell) *Discuss the connotation with a partner. What does the author want the reader to feel when reading the word* ballooned? (The author wants the reader to think of the score expanding, or going up quickly.)

Pages 8–9 *Why is Elisa working so hard?* (So that she can play forward in the tournament.) *What does this tell you about the theme of the story?* (Hard work is important to achieve success.)

Use Graphic Organizer

Pages 10–11 *Who do you think will win the tournament?* (Possible Answer: I think the Pumas will win because they have practiced very hard in order to get better.)

Pages 12–15 *Name an example of figurative language on page 14?* ("chasing shadows") *Why does the author use this language?* (To make the story interesting for the reader.) *Work with a partner to find another example of figurative language on page 15.* ("took the words right out of my mouth") *Did the Pumas succeed, even though they did not win?* (Yes) *What does this say about the theme of the story?* (Working hard can be a kind of success.)

After Reading

Respond to Reading Have students complete Respond to Reading on page 16 after they have finished reading.

Analytical Writing **Write About Reading** Have students use details in the text to summarize how Elisa became better at soccer. Make sure the summary is written in their own words.

Fluency: Rate

Model Model reading page 3 using the correct rate. Next, reread the page aloud and have students read along with you.

Apply Have students practice reading with a partner.

Leveled Reader

PAIRED READ

"Talent Show"

Make Connections:
Write About It ● *Analytical Writing*

Before reading, ask students to note that the genre of the text is narrative poetry.
A narrative poem tells a story. Then discuss the Essential Question. After reading, ask students to make connections between *The Final* and "Talent Show." How did the characters in both stories succeed?

FOCUS ON LITERARY ELEMENTS

Students can extend their knowledge of repetition by completing the activity on page 20.

Literature Circles

Ask students to conduct a literature circle using the Thinkmark questions to guide the discussion. You may wish to have a whole-class discussion on how success can mean different things.

Gifted and Talented

Synthesize Challenge students to think of a goal they would like to accomplish. Have students create a short outline explaining why they would like to accomplish their goal and how they plan to do it. Invite volunteers to share their goals with the class.

Beyond Level

Vocabulary

REVIEW DOMAIN-SPECIFIC WORDS

OBJECTIVES

 Acquire and use accurately grade-appropriate general academic and domain-specific words and phrases, including those that signal precise actions, emotions, or states of being and that are basic to a particular topic. **L.4.6**

 Model Use the **Visual Vocabulary Cards** to review the meanings of the words *triumph* and *attain*. Write sentences on the board using the words.

Write the words *conquest* and *successful* on the board and discuss the meanings with students. Then help students write sentences using these words.

 Apply Have students work in pairs to review the meanings of the words *celebration* and *victorious*. Then have partners write sentences using the words.

CONNOTATION AND DENOTATION

OBJECTIVES

 Demonstrate understanding of figurative language, word relationships, and nuances in word meanings. Use the relationship between particular words (e.g., synonyms, antonyms, homographs) to better understand each of the words. **L.5.5c**

Use connotation and denotation to determine the meanings of unfamiliar words.

 Model Read aloud the second stanza of the Comprehension and Fluency poem on **Beyond Reproducibles** page 193.

Think Aloud When I read the second stanza, I want to understand the connotation and denotation of the word *sags*. When I look up *sags,* I learn that it means to "sink or bend down." The poem tells me that "one last kid sags with his head/in his hands." These lines help me understand the idea that is associated with the word *sags* is to be scared or sad.

 Apply Have pairs of students read the rest of the poem. Ask them to use a dictionary to find out the denotation of *scribbled* in the fourth stanza. Then ask students to visualize what is happening in the poem to help them determine the connotation of the word.

 Gifted and Talented **Poem** Have students write a poem about a time they were successful. Remind students to include key details that can help readers determine the main message or theme they are trying to convey.

Comprehension

REVIEW THEME

OBJECTIVES

 Determine a theme of a story, drama, or poem from details in the text; summarize the text. **RL.4.2**

 Model Remind students that the theme of a poem is its main message or lesson. Explain that students must first identify key details in the poem to help them determine the theme.

Have students read the first three stanzas of the Comprehension and Fluency poem on **Beyond Reproducibles** page 193. Ask open-ended questions to facilitate discussion, such as *What is the speaker telling us in these stanzas? How does the speaker feel about the spelling bee?* Students should support their responses with key details.

 Apply Have students identify key details in the poem as they independently fill in a Theme Chart. Then have partners use the key details to determine the theme of the whole poem.

SELF-SELECTED READING

OBJECTIVES

 Determine a theme of a story, drama, or poem from details in the text; summarize the text. **RL.4.2**

Visualize the text to increase understanding.

Read Independently

Have students choose a narrative poem for sustained silent reading.

→ As students read, have them fill in a Theme Chart.

→ Remind them to look for key details in the poem that reveal the main message or theme.

→ Explain that students can close their eyes and try to form an image in their minds based on what they know from personal experience and the descriptive words and phrases in the poem.

Read Purposefully

Encourage students to keep a reading journal. Ask them to read different poems in order to learn about a variety of subjects and styles.

→ Students can write summaries of the poems in their journals.

→ Ask students to share their reactions to the poem with classmates.

 Analyze Have students discuss why people run for public office. Then ask them to name a public official that they most admire and tell why.

English Language Learners

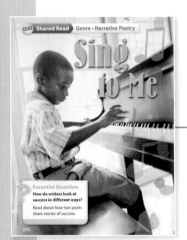

Reading/Writing Workshop

OBJECTIVES

 Determine a theme of a story, drama, or poem from details in the text; summarize the text. **RL.4.2**

LANGUAGE OBJECTIVE

 Demonstrate understanding of figurative language, word relationships, and nuances in word meanings. Explain the meaning of simple similes and metaphors (e.g., *as pretty as a picture*) in context. **L.4.5a**

ACADEMIC LANGUAGE

• *theme, poem, connotation, denotation*

• Cognates: *tema, poema, connotación, denotación*

Shared Read
"Sing to Me" and *"The Climb"*

Go Digital

View *"Sing to Me"* and *"The Climb"*

Before Reading

Build Background

Read the Essential Question: How do writers look at success in different ways?

→ Explain the meaning of the Essential Question. Help students understand that writers can use what they know and what has happened in their lives to write about success.

→ **Model an answer:** *Writers write about the small ways people succeed and the big, important ways people succeed. To some writers, success may be as simple as riding a bike for the first time. Others may write about the success of climbing a mountain or swimming across an ocean. Success can mean different things to different people.*

→ Ask students a question that ties the Essential Question to their own background knowledge: *Turn to a partner and discuss what success means to you. Think of a time you were successful. What did you try to do? How were you able to do it?* Call on several pairs.

During Reading

Interactive Question-Response

→ Ask questions that help students understand the meaning of the text after each paragraph.

→ Reinforce the meanings of key vocabulary.

→ Ask students questions that require them to use key vocabulary.

→ Reinforce strategies and skills of the week by modeling.

Pages 294–295

"Sing to Me"

Stanzas 1–3

Explain and Model Visualizing Explain that poets use descriptive language to help readers picture ideas and feelings in their minds. Ask students to picture the "cool white keys" of the piano stretching "for miles." *Does the phrase "stretched for miles" make you feel that the piano keys go on and on?* (yes) *How does the phrase "stretched for miles" show that the narrator is nervous about playing the piano?* (Possible answer: The boy feels the notes go on and on, making it hard to play the piano.)

Point out the simile in the second stanza. Draw a picture of an apple dangling from a tree. *Why does the narrator compare the melody, or music, to an apple dangling from a tree?* (Like the apple, the notes are out of reach.)

Explain and Model Repetition Chorally read the third stanza. *Writers use repetition to emphasize something or to show emotion. Why do you think the writer repeats the line, "I can't do this?"* (to show the narrator is frustrated) Have students find another example of repetition.

Stanzas 4–7

Reread stanzas four and five. Define and act out difficult words and phrases. *What words and phrases help you visualize what is happening?* (notes leaping; hovering briefly, only to crash; slowly fading away; forehead on keys; slender fingers plucking the notes from the air)

Explain and Model Theme *What is the narrator trying to do in the beginning of the poem?* (learn how to play the piano) *What key details tell you that he is having a hard time learning to play the piano?* (I practiced and practiced all day. I can't do this.) *How does the narrator learn to play the piano?* (His mom sits down with him and helps him practice until he can play the piano.) *What is the theme?* (Practice leads to success.)

Pages 296–297

"The Climb"

Stanzas 1 and 2

Model Narrative Poetry Ask two students to read the first two stanzas. One student reads the brother's words. *Whose voice do we hear first?* (the narrator's brother) *What do we learn about the characters?* (They are brother and sister and are waiting for the bus.) *What is the narrator trying to do in the second stanza?* (climb a tree) *Is the narrator successful?* (no)

Explain and Model Connotation and Denotation Point out the word *screech*. Explain that a screech is a loud, high pitched sound. Ask a volunteer to demonstrate *screeching. Is the sound of a screech a nice, pleasant sound?* (no) *The feeling we get from a word is called* connotation. Have a student recall its denotation.

Stanzas 3–5

Model Repetition *What word does the narrator repeat?* (Today) *How does the repetition help you understand the narrator's thoughts and feelings?* (At first, it shows that the narrator is having a bad day, but in the last stanza, it shows that the narrator feels successful about climbing the tree.)

Stanzas 6 and 7

Model Theme *Think about the narrator's thoughts and actions to help you understand the theme. Have you ever tried something over and over again until you succeeded? Complete the frame: The theme of the poem is _____.* (try until you succeed)

After Reading

Make Connections

→ Review the Essential Question: How do writers look at success in different ways?

→ Make text connections.

→ Have students complete **ELL Reproducibles** pages 193–195.

English Language Learners

Lexile 510
TextEvaluator™ 24

OBJECTIVES

CCSS Determine a theme of a story, drama, or poem from details in the text; summarize the text. **RL.4.2**

CCSS Demonstrate understanding of figurative language, word relationships, and nuances in word meanings. Recognize and explain the meaning of common idioms, adages, and proverbs. **L.4.5b**

ACADEMIC LANGUAGE

• *realistic fiction, narrative poem, ask and answer questions, theme, connotation, denotation*

• Cognates: *ficción realista, poema narrativo, tema, connotación, denotación*

Leveled Reader:
The Math-lete

Go Digital

Leveled Readers

Before Reading

Preview

→ Read the Essential Question: How do writers look at success in different ways?

→ Refer to Reaching For Success: *Why is it important to have a positive attitude if you want to succeed?*

→ Preview The Math-lete and "Running the Race": *Let's read about how a girl overcomes her fear of math by practicing until she feels confident.*

Vocabulary

Use the **Visual Vocabulary Cards** to pre-teach the ELL vocabulary: *district, struggling.* Use the routine found on the cards. Point out the cognate: *distrito.*

During Reading

Interactive Question-Response

Note Taking Have students use their graphic organizer in **ELL Reproducibles** page 192. Use the questions below as you read each section with students.

Pages 2–5 Have partners reread the dialogue on pages 2–3. *How do you know this story is realistic fiction?* (The characters say and do things that people in real life do and say.) *What is the problem?* (Abby does not want to be on the math team because she thinks math is hard.) *How does Mr. Nelson help Abby?* (He gives her extra worksheets and helps her solve the problems.)

Pages 6–7 Point out the idiom on page 7 "Abby's head was spinning." *Can a person's head spin?* (no) *Spinning makes people feel dizzy and confused. How do the math problems make Abby feel?* (confused)

Pages 8–9 *The denotation of the word* scribbling *is to write quickly.* Demonstrate scribbling for students. *Does the word* scribbling *help you visualize how Abby is writing a note?* (yes)

Use Graphic Organizer

Literature Circles

Ask students to conduct a literature circle using the Thinkmark questions to guide the discussion. You may wish to have a whole-class discussion, asking students what it means to succeed.

Pages 10–15 Chorally read the second paragraph on page 11. *How does Abby help her team?* (She tells them to stay focused and positive and she guides them through three problems.)

Pages 13–15 *Does Abby succeed in the competition?* (yes) *What helps her succeed?* (She practices math with Mr. Nelson until she feels confident.) *What is the theme of the story?* (Possible answers: Do not give up. Practicing something can help you succeed.)

After Reading

Respond to Reading Help students complete the graphic organizer in **ELL Reproducibles** page 192. Revisit the Essential Question. Have students pairs summarize and answer the Text Evidence Questions.

Analytical Writing **Write About Reading** Have partners write about how Abby succeeds in math. Encourage students to use their graphic organizers and cite evidence showing how Abby's feelings about math changed.

Fluency: Rate

Model Model reading page 7 using the correct rate. Next, reread the page aloud and have students read along with you.

Apply Have students practice reading with a partner.

Level Up

Level-up lessons available online.

IF students read the **ELL Level** fluently and answered the questions

THEN pair them with students who have proficiently read **On Level** and have students

- echo-read the **On Level** main selection with their partners.
- list words with which they have difficulty.
- discuss these words with their partners.

PAIRED READ

Leveled Reader

"Running the Race"

Make Connections:
Write About It *Analytical Writing*

Before reading, ask students to note that the genre of the text is narrative poetry. A narrative poem tells a story. Then discuss the Essential Question. After reading, ask students to make connections between the themes in *The Math-lete* and "Running the Race" and discuss how the characters succeed.

FOCUS ON LITERARY ELEMENTS

Students can extend their knowledge of repetition by completing the activity on page 20.

A C T Access Complex Text

The **On Level** challenges students by including more **academic language**.

English Language Learners
Vocabulary

PRETEACH VOCABULARY

OBJECTIVES

CCSS Acquire and use accurately grade-appropriate general academic and domain-specific words and phrases, including those that signal precise actions, emotions, or states of being and that are basic to a particular topic. **L.4.6**

LANGUAGE OBJECTIVE

Use vocabulary words.

 I Do Preteach weekly vocabulary by following the Vocabulary Routine on the **Visual Vocabulary Cards** for *attain, dangling, hovering,* and *triumph*. Then review the poetry terms *connotation, denotation, repetition,* and *stanza*.

 We Do After completing the Vocabulary Routine for each word, point to the word on the card and read the word aloud. Ask students to repeat the word.

 You Do Have partners ask a question using one of the vocabulary words. Then have another pair answer the question to show their understanding of the word. Repeat until at least four words have been used.

Beginning	Intermediate	Advanced/High
Help students write the questions and answers and read them aloud.	Ask students to write a sentence for each word that was used.	Have students create different questions and answers for each word.

REVIEW VOCABULARY

OBJECTIVES

CCSS Acquire and use accurately grade-appropriate general academic and domain-specific words and phrases, including those that signal precise actions, emotions, or states of being and that are basic to a particular topic. **L.4.6**

LANGUAGE OBJECTIVE

Use vocabulary words.

 I Do Review the previous week's vocabulary words. Divide the words into two groups and review over two days. Read each word aloud and point to the word on the **Visual Vocabulary Card**. Have students repeat after you. Then follow the Vocabulary Routine on the back of each card.

 We Do Write each word on an index card. Hold up one index card at a time and ask volunteers to write a definition on a separate paper.

 You Do Give one student an index card from above. Give all other students the definitions. Ask the student to find the matching definition. Repeat with all the words.

Beginning	Intermediate	Advanced/High
Help students pronounce and define each word.	Have students use the words in a sentence.	Challenge students to give a synonym, antonym, or example for each word.

CONNOTATION AND DENOTATION

OBJECTIVES

 Demonstrate understanding of figurative language, word relationships, and nuances in word meanings. Use the relationship between particular words (e.g., synonyms, antonyms, homographs) to better understand each of the words. **L.5.5c**

LANGUAGE OBJECTIVE

Determine connotations and denotations of words.

I Do Read aloud the first stanza of the Comprehension and Fluency poem on **ELL Reproducibles** page 193. Model how someone can *trip*. Explain that denotation is the exact, dictionary meaning of a word. Connotation is the feeling behind a word. Explain that we must use the ideas or feelings associated with a word to determine its connotation.

Think Aloud After looking up *trip* in a dictionary, I know that it means "to hit your foot against something, so that you fall or almost fall." This is the denotation. By reading the rest of the sentence, I can tell that the connotation of *trip* means to be in a rush.

We Do Point to the word *race* on page 193. Help students find the connotation and denotation of the word. Write the meanings on the board.

You Do Have pairs write the connotation and denotation of *march* on the board.

Beginning	Intermediate	Advanced/High
Help students look up the denotation of the words.	Ask students to write one sentence in which the connotation of the word is clear.	Have students explain how they used connotation and denotation to determine the meaning of each word.

ADDITIONAL VOCABULARY

OBJECTIVES

 Choose words and phrases to convey ideas precisely. **L.4.3a**

LANGUAGE OBJECTIVE

Use academic and high-frequency words.

I Do List academic and high-frequency words from the Shared Read poems and *The Math-lete: argue, compete, difficult, immense,* and *struggle.* Define each word: *Argue means to give reasons for or against something.*

We Do Model using the words in a sentence: *My brother and I always argue over which game to play.* Then provide sentence frames and complete them with students: *The student council argued for new ____.*

You Do Have pairs write a sentence for two words and then read their sentences to the class. Ask volunteers to explain the connotation of each word.

Beginning	Intermediate	Advanced/High
Have students look up the denotation of each word in a dictionary.	Have students write sentences for three of the words.	Have students write sentences for all of the words and explain the connotation for each.

English Language Learners
Writing/Spelling

WRITING TRAIT: WORD CHOICE

OBJECTIVES

 Use concrete words and phrases and sensory details to convey experiences and events precisely. **W.4.3d**

LANGUAGE OBJECTIVE

Identify sensory details in writing.

 I Do Explain that writers use sensory details to describe how something looks, sounds, smells, tastes, or feels. Read the Expert Model aloud. Point out that writers use sensory details, such as "a jaybird's repetitive screech" and "slither down the trunk," to help readers picture what is happening.

We Do Read aloud the first two stanzas from "Sing to Me." Point out the phrases "cool white keys" and "hung dangling/like an apple." Explain how these sensory details help readers visualize what the narrator feels and thinks.

You Do Have pairs write three or four sentences describing a time they succeeded at something. Encourage them to use sensory details. Then have them use the sentences to write a short poem. Edit each pair's writing.

Beginning	Intermediate	Advanced/High
Help students write sensory details.	Ask students to identify additional sensory details.	Have students add sensory details and edit for errors.

SPELL WORDS WITH VARIANT VOWEL /ô/

OBJECTIVES

 Spell grade-appropriate words correctly, consulting references as needed. **L.4.2d**

LANGUAGE OBJECTIVE

Spell words with the variant vowel /ô/.

 I Do Read aloud the Spelling Words on page T292, sounding out words with the variant vowel /ô/. Have students repeat the words. Point out and discuss the different spellings of the variant vowel /ô/ in each word.

We Do Read the Dictation Sentences on page T293 aloud for students. Read the underlined word slowly and point out the variant vowel /ô/ in each word. Have students repeat after you and write the word.

 You Do Display the words. Have partners exchange their lists to check the spelling and write the words correctly.

Beginning	Intermediate	Advanced/High
Have students copy the words correctly and say the words aloud.	After students have corrected their words, have pairs quiz each other.	After students have corrected their words, have pairs form sentences.

Grammar

PRONOUNS AND HOMOPHONES

OBJECTIVES

 Demonstrate command of the conventions of standard English grammar and usage when writing or speaking. Correctly use frequently confused words (e.g., *to, too, two; there, their*). **L.4.1g**

LANGUAGE OBJECTIVE

Write sentences using pronouns and homophones.

Language Transfers Handbook

In Cantonese, Haitian Creole, Hmong, Korean, and Spanish, the third-person pronoun is gender free, or the personal pronoun is omitted. Reinforce the use of pronouns and homophones by helping students use them to form sentences.

I Do Remind students that pronouns are nouns that take the place of the name of a person or thing. Write on the board: *They had pizza for dinner.* Underline the pronoun *they*. Explain that homophones are words that sound alike but have different spellings and meanings. Write on the board: *You're always early for practice.* Underline the homophone *you're*. Point out that homophones include contractions, such as *you're* and possessive pronouns such as *your*. Tell students that subject pronouns are often used in conjunction with verbs to form contractions. Write on the board: *She's the president of the student council.*

We Do Write the following sentence starters on the board and help students complete each sentence with the correct pronoun or homophone. Remind students that some possessive pronouns are also homophones. Choral-read the completed sentences with students.

_____ *team was first in the national championship. (Their, There)*

_____ *wanted to sing in the winter pageant this year. (It, She)*

_____ *baking cookies for the school bake sale. (He's, I)*

You Do Brainstorm a list of pronouns and homophones with students. Have students work in pairs to write four sentences using pronouns and homophones as taught in the lesson. Have pairs read their sentences aloud.

Beginning	Intermediate	Advanced/High
Help students identify and circle the pronouns and homophones. Read the sentences aloud for students to repeat after you.	Ask students to circle the pronouns and homophones and explain how they identified them in the sentences.	Have students proofread their sentences and explain how they used each pronoun and homophone correctly.

For extra support, have students complete the activities in the **Grammar Practice Reproducibles** during the week, using the routine below:

→ Explain the grammar skill.

→ Model the first activity in the Grammar Practice Reproducibles.

→ Have the whole group complete the next couple of activities, and then do the rest with a partner.

→ Review the activities with correct answers.

PROGRESS MONITORING

Weekly Assessment

✓ COMPREHENSION:	✓ VOCABULARY:	✓ WRITING:
Theme **RL.4.2**	Connotation and Denotation **L.4.5**	Writing About Text **RL.4.2, W.4.9a**

Assessment Includes

→ Pencil-and-paper administration

→ On-line administration

→ Approaching-Level Weekly Assessment also available

Fluency Goal 102 to 122 words correct per minute (WCPM)

Accuracy Rate Goal 95% or higher.

Administer oral reading fluency assessments using the following schedule:

→ **Weeks 1, 3, 5** Provide Approaching-Level students at least three oral reading fluency assessments during the unit.

→ **Weeks 2 and 4** Provide On-Level students at least two oral reading fluency assessments during the unit.

→ **Week 6** If necessary, provide Beyond-Level students an oral reading fluency assessment at this time.

Also Available: Selection Tests online PDFs

Go Digital! www.connected.mcgraw-hill.com

Using Assessment Results

TESTED SKILLS	If ...	Then ...
COMPREHENSION	Students answer 0–6 multiple-choice items correctly ...	... assign Lessons 34–36 on Theme from the *Tier 2 Comprehension Intervention online PDFs.*
VOCABULARY	Students answer 0–6 multiple-choice items correctly ...	... assign Lesson 172 on Connotation and Denotation from the *Tier 2 Vocabulary Intervention online PDFs.*
WRITING	Students score less than "3" on the constructed response ...	... assign Lessons 34–36 and/or Write About Reading Lesson 194 from the *Tier 2 Comprehension Intervention online PDFs.*
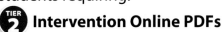	Students have a WCPM score of 94–101 ...	... assign a lesson from Section 1 or 7–10 of the *Tier 2 Fluency Intervention online PDFs.*
	Students have a WCPM score of 0–93 ...	... assign a lesson from Sections 2–6 of the *Tier 2 Fluency Intervention online PDFs.*

Response to Intervention

Use the appropriate sections of the **Placement and Diagnostic Assessment** as well as students' assessment results to designate students requiring:

TIER 2 Intervention Online PDFs

TIER 3 WonderWorks Intervention Program

WEEKLY OVERVIEW

The Big Idea: *How do different writers treat the same topic?*

REVIEW AND EXTEND

Reader's Theater

All the Money in the World

Genre Play

Fluency Accuracy, Rate, and Prosody

Reading Digitally

TIME. "Log On to Online Learning"

Comprehension Close Reading

Study Skills Skim and Scan

Research Navigate Links to Information

Go Digital!

Level Up Accelerating Progress

| From **APPROACHING** To **ON LEVEL** | From **ON LEVEL** To **BEYOND LEVEL** | From **ENGLISH LANGUAGE LEARNERS** To **ON LEVEL** | From **BEYOND LEVEL** To **SELF-SELECTED TRADE BOOK** |

Advanced Level **Trade Book**

ASSESS

Presentations

Research and Inquiry
Project Presentations
Project Rubric

Writing
Narrative Text Presentations
Writing Rubric

Unit Assessments

UNIT 4 TEST

FLUENCY

Evaluate Student Progress

Use the McGraw-Hill Reading Wonders eAssessment reports to evaluate student progress and help you make decisions about small group instruction and assignments.

→ Student and Class Assessment Report

→ Student and Class Standards Proficiency Report

→ Student Profile Summary Report

Vstock LLC/Getty Images

SUGGESTED LESSON PLAN

		DAY 1	**DAY 2**
READING			
Whole Group	Reader's Theater "All the Money in the World"	**Reader's Theater,** T326 "All the Money in the World" Assign Roles Model Fluency: Accuracy, Rate, and Prosody	**Reader's Theater,** T326 "All the Money in the World" Model Fluency: Accuracy, Rate, and Prosody **Reading Digitally,** T328 TIME. "Log On to Online Learning" **Research and Inquiry,** T330–T333 Relevant Facts
	"Log Onto Online Learning"		**Research and Inquiry Projects**

DIFFERENTIATED INSTRUCTION Level up to Accelerate

Small Group		**DAY 1**	**DAY 2**
Approaching Level		**Level Up to On Level** *Stargazing,* T336 **Spiral Review** Comprehension Skills Unit 4 PDFs Online *Analytical Writing*	**Level Up to On Level** *Stargazing,* T336 **Spiral Review** Comprehension Skills Unit 4 PDFs Online *Analytical Writing*
On Level		**Level Up to Beyond Level** *Stargazing,* T337	**Level Up to Beyond Level** *Stargazing,* T337
Beyond Level		**Level Up to Self-Selected Trade Book,** T339	**Level Up to Self-Selected Trade Book,** T339
English Language Learners		**Level Up to On Level** *Stargazing,* T338	**Level Up to On Level** *Stargazing,* T338

LANGUAGE ARTS

		DAY 1	**DAY 2**
Whole Group	**Writing**	**Share Your Writing, T334** Fictional Narrative/ Poetry Prepare to Present Your Writing	**Share Your Writing, T334** Fictional Narrative/ Poetry Discuss Peer Feedback

DAY 3	DAY 4	DAY 5
Reading Digitally, T328 TIME FOR KIDS. "Log On to Online Learning" Close Reading • *Analytical Writing*	**Reader's Theater,** T326 Performance	**Research and Inquiry,** T332–T333 Presentations ✓**Unit Assessment,** T340–T341
Research and Inquiry Projects	**Research and Inquiry Projects** • *Analytical Writing*	
Level Up to On Level *Stargazing,* T336 **Spiral Review** Comprehension Skills Unit 4 PDFs Online • *Analytical Writing*	**Level Up to On Level** "Orion the Hunter," T336	**Level Up to On Level** Literature Circles, T336
Level Up to Beyond Level *Stargazing,* T337	**Level Up to Beyond Level** "Orion the Hunter," T337	**Level Up to Beyond Level** Literature Circles, T337
Level Up to Self-Selected **Trade Book,** T339	**Level Up to Self-Selected** **Trade Book,** T339	**Level Up to Self-Selected** **Trade Book,** T339
Level Up to On Level *Stargazing,* T338	**Level Up to On Level** "Orion the Hunter," T338	**Level Up to On Level** Literature Circles, T338
Share Your Writing, T334 Fictional Narrative/ Poetry Rehearse Your Presentation	**Share Your Writing, T334** Present Your Fictional Narrative/ Poetry Evaluate Your Presentation	**Share Your Writing, T335** Fictional Narrative/ Poetry Portfolio Choice

Reader's Theater

ALL THE MONEY
IN THE WORLD

based on the novel by Bill Brittain
by Richard Holland

CAST:
Narrator
Vincent Arbor   General Mainwaring
Roselynn Peabody   Sergeant
Quentin Stowe   Mr. Milleridge
Flan   Mrs. Hobson
Mr. Stowe   Miss Draymore
Mrs. Stowe   Mayor
President   Mrs. Trussker

SETTING:
A small farming community

Go Digital!

**Teacher's Resource
PDF Online,
pp. 54–74**

OBJECTIVES

CCSS Read on-level text with purpose and understanding. **RF.4.4a**

CCSS Read on-level prose and poetry orally with accuracy, appropriate rate, and expression on successive readings. **RF.4.4b**

CCSS Use context to confirm or self-correct word recognition and understanding, rereading as necessary. **RF.4.4c**

All the Money in the World

Introduce the Play

Explain that *All the Money in the World* is a play set in a small farming community. In return for saving a leprechaun named Flan from a deep well, Quentin is granted three wishes. Quentin wishes for and gets all of the money in the world. Distribute scripts and the Elements of Drama handout from the **Teacher's Resource PDF Online, pp. 54–74**.

→ Review the features of a play.

→ Review the list of characters. Build background on the setting, defining the roles of Quentin, Roselynn, Vincent, and the other characters during the modern time period in a small farming community.

Shared Reading

Model reading the play as students follow along in their scripts.

Focus on Vocabulary Stop and discuss any vocabulary words that students may not know. You may wish to teach:

→ Olympics   → splendid

→ leprechaun   → eerie

→ due   → fie

Model Fluency As you read each part, state the name of each character. Read the part emphasizing the appropriate phrasing and expression.

Discuss Each Role

→ After reading each character's part, ask partners to note the traits of Quentin and Flan. Model how to find text evidence that tells about the characters.

→ After reading the part of the Narrator, ask students to identify what information the Narrator gives about the play.

Assign Roles

Depending on the number of students, you may wish to split the class into two groups. If you need additional roles you can assign the roles of Narrator, Quentin, and Flan to more than one student.

Practice the Play

Each day, allow students time to practice their parts in the play. Pair fluent readers with less fluent readers. Pairs can echo-read or choral-read their parts. As needed, work with less fluent readers to mark pauses in their script using one slash for a short pause and two slashes for longer pauses.

Throughout the week have students work on the Reader's Theater activities on the **Reading Workstation Activity Card 30**.

Once students have practiced reading their parts several times, allow students time to practice performing the script.

Perform the Reader's Theater

→ Discuss what it is like to be Flan. How would you perform Flan's role?

→ As a class, discuss how performing the play aloud is different from reading it silently. Have students list what they liked about performing the play and what they found difficult.

→ Lead a class discussion about different ways the changes in setting can be shown.

ACTIVITIES

PERFORMING WITH PIZZAZZ

There are several ways to make performing *All the Money in the World* spectacular for the audience. Audiotape the practices and listen to the performances. Compare how different groups present the story.

Then ask for suggestions about improving the performance. Some ideas to consider include:

1. What should the show sound like? Can you add background sounds, sound effects, or music?

2. How does adding physical expression to a role add to the video performance?

3. Discuss the expression "ham it up." How do readers who "ham it up," or present particularly dramatic readings, sound on the audio performance?

A SPRITELY IRISH FAIRY

All the Money in the World has an engaging, fanciful plot and lively characters. Have students examine the traits of the leprechaun Flan in the play. First, students should list Flan's characteristics: green, old man, partakes in mischief, has magical powers, grants a human three wishes in exchange for release, child-sized in height.

Next, students can identify his behavior, words, feelings, and actions in the play.

Students can then complete a character analysis chart for Flan.

Example: Flan

Appearance	Detail
Personality Traits	Detail
Challenge	Detail
Role in Play	Detail

ELL ENGLISH LANGUAGE LEARNERS

→ Review the definitions of difficult words including: *rickety, bass, lad, coattails, vibrate, citizens, allies.*

→ Team an ELL student with a fluent reader who is also reading the part of Quentin. Have each reader take turns reading the lines. Determine which reader will read which lines at the performance.

→ Encourage ELLs to retell the play, pointing out their favorite parts. Clarify the meanings of students' retellings as needed.

Reading Digitally

OBJECTIVES

 CCSS Interpret information presented visually, orally, or quantitatively (e.g., in charts, graphs, diagrams, time lines, animations, or interactive elements on Web pages) and explain how the information contributes to an understanding of the text in which it appears. **RI.4.7**

 CCSS Conduct short research projects that build knowledge through investigation of different aspects of a topic. **W.4.7**

 CCSS Paraphrase portions of a text read aloud or information presented in diverse media and formats, including visually, quantitatively, and orally. **SL.4.2**

TIME FOR KIDS

Log On to Online Learning

Before Reading

Preview Scroll through the online article "Log On to Online Learning" at www.connected.mcgraw-hill.com and have students identify text features. Clarify how to navigate through the article. Point out the interactive features, such as the **link, roll-over graph,** and **video**. Tell students that you will read the article together first and then access these features.

Close Reading Online

Take Notes Scroll back to the top and read the article aloud. As you read, ask questions to focus students on the similarities and differences between cyber school and traditional school. Have students take notes using **Graphic Organizer 67**. After each section, have partners paraphrase the main ideas, giving text evidence. Discuss words with Latin roots, such as *depends, report, supporters,* and *attract*.

Access Interactive Elements Help students access the interactive elements by clicking or rolling over each feature. Discuss what information these elements add to the text.

Tell students they will reread parts of the article to help them answer a specific question: *What is a day in cyber school like?* Remind them that they do not need to reread every word. Instead, they can

→ **skim** by reading quickly and focusing on topic sentences, or

→ **scan** by moving their eyes over the text quickly to spot key words.

Have students skim the article to find text detailing what a day in cyber school is like. Have partners share what they find.

Navigate Links to Information Review that online texts may include **hyperlinks**. Model using a hyperlink to jump to another Web page. Discuss any information on the new Web page related to the question *What is a day in cyber school like?* Remind students that bookmarking the page or adding it to their "Favorites" allows them to easily return to the page at another time.

WRITE ABOUT READING *Analytical Writing*

Summarize Review students' graphic organizers. Model using the information to summarize "Log On to Online Learning."

Ask students to write a summary of the article, comparing and contrasting cyber school with traditional school. Partners should discuss their summaries.

Make Connections Have students compare what they learned about the different points of view people have regarding cyber school with what they have learned about different points of view on other topics in texts they have read in this unit.

TAKE A STAND

Cyber School

Have students state their opinion about whether they would prefer to attend cyber school or traditional school. Tell them they should

→ Clearly state their opinion.

→ Organize their ideas logically.

→ Support their position with information from the online article or linked Web page.

→ End with a concluding statement that restates their opinion.

Have students with opposing viewpoints debate one another.

RESEARCH ONLINE

Key Words Explain that part of successful online research is choosing the correct search terms. Tell students to use only the most important words related to the topic and omit articles such as *an* and *the*. The more words they type, the narrower their results will be.

Search Results Model conducting an Internet search using key words related to cyber school. Then discuss the Results page. Point out that the most relevant results are usually listed first. Demonstrate clicking on the hyperlink at the top of a result to jump to that page and then using the Back button to return to Results.

INDEPENDENT STUDY

Investigate

Choose a Topic Students should brainstorm questions related to the article. For example, they might ask: *What technology is needed to take an online class?* Then have students choose a question to research. Help them narrow it.

Conduct Internet Research Review how to conduct an Internet search. Remind students to choose good search terms and to spell them correctly. Tell students to verify that they are using reliable sites and sources in their research.

Present Have groups give an informational or persuasive presentation on cyber schools.

RESEARCH AND INQUIRY

The Big Idea: *How do different writers treat the same topic?*

Assign the Projects Break students into five groups. Assign each group one of the five Projects that follow. Before students begin researching, present these minilessons.

Research Skill: Relevant Facts

OBJECTIVES

CCSS With some guidance and support from adults, use technology, including the Internet, to produce and publish writing as well as to interact and collaborate with others; demonstrate sufficient command of keyboarding skills to type a minimum of one page in a single sitting. **W.4.6**

CCSS Conduct short research projects that build knowledge through investigation of different aspects of a topic. **W.4.7**

CCSS Recall relevant information from experiences or gather relevant information from print and digital sources; take notes and categorize information, and provide a list of sources. **W.4.8**

CCSS Report on a topic or text, tell a story, or recount an experience in an organized manner, using appropriate facts and relevant, descriptive details to support main ideas or themes; speak clearly at an understandable pace. **SL.4.4**

Selecting and Organizing Relevant Facts

→ Explain to students that in order to research a topic, they need to collect information from multiple sources. They may look for facts about a topic in books, magazines, newspapers, online sources, maps, and interviews. Model evaluating a sentence that reveals an important fact about a topic students are researching.

→ Remind students that there are a number of ways to sort and organize information they have collected about their topics. They may place information in an outline, with a topic followed by a main idea and details. They may also group facts into different categories or put them in a graphic organizer with headings.

→ As students collect information about a topic, have them practice using different methods for sorting facts from at least two different sources. Have students decide which method works best for them.

Skimming and Scanning Techniques

Good writers skim and scan written materials to gather information about a topic. They create questions about the topic and look for the answers in multiple sources. By learning how to skim and scan, students can get the information they need quickly.

→ Explain to students that when they skim written materials, they glance over them paragraph by paragraph to get an idea of what they are about. The first and last sentences of paragraphs often tell the main idea and conclusion. When they scan a book or an article, they quickly look over the text to find specific information, such as key words or main ideas.

→ Remind students that a key idea is a main idea that authors develop in their writing. Headings or boldfaced words may signal a key idea.

→ Model using the skimming and scanning techniques to collect and evaluate information for a topic from at least two different sources.

Go Digital

COLLABORATE
Manage and assign Projects online. Students can also work with their group online.

Choose a Project!

1 Make an Educational Poster

ESSENTIAL QUESTION
Why do we need government?

Goal
Research teams will choose a department or committee at work in their state's government and create an educational poster about it.

2 Create an Illustrated Biography

ESSENTIAL QUESTION
Why do people run for public office?

Goal
Research teams will choose a previous president and present to the class an illustrated biography showing his or her early life, career path, and motivations for running for office.

3 Make a Time Line

ESSENTIAL QUESTION
How do inventions and technology affect your life?

Goal
Research teams will create a time line showing how a group of inventions, such as those involved with communications, came about. Time lines will show how the inventions developed over time.

STEM

4 Record a Newscast

ESSENTIAL QUESTION
How do you explain what you see in the sky?

Goal
Research teams will record a fictional newscast covering an eclipse. The newscast should include descriptions of the eclipse and mock interviews with people who witnessed the eclipse.

STEM

5 Write a Poem

ESSENTIAL QUESTION
How do writers look at success in different ways?

Goal
Research teams will write and present a poem about a successful person. Groups should accompany their poems with a piece of music or art.

RESEARCH AND INQUIRY

Distribute the Research Roadmap online PDF. Have students use the roadmap to complete the project.

Conducting the Research

STEP 1 Set Research Goals

Discuss with students the Essential Question and the research project. Each group should

→ make sure they are clear on their research focus and end product.

→ decide on each member's role. *Who will do the primary research? Who will organize the information? Who will write the poem? Who will illustrate the biography? Who will be in charge of technology? Who will speak during the presentation? Who will play which part in the newscast?*

STEP 2 Identify Sources

Have the group brainstorm where they can find the information. Sources might include

→ print works, such as informational texts and reference books.

→ digital media, such as online newspapers, maps, and community Web sites.

→ interviews with experts.

Remind them that using a variety of sources will ensure a more complete and accurate presentation.

STEP 3 Find and Record Information

Have students review the organizational strategies on page T330. Then have them research their topic. Remind them to list their sources carefully.

STEP 4 Organize

After team members have completed the research, they can review and analyze all the information they collected. First they should classify and categorize their notes in order to determine the most useful information. Then they can create a rough version of their end product as a way to clarify categories of information.

STEP 5 Synthesize and Present

Have team members synthesize their research and decide on their final message.

→ Encourage students to use all available technologies, such as audio recordings and visual displays, to enhance their presentations.

→ They should check that the key ideas are included in their presentations and that their findings relate to the Big Idea.

Audience Participation

→ Encourage the audience to make comments and ask clarifying questions.

→ Have students discuss how each presentation relates to the Essential Question.

Review and Evaluate

Distribute the online PDF of the checklists and rubrics. Use the following Teacher Checklist and rubric to evaluate students' research and presentations.

Student Checklist

Research Process

☑ Did you narrow the focus of your research?

☑ Did you take notes and sort the information into categories?

☑ Did you evaluate the information you collected?

Presenting

☑ Did you express your ideas clearly?

☑ Did you support your topic with appropriate facts and details?

☑ Did you answer the Essential Question and the Big Idea?

☑ Did you use appropriate audio recordings or visual displays to enhance your presentation?

Teacher Checklist

Assess the Research Process

☑ Selected a focus.

☑ Used multiple sources to gather information.

☑ Cited sources for information.

☑ Used time effectively and collaborated well.

Assess the Presentation

☑ Spoke clearly and at an appropriate pace and volume.

☑ Maintained eye contact.

☑ Established a main message that answered the Essential Question and the Big Idea.

☑ Used appropriate visuals and technology.

☑ Shared responsibility and tasks among all group members.

Assess the Listener

☑ Listened quietly and politely.

☑ Made appropriate comments and asked clarifying questions.

☑ Responded with an open mind to different ideas.

Project Rubric

4 Excellent	**3** Good	**2** Fair	**1** Unsatisfactory
The project	**The project**	**The project**	**The project**
→ presents the information clearly.	→ presents the information adequately.	→ attempts to present information.	→ may show little grasp of the task.
→ includes many details.	→ provides adequate details.	→ may offer few or vague details.	→ may present irrelevant information.
→ may include sophisticated observations.	→ includes relevant observations.	→ may include few or irrelevant personal observations.	→ may reflect extreme difficulty with research or presentation.

Celebrate Share Your Writing

Publishing Celebrations

Giving Presentations

Now is the time for students to share one of their pieces of narrative writing or poetry that they have worked on through the unit.

You may wish to invite parents or students from other classes to the Publishing Celebrations.

Preparing for Presentations

Tell students that they will be presenting their writing and that they will need to prepare in order to provide the best representation of their hard work.

Allow students time to rehearse their presentations. Ask them to reread their presentation piece until they feel familiar with it. Tell students that they should plan to look at the audience and make eye contact rather than simply reading straight from their paper. Remind them that the way they speak and present themselves is as important as the information they are presenting.

Students should also consider any visuals or digital elements that they want to use during their presentation. Discuss a few possible options with students.

→ Do they have photos they want to share? Can they illustrate an important part of the narrative or poem?

→ Are there flyers, souvenirs or other items that they would like to share that are related to their narrative or poem?

→ Is there a video they can show about the experience or poem's topic?

Students can practice presenting to a partner in the classroom. They can also practice with family members at home or in front of a mirror. Share the following checklist with students to help them focus on important parts of their presentation as they rehearse. Discuss each point on the checklist.

Speaking Checklist

Review the Speaking Checklist with students as they practice.

- ☑ Have all your notes and visuals ready.
- ☑ Take a few deep breaths.
- ☑ Stand up straight.
- ☑ Look at the audience.
- ☑ Speak clearly and slowly.
- ☑ Speak loudly enough that everyone can hear.
- ☑ Speak with excitement.
- ☑ Use appropriate gestures.
- ☑ Hold your visual aids so that everyone can see them.
- ☑ Remember to smile.

Vstock LLC/Getty Images

Listening to Presentations

Remind students that they will not only take on the role of a presenter, they will also be part of the audience for other students' presentations. As listeners, students have an important role. Review with students the following Listening Checklist.

Listening Checklist

During the presentation

- ☑ Pay attention to how the speaker uses the visuals in the presentation.
- ☑ Take notes on one or two things you liked about the presentation.
- ☑ Write one question or comment you have about the events presented.
- ☑ Listen to the speaker carefully.
- ☑ Do not talk during the presentation.

After the presentation

- ☑ Only comment on the presentation when it is your turn.
- ☑ Tell why you liked the presentation.
- ☑ If someone else makes the same comment first, tell why you agree.
- ☑ Ask your question.

Portfolio Choice

Ask students to select one finished piece of writing and two revised pieces to include in their writing portfolio. As students consider their choices, have them use the questions below.

Published Writing

Does your writing

→ Clearly express feelings and ideas?

→ Use organization in an effective way?

→ Use descriptive words that appeal to the senses?

→ Have few or no spelling and grammatical errors?

→ Have a neat, published appearance?

Writing Entry Revisions

Did you revise your writing to

→ Include figurative language or dialogue?

→ Introduce sensory language?

→ Express feelings, events, or ideas more clearly?

PORTFOLIO
Students can submit their writing to be considered for inclusion in their digital Portfolio. Students' portfolios can be shared with parents.

Level Up Accelerating Progress

Leveled Reader

 OBJECTIVES

CCSS By the end of year, read and comprehend informational texts, including history/ social studies, science, and technical texts, in the grades 4–5 text complexity band proficiently, with scaffolding as needed at the high end of the range. **RI.4.10**

Approaching Level to On Level

Stargazing

Level Up Lessons also available online

Before Reading

Preview Discuss what students remember about the things people have learned about outer space. Tell them they will be reading a more challenging version of *Stargazing*.

Vocabulary Use the routines on the **Visual Vocabulary Cards** to review the vocabulary.

A C T During Reading

▶ **Specific Vocabulary** Review with students the following vocabulary words that are new to this title: *distorts, galaxies,* and *infrared.* Model using context clues to find the meaning of *distorts.* Provide the meanings for *galaxies* and *infrared.*

▶ **Connection of Ideas** Students may need help connecting Earth's rotation with the reason the North Star doesn't appear to move. Read pages 5–7 with students. Use a ball to demonstrate Earth's rotation. Ask: *What is moving?* (the ball) *Does the ceiling above the ball move?* (no) *Imagine the ball is Earth and the ceiling above the ball is the North Star. Does the North Star move?* (no)

▶ **Sentence Structure** Students may need help understanding the use of complex sentences. Point out that commas separate words into clauses, or ideas. Read the last sentence on page 12. Have students echo read the sentence after you. Say: *In this sentence, the commas separate two related ideas. Let's look at the sentence again. What two ideas are found in this sentence?* (Earth's atmosphere is full of dust; the dust makes it hard to see things in space.)

After Reading

Ask students to complete the Respond to Reading on page 15. Have students complete the Paired Read and hold Literature Circles. Students should respond to the questions using the new information from the On Level version of *Stargazing*.

Leveled Reader

OBJECTIVES

(CCSS) By the end of year, read and comprehend informational texts, including history/ social studies, science, and technical texts, in the grades 4–5 text complexity band proficiently, with scaffolding as needed at the high end of the range. **RI.4.10**

On Level
to Beyond Level

Stargazing

Level Up Lessons also available online

Before Reading

Preview Discuss what students remember about the things people have learned about outer space. Tell them they will be reading a more challenging version of *Stargazing*.

Vocabulary Use the routines on the **Visual Vocabulary Cards** to review the vocabulary.

A C T During Reading

▸ **Specific Vocabulary** Review with students the following words that are new to this title: *depicts, magnified, mechanics.* Model how to use paragraph clues to find the meaning for *depicts* and *magnified.* Provide the definition for *mechanics.*

▸ **Sentence Structure** Students may need help understanding more complex sentence structures. Have pairs reread the second paragraph on page 9. Point out that information in parenthesis can help the reader better understand a point. Ask students to identify the two examples of time in the text. (about a month, 29.5 days) Then have students identify why the information within the parenthesis is important. (It tells the reader exactly how long "about a month" is.)

▸ **Connection of Ideas** Students may need help connecting and synthesizing new ideas and information. Read the caption on page 9 with students. Ask: *What additional information does the caption tell us about Pleiades?* (It is thought to have formed 100 million years ago.)

After Reading

Have students complete the Respond to Reading on page 15. Have students complete the Paired Read and hold Literature Circles. Students should respond to the questions using the new information from the Beyond Level version of *Stargazing.*

Level Up Accelerating Progress

Leveled Reader

English Language Learners to On Level

Stargazing

Level Up Lessons also available online

OBJECTIVES

By the end of year, read and comprehend informational texts, including history/ social studies, science, and technical texts, in the grades 4–5 text complexity band proficiently, with scaffolding as needed at the high end of the range. **RI.4.10**

Before Reading

Preview Remind students that expository text gives facts about a topic. Discuss with them what they remember about the things people have learned about outer space. Tell them they will be reading a more challenging version of *Stargazing*.

Vocabulary Use the routines on the **Visual Vocabulary Cards** to review the vocabulary. Point out the cognates: *astronomía, creciente, fases, serie, específico, telescopio.*

A C T During Reading

▶ **Specific Vocabulary** Show students how to use paragraph clues to help them figure out the meaning of difficult words such as *distorts* on page 12. Ask students to suggest another word that could replace *distorts*. Then provide a definition. Repeat for other words that students have difficulty understanding.

▶ **Sentence Structure** Point out pronouns as you read. For example, reread the first two sentences on page 7. Explain to students that the pronoun "it" refers to the North Star. Repeat the routine with the pronouns found on page 13.

▶ **Connection of Ideas** Students may need help connecting the information on Earth's orbit from page 5 with the changes in night's sky on page 8. Model the concept by selecting three students to represent the sun, Earth, and a constellation. Position the sun in the center and have Earth rotate the sun. Then have the constellation stand in a fixed place outside of Earth's orbit. At different points in Earth's orbit ask: *Can Earth see the constellation?*

After Reading

Respond to Reading Have students complete the Respond to Reading on page 15. Have students complete the Paired Read and hold Literature Circles.

Advanced Level **Trade Book**

Leveled Reader

OBJECTIVES

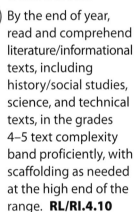

CCSS By the end of year, read and comprehend literature/informational texts, including history/social studies, science, and technical texts, in the grades 4–5 text complexity band proficiently, with scaffolding as needed at the high end of the range. **RL/RI.4.10**

Beyond Level
to Self-Selected Trade Book

Independent Reading

Level Up Lessons also available online

Before Reading

Together with students identify a particular focus for their reading based on the text they choose. Students who have chosen the same title will work in groups to identify the title's text structure.

Close Reading

Taking Notes Assign a graphic organizer for students to use to take notes as they read. Reinforce a specific comprehension focus from the unit by choosing the graphic organizer that best fits the book.

Examples:

Fiction	Informational Texts
Character, Setting, Plot	Main Ideas and Key Details
Graphic Organizer 109	Graphic Organizer 141

Ask and Answer Questions Remind students to ask questions as they read. They should write their questions on a separate sheet of paper. As students meet, have them share the questions that they noted and work together to find text evidence to support their answers. Have students write responses to their questions and note the text evidence they find to support their answers.

After Reading

Write About Reading

Have students work together to respond to the text using text evidence to support their writing.

Examples:

Fiction	Informational Text
How did the characters' actions change the events of the story?	What important details do you see? What do these details have in common with each other?

SUMMATIVE ASSESSMENT

Unit Assessment

 **TESTED SKILLS**

✔ COMPREHENSION:	**✔ VOCABULARY:**	**✔ ENGLISH LANGUAGE CONVENTIONS:**	**✔ WRITING:**
• Text Structure: Cause and Effect **RI.4.3**	• Latin Roots **L.4.4b**	• Pronouns and Antecedents **L.4.1a**	• Writing About Text **W.4.9a**
• Point of View **RL.4.6**	• Idioms **L.4.5b**	• Types of Pronouns **L.3.1a**	• Narrative **W.4.3a-e**
• Theme (narrative poetry) **RL.4.2**	• Context Clues: Synonyms **L.4.5c**	• Pronoun-Verb Agreement **L.3.1f**	
• Boldfaced Words **RI.4.7**	• Context Clues: Paragraph Clues **L.4.4a**	• Possessive Pronouns **L.3.2d**	
• Stanzas; Repetition **RL.4.5**	• Connotation and Denotation **L.4.5**	• Pronouns and Homophones **L.4.1g**	

 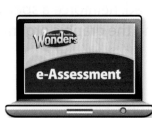

Assessment Includes

→ Pencil-and-paper administration

→ On-line administration

→ Performance Tasks

→ Writing Prompt

Additional Assessment Options

 Conduct assessments individually using the differentiated passages in **Fluency Assessment.** Students' expected fluency goal for this Unit is **102–122 WCPM** with an accuracy rate of 95% or higher.

Running Records

 Use the instructional reading level determined by the Running Record calculations for regrouping decisions. Students at Level 38 or below should be provided reteaching on specific Comprehension skills.

Using Assessment Results

TESTED SKILLS	If ...	Then ...
COMPREHENSION	Students answer 0–9 multiple-choice items correctly ...	... reteach tested skills using the *Tier 2 Comprehension Intervention online PDFs.*
VOCABULARY	Students answer 0–7 multiple-choice items correctly ...	... reteach tested skills using the *Tier 2 Vocabulary Intervention online PDFs.*
ENGLISH LANGUAGE CONVENTIONS	Students answer 0–7 multiple-choice items correctly ...	... reteach tested skills using the *Tier 2 Writing and Grammar Intervention online PDFs.*
WRITING	Students score less than "2" on short-response items and "3" on extended constructed response items ...	... reteach tested skills using appropriate lessons from the Strategies and Skills and/or Write About Reading sections in the *Tier 2 Comprehension Intervention online PDFs.*
	Students score less than "3" on the writing prompt ...	... reteach tested skills using the *Tier 2 Writing and Grammar Intervention online PDFs.*
FLUENCY	Students have a WCPM score of 0–101 ...	... reteach tested skills using the *Tier 2 Fluency Intervention online PDFs.*

Response to Intervention

Use the appropriate sections of the *Placement and Diagnostic Assessment* as well as students' assessment results to designate students requiring:

 **Intervention Online PDFs**

 **WonderWorks Intervention Program**

Reevaluate Student Grouping

View the *McGraw-Hill Reading Wonders e-Assessment* reports available for this Unit Assessment. Note students who are below the overall proficiency level for the assessment, and use the reports to assign small group instruction for students with similar needs.

Genre Writing: Narrative/Poetry

Reading Extended Complex Text

Program Information

For Additional Resources

Review Comprehension Lessons

Unit Bibliography

Word Lists

Literature and Informational Text Charts

Web Sites

Resources

www.connected.mcgraw-hill.com

NARRATIVE TEXT Fictional Narrative

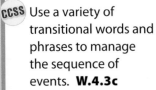

Writing Process Lesson 1

Exper... ...rrative • 61

Michael for School President
by James P.

I could barely sit still in my seat during the bus ride to school this morning. Today was Election Day, and I was running for school president. My mind drifted to last Thursday when someone had drawn silly faces all over my campaign posters. I knew it was Jared Fisher, but of course he denied it.

"Are you getting off the bus or are you going to stand there like we have all day?" Jared hissed. I shook my head and walked off the bus toward the front of the red brick school building.

Later that morning in the gym, Sadie Monroe walked up to me and said, "Well this is it, Michael."

"Yep, it sure is. We just have to wait and see if money talks or if students are really interested in changing things around here," I said.

"I hope you win, Michael. I really like your idea about bringing back our arts and music programs." Sadie smiled, and her braces gleamed under the gym lights.

"Thanks, Sadie. At least I'll have two votes--yours and mine," I said, smiling nervously as we walked toward the ballot box.

Next, I glanced to my left and saw Jared. He smiled at me and adjusted his tie. He even wore a dark blue pinstripe suit. He already looked presidential. I looked down at my white cotton shirt and khaki slacks.

**Expert Model
PDF Online**

OBJECTIVES

CCSS Orient the reader by establishing a situation and introducing a narrator and/or characters; organize an event sequence that unfolds naturally. **W.4.3a**

CCSS Use a variety of transitional words and phrases to manage the sequence of events. **W.4.3c**

CCSS Provide a conclusion that follows from the narrated experiences or events. **W.4.3e**

ACADEMIC LANGUAGE

fictional narrative, sequence, dialogue

Read Like a Writer

Point out that many of the stories students read are fiction, which means that they are made up. When you make up an entertaining story to share with others, you are using a form of writing known as a fictional narrative. Read and discuss the features of a fictional narrative.

Provide copies of the Expert Model "Michael for School President" and the features of a Fictional Narrative found online in Writer's Workspace.

Features of a Fictional Narrative

→ It tells a story that the writer has made up.

→ It has a beginning, middle, and end.

→ It has a setting, characters, and a plot.

→ The beginning establishes the situation and introduces the characters.

→ It uses sequence words to tell events in the order they happened.

→ It includes dialogue to develop the plot and characters.

Discuss the Expert Model

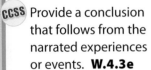

Use the questions below to prompt discussion of the features of fictional narratives.

→ Who are the characters in the story? (Michael, Jared, Sadie, Mr. Charles, and Ms. Freeman)

→ What is the setting? What is the plot? (Park Elementary School; Michael and Jared are running against each other to become school president of Park Elementary.)

→ Does the story have a beginning, middle, and end? What happens in the beginning of the story? (Yes; We learn that Michael is anxious about the election for school president and that he and Jared are rivals. The main characters, Michael and Jared, are introduced.)

→ What sequence words does the writer use? (*later that morning, next, then, finally, a few hours later*)

→ How does the dialogue develop the plot and characters? (It helps explain how much winning the election means to Michael. It also advances the plot by showing the tension between Jared and Michael.)

Go Digital

Writer's Workspace

PREWRITE

Discuss and Plan

Purpose Discuss with students the purpose for writing a fictional narrative. They can entertain readers by making up a story that has an interesting plot, setting, and cast of characters. They may also write a story that teaches a lesson or inspires readers in some way.

Audience Have students think about who will read their fictional narratives, such as friends, family members, and classmates. Ask: *How will your story entertain your readers?*

Teach the Minilesson

Sequence Explain that writers often tell the events in a story in the order they happened. This sequence of events helps readers understand what happened and why it happened. Writers use sequence words and phrases to signal the order of events. Sequence words include *later, next, then,* and *finally*.

Distribute copies of the Model Story Map found online in the Writer's Workspace. Point out that the events in James's fictional narrative unfold naturally, as they might happen in real life. He organizes the events in order by telling what happens in the beginning, middle, and end of the story.

Your Turn

Choose Your Topic Have students work in small groups to brainstorm ideas for a fictional narrative about someone who is running for mayor of a town. Remind them that their stories should have a setting, characters, and a plot. Ask questions to prompt thinking. Have students record their ideas in their Writer's Notebooks.

→ What characters, besides the mayor, will you include in your story?

→ Where will the story take place? What are some other details about the setting?

→ What happens in the beginning of the campaign? What happens next? What happens in the end?

Plan Provide copies of the blank Story Map found online in the Writer's Workspace. Ask students to put the important events in order, or sequence. The beginning should establish the situation and introduce the characters.

ENGLISH LANGUAGE LEARNERS

Beginning

Demonstrate Comprehension Have students draw pictures of or act out the events from their fictional narrative.

Intermediate

Explain Have students write a list of the details described in the sample fictional narrative.

Advanced/High

Expand Have partners ask and answer simple questions about their fictional narrative.

MODEL STORY MAP

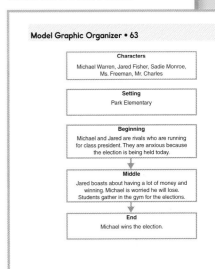

Model Graphic Organizer • 63

Characters
Michael Warren, Jared Fisher, Sadie Monroe, Ms. Freeman, Mr. Charles

Setting
Park Elementary

Beginning
Michael and Jared are rivals who are running for class president. They are anxious because the election is being held today.

Middle
Jared boasts about having a lot of money and winning. Michael is worried he will lose. Students gather in the gym for the elections.

End
Michael wins the election.

NARRATIVE TEXT Fictional Narrative

DRAFT

OBJECTIVES

 CCSS Use dialogue and description to develop experiences and events or show the responses of characters to situations. **W.4.3b**

CCSS Use concrete words and phrases and sensory details to convey experiences and events precisely. **W.4.3d**

ACADEMIC LANGUAGE

draft, sequence, descriptive details, dialogue, revise, peer review

Discuss the Student Model

Review the features of fictional narratives. Provide copies of the Student Model found online in the Writer's Workspace.

Teach the Minilesson

Description To make their fictional narratives more interesting, writers often use descriptive details. Descriptive details tell readers about the actions, thoughts, and feelings of the characters in the story. These details help readers picture the characters and the setting in their minds.

Discuss with students how the following descriptive details make the fictional narrative more interesting.

> The sky was gray
>
> wind as cold as ice
>
> leafless trees
>
> a huge menacing tabby cat purred with a smile

Invite students to share descriptive details from stories.

Your Turn

Write a Draft Have students review the Story Maps they prepared in Prewrite. Remind them to use descriptive details.

Go Digital

Writer's Workspace

Conferencing Routines

Teacher Conferences

STEP 1

Talk about the strengths of the writing.

The sequence words you used help me understand the order of events in your story.

STEP 2

Focus on how a writer uses a writing trait.

I can picture what is happening in the story because you used vivid, descriptive details to describe the characters and setting.

STEP 3

Make concrete suggestions for revision.

Your story would be more interesting if you added more dialogue to help the reader understand the characters' thoughts and feelings.

REVISE

Discuss the Revised Model

Distribute copies of the Revised Student Model found online in Writer's Workspace. Read the model aloud and have students note the revisions that Sunil made. Use the specific revisions to show how adding sequence words, descriptive details, and dialogue, and reviewing word choice help to make the fictional narrative more engaging.

Teach the Minilesson

Dialogue Explain that writers often use dialogue to help advance the story's plot and reveal the thoughts and feelings of characters.

Discuss with students how the following dialogue reveals Ruby's thoughts and feelings.

"It's empty," Ruby cried. "I'll never have the strength to fly south. I am in hot water."

"Wow! I'll be, you're my lucky star," Ruby gasped in surprise.

Your Turn

COLLABORATE

Revise Have students use the peer review routine and questions to review their partner's draft. Then have students select suggestions from the peer review to incorporate in their revisions. Provide the Revise and Edit Checklist from the Writer's Workspace to guide them as they revise. Circulate among students as they work and conference as needed.

REVISED STUDENT MODEL

Revised Student Model • Fictional Narrative • 66

Hitching a Ride
by Sunil K.

The sky was gray, and wind as cold as ice rusted through the leafless trees.

First, Ruby puffed up her feathers to keep out the chill as she flew toward the red blossom. She poked her long, thin bill inside the flower. Ruby started to cry.

"All the nectar is gone and the plants are dying. I should have gone south before Thanksgiving. Eat this acorn, little hungry hummingbird, a fluffy brown squirrel insisted from a nearby tree.

Next, Ruby sat on another tree. He didn't want to be rude, but she didn't dare get too close. "Thank you very much, squirrel. But I can't eat anything so big," Ruby said.

"I'd be happy to help," a huge menasing tabby cat purred with a sneaky smile. "I could bring up a little snack."

Then, Ruby flew off without answering, but hunger soon forced her down to a bird feeder. "It's empty," Ruby cried. "I'll never have the strength to fly south. I'm in hot water."

"Honk, honk, honk." Ruby looked up and saw a gigantic goose. "I overheard what you said," Goose explained politely. "I'm headed south myself. Want to hitch a ride?"

Peer Conferences

Review with students the routine for peer review of writing: Listen carefully as the writer reads his or her work aloud. Begin by telling what you liked about the writing. Then ask a question that will help the writer think more about the writing. Finally, make a suggestion that will make the writing stronger.

Use these questions for peer review.

☑ Does the story have a beginning, middle, and end?

☑ Are sequence words used to help readers understand the order of events?

☑ Are descriptive details included to help readers picture the events?

NARRATIVE TEXT Fictional Narrative

PROOFREAD/EDIT AND PUBLISH

ACADEMIC LANGUAGE

publish, multimedia, rubric

EDITED STUDENT MODEL

Edited Student Model • Fictional Narrative • 67

Hitching a Ride
by Sunil K.

¶The sky was gray, and wind as cold as ice rustled through the leafless trees.

¶First Ruby puffed up her feathers to keep out the chill as she flew toward the red blossom. She poked her long, thin bill inside the flower. Ruby started to cry.

¶"All the nectar is gone and the plants are dying. I should have gone south before Thanksgiving. Eat this acorn, little hungry hummingbird," a fluffy brown squirrel insisted from a nearby tree.

¶Next, Ruby sat on another tree. He didn't want to be rude, but she didn't dare get too close. "Thank you very much, squirrel. But I can't eat anything so big," Ruby said.

¶"I'd be happy to help," a huge menacing tabby cat purred with a smile. "I could bring up a little snack."

¶Then, Ruby flew off without answering, but hunger soon forced her down to a bird feeder. "It's empty," Ruby cried. "I'll never have the strength to fly south. I'm in hot water."

¶"Honk, honk, honk." Ruby looked up and saw a gigantic goose. "I overheard what you said," Goose explained politely. "I'm headed south myself. Want to hitch a ride?"

Discuss the Edited Model

Provide copies of the Edited Student Model found online in the Writer's Workspace. Read the model aloud and have students note the editing changes that Sunil made. Use the specific edits to show how editing for spelling, pronoun use, capitalization, and punctuation improves the fictional narrative.

Your Turn

Edit Have students use the edit questions on the Revise and Edit Checklist to guide them as they review and edit their drafts on their own. Remind them to read for one type of error at a time.

Publish

For the final presentation of their fictional narratives, have students choose a format for publishing. Students may want to consider:

Print Publishing	Digital Publishing
Personal Book	Writer's Workspace
Class Magazine	Class Blog
Class Newsletter	School Web site

Whether students handwrite or use a word-processing program, they should be sure to use standard margins and format their final drafts so that the text is easy for readers to follow. Make sure students demonstrate sufficient keyboarding skills to type at least one page of the narrative in one sitting.

Explain to students that adding visual and multimedia elements can strengthen their writing and presentation, making them more engaging for their readers and audience. Allow time for students to design and include illustrations, photos, videos, audio, slideshows, animations, and other multimedia elements that will enhance their fictional narratives.

Go Digital

Writer's Workspace

EVALUATE

Discuss Rubrics

Guide students as they use the Student Rubric found online in Writer's Workspace. Help them understand that using a rubric helps them identify and focus on areas that might need further work. Work with the class to review the bulleted points on the rubric.

→ **Focus and Coherence** Does the fictional narrative have an engaging beginning, middle, and end?

→ **Organization** Are events told in an order that makes sense? Are sequence words used?

→ **Ideas and Support** Is there dialogue that helps advance the plot and reveal the characters' thoughts and feelings?

→ **Word Choice** Are there descriptive details that help readers picture the characters and setting?

→ **Voice/Sentence Fluency** Is the narrative voice strong? Does the writing include a variety of sentence types and lengths?

→ **Conventions** Are errors in grammar, usage, spelling, punctuation, and capitalization corrected?

STUDENT RUBRIC

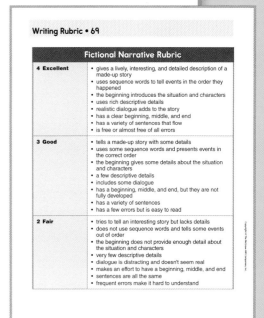

Your Turn

Reflect and Set Goals After students have evaluated their own fictional narratives, tell them to reflect on their progress as writers. Encourage them to consider areas where they feel they have shown improvement and to think about what areas need further improvement. Have them set writing goals to prepare for their conference with the teacher.

Conference with Students

Use the Rubric and Anchor Papers provided online in Writer's Workspace as you evaluate student writing. The anchor papers provide samples of papers that score from 1 to 4. These papers reflect the criteria described in the Rubric. Anchor papers offer a standard against which to judge writing.

Review with individual students the writing goals they have set. Discuss ways to achieve these goals and suggest any further areas of improvement students may need to target.

NARRATIVE TEXT Poetry

EXPERT MODEL

Catch
by Jeff B.

Dad tells me about the long day
his dad had. And those
of *his* dad. I understood then,
my roots snake
backwards—each pair, father and son,
sees itself in the one before,
two mirrors facing one another.
The image reflected and extending in both directions.
I can see backwards
and forwards (to when I might have a son).

We move slowly apart,
and the talk goes on,
but the ball carries our words
glove to hand
glove to hand—slap!
Each throw is the swipe of an eraser,
making the long day harder
to see until
we have a blank slate to carry
inside for tomorrow.

**Expert Model
PDF Online**

OBJECTIVES

CCSS Produce clear, coherent writing in which the development and organization are appropriate to task, purpose, and audience. **W.4.4**

CCSS Use concrete words and phrases and sensory details to convey experiences and events precisely. **W.4.3d**

ACADEMIC LANGUAGE

poetry, stanza, alliteration, figurative language, simile, metaphor

Read Like a Writer

Point out that everyone has feelings and ideas they can express in the form of a poem. There are many different kinds of poems you can write, but most poems have the same basic elements. Read and discuss the features of poetry.

Provide copies of the Expert Model "Catch" and the features of Poetry found online in Writer's Workspace.

Features of Poetry

→ It expresses feelings and ideas.

→ It is often organized into lines and stanzas.

→ It uses sound techniques, such as rhyme, rhythm, and alliteration.

→ It uses figurative language, such as similes and metaphors.

→ It uses language that appeals to the reader's senses.

Discuss the Expert Model

Use the questions below to prompt discussion of the features of poetry.

→ What feelings and ideas does the poet express in his poem? (He expresses feelings and ideas about his relationship with his father.)

→ How is the poem organized? (It has two stanzas. Each stanza has ten lines.)

→ What sound techniques are used in the poem? (The word "dad" is repeated in the first stanza, and the phrase "glove to hand" is repeated in the second stanza. This repetition adds rhythm to the poem.)

→ What figurative language does the poet use? (metaphors—father and son are compared to two mirrors facing each other, each throw of the ball is compared to the swipe of an eraser; personification—the ball carries their words)

→ How does the language in the poem appeal to the reader's senses? (Sensory details in the poem help the reader visualize what is happening between the boy and his father.)

Go Digital

Writer's Workspace

PREWRITE

Discuss and Plan

Purpose Discuss with students the purpose for writing poetry. They can express their feelings about an experience or their ideas about a topic. Poetry can also entertain the reader.

Audience Have students think about who will read their poems, such as friends, family members, and classmates. Ask: *How do you want readers to feel after reading your poem?*

Teach the Minilesson

Organization Explain that poets often organize their poems in lines and stanzas to make them easier to read. A stanza is one section of a poem. Stanzas in a poem often, but not always, have the same number of lines. The lines in a poem may or may not rhyme.

Distribute copies of the Model Word Web found online in the Writer's Workspace. Point out that Jeff used his word web to plan the feelings and ideas he wanted to include in his poem about the relationship between a boy and his father.

Your Turn

COLLABORATE

Choose Your Topic Have students work in pairs or small groups to brainstorm ideas for a poem about a leader they admire. Remind them that their poems should include language that appeals to the reader's senses. Ask questions to prompt thinking. Have students record their ideas in their Writer's Notebooks.

→ What qualities do you admire most in a leader?

→ What figurative language can you use to describe the leader you chose?

→ How many stanzas will your poem have? How many lines will each stanza have?

Plan Provide copies of the blank Word Web found online in the Writer's Workspace. Ask students to write the topic of their poem in the middle oval. Then have them add related details in the surrounding ovals.

MODEL WORD WEB

Model Graphic Organizer • 73

Dad tells his son about his day.

Boy learns about his roots.

Father and son play catch.

Boy sees himself in his father.

They talk until it's time to go inside.

NARRATIVE TEXT Poetry

DRAFT

OBJECTIVES

 CCSS Produce clear and coherent writing in which the development and organization are appropriate to task, purpose, and audience. **W.4.4**

CCSS Use concrete words and phrases and sensory details to convey experiences and events precisely. **W.4.3d**

ACADEMIC LANGUAGE

draft, concrete words and phrases, revise, peer review, sensory details

Discuss the Student Model

Review the features of poetry. Provide copies of the Student Model found online in the Writer's Workspace.

Teach the Minilesson

Concrete Words and Phrases Explain that poets often use concrete words and phrases to help readers clearly visualize the images in their poems. Concrete words and phrases include specific nouns, verbs, adjectives, and adverbs that precisely describe a person, thing, or action.

Discuss with students how the following concrete words and phrases help them clearly visualize the images in the poem.

> *punching the leather*
>
> *back into summer catch shape*
>
> *tossing underhanded lobs*
>
> *delicate as a pop up*

Invite students to share concrete words and phrases from poems they have read.

Your Turn

Write a Draft Have students review the Word Webs they prepared in Prewrite. Remind them to use concrete words and phrases.

Go Digital

Writer's Workspace

Conferencing Routines

Teacher Conferences

STEP 1

Talk about the strengths of the poem.

You did a good job of organizing your poem into stanzas. The stanzas make your poem easier to read and understand.

STEP 2

Focus on how a writer uses a writing trait.

The sensory details you used help me picture the leader you are describing clearly.

STEP 3

Make concrete suggestions for revision.

Your poem would be more interesting if you added some figurative language, such as a simile or metaphor.

REVISE

Discuss the Revised Model

Distribute copies of the Revised Student Model found online in Writer's Workspace. Read the model aloud and have students note the revisions that Jeff made. Use the specific revisions to show how adding details, improving word choice, and using correct pronoun form help to make the poem more engaging.

Teach the Minilesson

Sensory Details Remind students that sensory details tell how a subject looks, sounds, smells, tastes, or feels. These details help paint a vivid picture in the reader's mind. Discuss with students how the following sensory details paint a picture in the reader's mind and make the poem more interesting.

The sun leans back

On the horizon

splashing the sky with red and orange and pink

Your Turn
COLLABORATE

Revise Have students use the peer review routine and questions to review their partner's draft. Then have students select suggestions from the peer review to incorporate into their revisions. Provide the Revise and Edit Checklist from the Writer's Workspace to guide them as they revise. Suggest they consider adding sensory details to their poems.

REVISED STUDENT MODEL

Revised Student Model • Poetry • 76

Dad and I
by Jeff D.

Just before twylight, and Dad and I have
had our bad days seperate. Pulling our
brown mitts from beneath the winter
beanies in the closet,
we head to the alley behind the house,
punching the leather
back into summer catch shape.

The sun leans back
On the horizon
splashing the sky with red and orange and pink
We start only 2 arm length a part,
tossing underhanded lobs
delikate as a pop up. Him tells me
about the day he's had,
and I do the same.

Peer Conferences

Review with students the routine for peer review of writing: Listen carefully as the writer reads his or her work aloud. Begin by telling what you liked about the writing. Then, ask a question that will help the writer think more about the writing. Finally, make a suggestion that will make the writing stronger.

Use these questions for peer review.

- ✓ Does the poem express feelings and ideas?

- ✓ Is the poem organized into lines and stanzas?

- ✓ Are concrete words and phrases included to help you visualize images in the poem?

- ✓ Are sensory details and figurative language included?

NARRATIVE TEXT Poetry

PROOFREAD/EDIT AND PUBLISH

OBJECTIVES

CCSS With guidance and support from peers and adults, develop and strengthen writing as needed by planning, revising, and editing. **W.4.5**

CCSS With some guidance and support from adults, use technology, including the Internet, to produce and publish writing as well as to interact and collaborate with others; demonstrate sufficient command of keyboarding skills to type a minimum of one page in a single sitting. **W.4.6**

ACADEMIC LANGUAGE

publish, multimedia, rubric

EDITED STUDENT MODEL

Edited Student Model • Poetry • 77

Dad and I
by Jeff D.

twilight
Just before twilight, and Dad and I have
separate.
had our bad days separate. Pulling our
worn
brown mitts from beneath the winter
beanies in the closet,
we head to the alley behind the house,
punching the leather
Soft
back into summer catch shape.

The sun leans back
On the horizon
splashing the sky with red and orange and pink
We start only 2 arm length a part,
tossing underhanded lobs
delicate   He
delicate as a pop up, Him tells me
about the day he's had,
and I do the same.

Discuss the Edited Model

Provide copies of the Edited Student Model found online in the Writer's Workspace. Read the model aloud and have students note the editing changes that Jeff made. Use the specific edits to show how editing for spelling, pronoun use, capitalization, and punctuation improves the poem.

Your Turn

Edit Have students use the edit questions on the Revise and Edit Checklist to guide them as they review and edit their drafts on their own. Remind them to read for one type of error at a time.

Publish

For the final presentation of their poems, have students choose a format for publishing. Students may want to consider:

Print Publishing	Digital Publishing
School Newspaper	Class Blog
Class Magazine	Class Zine
Class Bulletin Board	Class Web site

Whether students handwrite or use a word processing program on the computer, they should be sure to use standard margins and format their final drafts so that the text is easy for readers to follow. Make sure students demonstrate sufficient keyboarding skills to type their poem in a single sitting.

Explain to students that adding visual and multimedia elements can strengthen their writing and presentation, making them more engaging for their readers and audience. Allow time for students to design and include illustrations, photos, videos, audio, slideshows, animations, and other multimedia elements that will enhance their poems.

Go Digital

Writer's Workspace

EVALUATE

Discuss Rubrics

Guide students as they use the Student Rubric found online in Writer's Workspace. Help them understand that using a rubric helps them identify and focus on areas that might need further work. Work with the class to review the bulleted points on the rubric.

→ **Focus and Coherence** Is the poem focused? Does the poem express feelings and ideas?

→ **Organization** Is the poem complete and thoughtfully organized? Is it organized into lines and stanzas?

→ **Ideas and Support** Are there concrete words and phrases to help readers visualize images?

→ **Word Choice** Does the poem include sensory details and figurative language to paint a picture in the reader's mind?

→ **Voice** Does the poem have an authentic and strong voice?

→ **Sentence Fluency** Are sound techniques such as rhythm, rhyme, and alliteration used in the poem?

→ **Conventions** Are errors in grammar, usage, spelling, punctuation, and capitalization corrected?

STUDENT RUBRIC

Writing Rubric • 79

	Poetry Rubric
4 Excellent	• expresses feelings and ideas in an original way; focus on subject is sustained • is complete and organized into lines and stanzas • uses vivid sensory details • uses figurative language in an effective, original way • uses a variety of sound techniques to enhance the meaning of the poem • has a clear, strong voice • has a variety of sentences • is free or almost free of all errors
3 Good	• expresses feelings and ideas with some originality; focus on subject is mostly sustained • is complete; inconsistent organization of lines and stanzas does not interfere with comprehension • a few sensory details • includes some figurative language • uses some sound techniques • has a voice but it is not strong • has some sentence variety • has a few errors but is easy to read
2 Fair	• tries to express feelings and ideas but lacks details, focus, and originality • is incomplete but mostly written in proper form; lines and stanzas are not well organized • very few sensory details • use of figurative language is not effective or original • very little use of sound techniques • voice is inconsistent • sentences are all the same • frequent errors make it hard to understand

Your Turn

Reflect and Set Goals After students have evaluated their own poems, tell them to reflect on their progress as poets. Encourage them to consider areas where they feel they have shown improvement and to think about what areas need further improvement. Have them set writing goals to prepare for their conference with the teacher.

Conference with Students

Use the Rubric and Anchor Papers provided online in Writer's Workspace as you evaluate student writing. The anchor papers provide samples of papers that score from 1 to 4. These papers reflect the criteria described in the Rubric. Anchor papers offer a standard against which to judge writing.

Review with individual students the writing goals they have set. Discuss ways to achieve these goals and suggest any further areas of improvement students may need to target.

Close Reading Routine

Read the Text | *What does the author tell us?*

Assign the Reading

Depending on the needs of your students, you can

→ ask students to read the text silently

→ read the text together with students

→ read the text aloud

Take Notes

Students generate questions and take notes about aspects of the text that might be confusing for them. Encourage students to note

→ difficult vocabulary words or phrases

→ details that are not clear

→ information that they do not understand

Students complete a graphic organizer to take notes on important information from the text.

Reread the Text | *What does the text mean?*

Ask Text-Dependent Questions/Generate Questions

Students reread and discuss and take notes on important shorter passages from the text. Students should

→ generate questions about the text

→ work with partners or small groups to answer questions using text evidence

Write About the Text | *Think about what the author wrote.*

Students write a response to the text, using evidence from the text to support their ideas or arguments.

Use the Literature Anthology

Getting Ready

Close Reading of *LaRue for Mayor*, pages 288–307

Use the suggestions in the chart to assign reading of the text and to chunk the text into shorter passages for rereading.

ESSENTIAL QUESTION   *Why do people run for public office?*

Ask students to discuss what they have learned about why people run for public office.

Suggested Pacing

Days 1–4   **Read**
          pp. 288–291
          pp. 292–297
          pp. 298–303
          pp. 304–307

Days 5–12 **Reread**
          pp. 288–289
          pp. 290–291
          pp. 292–294
          pp. 295–297
          pp. 298–301
          pp. 302–303
          pp. 304–305
          pp. 306–307

Days 13–15 **Write About**
          the Text

Read the Text   *What does the author tell us?*

Assign the Reading

Ask students to read the text independently. You may want to read pages 288–291 together with students due to difficult vocabulary used in the text.

Take Notes

As students read, ask them to generate questions and other notes on features of the text they find difficult to understand. For this selection, students may note:

→ information and details that are unclear

→ words they do not know

→ lack of knowledge about the content

→ confusion about the connection between ideas or events

Model for students how to take notes.

Think Aloud   On page 297, there is a letter from a concerned citizen. I wonder if the letter is from Ike. The letter sounds like it is from him, but the text doesn't say for sure.

> p. 297
>
> Is Ike the concerned citizen?

Use the Literature Anthology

Assign **Graphic Organizer 125** to help students take notes about the point of view in the story.

As students share their questions and notes, use the Access Complex Text suggestions on pages T89A–T89T to help address features about the text that students found difficult.

Reread the Text *What does the text mean?*

Ask Text-Dependent Questions/Generate Questions

Ask students to reread the shorter passages from the text, focusing on **how** the author entertains readers. Ask questions about

→ **Use of Text Features, pp. 288–289, 292–294**

→ How is information provided in visual features, such as illustrations?

→ What features of newspaper articles do you notice? What information do they give?

→ **Humor, pp. 292–294**

→ How does the author use humor in the story? Why might he use it?

→ **Literary Elements, pp. 304–305**

→ How does the author use personification? What effect does it create?

→ **Word Choice, pp. 290–291, 295–297, 298–301, 302–303**

→ When does the author use complex words? Why does he use them?

→ What kind of figurative language does the author use? What effect does it create?

→ When does the author use idioms? What tone do they create?

Use the prompts on Teacher Edition pages T89A–T89T for suggested text-dependent questions. Remind students that they are to look back into the text to cite evidence to support their answers.

Model citing text evidence as needed.

Is Ike keeping his campaign against Bugwort as positive as he claims he will in his letter to Mrs. LaRue?

Think Aloud On page 300, Ike calls Bugwort "vicious and unstable, if not insane." The illustration on the page shows Ike's supporters drawing on one of Bugwort's campaign posters and changing the words so they make fun of Bugwort. This text evidence shows me that Ike is not keeping his campaign positive.

As they reread each section, students should continue to generate their own questions about the text. As each student shares a question, ask all students to go back into the text to find text evidence to answer the question. Encourage students to

→ point out the exact place within the text they found evidence

→ reread and paraphrase the section of the text that they think supports their answer

→ discuss how well the cited evidence answers the question

→ identify when an answer to a question cannot be found in the text

Write About the Text   *Think about what the author wrote.*

Essential Question

Have students respond in writing to the Essential Question using evidence from the text.

Why do people run for public office?

Students should use their notes and graphic organizers to cite evidence from the text to support their answer.

Model how to use notes to respond to the Essential Question:

Think Aloud I can reread the notes I took during reading to find text evidence that can help me answer the question. After reading page 299, I wrote in my notes that Ike decides to run against Bugwort to stop him from continuing his "scurrilous attacks" on dogs. I can use that information in my answer. Then I'll look through the rest of my notes to find more text evidence that I can use to support my answer.

Students can work with a partner and use their notes and graphic organizer to locate evidence that can be used to answer the question. Encourage students to discuss the strength of the evidence cited and give arguments about what may be strong or weak about a particular citation.

READING Extended Complex Text

Use Your Own Text

Classroom Library

Classroom Library lessons available online.

or Choose from your own **Trade Books**

The Moon and I
Genre Nonfiction

Lexile 870
TextEvaluator™ 38

A Picture Book of Harry Houdini
Genre Nonfiction

Lexile 770
TextEvaluator™ 41

Project Mulberry
Genre Realistic Fiction

Lexile 690
TextEvaluator™ 39

Riding Freedom
Genre Realistic Fiction

Lexile 720
TextEvaluator™ 40

→ Use this lesson with a text of your own choice. Go online for title specific classroom library book lessons.

→ Assign reading of the text. You may wish to do this by section or chapters.

→ Chunk the text into shorter important passages for rereading.

→ Present an Essential Question. You may want to use the Unit Big Idea.

Read the Text *What does the author tell us?*

Assign the Reading

Ask students to read the assigned sections of the text independently. For sections that are more difficult for students, you may wish to read the text aloud or ask students to read with a partner.

Take Notes

As students read, ask them to take notes on difficult parts of the text. Model how to take notes on

→ details or parts that are unclear

→ words they do not know

→ information they feel is important

→ ways in which information or events are connected

→ the genre of the text

You may wish to have students complete a graphic organizer, chosen from within the unit, to take notes on important information as they read. The graphic organizer can help them summarize the text.

Help students access the complex features of the text. Scaffold instruction on the following features as necessary:

→ Purpose

→ Genre

→ Specific Vocabulary

→ Sentence Structure

→ Connection of Ideas

→ Organization

→ Prior Knowledge

Reread the Text *What does the text mean?*

Ask Text-Dependent Questions/Generate Questions

 Ask students to reread the shorter passages from the text, focusing on how the author provides information or develops the characters, setting, and plot. Focus questions on the following:

Literature Selections

Character, Setting, and Plot Development

Word Choice

Genre

Point of View

Informational Text

Main Idea and Supporting Key Details

Word Choice

Text Structure

Text Features

Genre

Have students discuss questions they generated. As each student shares a question, ask all students to go back into the text to find text evidence to answer the question. Encourage students to

→ point out the exact place within the text they found the evidence

→ reread and paraphrase the section of the text that they think supports their answer

→ discuss how well the cited evidence answers the question

→ identify when an answer to a question cannot be found in the text

Write About the Text *Think about what the author wrote.*

Essential Question

Have students respond in writing to the Essential Question, considering the complete text. Students can work with a partner and use their notes and graphic organizer to locate evidence that can be used to answer the question.

 SCOPE & SEQUENCE

	K	1	2	3	4	5	6
READING PROCESS							
Concepts About Print/Print Awareness							
Recognize own name							
Understand directionality (top to bottom; tracking print from left to right; return sweep, page by page)	✔						
Locate printed word on page	✔						
Develop print awareness (concept of letter, word, sentence)	✔						
Identify separate sounds in a spoken sentence	✔						
Understand that written words are represented in written language by a specific sequence of letters	✔						
Distinguish between letters, words, and sentences	✔						
Identify and distinguish paragraphs							
Match print to speech (one-to-one correspondence)	✔						
Name uppercase and lowercase letters	✔						
Understand book handling (holding a book right-side-up, turning its pages)	✔						
Identify parts of a book (front cover, back cover, title page, table of contents); recognize that parts of a book contain information	✔						
Phonological Awareness							
Recognize and understand alliteration							
Segment sentences into correct number of words							
Identify, blend, segment syllables in words		✔					
Recognize and generate rhyming words	✔	✔					
Identify, blend, segment onset and rime	✔	✔					
Phonemic Awareness							
Count phonemes	✔	✔					
Isolate initial, medial, and final sounds	✔	✔					
Blend spoken phonemes to form words	✔	✔					
Segment spoken words into phonemes	✔	✔					
Distinguish between long- and short-vowel sounds	✔	✔					
Manipulate phonemes (addition, deletion, substitution)	✔	✔					
Phonics and Decoding /Word Recognition							
Understand the alphabetic principle	✔	✔					
Sound/letter correspondence	✔	✔	✔	✔			
Blend sounds into words, including VC, CVC, CVCe, CVVC words	✔	✔	✔	✔			
Blend common word families	✔	✔	✔	✔			

KEY	✔ = Assessed Skill Tinted panels show skills, strategies, and other teaching opportunities.

	K	1	2	3	4	5	6
Initial consonant blends		✔	✔	✔			
Final consonant blends		✔	✔	✔			
Initial and medial short vowels	✔	✔	✔	✔	✔	✔	✔
Decode one-syllable words in isolation and in context	✔	✔	✔	✔			
Decode multisyllabic words in isolation and in context using common syllabication patterns		✔	✔	✔	✔	✔	✔
Distinguish between similarly spelled words	✔	✔	✔	✔	✔	✔	✔
Monitor accuracy of decoding							
Identify and read common high-frequency words, irregularly spelled words	✔	✔	✔	✔			
Identify and read compound words, contractions		✔	✔	✔	✔	✔	✔
Use knowledge of spelling patterns to identify syllables		✔	✔	✔	✔	✔	✔
Regular and irregular plurals	✔	✔	✔	✔	✔	✔	✔
Long vowels (silent e, vowel teams)	✔	✔	✔	✔	✔	✔	✔
Vowel digraphs (variant vowels)		✔	✔	✔	✔	✔	✔
r-Controlled vowels		✔	✔	✔	✔	✔	✔
Hard/soft consonants		✔	✔	✔	✔	✔	✔
Initial consonant digraphs		✔	✔	✔	✔	✔	
Medial and final consonant digraphs		✔	✔	✔	✔	✔	
Vowel diphthongs		✔	✔	✔	✔	✔	✔
Identify and distinguish letter-sounds (initial, medial, final)	✔	✔	✔				
Silent letters		✔	✔	✔	✔	✔	✔
Schwa words				✔	✔	✔	✔
Inflectional endings		✔	✔	✔	✔	✔	✔
Triple-consonant clusters		✔	✔	✔	✔	✔	
Unfamiliar and complex word families				✔	✔	✔	✔
Structural Analysis/Word Analysis							
Common spelling patterns (word families)		✔	✔	✔	✔	✔	✔
Common syllable patterns		✔	✔	✔	✔	✔	✔
Inflectional endings		✔	✔	✔	✔	✔	✔
Contractions		✔	✔	✔	✔	✔	✔
Compound words		✔	✔	✔	✔	✔	✔
Prefixes and suffixes		✔	✔	✔	✔	✔	✔
Root or base words			✔	✔	✔	✔	✔
Comparatives and superlatives			✔	✔	✔	✔	✔
Greek and Latin roots			✔	✔	✔	✔	✔
Fluency							
Apply letter/sound knowledge to decode phonetically regular words accurately	✔	✔	✔	✔	✔	✔	✔
Recognize high-frequency and familiar words	✔	✔	✔	✔	✔	✔	✔
Read regularly on independent and instructional levels							
Read orally with fluency from familiar texts (choral, echo, partner, Reader's Theater)							
Use appropriate rate, expression, intonation, and phrasing		✔	✔	✔	✔	✔	✔
Read with automaticity (accurately and effortlessly)		✔	✔	✔	✔	✔	✔
Use punctuation cues in reading		✔	✔	✔	✔	✔	✔

	K	1	2	3	4	5	6
Adjust reading rate to purpose, text difficulty, form, and style							
Repeated readings							
Timed readings		✔	✔	✔	✔	✔	✔
Read with purpose and understanding		✔	✔	✔	✔	✔	✔
Read orally with accuracy		✔	✔	✔	✔	✔	✔
Use context to confirm or self-correct word recognition		✔	✔	✔	✔	✔	✔

READING LITERATURE

Comprehension Strategies and Skills

	K	1	2	3	4	5	6
Read literature from a broad range of genres, cultures, and periods		✔	✔	✔	✔	✔	✔
Access complex text		✔	✔	✔	✔	✔	✔
Build background							
Preview and predict							
Establish and adjust purpose for reading							
Evaluate citing evidence from the text							
Ask and answer questions	✔	✔	✔	✔	✔	✔	✔
Inferences and conclusions, citing evidence from the text	✔	✔	✔	✔	✔	✔	✔
Monitor/adjust comprehension including reread, reading rate, paraphrase							
Recount/Retell	✔	✔					
Summarize			✔	✔	✔	✔	✔
Story structure (beginning, middle, end)	✔	✔	✔	✔	✔	✔	✔
Visualize							
Make connections between and across texts		✔	✔	✔	✔	✔	✔
Point of view		✔	✔	✔	✔	✔	
Author's purpose							
Cause and effect	✔	✔	✔	✔	✔	✔	✔
Compare and contrast (including character, setting, plot, topics)	✔	✔	✔	✔	✔	✔	✔
Classify and categorize		✔	✔				
Literature vs informational text	✔	✔	✔				
Illustrations, using	✔	✔	✔	✔			
Theme, central message, moral, lesson		✔	✔	✔	✔	✔	✔
Predictions, making/confirming	✔	✔	✔				
Problem and solution (problem/resolution)		✔	✔	✔	✔	✔	✔
Sequence of events	✔	✔	✔	✔	✔	✔	✔

Literary Elements

	K	1	2	3	4	5	6
Character	✔	✔	✔	✔	✔	✔	✔
Plot development/Events	✔	✔	✔	✔	✔	✔	✔
Setting	✔	✔	✔	✔	✔	✔	✔
Stanza				✔	✔	✔	✔
Alliteration						✔	✔
Assonance						✔	✔
Dialogue							
Foreshadowing						✔	✔

KEY	✔ = Assessed Skill
	Tinted panels show skills, strategies, and other teaching opportunities.

	K	1	2	3	4	5	6
Flashback						✔	✔
Descriptive and figurative language		✔	✔	✔	✔	✔	✔
Imagery					✔	✔	✔
Meter					✔	✔	✔
Onomatopoeia							
Repetition		✔	✔	✔	✔	✔	✔
Rhyme/rhyme schemes		✔	✔	✔	✔	✔	✔
Rhythm		✔	✔				
Sensory language							
Symbolism							

Write About Reading/Literary Response Discussions

	K	1	2	3	4	5	6
Reflect and respond to text citing text evidence		✔	✔	✔	✔	✔	✔
Connect and compare text characters, events, ideas to self, to other texts, to world							
Connect literary texts to other curriculum areas							
Identify cultural and historical elements of text							
Evaluate author's techniques, craft							
Analytical writing							
Interpret text ideas through writing, discussion, media, research							
Book report or review							
Locate, use, explain information from text features		✔	✔	✔	✔	✔	✔
Organize information to show understanding of main idea through charts, mapping							
Cite text evidence	✔	✔	✔	✔	✔	✔	✔
Author's purpose/ Illustrator's purpose							

READING INFORMATIONAL TEXT

Comprehension Strategies and Skills

	K	1	2	3	4	5	6
Read informational text from a broad range of topics and cultures	✔	✔	✔	✔	✔	✔	✔
Access complex text		✔	✔	✔	✔	✔	✔
Build background							
Preview and predict	✔	✔	✔				
Establish and adjust purpose for reading							
Evaluate citing evidence from the text							
Ask and answer questions	✔	✔	✔	✔	✔	✔	✔
Inferences and conclusions, citing evidence from the text	✔	✔	✔	✔	✔	✔	✔
Monitor and adjust comprehension including reread, adjust reading rate, paraphrase							
Recount/Retell	✔	✔					
Summarize			✔	✔	✔	✔	✔
Text structure	✔	✔	✔	✔	✔	✔	✔
Identify text features		✔	✔	✔	✔	✔	✔
Make connections between and across texts	✔	✔	✔	✔	✔	✔	✔
Author's point of view				✔	✔	✔	✔
Author's purpose		✔	✔				
Cause and effect	✔	✔	✔	✔	✔	✔	✔

	K	1	2	3	4	5	6
Compare and contrast	✔	✔	✔	✔	✔	✔	✔
Classify and categorize		✔	✔				
Illustrations and photographs, using	✔	✔	✔	✔			
Instructions/directions (written and oral)		✔	✔	✔	✔	✔	✔
Main idea and key details	✔	✔	✔	✔	✔	✔	✔
Persuasion, reasons and evidence to support points/persuasive techniques						✔	✔
Predictions, making/confirming	✔	✔					
Problem and solution		✔	✔	✔	✔	✔	✔
Sequence, chronological order of events, time order, steps in a process	✔	✔	✔	✔	✔	✔	✔

Writing About Reading/Expository Critique Discussions

	K	1	2	3	4	5	6
Reflect and respond to text citing text evidence		✔	✔	✔	✔	✔	✔
Connect and compare text characters, events, ideas to self, to other texts, to world							
Connect texts to other curriculum areas							
Identify cultural and historical elements of text							
Evaluate author's techniques, craft							
Analytical writing							
Read to understand and perform tasks and activities							
Interpret text ideas through writing, discussion, media, research							
Locate, use, explain information from text features		✔	✔	✔	✔	✔	✔
Organize information to show understanding of main idea through charts, mapping							
Cite text evidence		✔	✔	✔	✔	✔	✔
Author's purpose/Illustrator's purpose							

Text Features

	K	1	2	3	4	5	6
Recognize and identify text and organizational features of nonfiction texts		✔	✔	✔	✔	✔	✔
Captions and labels, headings, subheadings, endnotes, key words, bold print	✔	✔	✔	✔	✔	✔	✔
Graphics, including photographs, illustrations, maps, charts, diagrams, graphs, time lines	✔	✔	✔	✔	✔	✔	✔

Self-Selected Reading/Independent Reading

	K	1	2	3	4	5	6
Use personal criteria to choose own reading including favorite authors, genres, recommendations from others; set up a reading log							
Read a range of literature and informational text for tasks as well as for enjoyment; participate in literature circles							
Produce evidence of reading by retelling, summarizing, or paraphrasing							

Media Literacy

	K	1	2	3	4	5	6
Summarize the message or content from media message, citing text evidence							
Use graphics, illustrations to analyze and interpret information	✔	✔	✔	✔	✔	✔	✔
Identify structural features of popular media and use the features to obtain information, including digital sources					✔	✔	✔	✔
Identify reasons and evidence in visuals and media message							
Analyze media source: recognize effects of media in one's mood and emotion							
Make informed judgments about print and digital media							
Critique persuasive techniques							

KEY ✔ = Assessed Skill
Tinted panels show skills, strategies, and other teaching opportunities.

WRITING

	K	1	2	3	4	5	6
Writing Process							
Plan/prewrite							
Draft							
Revise							
Edit/proofread							
Publish and present including using technology							
Teacher and peer feedback							
Writing Traits							
Conventions		✔	✔	✔	✔	✔	✔
Ideas		✔	✔	✔	✔	✔	✔
Organization		✔	✔	✔	✔	✔	✔
Sentence fluency		✔	✔	✔	✔	✔	✔
Voice		✔	✔	✔	✔	✔	✔
Word choice		✔	✔	✔	✔	✔	✔
Writer's Craft							
Good topic, focus on and develop topic, topic sentence			✔	✔	✔	✔	✔
Paragraph(s); sentence structure			✔	✔	✔	✔	✔
Main idea and supporting key details			✔	✔	✔	✔	✔
Unimportant details							
Relevant supporting evidence			✔	✔	✔	✔	✔
Strong opening, strong conclusion			✔	✔	✔	✔	✔
Beginning, middle, end; sequence		✔	✔	✔	✔	✔	✔
Precise words, strong words, vary words			✔	✔	✔	✔	✔
Figurative and sensory language, descriptive details							
Informal/formal language							
Mood/style/tone							
Dialogue				✔	✔	✔	✔
Transition words, transitions to multiple paragraphs				✔	✔	✔	✔
Select focus and organization			✔	✔	✔	✔	✔
Points and counterpoints/Opposing claims and counterarguments							
Use reference materials (online and print dictionary, thesaurus, encyclopedia)							
Writing Applications							
Writing about text	✔	✔	✔	✔	✔	✔	✔
Personal and fictional narrative (also biographical and autobiographical)	✔	✔	✔	✔	✔	✔	✔
Variety of expressive forms including poetry	✔	✔	✔	✔	✔	✔	✔
Informative/explanatory texts	✔	✔	✔	✔	✔	✔	✔
Description	✔	✔	✔	✔			
Procedural texts			✔	✔	✔	✔	✔
Opinion pieces or arguments	✔	✔	✔	✔	✔	✔	✔
Communications including technical documents			✔	✔	✔	✔	✔
Research report	✔	✔	✔	✔	✔	✔	✔
Responses to literature/reflection				✔	✔	✔	✔

	K	1	2	3	4	5	6
Analytical writing							
Letters		✔	✔	✔	✔	✔	✔
Write daily and over short and extended time frames; set up writer's notebooks							

Penmanship/Handwriting

	K	1	2	3	4	5	6
Write legibly in manuscript using correct formation, directionality, and spacing							
Write legibly in cursive using correct formation, directionality, and spacing							

SPEAKING AND LISTENING

Speaking

	K	1	2	3	4	5	6
Use repetition, rhyme, and rhythm in oral texts							
Participate in classroom activities and discussions							
Collaborative conversation with peers and adults in small and large groups using formal English when appropriate							
Differentiate between formal and informal English							
Follow agreed upon rules for discussion							
Build on others' talk in conversation, adding new ideas							
Come to discussion prepared							
Describe familiar people, places, and things and add drawings as desired							
Paraphrase portions of text read alone or information presented							
Apply comprehension strategies and skills in speaking activities							
Use literal and nonliteral meanings							
Ask and answer questions about text read aloud and about media							
Stay on topic when speaking							
Use language appropriate to situation, purpose, and audience							
Use nonverbal communications such as eye contact, gestures, and props							
Use verbal communication in effective ways and improve expression in conventional language							
Retell a story, presentation, or spoken message by summarizing							
Oral presentations: focus, organizational structure, audience, purpose							
Give and follow directions							
Consider audience when speaking or preparing a presentation							
Recite poems, rhymes, songs							
Use complete, coherent sentences							
Organize presentations							
Deliver presentations (narrative, summaries, research, persuasive); add visuals							
Speak audibly (accuracy, expression, volume, pitch, rate, phrasing, modulation, enunciation)							
Create audio recordings of poems, stories, presentations							

Listening

	K	1	2	3	4	5	6
Identify musical elements in language							
Determine the purpose for listening							
Understand, follow, restate, and give oral directions							
Develop oral language and concepts							
Listen openly, responsively, attentively, and critically							

KEY	✔ = Assessed Skill
	Tinted panels show skills, strategies, and other teaching opportunities.

	K	1	2	3	4	5	6
Listen to identify the points a speaker makes							
Listen responsively to oral presentations (determine main idea and key details)							
Ask and answer relevant questions (for clarification to follow-up on ideas)							
Identify reasons and evidence presented by speaker							
Recall and interpret speakers' verbal/nonverbal messages, purposes, perspectives							

LANGUAGE

Vocabulary Acquisition and Use

	K	1	2	3	4	5	6
Develop oral vocabulary and choose words for effect							
Use academic language		✔	✔	✔	✔	✔	✔
Identify persons, places, things, actions		✔	✔	✔			
Classify, sort, and categorize words	✔	✔	✔	✔	✔	✔	✔
Determine or clarify the meaning of unknown words; use word walls		✔	✔	✔	✔	✔	✔
Synonyms, antonyms, and opposites		✔	✔	✔	✔	✔	✔
Use context clues such as word, sentence, paragraph, definition, example, restatement, description, comparison, cause and effect		✔	✔	✔	✔	✔	✔
Use word identification strategies		✔	✔	✔	✔	✔	✔
Unfamiliar words		✔	✔	✔	✔	✔	✔
Multiple-meaning words		✔	✔	✔	✔	✔	✔
Use print and online dictionary to locate meanings, pronunciation, derivatives, parts of speech		✔	✔	✔	✔	✔	✔
Compound words		✔	✔	✔	✔	✔	✔
Words ending in -er and -est		✔	✔	✔	✔	✔	
Root words (base words)		✔	✔	✔	✔		✔
Prefixes and suffixes		✔	✔	✔	✔	✔	✔
Greek and Latin affixes and roots			✔	✔	✔	✔	✔
Denotation and connotation					✔	✔	✔
Word families		✔	✔	✔	✔	✔	✔
Inflectional endings		✔	✔	✔	✔	✔	✔
Use a print and online thesaurus			✔	✔	✔	✔	✔
Use print and online reference sources for word meaning (dictionary, glossaries)		✔	✔	✔	✔	✔	✔
Homographs				✔	✔	✔	✔
Homophones			✔	✔	✔	✔	✔
Contractions		✔	✔	✔			
Figurative language such as metaphors, similes, personification			✔	✔	✔	✔	✔
Idioms, adages, proverbs, literal and nonliteral language			✔	✔	✔	✔	✔
Analogies							
Listen to, read, discuss familiar and unfamiliar challenging text							
Identify real-life connections between words and their use							
Use acquired words and phrases to convey precise ideas							
Use vocabulary to express spatial and temporal relationships							
Identify shades of meaning in related words	✔	✔	✔	✔	✔	✔	✔
Word origins				✔	✔	✔	✔
Morphology				✔	✔	✔	✔

	K	1	2	3	4	5	6
Knowledge of Language							
Choose words, phrases, and sentences for effect							
Choose punctuation effectively							
Formal and informal language for style and tone including dialects							
Conventions of Standard English/Grammar, Mechanics, and Usage							
Sentence concepts: statements, questions, exclamations, commands		✔	✔	✔	✔	✔	✔
Complete and incomplete sentences; sentence fragments; word order		✔	✔	✔	✔	✔	✔
Compound sentences, complex sentences				✔	✔	✔	✔
Combining sentences		✔	✔	✔	✔	✔	✔
Nouns including common, proper, singular, plural, irregular plurals, possessives, abstract, concrete, collective		✔	✔	✔	✔	✔	✔
Verbs including action, helping, linking, irregular		✔	✔	✔	✔	✔	✔
Verb tenses including past, present, future, perfect, and progressive		✔	✔	✔	✔	✔	✔
Pronouns including possessive, subject and object, pronoun-verb agreement, indefinite, intensive, reciprocal; correct unclear pronouns		✔	✔	✔	✔	✔	✔
Adjectives including articles, demonstrative, proper, adjectives that compare		✔	✔	✔	✔	✔	✔
Adverbs including telling how, when, where, comparative, superlative, irregular		✔	✔	✔	✔	✔	✔
Subject, predicate; subject-verb agreement		✔	✔	✔	✔	✔	✔
Contractions		✔	✔	✔	✔	✔	✔
Conjunctions				✔	✔	✔	✔
Commas			✔	✔	✔	✔	✔
Colons, semicolons, dashes, hyphens						✔	✔
Question words							
Quotation marks			✔	✔	✔	✔	✔
Prepositions and prepositional phrases, appositives		✔	✔	✔	✔	✔	✔
Independent and dependent clauses						✔	✔
Italics/underlining for emphasis and titles							
Negatives, correcting double negatives					✔	✔	✔
Abbreviations			✔	✔	✔	✔	✔
Use correct capitalization in sentences, proper nouns, titles, abbreviations		✔	✔	✔	✔	✔	✔
Use correct punctuation		✔	✔	✔	✔	✔	✔
Antecedents				✔	✔	✔	✔
Homophones and words often confused			✔	✔	✔	✔	✔
Apostrophes				✔	✔	✔	✔
Spelling							
Write irregular, high-frequency words	✔	✔	✔				
ABC order	✔	✔					
Write letters	✔	✔					
Words with short vowels	✔	✔	✔	✔	✔	✔	✔
Words with long vowels	✔	✔	✔	✔	✔	✔	✔
Words with digraphs, blends, consonant clusters, double consonants		✔	✔	✔	✔	✔	✔
Words with vowel digraphs and ambiguous vowels		✔	✔	✔	✔	✔	✔
Words with diphthongs		✔	✔	✔	✔	✔	✔

KEY   ✔ = Assessed Skill
Tinted panels show skills, strategies, and other teaching opportunities.

	K	1	2	3	4	5	6
Words with r-controlled vowels		✔	✔	✔	✔	✔	✔
Use conventional spelling		✔	✔	✔	✔	✔	✔
Schwa words				✔	✔	✔	✔
Words with silent letters			✔	✔	✔	✔	✔
Words with hard and soft letters			✔	✔	✔	✔	✔
Inflectional endings including plural, past tense, drop final e and double consonant when adding -ed and -ing, changing y to i	✔	✔	✔	✔	✔	✔	✔
Compound words		✔	✔	✔	✔	✔	✔
Homonyms/homophones			✔	✔	✔	✔	✔
Prefixes and suffixes	✔	✔	✔	✔	✔	✔	✔
Root and base words (also spell derivatives)				✔	✔	✔	✔
Syllables: patterns, rules, accented, stressed, closed, open				✔	✔	✔	✔
Words with Greek and Latin roots						✔	✔
Words from mythology						✔	✔
Words with spelling patterns, word families	✔	✔	✔	✔	✔	✔	✔

RESEARCH AND INQUIRY

Study Skills

	K	1	2	3	4	5	6
Directions: read, write, give, follow (includes technical directions)			✔	✔	✔	✔	✔
Evaluate directions for sequence and completeness				✔	✔	✔	✔
Use library/media center							
Use parts of a book to locate information							
Interpret information from graphic aids		✔	✔	✔	✔	✔	✔
Use graphic organizers to organize information and comprehend text		✔	✔	✔	✔	✔	✔
Use functional, everyday documents				✔	✔	✔	✔
Apply study strategies: skimming and scanning, note-taking, outlining							

Research Process

	K	1	2	3	4	5	6
Generate and revise topics and questions for research				✔	✔	✔	✔
Narrow focus of research, set research goals				✔	✔	✔	✔
Find and locate information using print and digital resources		✔	✔	✔	✔	✔	✔
Record information systematically (note-taking, outlining, using technology)				✔	✔	✔	✔
Develop a systematic research plan				✔	✔	✔	✔
Evaluate reliability, credibility, usefulness of sources and information						✔	✔
Use primary sources to obtain information					✔	✔	✔
Organize, synthesize, evaluate, and draw conclusions from information							
Cite and list sources of information (record basic bibliographic data)					✔	✔	✔
Demonstrate basic keyboarding skills							
Participate in and present shared research							

Technology

	K	1	2	3	4	5	6
Use computer, Internet, and other technology resources to access information							
Use text and organizational features of electronic resources such as search engines, keywords, e-mail, hyperlinks, URLs, Web pages, databases, graphics							
Use digital tools to present and publish in a variety of media formats							

INDEX

A

H

Haiku, 2: T268–T269, T274–T275

Higher-level thinking. *See* Comprehension skills; Comprehension strategies; Text connections.

Historical fiction. *See under* Genre: fiction.

Homographs. *See* Vocabulary: homographs.

Homophones. *See* Phonics/Word Study: homophones.

Hyperbole, 5: T86–T87, T89E

I

Idioms. *See under* Vocabulary: figurative language.

Illustrations/photographs, using,
1: T25B, T89D, T153B, T217B, 217C, T217Q, 2: T25B, T25F, T25L, T89G, T153B, T153D, T153L, T153M, T153N, T153Q, T217B, 3: T23, T25B, T25N, T89B, T153B, 4: T86–T87, T89B, T153B, T153C, T153F, T209, T217B, 5: T25B, T89B, T153B, T153C, T153N, 6: T89B, T153A, T153B, T153J, T217B

Illustrators and photographers,
Alarcão, Renato, 2: T89Q
Andrews, Benny, 3: T153S
Auch, Herm, 1: T25Q
Auch, Mary Jane, 1: T25Q
Bishop, Nic, 2: T217Q
Carpenter, Nancy, 5: T89Q
Drummond, Allan, 6: T153S
Erwin, Steve, 1: T217Q
Gallagher, S. Saelig, 5: T25Q
Garth, Williams, 3: T25Q
Minor, Wendell, 2: T153Q
Nelson, Kadir, 3: T217U
Parra, John, 3: T89M
Pinkney, Jerry, 4: T153Q
Rodanas, Kristina, 6: T89O
Schanzer, Rosalyn, 5: T153Q
Spector, Joel, 6: T25M
Smith, Elwood, 4: T25M
Teague, Mark, 4: T89U
Whatley, Bruce, 2: T25O

Imagery, 6: T278–T279, T281B, T281C

Independent reading. *See* Reading independently.

Inferences, drawing, 1: S12–S14, S25, T25F, T153H, **2:** T25F, T25I, T153E, T153L, T217H, **3:** T25C, T25E, T25I, T25N, T153N, T217H, **4:** T25I, T25K, T89L, T217E, **5:** T25D, T25G, T25J, T89O, T153D, T153J, T217H, T217M, **6:** T25F, T89K

Inflectional endings. *See* Spelling: inflectional endings.

Information and Media Literacy. *See* Computer Literacy; Informational text; Media Literacy; Research and Inquiry; Technology.

Informational text. *See* Genre: informational text.

Integrate knowledge and ideas,
1: S35, T28–T29, T92–T93, T156–T157, T220–T221, T284–T285, 2: T28–T29, T92–T93, T156–T157, T220–T221, T284–T285, 3: T28–T29, T92–T93, T156–T157, T220–T221, T284–T285, 4: T28–T29, T92–T93, T156–T157, T220–T221, T284–T285, 5: T28–T29, T92–T93, T156–T157, T220–T221, T284–T285, 6: T28–T29, T92–T93, T156–T157, T220–T221, T284–T285

Internet. *See* Computer Literacy.

Interview, 1: S35, T28, **3:** T28, **4:** T183, **6:** T284

J

Journal writing. *See* Writer's Notebooks.

K

Key details. *See* Comprehension Skills: Main idea and key details.

L

Language arts, 1: T30–T39, T94–T103, T158–T167, T222–T231, T286–T295, **2:** T30–T39, T94–T103, T158–T167, T222–T231, T286–T295, **3:** T30–T39, T94–T103, T158–T167, T222–T231, T286–T295, **4:** T30–T39, T94–T103, T158–T167, T222–T231, T286–T295, **5:** T30–T39, T94–T103, T158–T167, T222–T231, T286–T295, **6:** T30–T39, T94–T103, T158–T167, T222–T231, T286–T295

Latin roots. *See under* Vocabulary: base words/root words.

Legend. *See under* Genre: fiction.

Lesson Plans, 1: T6–T7, T70–T71, T134–T135, T198–T199, T262–T263, T324–T325, **2:** T6–T7, T70–T71, T134–T135, T198–T199, T262–T263, T324–T325, **3:** T6–T7, T70–T71, T134–T135, T198–T199, T262–T263, T324–T325, **4:** T6–T7, T70–T71, T134–T135, T198–T199, T262–T263, T324–T325, **5:** T6–T7, T70–T71, T134–T135, T198–T199, T262–T263, T324–T325, **6:** T6–T7, T70–T71, T134–T135, T198–T199, T262–T263, T324–T325

Letters,
expository, 5: T344–T349
friendly, 1: T344–T349

Level Up, 1: T41, T49, T59, T105, T113, T123, T169, T177, T187, T233, T241, T251, T297, T305, T315, T336–T339, **2:** T41, T49, T59, T105, T113, T123, T169, T177, T187, T233, T241, T251, T297, T305, T315, T336–T339, **3:** T41, T49, T59, T105, T113, T123, T169, T177, T187, T233, T241, T251, T297, T305, T315, T336–T339, **4:** T41, T49, T59, T105, T113, T123, T169, T177, T187, T233, T241, T251, T297, T305, T315, T336–T339, **5:** T41, T49, T59, T105, T113, T123, T169, T177, T187, T233, T241, T251, T297, T305, T315, T336–T339, **6:** T41, T49, T59, T105, T113, T123, T169, T177, T187, T233, T241, T251, T297, T305, T315, T336–T339

Leveled Reader Lessons. *See under* Approaching Level Options; Beyond Level Options; English Language Learners; On Level Options.

Library or media center, using. *See under* Study skills. *See also* Theme projects.

Listening,
develop skills in speaking/listening,
1: S6, S20, T28, T92, T138, T156, T204–T205, T220, T268–T269, T284, 2: T28, T92, T138, T156, T204–T205, T220, T268–T269, T284, 3: T28, T92, T138, T156, T204–T205, T220, T268–T269, T284, 4: T28, T92, T138, T156, T204–T205, T220, T268–T269, T284, 5: T28, T92, T138, T156, T204–T205, T220, T268–T269, T284, 6: T28, T92, T138, T156, T204–T205, T220, T268–T269, T284

for a purpose, 1: T12–T13, T76–T77, T140–T141, T204–T205, T268–T269, 2: T12–T13, T76–T77, T140–T141, T204–T205, T268–T269, 3: T12–T13, T76–T77, T140–T141, T204–T205, T268–T269, 4: T12–T13, T76–T77, T140–T141, T204–T205, T268–T269, 5: T12–T13, T76–T77, T140–T141, T204–T205, T268–T269, 6: T12–T13, T76–T77, T140–T141, T204–T205, T268–T269

M

N

O

R

S

Key **4** = Unit 4

W

Common Core State Standards Correlations

English Language Arts

College and Career Readiness Anchor Standards for READING

The K-5 standards on the following pages define what students should understand and be able to do by the end of each grade. They correspond to the College and Career Readiness (CCR) anchor standards below by number. The CCR and grade-specific standards are necessary complements—the former providing broad standards, the latter providing additional specificity—that together define the skills and understandings that all students must demonstrate.

Key Ideas and Details

1. Read closely to determine what the text says explicitly and to make logical inferences from it; cite specific textual evidence when writing or speaking to support conclusions drawn from the text.

2. Determine central ideas or themes of a text and analyze their development; summarize the key supporting details and ideas.

3. Analyze how and why individuals, events, and ideas develop and interact over the course of a text.

Craft and Structure

4. Interpret words and phrases as they are used in a text, including determining technical, connotative, and figurative meanings, and analyze how specific word choices shape meaning or tone.

5. Analyze the structure of texts, including how specific sentences, paragraphs, and larger portions of the text (e.g., a section, chapter, scene, or stanza) relate to each other and the whole.

6. Assess how point of view or purpose shapes the content and style of a text.

Integration of Knowledge and Ideas

7. Integrate and evaluate content presented in diverse media and formats, including visually and quantitatively, as well as in words.

8. Delineate and evaluate the argument and specific claims in a text, including the validity of the reasoning as well as the relevance and sufficiency of the evidence.

9. Analyze how two or more texts address a number of similar themes or topics in order to build knowledge or to compare the approaches the authors take.

Range of Reading and Level of Text Complexity

10. Read and comprehend complex literary and informational texts independently and proficiently.

Common Core State Standards
English Language Arts

Grade 4

Each standard is coded in the following manner:

Strand	Grade Level	Standard
RL	4	1

Reading Standards for Literature

Key Ideas and Details		*McGraw-Hill Reading Wonders*
RL.4.1	Refer to details and examples in a text when explaining what the text says explicitly and when drawing inferences from the text.	**READING/WRITING WORKSHOP:** Unit 1: 26, 27, 40, 41 **Unit 2:** 98, 99, 112, 113 **Unit 3:** 170, 171, 184, 185 **Unit 4:** 256, 257, 270, 271 **Unit 5:** 314, 315, 328, 329 **Unit 6:** 386, 387, 400, 401 **YOUR TURN PRACTICE BOOK:** 3–4, 53–54, 103–104, 153–154, 203–204, 253–254 **READING WORKSTATION ACTIVITY CARDS:** 12 **TEACHER'S EDITION: Unit 1:** T25B, T25F, T25L, T25P, T80, T82 **Unit 2:** T18, T25F, T25I, T25J, T25L, T25P **Unit 3:** T25L, T25O, T25P, T25R, T81, T82, T89D **Unit 4:** T76, T80, T82, T89B, T89D, T89G, T89L, T89S **Unit 5:** T89B, T89H, T89K, T89O, T217V, T217W **Unit 6:** T18, T25F, T25K, T82, T89K, T278 www.connected.mcgraw-hill.com: **RESOURCES** **Student Resources:** Comprehension Interactive Games and Activities **Teacher Resources:** Interactive Read Aloud Images
RL.4.2	Determine a theme of a story, drama, or poem from details in the text; summarize the text.	**READING/WRITING WORKSHOP: Unit 2:** 94–97, 99, 108–111, 113 **Unit 4:** 294–297, 299 **Unit 6:** 382–385, 387, 438–441, 443 **LITERATURE ANTHOLOGY: Unit 2:** 90–105, 108–125, 172–175 **Unit 4:** 356–359, 360–361 **Unit 6:** 458–471, 534–537, 538–539 **LEVELED READERS: Unit 2, Week 1:** *The Cockroach and the Mouse* (A), *The Badger and the Fan* (O, ELL), *The Wings of the Butterfly* (B) **Unit 2, Week 2:** *Saving the Green Bird* (A), *The Prince Who Could Fly* (O, ELL), *Behind the Secret Trapdoor* (B) **Unit 6, Week 1:** *The Visit* (A), *Our Teacher, the Hero* (O, ELL), *Continuing On* (B) **YOUR TURN PRACTICE BOOK:** 53–55, 63–65, 253–255 **READING WORKSTATION ACTIVITY CARDS:** 4 **TEACHER'S EDITION: Unit 1:** T25R, T51, T76, T84, T89L **Unit 2:** T12, T20, T25C, T25H, T25K, T25M, T25P, T28, T46, T47, T51, T55, T76, T84, T89C, T89F, T89I, T89M, T89O, T89R, T110, T111, T115, T119 **Unit 3:** T12, T25R, T76 **Unit 4:** T76, T89Q, T276, T281B, T303, T307 **Unit 5:** T12, T16, T20, T25O, T25R **Unit 6:** T20, T25D, T25H, T276, T281C, T303, T307 www.connected.mcgraw-hill.com: **RESOURCES** **Student Resources:** Comprehension Interactive Games and Activities **Teacher Resources:** Graphic Organizers, Interactive Read Aloud Images, Skills Review

Reading Standards for Literature

Key Ideas and Details	*McGraw-Hill Reading Wonders*
RL.4.3 Describe in depth a character, setting, or event in a story or drama, drawing on specific details in the text (e.g., a character's thoughts, words, or actions).	**READING/WRITING WORKSHOP:** Unit 1: 22–25, 27, 36–39, 41 **Unit 5:** 310–313, 315, 324–327, 329 **LITERATURE ANTHOLOGY:** Unit 1: 10–27, 32–43 **Unit 5:** 362–379, 384–401 **LEVELED READERS:** Unit 1, Week 1: *Clever Puss* (A), *Jack and the Extreme Stalk* (O, ELL), *Charming Ella* (B) **Unit 1, Week 2:** *The Dream Team* (A), *Rosa's Garden* (O, ELL), *Saving Grasshopper* (B) **Unit 5, Week 1:** *Saving Stolen Treasure* (A), *The Perfect Present* (O, ELL), *First Edition* (B) **Unit 5, Week 2:** *The Adventures of Sal Fink* (A), *The Great Man of Nebraska* (O, ELL), *The Tale of John Henry* (B) **YOUR TURN PRACTICE BOOK:** 2–5, 13–15, 23–25, 203–205, 213–215 **READING WORKSTATION ACTIVITY CARDS:** 1, 2, 3 **TEACHER'S EDITION:** Unit 1: T12, T20, T25I, T25M, T25O, T25R, T46, T47, T51, T55, T76, T81, T84, T85, T89A, T89C, T89E, T89G, T89I, T104, T110, T111, T112, T115, T116 **Unit 2:** T28, T89D, T89H, T89J, T92 **Unit 3:** T12, T18, T82, T86 **Unit 4:** T89M, T89O **Unit 5:** T12, T18, T20, T25C, T25F, T25G, T25H, T25I, T25J, T25K, T25N, T76, T80, T82, T84, T89C, T89F, T89G, T89H, T89I, T89K, T89N, T89O **Unit 6:** T12, T76 www.connected.mcgraw-hill.com: **RESOURCES** **Student Resources:** Comprehension Interactive Games and Activities **Teacher Resources:** Graphic Organizers, Skills Review

Craft and Structure	*McGraw-Hill Reading Wonders*
RL.4.4 Determine the meaning of words and phrases as they are used in a text, including those that allude to significant characters found in mythology (e.g., Herculean).	**READING/WRITING WORKSHOP:** Unit 1: 22–25 **Unit 2:** 94–97 **Unit 5:** 324–327 **READING WORKSTATION ACTIVITY CARDS:** 13 **TEACHER'S EDITION:** Unit 1: T24, T25E, T25N, T25R, T88, T89F, T120, T145 **Unit 3:** T24, T25E, T25G, T25I, T25R, T81, T88, T89E, T89N **Unit 4:** T88, T89C, T89H, T89P, T89V, T145, T217R **Unit 5:** T25U, T88, T89E, T89J, T89K, T217W **Unit 6:** T25C, T88, T89K, T154, T171 www.connected.mcgraw-hill.com: **RESOURCES** **Student Resources:** Comprehension Interactive Games and Activities, Vocabulary Interactive Games and Activities **Teacher Resources:** Graphic Organizers
RL.4.5 Explain major differences between poems, drama, and prose, and refer to the structural elements of poems (e.g., verse, rhythm, meter) and drama (e.g., casts of characters, settings, descriptions, dialogue, stage directions) when writing or speaking about a text.	**READING/WRITING WORKSHOP:** Unit 1: 42 **Unit 2:** 114, 154 **Unit 4:** 298 **Unit 6:** 442 **LITERATURE ANTHOLOGY:** Unit 2: 108–125, 172–175, 176–177 **Unit 4:** 356–359 **LEVELED READERS:** Unit 2, Week 2: *Saving the Green Bird* (A), *The Prince Who Could Fly* (O, ELL), *Behind the Secret Trapdoor* (B) **YOUR TURN PRACTICE BOOK:** 6, 16, 63–65 **READING WORKSTATION ACTIVITY CARDS:** 25, 27, 28 **TEACHER'S EDITION:** Unit 1: T25J, T25T, T86 **Unit 2:** T12, T22, T76, T81, T82, T86, T89C, T89I, T89T, T89U, T89V, T268, T274, T278, T281C **Unit 3:** T22, T25D, T86 **Unit 4:** T76, T140, T150, T274, T278, T281A, T281C, T281E **Unit 5:** T22, T76 **Unit 6:** T268, T274, T281B www.connected.mcgraw-hill.com: **RESOURCES** **Student Resources:** Comprehension Interactive Games and Activities **Teacher Resources:** Genre Study Reproducibles, Graphic Organizers
RL.4.6 Compare and contrast the point of view from which different stories are narrated, including the difference between first- and third-person narrations.	**READING/WRITING WORKSHOP:** Unit 2: 150–153, 155 **Unit 3:** 166–169, 171, 180–183, 185 **Unit 4:** 252–255, 257, 266–269, 271 **LITERATURE ANTHOLOGY:** Unit 3: 178–195, 198–211 **Unit 4:** 288–309, 314–331 **LEVELED READERS:** Unit 3, Week 1: *A New Bear in the Forest* (A), *Not From Around Here* (O, ELL), *Cara and the Sky Kingdom* (B) **Unit 3, Week 2:** *Playground Buddy* (A), *Brick by Brick* (O, ELL), *Standing Guard* (B) **Unit 4, Week 2:** *Floozle Dreams* (A), *The Wolves of Yellowstone* (O, ELL), *Krillville* (B) **Unit 4, Week 3:** *Ron's Radio* (A), *The Freedom Machine* (O, ELL), *A Better Way* (B) **YOUR TURN PRACTICE BOOK:** 103–105, 113–115, 163–165, 183–185 **READING WORKSTATION ACTIVITY CARDS:** 5 **TEACHER'S EDITION:** Unit 1: T89K **Unit 2:** T276, T281E, T281F **Unit 3:** T20, T29, T47, T51, T55, T84, T89N **Unit 4:** T84, T89O, T89R, T89U, T89V, T111, T115, T119, T148, T174, T175, T179, T183 www.connected.mcgraw-hill.com: **RESOURCES** **Student Resources:** Comprehension Interactive Games and Activities

Reading Standards for Literature

Integration of Knowledge and Ideas		*McGraw-Hill Reading Wonders*
RL.4.7	Make connections between the text of a story or drama and a visual or oral presentation of the text, identifying where each version reflects specific descriptions and directions in the text.	**YOUR TURN PRACTICE BOOK:** 6, 106, 166 **READING WORKSTATION ACTIVITY CARDS:** 14 **TEACHER'S EDITION: Unit 1:** T22, T25B, T40, T58, T89D **Unit 2:** T25B, T25G, T89G, T89Q **Unit 3:** T22, T23, T25N, T89B **Unit 4:** T86, T89B, T89F, T89U, T153B, T153C, T153F **Unit 5:** T89C, T89E **Unit 6:** T89B **www.connected.mcgraw-hill.com: RESOURCES** **Student Resources:** Comprehension Interactive Games and Activities, Music/Fine Arts Activities **Teacher Resources:** Interactive Read Aloud Images, Music/Fine Arts Activities
RL.4.8	(Not applicable to literature)	(Not applicable to literature)
RL.4.9	Compare and contrast the treatment of similar themes and topics (e.g., opposition of good and evil) and patterns of events (e.g., the quest) in stories, myths, and traditional literature from different cultures.	**LITERATURE ANTHOLOGY: Unit 4:** 352–355 **READING WORKSTATION ACTIVITY CARDS:** 15 **TEACHER'S EDITION: Unit 1:** T25T, T25V, T29, T93 **Unit 2:** T17, T20, T25R, T29, T55, T74, T89V, T93, T217S, T217T **Unit 3:** T17, T25S, T25T, T29 **Unit 4:** T93, T157, T217T **Unit 5:** T25T, T25V, T29, T93, T217X **Unit 6:** T29, T153X, T281F, T217N **www.connected.mcgraw-hill.com: RESOURCES** **Student Resources:** Comprehension Interactive Games and Activities

Range of Reading and Level of Text Complexity		*McGraw-Hill Reading Wonders*
RL.4.10	By the end of the year, read and comprehend literature, including stories, dramas, and poetry, in the grades 4–5 text complexity band proficiently, with scaffolding as needed at the high end of the range.	**READING/WRITING WORKSHOP:** These units reflect the range of text complexity found throughout the book. **Unit 2:** 108–111, 150–153 **Unit 6:** 438–441 **LITERATURE ANTHOLOGY:** These units reflect the range of text complexity found throughout the book. **Unit 2:** 90–95, 108–125, 172–175 **Unit 4:** 288–309, 314–331, 356–359 **Unit 5:** 362–367, 406–423 **Unit 6:** 534–537 **LEVELED READERS: Unit 2, Week 2:** *Saving the Green Bird* (A), *The Prince Who Could Fly* (O, ELL), *Behind the Secret Trapdoor* (B) **Unit 3, Week 1:** *A New Bear in the Forest* (A), *Not From Around Here* (O, ELL), *Cara and the Sky Kingdom* (B) **Unit 4, Week 3:** *Ron's Radio* (A), *The Freedom Machine* (O, ELL), *A Better Way* (B) **Unit 6, Week 1:** *The Visit* (A), *Our Teacher, the Hero* (O, ELL), *Continuing On* (B) **READING WORKSTATION ACTIVITY CARDS:** 22, 25, 27, 28 **TEACHER'S EDITION: Unit 1:** T22, T25A, T25S, T47, T51, T55, T86 **Unit 2:** T47, T51, T55, T86, T89A, T89S, T120, T274, T281A, T281E **Unit 3:** T51, T86, T89A, T111, T115, T119 **Unit 4:** T153A, T175, T179, T183, T217Q, T274, T281A, T281E **Unit 5:** T16, T22, T25A, T25S, T80, T86, T89A, T217U **Unit 6:** T22, T25A, T86, T89A, T153U, T217M, T274, T281A, T281E **www.connected.mcgraw-hill.com: RESOURCES** **Student Resources:** Comprehension Interactive Games and Activities

Reading Standards for Informational Text

Key Ideas and Details		*McGraw-Hill Reading Wonders*
RI.4.1	Refer to details and examples in a text when explaining what the text says explicitly and when drawing inferences from the text.	**READING/WRITING WORKSHOP: Unit 1:** 54, 55, 68, 69, 82, 83 **Unit 2:** 126, 127, 140, 141 **Unit 3:** 198, 199, 212, 213, 226, 227 **Unit 4:** 242, 243, 284, 285 **Unit 5:** 342, 343, 356, 357, 370, 371 **Unit 6:** 414, 415, 428, 429 **LEVELED READERS: Unit 3, Week 3:** *Jacob Riis: Champion of the Poor* (A, O, ELL, B) **YOUR TURN PRACTICE BOOK:** 123–125 **READING WORKSTATION ACTIVITY CARDS:** 12 **TEACHER'S EDITION: Unit 1:** T890, T144, T146, T153F, T153H, T153J **Unit 2:** T153R, T153U, T217H, T217R **Unit 3:** T204, T209, T212, T217H, T217V **Unit 4:** T12, T18, T25F, T25H, T25I, T25N, T25P, T25Q, T89X, T89Y **Unit 5:** T89T, T89U, T153B, T153D, T153G, T153J, T153T **Unit 6:** T153D, T153G, T153P, T217C, T217H www.connected.mcgraw-hill.com: **RESOURCES** **Student Resources:** Comprehension Interactive Games and Activities **Teacher Resources:** Interactive Read Aloud Images
RI.4.2	Determine the main idea of a text and explain how it is supported by key details; summarize the text.	**READING/WRITING WORKSHOP: Unit 1:** 78–81, 83 **Unit 2:** 122–125, 127, 136–139, 141 **Unit 6:** 396–399, 401, 410–413, 415, 424–427, 429 **LITERATURE ANTHOLOGY: Unit 1:** 84–87 **Unit 2:** 130–147, 152–169 **Unit 6:** 476–491, 496–515, 520–531 **LEVELED READERS: Unit 2, Week 3:** *Saving San Francisco Bay* (A, O, ELL, B) **Unit 2, Week 4:** *Extreme Animals* (A, O, ELL, B) **Unit 6, Week 3:** *Planet Power* (A, O, ELL, B) **Unit 6, Week 4:** *The Bike Company* (A, O, ELL, B) **YOUR TURN PRACTICE BOOK:** 73–75, 83–85, 273–275, 283–285 **READING WORKSTATION ACTIVITY CARDS:** 6 **TEACHER'S EDITION: Unit 1:** T140, T148, T153L **Unit 2:** T140, T146, T148, T153C, T153D, T153F, T153G, T153H, T153J, T153K, T153N, T153O, T153P, T208, T210, T212, T217C, T217D, T217E, T217G, T217I, T217J, T217K, T217L, T217N, T217M, T217O **Unit 3:** T140, T153R **Unit 4:** T25J, T25L **Unit 5:** T140, T144, T153E, T153J, T153K, T153R **Unit 6:** T148, T153C, T153E, T153I, T153L www.connected.mcgraw-hill.com: **RESOURCES** **Student Resources:** Comprehension Interactive Games and Activities **Teacher Resources:** Graphic Organizers, Interactive Read Aloud Images, Skills Review
RI.4.3	Explain events, procedures, ideas, or concepts in a historical, scientific, or technical text, including what happened and why, based on specific information in the text.	**READING/WRITING WORKSHOP: Unit 4:** 238–241, 243, 280–283, 285 **Unit 5:** 338–341, 343, 352–355, 357 **LITERATURE ANTHOLOGY: Unit 4:** 270–283, 336–351 **Unit 5:** 428–447 **LEVELED READERS: Unit 4, Week 1:** *A Day in the Senate* (A, O, ELL, B) **Unit 4, Week 4:** *Stargazing* (A, O, ELL, B) **Unit 5, Week 4:** *Secrets of the Ice* (A, O, ELL, B) **YOUR TURN PRACTICE BOOK:** 153–155, 183–185, 233–235 **READING WORKSTATION ACTIVITY CARDS:** 7, 8, 9, 10, 17 **TEACHER'S EDITION: Unit 1:** T217E, T217G **Unit 2:** T212, T217I, T217K **Unit 3:** T146, T153C, T210, T217C, T217K **Unit 4:** T18, T204, T212, T217E, T217F, T217G, T217H, T217J, T217K, T217L **Unit 5:** T146, T148, T153F, T153H, T153M, T153U, T210, T212, T217C, T217F, T217I, T217K, T217Q **Unit 6:** T140, T146, T210 www.connected.mcgraw-hill.com: **RESOURCES** **Student Resources:** Comprehension Interactive Games and Activities **Teacher Resources:** Graphic Organizers, Skills Review
Craft and Structure		*McGraw-Hill Reading Wonders*
RI.4.4	Determine the meaning of general academic and domain-specific words or phrases in a text relevant to a grade 4 topic or subject area.	**READING/WRITING WORKSHOP: Unit 1:** 50–53, 64–67 **Unit 2:** 122–125, 136–139 **Unit 4:** 280–283 **Unit 5:** 338–341 **Unit 6:** 410–413, 424–427 **READING WORKSTATION ACTIVITY CARDS:** 21 **TEACHER'S EDITION: Unit 1:** T152, T153E, T216, T217H, T280 **Unit 2:** T152, T153I, T153O, T216, T217N **Unit 4:** T216, T217E, T217P **Unit 5:** T152, T153G, T153I, T153K, T216, T217H, T217I **Unit 6:** T152, T153G, T153K, T217E www.connected.mcgraw-hill.com: **RESOURCES** **Student Resources:** Comprehension Interactive Games and Activities, Vocabulary Interactive Games and Activities **Teacher Resources:** Graphic Organizers

Reading Standards for Informational Text

Craft and Structure		McGraw-Hill Reading Wonders
RI.4.5	Describe the overall structure (e.g., chronology, comparison, cause/effect, problem/solution) of events, ideas, concepts, or information in a text or part of a text.	**READING/WRITING WORKSHOP:** Unit 1: 50–53, 55, 64–67, 69 **Unit 5:** 338–341, 343, 366–369, 371 **LITERATURE ANTHOLOGY:** Unit 1: 48–59, 62–79 **Unit 5:** 406–423, 452–455 **LEVELED READERS:** Unit 1, Week 3: *Changing Landscapes* (A, O, ELL, B) **Unit 1, Week 4:** *George's Giant Wheel* (A, O, ELL, B) **Unit 5, Week 3:** *The Inventive Lewis Latimer* (A, O, ELL, B) **YOUR TURN PRACTICE BOOK:** 23–25, 33–35, 223–225 **READING WORKSTATION ACTIVITY CARDS:** 7, 8, 9, 10 **TEACHER'S EDITION:** Unit 1: T148, T153C, T153G, T153I, T174, T175, T179, T183, T212, T217E, T217G, T217I, T217K, T217L, T217O **Unit 2:** T153E, T153M **Unit 3:** T153M **Unit 4:** T20, T25C, T212, T217F, T217H, T217J **Unit 5:** T148, T153F, T153H, T153M, T212, T217C, T217E, T217F, T217G, T217I, T217K, T217L, T217Q www.connected.mcgraw-hill.com: **RESOURCES** **Student Resources:** Comprehension Interactive Games and Activities **Teacher Resources:** Graphic Organizers, Skills Review
RI.4.6	Compare and contrast a firsthand and secondhand account of the same event or topic; describe the differences in focus and the information provided.	**LITERATURE ANTHOLOGY:** Unit 3: 216–235 **LEVELED READERS:** Unit 3, Week 3: *Jacob Riis: Champion of the Poor* (A, O, ELL, B) **YOUR TURN PRACTICE BOOK:** 123–125 **READING WORKSTATION ACTIVITY CARDS:** 11, 18 **TEACHER'S EDITION:** Unit 1: T153D **Unit 3:** T153V, T153W, T153X, T174, T217C, T217F, T217I, T217O, T217R www.connected.mcgraw-hill.com: **RESOURCES** **Student Resources:** Comprehension Interactive Games and Activities

Integration of Knowledge and Ideas		McGraw-Hill Reading Wonders
RI.4.7	Interpret information presented visually, orally, or quantitatively (e.g., in charts, graphs, diagrams, time lines, animations, or interactive elements on Web pages) and explain how the information contributes to an understanding of the text in which it appears.	**READING/WRITING WORKSHOP:** Unit 1: 50–53, 64–67, 78–81 **Unit 2:** 122–125, 136–139 **Unit 3:** 194–197, 208–211, 222–225 **Unit 4:** 280–283 **Unit 5:** 338–341, 352–355, 366–369 **Unit 6:** 410–413 **LITERATURE ANTHOLOGY:** Unit 1: 48–59, 84–87, 88–89 **Unit 2:** 148–151, 152–169 Unit 3: 212–215, 236–239, 264–267 **Unit 4:** 284–287, 310–313, 336–351 **Unit 5:** 402–405, 424–427, 428–447, 452–455, 456–457 **Unit 6:** 472–475, 492–495, 496–515, 520–531 **LEVELED READERS:** Unit 1, Week 3: *Changing Landscapes* (A, O, ELL, B) **Unit 4, Week 1:** *A Day in the Senate* (A, O, ELL, B) **Unit 5, Week 4:** *Secrets of the Ice* (A, O, ELL, B) **Unit 6, Week 3:** *Planet Power* (A, O, ELL, B) **YOUR TURN PRACTICE BOOK:** 23–25, 153–155, 233–235, 273–275 **READING WORKSTATION ACTIVITY CARDS:** 16, 23 **TEACHER'S EDITION:** Unit 1: T10, T74, T138, T150, T151, T153B, T328–T329 **Unit 2:** T153B, T157, T202, T214, T217B, T328–T329 **Unit 3:** T10, T74, T138, T150, T153J, T328–T329 **Unit 4:** T217B, T217D, T217M, T217O, T328–T329 **Unit 5:** T150, T153B, T153C, T153N, T153Q, T153U, T328–T329 **Unit 6:** T10, T74, T138, T153J, T217B, T266 www.connected.mcgraw-hill.com: **RESOURCES** **Student Resources:** Comprehension Interactive Games and Activities, Music/Fine Arts Activities **Teacher Resources:** Graphic Organizers, Interactive Read Aloud Images, Music/Fine Arts Activities
RI.4.8	Explain how an author uses reasons and evidence to support particular points in a text.	**READING/WRITING WORKSHOP:** Unit 3: 194–197, 199, 208–211, 213, 222–225, 227 **LITERATURE ANTHOLOGY:** Unit 3: 240–261, 264–267 **LEVELED READERS:** Unit 3, Week 4: *Nellie Bly: Reporter for the Underdog* (A, O, ELL, B) **YOUR TURN PRACTICE BOOK:** 133–135 **READING WORKSTATION ACTIVITY CARDS:** 11, 19 **TEACHER'S EDITION:** Unit 2: T153K, T153R **Unit 3:** T148, T153C, T153E, T153G, T153I, T153K, T153O, T153Q, T157, T174, T175, T179, T183, T212, T214, T217C, T217E, T217G, T217J, T217K, T217Q, T217R, T239, T243, T247 **Unit 4:** T17, T22, T208 **Unit 5:** T145, T153R www.connected.mcgraw-hill.com: **RESOURCES** **Student Resources:** Comprehension Interactive Games and Activities **Teacher Resources:** Graphic Organizers, Skills Review

Reading Standards for Informational Text

Integration of Knowledge and Ideas	McGraw-Hill Reading Wonders
RI.4.9 Integrate information from two texts on the same topic in order to write or speak about the subject knowledgeably.	**READING WORKSTATION ACTIVITY CARDS:** 20 **TEACHER'S EDITION: Unit 1:** T89P, T105, T113, T117, T123, T153M, T153N, T157, T217V, T221 **Unit 2:** T153T, T153V, T157, T209, T221 **Unit 3:** T89P, T89R, T93, T153V, T153X, T157, T217W, T217X, T221 **Unit 4:** T25P, T25R, T29, T89X, T89Z, T153T, T153V, T221 **Unit 5:** T89T, T89V, T153T, T153V, T157, T221 **Unit 6:** T25R, T89T, T157, T221 www.connected.mcgraw-hill.com: **RESOURCES** **Student Resources:** Comprehension Interactive Games and Activities

Range of Reading and Level of Text Complexity	McGraw-Hill Reading Wonders
RI.4.10 By the end of year, read and comprehend informational texts, including history/social studies, science, and technical texts, in the grades 4–5 text complexity band proficiently, with scaffolding as needed at the high end of the range.	**READING/WRITING WORKSHOP:** These units reflect the range of text complexity found throughout the book. **Unit 1:** 40–53 **Unit 2:** 136–139 **Unit 3:** 194–197 **Unit 4:** 280–283 **Unit 5:** 338–341 **Unit 6:** 410–413 **LITERATURE ANTHOLOGY:** These units reflect the range of text complexity found throughout the book. **Unit 1:** 48–59 **Unit 2:** 152–169 **Unit 3:** 216–235 **Unit 4:** 270–283 **Unit 5:** 406–423 **Unit 6:** 520–531 **LEVELED READERS: Unit 2, Week 4:** *Extreme Animals* (A, O, ELL, B) **Unit 3, Week 4:** *Nellie Bly: Reporter for the Underdog* (A, O, ELL, B) **Unit 4, Week 1:** *A Day in the Senate* (A, O, ELL, B) **Unit 6, Week 4:** *The Bike Company* (A, O, ELL, B) **READING WORKSTATION ACTIVITY CARDS:** 22, 26 **TEACHER'S EDITION: Unit 1:** T89M, T150, T153A, T153M, T214, T217A, T278, T281A, T281E **Unit 2:** T150, T153A, T153S, T175, T179, T183, T214, T217A **Unit 3:** T890, T150, T153A, T153U, T175, T179, T214, T217A, T217W, T248, T278, T281A, T281E **Unit 4:** T22, T25A, T250, T47, T51, T55, T89W, T153S, T208, T214, T217A **Unit 5:** T153A, T153S, T208, T214, T217A, T278, T281A, T281E **Unit 6:** T250, T89Q, T150, T153A, T214, T217A www.connected.mcgraw-hill.com: **RESOURCES** **Student Resources:** Comprehension Interactive Games and Activities

Reading Standards: Foundational Skills

There are no standards for Print Concepts (1) or Phonological Awareness (2) in Foundational Skills for Grade 4.

Phonics and Word Recognition	*McGraw-Hill Reading Wonders*
RF.4.3	Know and apply grade-level phonics and word analysis skills in decoding words.

| **RF.4.3a** | Use combined knowledge of all letter-sound correspondences, syllabication patterns, and morphology (e.g., roots and affixes) to read accurately unfamiliar multisyllabic words in context and out of context. | **READING/WRITING WORKSHOP:** Unit 1: 85 Unit 2: 143
 YOUR TURN PRACTICE BOOK: 8, 18, 28, 38, 47, 48, 78, 87, 88, 108, 148, 168, 198, 208, 228, 258, 268, 298
 PHONICS/WORD STUDY WORKSTATION ACTIVITY CARDS: 5, 8, 16, 18, 23, 27, 30
 TEACHER'S EDITION: Unit 1: T26, T27, T42, T43, T90, T91 Unit 2: T43, T90, T106, T107, T154, T155, T170, T171 Unit 3: T217L, T218, T219, T234, T235 Unit 4: T107, T154, T155, T170, T171, T218, T219 Unit 5: T27, T90, T91, T152, T153G, T154, T155, T218 Unit 6: T26, T42, T43, T90, T106, T282

 www.connected.mcgraw-hill.com: **RESOURCES**
 Student Resources: Word Study Interactive Games and Activities
 Teacher Resources: Decodable Passages |

Fluency	*McGraw-Hill Reading Wonders*
RF.4.4	Read with sufficient accuracy and fluency to support comprehension.

| **RF.4.4a** | Read on-level text with purpose and understanding. | **READING WORKSTATION ACTIVITY CARDS:** 2, 7, 10, 14, 18, 22, 27, 29, 30
 TEACHER'S EDITION: Unit 1: T44, T108, T172, T236, T326–T327 Unit 2: T44, T91, T108, T172, T236, T326–T327 Unit 3: T27, T44, T108, T172, T219, T236, T326–T327 Unit 4: T27, T44, T108, T155, T172, T236, T326–T327 Unit 5: T27, T91, T326–T327 Unit 6: T26, T44, T90, T108, T326–T327

 www.connected.mcgraw-hill.com: **RESOURCES**
 Student Resources: Fluency Interactive Games and Activities |

| **RF.4.4b** | Read on-level prose and poetry orally with accuracy, appropriate rate, and expression on successive readings. | **READING WORKSTATION ACTIVITY CARDS:** 3, 8, 12, 13, 15, 20, 26, 28, 29, 30
 YOUR TURN PRACTICE BOOK: 3–5, 63–65, 133–135, 173–175, 213–215, 263–265
 TEACHER'S EDITION: Unit 1: T27, T46, T91, T105, T110, T113, T117, T123, T219, T238, T326–T327 Unit 2: T27, T46, T91, T110, T155, T174, T219, T238, T282, T302, T326–T327 Unit 3: T27, T46, T91, T110, T155, T174, T219, T238, T326–T327 Unit 4: T27, T46, T91, T110, T155, T174, T218, T238, T282, T302, T326–T327 Unit 5: T27, T155, T219, T326–T327 Unit 6: T26, T41, T90, T282, T302, T326–T327

 www.connected.mcgraw-hill.com: **RESOURCES**
 Student Resources: Fluency Interactive Games and Activities |

| **RF.4.4c** | Use context to confirm or self-correct word recognition and understanding, rereading as necessary. | **READING/WRITING WORKSHOP:** Unit 1: 29, 57, 71 Unit 2: 115, 129 Unit 3: 173, 187 Unit 4: 273, 287 Unit 5: 359
 YOUR TURN PRACTICE BOOK: 7, 27, 37, 67, 77, 107, 117, 177, 187, 237
 READING WORKSTATION ACTIVITY CARDS: 3, 8, 13, 18, 23, 28
 TEACHER'S EDITION: Unit 1: T155, T174 Unit 2: T155, T174 Unit 3: T155, T174 Unit 4: T218, T238 Unit 5: T155, T174 Unit 6: T46, T218, T238

 www.connected.mcgraw-hill.com: **RESOURCES**
 Student Resources: Fluency Interactive Games and Activities |

College and Career Readiness Anchor Standards for WRITING

The K-5 standards on the following pages define what students should understand and be able to do by the end of each grade. They correspond to the College and Career Readiness (CCR) anchor standards below by number. The CCR and grade-specific standards are necessary complements—the former providing broad standards, the latter providing additional specificity—that together define the skills and understandings that all students must demonstrate.

Text Types and Purposes

1. Write arguments to support claims in an analysis of substantive topics or texts, using valid reasoning and relevant and sufficient evidence.

2. Write informative/explanatory texts to examine and convey complex ideas and information clearly and accurately through the effective selection, organization, and analysis of content.

3. Write narratives to develop real or imagined experiences or events using effective techniques, well-chosen details, and well-structured event sequences.

Production and Distribution of Writing

4. Produce clear and coherent writing in which the development, organization, and style are appropriate to task, purpose, and audience.

5. Develop and strengthen writing as needed by planning, revising, editing, rewriting, or trying a new approach.

6. Use technology, including the Internet, to produce and publish writing and to interact and collaborate with others.

Research to Build and Present Knowledge

7. Conduct short as well as more sustained research projects based on focused questions, demonstrating understanding of the subject under investigation.

8. Gather relevant information from multiple print and digital sources, assess the credibility and accuracy of each source, and integrate information while avoiding plagiarism.

9. Draw evidence from literacy or informational texts to support analysis, reflection, and research.

Range of Writing

10. Write routinely over extended time frames (time for research, reflection, and revision) and shorter time frames (a single sitting or a day or two) for a range of tasks, purposes, and audiences.

CCSS Common Core State Standards
English Language Arts
Grade 4

Each standard is coded in the following manner:

Strand	Grade Level	Standard
W	4	1

Writing Standards

Text Types and Purposes	*McGraw-Hill Reading Wonders*
W.4.1	Write opinion pieces on topics or texts, supporting a point of view with reasons and information.
W.4.1a Introduce a topic or text clearly, state an opinion, and create an organizational structure in which related ideas are grouped to support the writer's purpose.	**READING/WRITING WORKSHOP:** Unit 3: 230–231 Unit 5: 318–319 **YOUR TURN PRACTICE BOOK:** 150, 210 **WRITING WORKSTATION ACTIVITY CARDS:** 3, 7 **TEACHER'S EDITION:** Unit 3: T344, T346, T350, T352 Unit 4: T30, T32–T33 Unit 5: T30, T32, T33, T62 Unit 6: T344, T346, T350, T352 www.connected.mcgraw-hill.com: **RESOURCES** **Student Resources:** Writer's Workspace
W.4.1b Provide reasons that are supported by facts and details.	**READING/WRITING WORKSHOP:** Unit 3: 202–203 **YOUR TURN PRACTICE BOOK:** 30, 130 **WRITING WORKSTATION ACTIVITY CARDS:** 3, 9, 23, 26 **TEACHER'S EDITION:** Unit 1: T93 Unit 2: T29, T93, T221 Unit 3: T93, T158, T160–T161, T190, T344, T352 Unit 6: T93, T344, T346, T350, T352 www.connected.mcgraw-hill.com: **RESOURCES** **Student Resources:** Writer's Workspace
W.4.1c Link opinion and reasons using words and phrases (e.g., *for instance, in order to, in addition*).	**READING/WRITING WORKSHOP:** Unit 5: 346–347 Unit 6: 418–419 **YOUR TURN PRACTICE BOOK:** 230, 280 **WRITING WORKSTATION ACTIVITY CARDS:** 13 **TEACHER'S EDITION:** Unit 3: T350, T352 Unit 5: T93, T95, T96, T97, T158 Unit 6: T158, T160, T161, T350, T352 www.connected.mcgraw-hill.com: **RESOURCES** **Student Resources:** Writer's Workspace
W.4.1d Provide a concluding statement or section related to the opinion presented.	**READING/WRITING WORKSHOP:** Unit 3: 216–217 **WRITING WORKSTATION ACTIVITY CARDS:** 10 **TEACHER'S EDITION:** Unit 3: T222, T224–T225, T346, T350 Unit 6: T346 www.connected.mcgraw-hill.com: **RESOURCES** **Student Resources:** Writer's Workspace
W.4.2	Write informative/explanatory texts to examine a topic and convey ideas and information clearly.
W.4.2a Introduce a topic clearly and group related information in paragraphs and sections; include formatting (e.g., headings), illustrations, and multimedia when useful to aiding comprehension.	**READING/WRITING WORKSHOP:** Unit 2: 144–145 Unit 4: 246–247 **YOUR TURN PRACTICE BOOK:** 90, 160 **WRITING WORKSTATION ACTIVITY CARDS:** 6, 11 **TEACHER'S EDITION:** Unit 2: T157, T222, T224–T225, T346, T348, T350, T352, T354 Unit 4: T30, T32–T33, T62, T221 Unit 5: T221, T348 www.connected.mcgraw-hill.com: **RESOURCES** **Student Resources:** Writer's Workspace

Writing Standards

Text Types and Purposes		*McGraw-Hill Reading Wonders*
W.4.2b	Develop the topic with facts, definitions, concrete details, quotations, or other information and examples related to the topic.	**READING/WRITING WORKSHOP:** Unit 1: 58–59 Unit 2: 130–131 Unit 3: 202–203 **YOUR TURN PRACTICE BOOK:** 30, 80, 160 **WRITING WORKSTATION ACTIVITY CARDS:** 6, 11 **TEACHER'S EDITION:** Unit 1: T29, T158, T160–T161, T190 Unit 2: T158, T161, T160, T190, T344, T352 Unit 5: T346 www.connected.mcgraw-hill.com: **RESOURCES** **Student Resources:** Writer's Workspace
W.4.2c	Link ideas within categories of information using words and phrases (e.g., *another, for example, also, because*).	**READING/WRITING WORKSHOP:** Unit 6: 418–419 **YOUR TURN PRACTICE BOOK:** 280 **WRITING WORKSTATION ACTIVITY CARDS:** 6, 19 **TEACHER'S EDITION:** Unit 1: T157 Unit 2: T344, T350 Unit 5: T158, T160–T161, T190, T344, T350, T352 Unit 6: T94, T96–T97 www.connected.mcgraw-hill.com: **RESOURCES** **Student Resources:** Writer's Workspace
W.4.2d	Use precise language and domain-specific vocabulary to inform about or explain the topic.	**READING/WRITING WORKSHOP:** Unit 2: 158–159 Unit 6: 390–391 **YOUR TURN PRACTICE BOOK:** 100, 260 **WRITING WORKSTATION ACTIVITY CARDS:** 1, 14, 15, 18, 27 **TEACHER'S EDITION:** Unit 1: T156 Unit 2: T286, T288, T346 Unit 4: T222, T224–T225 Unit 5: T222, T224–T225, T344 Unit 6: T222, T224–T225 www.connected.mcgraw-hill.com: **RESOURCES** **Student Resources:** Writer's Workspace
W.4.2e	Provide a concluding statement or section related to the information or explanation presented.	**READING/WRITING WORKSHOP:** Unit 5: 374–375 **YOUR TURN PRACTICE BOOK:** 250 **WRITING WORKSTATION ACTIVITY CARDS:** 10 **TEACHER'S EDITION:** Unit 1: T84, T221 Unit 2: T346 Unit 3: T222, T224–T225 Unit 5: T221, T286, T288–T289, T344, T346 www.connected.mcgraw-hill.com: **RESOURCES** **Student Resources:** Writer's Workspace
W.4.3	Write narratives to develop real or imagined experiences or events using effective technique, descriptive details, and clear event sequences.	
W.4.3a	Orient the reader by establishing a situation and introducing a narrator and/or characters; organize an event sequence that unfolds naturally.	**READING/WRITING WORKSHOP:** Unit 2: 102–103 Unit 4: 274–275 **YOUR TURN PRACTICE BOOK:** 60, 180 **WRITING WORKSTATION ACTIVITY CARDS:** 2, 5, 7, 8 **TEACHER'S EDITION:** Unit 1: T94, T222, T224–T225, T254, T344, T346, T350 Unit 2: T30, T32–T33, T62 Unit 4: T158, T160–T161, T190, T344 www.connected.mcgraw-hill.com: **RESOURCES** **Student Resources:** Writer's Workspace
W.4.3b	Use dialogue and description to develop experiences and events or show the responses of characters to situations.	**READING/WRITING WORKSHOP:** Unit 1: 30–31 Unit 4: 260–261 **YOUR TURN PRACTICE BOOK:** 10, 170 **WRITING WORKSTATION ACTIVITY CARDS:** 4 **TEACHER'S EDITION:** Unit 1: T94, T96–T97, T126, T352 Unit 2: T94, T96–T97, T126 Unit 4: T94, T96–T97, T126, T158, T160–T161, T344, T346 Unit 6: T30, T32–T33 www.connected.mcgraw-hill.com: **RESOURCES** **Student Resources:** Writer's Workspace
W.4.3c	Use a variety of transitional words and phrases to manage the sequence of events.	**READING/WRITING WORKSHOP:** Unit 1: 72–73 Unit 3: 174–175 **YOUR TURN PRACTICE BOOK:** 40, 110 **WRITING WORKSTATION ACTIVITY CARDS:** 19, 25 **TEACHER'S EDITION:** Unit 1: T222, T224–T225, T254, T344, T352 Unit 3: T30, T32–T33, T62 Unit 4: T344 Unit 6: T94, T96–97, T126 www.connected.mcgraw-hill.com: **RESOURCES** **Student Resources:** Writer's Workspace

Writing Standards

Text Types and Purposes		McGraw-Hill Reading Wonders
W.4.3d	Use concrete words and phrases and sensory details to convey experiences and events precisely.	**READING/WRITING WORKSHOP:** Unit 1: 30–31, 44–45 Unit 3: 188–189 Unit 4: 302–303 Unit 6: 446–447 **YOUR TURN PRACTICE BOOK:** 10, 20, 120, 200, 300 **WRITING WORKSTATION ACTIVITY CARDS:** 2, 16, 17 **TEACHER'S EDITION:** Unit 1: T30, T32–T33, T62, T346 Unit 2: T94, T96–T97 Unit 3: T94, T96–T97, T126 Unit 4: T222, T224–T225, T254, T286, T288–T289, T350, T352 Unit 6: T30, T32–T33, T286, T288–T289 www.connected.mcgraw-hill.com: **RESOURCES** **Student Resources:** Writer's Workspace
W.4.3e	Provide a conclusion that follows from the narrated experiences or events.	**READING/WRITING WORKSHOP:** Unit 3: 216–217 **YOUR TURN PRACTICE BOOK:** 140 **TEACHER'S EDITION:** Unit 1: T222, T224–T225, T346 Unit 3: T222, T224–T225, T254 Unit 4: T158, T160–T161, T344 www.connected.mcgraw-hill.com: **RESOURCES** **Student Resources:** Writer's Workspace

Production and Distribution of Writing		McGraw-Hill Reading Wonders
W.4.4	Produce clear and coherent writing in which the development and organization are appropriate to task, purpose, and audience. (Grade-specific expectations for writing types are defined in standards 1–3 above.)	**READING/WRITING WORKSHOP:** Unit 2: 116–117 Unit 3: 230–231 Unit 5: 360–361 Unit 6: 404–405 **YOUR TURN PRACTICE BOOK:** 70, 150, 240, 270 **WRITING WORKSTATION ACTIVITY CARDS:** 20, 21, 22 **TEACHER'S EDITION:** Unit 1: T32–T33, T96–T97, T160–T161, T224–T225 Unit 2: T32–T33, T96–T97, T160–T161, T224–T225, T254 Unit 3: T32–T33, T96–T97, T160–T161, T224–T225 Unit 4: T32–T33, T96–T97, T160–T161, T224–T225, T350, T352 Unit 5: T32–T33, T96–T97, T160–T161, T224–T225 Unit 6: T32–T33, T96–T97, T160–T161, T224–T225 www.connected.mcgraw-hill.com: **RESOURCES** **Student Resources:** Writer's Workspace
W.4.5	With guidance and support from peers and adults, develop and strengthen writing as needed by planning, revising, and editing.	**READING/WRITING WORKSHOP:** Unit 1: 31, 45, 59, 73, 87 Unit 2: 103, 117, 131, 145, 159 Unit 3: 175, 189, 203, 217, 231 Unit 4: 247, 261, 275, 289, 303 Unit 5: 319, 333, 347, 361, 375 Unit 6: 391, 405, 419, 433, 447 **TEACHER'S EDITION:** Unit 1: T32–T33, T96–T97, T160–T161, T224–T225, T344–T349, T350–T355 Unit 2: T32–T33, T96–T97, T160–T161, T224–T225, T344–T349 Unit 3: T32–T33, T96–T97, T160–T161, T220, T224–T225, T350–T355 Unit 4: T32–T33, T96–T97, T156, T160–T161, T224–T225, T344–T349, T350–T355 Unit 5: T32–T33, T96–T97, T156, T160–T161, T224–T225 Unit 6: T32–T33, T96–T97, T160–T161, T224–T225, T344–T349, T350–T355 www.connected.mcgraw-hill.com: **RESOURCES** **Student Resources:** Writer's Workspace
W.4.6	With some guidance and support from adults, use technology, including the Internet, to produce and publish writing as well as to interact and collaborate with others; demonstrate sufficient command of keyboarding skills to type a minimum of one page in a single sitting.	**TEACHER'S EDITION:** Unit 1: T332, T348, T354 Unit 2: T332, T348, T354 Unit 3: T156, T332, T348, T354 Unit 4: T156, T332, T348, T354 Unit 5: T156, T332, T348, T354 Unit 6: T156, T332, T348, T354 www.connected.mcgraw-hill.com: **RESOURCES** **Student Resources:** Writer's Workspace

Writing Standards

	Research to Build and Present Knowledge	*McGraw-Hill Reading Wonders*
W.4.7	Conduct short research projects that build knowledge through investigation of different aspects of a topic.	**TEACHER'S EDITION: Unit 1:** T28, T92, T156, T220, T328–T329, T330–T333 **Unit 2:** T28, T92, T156, T220, T330–T333 **Unit 3:** T28, T92, T156, T220, T328–T329, T330–T333 **Unit 4:** T28, T92, T156, T220, T328–T329, T330–T333 **Unit 5:** T28, T92, T156, T220, T328–T329, T330–T333 **Unit 6:** T28, T92, T156, T220, T328–T329, T330–T333 www.connected.mcgraw-hill.com: **RESOURCES** **Student Resources:** Research and Inquiry, Writer's Workspace **Teacher Resources:** Graphic Organizers, Research and Inquiry
W.4.8	Recall relevant information from experiences or gather relevant information from print and digital sources; take notes and categorize information, and provide a list of sources.	**TEACHER'S EDITION: Unit 1:** T28, T92, T156, T220, T330–T333 **Unit 2:** T28, T92, T156, T220, T328–T329, T330–T333 **Unit 3:** T28, T92, T156, T220, T330–T333 **Unit 4:** T28, T92, T156, T220, T330–T333 **Unit 5:** T28, T92, T156, T220, T330–T333, T350, T352 **Unit 6:** T28, T92, T156, T220, T330–T333 www.connected.mcgraw-hill.com: **RESOURCES** **Student Resources:** Research and Inquiry, Writer's Workspace **Teacher Resources:** Graphic Organizers, Research and Inquiry
W.4.9	Draw evidence from literary or informational texts to support analysis, reflection, and research.	
W.4.9a	Apply *grade 4 Reading standards* to literature (e.g., "Describe in depth a character, setting, or event in a story or drama, drawing on specific details in the text [e.g., a character's thoughts, words, or actions].").	**YOUR TURN PRACTICE BOOK:** 9, 19, 59, 69, 109, 119, 169, 179, 209, 219, 259, 269 **WRITING WORKSTATION ACTIVITY CARDS:** 26 **TEACHER'S EDITION: Unit 1:** T29, T93 **Unit 2:** T28, T29, T92, T93 **Unit 3:** T29, T93 **Unit 4:** T93, T157 **Unit 5:** T29, T93 **Unit 6:** T29, T93 www.connected.mcgraw-hill.com: **RESOURCES** **Student Resources:** Writer's Workspace
W.4.9b	Apply *grade 4 Reading standards* to informational texts (e.g., "Explain how an author uses reasons and evidence to support particular points in a text").	**YOUR TURN PRACTICE BOOK:** 29, 39, 49, 79, 89, 129, 139, 159, 189, 229, 239, 249, 279, 289 **WRITING WORKSTATION ACTIVITY CARDS:** 26 **TEACHER'S EDITION: Unit 1:** T157, T221, T285 **Unit 2:** T157, T220, T221 **Unit 3:** T157, T221 **Unit 4:** T29, T221 **Unit 5:** T157, T221, T285 www.connected.mcgraw-hill.com: **RESOURCES** **Student Resources:** Writer's Workspace
	Range of Writing	*McGraw-Hill Reading Wonders*
W.4.10	Write routinely over extended time frames (time for research, reflection, and revision) and shorter time frames (a single sitting or a day or two) for a range of discipline-specific tasks, purposes, and audiences.	**READING/WRITING WORKSHOP: Unit 1:** 72–73 **Unit 2:** 116–117 **Unit 3:** 216–217 **Unit 4:** 246–247 **Unit 5:** 318–319 **Unit 6:** 446–447 **WRITING WORKSTATION ACTIVITY CARDS:** 20, 21, 22, 23, 24, 25, 26, 27, 28, 29 **TEACHER'S EDITION: Unit 1:** T25R, T25T, T29, T30, T89N, T94, T157, T158, T222, T286, T344–T349, T350–T355 **Unit 2:** T25P, T29, T30, T89R, T94, T153R, T158, T222, T286, T344–T349, T350–T355 **Unit 3:** T25R, T30, T89N, T94, T158, T222, T344–T349, T350–T355 **Unit 4:** T25N, T30, T89V, T94, T153R, T158, T217P, T222, T286, T344–T349, T350–T355 **Unit 5:** T25R, T28, T89R, T220, T286, T344–T349, T350–T355 **Unit 6:** T25N, T30, T94, T153T, T158, T222, T344–T349, T350–T355 www.connected.mcgraw-hill.com: **RESOURCES** **Student Resources:** Research and Inquiry, Writer's Workspace **Teacher Resources:** Research and Inquiry

College and Career Readiness Anchor Standards for
SPEAKING AND LISTENING

The K-5 standards on the following pages define what students should understand and be able to do by the end of each grade. They correspond to the College and Career Readiness (CCR) anchor standards below by number. The CCR and grade-specific standards are necessary complements—the former providing broad standards, the latter providing additional specificity—that together define the skills and understandings that all students must demonstrate.

Comprehension and Collaboration
1. Prepare for and participate effectively in a range of conversations and collaborations with diverse partners, building on others' ideas and expressing their own clearly and persuasively.
2. Integrate and evaluate information presented in diverse media and formats, including visually, quantitatively, and orally.
3. Evaluate a speaker's point of view, reasoning, and use of evidence and rhetoric.
Presentation of Knowledge and Ideas
4. Present information, findings, and supporting evidence such that listeners can follow the line of reasoning and the organization, development, and style are appropriate to task, purpose, and audience.
5. Make strategic use of digital media and visual displays of data to express information and enhance understanding of presentations.
6. Adapt speech to a variety of contexts and communicative tasks, demonstrating command of formal English when indicated or appropriate.

CCSS Common Core State Standards
English Language Arts
Grade 4

Each standard is coded in the following manner:

Strand	Grade Level	Standard
SL	4	1

Speaking and Listening Standards

Comprehension and Collaboration	McGraw-Hill Reading Wonders
SL.4.1 Engage effectively in a range of collaborative discussions (one-on-one, in groups, and teacher-led) with diverse partners on *grade 4 topics and texts*, building on others' ideas and expressing their own clearly.	
SL.4.1a Come to discussions prepared, having read or studied required material; explicitly draw on that preparation and other information known about the topic to explore ideas under discussion.	**READING/WRITING WORKSHOP:** Unit 1: 26, 27, 40, 41, 54, 55, 68, 69, 82, 83 **Unit 2:** 98, 99, 112, 113, 126, 127, 140, 141 **Unit 3:** 170, 171, 184, 185, 198, 199, 212, 213, 226, 227 **Unit 4:** 242, 243, 256, 257, 270, 271, 284, 285 **Unit 5:** 314, 315, 328, 329, 342, 343, 356, 357, 370, 371 **Unit 6:** 386, 387, 400, 401, 414, 415, 428, 429 **READING WORKSTATION ACTIVITY CARDS:** 24 **TEACHER'S EDITION:** Unit 1: T29, T93, T157, T221, T285 **Unit 2:** T29, T93, T157, T221, T285 **Unit 3:** T22, T28, T29, T93, T157, T221 **Unit 4:** T29, T93, T157, T221 **Unit 5:** T29, T93, T157, T221, T266, T285 **Unit 6:** T29, T93, T157, T221, T285 www.connected.mcgraw-hill.com: **RESOURCES** **Teacher Resources:** Build Background Videos
SL.4.1b Follow agreed-upon rules for discussions and carry out assigned roles.	**READING WORKSTATION ACTIVITY CARDS:** 24 **TEACHER'S EDITION:** Unit 1: T10, T138 **Unit 2:** T10, T202 **Unit 3:** T10, T74, T202, T266 **Unit 4:** T10, T138, T266 **Unit 5:** T10, T138 **Unit 6:** T10, T266 www.connected.mcgraw-hill.com: **RESOURCES** **Teacher Resources:** Build Background Videos
SL.4.1c Pose and respond to specific questions to clarify or follow up on information, and make comments that contribute to the discussion and link to the remarks of others.	**READING/WRITING WORKSHOP:** Unit 1: 18–19, 32–33, 46–47, 59–60, 74–75 **Unit 2:** 90–91, 104–105, 118–119, 132–133, 146–147 **Unit 3:** 162–163, 176–177, 190–191, 204–205, 218–219 **Unit 4:** 234–235, 248–249, 262–263, 276–277 **Unit 5:** 306–307, 320–321, 334–335, 348–349, 362–363 **Unit 6:** 378–379, 392–393, 406–407, 420–421, 434–435 **READING WORKSTATION ACTIVITY CARDS:** 24 **TEACHER'S EDITION:** Unit 1: T28, T74, T92, T202, T332 **Unit 2:** T266, T332 **Unit 3:** T138, T332 **Unit 4:** T74, T138, T202, T332 **Unit 5:** T74, T332 **Unit 6:** T74, T138, T202, T332 www.connected.mcgraw-hill.com: **RESOURCES** **Student Resources:** Research and Inquiry **Teacher Resources:** Build Background Videos, Research and Inquiry
SL.4.1d Review the key ideas expressed and explain their own ideas and understanding in light of the discussion.	**READING WORKSTATION ACTIVITY CARDS:** 24 **TEACHER'S EDITION:** Unit 1: T28, T29, T93, T138, T157 **Unit 2:** T29, T74, T138, T157, T221 **Unit 3:** T29, T93, T157, T221 **Unit 4:** T29, T93, T157, T221 **Unit 5:** T29, T93, T157, T202, T221 **Unit 6:** T29, T93, T157, T221 www.connected.mcgraw-hill.com: **RESOURCES** **Teacher Resources:** Build Background Videos

Speaking and Listening Standards

Comprehension and Collaboration		McGraw-Hill Reading Wonders
SL.4.2	Paraphrase portions of a text read aloud or information presented in diverse media and formats, including visually, quantitatively, and orally.	**TEACHER'S EDITION:** Unit 1: T10, T12, T16, T74, T92, T104, T112, T116, T122, T140, T168, T176, T208 **Unit 2:** T10, T12, T76, T140, T202, T204 **Unit 3:** T12, T74, T76, T138, T150, T202, T204 **Unit 4:** T10, T12, T74, T76, T140, T202, T204 **Unit 5:** T10, T12, T76, T140, T150, T204 **Unit 6:** T10, T74, T138, T202 www.connected.mcgraw-hill.com: **RESOURCES** **Student Resources:** Music/Fine Arts Activities **Teacher Resources:** Interactive Read Aloud Images, Music/Fine Arts Activities
SL.4.3	Identify the reasons and evidence a speaker provides to support particular points.	**TEACHER'S EDITION:** Unit 1: T29, T93, T157, T221 **Unit 2:** T29, T93, T157, T221 **Unit 3:** T29, T93, T157, T221 **Unit 4:** T29, T93, T157, T221 **Unit 5:** T29, T93, T157, T221 **Unit 6:** T29, T93, T157, T221 www.connected.mcgraw-hill.com: **RESOURCES** **Student Resources:** Research and Inquiry **Teacher Resources:** Research and Inquiry
Presentation of Knowledge and Ideas		*McGraw-Hill Reading Wonders*
SL.4.4	Report on a topic or text, tell a story, or recount an experience in an organized manner, using appropriate facts and relevant, descriptive details to support main ideas or themes; speak clearly at an understandable pace.	**TEACHER'S EDITION:** Unit 1: T28, T29, T92, T156, T220, T284, T332, T334–T335 **Unit 2:** T28, T156, T284, T332, T334–T335 **Unit 3:** T28, T92, T221, T332, T334–T335 **Unit 4:** T28, T92, T156, T220, T332, T334–T335 **Unit 5:** T28, T92, T220, T332, T334–T335 **Unit 6:** T28, T156, T220, T284, T332, T334–T335 www.connected.mcgraw-hill.com: **RESOURCES** **Student Resources:** Research and Inquiry **Teacher Resources:** Research and Inquiry
SL.4.5	Add audio recordings and visual displays to presentations when appropriate to enhance the development of main ideas or themes.	**TEACHER'S EDITION:** Unit 1: T156, T220, T284, T332, T334–T335 **Unit 2:** T156, T220, T284, T332, T334–T335 **Unit 3:** T92, T156, T332, T334–T335 **Unit 4:** T92, T156, T220, T332, T334–T335 **Unit 5:** T28, T92, T220, T332, T334–T335 **Unit 6:** T28, T220, T332, T334–T335 www.connected.mcgraw-hill.com: **RESOURCES** **Student Resources:** Research and Inquiry **Teacher Resources:** Research and Inquiry
SL.4.6	Differentiate between contexts that call for formal English (e.g., presenting ideas) and situations where informal discourse is appropriate (e.g., small-group discussion); use formal English when appropriate to task and situation. (See grade 4 Language standards 1 for specific expectations.)	**TEACHER'S EDITION:** Unit 1: T28, T220 **Unit 2:** T28 **Unit 4:** T92 **Unit 5:** T92 www.connected.mcgraw-hill.com: **RESOURCES** **Student Resources:** Research and Inquiry **Teacher Resources:** Research and Inquiry

College and Career Readiness Anchor Standards for LANGUAGE

The K-5 standards on the following pages define what students should understand and be able to do by the end of each grade. They correspond to the College and Career Readiness (CCR) anchor standards below by number. The CCR and grade-specific standards are necessary complements—the former providing broad standards, the latter providing additional specificity—that together define the skills and understandings that all students must demonstrate.

Conventions of English

1. Demonstrate command of the conventions of standard English grammar and usage when writing or speaking.

2. Demonstrate command of the conventions of standard English capitalization, punctuation, and spelling when writing.

Knowledge of Language

3. Apply knowledge of language to understand how language functions in different contexts, to make effective choices for meaning or style, and to comprehend more fully when reading and listening.

Vocabulary Acquisition and Use

4. Determine or clarify the meaning of unknown and multiple-meaning words and phrases by using context clues, analyzing meaningful word parts, and consulting general and specialized reference materials, as appropriate.

5. Demonstrate understanding of figurative language, word relationships, and nuances in word meanings.

6. Acquire and use accurately a range of general academic and domain-specific words and phrases sufficient for reading, writing, speaking, and listening at the college and career readiness level; demonstrate independence in gathering vocabulary knowledge when encountering an unknown term important to comprehension or expression.

CCSS Common Core State Standards
English Language Arts

Grade 4

Each standard is coded in the following manner:

Strand	Grade Level	Standard
L	4	1

Language Standards

Conventions of English		*McGraw-Hill Reading Wonders*
L.4.1	Demonstrate command of the conventions of standard English grammar and usage when writing or speaking.	
L.4.1a	Use relative pronouns (*who, whose, whom, which, that*) and relative adverbs (*where, when, why*).	**READING/WRITING WORKSHOP:** Grammar Handbook: 463–465, 468–469 **TEACHER'S EDITION:** Unit 1: T225, T226 Unit 4: T29, T34 Unit 6: T32, T33, T34, T63 www.connected.mcgraw-hill.com: **RESOURCES** **Student Resources:** Grammar Interactive Games and Activities, Music/Fine Arts Activities **Teacher Resources:** Music/Fine Arts Activities
L.4.1b	Form and use the progressive (e.g., *I was walking; I am walking; I will be walking*) verb tenses.	**READING/WRITING WORKSHOP:** Grammar Handbook: 458 **TEACHER'S EDITION:** Unit 3: T93, T96, T97, T98, T127 www.connected.mcgraw-hill.com: **RESOURCES** **Student Resources:** Grammar Interactive Games and Activities, Music/Fine Arts Activities **Teacher Resources:** Music/Fine Arts Activities
L.4.1c	Use modal auxiliaries (e.g., *can, may, must*) to convey various conditions.	**READING/WRITING WORKSHOP:** Grammar Handbook: 460–461 **TEACHER'S EDITION:** Unit 3: T157, T160, T161, T162, T191 www.connected.mcgraw-hill.com: **RESOURCES** **Student Resources:** Grammar Interactive Games and Activities, Music/Fine Arts Activities **Teacher Resources:** Music/Fine Arts Activities
L.4.1d	Order adjectives within sentences according to conventional patterns (e.g., a *small red bag* rather than a *red small bag*).	**READING/WRITING WORKSHOP:** Grammar Handbook: 466–467 **TEACHER'S EDITION:** Unit 5: T29, T32, T33, T34, T63 www.connected.mcgraw-hill.com: **RESOURCES** **Student Resources:** Grammar Interactive Games and Activities, Music/Fine Arts Activities **Teacher Resources:** Music/Fine Arts Activities
L.4.1e	Form and use prepositional phrases.	**READING/WRITING WORKSHOP:** Grammar Handbook: 471 **TEACHER'S EDITION:** Unit 6: T224, T225, T226, T255, T290, T319 www.connected.mcgraw-hill.com: **RESOURCES** **Student Resources:** Grammar Interactive Games and Activities, Music/Fine Arts Activities **Teacher Resources:** Music/Fine Arts Activities
L.4.1f	Produce complete sentences, recognizing and correcting inappropriate fragments and run-ons.	**READING/WRITING WORKSHOP:** Grammar Handbook: 450–451 **YOUR TURN PRACTICE BOOK:** 50 **TEACHER'S EDITION:** Unit 1: T29, T32, T34, T63, T93, T96, T98, T127, T160, T162, T191, T224, T225, T288, T289, T290, T291, T319 www.connected.mcgraw-hill.com: **RESOURCES** **Student Resources:** Grammar Interactive Games and Activities, Music/Fine Arts Activities **Teacher Resources:** Music/Fine Arts Activities

Language Standards

Conventions of English		*McGraw-Hill Reading Wonders*
L.4.1g	Correctly use frequently confused words (e.g., *to, too, two; there, their*).	**PHONICS/WORD STUDY WORKSTATION ACTIVITY CARDS:** 13, 14 **TEACHER'S EDITION:** Unit 4: T226, T282, T290, T299, T319 Unit 5: T219, T235 www.connected.mcgraw-hill.com: **RESOURCES** **Student Resources:** Grammar Interactive Games and Activities, Music/Fine Arts Activities **Teacher Resources:** Music/Fine Arts Activities
L.4.2	Demonstrate command of the conventions of standard English capitalization, punctuation, and spelling when writing.	
L.4.2a	Use correct capitalization.	**READING/WRITING WORKSHOP:** Grammar Handbook: 474–476 **TEACHER'S EDITION:** Unit 1: T35 Unit 2: T29, T32, T33, T34 Unit 3: T34 Unit 6: T98 www.connected.mcgraw-hill.com: **RESOURCES** **Student Resources:** Grammar Interactive Games and Activities, Music/Fine Arts Activities **Teacher Resources:** Music/Fine Arts Activities
L.4.2b	Use commas and quotation marks to mark direct speech and quotations from a text.	**READING/WRITING WORKSHOP:** Grammar Handbook: 479, 480 **TEACHER'S EDITION:** Unit 1: T226 Unit 4: T162 Unit 5: T32, T33, T34 Unit 6: T98, T226 www.connected.mcgraw-hill.com: **RESOURCES** **Student Resources:** Grammar Interactive Games and Activities, Music/Fine Arts Activities **Teacher Resources:** Music/Fine Arts Activities
L.4.2c	Use a comma before a coordinating conjunction in a compound sentence.	**READING/WRITING WORKSHOP:** Grammar Handbook: 479 **TEACHER'S EDITION:** Unit 1: T161, T162, T191, T225, T226, T255 Unit 5: T226, T290 Unit 6: T98 www.connected.mcgraw-hill.com: **RESOURCES** **Student Resources:** Grammar Interactive Games and Activities, Music/Fine Arts Activities **Teacher Resources:** Music/Fine Arts Activities
L.4.2d	Spell grade-appropriate words correctly, consulting references as needed.	**TEACHER'S EDITION:** Unit 1: T36, T62, T100, T126, T164, T190, T228, T254 Unit 2: T36, T62, T100, T126, T164, T190, T228, T254 Unit 3: T36, T62, T100, T126, T164, T190, T228, T254 Unit 4: T36, T62, T100, T126, T164, T190, T228, T254 Unit 5: T36, T62, T100, T126, T164, T190, T228, T254 Unit 6: T36, T62, T100, T126, T164, T190, T228, T254 www.connected.mcgraw-hill.com: **RESOURCES** **Student Resources:** Grammar Interactive Games and Activities, Music/Fine Arts Activities **Teacher Resources:** Music/Fine Arts Activities
Knowledge of Language		*McGraw-Hill Reading Wonders*
L.4.3	Use knowledge of language and its conventions when writing, speaking, reading, or listening.	
L.4.3a	Choose words and phrases to convey ideas precisely.	**READING/WRITING WORKSHOP:** Unit 1: 30–31, 44–45 Unit 2: 158–159 Unit 3: 188–189 Unit 4: 302–303 Unit 6: 390–391, 446–447 **YOUR TURN PRACTICE BOOK:** 10, 20, 100, 120, 200, 260, 300 **TEACHER'S EDITION:** Unit 1: T30, T61, T94, T125, T156, T189 Unit 2: T61, T94, T125, T189 Unit 3: T61, T94, T118, T125, T189, T253 Unit 4: T61, T92, T125, T156, T189, T222, T253 Unit 5: T28, T61, T125, T189, T253 Unit 6: T61, T92, T125, T189 www.connected.mcgraw-hill.com: **RESOURCES** **Student Resources:** Writer's Workspace
L.4.3b	Choose punctuation for effect.	**READING/WRITING WORKSHOP:** Grammar Handbook: 477 **TEACHER'S EDITION:** Unit 1: T34, T63 Unit 2: T94 Unit 6: T92 www.connected.mcgraw-hill.com: **RESOURCES** **Student Resources:** Writer's Workspace
L.4.3c	Differentiate between contexts that call for formal English (e.g., presenting ideas) and situations where informal discourse is appropriate (e.g., small-group discussion).	**TEACHER'S EDITION:** Unit 2: T28, T92, T94 Unit 3: T28, T220 Unit 4: T156 Unit 5: T156, T222, T224–T225 www.connected.mcgraw-hill.com: **RESOURCES** **Student Resources:** Writer's Workspace

Language Standards

Vocabulary Acquisition and Use		McGraw-Hill Reading Wonders
L.4.4	Determine or clarify the meaning of unknown and multiple-meaning words and phrases based on grade 4 reading and content, choosing flexibly from a range of strategies.	
L.4.4a	Use context (e.g., definitions, examples, or restatements in text) as a clue to the meaning of a word or phrase.	**READING/WRITING WORKSHOP:** Unit 1: 29, 57, 71 Unit 2: 115, 129 Unit 3: 173, 187 Unit 4: 273, 287 Unit 5: 359 **YOUR TURN PRACTICE BOOK:** 7, 27, 37, 67, 77, 107, 117, 177, 187, 237 **PHONICS/WORD STUDY WORKSTATION ACTIVITY CARDS:** 1, 3, 4, 7 **TEACHER'S EDITION:** Unit 1: T38, T54, T152, T153E, T166, T173, T178, T182, T189, T216, T217H, T230, T237, T242, T246, T253 Unit 2: T25P, T38, T88, T152, T153R, T166, T173, T178, T182, T189 Unit 3: T24, T25E, T25G, T25I, T25R, T38, T45, T50, T54, T61, T88, T89E, T102, T109, T114, T118, T125, T166 Unit 4: T38, T102, T153R, T166, T216, T217E, T217P, T230, T237, T242, T246, T253 Unit 5: T25U, T88, T89E, T89J, T153K, T216, T217H Unit 6: T88, T102, T109, T114, T118, T125 www.connected.mcgraw-hill.com: **RESOURCES** **Student Resources:** Vocabulary Interactive Games and Activities
L.4.4b	Use common, grade-appropriate Greek and Latin affixes and roots as clues to the meaning of a word (e.g., *telegraph, photograph, autograph*).	**READING/WRITING WORKSHOP:** Unit 3: 215, 229 Unit 4: 245 Unit 5: 345 Unit 6: 417 **YOUR TURN PRACTICE BOOK:** 137, 147, 157, 227, 277 **PHONICS/WORD STUDY WORKSTATION ACTIVITY CARDS:** 10, 11, 15 **TEACHER'S EDITION:** Unit 2: T26, T216, T217N, T217R, T219, T237, T242, T246, T253 Unit 3: T166, T216, T217L, T230, T237, T242, T246, T253 Unit 4: T38, T45, T50, T54, T61, T166, T219, T230, T235 Unit 5: T27, T152, T153G, T153R, T155, T166, T209 Unit 6: T91, T107, T152, T153G, T219, T230 www.connected.mcgraw-hill.com: **RESOURCES** **Student Resources:** Vocabulary Interactive Games and Activities
L.4.4c	Consult reference materials (e.g., dictionaries, glossaries, thesauruses), both print and digital, to find the pronunciation and determine or clarify the precise meaning of key words and phrases.	**READING/WRITING WORKSHOP:** Unit 6: 424–427 **TEACHER'S EDITION:** Unit 1: T24, T153G, T216, T217T Unit 2: T24, T25B, T216 Unit 3: T24, T152, T217K Unit 4: T24, T92, T152, T280, T284 Unit 5: T88, T152 Unit 6: T25B, T92, T214, T216 www.connected.mcgraw-hill.com: **RESOURCES** **Student Resources:** Vocabulary Interactive Games and Activities
L.4.5	Demonstrate understanding of figurative language, word relationships, and nuances in word meanings.	
L.4.5a	Explain the meaning of simple similes and metaphors (e.g., *as pretty as a picture*) in context.	**READING/WRITING WORKSHOP:** Unit 2: 157 Unit 5: 317 Unit 6: 445 **YOUR TURN PRACTICE BOOK:** 97, 207, 297 **PHONICS/WORD STUDY WORKSTATION ACTIVITY CARDS:** 9 **LITERATURE ANTHOLOGY:** Unit 2: 172–175, 176–177 Unit 6: 534–537, 538–539 **TEACHER'S EDITION:** Unit 2: T25F, T153L, T280, T281B, T281C Unit 3: T25K, T89I, T217F Unit 4: T153K, T153N Unit 5: T24, T25D, T25E, T25L, T25Q, T25R, T153L, T217O Unit 6: T25C, T89J, T280, T294 www.connected.mcgraw-hill.com: **RESOURCES** **Student Resources:** Vocabulary Interactive Games and Activities
L.4.5b	Recognize and explain the meaning of common idioms, adages, and proverbs.	**READING/WRITING WORKSHOP:** Unit 1: 43 Unit 4: 259 Unit 5: 373 Unit 6: 431 **LITERATURE ANTHOLOGY:** Unit 1: 37, 43 **YOUR TURN PRACTICE BOOK:** 17, 167, 247, 287 **PHONICS/WORD STUDY WORKSTATION ACTIVITY CARDS:** 2 **TEACHER'S EDITION:** Unit 1: T25H, T88, T89F, T102, T109, T114, T118, T125, T166 Unit 2: T25R, T28 Unit 4: T25F, T88, T89, T89H, T89P, T89V, T102, T109, T114, T118, T125 Unit 5: T89D, T153L, T280, T294, T301, T306, T310 Unit 6: T166, T216, T217G, T230 www.connected.mcgraw-hill.com: **RESOURCES** **Student Resources:** Vocabulary Interactive Games and Activities

CORRELATIONS

Language Standards

Vocabulary Acquisition and Use		McGraw-Hill Reading Wonders
L.4.5c	Demonstrate understanding of words by relating them to their opposites (antonyms) and to words with similar but not identical meanings (synonyms).	**READING/WRITING WORKSHOP:** Unit 1: 29 Unit 2: 115 Unit 3: 201 Unit 4: 273 Unit 5: 359 **YOUR TURN PRACTICE BOOK:** 7, 67, 127, 177, 237 **PHONICS/WORD STUDY WORKSTATION ACTIVITY CARDS:** 1, 7 **TEACHER'S EDITION:** Unit 1: T24, T38, T45, T50, T54, T61, T102, T109, T237 Unit 2: T88, T89K, T89R, T102, T109, T114, T118, T125, T166, T237 Unit 3: T45, T152, T153H, T153T, T166, T173, T178, T182, T189, T230 Unit 4: T38, T45, T152, T153K, T166, T173, T178, T182, T189 Unit 5: T216, T217H, T217T, T230, T237, T242, T246, T253 Unit 6: T173 www.connected.mcgraw-hill.com: **RESOURCES** **Student Resources:** Vocabulary Interactive Games and Activities
L.4.6	Acquire and use accurately grade-appropriate general academic and domain-specific words and phrases, including those that signal precise actions, emotions, or states of being (e.g., *quizzed, whined, stammered*) and that are basic to a particular topic (e.g., *wildlife, conservation,* and *endangered* when discussing animal preservation).	**READING/WRITING WORKSHOP:** Unit 1: 20–21, 34–35, 48–49, 61–62, 76–77 Unit 2: 92–93, 106–107, 120–121, 134–135, 148–149 Unit 3: 164–165, 178–179, 192–193, 206–207, 220–221 Unit 4: 236–237, 250–251, 264–265, 278–279, Unit 5: 308–309, 322–323, 336–337, 350–351, 364–365 Unit 6: 380–381, 394–395, 408–409, 422–423, 436–437 **YOUR TURN PRACTICE BOOK:** 1, 11, 51, 61, 101, 111, 151, 161, 201, 211, 251, 261 **TEACHER'S EDITION:** Unit 1: T14, T38, T44, T45, T50, T54, T60, T173, T178, T182, T188, T206, T230, T236 Unit 2: T38, T44, T45, T50, T54, T60, T78, T102, T108, T109, T114, T118, T124, T142, T166, T172, T173, T178 Unit 3: T14, T38, T44, T50, T54, T60, T78, T102, T108, T109, T236, T237, T242, T246, T252 Unit 4: T114, T118, T124, T142, T172, T173, T178, T182, T188, T206, T236, T237 Unit 5: T14, T44, T45, T50, T54, T60, T78, T142, T206 Unit 6: T14, T44, T45, T50, T60, T78, T108, T142, T172, T178, T182 www.connected.mcgraw-hill.com: **RESOURCES** **Student Resources:** Vocabulary Interactive Games and Activities **Teacher Resources:** Build Background Videos, Graphic Organizers

CCSS Language Progressive Skills

Below are the grade 3 Language standards indicated by CCSS to be particularly likely to require continued attention in grade 4 as they are applied to increasingly sophisticated writing and speaking.

Language Progressive Skills

Standard		*McGraw-Hill Reading Wonders*
L.3.1f	Ensure subject-verb and pronoun-antecedent agreement.	**READING/WRITING WORKSHOP:** Grammar Handbook: 459, 463 **TEACHER'S EDITION: Unit 2:** T319 **Unit 3:** T98, T127, T162, T226, T255 **Unit 4:** T34, T63, T98, T162, T191, T255 www.connected.mcgraw-hill.com: **RESOURCES** **Student Resources:** Grammar Interactive Games and Activities, Music/Fine Arts Activities **Teacher Resources:** Music/Fine Arts Activities
L.3.3a	Choose words and phrases for effect.	**READING/WRITING WORKSHOP: Unit 1:** 30–31, 44–45 **Unit 2:** 158–159 **Unit 3:** 188–189 **Unit 4:** 302–303 **Unit 6:** 390–391, 446–447 **YOUR TURN PRACTICE BOOK:** 10, 20, 100, 120, 200, 260, 300 **TEACHER'S EDITION: Unit 4:** T92, T156, T222 **Unit 5:** T28 **Unit 6:** T92 www.connected.mcgraw-hill.com: **RESOURCES** **Student Resources:** Grammar Interactive Games and Activities, Music/Fine Arts Activities **Teacher Resources:** Music/Fine Arts Activities